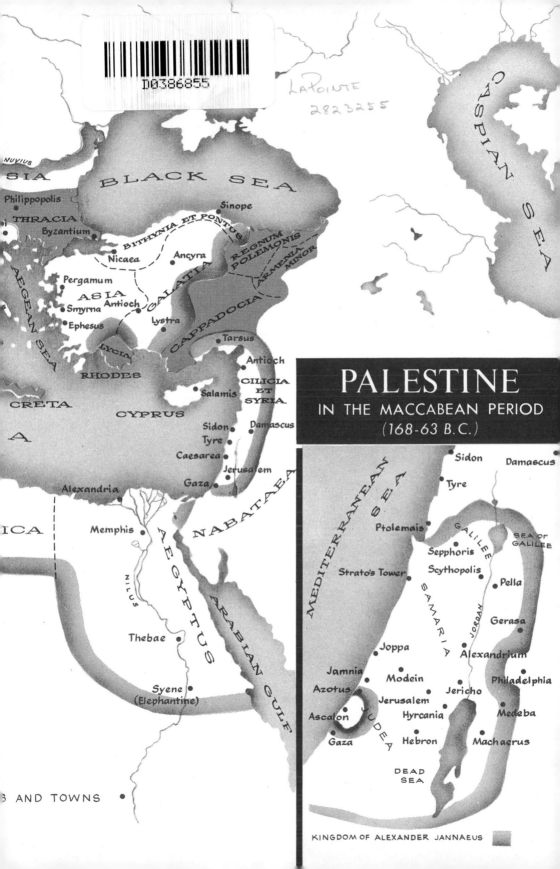

LAPOINTE
2823255

NUVIUS

SIA

Philippopolis

THRACIA

Byzantium

AEGEAN SEA

Pergamum

ASIA

Smyrna
Antioch

Ephesus

LYCIA

RHODES

CRETA

A

BLACK SEA

Sinope

BITHYNIA ET PONTUS

Nicaea
Ancyra

GALATIA

REGNUM
POLEMONIS

ARMENIA
MINOR

CAPPADOCIA

Lystra

Tarsus

Antioch

CILICIA
ET
SYRIA

Salamis

CYPRUS

Damascus

Sidon
Tyre

Caesarea

Jerusalem
Gaza

Alexandria

NABATAEA

ICA

Memphis

AEGYPTUS

NILUS

ARABIAN GULF

Thebae

Syene
(Elephantine)

CASPIAN SEA

B AND TOWNS

PALESTINE
IN THE MACCABEAN PERIOD
(168-63 B.C.)

Sidon
Damascus

MEDITERRANEAN SEA

Tyre

Ptolemais

GALILEE

SEA OF
GALILEE

Sepphoris

Strato's Tower

Scythopolis

Pella

SAMARIA

JORDAN

Gerasa

Joppa

Alexandrium

Jamnia

Modein

Philadelphia

Azotus

Jericho

Ascalon

Jerusalem

Hyrcania

Medeba

JUDEA

Gaza

Hebron

Machaerus

DEAD
SEA

KINGDOM OF ALEXANDER JANNAEUS

UNDERSTANDING THE NEW TESTAMENT

HOWARD CLARK KEE

Professor of the History of Religion
Bryn Mawr College

FRANKLIN W. YOUNG

Professor of New Testament and Patristic Studies
The Divinity School, Duke University

KARLFRIED FROEHLICH

Associate Professor of Church History
Princeton Theological Seminary

PRENTICE-HALL, INC., *Englewood Cliffs, New Jersey*

THIRD EDITION

UNDERSTANDING
THE NEW TESTAMENT

Library of Congress Cataloging in Publication Data

Kee, Howard Clark.
   Understanding the New Testament.

   Bibliography: p. 411
    1. Bible. N.T.–History of Biblical events.
2. Bible. N.T.–Introductions. I. Young, Franklin
W., joint author. II. Froehlich, Karlfried, joint
author. III. Title.
BS2407.K37 1973   225.6'6   72–13877
ISBN 0–13–936104–9

UNDERSTANDING THE NEW TESTAMENT
Third Edition
Howard Clark Kee / Franklin W. Young / Karlfried Froehlich

10 9

PRENTICE-HALL INTERNATIONAL, INC., *London*
PRENTICE-HALL OF AUSTRALIA, PTY. LTD., *Sydney*
PRENTICE-HALL OF CANADA, LTD., *Toronto*
PRENTICE-HALL OF INDIA PRIVATE LIMITED, *New Delhi*
PRENTICE-HALL OF JAPAN, INC., *Tokyo*

Preface

Nearly twenty years have passed since, on the initiative of the Society for Religion in Higher Education, the initial conversations began that led to the publication of the first edition of this book. Inevitably the changes in attitudes toward the study of religion have been reflected in each of the three editions of this work. The fifties called for synthesis and certainties; the sixties demanded analysis and scholarly objectivity. In the seventies, though institutional religion faces an uncertain future, there is a widespread mood of searching and a willingness to examine religious claims that is serious and, to those of us who teach in the field of academic study of religion, gratifying. The professional biblical scholar who may read these pages will sense our reaction to trends in the field, but we hope we have not been merely faddish. There has been no attempt to "make religion relevant"; rather we have sought to set forth the story of Christian origins against the background of its own social, political, and cultural setting, in the expectation that the bearing of this movement on our own time will be apparent without being coerced into a contemporary mold. With this aim in view, the factor of "understanding" has been given more explicit prominence than in the previous editions.

Special thanks are due to Darryl Jones and Karl Dimler for their help with photographs, and to Hilda Tauber, of the Prentice-Hall editorial staff, for her perceptive assistance at every stage of the revision. Colleagues have kindly drawn attention to errors in the earlier editions and have offered suggestions which have been taken into account in this revision.

HOWARD CLARK KEE

FRANKLIN W. YOUNG

KARLFRIED FROEHLICH

Contents

ILLUSTRATIONS

MAPS

End-paper maps and all maps listed above, except *Plan of the Temple
Area* and *Ancient Rome*, are based on maps in *The Westminster
Historical Atlas to the Bible* (Revised Edition), edited by George
Ernest Wright and Floyd Vivian Filson, copyright 1956 by W. L.
Jenkins, copyright 1945 by The Westminster Press, and are used by
permission.

Plan of the Temple Area is based on the plan in *Sacred Sites and
Ways*, by Gustaf Dalman, copyright 1935 by The Macmillan Com-
pany, and is used by permission of the Society for Promoting
Christian Knowledge, London.

PART ONE

COMMUNITY
AND
IDENTITY

It might seem obvious that the way to understand the New Testament is to handle it like any other writing: read it carefully and thoughtfully, seeking to determine the aims of its writers and the effectiveness with which those aims are stated. But for a range of reasons the task of understanding the New Testament is more complex than is the case with most other books.

The New Testament has been and is regarded by many people as inspired and authoritative scripture. For those who share this view, the New Testament writings are set apart from all others in that they are not appropriate subjects for critical examination or evaluation. They are to be heard and inwardly digested; any difficulties or seeming discrepancies are not to be thought of as a concern for faith, but rather as evidence of the limits of human comprehension. For those who do not regard the New Testament as divinely inspired, the reaction to the notion of inspiration may be annoyance at those who claim to possess the special revelation and amazement at their obscurantism and gullibility.

3

Both groups, however, as well as the majority of thoughtful persons who are neither skeptics nor true believers, experience major problems in trying to comprehend the New Testament. The believers gloss over the difficulties; the doubters are often put off by them. Of course nearly all modern men who read ancient texts are aware of the cultural differences between the situation of the writer and their own; but the nature of the New Testament writings is such that the difficulties are compounded, and it is essential that the modern reader be aware of the interpretive problems.

Fundamental is the recognition that the New Testament is a collection of writings and not a "book" in the ordinary sense. Each of the twenty-seven writings included in the New Testament arose under different circumstances, and among themselves they differ widely in time, place, circumstance of origin, and in the aim of the author. Only a few are self-conscious literary products such as the Letter to the Hebrews and the originally two-volumed work, the Gospel of Luke and the Book of Acts (now separated by the Gospel of John). Many are genuine letters, written by a single individual (Paul) to a specific group of intended readers in one of the churches he founded, such as Corinth or Philippi. The writer could use terms and make allusions that were fully comprehensible to the original readers, but which are puzzling or even meaningless to anyone who does not share the common experiences and perspective of the original sender and recipients. Other writings of the New Testament served as evangelistic propaganda (for example, the Gospel of Mark and the Gospel of John), or were intended to provide moral or organizational instruction for the young churches (the Letters of Paul, the Gospel of Matthew, the Letters of John).

The response of Christians in the years immediately following the writing of these books and for many centuries later—certainly from the mid-second century down to the rise of modern historical consciousness in the eighteenth and early nineteenth centuries, and even now among many devout Christians—has been strongly influenced by their belief that the scriptures are not only inspired but also canonical. That is, the twenty-seven books of the New Testament as we now know it were considered to be authoritative in matters of faith and practice in the Church. They were a rule—*canon*, meaning "measuring rod"—by which the claims of faith were to be tested and with which the Church's faith was believed to be wholly compatible. Possibly the earliest canonical lists were drawn up in reaction to proposals from forceful leaders in the Church who were regarded by most other Christians as radical or even heretical. For example, Marcion, a rich shipowner and son of the bishop of the Black Sea city of Sinope, some time after he came to Rome (about A.D. 139) began to exert great influence in the Church there on the subject of scriptural authority. He proposed that the Christian scriptures omit the Old Testament but include a single gospel (his own abridged edition of Luke) and the Letters of Paul. The mainstream of the Church rejected this proposal, however, and came to recognize as authoritative all four of the gospels now in the New Testament, later adding the Letters of Paul. Among the latter were included not only those now regarded as genuinely Pauline, but second-century writings that were claimed to be by Paul (I and II Timothy and Titus) and, with considerable hesitancy, the Letter to the Hebrews, as the lists of authoritative writings given by the great theologians of the second century—Clement of Alexandria, Irenaeus of Lyons, and Tertullian of North Africa—attest. Such a list, found in a library in Milan in the eighteenth century and designated the Muratorian Canon in honor of its founder, is believed to be a copy of a late second-century document. It includes our present canon, the Wisdom of Solomon (a Hellenistic Jewish document of the second century B.C.) and an Apocalypse of Peter, which it cautions against reading in the churches.

It was not until the fourth century that the present form of the canon with its three groups of writings was organized to constitute the authoritative list: (1) "gospel": Matthew, Mark, Luke, and John; (2) "apostle": Acts and the Pauline letters: Romans, I and II Corinthians, Galatians, Ephesians, Philippians, Colossians, I and II Thessalonians, I and II Timothy, and Titus;[1] (3) "Catholics": Hebrews, James, I and II Peter, I, II, and III John, Jude, and Revelation. Disputes continued about some of these books, especially Hebrews, whose Pauline authorship was rightly doubted, and Revelation, whose theology did not fit neatly with the other Johannine writings or indeed with most of the rest of the New Testament. Some lists included the first- and early second-century writings such as the Shepherd of Hermas and the Epistle of Barnabas. Even when Athanasius, Bishop of Alexandria, set out in his Easter letter of 367 a list of authoritative books that coincides exactly with our present New Testament, he went on to encourage Christians to read the Shepherd of Hermas and the Didache (Teaching of the Twelve Apostles), which were never accepted into the canon.[2]

Rational factors were invoked by the Church in the early centuries to justify both the list and the Church's refusal to extend it. To be able to link a book with an apostle, either as the writer or as the master whose memoirs or thoughts the writer reproduces, was thought to be a primary guarantee of

---

[1]Only in relatively recent times, with the rise of refined techniques of historical and literary criticism, has the authenticity of such purportedly Pauline letters as Colossians, Ephesians, and II Corinthians been questioned. These issues are discussed later on in this book.

[2]All the books in this list are discussed at the appropriate points in the present work (see the Table of Contents and the Index). For a fuller discussion of the canon, see the articles by A. C. Sundberg in *Interpreter's One-Volume Commentary on the Bible* (New York and Nashville: Abingdon, 1971); by F. C. Beare in *Interpreter's Dictionary of the Bible* (New York and Nashville: Abingdon, 1962); and the superb essay by Ph. Vielhauer in *New Testament Apocrypha*, ed. W. Schneemelcher, tr. and ed. R. McL. Wilson (Philadelphia: Westminster Press, 1963), Vol. I.

authority. But the power of these writings lay not in an external claim of apostolic authority but rather in what they say and how they have addressed successive generations with personal and religious questions that demand decisions.

All of the New Testament writers—whatever their aims—assumed that their readers shared with them certain religious concepts and that they comprehended the language and terminology in which the ideas were expressed. They all presupposed that their readers knew what the political situation was in Rome or in Greece or in the eastern provinces, where the New Testament was written. The forms of religious aspiration and practice with which the early Christians had to compete were a matter of common knowledge. But of course, the modern reader's experience is vastly different, and the presuppositions are not shared.

Perhaps some specific examples of what is presupposed by the New Testament writers will bring the difficulties into focus. The narrative sections of the gospels and the Book of Acts might be expected to offer more or less straightforward accounts of the events which they recount. But the casual way in which the narrator introduces supernatural elements such as hymns sung by angels, temptations by Satan, and performance of miracles shows the reader that he is not here dealing with natural, historical circumstances. A careful comparison of events told by more than one gospel writer shows further that the accounts do not always agree in detail, such as whether Jesus' cleansing the Temple courts took place at the outset of his public ministry (so John) or at the end (so the other three gospels). More important, there is evidence that the stories about Jesus and some of the incidents reported in Acts were transmitted orally or in earlier documents before they were placed by the writers in the positions they now occupy in the Gospels and the Acts. This means that the sequence of events in the lives of Jesus and Paul cannot be accepted uncritically as it stands in the New Testament, any more than the events themselves can be regarded as objective historical accounts.

With regard to the sayings and teaching material, the problems are of a different sort. Many of the basic terms such as "kingdom of God" and "son of man" are never defined by the writers who use them, since they could assume that their readers knew what they meant. The legal points at issue between Jesus and the Pharisees or between Paul and his Jewish-Christian opponents were self-evident in the first century, but they clearly no longer are. We are presented with the solutions to issues the nature of which we have to infer or conjecture. It is essential, therefore, that we attempt to reconstruct the religious situation in Judaism from which the controversies arose. There is also evidence that some of the controversies in the form reflected in the gospels originated not during the lifetime of Jesus but in the later conflict between nascent Christianity and its Jewish opponents. And yet the New Testament itself is our primary resource for reconstructing the development of Christianity in the first and second generations of its existence, so that problem and potential solution both arise from the same source. Unfortunately, there are nearly no references to Christian origins in either Jewish or pagan sources of the period, and the non-Biblical Christian sources date from the end of the first century A.D. and later. We are obliged, therefore, to work largely within the New Testament for our study of Christian origins, drawing where possible on contemporary sources and documents to enrich our meager knowledge of the setting in which Christianity arose.

To deal responsibly with these problems, the following series of guidelines for the study of the New Testament is offered. The proposals begin with the more abstract questions about sources and method and move to the personal issues of faith and religious identity.

SOURCES AND METHODS FOR ANALYZING
THE NEW TESTAMENT AGAINST ITS BACKGROUND

As we have noted, our sources of direct information about Jesus and the early Church, apart from the New Testament itself, are extremely limited and do not significantly supplement what we know from Christian sources. But historical work always proceeds by the perilous route of analogy, according to which the historian compares and contrasts what is historically known about other events and phenomena with the event that he is seeking to analyze historically. The historical study of the New Testament is no exception. We must search over as wide a range of information as possible about developments in the first century A.D. and earlier that might be analogous to the literary, conceptual, religious, and social forms of the New Testament. We must study how letters were written in the first century in order to see what is distinctive about the Letters of Paul, and specifically to learn how he used the letter form, adapting it to serve his peculiar aims in rebuking and strengthening the churches. Fortunately, copies of the Letters have been preserved from this period and are available for comparative study.

When we seek for analogies between the teachings of Jesus and the Jewish interpretation of Torah (the Law of Moses, comprising the first five books of the Jewish Bible), however, we find that the rabbinic interpretations of scripture and law were not written down until the period from the second to the sixth century A.D., and we have no guarantee as to how accurately this later documentation represents the interpretive process that was current in Jesus' day. The viewpoint associated with the Pharisees was only one of several open to Jews in Jesus' lifetime, but it was the one that prevailed after the destruction of the Jerusalem Temple in A.D. 70 and the crushing of the second Jewish revolt in A.D. 135. As a result, it is the only view that is given full and sympathetic treatment in the rabbinic sources, which have been nearly our only access to Judaism of this period. That situation was altered, however, by the discovery about 1950 near the Dead Sea, at a site called Qumran, of a library of Jewish writings from the first century A.D. and earlier, in which is fully documented a kind of Judaism that is sharply at variance with rabbinic thought, and at the same time has many remarkable points of contact with early Christian views and writings. (See pp. 57–66.)

Similarly, there are traces in the New Testament of a kind of religious philosophy which in its fully developed form in the second century A.D. was known as Gnosticism, from the Greek word *gnosis*, "knowledge." Gnostics claimed to have been given superior information about the nature of reality. They believed that man had his origins in the celestial realms where only pure spirits dwell. He had fallen, however, and had become ensnared in a material body, bound to the material world and its values and motives. Escape was possible for him if he would follow the path of truth that had been opened up for him and for all true Gnostics by a redeemer who had come from heaven, who had overcome the world of matter, and whose release made possible salvation and return to heaven for all who followed him. In broad outline, this view of man's nature and destiny was known to historians chiefly from critical denunciations of Gnosticism in the writings of some major thinkers of the Church in the second and subsequent centuries. In 1945, however, a library of Gnostic documents was found in upper Egypt, at Nag Hammadi, which was composed of copies of many original Gnostic works, some of which date back to the second century A.D. Now Gnosticism can be studied from works written by and for Gnostics, rather than solely from polemics against them. The publication of the Nag Hammadi materials has continued since the 1950s, and has spurred the publication of other related Gnostic documents that had been known to a few specialists but inadequately studied. The study of Gnosis has been placed on a new and far firmer basis. Yet the problem remains: When did Gnosticism originate? Can we reason backward from the second-century documents to suppose that this system existed in the time of Jesus and Paul? Or did some of the constituent elements of what became Gnosticism in the second century affect religious thinking in the first century as well? The language of Paul at some points resembles the vocabulary of Gnosticism, and the writings of the later Pauline school (for example in Ephesians and II Timothy) give even clearer evidence of Gnostic influence. Ironically, the best sources available for providing answers to these questions are the New Testament writings—precisely the documents that we must assess for possible Gnostic influence. But what is the relationship between the New Testament and Gnosticism? Is the redeemer figure of later Gnosticism a perversion of the Word-made-flesh of John 1? Or did John adapt his interpretation of Jesus to fit an existing model, the heavenly redeemer of Gnosis?

Once we begin to raise such questions about the sources of the gospels, we come against another issue: Did the gospel writers develop their writings by starting from scratch, or did they combine existing sources, putting their own distinctive touch on the finished product? As we shall consider in Chapter Three, there do seem to have been collections of saying of Jesus and possibly of miracles of Jesus before there were gospels as we know them. And before those collections were written down, the material they incorporate seems to have circulated orally and received certain modifications and stylization in the process. Yet once more, the only evidence we have for this process is the end result: the gospels themselves, although some help is provided by studies of other material of a folk nature originally transmitted orally. The form-critical, or tradition-historical, method employed in the chapters below dealing with the gospels shows what the results of such an approach are.

THE SOCIOPOLITICAL SETTING OF EARLY CHRISTIANITY

Although there are frequent allusions to political rulers in Palestine and the provinces of Asia Minor and Greece visited by Paul, the whole pattern of political power as experienced by the early Christians as well as the social structures within which they lived are simply presupposed by the New Testament writers without explanation. Some aspects of the first Christians' social and political situation can be inferred from the writings themselves, but most details of this kind must be reconstructed from other sources. The cities and villages of the eastern Mediterranean were a mixture of indigenous social and cultural patterns and were influenced by the Hellenization process from the time of Alexander the Great onward. There are the specific questions to be considered about how Jewish life was affected by these forces. It is usually assumed that the Jews in Palestine were somewhat more conservative in their response to Hellenism than the Jews in Egypt, for example. In the writings of Philo of Alexandria and the Wisdom Literature produced in that city we have abundant evidence of the extent to which Judaism there assimilated aspects of Hellenism, while from Palestine we learn of the resistance to Hellenization from the days of the Maccabees down through the first and second Jewish revolts. This is not to say, however, that Palestinian Jews were impervious to the influences of Graeco-Roman culture, but it is necessary to survey the range of responses to pagan culture in order to see how this in turn affected the forms that Christianity took as it grew on Jewish soil, both in Palestine and among the Jews of the Diaspora (Dispersion).

Another aspect of the political context of early Christianity that needs to be investigated, if the reaction of the New Testament writers to the political realities of their time is to be understood, is the growing conflict between the Church and the Roman Empire, as the emperors began to press with mounting seriousness their claims to divinity and the Church began to resist and then to reject these claims. The reader of the New Testament cannot assume that there is a single stance toward the empire in these writings, but rather he must seek to discover how that stance constantly shifted as the empire's attitude toward the infant Church began to change.

Similarly, the Church itself underwent fundamental changes as it became less of a movement and more of an institution. These changes are nowhere spelled out explicitly by the writers of the New Testament, but must be inferred in each instance from the documents themselves. Only when these factors are adequately assessed does it become apparent what lies behind the struggles over authority and norms that appear on so many of the later pages of the New Testament.

RELIGIOUS LANGUAGE AND CONCEPTS IN FIRST-CENTURY JUDAISM AND AMONG THE HELLENISTIC RELIGIONS

Because it originated from a Jewish matrix and grew in competition with the flourishing religions of the Graeco-Roman world, Christianity had to be culturally bilingual: it had to be able to speak the language of Judaism, so that it could interpret to its first adherents as well as to its original opponents how it concurred with and differed from the interpretation of the Jewish tradition. And when it began to convert the Gentile world, it had to learn to speak to the needs of non-Jews whose religious forms and aspirations were a mixture of Hellenistic mysticism and oriental cults, of Stoic ethics and revealed laws. The New Testament writers could assume a common basis of understanding with their readers, but the modern reader must strive to reconstruct the thought-worlds in which this ancient communication took place. He must recognize that such basic words as "faith," "church," "righteousness," "kingdom" did not have an unalterable meaning, but that the meaning can only be determined by examining not merely the literary context in which the term appears but by becoming familiar as well with the larger context—cultural and religious—in which the words were penned. This aspect of interpretation is complicated by the fact that most readers of the New Testament know it only in translation, which is at best never more than an approximation of the original. There exist many fine modern translations, but these cannot convey a feel for the wider context which lies behind the texts. Even for those who can read the New Testament in the Greek original, or who have sufficient knowledge of Semitic languages to be able to reconstruct the Aramaic in which Jesus may have uttered the sayings attributed to him in the gospels, the study of the New Testament must still be carried out with careful attention to the specific connotations of the language.

THE LIFE-STYLE AND CONCEPT OF COMMUNITY
OF THE ORIGINAL WRITERS AND HEARERS

More is at work in the New Testament than exchange of information, however: the writers are concerned to convert unbelievers and to confirm believers
in the faith. They do not attempt to present facts objectively for the detached
scrutiny of the reader; rather, they aim to persuade the reader of the truth,
whether the subject be evangelism, moral instruction, polemical attack against
error or misbehavior, liturgical rules, organizational regulations. Even Paul's
travel plans are presented to his Roman readers (Rom. 16) as evidence of
divine providence at work in extending the gospel to the whole inhabited
world. The modern reader, if he is to "understand" the dynamics at work in
the writings and in the movement that produced them, must put himself in
the place of the community of faith that produced these works.

Two aspects of the self-understanding of this community must be perceived
if more than the external meaning of the New Testament is to be grasped: (1)
the way in which the community defines itself in relation to the covenant
people, Israel; and (2) the way the community interprets the Jewish scriptures
and even its own oral traditions in the light of its developing self-understanding. Neither of these factors is static, since both undergo change and even
develop in different directions in different sectors of the nascent Church.
Only in the later books of the New Testament do norms of faith and practice
begin to appear; and only in the second century does a fixed body of orthodox
truths begin to develop. Both the redefinition of community and the rein
terpretation of tradition are factors which play upon each other, so that how
the community reads and interprets the Jewish scriptures directly affects how
it sees itself as the community of faith. And as the community changes, and
its needs and constituents change, it comes to see new meanings in the scriptures and to appropriate in new ways the Jesus tradition it has received from
the first generation of his followers. In one situation, the community will see
itself as a mystical communion, as in the Gospel of John; in other circumstances,
it will strive for careful delineation of duties and obligations, as in the Gospel
of Matthew. Paul regards the empire as guarantor of stability and protector
of the peace; the author of Revelation, writing a generation later, sees the
emperor as the tool of Satan, and summons his readers to unyielding opposition
to the idolatry of the imperial cult.

Throughout our study, therefore, it will be essential to see how the two
factors of community and scriptural interpretations help to shape the New
Testament writings. There are no objective criteria by which it can be determined that one definition of the community is "right" or that one interpretation

of the tradition is "true." What the search for understanding requires is sensitivity to the dynamic and diverse processes by which these forces worked in the rise of Christianity during the New Testament period.

THE STANDPOINT OF FAITH

In the early generations of its existence, the Church was much more of a voluntary association than it has been since that time. Once it became an established part of society, even before it became the official religion of the later Roman Empire, children were born into Christian families, were expected to take part in the life of the Church, and were automatically identified as Christians. But it was not so at the outset: then, a commitment of faith was required, and in making that commitment the individual cut himself off from the religious or social traditions in which he had been reared and took his stand within the new community of faith. It was essential that the decisional element be foremost in the writings of the beginning Church. We have already considered in the preceding section the aim of the New Testament writers to call together an association of persons of similar persuasion. But such a social group is inevitably composed of individuals who have made certain decisions and commitments. The New Testament writers seem convinced that only those who share the faith can fully understand its claims to truth.

In its method of conveying truth, therefore, the New Testament does not employ rigid logical or catechetical methods. Paul, for example, does utilize the terminology of Stoic ethics and the rhetoric of the Cynic-Stoic diatribes. He does develop his arguments with care, but by pleading, sarcasm, scriptural analogy rather than by syllogisms or deductions. The teachings of Jesus and the laws of the early Church either carry the power to persuade or they do not; there is no appeal to external authority as sanction or proof. Indeed, in some cases the teachings of Jesus raise as many difficulties as they illumine. For example, the Parable of the Lost Son (Lk. 15) is unambiguous in its praise of the loving father who welcomes home the itinerant and profligate son, but it leaves unanswered the seemingly justifiable complaints of the stay-at-home brother whose faithful service goes unacknowledged, much less rewarded. The teachings of Jesus, therefore, are not so much answers as challenges. The resolution of the difficulties in human behavior to which they speak is not handed to the hearer (or reader), but the problem is illumined more clearly and tossed back into the reader's lap.

The New Testament writers call their readers to make a decision about what is being claimed or declared. In some cases, it is claimed that man's eternal destiny hangs on the decision of faith, as in John 8:24, ". . . You will die in your sins unless you believe that I am he." The reader today may react to these calls to decision in various ways. He may be challenged by the concept of neighbor love at the ethical level while rejecting the claims made in behalf of Jesus, from whose teachings this concept arose and in whose life it was embodied. On the other hand, another contemporary reader of the New Testament may perceive very clearly what ethical challenges are being offered and what faith-claims are made, and yet reject the whole. Or what is most likely, he will react variously, selecting certain aspects of the New Testament concepts and aspirations that he can affirm or at least admire, while rejecting others. In the academic study of the New Testament there is no place for pressing the claims of faith or of persuading the reader concerning the truth of what is set forth in the New Testament. Critical study of the New Testament can clarify the issues and shed light on obscurities, but it cannot coerce or even invite decisions of faith. But whether the reader shares the faith or not—*in toto* or on a selective basis—it is hoped that the study of the New Testament with these factors in view will contribute to facilitate more sympathetic and better informed insight into the dynamics of the life and convictions of the early generation of Christians who produced the New Testament.

Quests for Community and Identity in the Early Roman Empire

Every age is an age of transition, for the world never stands still. But in some ages the rate of change seems to speed up. Ideas move swiftly from place to place, the population shifts about restlessly, social classes become more mobile, loyalties are made and unmade overnight, and political and economic institutions are dramatically reshaped. Rapid changes of this sort always dislocate groups and individuals, creating an atmosphere of uneasiness or even of anxiety. Life seems to be open at both ends; the past seems to be crumbling and the shape of the future has not yet become clear. Fascination with new developments breeds insecurity, and men and women tend to cling uncertainly to the discredited beliefs of the past or else grasp frantically at any new proposal that offers a solution to the perennial problems of life. It is as though some sinister hand had written across the face of the present: "Subject to change without notice."

Unsettled by the insecurity of such an age, men search for certainty. Some seek for a more profound understanding of the nature of the universe and the ultimate meaning of life. Others may shun the search, preferring rather to put their confidence in the fantastic promises of would-be saviors, or in the secret formulas of those who purvey quick and easy answers. An age of transition is a flourishing time for religions and philosophies that promise security and for governments that promise stability. When the old patterns of society break up and men are set adrift in a hostile, unpredictable world, they seek for security in some group that is bound together by common concerns and common aspirations. They search for true community—that is, for community of interest, for a common destiny, and for a sense of belonging.

It was in such an age of transition and searching that Jesus was born and that the movement which became Christianity had its origins. The literary remains left by the beginnings of this movement are what we know as the New Testament. In this collection are included reports of oral traditions that go back to the time of Jesus as well as documents that reflect later developments in the movement over a period reaching well into the second century A.D. By their diversity these writings manifest the different ways in which the young movement developed conceptually, culturally, and institutionally.

Like other religious movements before and since, the people who produced the New Testament did not think of themselves as innovators so much as the true heirs of past hopes and aspirations. However, they were convinced that the promises made to ancient Israel through the Law and the prophets were in process of fulfillment in their midst and were about to be consummated. Two factors were powerfully operative within this community, in spite of a diverse range of viewpoints represented by the various subgroups among the early Christians: (1) the community of God's people must be redefined, and (2) the religious tradition must be appropriated and interpreted in new ways. Specifically, the New Testament community saw itself as the fulfillment of the hope uttered by the prophet Jeremiah (Jer. 31) that God would create a New Covenant people in place of the Old Covenant people, Israel. As a corollary of this claim, the Christians believed that they had the proper means for interpreting the scriptures of ancient Israel, which were the deposit of that people's own developing religious tradition. Thus, a New Covenant people presupposes an Old Covenant people, just as a New Testament points back to an Old Testament; and this is the somewhat condescending way in which the Christians came to refer to the reappropriated traditions that they took over from ancient Israel. The redefinition of community and the reappropriation of tradition provide twin poles around which the whole of the New Testament and this present introductory volume revolve.

WAR AND PEACE: FROM ALEXANDER TO AUGUSTUS

One of the most familiar stories in the New Testament—the birth of Jesus according to the Gospel of Luke (Lk. 2:1ff.)—reminds us that Christianity began during the reign of Octavian (27 B.C.–A.D. 14), better known by his title of Caesar Augustus, the first and in many ways the greatest of the Roman emperors. "In those days a decree went out from Caesar Augustus that all the world should be enrolled." Augustus was acclaimed by many throughout the empire as a deliverer and savior. And it is true that he had brought to an end the power struggle among the Roman leaders that had led to the murder of Julius Caesar in 44 B.C. He had driven the pirates from the seas, making them safe once more for travel and commerce. He had quelled Rome's enemies, some of whom had harassed her borders for decades. Above all, he had managed to create an atmosphere of peace and unity throughout the far reaches of the empire. On landing at ports, sailors gave thanks to Augustus that they had been able to sail unmolested by pirates. The Italian peasants, with their strong sense of morality, were profoundly grateful to Augustus for combating the immorality that had become rampant among the upper classes of Rome in the years before his rise.

Caesar as Savior and Divine King

The people of the empire acclaimed Augustus not merely as a human deliverer from conflict and struggle, but as a divine savior-king. Temples were erected in his honor; sacrifices were made and incense was burned on the altars. In Palestine, for example, the fawning puppet king, Herod, built an imposing seaport in honor of Augustus. From it one could see glistening on the distant Samaritan hills white limestone columns of the Temple of Augustus, which stood at the west gate of the city that Herod had built on the site of ancient Samaria and had named Sebaste (the Greek equivalent of Augustus). Although the Jews themselves did not pay divine honors to Augustus, most of the other eastern peoples accepted him as divine, in keeping with their ancient tradition of regarding the king as a god. Augustus carefully avoided accepting the title of king, and even tried to preserve the fiction that he was no more than the leading citizen (*princeps*) among equals in the empire.

The worldwide acclaim given Augustus was not without precedent: in the fourth century before Christ a young Macedonian prince named Alexander had been hailed as a divine king in Egypt, in Asia Minor, and throughout much of western Asia. The military conquests of Alexander the Great, as he came to be called, were aided by the popular belief that he was a divine ruler before whom resistance would be useless and impious.

Although Augustus did not publicly seek divine honors as had Alexander the Great (356–323 B.C.), he benefited from Alexander's success in establishing himself in the minds of men from the Mediterranean basin to the borders of India as a divine king destined to unify the civilized world. Even the three centuries that intervened between the time of Alexander and that of Augustus had not tarnished the popular image of the divine ruler; so Augustus took on

AUGUSTUS CAESAR,
whose name was actually Gaius Octavius, was given the title "Augustus" by the Roman senate in gratitude for the peace and prosperity that he brought to the Roman lands. He was the first to be designated emperor. (Fototeca Architettura e Topografia dell'Italia Antica)

a familiar role when he set about extending the empire from the Nile to the Seine and from Gibraltar to Jerusalem.

Caesar Re-creates Alexander's One World

But Augustus inherited from Alexander more than the tradition of divine kingship; the atmosphere of outward peace and inner unrest that characterized the age of Augustus was a direct development of forces that had been set in motion in the time of Alexander.

Alexander's conquests had begun in Greece at a time when the city-states were in decline (336 B.C.). The weakening of the Greek social and political structure resulted in both military weakness and a breakdown in the sense of group loyalty that had reached its height in the golden age of the city-states. Although Alexander managed to build up an administrative unity among the Greek cities, he failed to create a common allegiance to himself to take the place of the old devotion to the city-states. In the eastern territories, however, where the tradition of divine kingship reached back for centuries, Alexander did succeed in winning great personal devotion from the conquered peoples.

A story arose that the tide along the coast of Asia Minor had retreated at his coming to enable him to pass along a narrow beach between sea and cliff. Since there was an ancient legend that the sea would recede at this point to herald the coming of a world ruler, word of the event sped before him and prepared the way for his acceptance in the East as a divine king. Had Alexander lived, there is little doubt that he could have developed tremendous support and affection—even veneration—from the peoples he had conquered, for legends of his divinity had begun to flourish even during his brief lifetime. But his efforts to create a politically unified world were cut short by his death in 323 B.C.

ALEXANDER THE GREAT
on a silver coin (tetradrachm) minted during his reign. (James T. Stewart)

Alexander's vision of one world stretched far beyond the political sphere, however; he took with him a small army of scholars to record descriptions of the peoples, customs, animals, plant life, and terrain that he and his armies encountered. He had caught from his old teacher, Aristotle, a love of knowledge and an insatiable curiosity about the world around him. And he shared Aristotle's conviction that Greek learning was superior to all other, and that it was his responsibility as a leader of men to spread Greek culture wherever he went. This process of "Greek-izing" the world became known as *Hellenizing*, since the Greeks called their own land *Hellas* and themselves *Hellenes*. In their intensive efforts to disseminate Greek culture, Alexander and his followers established Greek-style cities as far east as the Indus Valley and as far north as the territory now included in the Central Asia states of the Soviet Union. Reports have come down to us of petty monarchs in Central Asia who staged Greek tragedies as entertainments for their courtiers. Alexander did not present himself to the world as an innovator but as the conservator of the great traditions of the past, both of Greece and of the East. The new element in his Hellenizing enterprise was that the benefits of Hellenic culture were now to be available not merely to the peoples of the Greek city-states, but to the whole inhabited world.

Yet Hellenization never succeeded in laying more than a thin veneer of Greek culture over the oriental parts of Alexander's realm, either during his reign or after his death. The mass of the people in the subject lands remained faithful to their native customs and ways of life. Among the aristocracy, however, there was a strong desire to ape the ways of the Greeks. The aristocrats changed the names of their temples to honor local gods under new Greek titles. They built gymnasia and hippodromes and theaters to provide a setting for Greek-style entertainment. The upper classes even adopted Greek dress. But most of the people in these conquered lands continued to live and amuse themselves much as they had before Alexander began his Hellenizing conquests.

In one area of life, however, Hellenization had a profound and lasting effect, for Greek was widely accepted as the common language of commerce and international correspondence. Although men continued to speak their native language among themselves, Greek became the *lingua franca* of the Hellenistic world. So readily did it gain acceptance that some colonies of expatriates—such as the Jews living in Alexandria—stopped using their native tongues altogether and spoke only Greek. The Alexandrian Jews finally had to translate their Hebrew Bible into Greek so that their own people could understand it. This translation, known as the Septuagint (*i.e.*, seventy, since a Jewish legend claimed that seventy men had prepared independent translations that miraculously turned out to be identical), was widely used by Jews and was known to educated Gentiles throughout the world.

With Alexander's death in 323 B.C., all appearances of political unity vanished. His generals vied with one another to gain power over their dead leader's domain, and conflict among them and their successors raged on until the rise of Rome in the middle of the first century B.C. Only two relatively stable centers of power remained in the Hellenistic empires: one was Syria, where the Seleucids (successors of Seleucus, one of Alexander's generals) ruled, and the other was Egypt, where Ptolemy (another general) established the Ptolemaic dynasty. But in Asia Minor and Greece there was an unending series of wars and dynastic disputes.

In spite of the widespread disruption created by the continuing struggles, important centers of learning managed to grow up during the period between Alexander and Augustus. Athens had already begun to decline as the center of philosophical thought, although the Academy founded by Plato (427–347 B.C.) continued to exist until A.D. 529, eight centuries after his death. Tarsus, on the southern coast of Asia Minor, however, became an important university city. But most significant of all was Alexandria, the city that Alexander had founded at the western edge of the Nile Delta as a center for commercial and cultural interchange between East and West. There Alexander had founded the Museum, by definition a shrine to the Muses, but in actuality a great library with more than half a million volumes, and a center of learning and research unparalleled in the ancient world. It was there that Euclid developed his principles of plane geometry, that Archimedes performed his famous experiments with water, and that Eratosthenes discovered the formula by which he was able to calculate the circumference of the earth.

At the eastern end of the Mediterranean Sea there was continual conflict between the Seleucids and the Ptolemies. As we shall see later, one victim of this conflict was the Jewish nation, situated as it was in the buffer zone between the two great centers of power. The Ptolemaic kingdom enjoyed a high degree of stability because of the great desert that protected it on three sides and because of the immense wealth that it acquired, both through the agricultural produce of its own lush valley and through the luxuries that were shipped across it on the way from India to the Mediterranean cities. The Seleucids, on the other hand, had vast territories to the east over which they exercised only feeble control and beyond which lived powerful hostile tribes who constantly threatened to engulf them. Except for a century of relative independence, Palestine, from the time of Alexander until the coming of the Romans in 63 B.C., was subject to either Egypt or Syria, the one rich and indolent, and the other aggressive but insecure.

The Failure to Create Unity

In spite of the efforts of Alexander's successors to bring unity to their realms, they succeeded only in creating profound unrest. The simpler units of society, like the Greek city-states and the petty oriental kingdoms, had been ruined by the military and cultural conquests of Alexander and his successors. And nothing had risen to fill the void. Merchants could no longer look ahead in the certainty that their business would continue as usual. Villagers never knew when a pillaging army might sweep through and leave them impoverished. The old worship of local gods had been disrupted by attempts to make all men worship universal deities, or at least to give new and unfamiliar names to the old ones. Politically, a man's allegiance to his city or to his petty prince was irreparably shaken; religiously, the world revealed by these widening horizons was too vast to be controlled by local gods.

In Rome itself even the most skeptical citizens felt it was important to maintain the elaborate rituals of the state cult, since they felt that proper sacrifices to Rome's patron deities guaranteed the security of the Roman state. Any extraordinary event—ranging from a lightning bolt out of a clear sky to the birth of a deformed calf—was seen as a sign from the gods and called for careful investigation by the augurs, whose task it was to interpret the signs, and for propitiatory offerings to appease the gods and thus preserve the health of the state. Efforts to import into Rome more emotional and personal modes of worship (especially from the eastern Mediterranean) were resisted but were agreed to by the Roman authorities when it could be shown that the presence of a shrine to a particular deity was in the best interests of the state. Thus, the worship of the Great Mother was introduced at Rome from Asia Minor when it was determined that her coming would help bring an end to the Punic Wars at the close of the third century B.C. The goddess was welcomed at the mouth of the Tiber by distinguished Roman citizens and turned over to certain women who were in charge of maintaining the cult in her honor. Even though this precedent was established, there was great reluctance to allow the worship of foreign deities in Rome; and during the power struggle with Cleopatra, Augustus forbade the worship of Egyptian deities within a mile of the city limits.

The worship of foreign gods was enormously attractive to many Romans, however, and the Council of Fifteen which supervised religion in Rome was forced several times to expel the devotees of this or that eastern deity. But the cult of Mithra, which was more concerned with personal devotion than public ceremony, was tolerated. Developed on the basis of Persian religion but with mystical elements added from other sources—the devotee passed through stages of initiation and thereby prepared his soul to move through the heavenly spheres on its ascent to the god of light—Mithraism was allowed to flourish, and became a favorite religion of the common people and the soldiers. Mithraic shrines have been uncovered in the heart of Rome and in its port of Ostia, as well as at the sites of Roman military outposts from the Taunus Range in Germany to the banks of the Thames.

The insistence on preserving the state cult in Rome in spite of the appeal of the oriental cults should not be considered as mere mindless conservatism; rather, it was believed to be essential for the welfare of the state and the identity of the Roman people. But as Rome became an empire of diverse peoples and cultures, it was impossible for its subjects to find their identity in Roman tradition or indeed to find any sense of belonging or of personal security in the vast world in which they were engulfed. The close-knit groups of worshippers, the promises of security in this life and the life to come, the sense of awe that the exotic rites provided combined to offer the sense of identity and certainty that all else lacked. Even the adherents of some of the Hellenistic philosophies, notably those who revived the teachings of the sixth-century B.C. mathematician-musician, Pythagoras, organized themselves into brotherhoods and constructed chapels where study and meditation could be pursued. The spirit of the Neo-Pythagoreans was to be an important factor in the rapid development of ascetic and even monastic life among Christians of subsequent centuries.

Rome's contact with the religious philosophy of Greece and the gods of the East was an outcome of her commercial and military operations in the eastern

Mediterranean. For centuries, Romans had modestly busied themselves developing and safeguarding agriculture and commerce within the limits of the Italian peninsula. But in the process of extending their power over all of Italy, they fell into conflict with the Phoenicians, who dominated the sea from their capital, Carthage, across the Mediterranean in North Africa. In the course of her long struggle with Carthage (264–146 B.C.), Rome gained control of the southern coast of France and Spain, and became mistress of the western Mediterranean. Only then was she ready to extend her power to the east.

Rome's sympathy with the democratic ideals of the Greek city-states moved her to aid Greece in her struggles during the early second century B.C. against the Macedonians and other Hellenistic kingdoms that were competing for the opportunity to absorb her. But Rome's motives in turning to the aid of Greece were not altogether unselfish, for her commercial success in the West had led her to cast ambitious eyes toward the East. When a Seleucid ruler (Antiochus the Great) intervened to support Macedonia in an invasion of Greece, he was defeated by the Roman army and driven back into Syria (192–190 B.C.). Now Rome was in control of Greece, Illyria (modern Yugoslavia), and Asia Minor as far east as the Taurus Mountains. By treaty and military conquest, her expansion continued steadily for more than a century (200–63 B.C.), until at last Syria herself, including Palestine, became a Roman province. Egypt continued her independence under the Ptolemies, although Rome had to intervene in 168 B.C. to keep the Seleucids from taking over. The final round in Rome's battle for the East came in 30 B.C., when, following the defeat of Anthony by Octavian (Augustus) and the suicide of Cleopatra, Egypt too became a part of the Roman Empire. Augustus' victory was the crowning one; the Mediterranean had become a Roman lake; what began as a defense of democracy had ended in the establishment of the most powerful empire the world had ever seen.

The calm that fell after Augustus' destruction of his enemies brought peace to the empire but not peace of mind to its peoples. In the long struggle for power, the Roman ideals of democracy had been crushed. Public and private morality had declined appallingly in the presence of new wealth and power. The local Roman gods had been offered up on the altar of political expediency, for over and over again the Roman leaders had honored foreign gods in order to win the favor of subject peoples. The strict moral philosophy that the Roman ruling classes had borrowed from the Greeks had withered away. And, in spite of efforts to create a kind of universal religion by identifying the Greek and Roman gods with those, for example, of Egypt, men everywhere were left with no sense of religious certainty. Instead of worshiping the gods who were meant to keep things as they were, men searched for a religion that would deliver them from the evils of this world and would provide a promise of new life in the next.

THE DECLINE OF PHILOSOPHY

Although the Greeks tried hard to spread their culture throughout the civilized world, the rich tradition of Greek philosophy degenerated on foreign soil. And even at home, the lofty heights of philosophy reached by Plato were never attained by any of his successors in the Academy.

The Decline of Platonism

In the golden age of Greek philosophy, Plato had taught that reality does not consist of specific, tangible objects or observable activities like houses, men, and good or evil deeds. Rather, reality consists of *the idea or universal pattern of any particular class of object.* For example, the *idea* of "house" exists independently of whether or not a particular house exists; the *idea* of "goodness" exists independently of whether or not men do in fact perform good deeds. These "ideas," Plato suggested, exist eternally; they are not concepts that exist only in men's minds; they are the true and perfect realities of which the objects and actions we know in this world are only imperfect copies. Even though by the beginning of the Christian Era philosophers who claimed to subscribe to Plato's thought had debased his system, his understanding of reality had an important influence on Christian thinking almost from the start.

The Appeal of Stoicism

The name Stoic was originally given to the philosophical school founded by Zeno (336–264 B.C.), who instead of giving his lectures in a hall, as did other teachers of the day, gathered his pupils around him in one of the colonnades or *stoas* adjoining the public market place of Athens. During Zeno's lifetime, and for centuries after his death, the Stoic way of life continued to attract a large following among both aristocrats and the common people. Perhaps the chief appeal of the great Stoic figures was their personal character and quality of mind, for they were earnest men of great moral integrity. Their outlook on life was one of quiet joy and serenity, and they accepted suffering and tragedy with calmness. Although their ascetic ways discouraged pleasure-seekers from following them, their ability to discipline themselves appealed to many in an age when the moral standards of public officials and private individuals were notoriously low.

The Stoics rejected the Platonic belief that ideas exist independently of man and of the physical universe, and affirmed instead that the real world is the world of material bodies acting and reacting upon one another. They believed

THE AGORA AT ATHENS
was the marketplace and main gathering point of the city. The Acropolis is the hill on the right; the reconstructed portico known as the Stoa of Atallos is in the center; and the temple of Haephestus, commonly but erroneously called "The Theseum" is the well-preserved building on the extreme left. (American School of Classical Studies, Athens)

that the universe is a single organism energized by a world-soul, just as man is a body energized by a human soul. Soul itself is an extremely fine bodily substance that penetrates everything and is to be found in greater degree in man, in lesser degree in animals and inanimate objects. This world-soul is Reason, an impersonal force that operates throughout the universe, shaping its destiny, and bringing it to its predetermined goal. Then evil will be overcome, and great happiness unknown since the legendary past will again prevail. The true unity of man will be realized in the establishment of a great brotherhood of mankind. The world will be absorbed by God, who is all in all; a great conflagration will purge the universe, and a new cycle of the ages will begin.

Critics of the Stoics scoffed at the notion that the history of the world is the unfolding of a divine purpose, claiming instead that man is free to make his own decisions on the basis of what serves his natural desires, and that there are, after all, no certainties in this world, only degrees of probability.

In spite of critical attacks, Stoicism continued to exert a powerful influence down into the Christian Era. The two greatest figures in the later period of Stoic thought were Epictetus, a contemporary of Paul the Apostle, and Marcus Aurelius, the philosophizing Roman emperor of the second century A.D.

Epicurus' Vision of the Pleasant Life

A more sophisticated philosophy than Stoicism was that of Epicurus (341–270 B.C.), whose views were adopted by such outstanding Roman thinkers of the first century B.C. as Lucretius and the Latin poet, Horace. Epicureanism never exercised a wide popular appeal, however, largely because it pictured the gods as far removed from the world and utterly indifferent to human affairs. Contrary to popular misconception, Epicureanism did not teach self-indulgence; rather, it taught peace of mind based on the conviction that the universe operates according to fixed laws over which man has no control, and in which the gods have no interest. Its chief concern was to free man from anxieties over the terrors of hell, and from fear of the acts of capricious gods. Although the scientific treatises of the Epicureans (like Lucretius' *On the Nature of Things*) are filled with quaint and fascinating speculations on the natural world, their ethical and religious statements sound like commonplaces from the pen of some contemporary writer telling his readers how to stop worrying, how to find inner peace, how to live bravely in the face of adversity, and so on.

The Hybrid Philosophies

None of these philosophies continued for long in a pure form. As the years passed, elements from all of them were merged into a kind of generalized religious philosophy, which became immensely popular among self-styled intellectuals during the last century B.C. and the first Christian century. To this philosophical mixture each of the philosophical schools contributed some facet of its thought. Stoicism provided its stress on reason, thereby permitting the hybrid philosophers to claim that they were essentially rational in their approach to truth. From Platonism came the yearning for a vision of the eternal world. But Platonism itself provided no mediators to bridge the gap between the finite world, known to human senses, and the eternal world. Accordingly, the popular philosophies developed hypotheses about ways of mediation through which men might attain direct knowledge of the eternal. From Stoicism and Epicureanism came curiosity about the physical world; so the composite philosophy had its quasi-scientific interests as well.

One of the best-known of the eclectics (*i.e.*, a thinker who chooses what suits his fancy from a variety of philosophical systems) was Seneca (4 B.C.–A.D. 65), a chief adviser at the court of the Emperor Nero. Even though his basic viewpoint was a modified Stoicism, Seneca drew heavily on Plato and Epicurus and on anyone else whose moral teachings happened to appeal to him at the moment.

Perhaps the most prolific of the eclectic philosophers of the first Christian century was a Jew named Philo. Born into a prominent family among the nearly third of a million Jews of Alexandria, Philo distinguished himself in public affairs as leader of an embassy to the court of the Emperor Gaius Caligula (A.D. 37–41), and in intellectual circles as the first thinker to join together in thoroughgoing fashion rational philosophy and the revealed religion of the Jews.

Philo's voluminous writings consist chiefly of long treatises on the spiritual (*i.e.*, philosophical) meaning of the narratives and laws included in the Hebrew Bible. For example, Abraham's journey from Ur in Mesopotamia to Hebron in Palestine is really not a narrative of ancient Semitic nomads, but a description of the spiritual journey of the seeker after truth, who moves from the world of the sense (Ur) to the place where he has a direct vision of God (the promised land of Palestine. By fanciful explanations of Old Testament stories, names, and numbers, Philo tried to show that the sacred books of the Old Testament were really saying the same things as the religious philosophers of his own day. Although we have no evidence that Philo's writings attracted a wide following among Gentiles, they do show how eager the Jews of the first century A.D. were to find in the Bible some knowledge of God that would be rationally defensible and that would at the same time provide an experience of God's living presence. In his interpretations of the Old Testament, Philo uses many of the commonplaces of Stoic and Platonic philosophy as they had come to be understood in his time.

Growing rapidly alongside these movements in philosophy, and at times overlapping them, were three other closely related approaches to the universe: astrology, magic, and Gnosticism.

EFFORTS TO CONTROL A HOSTILE UNIVERSE

Astrology developed in Mesopotamia, where for centuries men had observed and recorded the orderly movements of the stars and planets. At last they had come to the conclusion that the stars possessed power over human affairs, and that the particular configuration of the stars at the time of a man's birth shaped his destiny. To gain happiness in life, therefore, man must try to understand and, if necessary, to placate the star spirits. Plato's belief that the stars were gods (*Timaeus*, Section 40) had provided a link between those astrological speculations and the Greek philosophical tradition. Other Hellenistic philosophers, by combining astrology with Greek mathematics, heightened the sense of order and precision with which the stars moved. As a result, men of the late Hellenic and early Roman periods grew apprehensive about the power of the stars, and more eager than ever to learn their secrets in order to gain the favor of the star spirits. Only in this way could men guarantee that the fate ordained for them by the stars would be a happy one.

The intense desire to curry the favor of the star spirits, and of other seem-

THE ORACLE AT DELPHI
was the site where the priestess of Apollo, after ceremonial preparation, uttered statements, often enigmatic, which were understood to be answers to questions addressed to her concening momentous personal and political problems. (Darryl Jones)

ingly hostile forces of nature, gave rise to formulas by which one could ward off evil, drive away pain, avert accidents. Societies sprang up that claimed to possess such secrets as astral knowledge, or the trick of staying on the right side of Asclepius, the god of healing. The magic formulas invoked the name of as many deities as possible in order to assure a happy outcome. One crudely written manuscript has been discovered in which the name of Jehovah (or Yahweh), the God of the Hebrews, is linked with Zeus, the chief god of the Greeks, and with the Egyptian god, Serapis. Presumably the man who knew the most magical words and how to invoke the greatest number of deities stood the best chance of gaining happiness in this world and the next.

As kingdoms fell and as life grew more uncertain, people of every class became more interested in life beyond the grave and more anxious to escape the catastrophes of life on this side of it. Even the magic formulas fell into disrepute, and many people turned elsewhere in their search for the secrets of life and death. Some believed that they possessed superior knowledge of history and secrets of the universe that had been revealed to them through visions of divine oracles. They claimed that they could help a man to learn his own fate, or, better still, to secure a happier one; they offered to teach the topography of the underworld to aid men on their journey back from death to the next life.

THE RISE OF GNOSTICISM

During the first century of the Christian Era, the Church carried on a running battle with groups within and outside the Church organization who claimed that they possessed superior knowledge of God and his purposes. In the second century A.D. these groups came to be known as *Gnostics,* a name taken from the Greek word *gnosis,* meaning "knowledge." They were the ones who were "in the know." We have no certain information about the origins of these groups, nor even whether the beginnings of this movement were among Jews or pagans. That Gnosticism was strongly influenced by pagan religious and philosophical developments cannot be doubted. The sharp dualism of the Gnostics, according to which light and darkness, good and evil, matter and spirit are set in sharpest contrast, seems to have arisen under the impact of Persian thought, within whose bounds precisely these pairs of realities were central. But whether there was a pre-Christian Gnosticism, as is often assumed,[1] we cannot determine. Indeed, it is even difficult to decide on a definition of Gnosticism.

If we were to content ourselves with some such minimal definition of Gnosticism as that it is "a dualistic-mythological religion of redemption through revelation and knowledge,"[2] then surely such religious ideas were abroad in pre-Christian times. What is distinctive about Gnosticism in its fully developed form, however, is (1) that it considers the supreme God to be utterly removed from the world and in no way responsible for its creation, which was accomplished by fallen angels or by one of a series of emanations from the supreme God; (2) that man's original being was purely spiritual but that the fall of man resulted in his imprisonment in a material body from which he required a redemptive agent to release him; and (3) that only through possession of this spiritual knowledge—which is not the same as either rational or empirical modes of cognition—can man liberate himself from this alien world and return to the realm of his origin. The mythological details of the later Gnostic systems vary widely, as do the ethical norms, which range from the ascetic to the libertine. But although the three elements listed above are constants in the verified Gnostic literature, they are not combined in religious writings of the pre-Christian period or even in writings that incorporate ideas largely originating in pre-Christian times. The Dead Sea Scrolls, for example, have been claimed

---

[1]This is the assumption of Rudolf Bultmann, as is evident in his *Theology of the New Testament,* I (New York: Scribner's, 1951), 164–183. This point of view, which has been taken by many New Testament scholars as self-evident, has been discredited by the work of Carsten Colpe, *Die Religionsgeschichtliche Schule,* I (Göttingen: Vandenhoeck & Ruprecht, 1961), who has shown that all the documentation we have for the Gnostic redeemer myth—the existence of which in pre-Christian times has been so widely assumed—is from the Christian Era.

[2]This definition of Gnosticism is offered by W. G. Kümmel in his *Introduction to the New Testament* (New York and Nashville: Abingdon, 1966), p. 159.

as evidence for pre-Christian Gnosticism, but there is no hint in them of the Creation as evil, no pejorative attitude toward the material world as such, no notion of a heavenly redeemer figure, and no conception of the fall of man as imprisonment in a body or of his redemption as release from a material body. In our study of Christian origins, therefore, we shall restrict the terms Gnostic and Gnosticism to those religious systems that include the three core elements mentioned above, on the assumption that the ingredients of Gnosticism were present in Hellenistic and even in Jewish thought before the first century A.D., but that they did not evolve into what is distinctively Gnostic until the second century.

Until recently, the oldest evidence available to us concerning Gnosticism was in the form of polemical attacks on Gnostics contained in the writings of second-century Fathers of the Church. Chief among these was Irenaeus, who left his native Asia Minor in the middle of the second century A.D. to become Bishop of Lyons in France. His best-known work was titled *Refutation and Overthrow of Gnosis Falsely So-Called* (usually known as *Against Heresies*). In this writing he quoted at length from Gnostic writings and refuted their claims by appeal to scripture and Church tradition.[3] Gnosticism, as depicted in its various forms by Irenaeus, was elaborately mythological, with multiple heavens and complex patterns of deities and celestial powers. In the teachings of one group called Sethians (for Seth, one of the sons of Adam and Eve, through whom these Gnostics traced their origin) or Ophites (since the serpent —in Greek, *ophis*—was worshiped by them) there is an elaborate account of the origins of the Trinity and of seven lesser deities generated by the Son. After giving their names, which are Greek versions of Hebrew names of God, the account continues:

> These heavens and excellences and powers and angels have places in heaven according to the order of their generation, and they invisibly reign over things celestial and terrestrial. When they had been made, his sons turned to a struggle for the primacy. Therefore in grief and despair Ialdaboth [the first of the lesser divinities] looked down on the dregs of matter and solidified his desire into it and generated a son. This son is Mind, twisted in the form of a serpent and is also Spirit and Soul and everything worldly. From him were generated all forgetfulness and wickedness and jealousy and envy and death.[4]

From even this brief excerpt, which differs in detail from the other Gnostic systems, it is evident that the basic problem with which the Gnostics were

---

[3]The full text (in translation) of Irenaeus' *Against Heresies* is found in *Ante-Nicene Fathers*, I (Grand Rapids, Mich.: Eerdmans, n.d.), 315–358. Excerpts from Irenaeus, together with translations of most of the available material relating to Gnostic origins, are given in *Gnosticism: A Sourcebook*, ed. R. M. Grant (New York: Harper & Row, 1961).

[4]Quoted from *Gnosticism: A Sourcebook*, ed. R. M. Grant (New York: Harper & Row, 1961), p. 54.

struggling was the involvement of man in the material world, subject as it is to decay, death, and defeat. As a part of the Creation, man is to some extent composed of matter, and the world of matter is subject to catastrophe and destruction. How can one believe in a just God and see the evil and disintegration that pervades the created world? Stated more personally, how can man become free from this involvement?

The divine process as seen by the Gnostics was one in which the lesser deities made unwitting errors, or in which their offspring became filled with pride and sought to usurp the powers of their betters. Man was considered to be a divided being: on the one hand he was imprisoned in the world of matter; on the other hand, the ultimate source of his being was the supreme deity, who was free of involvement in the Creation, dwelling in eternal light. The promise of the Gnostics was that by heeding secret knowledge and by the appropriate worship of the deities, man could ascend to the realms of light. In most of the Gnostic systems there was a redemptive figure who had come from the heavenly regions and had become ensnared and suffered in the material world, but who, having triumphed over these adversities, could lead the faithful back to the realm of pure spirit.

Until 1945, all that was available for the study of Gnosticism consisted of quotations from Irenaeus and other Church Fathers, in addition to some rather late (fifth-century) manuscripts, which unfortunately were not published until 1955 and subsequently. But in 1945 there was found in upper Egypt a large clay jar containing a number of manuscripts. Although it was nearly a decade before they began to become available for scholarly study, it was soon learned that the manuscripts were part of a library of works, written in Coptic,[5] which had once belonged to a church or monastery, the ruins of which were near the site of the discovery. It was obvious from the first information that was released concerning these finds that they were preserved by a Gnostic group, and that several of the documents were first-hand Gnostic writings. Others showed Gnostic tendencies. There are about fifty different treatises in the collection, some of them known previously only by title, some by quotations in the Church Fathers or from translations in other languages, and some not known at all. One writing, called the Gospel of Truth, is a thoroughly Gnostic document, and may have been written by Valentinus, one of the leading Gnostics whose ideas were attacked by Irenaeus. The Gospel of Thomas, which was known from a few quotations, and a few fragments of which had been found among other Egyptian papyri, was discovered apparently complete. Although it is not a gospel in the sense that it describes the ministry of Jesus, culminating in his crucifixion—no activities of Jesus are depicted at all, only

---

[5]Coptic is a language descended from ancient Egyptian, written in the Greek alphabet, with the necessary addition of extra letters to cover sounds not provided for in Greek.

his sayings—it does parallel many of the sayings in our New Testament gospels, and at some points it may preserve an older form of the sayings of Jesus than those found in the gospels as we know them.[6] Together with the fragmentary collections of sayings of Jesus discovered nearly a century ago in Egypt, the Gospel of Thomas, with its exclusive interest in the sayings of Jesus (as contrasted with his activity), confirms the thesis that in some segments of the early Church Jesus was conceived as the bearer of divine wisdom.[7] By the middle of the second century, the Gnostics had transformed this view of Jesus into one that portrayed him as essentially the supreme manifestation of divine wisdom or Sophia, rather than as a historical person.

We may ask what light these discoveries shed on the origins of Gnosticism. The answer cannot be categorical, but the fact that all these documents employ Jewish-Christian vocabulary in spite of their heterodox views would suggest that Gnosticism as an organized movement arose on Christian soil. It is an aberration from, or rose concurrently with, Christian teaching. A major ingredient in the development of Gnostic thought, however, seems to have been the Jewish apocalyptic writings,[8] since the names of the demons and angels and the elaborate descriptions of the celestial regions in the Gnostic writings closely resemble or are in some cases identical with those found in the apocalyptic writings. We have already noted that the dualistic view of the world that is expressed in apocalypticism came into Judaism under pagan (Persian) influence, but the Gnostic movement itself seems to have developed from Jewish and Christian sources. Although our sources are late and fragmentary, there is evidence that the Jewish sects in the east Jordan and southern Syria regions were or became Gnostic by the second century A.D. One such group, the Mandaeans—whose name means "knowers" (Gnostics)—originated in this area, and then moved to Iraq, where they still exist as a small practicing

---

[6]Already an extensive literature has appeared dealing with these Gnostic documents. A brief, reliable account of the discovery and contents is by W. Van Unnik, in *Newly Discovered Gnostic Writings* (London: SCM Press, 1960). A fuller description of the discovery, together with a translation of the Gospel of Thomas, was written by J. Doresse, *The Secret Books of the Egyptian Gnostics* (New York: Viking, 1960). *The Gospel of Truth* was edited and translated by K. Grobel (New York: Abingdon, 1960). The text and translation of *The Gospel of Thomas* was published by Harper & Row in 1959.

[7]See H.-Ch. Puech in *New Testament Apocrypha*, I, ed. W. Schneemelcher, tr. R. McL. Wilson (Philadelphia: Westminster, 1963), p. 286.

[8]Apocalyptic, from the Greek *apocalypto*, meaning "reveal, disclose," is used with reference to a body of literature that arose in the last centuries before the birth of Christ and in the first century A.D. These writings purport to predict how God will act in the future in behalf of his Chosen People. The picture of the future is given in elaborate imagery and symbols, often recounted in the form of dreams. It is a primitive way of viewing history, the consummation of which is expected in the near future. A discussion of the historical situation in Judaism out of which this literature arose is given in the next chapter.

Gnostic group.[9] But the only Gnostic writings we have that go back to the early stages of the movement are based on Christian and Old Testament ideas and language, even though the whole complex of ideas has been set in a new framework.

One explanation which has been offered for the emergence of the new framework in which Gnosticism placed old material is the failure of the expectation held by Jews and early Christians that God was very soon going to establish a New Age.[10] Instead of locating the fulfillment of redemptive hope in the Future Age, as Jewish prophetism and apocalypticism did, it was now envisioned as occurring in another sphere of existence in a timeless present. Instead of taking place on the plane of world history, the redemption was seen as happening in cosmic history—or perhaps in the realm of man's own personal history as an inner experience. Indeed, the fruitfulness of Gnostic perspectives for providing man with an understanding of himself is evident even today in the interest of existentialist philosophers[11] and theologians,[12] as well as depth psychologists,[13] in Gnostic literature.

Although we cannot regard developed Gnosticism as an antecedent of Christianity, we can see that the use of Gnostic modes of interpretation in the early centuries of the Church's life was of profound importance in enabling Christian propagandists to appeal to sophisticated pagans. Unfortunately, the Gnostic modes very soon crowded out the essence of Christian faith, so that Gnosticism in its fully developed forms had to be repudiated by the Church. Yet, even over the span of centuries, we can sense what an enormous appeal it must have exerted for men foundering in an uncertain or even meaningless world. It gave

---

[9]For a sympathetic account of this group, see E. S. Drower, *The Mandaeans of Iraq and Iran* (Leiden: E. J. Brill, 1962). The Mandaean literature has been pointed to as preserving pre-Christian Gnostic material, but in its present form we cannot with any confidence go behind the fifth- or sixth-century stage of development of the Mandaeans. It sheds little light on Gnostic origins.

[10]The theory that Gnosticism arose through the transformation of apocalyptic eschatology in the speculative climate of the Hellenistic world is developed by R. M. Grant, *Gnosticism and Early Christianity* (New York: Columbia University Press, 1959), especially pp. 150–185.

[11]A comprehensive survey of the rise of Gnosticism by a sympathetic philosopher is presented in Hans Jonas, *The Gnostic Religion* (Boston: Beacon Press, 1958). Unfortunately, this penetrating survey relies too heavily on the late Mandaean materials for its reconstruction of what is presented as pre-Christian Gnosis.

[12]Especially R. Bultmann, whose two-volume *Theology of the New Testament* (New York: Scribner's, 1951) shows how attractive the Gnostic attempt at providing man with an understanding of his existence can be for modern man. It is significant that Bultmann's *Commentary on John* (Philadelphia: Westminster, 1970) interprets the central Christian message along lines that are wholly sympathetic with the Gnostic motifs that Bultmann sees at work in John's gospel.

[13]Psychologists of the Jungian school have long been attracted to Gnostic writings in their search for the "master images" in terms of which C. C. Jung set forth his analysis of man's collective history, his self-consciousness, and his place in the universe. It is not surprising that one of the most important of the Egyptian Coptic manuscripts, the Gospel of Truth, was purchased for the Jung Institute and named the Jung Codex.

them a sense of identity with an elect community to whom God had granted secret knowledge of the reality behind the present world and a sense of assurance about the world to come.

THE RISE OF THE MYSTERY RELIGIONS

Among those who claimed access to the secrets of life were the groups of worshipers who made up the so-called mystery cults. Through participation in religious dramas and other ceremonies, the initiates of these cults believed that they could share in the life of the gods. The myths on which the mysteries were based varied from country to country, but the basic intent and the general pattern of the myths were common to all. In most cases there is a wife (or mother) who grieves for her lost husband (or child). After a period of suffering, the son or daughter is restored to the mother—usually from the dead —and begins a new life.

The Mystery of Osiris

In the Egyptian cults, the myth tells of Isis and her consort Osiris, a divine king of ancient Egypt. Osiris was seized by his enemies, killed, and dismembered, and Isis wandered over the earth searching for his body, burying each part as she found it. Part of Osiris' corpse was eaten by the fish in the Nile, which the Egyptians believed to flow into the underworld; as a result, Osiris became god of the underworld, where he ruled over the dead. In a series of elaborate ceremonies, described in detail in the *Metamorphoses* of Apuleius, a Latin writer of the second century A.D., an initiate re-enacts the suffering and journey to death that Osiris experienced. As a result of the initiate's union with Osiris, the king of the dead, death has no more fears for him and he is assured of life beyond death. The dignity of the cultic ritual, the splendor of the robes worn by the priests, and the awesomeness of the drama combined to give the worship of Isis and Osiris a tremendous appeal, not only in Egypt but in Rome and throughout the empire as well.

Greek Mystic Saviors

In Greece, the mystery cults developed around the myth of Dionysus, the god of wine, and Demeter, the goddess of grain. Dionysus was the son of Zeus, the father of the gods, and was destroyed and devoured by the Titans. His heart, however, was snatched from them and given to Semele, one of the wives of Zeus, who bore another Dionysus to the father of the gods. Since the race of man sprang from the Titans, the divine spark that the Titans took in by eating Dionysus was also present in man. Through mystical union with

Dionysus, man could purge away the earthly aspect of his existence and, by rekindling the divine spark, could enter more closely into the life of the gods. From the classical era of Greece down into the Roman period, union with Dionysus was sought by groups of people—especially women—who through night-long ceremonies and the drinking of wine entered into a state of frenzy in which the god allegedly appeared to them. A gruesome account of one such ecstasy is preserved in the *Bacchae*, by Euripides (*ca.* 485–406 B.C.), one of classical Greece's greatest dramatists.

DIONYSUS, *the god of wine, with a procession of his devotees. Fifth century* B.C. *vase.* (Metropolitan Museum of Art)

In the cluster of myths that have survived, Demeter is pictured as the goddess of earth, whose daughter, Persephone, was stolen from her by the god of the underworld. In her grief, she neglects the earth, and all vegetation withers and dies. Through the intervention of other gods, Persephone is restored to her, but since Persephone has eaten food in the lower world she must return there for a part of each year. During the months of the year when mother and daughter are united, the earth rejoices and vegetation flourishes; but during the winter months Demeter mourns her lost child. While Demeter was searching for her daughter, she disguised herself as a child's nurse and stayed at Eleusis, a town about twelve miles from Athens. From early Greek times, a series of ceremonies was conducted here every year, beginning with a procession from Athens, and including the reenactment of the mourning of Demeter, the journey of Persephone into the underworld, and her joyous return.

Only the general outline of the Eleusinian and other mysteries is known, but we know they were attended by thousands every year from all over the civilized world. From the time of Caligula (A.D. 37–41), who granted permission for the worship of Isis to be carried on in Rome, to the initiation of Julian (A.D. 331–363) into the cult of Attis, the mysteries found support in high places in the empire.

Scholars have offered various theories to account for the origin of the mysteries. The fact that one of the most important of the sacred objects displayed to the initiates at Eleusis was a stalk of grain suggests that the rites originated as a magical means of guaranteeing good grain crops. This conjecture is confirmed by the way in which the sacred mystery dramas follow the pattern of recurrent death (sowing), mourning (the winter period when seeds are dormant), and life from the dead (growth and harvest). In one of the cultic liturgies, the priest shouted at the sky, "Hu-eh" (meaning "rain"), and at the earth, "Ku-eh" (meaning "bring forth"). The myth of Isis was clearly associated with the annual flooding by the Nile, which was the sole source of fertility for the land of Egypt.

But it is obvious that by Hellenistic times the ceremonies had become far more than rituals performed to insure good crops. The crops' cycle of life and death had become a symbol of man's cycle of life and death, and the intent of the mystery drama was to assure new life not for the crops, but for the worshiper. In an age when the future held so little promise, and when the old order had broken down, men turned with enthusiasm to these cults with their secrets of life beyond death and their guarantees of immortality.

The mystery religions had another strong appeal: the initiates of each cult were united in a brotherhood from which the barriers of race and social standing were erased. All presented themselves to the deity on the same level, and through participation in the sacramental rites all were united into a fellowship that was to endure forever. That the mysteries were ridden with superstition, that the myths on which they were based were jumbled and contradictory, and that they provided no basis for social or individual morality seem to have mattered only to cynics and critical satirists. Slaves and freedmen, middle-class merchants and artisans, men and women of the upper classes—all flocked to the mystery cults in their search for security and a sense of community in an age of uncertainty.

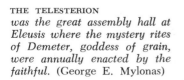

THE TELESTERION
was the great assembly hall at Eleusis where the mystery rites of Demeter, goddess of grain, were annually enacted by the faithful. (George E. Mylonas)

Ironically, the effort to create one world, begun by Alexander and achieved by Augustus, produced the opposite of what was intended. By melting nations and peoples together in a single vast empire, individuals felt lost in a universe beyond their comprehension or control. As an antidote to this depersonalization, the voluntary communities created by the religious cults and the philosophizing sects offered new forms of identity and enabled their adherents to reappropriate old traditions in new ways.

The People
of the Book
and Their Destiny

CHAPTER TWO

To the inhabitants of most major cities of the Roman Empire in the first century A.D. there was one religious community in particular that was notable for its cohesive life. This was the Jewish community which, though it looked to Jerusalem as its religious capital, had thriving settlements throughout the Graeco-Roman world. To the outsider, no religious group seemed more zealous for its religious convictions and way of life.

Some Gentiles were attracted to the beliefs and practices of the Jewish people. Their monotheistic faith and their rigorous concern for ethics led some into various modes of affiliation with the Jewish community. The efforts of such Jews as Philo of Alexandria (see pp. 25–26) to bridge the gap between Judaism and certain religious and philosophical beliefs of the Hellenistic world enhanced the possibility for such affiliation. But in a world where many minds were dominated largely by polytheistic tendencies, and where the close relation between religion and ethics was not consistently affirmed, disdainful and even hostile attitudes toward the Jewish faith were not uncommon. The resistance of the Jews to the popular religious beliefs was intolerable to most Gentiles, since they believed that prosperity and good fortune, in both civic and private affairs, depended upon the good favors of the popular deities. Resentment toward the Jews could be sharp, particularly in times of public crisis.

The religious zeal of the Jews as shown by their resistance to surrounding religious cultures was no new phenomenon; in varying degrees of intensity it had characterized the lives of many of their forebears for centuries. At the very heart of their religious faith was the conviction that the one and only God, Yahweh, had chosen and elected them as a people to bear faithful witness to him. Their destiny as a people, they believed, was inseparable from this faithful and singular witness. Their sacred writings preserved the record of their election in God's revelation to Moses; these writings told the story of the continuous appropriation of this central conviction by succeeding genera-tions of Jewish people. The persistent vitality of this conviction is clearly demonstrated in the way it flourished even more vigorously in the wake of historical events that seemed to threaten the existence of the Jewish community. Their reappropriation of the faith always involved the effort to understand what God was saying to them in the events of history, particularly in disastrous events. For they believed that their God was the Lord of history, confronting them as the living God and calling them to obedience and faithful witness to his will in the historical circumstances in which they found themselves.

Since the Jews believed that their God had spoken to their forebears throughout previous generations, and the record of his word was found in their sacred writings, they considered these writings the primary source for gui-dance in their efforts to understand their times and God's will. Therefore, to understand better Jewish religious life in the first century A.D., we will consider the important events that affected them and the religious beliefs, hopes, practices, and institutions that emerged over a period of several centuries.

THE JEWS UNDER FOREIGN DOMINATION: THE PERSIANS AND THE GREEKS

In the early sixth century B.C. occurred one of the most devastating events in the memory of the Jewish people. At that time the Babylonians destroyed Jerusalem and the Temple (in 586 B.C.), laid waste much of the land of Judah, and led into captivity in Babylonia the religious and political leaders of the Jews, along with thousands of their countrymen. To all appearances their religious and political existence had been dealt a mortal blow. The conse-quences of this event played a major role in shaping Jewish life and thought during later centuries. In the late sixth century, Persia overthrew the Baby-lonians and granted the Jewish exiles permission to return to their home-land (538 B.C.). Many of them were content to remain where they were, but others began a slow migration homeward that continued for a century. By

516 B.C., the Temple in Jerusalem had been reconstructed and work had been started on rebuilding the city and its walls. Because of opposition from hostile neighbors, however, the walls were not completed until shortly after 450 B.C.

By the end of the fifth century B.C., then, Jerusalem had once again become the center of Jewish national and religious life, even though the Jews were the political subjects of Persia. Though stripped of political power, the Jews were free to develop their religious life and thought with little interference from the Persian authorities. Under the leadership of their High Priest they developed into a small theocracy set within the confines of the Persian Empire.

When the Greeks under Alexander made their conquest of Persia and her territories, the Jews, like most of the oriental subjects of Persia, welcomed him as a liberator. During the period following Alexander's death, when the Jews were subjected first to the Ptolemies and then to the Seleucids, they enjoyed the same religious toleration they had experiencd under Persia. So long as they paid their tribute and offered no resistance to their rulers this condition continued—until the reign of the Seleucid king, Antiochus IV Epiphanes (175–164 B.C.). It was at this time that the Jewish people experienced the most serious threat to their existence that had arisen since the Babylonian Captivity.

The Maccabean Revolt

Ancient and modern historians have offered many reasons for Antiochus IV's attack on the Jews. Among them was a very practical economic reason. For some time, the Seleucids had been hard pressed for funds not only to carry on their feud with the Ptolemies, but also to maintain control over their vast holdings in the East. One of their sources of revenue was the Jewish nation. In addition to increasing the taxes levied on the Jews, Antiochus decided to offer the Jewish office of High Priest to the highest bidder. He deposed the rightful High Priest, Onias, and in his place appointed a man named Jason, who offered large sums of money for the office and agreed to support Antiochus in the Hellenization of the Jewish nation. Antiochus, who fancied himself a true representative of Hellenistic culture, was eager to force this culture upon all his subjects. It was this effort, in which Jason joined, that led to conflict between Antiochus and the Jews.

Jason built a gymnasium in the heart of Jerusalem in which young Jews, some of them from priestly families, exercised in the nude according to Greek custom. Some Jews even submitted to surgery to remove the distinctive marks of circumcision. These Greek practices horrified many of the Jews, who regarded them as contrary to their Law and in violation of their covenant with God. Consequently, a strong opposition party called the Hasidim (pious ones) arose in opposition to Jason and to the Jews who were sympathetic to Hellenization. The Hasidim fought against all efforts to adopt Greek ways, for to them these customs were inseparably bound up with the idolatry and immorality that they associated with the Greek religion and way of life.

ANTIOCHUS IV

(Epiphanes) on a Greek coin. The reverse side carries the Greek words: Basileos Antiochou, Theou Epiphanous, Nikephorou—*"(coinage) of King Antiochus, God Manifest, Bearer of Victory." The king represents himself as Zeus, seated on a throne, holding in his left hand a royal staff and in his right the figure of the goddess of victory, Nike, who holds in her hand the laurel wreath, symbol of victory.* (American Numismatic Society)

Antiochus finally realized that he could not bend the Jews to his will until he had first destroyed their religion. So in 168 B.C. he issued an edict of proscription. Under penalty of death all Jews were forbidden to circumcise, to celebrate religious festivals, or to observe the Sabbath. He ordered all copies of the Law to be destroyed, and anyone found in possession of it to be punished. Antiochus' men set up a Greek altar to Zeus in the Temple in Jerusalem, and sacrificed swine upon it. Heathen altars were erected throughout the land, and the Jews were compelled to worship heathen gods. To enforce his edict, Antiochus stationed troops throughout Israel.

Although the Jews who had favored Hellenization in the first place acceded to Antiochus' demands, the stubborn Hasidim refused to comply with the edict even though they were faced with martyrdom. Finally, the Jews revolted under the leadership of a priest named Mattathias (from the Hasmon family —Hasmoneans), who came from the village of Modin. After killing a Jew who was in the act of sacrificing on a pagan altar, Mattathias fled with his five sons to the rugged hill country outside Jerusalem. There they gathered around them followers who were ready to fight the Syrian oppressors in the name of God and in defense of their right to live according to their Law.

This action marked the beginning of the Maccabean Revolt, named for Judas Maccabeus, Mattathias' son who assumed command of the forces when his father died. The Syrians were little disturbed by the uprising, for the Jews had no trained militia, no arms, and almost no financial backing. But Antiochus underestimated their religious zeal, their bravery, and their ingenuity. Since the Jews were greatly outnumbered and had only crude weapons, they turned to guerrilla tactics against the Syrians. After suffering a number of discouraging defeats, Judas and his men made a heroic effort and finally managed to win a peace treaty from Antiochus' general, Lysias. In December, 165 B.C.,

PALESTINE
IN 30 A.D.

TETRARCHY OF
HEROD ANTIPAS
TETRARCHY OF PHILIP
UNDER PONTIUS PILATE
CITIES OF THE DECAPOLIS ✦
CITIES AND TOWNS ○

SEA

Sidon
Sarepta
Damascus

Tyre

PHOENICIA
Caesarea Philippi
PANIAS
ITURAEA
TRACHONITIS

Gischala
Meroth
GALILEE
GAULANITIS

Ptolemais
Chorazin
Bethsaida Julius
Gergesa?
BATANAEA
Raphana?

Cana
Capernaum
Magdala
Sepphoris
Tiberias
Gaba
SEA OF
GALILEE
Hippos
Dion
Canatha

Nazareth
Nain
Abila

Caesarea
Gadara

Scythopolis
Pella

Salim?
DECAPOLIS

Samaria, Sebaste
Sichem
Sychar?
JACOB'S WELL

SAMARIA
PERAEA

Joppa
Antipatris
Borcaeus
Gerasa

Lydda
Phasaelis

Emmaus
Archelais
Philadelphia

Jamnia
Jerusalem
Bethphage?
Jericho

Azotus
Bethlehem
(Qumram)
Bethany
Bethany Beyond Jordan?

Ascalon
JUDAEA

Gaza
Machaerus

Jorda
Hebron

Raphia
IDUMAEA
Masada

MEDITERRANEAN

DEAD SEA

Judas entered the Temple in Jerusalem, cleansed it, and reestablished the traditional Jewish worship. To the present day, Jews commemorate this triumphant event in the festival of Hanukkah (Rededication), the Feast of Lights.

Now that religious liberty had been restored, many of the Hasidim were apparently ready to withdraw from the revolt. But Judas and his followers carried on raids against the Ammonites and Idumeans, traditional enemies of the Jews, and led expeditions to Galilee and Gilead to rescue Jews who were suffering retaliation at the hands of Gentiles. The fact that the Syrians still were in control of strong fortifications in Judaea and in Jerusalem itself (the Acra) also must have increased Judas' reluctance to disband his forces. Furthermore, there was still an active Hellenizing party among the Jews that continued to seek the high priestly office and was quite ready to call upon the Seleucid king for assistance.

What had begun as a revolt for religious liberty now became a struggle for political freedom, a struggle that was carried on by the brothers of Judas after his death. Under the leadership of Simon (142–135 B.C.), the Jews took several strategic Syrian fortresses, including the Acra in Jerusalem, and thereby gained virtual independence. The people acknowledged Simon's success by naming him the legitimate High Priest, even though he was not a member of a high priestly family. As the years passed, efforts were made to enlarge the boundaries of the kingdom, and the Hasmonean rule became more obviously political. John Hyrcanus (135–104 B.C.), Hyrcanus' son, made notable strides toward his goal of restoring the boundaries of the former kingdom of David. This ambition was more nearly realized by Simon's son, Alexander Jannaeus (103–76 B.C.), who was more ambitious than his father and more ruthless in his tactics. Using mercenary troops, he even attacked fellow Jews who opposed his insatiable desire for expansion, and put to death many of the Jewish leaders. Under Alexander Jannaeus, the religious aims of the original Maccabean Revolt were all but obliterated, and most Jews looked upon him as disloyal to the cause of the original Maccabean heroes.

After Alexander Jannaeus' death, his widow Alexandra (76–67 B.C.) restored some degree of stability to the Jewish nation. But when she died, a dispute sprang up between her two sons over the succession. Each had his following among the Jews, and each sent an embassy to Pompey, in Syria, to seek Roman support. A third embassy, representing the Jewish people, requested that Pompey reject the monarchy altogether and restore the Jewish nation to its pre-Maccabean nonpolitical status.

UNDER ROMAN RULE: THE HERODIANS

In 63 B.C., with Pompey's arrival in Jerusalem, the political independence of the Jews was cut off once again. The territory now passed under Roman rule, and was made subject to Rome's representative in the territory of Syria.

Hyrcanus II, a son of Alexandra who was appointed High Priest by Pompey, faithfully carried out Rome's policy with the help of his minister, Antipater, an Idumean who was clearly motivated by personal ambition. During the long period of disturbances in Rome at the close of the Republican period, Antipater and his son Herod, through political astuteness and cunning, managed to stay in favor with a succession of Roman leaders. In 40 B.C., Rome named Herod ruler of both Judea and Samaria, with the title of king, although disturbances in Jerusalem made it impossible for him to ascend the throne until 37 B.C. Herod's rule (37–4 B.C.) was confirmed by Augustus Caesar in 30 B.C. Before Herod died, his kingdom had come to include not only Idumea, Judea, and Samaria, but also Perea in Transjordan, Galilee, and a territory north and east of the Sea of Galilee. It was this Herod who was ruler at the time of Jesus' birth.

Herod proved one of the most successful of Rome's puppet rulers, and he came to be known as Herod the Great. He restored some degree of law and order to troubled Palestine and set it up as a buffer state between Rome's territories and the marauding Arab peoples who constantly threatened the peace and Rome's lines of communication. Furthermore, in the fashion of a true Hellenistic monarch, he tried to foster in his kingdom Augustus' hopes for a common Graeco-Roman culture throughout the Roman Empire. Herod, as we noted above, gave support to the imperial cult and built temples honoring Augustus in cities of Palestine and Asia Minor. He rebuilt many old cities according to the Hellenistic pattern, and throughout the land he constructed gymnasia, theaters, and stadia to encourage the Hellenistic way of life.

But most of the Jews despised Herod for his Idumean ancestry and for his tireless efforts to Hellenize the kingdom. Furthermore, his ambitious building programs cost money that had to be raised by excessive taxation. Desperately jealous of his power and fearful lest he lose it, Herod filled the land with secret police and severely punished any Jew who aroused the least suspicion of disloyalty. He went so far as to have his mother-in-law, two of his sons, and his favorite wife (he had nine others) murdered because he suspected their loyalty. Herod did try, though in vain, to conciliate the Jews, for in hard times he eased their taxes and during famine he provided food. And he began the construction of a beautiful new Temple in Jerusalem (20 B.C.), though it was not completed until after his death. But all these efforts were to no avail. The land was seething with parties of dissatisfaction, and there is evidence that Herod shrewdly played one off against the other to heighten the internal unrest.

It is not surprising, then, that when Herod died in 4 B.C. the Jews sent an embassy to Augustus imploring that Rome refuse to execute Herod's will, in which he had appointed his sons as successors. When riots broke out in Judea, Varus, the Roman governor of Syria, was sent to quell them, and Augustus shortly approved Herod's will dividing the kingdom among his three sons. Archelaus was appointed ethnarch in Judea (4 B.C.–A.D. 6), Herod Antipas tetrarch of Galilee, Perea (4 B.C.–A.D. 39), and Philip tetrarch of Iturea, Tra-

WESTERN WALL
OF THE JERUSALEM TEMPLE,
*recently undergoing excavation,
is actually the lower part of the
enormous platform on which
the Temple was constructed by
Herod the Great.* (Khalil Rissas)

chonitis, Batanea, Auranitis, Gaulinitis, and Panias. Philip, most of whose subjects were Gentile, enjoyed a very successful rule. Herod Antipas was relatively successful in the eyes of Rome but distasteful to the Jews; it was under his rule that John the Baptist and Jesus carried on their ministries. Archelaus, who proved totally incompetent, was deposed after offending both Jews and Romans. Following Archelaus' deposition, Jerusalem and Judea passed under direct Roman rule administered by a succession of procurators. There was just one short break in the administration (from A.D. 41 to 44), when Herod Agrippa I, Herod the Great's grandson, was granted the rule of his grandfather's entire territory. Since the welfare of the Jewish nation during the years of Roman rule depended directly on the relations between the people and the procurators, we must consider more carefully the events of this period.

The Procurators (A.D. 6–66)

No less than fourteen procurators were sent to Judea during the sixty-year period from A.D. 6 to 66. As the years passed, tension between Rome and the Jewish people increased steadily, partly because of the character of the

44

procurators themselves. With few exceptions, these men failed to measure up to the highest standards of Roman administrative personnel, and their caliber seemed to decline with each successive appointment. Repeatedly, they made foolish judgments in administration, and often they were guilty of inordinate cruelty in carrying out official policies.

But the lot of the procurators was not easy, for they were appointed to govern one of the most troublesome territories under Roman rule—a territory that had grown increasingly resentful under years of alien control. Furthermore, they could not understand the Jews' stubborn resistance to Hellenistic religion and customs, and their persistent loyalty to their own religious faith— a faith that procurators looked upon as superstitious and barbarous. In the name of that faith, minor figures arose time and time again promising release from Roman rule. To the Romans, such promises carried with them the threat of political treason. A good example of the procurators' failure to understand the Jews occurred under Pontius Pilate (A.D. 26–36), before whom Jesus stood trial. On one occasion, in order to build a new aqueduct, Pilate appropriated funds from the Temple treasury in Jerusalem that were specifically designated for maintaining sacrifices. Then, when the people protested this outrage against their religion, he turned them away by force of arms. On another occasion, he offended the religious sensitivity of the Jews by bringing military insignia bearing the emperor's image into the city of Jerusalem. Pilate finally had to be removed from office when he commanded his soldiers to attack a crowd of defenseless Samaritans who had gathered to watch a self-styled prophet perform a miracle on Mt. Gerizim.

As time went by, an increasing number of Jews were drawn into groups (Zealots) that openly or secretly favored armed rebellion. Open hostility often flared up. Under Felix (A.D. 51–60), before whom the Apostle Paul was brought for a hearing, the Jewish reactionary groups became even more fanatical, and assassinations on both sides were common. Felix's ruthless reaction to his opponents drove still more Jews to adopt radical ways of showing their hatred. Albinus (A.D. 62–64), who was recalled by Rome because of his graft and his maltreatment of innocent people, emptied the jails of prisoners before he left Judea, flooding the country with brigands who added to the confusion of the times. By the time of Florus (A.D. 64–66), the last of the procurators, open fighting had become common. To add to the fury, Florus plundered the Temple treasury, and when the people demonstrated against his action he ordered many of them crucified. By A.D. 66, the situation had become so critical and the promise of improvement so remote that organized revolt against Rome finally broke out. (See pp. 133–134 for further discussion.)

But the rebellion of the Jews against the Romans was lost before it began, for the trained and powerful forces of Rome could not be overcome. Under the Roman generals Vespasian and Titus, the war was successfully concluded by Rome in A.D. 70, though the last remnants of resistance were not wiped out until A.D. 73. The city of Jerusalem suffered heavy damage during the fighting, and the Temple itself was destroyed. For the third time in their history, the Jews had suffered what appeared to be annihilating defeat; yet once again they managed to survive.

Although political, social, and economic factors contributed to the outbreak of the Jewish War, the desperate venture sprang primarily from religious motives. Most of the leaders of the revolt saw themselves as the true successors of the Maccabean heroes, and they fought the enemy for the sake of their faith. Like the revolt itself, the Jews' survival as a community can be understood only in terms of faith. And, since it was the religious development within the community that determined to a large degree the community's development, we must turn now to the faith of the Jewish community that sustained its life through these decisive periods in its history.

THE FAITH OF THE JEWISH COMMUNITY

After the calamity wrought by the Babylonians in 587 B.C., it was a resurgence of religious faith that had brought about the reconstitution of the Jewish community. The Jewish prophets and leaders during the Exile boldly declared that the victory of the Babylonians was not a sign of the weakness of their God Yahweh, but rather the means whereby he had revealed his judgment on his people for their sins. Looking back to the words of the great prophets Amos, Hosea, Isaiah, and Jeremiah, the Jews saw that through them God had repeatedly warned his people that continual refusal to obey his commands would lead to destruction. In the Exile, destruction had indeed come as testimony to the truth of all that the prophets had said.

The prophet whose words are found in the last chapters of the Book of Isaiah (40–66) saw in Cyrus' permission to the Jews to return to their homeland a sign of God's continuing concern for his people. By granting them an opportunity to renew their loyalty to him, God had provided the Jews with further evidence that he was not only their God but the only true God in all the universe. It was the mission of his people to bear witness to him to all the nations through their loyalty and obedience.

When the leaders of the returning Jews tried to understand just how the people had sinned and had brought down the judgment of God, they emphasized three major failures: First, the Jews had succumbed to idolatry and had turned to foreign gods rather than to Yahweh alone. Second, they had not worshiped Yahweh in purity, but had permitted their worship to become corrupted by all manner of foreign practices. Third, they had not obeyed the commandments that he had given them. With these failures in mind, the postexile Jews determined to guard against any intrusion into their religious belief and life that might turn them from worshiping God as he ought to be worshiped. They realized that all through their history God had been seeking to lead them to what they fully came to understand only through the Babylonian Captivity. They had been chosen by the one true God to know him, to worship him, and to live according to his commandments.

These convictions led to what has been called Jewish "particularism" or "exclusivism." It was not merely their belief that they were God's Chosen People that set the Jews apart from all other people. Given their firm conviction that belief, conduct, and worship were all of one piece, it was inevitable that they would seek to separate themselves from any mode of life that threatened the purity of any of the three. The Books of Ezra and Nehemiah show the lengths to which this particularism was carried, for in them the Jews returning to Judea after the captivity are forbidden to marry foreigners, and those who have married non-Jews are asked to put them aside. Such exclusivism can be understood only in the light of the religious zeal that prompted it—the earnest desire to avoid at all costs the disloyalty of their fathers. And since loyalty to Yahweh involved every aspect of life, it was dangerous to enter into close relations with those who lived in accordance with other ways. This exclusivism at its worst could become a cloak for the derision and hatred of other peoples. But at its best it was the Jews' testimony to the reality of the God they worshiped and the way of life into which faithfulness to him inescapably led them.

In the Hellenistic Age, when polytheism and idolatry were commonplace, and when religion and morality were not so clearly related as they were in Judaism, the exclusivism of the Jews stood out sharply against the pagan world. Concerted efforts to Hellenize the Jews, by such rulers as Antiochus Epiphanes, drove loyal Jews to defiance, since they felt that their way of life had been given by God himself, in the form of the Jewish Law. More than anything else, it was the Law that provided the bond between Jews and that distinguished them as a community from all other people.

THE CENTRALITY OF THE TORAH: THE AUTHORITY OF THE SCRIPTURES

The Jews were convinced that to avoid the recurrence of such a tragedy as the Babylonian Exile, they must know God's will as revealed in the Law of Moses and live in accordance with it. The Jews fervently believed that his Law had been given by divine revelation through Moses and was contained in the Pentateuch (the first five books of the Old Testament). It is now common knowledge that these books contain materials that were gradually brought together over many centuries and that it was not until the end of the fifth century B.C. that they reached their present state.

By the end of the third century B.C., the prophetic books (Amos, Hosea, Isaiah, and so forth) had also assumed the form in which they now appear and had been accepted as part of God's divine revelation to his people. In the New Testament, the phrase "the Law and the Prophets" is a reference to God's revelation to his people as it was contained in these holy scriptures. By the end of the first century B.C., all the books in the Old Testament, except for a very few, were regarded as divine revelation.

The English term *law* is not an adequate translation of the Hebrew word *Torah*, a fact that is obvious to anyone who reads the Pentateuch carefully. For the Pentateuch contains a great deal of legend, history, and myth, as well as specific rules or regulations. To the Jews, Torah was a very inclusive term that referred to all that God had revealed about himself, their history, and the conduct that was required of them. In time, the entire written revelation came to be referred to as Torah, though in the more narrow sense Torah always meant the Pentateuch, and often specifically God's commandments.

It is this centrality of the Torah in Judaism that accounts for the rise of a body of Jewish scholars known as the Scribes (*Sopherim*). Since knowledge of the Torah was so essential, there had to be authorities who were competent to interpret the meaning of Torah to the people. In the early post-exile period, the priests had been the learned men who were looked to as authorities. By the end of the third century B.C., some laymen had become Scribes charged with the responsibility of preserving the writings and giving the official interpretation of them. The conviction had arisen by that time that God was no longer revealing his will through prophets but that the authority for understanding and interpreting God's will now resided largely with the Scribes, who accordingly thought of themselves as the successors to the prophets.

The Torah, then, provided the basis for the common belief and conduct that characterized Jewish life and bound Jews together wherever they might be. But no institution in Judaism was more important in transmitting knowledge of the Torah and in nurturing deep reverence for it than the synagogue (transliterated from a Greek word meaning *assembly*). It is impossible to speak with certainty of the precise origins of the synagogue. It may have had its inception during the exile in Babylonia, when the Temple no longer stood and the Jews, far from their home, came together for worship, deliberation, and mutual support. Long before the end of the first century B.C., the synagogue had become a well-established institution, though its significance had evolved gradually. In the lands where Jews were dispersed, Greek became their common language, so that the scriptures were translated into Greek and read in the synagogues. A legend that this version was made by 70 inspired translators gave it the name Septuagint, abbreviated as LXX. Whenever Jews lived throughout the Graeco-Roman world, the synagogue served as the center of Jewish life and thought. Indeed, the term *synagogue* referred not so much to a place of meeting as to the coming together of Jews in any locality. It was an assembly for worship for Jews who had no temple, an occasion to read and interpret the Torah in the presence of the community. And it was in the synagogue that the "elders," the respected counselors of the local Jewish community, sought ways in which the Jews could adjust to an alien environment

destiny. They endeavored in their reading of the Torah to interpret and express their expectations for their own times.

Popular thought was increasingly dominated by the coming of the Kingdom of God. While the coming of the Kingdom meant essentially the establishment of God's rule and sovereignty over the world, there was considerable variation in the beliefs regarding the nature of his rule, how he would establish it, and the conditions in which it would become a reality. One line of such expectation had its roots in the time before the exile. This was the hope for the coming of an ideal ruler who would establish a reign of righteousness and peace throughout the world. As time passed the Jews came to believe that this ruler would be a descendant of David the King, and that he would restore the Kingdom of David, which the Jews increasingly tended to idealize. A corollary of this hope was the belief that the Jewish nation would regain the political prestige it had once enjoyed, but its ultimate meaning was that the nation's resurgence would vindicate the faith of the Jews and the righteousness of God.

Emerging into prominence during the second and first centuries B.C., however, was a more radical mode of thinking about the meaning of the Kingdom of God and its coming. It was radical in that it envisaged God's bringing about a complete transformation of man and the world as the only context in which his rule could be realized. The reasons for this evolving mode of envisaging the Kingdom are complex, but two influences were undeniably important. First, as the result of repeated defeats by the Seleucids, the continuing disillusionment over the political-minded Hasmoneans, and the subjection and oppression at the hands of Rome, many Jews came to believe that only through some radically transforming act of God himself could they ever be vindicated and the oppressors brought under judgment. Second, there was the growing belief that the world and man lay in the power of evil spirits who could not be defeated by human agencies alone. Under the impact of Persian religious thought, which had first made a strong impression on the Jews during the exile in Babylonia, dualistic tendencies influenced their thinking. They conceived of the world as the battleground of two opposing realms, the realm of God and the realm of Satan, with all men divided between those who fought in faithfulness for God and those who served Satan. Although the powers of evil seemed to have the upper hand for the time being, the Jews were confident that God's rule would prevail. The day was coming when he would once and for all destroy the realm of Satan and bring in a new age in which his people would be vindicated in the Kingdom of God.

During the last two centuries B.C. there emerged a whole body of literature[1] dealing with the conflict between the kingdom of God and the kingdom of

---

[1]Such writings have been brought together in modern times into two great collections, called *The Apocrypha* and *The Pseudepigrapha*. See R. H. Charles, *The Apocrypha and Pseudepigrapha of the Old Testament*, 2 vols. (Oxford: Clarendon Press, 1963). The literature has been expanded with the discovery of the Dead Sea Scrolls.

Satan, and with the great victory that God would eventually bring about. In general, the struggle was portrayed as growing increasingly worse until a violent conflict broke out among mankind, accompanied by violent disruptions in the whole natural order. Finally, in a totally renewed order of existence, God's kingdom would prevail, God's faithful servants who had died would be raised up to live in joy and peace, and God's purposes in creating the world would be brought to fulfillment.

Although the Jews felt that it was God himself who would bring about this final renewal, there was a growing tendency to think that it would be accomplished by the Messiah, one anointed by God as his agent in carrying out his purposes. Not all the Jews thought of the Messiah in the same way. Some expected him to be a human being who would emerge from the Jewish people, perhaps the long-expected ruler from the Davidic line. Others believed the origin of the Messiah to be cloaked in mystery. Some texts suggest the expectations of a divine being who would descend from heaven and lead the righteous to a transformed life in the kingdom of heaven. The messianic figure of the Son of Man in the Book of Enoch might be such a Messiah. But most Jews agreed that the Messiah's coming would mark the beginning of God's victory over the powers of evil.

This type of thinking about the events related to God's final judgment on evil is referred to technically as *eschatological,* a term that comes from the Greek word meaning "final" or "end." Another term used to describe such speculative thought is *apocalyptic,* derived from a Greek term meaning "revelation." Writers who dealt with eschatology presented revelations regarding the end that purportedly had been given to ancient worthies such as Enoch, Noah, and Abraham. Although the various apocalyptic and eschatological writers made use of a wide range of mythological images, they were all interested in making one point: that God would triumph over evil and bring to completion his purposes.

Throughout the period from the Maccabean Revolt to the end of the war with Rome, the eschatological hopes of the Jews fanned the flames of their religious zeal and held them firm in their resistance to any violation of the Torah. Soon after the Maccabean War broke out, the apocalyptic Book of Daniel was written, urging the Jews to stand firm in their faith since God's kingdom was at hand and the kingdom of evil was about to be destroyed. Appropriately, evil was personified in the Seleucid kingdom. Later, under Roman domination, other apocalyptic writings appeared in which Rome was identified with the reign of evil. The sharper the crisis, the more brightly the Jewish hopes flamed.

When the final battle with Rome took place in A.D. 66, these hopes undoubtedly played a major role in rallying the Jews to action. Those who thought of God's victory in political terms stood side by side with those who looked for some cataclysmic transformation of the world and a renewed order of existence. For Rome was both the political enemy of the Jewish nation and a personification of the evil that thwarted the rule of God himself. But it was primarily the religious hope that led the Jews to throw themselves into conflict with Rome. This was a hope common to all Jews, for all had been nourished on the conviction that God would vindicate their faithfulness to him before the eyes of the whole world.

JEWISH SECTARIAN GROUPS

Although the worldwide Jewish community was bound together by Torah and Temple, certain differences did spring up on the basis of divergent interpretations of Torah. Disagreements arose between the Jews of Palestine and those of the Diaspora, such as Philo of Alexandria. Under the influence of Hellenistic thinking and the necessity of living among predominantly Gentile populations, the non-Palestinian Jews had made various modifications and accommodations in their religious thought and practice. But·even in Palestine differences in the interpretation of Torah occurred. These differences are clearly illustrated by three important sectarian groups which on numerous points of belief and practice were at odds with one another: the Sadducees, the Pharisees, and the Essenes. Recognition of these differences is essential for anyone who would understand the flexibility, diversity, and serious tensions of Judaism in the first century of our era.

The Sadducees

Concerning the origin of the term *Sadducee*, and of the sect itself, there is considerable uncertainty. The first mention of the sect is given by the Jewish historian, Josephus, discussing events in the time of John Hyrcanus (135–104 B.C.). According to one hypothesis which has received considerable support, the term *Sadducee* was derived from *Zadok (Zadokite)*. In the Old Testament the legitimate priestly office of Aaron is said to have been given to Zadok and his descendants. According to this hypothesis, since the principal claim and concern of the Sadducees was the legitimate succession of the priestly office, this derivation of the name and the movement seems justified.

Since no literature of the Sadducees is extant, and our knowledge about them is derived from the writings of rival movements, it is difficult to reconstruct a full and accurate account of their beliefs and practices. In comparison with the *Pharisees* and the *Essenes* their religious outlook was conservative. Their central guide in religious matters was the Law of Moses, the first five books of the Old Testament. In these books are contained the basic rules and regulations governing the Temple, the priesthood, and the sacrificial rites. How the Scribes of the Sadducees interpreted the meaning of the sacrifices cannot be known. This much seems clear: they believed that faithful and literal fulfillment of God's provision for sacrificial worship in the Temple was the crucial requirement in maintaining Israel's covenant relationship with God. Here was their focus of religious piety.

The influence and prerogatives of the Sadducees reached beyond the confines and activities of the Temple and its priesthood. They enjoyed a dominant position in the Sanhedrin, whose presiding officer was the High Priest. Considering the authority of the Sanhedrin, the potential for wielding influence over the life of the Jews is quite obvious. Only the Pharisees, who gradually increased in strength, were powerful enough to challenge both their influence and their interpretation of the Torah. The sphere of Sadducean involvement and influence was even broader. Through their dominant role in the Temple and the Sanhedrin, the Sadducean priesthood and its supporters were the official spokesmen for the Jews in their dealings with Rome. Drawn largely from the wealthy, aristocratic, priestly families, they were concerned and in close touch with both the economic and political problems of the harassed nation. When possible they followed the road of peaceful coexistence with the civil authorities. Nevertheless, on occasion they were capable of resistance when a political authority ventured to control and manipulate the office of High Priest, or plundered the treasury of the Temple.

Placing supreme value upon the Law of Moses, the Sadducees relegated the prophetic and other writings of the Old Testament to a place of secondary importance. They were particularly opposed to apocalyptic and eschatological thought, on the grounds that such speculation was not compatible with the Torah. For the same reason, they disavowed the popular belief in angels, demons, evil spirits, and the resurrection of the dead. Firmly ensconced in their theocratic conservatism, which saw the life blood of Judaism pulsing in the Temple cult, they looked with particular fear and horror on eschatological speculation and apocalyptic hopes, especially when these fanned the flames of anti-Roman nationalism. While the Sadducees' political sagacity undoubtedly was an important factor in keeping a potentially hot war cold, the succeeding years were to show that the Sadducees had cut themselves off from those vital movements in Jewish religious life and thought that were to play such a decisive role in the resurgence of Judaism after the tragedy of 70 A.D. From that date, when the Romans sacked Jerusalem and destroyed the Temple, the Sadducees quickly disappeared from the Jewish scene. Their understanding of the Torah was so literalistically and unimaginatively limited, and their religious piety was so narrowly centered in the Temple, that once the Temple was destroyed their reason for existence ceased. The disappearance of the Sadducees marked the triumph of their chief rivals, the Pharisees.

The Pharisees

The origin of the Pharisees was closely related to the revolt of the Hasidim in the Maccabean period, and, like them, they were rigorous supporters of the Torah. According to their own traditions they looked back to the time of Ezra as the formative period. But even if they could legitimately claim such early antecedents for their movement, it was not until after the Maccabean Revolt that the patterns of thinking emerged that were to be determinative for the later development of the movement. It was also in this period that they became a coherent force in Jewish life. Concerning the derivation of the name, Pharisee, there is even less agreement among scholars than in the case of the Sadducees. One plausible hypothesis derives the name from a Hebrew word meaning "separatists." Whether this was a self-designation or a derogatory label of their opponents is uncertain. The problem of determining specifically what it was from which they were separated is likewise difficult to decide. One possibility would be the group's withdrawal of support from the Hasmonean monarchy, when in the second century B.C. it pursued a more decidedly political course and tended to veer from a distinctly religious orientation.

Pharisaism was a nonpriestly lay movement in Judaism. Whatever its background in pre-Maccabean times, during the second century B.C. there appeared a succession of prominent teachers and scholars whose teachings, along with those of their successors, were the beginning of that vast body of religious literature known as the *Mishnah* and the *Palestinian* and *Babylonian Talmuds*. Though this literature took written form only after the second century A.D., it contains much earlier tradition which had been orally preserved, and from which the expert can learn much about the origins and development of the movement.

Like the Sadducees, the Pharisees looked upon the Torah of Moses as a definitive revelation of God's will. Unlike the Sadducees, they paid great respect to the prophetic writings, and to another group called "holy writings" (*hagiographa*) that were eventually to be accepted as authoritative. Indeed, it was the Pharisees who finally (about 90 A.D.) determined the contents of the Hebrew Bible. But the Pharisees went a step further, for they also acknowledged the existence and validity of an Oral Torah (Oral Tradition). According to rabbinic tradition it had its inception with Moses himself. In this point they were in radical conflict with the Sadducees, who rejected the Oral Torah and all doctrines not found in the Written Law.

In their insistence on the validity of the Oral Torah, the Pharisees exercised a liberalizing influence on Judaism; through the Oral Torah it was possible for Judaism to keep the Written Torah relevant to changing conditions. The Pharisees believed that God had fully revealed his will in the Written Torah, but that new rules of conduct had to be worked out if the Written Torah were to be understood and obeyed in the face of ever-changing external circumstances. It was their firm conviction that every decision in life must be governed by Torah (the revelation of God's will) that led them to develop elaborate principles of interpretation whereby they could derive specific rules to govern conduct in every conceivable situation. A rule or instruction so derived to set forth the relevant meaning of the Written Torah was called a *halakah.* In the development of these *halakoth* (plural) the Pharisees employed an important principle called the "hedge." According to their tradition an important early Pharisaic teacher had said, among other things, "Build a hedge around the Torah." In practice this meant the formulation of additional *halakoth* to assist in faithfully obeying the requirement of some injunction of Written Torah or previously formulated *halakah.* But the Oral Torah consisted of more than these succinct instructions. It also contained *haggadah.* *Haggadah* could take a variety of forms, such as a parable, simile, legend, myth, historical reminiscence. Its purpose might be to illustrate and elicit response to the moral injunctions of Written or Oral Torah. But its range of concern was much broader. In it such subjects as the relation of God to Israel and the world, the meaning of Israel's past, present, and future, the problems of life, death, sin, temptation, etc., were dealt with in an imaginative way. If the *halakah* served as an arrow pointing to God and his will, the *haggadah* was intended not only to emphasize the urgency of following the arrow, but to evoke the faith, understanding, and motivation that brought active response.

Through the Oral Tradition the Pharisees found an outlet for their religious imagination, always of necessity oriented toward the Written Torah. Among other things, it enabled the Pharisees to incorporate into their thinking the apocalyptic and eschatological insights which became increasingly important during the second century B.C. and later. Such expectations as the victorious coming of God's kingdom, the coming of the Messiah, and the resurrection of the dead, assumed an important place in Pharisaic thought. They were accustomed to thinking of the history of Israel and all men in terms of the "two Ages": "this Age," and the "Age to Come." By "this Age" they referred to the then present world situation, wherein evil powers and lawless men sought to frustrate God's purposes and God's will. Within "this Age" the one certain path was that of obedience to the Torah through which the powers of temptation and sin could be overthrown and overcome. In God's own time he would bring the "Age to Come," in which his final victory over sin and evil would be disclosed to mankind, and a new order of existence would characterize human life. But compared with such a sect as the Essenes, most Pharisees were restrained in their attitude toward eschatological speculation.

If the piety of the Sadducees was centered in the Temple, that of the Pharisees was centered in the Torah. Even their hopes for the "Age to Come" were understood basically from the standpoint of obedience to the law. There were some Pharisees who could say that if Israel should obey the Torah for one day then the Kingdom of God would come. And so, their zeal for the Torah was conditioned not only by their desire for Israel not to be faithless as in the past, but also by their belief that obedience was determinative for the future. It is in this context that their rigorous emphasis on obedience to the Law must be understood.

To the Pharisees, the Torah was God's great gift to Israel, and through Israel, to all men. They emphatically taught that it was sin that stood between man and God. Residing in each man's heart is an evil and a good desire, the former leading to sin, the latter to obedience and good deeds. God gave the Torah in order that his good desire might overcome the evil. When the Pharisee spoke of the "joy of the Law" he meant not only its ability to show man what God requires, but also its power to lead man to overcome his evil desire. And if he failed, God in his mercy had also offered man the gift of repentance. The power of the Law and the power of repentance were two of the great themes of Pharisaic teaching.

The Pharisees set a rigid standard of adherence to Torah that few could follow. But there is no doubt that many respected them. Their influence was dominant in the synagogue, whose existence and worship was validated by Oral Tradition, and in the home, where they encouraged study and obedience to the Torah. On the other hand, it was inevitable that their rigorous attitude would tend to cut them off from many of their fellow Jews, and bring with it the danger of self-righteousness, a problem they recognized and combated in their teachings.

It was the Pharisees who led the Jewish community to recovery after the fall of Jerusalem and the destruction of the Temple. The Pharisees had lost no love on Rome or her puppet rulers in Palestine, but the majority of leaders seem to have cautioned against open revolt as demanded by the more radical elements of the population. They were not motivated by political or economic ambitions, but by their understanding of Torah and their belief that the destiny of the Jews was religious rather than political. Pharisees rallied to the support of the nation once Rome attacked. But even as the terrible seige of Jerusalem was on, they managed to smuggle out of Jerusalem Johannan ben Zacchai, the famous teacher who was later to play a major role in recovery. Strengthened by a religious faith and piety so deeply grounded in the Torah, by applying the Oral Torah to the new situation they confronted after the destruction of the Temple, they were able to withstand the shock and proceed to create an even greater unity of life in the Jewish community—a unity that has persisted to the present day.

The Essenes

The Essenes were the third important sectarian group to develop in the Jewish community during the last two centuries B.C. Although they are not mentioned in the New Testament, they have long been known from the writings of both Philo and Flavius Josephus, the Jewish historian of the first century A.D. Until recently, many questions regarding the Essenes and their origins had never been answered. However, a new flood of light has been thrown on the Essene movement with the discovery (beginning in 1947) of the now famous Dead Sea Scrolls, more recently called the Qumran Scrolls after the name of the site (Khirbet Qumran) of the community's dwelling adjacent to the caves where the scrolls were stored. From the beginning, scholars recognized certain differences and omissions in the accounts of Philo and Josephus, as compared with the Scrolls themselves. There is now general agreement that these discrepancies can be explained, and there is little doubt that the community which composed and treasured these scrolls belonged to the Essene movement. Since the day when a shepherd accidentally stumbled upon the first cave in the rugged hills on the western shore of the Dead Sea, numerous caves (eleven are of major importance for the sect) have been found and their valuable manuscripts and fragments of manuscripts recovered. The task of publication and research is far from complete. Nevertheless, study of the literature has proceeded sufficiently to provide a tentative reconstruction of the beliefs, practices, and history of the sect. The information derived from the

SITE OF THE DEAD SEA COMMUNITY:
The excavated ruins, with the Dead Sea in the background. The cave in the cliff in the right center foreground is one of many in the area that contained manuscript fragments of the Dead Sea Scrolls. (Israel Department of Antiquities and Museums)

QUMRAN WRITING MATERIALS
Tables or benches on which scribes of the Qumran sect copied manuscripts. Inkwells found nearby contain traces of dried ink. At the far end is a ceremonial basin in which the scribes washed their hands before copying the sacred writings. (Israel Department of Antiquities and Museums)

documents has been enhanced by the knowledge gained from archeological excavation and study of the ruins at Khirbet Qumran.[2]

The Essenes, just as the Pharisees, were spiritual descendants of the movement of religious protest generated by the Hasidim. In the case of the Essenes this protest, culminating in the establishment of the community at Qumran, entailed a radical withdrawal from normal social and religious associations. Scholars continue to debate the date of the sect's origins; suggestions range widely from the beginning of the Maccabean Revolt (167–165 B.C.) to the reign of Alexander Jannaeus (103–76 B.C.). If its beginnings were contemporaneous with the settlement at Qumran, we arrive at a date either during, or shortly before or after, the reign of John Hyrcanus (135–104 B.C.). Archeological evidence points decisively to settlement within this period. On the basis of the primary literary evidence, mainly Josephus' works and the historical allu-

---

2There is an immense bibliography for Qumran studies. Among the many excellent works, the following are notable for their conciseness as well as their dependability: Frank M. Cross, *The Ancient Library at Qumran and Modern Biblical Studies* (Garden City, N.Y.: Doubleday, 1958); J. T. Milik, *Ten Years of Discovery in the Wilderness of Judaea* (Naperville, Ill.: Allenson, Inc., 1959); and Helmer Ringgren, *The Faith of Qumran* (Philadelphia: Fortress Press, 1963). For a translation of the documents that were accessible at the time of its publication, see Theodor H. Gaster, *The Dead Sea Scriptures* (Garden City, N.Y.: Doubleday, 1964); and G. Vermes, *The Dead Sea Scrolls in English* (Middlesex, Eng.: Penguin Books, Ltd., 1962). Many of the important documents are included.

sions in the Scrolls, events which motivated the sect's withdrawal to Qumran can be satisfactorily harmonized, through several alternative interpretations, with what is known of Jewish history at that time. There are good grounds, however, for believing that the Essene movement antedated the withdrawal to Qumran. According to one interpretation of an important Essene writing, the *Damascus Document,* the sect existed for "twenty years" before the crisis that sparked the withdrawal to Qumran. It is quite possible, however, that "twenty" has a symbolical meaning. On one fact there is general agreement: the establishment of the community at Qumran, and the circumstances accompanying that event, were decisive in the formation of Essene religious life and thought as they are described in the Qumran Scrolls.

The withdrawal of the sect to Qumran represented a drastic reaction to the increased Hellenizing and secularizing tendencies of the Hasmonean rulers, and a repudiation of their illegitimate claims to the high priesthood. The specific event which provoked the departure was the persecution of the Righteous Teacher, whom the sect venerated as its founder, by a "wicked priest." Efforts to identify these persons with known historical figures has produced a flood of hypotheses. This much seems certain: the wicked priest was one of the Hasmonean rulers. Concerning the Righteous Teacher, there has been less success in overcoming his anonymity. His significance for the development of the Essene movement is acknowledged by all, but most interpreters are inclined to limit our knowledge about him to the information contained in the sectarian writings. Specific references are scarce, and in certain cases, downright controversial. Fortunately, the writings are clear on two essential facts about the Teacher. In the first place, his followers believed that he was the true representative of the legitimate line of priesthood, the Zadokite. This, in part, accounts for the priestly character of the sect and its violent opposition to the established priesthood in Jerusalem. In the second place, they believed that

BAPTISMAL POOLS AT QUMRAN
(Israel Department of Antiquities and Museums)

God had revealed to the Teacher a new interpretation which was the true interpretation of the Law and the Prophets. According to their *Habakkuk Commentary*, God had revealed to the Righteous Teacher "all the secrets of the words of his servants the prophets." Through their inspired Teacher the Essenes were constituted as the community who alone possessed and exercised the legitimate priestly offices, and alone had received the authoritative interpretation of the Torah.

INTERPRETATION OF AND OBEDIENCE TO SCRIPTURE.   Like the Hasidim, who rallied in Maccabean times to the defense of the Torah, the Essenes ardently sought to understand and obey the holy scriptures. However, it was their peculiar mode of interpretation which made for the distinctive features of their life and thought. Fortunately, among the Scrolls are several commentaries on Biblical books, the earliest extant literature of this type, and from these, in particular, their peculiar way of interpreting the sacred writings can be discerned. While it is questionable if any of these writings can be attributed to the Teacher, the method of interpretation, which the sect called the *pesher*, undoubtedly derives from him. Simply stated, the sect read the sacred writings, especially the prophetic books, in the belief that the words and events contained in them were written with specific reference to the events occurring in their own time. For example, their understanding of a passage from Isaiah (40:3) was of crucial importance: "Prepare in the wilderness a way . . . make straight in the desert a highway for our God." It is clear that they read these words as if they were spoken to them, and their retreat to Qumran was seen as the obedient response to prepare in the wilderness for the coming of God's kingdom. It was not only their belief that the prophets were to be understood in terms of the sect's contemporary history that was important. Equally significant was the conviction that the prophets' words referred to the last days before the final victory of God's kingdom. The Essenes believed they were living in those last days. Their religious outlook was eschatological, and this way of viewing history exercised a decisive influence over all they thought and did. The Essenes were an eschatological community; more than any other Jewish sect they were nourished on the eschatological hopes that touched the lives of so many Jews during the troubled times of Hasmonean, Herodian, and Roman domination. The strength of these hopes was manifested in their rigorously disciplined life, which they believed was God's true way for his people during the short interval before his long-expected deliverance.

The sect was organized on the pattern of the early days of Israel's history when the people paused on the edge of the wilderness, preparing to enter into the inheritance of the Promised Land as a sequel of God's covenant with them. The Essenes clearly thought that the end of Israel's earthly pilgrimage would be a recapitulation of her beginnings under Moses and Aaron and Joshua. But they were forced to recognize the actual situation in their day—

as they saw it. The Promised Land was in the hands of the wicked, who were unfaithful to the covenant and ignorant of the truth of the Law and the Prophets. But now God was about to bring to fulfillment the establishment of a new covenant which he had promised through his prophets. It was an eternal covenant. If its fulfillment involved the defeat of the enemies both within and without Israel, its culmination was eternal life. The Essenes believed God had called them into the wilderness in order to lead them out by way of the new covenant; indeed, they called themselves the *Community of the New Covenant*. They alone were the true Israel, the faithful remnant, who in their way of life already celebrated the anticipated fulfillment of God's promises.

THE DISCIPLINE AND ROUTINE OF THE COMMUNITY.   The Essenes residing at Qumran lived, as we have said, a life of strict discipline. The character of this discipline is reflected throughout their writings, but particularly in the *Rule of the Community* (or, *Manual of Discipline*), a document which sets forth the sect's principal doctrines, rites, and governing rules and regulations, with precise penalties for infractions. The community was tightly organized into groups of Priests, Levites, and Laymen, each enjoying a special status determined by specific privileges and responsibilities. A central council consisting of twelve Laymen and three Priests served as a judiciary body to deal with certain well-defined problem areas. The superior status of the Priests clearly indicates the priestly character of the community's organization. This division into orders was set within the context of a strong sense of unity. Indeed, the characteristic Hebrew word used by the Qumran sect to designate themselves can be translated *unity* as well as *community*.

The daily life of the sect included work, assemblies for prayer and worship, study of the Law, and meals of a distinctly religious significance. Members engaged in those trades necessary to furnish a modest subsistence for the group, each in return drawing on the communal goods for his needs. In the ruins of Qumran were found the remains of a smith shop, pottery kilns and shop, bakery, grain mills, and storage silos. The sect also appears to have occupied an additional site at 'Ain Feshka, about two miles south of Qumran, where they engaged in small-scale irrigation farming, and maintained their herds. Those who entered the community pooled their possessions voluntarily. A vow of poverty was a feature of their discipline—they called themselves the *Congregation of the Poor*. As the sect's commentary on Psalm 37 shows, they were the "meek [who] shall inherit the earth"—of course, in the eschatological sense in which they understood "inheritance."

Early in the morning, before going about their work, and again in the evening, the sect assembled for prayers, probably in the large assembly hall which was located in the central building at Qumran. The many original psalms found in the Scrolls, especially the *Thanksgiving Scroll*, and remains of liturgical texts, suggest the liturgical form of their worship. Considering their zeal for the

Torah and its interpretation, it is probable that reading and exposition of the Torah was an important part of their worship. Study of the Torah absorbed much more of their time. The discovery of a large *scriptorium* at the Qumran site, as well as the many remains of Biblical texts, bear witness to the energy they devoted daily to studying, copying, preserving, and commenting upon the scriptures. According to the *Rule of the Community,* the Torah was to be read throughout the night for one-third of the nights of the year, in the wakeful presence of the whole community.

The two daily meals of the sect, at noontime and evening, were central to their life of religious devotion. The *Rule of the Community* designates participation as one of the culminating privileges of full membership; it was one of their principal religious rites. The *Rule* stipulates that these meals were to take place in the presence of an officiating priest, whose prayer of blessing was of primary importance. It is generally maintained that these meals should be understood within the eschatological framework of their thinking. They were eaten in anticipation of the great Messianic Feast in which the Essenes expected to participate when God's final victory had been achieved. In the present, their meals were an anticipation and celebration of the certain joys of the impending future, which were symbolized by that banquet.

Throughout the year the Essenes celebrated the great religious festivals of the Jews, such as Sabbath, Passover, Pentecost, and the Day of Atonement. However, they followed a religious calendar at variance with the authoritative calendar of the Jerusalem Temple—undoubtedly an important source of contention in their continuing conflict with the established priesthood. To understand the significance of this feud it is necessary to recognize the Essenes' strong conviction that the times for the great religious festivals were ordained by God for the world, and fixed according to the movements of the heavenly bodies. Since a solar calendar was employed at Qumran, and a lunar calendar in Jerusalem, serious discrepancies were inevitable. To the Essenes, irregularities at Jerusalem were a defiance of God's will.

In view of the freedom and ingenuity which marked their scriptural interpretation, and their absence from the Temple, the Essenes' rites probably varied from those of the Jerusalem Temple. One important problem concerns their attitude toward sacrifices. There is no clear evidence that they performed sacrifices at Qumran, and good reason to believe that they tended to "spiritualize" the concept of sacrifice. How far they went in this direction remains a highly controversial question. Did they abstain from sacrifices at Jerusalem merely because of their opposition to the priesthood? Or did their abstention reflect a radical reinterpretation of sacrifice, consequently reflected in their theology and rites?

INITIATION, RITES, AND DOCTRINE.   Entrance into the community was preceded by a two-year-long novitiate of instruction and of testing the candidate's "knowledge," culminating in full membership. The *Rule of the Com-*

munity describes the ceremonial rite of initiation, in which each of the orders —Priests, Levites, and Laymen—had its special part to play. The new members were placed under the solemn oath of secrecy, and confronted with an impressive recitation of curses and blessings, a testimony to the alternate consequences of disobedience or obedience to their vows. Apparently the admission of new members was an annual event, at which time the old members submitted to an examination of their obedience, and renewed their entrance into the New Covenant. Such a ceremony surely augmented the solemnity of the occasion. The initiation was climaxed by a purificatory rite of baptism, in which the baptized was purified by the Holy Spirit. The Essene writings, as well as the discovery of cisterns and water channels fed by aqueduct from Wadi Qumran, testify to the importance of ritual ablutions and baptisms. From the time of his initial baptism the Essene was admitted to the privilege of, and obligation for, such ritual ablutions.

The zeal with which the Essenes embraced their rigoristic discipline is to be understood in the context of their dualistic interpretation of the world and their eschatologically determined hopes. Beyond the visible world there existed a host of wicked angels or spirits under the dominion of their ruler, Belial, also called the Spirit of Wickedness and the Prince of Darkness. Arrayed against them were the heavenly hosts of God, led by the Spirit of Truth, also named the Prince of Lights and the Angel of Truth. God, they believed, had permitted Belial and his forces to pursue their wicked course, but only for an allotted time. Why God had permitted this was one of the deep mysteries known only to God. But there is no suggestion that Belial existed outside God's ultimate sovereignty. There is no hint of an absolute or metaphysical dualism. This has led scholars to coin the phrase "eschatological dualism" to describe it. The wicked course of Belial was manifested principally through men of Belial's lot, Sons of Darkness, who rejected God and his will. These men of Belial's lot were identified not only with the enemies of the Jews, such as the Roman oppressors, but also with Jews who were not a part of the true remnant. Against these angelic and human forces were arrayed the angels of God's lot, and the men of God's lot, the Sons of Light, the *Community of the New Covenant.*

According to the Essenes, God had predestined each man's lot. Entrance into the community was evidence of being in God's lot, and assured a man of the support of the Spirit of Truth in fulfilling his destiny. That destiny for the Essene would be fulfilled when Belial's allotted time came to an end, and he and those of his lot were destroyed. For the Essene, life was already a battle against the Spirit of Wickedness which sought to overcome him; the struggle served as a discipline and preparation for the final conflict. For the end of Belial's lot was to come in a mighty battle. In one of their writings, the *War of the Children of Light Against the Children of Darkness*, the details of the progressive stages in that Holy War, and the military organization of the community, are meticulously described. The Essenes with the hosts of God would prevail in the battle which marked the end of the hosts of wickedness, both angelic and human.

THE ESCHATOLOGICAL HOPE OF THE COMMUNITY.   Messianic speculation played an important role in the sect's eschatological expectations. Their preoccupation with messianism is especially evident in their *Testimonia Document*, a collection of scriptural verses which they interpreted as messianic prophecies. Like many other Jews, the Essenes looked forward to the coming of a prophet as the forerunner of the Messianic Age. They were distinctive in their expectation of *two* Messiahs, the Messiah of Aaron and the Messiah of Israel, the former from the priestly line, the latter from the royal line. The Messiah of Israel was to be instrumental in leading the community in its victorious war; the Messiah of Aaron was to be instrumental in the establishment of the New Jerusalem and the New Temple. It is significant that the Messiah of Aaron takes precedence over the Messiah of Israel. This precedence undoubtedly harks back to the centrality of the priesthood in the theocratic pattern of Israel's early history. No doubt it was further strengthened as a result of the disillusion over the secularistic tendencies of the Hasmoneans, and the later despair of the this-worldly victory over the Romans. The priestly ascendancy is clearly seen in the sect's expectation of the great Messianic Feast, participation in which was the privilege of those who entered into the New Age. Among the writings, the *Rule of the Congregation* contains a description of the feast, in which the priestly Messiah plays the primary, and the royal Messiah a secondary, role. This messianic speculation regarding Israel in the New Age was consistent with the Essenes' belief concerning God's purpose for Israel throughout her history. She was to be a priestly people whose only king was God, and a holy people whose only Law was Torah. On the basis of this conviction the sect withdrew to achieve the life which such a purpose demanded.

A very important question concerns the extent to which the Righteous Teacher was the subject of the Essenes' messianic speculation. Since the discovery of the Scrolls many theories regarding the Teacher have been promulgated—such as the theory that he had been crucified and had risen from the dead. Further study has decisively shown that this particular theory was founded on a mistaken reading of the texts. On somewhat firmer grounds other scholars have assigned a messianic role to the Teacher, identifying him with the expected prophet or even one of the messiahs. But such identifications are not generally maintained any longer. Most interpreters do acknowledge that his role as the herald of the Last Days, of the Messianic Age and its messianic figures, must be described as eschatological, if not messianic.

Nurtured on their eschatological hopes, the Essenes viewed the present world order pessimistically. We have already noted that, staunch in their Biblical doctrine of God the Creator and sovereign over his Creation, they avoided anything approaching a metaphysical dualism. But in their writings, especially their psalms, there is an emphasis on the lowliness of man which goes beyond the Biblical writings in intensity. At points it seems to exude the pessimism expressed in the body-spirit dualism found in the religious thought of the Hellenistic world. However, it is not so much the problem of the weakness of the body or flesh as such that troubles them; it is the perverseness of the heart, mind, and will—the inadequacy of all human righteousness, the hopelessness of man apart from the righteousness of God—without God's justification of man. Such thinking stands in an unresolved tension with their predestinarian tendencies; but it also mitigates clear-cut legalistic tendencies. It is also in harmony with their confession that only through the guidance of the Holy Spirit do they achieve purity, obedience, and salvation. However much their pessimism must have been accentuated by the repeated political and religious frustrations of the Jewish people during 200 troubled years, it was basically rooted in their conviction of man's moral weakness and the necessity of God's action to displace the grounds of pessimism.

The monastic life of the Essenes at Qumran must have had a peculiar appeal for many Jews who were world-weary, and looked to God for a new understanding of his ways with his people, Israel. The fact that there were Essene communities in places other than Qumran has long been known from Josephus' account. One of their writings, the *Damascus Document*, describes the organization of these camps, which were founded on a nucleus of ten persons, provided one was a priest. Obviously, accommodations in religious practices were necessary for the dispersed communities that did not enjoy the seclusion of Qumran. But the monastic life and thought at Qumran surely exercised a continuous influence upon them. Numerically the movement was small (Josephus says 4,000). However, the Essenes must have played an important role in spreading and nurturing the eschatological hopes and apocalyptic visions that pervaded the atmosphere of Jewish religious thought. This is one of the most important aspects of the discovery of the Dead Sea Scrolls. Now, in a way that was not possible before, we can better understand this atmosphere. It is significant that the sect's library included a number of writings which are either identical with, or bear a literary relationship to, writings of the *Apocrypha* and *Pseudepigrapha*. Essenes, undoubtedly, were the authors of many such writings. It is particularly important for the student of the New Testament to have some understanding of the eschatological mode of thought represented by the Essenes. For it was just this mode that was one major characteristic of the thought of Jesus and the New Testament writers.

THE END OF THE COMMUNITY.   The conclusions of the archeologists point to the grim fact that sometime during the siege of Jerusalem (probably in 68 A.D.) Roman legionaires attacked and devastated the settlement at Qumran. The disappearance of the sect after 70 A.D. affords persuasive evidence that the community pinned its hopes on the expectation that this was the Holy War for which they had waited. It appears that those who did not suffer death in the tragic war with Rome came to the shocking and disillusioning conclusion that their way of understanding Torah had been wrong. Their precious library, which they managed to conceal in their caves before the Roman onslaught, bears testimony to their incredible zeal for God and his Torah, and their consuming desire to be the faithful community established by his covenant.

The existence of the sectarian movements we have discussed shows a degree of flexibility in Judaism that is often overlooked. Although each movement in its own way claimed the Torah as the basis of its life, common loyalty to Torah helped provide the Jewish community with its sense of unity. This unity of life and thought must have attracted non-Jews by its religious and ethical fervor, and repelled them by its exclusiveness.

Earlier we saw that men and women in the Hellenistic age sought eagerly for membership in a religious community, but the Jews seemed to have been *born into* such a community. The Jews had made efforts to share their religious life with Gentiles, but with little success. Now, however, there arose out of Judaism a new movement—one that succeeded where the parent had failed. We turn next to a consideration of this new community: the Christian Church, which, like the Dead Sea sect, considered itself to be the heir of the New Covenant.

PART TWO

THE COMMUNITY
OF THE
NEW COVENANT

About the year thirty A.D. there appeared in Palestine a Jewish community that, like much of Judaism, hoped for the New Age that God had promised through the prophets and seers. But it differed radically from the rest of Judaism on one point: it was convinced that the New Age had already begun to dawn. More specifically it believed that God had acted in Jesus of Nazareth, whom its acclaimed as Messiah, to inaugurate a New Age, and that the community itself was the nucleus of the people of the New Age.

Who was this Jesus of Nazareth? What did he say? What did he do? What do we know about his life? Such questions are undoubtedly stirring in the mind of the reader whose historical imagination is stimulated by the underlying question: what motivated this small group of Jews to acclaim Jesus as the Messiah? The quest for knowledge about his life, words, and deeds, is pertinent and understandable. But the character of the sources upon which we have to depend poses many problems. In the latter part of this chapter we will consider these sources in order to better understand these problems and the difficulties they pose.

As background it is important first to recognize that, insofar as the earliest Christian community was concerned, it was not solely, or even primarily, Jesus' words and deeds that led them to acclaim him Messiah and the inaugurator of the New Age. What was the principal ground for their claims?

JESUS AND THE GOSPEL

The principal ground for the earliest Christian community's claims regarding Jesus was the belief that God had raised him from the dead. In the resurrection of Jesus, God had authenticated him as Messiah and inaugurated the New Age. Consideration of the various modes of understanding the meaning of Jesus' resurrection and the informative role it played in shaping the community's life and thought must await our study of the various writings of the New Testament. For the present we are mainly concerned to understand the resurrection faith as the context in which the traditions of the words and deeds of Jesus were remembered, interpreted, and transmitted in the community.

When we later turn to the writings of the New Testament, we will find two important terms employed to designate the message which the community believed God had given them in Jesus: *gospel* and *kerygma*. The English word, gospel, translates a Greek word meaning "good news." Kerygma is the English transliteration of a Greek term meaning *proclamation*. In New Testament usage kerygma may refer to both the content of the proclamation and the act of proclaiming. Some scholars have believed that the writings of the New Testament reveal a relatively definite pattern of contents which characterized the Gospel or kerygma of the Christian community from the earliest days.[1] But most scholars are dubious about this. They are more inclined to believe that from the beginning there were variations in the content of the good news which the community proclaimed. But if there is reluctance to posit a well-defined and uniform content of the Gospel message, there is general agreement on this point: the gospel, whatever the diverse language in which it was presented, was grounded in the resurrection of Jesus. The focal point of the gospel was Jesus, the living Lord of the community.

The implications of this latter point are many, but two are most important. First, since the early Christian community lived in the belief that Jesus was its living Lord, it was not concerned with him primarily as a figure in past history. Furthermore, since it also believed in the imminent return of the resurrected Lord, its interests and expectations were drawn to the future of Jesus, rather than his past. The first Christians were not preoccupied with researching the biographical details of his life. In the second place, because

---

[1]The classic effort to defend this thesis is found in C. H. Dodd, *The Apostolic Preaching and Its Development* (New York: Harper & Row, 1951), especially pp. 7–35.

the community believed that in the resurrection of Jesus God had affirmed him to be the Messiah who would bring to fulfillment his promises to the Jewish people, the community's primary concern was to understand and interpret the person of Jesus, his words and deeds, his death and resurrection, in the light of these promises. From the beginning, then, the traditions regarding Jesus, which were transmitted by the community, already bore the stamp of the community's interpretation. And in this form the traditions were revered and communicated as the gospel.

These sources for the life and words of Jesus are principally the four anonymous writings in the New Testament known as gospels and traditionally attributed to Matthew, Mark, Luke, and John. As we consider the contents and the aims of each of the Gospels in succeeding chapters (Chapter Three on the origins of the gospels; Chapter Five on Mark; Chapter Twelve on Matthew; Chapter Thirteen on John; Chapter Fourteen on Luke), we shall examine the evidence for the kind of person or community that lies behind these writings. In his *Ecclesiastical History*, the fourth-century historian Eusebius has collected ancient traditions about the authorship of the Gospels, and in each case he attributes them to an apostle (Matthew and John) or the companion of an apostle (Luke is linked with Paul, and Mark with Peter). But with the possible exception of Mark, all the gospels were written in the later first century, and none of them is from a first-hand apostolic writer. We use the traditional titles, but treat the works for what they are: witnesses to the ways in which the Jesus tradition was understood by certain persons or groups in the Church at that time or even somewhat later. Apart from these documents, the information we have about the life and ministry of Jesus is relatively negligible.[2] Each of these authors was dependent on the traditions which had been preserved by the Christian community, and these traditions already bore the stamp of the community's interpretation. Furthermore, the intention of the four authors was similar to that of the community: to present an interpretation of the person of Jesus as the gospel for Christians in their own day. When later, in the second century A.D., Christians began to designate each of these four literary documents by the term gospel, it was appropriate to the intention of the authors and the substance of their writings. The gospels were not composed for the primary purpose of presenting biographies of Jesus, but rather as proclamations of the Gospel, which it was believed had been revealed in and through the person of Jesus.

---

[2]For a discussion of the non-Biblical sources, see Howard C. Kee, *Jesus in History: An Approach to the Study of the Gospels* (New York: Harcourt Brace Jovanovich, 1970), especially pp. 29–43.

The Gospel
and the Gospels

CHAPTER THREE

So far we have offered a number of general assertions that might serve as answers to the questions: Who was Jesus? What did he say? What did he do? Undoubtedly, one could question the validity of these assertions and the historical methods on which they are based. Consequently, we shall now consider the critical study of the gospels that has been pursued over the last century and a half; both the assertions and the perspective on the life and message of Jesus derive mainly from the discoveries and conclusions of this critical research.

THE SYNOPTIC PROBLEM

When a close comparison is made between the general outline and content of the four gospels, two major problems emerge. First, there are striking differences between John and the other three gospels. Very few of the events in Jesus' life recorded in the latter are to be found in John. Those missing include such important events as the Temptation of

Jesus, the Transfiguration at Caesarea Philippi, Jesus' words at the Last Supper, the Gethsemane scene, to mention only a few. The place and chronology of Jesus' ministry are different in John, and the style and language of Jesus' message contrasts markedly with that of the other three. The problem of accounting for these differences has challenged scholars for years. Later (Chapter Thirteen) when the Gospel of John is considered in detail, attention will be given to this enigmatic problem of differences. For the present it is sufficient to note that for purposes of reconstructing the life and teachings of Jesus, Matthew, Mark, and Luke have been given priority in the work of critical scholarship.

Another problem is posed by a comparative examination of the Gospels of Matthew, Mark, and Luke.[1] Attention has already been called to certain similarities between them in contrast to John. Each of these gospels is constructed on a common arrangement which underlies any variations. For example, the beginning of Jesus' ministry is associated with John the Baptist, for the most part its scene is Galilee, and it concludes with a final trip to Jerusalem where, after a brief period, Jesus dies. In addition to this agreement in general content and plan it is apparent that in long individual passages not only is subject matter similar, but phrase after phrase of the Greek texts are identical.[2] When it is remembered that the original oral tradition was in the Aramaic language, it is incredible that the agreements between the synoptic gospels could have resulted from independent translations of this original tradition. The conclusion is inescapable that there must be some other explanation for the close literary relationship between the three gospels. Because of the broad agreement in content and outline, these gospels have come to be called the *synoptic gospels,* or *the Synoptics.* And the problem of accounting for their literary relationship is an important aspect of what is known as the *Synoptic problem.*

The Priority of the Gospel of Mark

One of the most widely accepted conclusions of gospel studies is the hypothesis that Mark was the earliest written gospel and that Matthew and Luke used Mark as the basis for writing their gospels.[3] This provides the clue

---

[1]Serious comparative study of the Gospels of Matthew, Mark, and Luke requires the constant use of a text which presents the three in parallel columns. The following discussion will be enhanced by reference to such a text. The text based on the Revised Standard Version (1952) is *Gospel Parallels: A Synopsis of the First Three Gospels* (New York: Nelson, 1957).

[2]Usually reflected in English translations.

[3]This is true of both Protestant and Roman Catholic scholarship. For a Roman Catholic interpretation see Alfred Wikenhauser, *New Testament Introduction* (New York: Herder & Herder, 1963), pp. 239–252. An elaborate attempt to demonstrate that Mark was dependent on Matthew is in W. R. Farmer, *The Synoptic Problem* (New York: Macmillan, 1964).

for understanding the literary relationship between the three synoptic gospels. More than a century of intensive research has amassed such overwhelming evidence in support of this hypothesis that alternative explanations have been given up. While we cannot survey all the arguments which have been given to support this hypothesis, a few of the most important ones will be considered to illustrate the nature and weight of the evidence.

The first and most obvious argument is based on the recurrence of Mark's subject matter in Matthew and Luke. Most of Mark, with the exception of eight brief passages, is found in Matthew, and all but twelve Markan passages are found in Luke. Dependence on Mark seems necessary since it is usually the case that when a Markan passage is missing in either Matthew or Luke it is found in the other gospel. This is one of the major arguments against the older view that Mark was an abridgment of Matthew. Further evidence against such a possibility is the fact that on actual word count in many passages Mark is the longer. In the analysis of such passages there is convincing evidence that Matthew and Luke have abridged, and the reason is not obscure. Stylistic changes and the elimination of redundancies are everywhere evident, and the presence of a good deal of non-Markan material in both Matthew and Luke suggests that these authors intentionally abridged Mark in order to include these non-Markan traditions.

The arrangement and sequence of material also supports the theory of dependence on Mark. It is not just the fact that the Markan sequence regularly recurs. In most instances when one of the two gospels varies from Mark in sequence, the other follows Mark. Sometimes such variations from Mark do not make good sense. For example, Mark gives an account of a visit of Jesus to Nazareth some time after the beginning of his ministry (Mk. 6:1–6). Luke places this episode at the very outset of the ministry (Lk. 4:16–30). In Luke's account Jesus says: "Doubtless you will quote to me this proverb, 'Physician, heal yourself; what we have heard you did at Capernaum, do here also in your own country.' " But according to Luke's sequence Jesus had not carried on a ministry in Capernaum before this time; the saying seems out of place. In Mark, however, the same words occur and make sense. According to the Gospel of Mark, Jesus has already been active in Capernaum (Mk. 1:21ff.; 2:1ff.). Luke's passage must presuppose Mark's sequence to make sense out of the content of the passage. That Luke has actually relocated a Markan passage is further substantiated by the fact that Matthew follows Mark in his order.

Another argument supporting dependence on Mark is based on the numerous parallel passages where the Greek of Matthew or Luke, or both, exhibits a refinement of style in contrast with Mark. In some instances Aramaisms of Mark are missing; in other passages the phraseology of Mark contrasts with the more "literary" style or language of Matthew or Luke. This strongly suggests that the latter authors have consciously improved upon the Markan original. There are occasions when the differences represent substantive modifications. For example, phrases in Mark which describe emotional states of Jesus frequently are either modified or omitted in Matthew and Luke. It is a good guess that the religious sensitivity of the latter has prompted such revisions. In certain cases more radical differences are to be found. In the story of the Rich Young Man (Mk. 10:17–22), according to Mark's account Jesus is addressed by the young man as "Good Teacher," and Jesus responds, "Why do you call me good?" In Matthew's version of this story, Jesus' question is missing in a complete recasting of the dialogue (Mt. 19:16–22). That Matthew has purposely reworked the Markan passage is further substantiated by the fact that Luke follows the Markan story (Lk. 18:18–23).

No one of these several arguments is sufficient in itself to support the theory of dependence on Mark. It is the accumulative weight of the evidence and the inadequacy of alternative explanations which demand explanation.

Fig. 1. A Selection from the Synoptic Gospels in Parallel

THE RICH YOUNG MAN

MATTHEW 19:16–22	MARK 10:17–22	LUKE 18:18–23
	17And as he was setting out on his journey, a man ran up	
16And behold, one came up to him,	and knelt before him, and askedhim, "GoodTeacher,what	18And a ruler askedhim, "GoodTeacher,what
saying, "Teacher, what good deed must I do, to have eternal life?" 17And he said to	must I do to inherit eternal life?" 18And Jesus said to	shall I do to inherit eternal life?" 19And Jesus said to
him, "Why do you ask me about what is good? One there is who	him, "Why do you call me good? No one is good	him, "Why do you call me good? No one is good
is good. If you would enter life, keep the commandments."	but God alone. 19You know the command-	but God alone. 20You know the command-
18He said to him, "Which?" And Jesus said, "You shall not	ments:	ments:
kill, You shall not commit adultery, You shall not steal,	'Do not kill, Do not commit adultery, Do not steal,	'Do not commit adultery, Do not kill, Do not steal,
You shall not bear false wit- ness, 19Honor	Do not bear false wit- ness, Do not defraud, Honor	Do not bear false wit- ness, Honor
your father and mother, and, You shall love your neigh-	your father and mother.' "	your father and mother.' "
bor as yourself." 20The young man said to him, "All	20And he said to him, "Teacher, all	21And he said, "All
these I have observed; what do I still lack?"	these I have observed from my youth." 21And Jesus looking	these I have observed from my youth." 22And when Jesus
21Jesus said to him, "If you would be	upon him loved him, and said to him, "You lack one thing;	heard it, he said to him, "One thing you still
perfect, go, sell what you possess and give to the	go, sell what you have, and give to the	lack. Sell all that you have and distribute to the
poor, and you will have treasure in heaven; and	poor, and you will have treasure in heaven; and	poor, and you will have treasure in heaven; and
come, follow me." 22When the young man heard this	come, follow me." 22At that saying his countenance fell,	come, follow me." 23But when he heard this
he went away sorrowful; for he had great possessions.	and he went away sorrowful, for he had great possessions.	he became sad, for he was very rich.

The Two-Source Hypothesis

There is another side to the Synoptic problem. Examination of these three gospels not only shows a large body of material common to all three; a little more than one-third of Matthew and one-fourth of Luke consists of material common to these two but missing in Mark. The question immediately arises: How can we account for the absence of this material in Mark and its presence in the other two? It is not impossible that Luke borrowed the material from Matthew, or vice versa. But there are such serious arguments against this solution that it is commonly rejected. For example, the different arrangement of the material in each gospel weighs heavily against it. In Luke this common material is incorporated in two insertions in the Markan narrative; these are called the "Little Insertion" (Lk. 6:20–8:3) and the "Great Insertion" (Lk. 9:51–18:14). Matthew, on the other hand, includes most of the material in five major discourses by Jesus in Chapters 5–7, 10, 13, 18, and 23–25, working his material into either the narrative or the specific sayings as presented in Mark. Such treatment of the material points more forcefully to an independent source rather than mutual dependence.

A more telling argument against the possibility that one author borrowed from the other is the fact that in various passages where there are variations of a minor sort, in some cases Matthew seems the more original, in others, Luke. It may be asked on what grounds one version can be determined the more original, since the only versions we have are those found in Matthew and Luke. Of course, there can be no absolute determination. However, a number of helpful principles have been developed in an effort to deal with the problem. For example, on the basis of the analysis of the linguistic style and religious interests of both Gospels, constructions and religious motifs characteristic of one author may be identified in his version of the common material. This suggests that the version in which such obvious evidences of the author's hand are absent *may be* the more original. Since the more original version of the common material is not confined to either one of the gospels, it would appear more reasonable to assume that both authors have made use of an independent source rather than that either borrowed from the other.

On the basis of such analyses it is commonly acknowledged today that Matthew and Luke did have access to a separate source which each employed in his own way, in addition to Mark, in the composition of his gospel. In gospel studies this source is designated "Q," a symbol introduced by nineteenth-century German scholars as an abbreviation of the German *Quelle*, meaning source. The Two-Source Hypothesis maintains that both Matthew and Luke used two sources, Mark and Q, in composing their gospels. While the hypothesis continues to be tested, even challenged, it is normally accepted as a basic working hypothesis in the study of the synoptic gospels.

When it comes to the matter of reconstructing the hypothetical Q source, there is anything but unanimous agreement. The problem is obvious. While Matthew and Luke verbally agree at many points, in many instances they differ (see Fig. 2, below). The problem of determining which is the more original is greater. Furthermore, there is always the possibility that Q consisted of more than has been preserved by Matthew and Luke. But on the basis of what they have incorporated in their gospels the contents of Q are fairly clear. While it consisted largely of sayings of Jesus, it also included traditions about John

Fig. 2. A Selection from Q

THE WATCHFUL HOUSEHOLDER

MATTHEW 24:43–44	LUKE 12:39–40
43But know this, that if the householder had known in what part of the night the thief was coming, he would have watched and would not have let his house be broken into. 44Therefore you also must be ready; for the Son of man is coming at an hour you do not expect.	39But know this, that if the householder had known at what hour the thief was coming, he would have been awake and would not have left his house to be broken into. 40You also must be ready; for the Son of man is coming at an hour you do not expect.

the Baptist, several parables, an account of the Temptation of Jesus, several controversy stories and miracles. Some scholars would include in Q materials found only in Matthew or Luke, but such decisions are highly subjective. It is commonly agreed that Q was not a gospel in form. It is quite certain that it contained little, if any, connective narrative. Matthew and Luke apparently knew it and used it in Greek translation; but it is almost certain that it first circulated in Aramaic.

One of the continuing debates centers on the question of whether Matthew and Luke had access to a written document or knew Q as an oral tradition. The strongest argument for its existence as a written source is the frequency of verbal agreements between the two gospels. Whether Matthew and Luke used two versions of Q, whether oral or written, is also a much debated question. The collection of traditions known as Q undoubtedly existed prior to the composition of Mark, perhaps as early as A.D. 50. Indeed, there are some scholars who believe that Mark used Q, and explain certain peculiarities in passages common to Matthew, Mark, and Luke as evidences of the text of Q.

There has been a good deal of speculation regarding the explanation of why the Q collection was first created. One very attractive hypothesis maintains that it was brought together for the purpose of instruction of newly baptized Christians. However its origin may be explained, its function was not primarily biographical. A typical reconstruction of Q can be seen in Appendix II.

The Problem of Additional Sources

When all the Markan material, as well as the Q material, has been isolated from Matthew and Luke, we find that there remains a considerable amount of material in each gospel. On examination it will be found that this material is peculiar to each gospel. For example, while both gospels have birth stories, they are quite different in content. Such familiar parables as the Prodigal Son (Lk. 15:11–32), the Good Samaritan (Lk. 10:29–37), and the Pharisee and the Publican (Lk. 18:9–14), and the story of the Rich Man and Lazarus (Lk. 16:19–31) are found only in Luke. Such parables as the Weeds (Mt. 13:24–30), the Hidden Treasure (Mt. 13:44), the Pearl (Mt. 13:45–46), and the Last Judgment (Mt. 25:31–46) are found only in Matthew. Luke alone has the story of John the Baptist's birth (Lk. 1:5–25; 57–80), the raising of the widow's son at Nain (Lk. 7:11–17), and Mary and Martha (Lk. 10:38–42). Matthew alone has such sayings of Jesus as that concerning alms (Mt. 6:1–4) and fasting (Mt. 6:16–18), and the description of Judas' death (Mt. 27:3–10; cf. Acts 1:15–20).

No one disputes that Matthew and Luke had access to independent sources; there is, however, no unanimity as to the character of these sources. In the first place, it is possible that some of the material peculiar to either Gospel came from the Q source. But after allowance is made for such possibilities, a large body of material remains to be accounted for. Perhaps some of these materials are the outright composition of the author of the Gospel. The genealogy of Jesus in Matthew may be an example of such a composition (Mt. 1:1–17). However, after allowance is made for such creativity on the part of the author, there is still a considerable bulk of material remaining. The dispute does not revolve around whether there were sources; the question is whether there were two written documents that were roughly equivalent to the special material in each Gospel. A number of years ago this thesis was strongly maintained as integral to what has been called the Four-Document Hypothesis.[4] Simply stated, this theory presupposed four written documents behind the Gospels of Matthew and Luke: Mark, Q, a written source peculiar to Matthew, and a written source peculiar to Luke. Matthew's special source was designated "M," and Luke's "L." In recent years there has been increasing skepticism regarding the existence of such written documents.

In recognition of the divergence of scholary opinion regarding sources, it is preferable to presuppose that each author had access to *several* sources, perhaps written and oral, from which he incorporated material into his gospel. This does not eliminate the possibility that among the sources, in the case of each author, there might have been one collection of traditions from which he drew

---

[4]The classic statement of this position is found in B. H. Streeter's *The Four Gospels*, rev. ed. (London: Macmillan, 1930).

heavily in writing his gospel. The symbols M and L have become convenient terms to designate the special material of Matthew and Luke rather than any specific theory about the character of the sources. The reader can consult Appendix III for the contents of M and L.

Up to this point in our consideration of the Synoptic Gospels we have dealt with the major conclusions reached during a century and a half in the effort to explain the similarities and differences among them. The conclusions of this particular discipline of study, technically known as *source criticism*, can be summarized diagrammatically as follows:

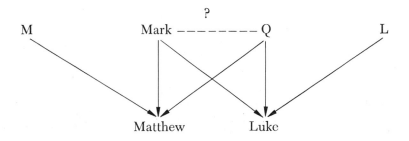

BEHIND THE WRITTEN SOURCES

The intensive examination of the Synoptic Gospels eventually led to a question opening the door to a new epoch in gospel studies. It was actually certain startling conclusions with respect to the character of the Gospel of Mark which prompted the new departure. On the basis of a close scrutiny of the connective narrative in Mark's gospel, attention was called to the generally vague notices of time (*e.g.*, "after John was arrested," 1:14; "one Sabbath," 2:23; "again," 3:1; "in those days," 8:1, etc.) and place (*e.g.*, "Galilee," 1:14; "by the Sea of Galilee," 1:16; "a lonely place," 1:35; "beside the sea," 2:13; "the grainfields," 2:23; "the sea," 3:7; "his own country," 6:1; "among the villages," 6:6, etc.). These investigations led to a conclusion that was to find general acceptance among critical scholars: generally speaking, the chronological and topographical narrative framework of Mark's gospel was the creation of the author. This literary analysis was supported by the further argument that the selection and arrangement of materials bore the marks of the author's religious insights and purposes. Concerning this important aspect of the argument more must be said. When the Gospel of Mark is considered in detail (Chapter Five), the reader's own conclusions must be drawn in view of that discussion. For the present, attention must be given to the implications of the conclusion. If the author of Mark himself supplied the general chronological and topographical framework, then obviously the traditions which he incorporated into his Gospel, with few exceptions, came to him devoid of any framework. This conclusion shattered a long-accepted tradition that Mark had preserved in his gospel a reliable and accurate account of the life of Jesus, dependable in its general chronological sequence and place setting for the events in Jesus' life. Now it was acknowledged that Mark had been the first to bring the early traditions about Jesus into a sequential pattern, endeavoring to provide the setting of time and place. Before Mark the traditions circulated independent of such a framework.

With this development a new epoch in gospel studies was launched. Attention now moved on from a preoccupation with the literary relations between the Synoptic Gospels—that is, from *source criticism*—to *form criticism*, the new discipline which continues to play an important role. Basically, form criticism has been concerned with the study of the period of oral transmission before the gospel traditions reached their written stage in the Synoptic Gospels. It is a basic thesis of form criticism that the traditions contained in the written gospels are analyzable in terms of definite forms in which they circulated orally. Form criticism also maintains that in the course of transmission there were changes and developments in these forms, and it is part of its task to identify and account for these changes. Insofar as the discipline is concerned with this latter investigation, it is more appropriately called *form history*.

From the beginning there have been, and still are, important differences of interpretation among those who acknowledge the importance of form criticism.[5] But there are broad agreements which must be seriously considered in any effort to understand the history and transmission of the traditions now contained in the gospels. In the first place, it is agreed that, generally speaking, at the beginning the traditions about Jesus circulated orally as independent units. That is, in most cases they were not specifically set within a chronological or sequential or topographical framework of his ministry. The major exception is the Passion narrative in its basic outline of Last Supper, arrest, trial of Jesus before the High Priest and Pilate, Crucifixion, and Resurrection appearances. In the second place, it is acknowledged that the situation in life (*Sitz im Leben*) or the needs of the first Christians to transmit the traditions, played an important role in the selection, formation, and transmission. What these needs were presupposes some understanding of the beliefs and activities of the earliest Christians. Such understanding depends not only on careful interpretation of the gospels but interpretation of the rest of the New Testament writings as well. In the reconstruction there are differences in emphasis, but consideration

---

[5]See Martin Dibelius, *From Tradition to Gospel* (New York: Scribner's, 1935); and R. Bultmann, *History of the Synoptic Tradition* (New York: Harper & Row, 1963). Both works appeared in post-World War I Germany (1919 and 1921, respectively); both have passed through several editions and have subsequently been translated into English. For another important evaluation of form criticism, see Vincent Taylor, *The Formation of the Gospel Tradition* (London: Macmillan, 1953).

would have to be given to the following: (1) Christian preaching; (2) teaching or instruction; (3) community worship; (4) debate with the Jews (and Gentiles when the mission of the Gentiles began); (5) community organization and discipline. The traditions about Jesus were remembered and transmitted not primarily to perpetuate the memory of past happenings, but to guide the community in its daily life in the world. Earlier we saw that central to the *kerygma* of the earliest Church were the death and resurrection of Jesus whom they believed to be God's Messiah. Therefore, form criticism's conclusion that the Passion narrative was the one episode in the life of Jesus which from the beginning consisted of a minimal sequence of events is not surprising. Not only would the occurrences surrounding Jesus' death have left an indelible mark upon the memories of the first disciples; just these events were at the heart of the message which they proclaimed as the Gospel.

The Forms of the Oral Tradition

Form critics have generally agreed in their classification of the units in which the tradition circulated during the period of oral transmission. They have differed in their choice of the technical terms by which they designate the forms, and to a certain extent there has been disagreement in their identification of the forms where, for various reasons, certain passages seem to fit the definition of more than one form. While these divergencies cannot be overlooked, the areas of agreement are impressive and provide the consensus which commends the form-critical method as an essential tool for understanding the period of oral transmission. In the present discussion of the various forms the nomenclature of Vincent Taylor[6] will be employed; the comparable terminology of two other form critics, Rudolf Bultmann and Martin Dibelius, will be given in footnotes.

PRONOUNCEMENT STORIES. *Pronouncement stories*[7] (see Fig. 3, below) are brief narratives purporting to describe an encounter between Jesus and one or more persons. The setting, which is regularly general and often vague, contains details sufficient only to provide the setting for the distinctive feature of the story: a culminating statement or pronouncement of Jesus which occurs at the end. While the pronouncement of Jesus can be understood in the immediate context of the story (often a conflict between Jesus and other persons), it is of such a nature as to lend itself to more general application. These stories were remembered and transmitted basically because of the pronouncements which the Christian community valued as an authoritative guide for their own lives.

---

[6]Taylor, *The Formation of the Gospel Tradition.*
[7]Dibelius uses the term *Paradigm*, and Bultmann *Apophthegmata*.

Fig. 3. A Pronouncement Story

And they sent to him some of the Pharisees and some of the Herodians, to entrap him in his talk. And they came and said to him, "Teacher, we know you are true, and care for no man; for you do not regard the position of men, but truly teach the way of God. Is it lawful to pay taxes to Caesar, or not? Should we pay them, or should we not?" But knowing their hypocrisy, he said to them, "Why put me to the test? Bring me a coin, and let me look at it." And they brought one. And he said to them, "Whose likeness and inscription is this?" They said to him, "Caesar's." Jesus said to them, "Render to Caesar the things that are Caesar's and to God the things that are God's."

MIRACLE STORIES.   *Miracle stories*[8] (Fig. 4, below) have as their principal point the narration of a miraculous act of Jesus. With rare exceptions the narrative contains a threefold pattern of development: (1) a description of the situation which prompts the miracle (*e.g.*, in the case of a healing this would involve the description of the condition of the person to be healed); (2) a description of the miraculous act; (3) a description of the consequences of the miracle (*e.g.*, the reaction of those who witnessed the miracle). The focus of the miracle story is the miracle itself, and when the narrative follows the above outline it is a *proper* miracle story. There are, however, certain narratives which appear to be a mixture of a pronouncement story and a miracle story (*e.g.*, Mk. 2:3–12). And in at least one instance we find two miracle stories combined in one narrative (Mk. 5:21–43). Like the pronouncement stories, the miracle stories circulated independently at first, though it is possible that in the period of oral transmission they already circulated in collections.

Fig. 4. A Miracle Story

And a leper came to him beseeching him, and kneeling said to him, "If you will, you can make me clean." And being moved with pity, he stretched out his hand and touched him, and said to him, "I will; be clean." And immediately the leprosy left him, and he sternly charged him, and sent him away at once, and said to him, "See that you say nothing to anyone; but go, show yourself to the priest, and offer for your cleansing what Moses commanded, for a proof to the people." But he went out and began to talk freely about it, and to spread the news, so that Jesus could no longer openly enter a town, but was out in the country; and the people came to him from every quarter.

---

[8]Dibelius designates these *Novellen* and Bultmann *Wundergeschichten*.

SAYINGS.   The oral tradition included a large number of sayings[9] of Jesus which originally circulated independently, without a narrative framework relating them to the specific occasion in Jesus' ministry when they were uttered. During the oral period there already was a tendency for these sayings to be grouped in small collections as illustrative of a common theme (see Fig. 5). In some instances, certain important sayings continued to be transmitted independently, as can be seen from the different contexts in which such sayings are found in the written gospels (see Mt. 23:12; Lk. 14:11; 18:14). It is likely that in certain instances the gospels retain a sequence of sayings which were originally uttered in that form by Jesus and were transmitted as a cluster throughout the oral period.[10] Luke's shorter version of the Beatitudes may reflect such an original cluster (Lk. 6:20–22; cf. Mt. 5:3–11). Such instances are the exception to the rule that in general the collections were made by the community in the course of oral transmission.

Fig. 5. A Cluster of Sayings

MARK 8:34–9:1

[And he called to him the multitude with his disciples, and said to them,] "If any man would come after me, let him deny himself and take up his cross and follow me. For whoever would save his life will lose it; and whoever loses his life for my sake and the gospel's will save it. For what does it profit a man, to gain the whole world and forfeit his life? For what can a man give in return for his life? For whoever is ashamed of me and of my words in this adulterous and sinful generation, of him will the Son of man also be ashamed when he comes in the glory of his Father with the holy angels." [And he said to them,] "Truly, I say to you, there are some standing here who will not taste death before they see the kingdom of God come with power."

PARABLES.   One of the most characteristic forms of Jesus' words preserved by the oral tradition was the parable.[11] A parable is a narrative which vividly describes a commonplace incident or experience (see Fig. 6). A lifelike quality is essential to the parable. It was important that the hearer recognize the incident described as something he had already seen occur, or at least, could imagine the incident as within the realm of possibility. The parables were originally intended to call attention to some truth by comparing the

---

[9]Dibelius prefers the term *Paranesis*. Bultmann classifies "saying" in five categories. His most comprehensive term is *Logia*.

[10]See C. F. Burney, *The Poetry of Our Lord* (Oxford: Oxford University Press, 1925). The author endeavors to recover the original sayings of Jesus by a retranslation of the Greek into original Aramaic.

[11]Both Dibelius and Bultmann use the term *Gleichnis*.

Fig. 6. A Parable

MARK 4:3–8

[Listen!] A sower went out to sow. And as he sowed, some seed fell along the path, and the birds came and devoured it. Other seed fell on rocky ground, where it had not much soil, and immediately it sprang up, since it had no depth of soil; and when the sun rose it was scorched, and since it had no root it withered away. Other seed fell among thorns and the thorns grew up and choked it, and it yielded no grain. And other seeds fell into good soil and brought forth grain, growing up and increasing and yielding thirtyfold and sixtyfold and a hundredfold.

principal impression left by the parable with that truth. For example, many of the parables were told to suggest some truth about the kingdom of God. The parable is a story employed to illustrate a truth which is independent of the parable itself. In oral transmission, parables tended to be allegorized. In some instances the parable itself maintained its internal structure and was accompanied by an allegorical interpretation; an example of this is the Parable of the Sower (Mk. 4:1–9), with its accompanying interpretation (Mk. 4:13–20). But in numerous instances the allegorizing has already affected the internal structure of the parable (*e.g.*, Mt. 22:1–14).

In another case we have a parable which already bears the marks of allegorizing, but is nevertheless accompanied by an allegorical interpretation (Mt. 13:24–30; 36–43). There were two primary reasons for this tendency toward allegorization. First, a proper understanding of the parable depended upon the concrete situation to which it was addressed. Since most of the parables soon circulated in isolation from the specific situation to which they were addressed by Jesus, one way to read them meaningfully was to allegorize them, for example, through understanding them as symbolic stories describing the early Church's situation. Second, allegorizing apparently resulted from a tendency to look for esoteric meaning in the words of Jesus.

While parables circulated as independent units it is likely that at the oral stage of transmission some were already transmitted in groups of two or more. For example, it is likely that Mark found in oral tradition the group of three parables he presents in 4:26–32.

Before leaving the parables, attention must be given to one literary form which stands in close relation to them. I refer to the *simile*, a term regularly used to designate a brief saying which, like the parable, implies a comparison, but unlike it does not have the extended narrative form. Since the similes, like the parables, were first uttered to provide clarification of some specific point Jesus was endeavoring to make by comparison, when they were detached from their original setting in oral transmission they posed problems for understanding. Like other sayings, they were often preserved in groups (see Fig. 7). The group of two similes found in Mk. 2:21–22 may have been found by the author in the oral tradition.

Fig. 7. A Cluster of Similes

MARK 2:21–22

No one sews a piece of unshrunk cloth on an old garment; if he does, the patch tears away from it, the new from the old, and a worse tear is made. And no one puts new wine into old wineskins; if he does, the wine will burst the skins, and the wine is lost, and so are the skins; but new wine is for fresh skins.

STORIES ABOUT JESUS.   These stories,[12] unlike the pronouncement story, have no special features which constitute a definable literary form. The category is intended to designate a sizable number of stories of wide-ranging subject matter which fail to fall clearly under other classifications (see Fig. 8, below). They include such stories as the birth stories of Jesus in Matthew and Luke (Mt. 1:18–25; Lk. 2:1–20), the Temptation of Jesus (Mt. 4:1–11; Lk. 4:1–13), the call of the disciples (Mk. 1:16–20), the Transfiguration (Mk. 9:2–8), the guard at Jesus' tomb (Mt. 27:62–66), and many others. To be exact, numbered among these are stories about persons other than Jesus: for example, the story of the birth of John the Baptist (Lk. 1:57–80). These stories generally circulated as independent units of the oral tradition; there are possible exceptions, such as each of the two independent cycles of stories concerning the birth of Jesus and John the Baptist which probably were transmitted together.

Fig. 8. A Story About Jesus

MARK 11:15–18

[And they came to Jerusalem.] And he entered the temple and began to drive out those who sold and those who bought in the temple, and he overturned the tables of the money-changers and the seats of those who sold pigeons; and he would not allow any one to carry anything through the temple. And he taught, and said to them, "Is it not written, 'My house shall be called a house of prayer for all the nations'? But you have made it a den of robbers."

---

[12]Dibelius uses the terms *Mythen* and *Legende*; Bultmann uses *Geschichtserzählung* and *Legende*.

THE GOSPEL WRITERS AS AUTHORS

We have been considering the contribution of form criticism to our under-standing of the traditions about Jesus during the period of oral transmission. Form-critical studies have reexamined the gospels to discover the extent to which their authors left the marks of their interpretations upon the traditions they wrote about. An acute awareness of the important role of the authors of the Gospels followed from the realization that in the oral period the tradi-tions circulated as independent units. The question was asked: Did the first author, Mark, and his successors merely take the oral traditions and such written traditions as were available, and with a minimum of organizing prin-ciples set them down as they found them? Study of the Gospels has made it increasingly clear that they did not. The validity of this judgment will be substantiated in later chapters when we examine the structure and content of each of the gospels. For the present, we shall consider the procedures employed in this particular phase of gospel research.

The text of any one gospel is studied for its divergencies from the sources which the author is believed to have used. These divergencies may involve such phenomena as changes made in the sequence of passages, in the context of short units of tradition, in the narrative sections joining passages, or in phraseology and vocabulary. This particular phase of gospel studies is com-monly called *redaction criticism*.[13] Redaction criticism seeks an explanation for all these variations in order to better understand the meaning of the partic-ular text and its place in the total structure of the gospel. Redaction criticism assumes that the author made his changes intentionally and purposefully to effect his own particular interpretation of his sources. But the detailed study of specific changes throughout the gospel must be carried on from the per-spective of the entire gospel. For the study proceeds on the assumption that the entire gospel, as a literary unity, coheres on the basis of some overall plan or purpose. This plan is revealed principally by certain recurring themes or motifs that conjoin to determine the structure and arrangement of the gospel and give it coherence.

To trace this process requires two concurrent types of analysis. On the one hand, constant attention must be given to the author's divergencies from his sources in specific incidents in order to discover what cumulative light these shed on his overall plan or purpose, his principal themes or motifs; on the other, the gospel must be considered as a literary unity, and its structure and recurring themes may become apparent from this wider perspective.

Insofar as redaction criticism involves the study of the changes which a Gospel writer imposes on his sources, the greater the knowledge of the specific content of his sources, the greater the possibility of determining the changes.

---

[13]See N. Perrin, *What is Redaction Criticism?*, Facet Books (Philadelphia: Fortress Press, 1969).

For example, if it is assumed that Matthew and Luke each made use of a text of Mark that approximates the text we now know, then study of the divergencies in Matthew and Luke from Mark may enjoy considerable precision. If it is assumed that Matthew and Luke each used source Q, precision is limited by the fact that we do not possess the original Q source, but only the Matthean and Lukan versions of it. Nevertheless, comparison of the texts can be made on the basis of a hypothetical reconstruction of the Q source. However, Matthew and Luke employed sources peculiar to each (M and L), and any conclusions regarding changes made by Matthew and Luke are highly speculative, since we have no knowledge of these sources outside Matthew and Luke. Finally, since there is no extant external evidence for Mark's sources on the basis of which to make a comparison with his text, conclusions regarding Mark's divergencies from his sources, as in the case of M and L, are far more hypothetical. Study of Mark is therefore highly dependent upon the careful analysis of the document as a literary unity.

This is an admittedly oversimplified description of the procedures followed by contemporary scholars to examine, explain, and expound the very important role of the Gospel authors in interpreting the traditions they utilized.[14] For example, all scholars bring to their study of the Gospels some understanding of the history and development of the early Christian community's life, thought, and traditions—an understanding that largely derives from the other writings of the New Testament, as well as from the Gospels. The particular understanding of each scholar inevitably informs his redaction criticism; the reader will be able to explore this further when we study each gospel.

By way of summary and reminder, it is important to make two observations: first, that the gospels mark the final stage in the earliest cycle of interpretations of the original traditions about Jesus; and second, as form criticism has made abundantly clear, the traditions at the disposal of the authors did not provide the kind of information that would enable them to compose biographies of Jesus even if they had desired to do so. But they did not. Their intentions in preserving and transmitting the traditions were more nearly in harmony with the community which passed on the oral tradition from the beginning than with those of modern biographers.

THE GOSPELS AND THE JESUS OF HISTORY

By now the reader is undoubtedly aware of the problems which confront the task of reconstructing the life and teachings of the historical Jesus. It is difficult to assess fully the change which has come about since the nineteenth century, when scholars labored in a confidence inspired by the recent achieve-

---

[14]A book which has become a classic representative of the contemporary interest in the importance of the gospel writers as authors, and the employment of redaction criticism is *The Theology of St. Luke* by Hans Conzelmann (London: Faber & Faber, 1960).

ments of source criticism. Accompanying the conclusion that Mark was the earliest Gospel was the conviction (now known to have been unjustified) that in Mark they possessed an account of the life and ministry of Jesus which reliably reported the sequence and progress of Jesus' ministry. In Q they believed they possessed an early source containing sayings of Jesus which were close to the very words (*ipsissima verba*) of Jesus. Many believed it was possible through Mark and Q not only to reconstruct the progress of Jesus' ministry, but to explore the consciousness of his mission, even to trace a development in that consciousness from the beginning to the end of his ministry.

The story of the quest of nineteenth-century scholars to write the life of the historical Jesus, and the many "Lives" that were produced, has been thoroughly told by Albert Schweitzer in a book that is now one of the great landmarks of New Testament studies, *The Quest of the Historical Jesus*.[15] Schweitzer leveled a severe criticism on much of their efforts. His criticism was based mainly on his contention that the efforts were misguided because of the neglect of the eschatological character of Jesus' message and mission.[16] It had receded into insignificance, he claimed, as scholars uncritically interpreted Jesus' life and teachings on the basis of their own ideas, which were derived mainly from nineteenth-century theology and philosophy. They had wrenched Jesus from his historical environment and clothed him in the garb of their own age.

The substance of Schweitzer's criticism of the nineteenth-century scholars continues to be a decisive factor in the differences between studies of Jesus in the nineteenth and twentieth centuries.[17] The truly decisive factor was yet to come. Schweitzer himself in one important respect continued the tradition of nineteenth-century scholarship. At the conclusion of his book, with a confidence as great as that of any of his predecessors, he sought on the basis of the content and sequence of events in the gospels to penetrate and explain the intentions, purposes, and decisions of Jesus' inner life. And on the basis of this he presented his own detailed "historical" analysis of the development of Jesus' life and message from its beginning to its earthly end. Schweitzer's critique of the nineteenth-century studies, and his stress on the importance of eschatology in Jesus' message, were supremely significant in determining the future direction of interpretations of the historical Jesus. But it was the conclusions of the form critics which drove the final wedge between the hopes and aims of the nineteenth- and mid-twentieth-century study of Jesus. Not only

---

[15]Albert Schweitzer, *The Quest of the Historical Jesus*, tr. W. Montgomery (New York: Macmillan, 1948). The original German title was *Von Reimarus zu Wrede: Eine Geschichte der Leben Jesu Forschung* (Tübingen: J. C. B. Mohr, 1906).

[16]Schweitzer was not the first or only scholar to make this criticism. Equally important in the scholarly world was the earlier work of Johannes Weiss, *Die Predigt Jesu vom Reiche Gottes* (Göttingen: Vandenhoeck & Ruprecht, 1900). Schweitzer's work was so important because of his review of the nineteenth century and because of the wider reading his book received.

[17]An account of the study of the historical Jesus in the twentieth century is presented in C. C. McCown, *The Search for the Real Jesus* (New York: Scribner's, 1940).

was the possibility of writing a full biography or life of Jesus called into question, but all pretensions to be able to penetrate recorded traditions to his life
and thought were shown to be beyond the realm of historical research.

THE NEW QUEST FOR THE HISTORICAL JESUS

One of the first fruits of form-critical studies was a profound skepticism.
Not only was the possibility of writing a life of Jesus discarded; it was seriously
believed that only a minimal content of Jesus' message could be recovered with
any certainty. In the words of one form critic, only a "whisper" remained.[18]
The crucial issue was the extent to which the Christian community not only
interpreted the traditions about Jesus, but created them. Dibelius and Bultmann
tended to assign a major creative role to the early Church. For example,
Dibelius believed that the pronouncement stories were largely the creation of
the non-Palestinian Christian community and served mainly as illustrative stories in the preaching mission to the Gentiles. Bultmann, on the other hand, was
inclined to trace the origin of the stories to Palestinian Christian communities.
But he believed the settings which provided the context for the pronouncements
were the creation of the community and reflected the conflicts in which the
community found itself engaged. Both scholars believed that the miracle
stories were largely the product of the religious imagination of the Gentile
churches. And both likewise considered that most of the stories about Jesus,
which they chose to describe as myths, legends, or tales, were the creation of
the community, many for the purpose of transferring the origin of later beliefs
and practices to the ministry of the historical Jesus. Many of the sayings, and
even the parables, were similarly viewed through skeptical eyes.

The reaction to the form critics was varied. Some scholars, shocked by their
skeptical conclusions, refused to take them seriously. There were from the beginning, however, many thoughtful scholars who after serious examination recognized the validity of certain basic claims of form criticism. But there were
serious objections made against certain historical judgments, principally the
creative role assigned to the early Christian community.[19] Among the many
criticisms of form criticism which have been made from the beginning, two
have particular importance in the eyes of many. First, it has been charged that
the more extreme form critics have neglected the impact of the words and
deeds of Jesus on those followers who after his death and resurrection formed
the nucleus of the earliest Christian community. Second, they have neglected
the importance of the presence of these eyewitnesses in the early Christian

---

[18]R. H. Lightfoot, *History and Interpretation in the Gospels* (London: Hodder &
Stoughton, 1935).

[19]One of the early responsible reactions to the form critics which is both appreciative
and critical is found in B. S. Easton, *The Gospel Before the Gospels* (New York: Scribner's,
1928).

community during the formative period when the traditions about Jesus were remembered, interpreted, and transmitted. Recently, reaction to this neglect has been expressed in the form of theories which suggest that the character of Jesus' teaching and the religious awe in which his words were held were such as to guarantee their almost inviolable transmission.[20] Such conclusions have not found a widely favorable response; nevertheless, a more moderate yet persistent insistence on the relative historical reliability of the Gospel tradition is increasingly evident among many scholars,[21] who at the same time acknowledge the indispensability of the contribution and method of form criticism in research into the mission and message of Jesus.

The contemporary trend of research into the words and deeds of Jesus is characterized by a positive attitude toward the possibilities for new understanding afforded by the advances in the field of source- and form-critical studies. If form criticism has established the fact that the gospel traditions continually bear witness to the interpretation of the early Church, its intensive study of the theological and practical interests of the emerging Church has enhanced the possibility of arriving at a more proximate, if not an absolute, understanding of the bedrock traditions of the historical Jesus. This increasing knowledge of the early Church's beliefs and practices has been supplemented by an ever-expanding knowledge of the Jewish background of Jesus' ministry. The sudden discovery of such unexpected evidence as the Dead Sea Scrolls, as well as a more adequate knowledge of various sects and the general historical situation in Palestine, provide a context most favorable to historical research.

It is common today to speak of a "new quest" for the historical Jesus.[22] It differs from the old nineteenth-century quest in its disavowal of any hopes to write a biography of Jesus.[23] It is generally agreed that methodological problems are far from solved. What is striking is the areas in which agreement is to be found.[24] A pioneering work in the new quest has been written,[25] and an

[20]See Harold Riesenfeld, *The Gospel Tradition and Its Beginnings* (London: A. R. Mowbray & Co., 1957); and B. Gerhardsson, *Memory and Manuscript: Oral Tradition and Written Transmission in Rabbinic Judaism and Early Christianity* (Uppsala: C. W. K. Gleerup, 1961).

[21]See Amos Wilder, "Form-History and the Oldest Tradition," in *Neotestamentica et Patristica*, supplements to *Novum Testamentum*, VI (Leiden: E. J. Brill, 1962), 3–13; W. D. Davies, "Reflections on a Scandinavian Approach to 'The Gospel Tradition'" in *Neotestamentica et Patristica*, supplements to *Novum Testamentum*, VI, 14–46. The latter article is a critique of Gerhardsson (see previous footnote).

[22]See J. M. Robinson, *A New Quest of the Historical Jesus* (Naperville, Ill.: Allenson, 1959). The major impetus for this quest came from an address by Ernst Kaesemann now in English translation, in *Essays on New Testament Themes* (Naperville: Allenson, 1964).

[23]There are also major differences created by the new theological context in which the quest is pursued. We have not dealt with these. For a discussion see J. M. Robinson, *op. cit.*

[24]See the stimulating essay by J. M. Robinson, "The Formal Structure of Jesus' Message," in *Current Issues in New Testament Interpretation*, William Klassen and Graydon F. Snyder, eds. (New York: Harper & Row, 1962), pp. 91–110.

[25]Gunther Bornkamm, *Jesus of Nazareth* (New York: Harper & Row, 1956). A more recent example of contemporary approach to the problem is Norman Perrin, *Rediscovering the Teachings of Jesus* (New York: Harper & Row, 1967), especially pp. 39–43, where he discusses his criteria.

increasing number of specialized studies, utilizing the critical insights of form criticism, but turning them to the positive task of understanding the words and deeds of Jesus, have appeared. One of the most important developments has been a critical but positive reaffirmation of the authenticity of the parables of Jesus in the synoptic tradition; important progress in their interpretation has shed new light on both the content of Jesus' message and the meaning of his mission.[26] There is a fresh new critical-but-appreciative understanding of the miracle tradition[27] in the gospels, and significant strides have been taken toward further illumination of the content and meaning of the ethical teaching of Jesus in the historical setting of his ministry.[28] It is within the limitations as well as the possibilities provided by the new situation in gospel studies that we now turn to a consideration of what can be said regarding the mission and message of Jesus at Nazareth.

[26]Consult the monumental work of J. Jeremias, *The Parables of Jesus*, 6th ed., tr. S. H. Hooke (New York: Scribner's, 1962).

[27]E.g., Reginald H. Fuller, *Interpreting the Miracles* (Philadelphia: Westminster, 1963).

[28]Representative of these new studies in the English-speaking world are Harvey K. McArthur, *Understanding the Sermon on the Mount* (New York: Harper & Row, 1960); T. W. Manson, *Ethics and the Gospel* (New York: Scribner's, 1960); W. D. Davies, *The Setting of the Sermon on the Mount* (Cambridge, England: Cambridge University Press, 1964).

Jesus, Prophet
of the New Age

CHAPTER FOUR

Among non-Christian historians and writers of the first century A.D., the career of Jesus of Nazareth passed all but unnoticed. The only references to him in the *Antiquities of the Jews,* by the first-century Jewish historian Josephus, mention his death along with other insurrectionists and troublemakers in Palestine whom Rome executed in order to preserve the peace (*Ant.,* 18.63) and allude to him as the brother of James, who became leader of the Church in Jerusalem in the middle of the first century (*Ant.,* 20.200). The Roman historian, Tacitus, in his *Annals* refers to Jesus as the founder of one of the religious sects that had found its way to Rome in the later first century, and by way of dismissing the group, mentions the fact that its leader had been executed under the Roman governor, Pontius Pilate (*Annals,* 15.44). The rabbinic sources from this period content themselves with denouncing Jesus (whom they refer to by epithet[1] rather than name) as a magician and a de-

---

[1]Common designations of Jesus in the rabbinic sources are "Ben-Pandira" or "Ben-Panthera," meaning "son of Pantheros," which implies that Jesus was the illegitimate son of a Roman soldier. Other rabbinic sources refer to him simply as "such a one."

94

ceiver of the people. When we take into account the polemical nature of these references, there is nothing in them that conflicts with the New Testament portrayals of Jesus, but they provide no supplement to the gospel narratives nor do they even furnish an objective perspective on the Biblical accounts. For reconstructing the career of Jesus, therefore, we are left to assess the Gospel materials themselves by critical methods.

The results of this kind of analysis are surprisingly clear and full. As we saw in the preceding chapter, one of the oldest—perhaps the very oldest— written source for our knowledge of Jesus is the Q document, which consists of cycles of sayings material. We have already noted the existence of similar collections which developed in Judaism in connection with the Wisdom tradition, although there were precedents and parallels in Wisdom traditions from other sources in the ancient Near East. In the material peculiar to Luke we have a very old tradition as well, so that by a judicious use of Q and L tradition, differentiating traditional material from the use to which the evangelists have put it, we can arrive at a clear and consistent reconstruction of Jesus' message as prophet of the New Age, though we can say only in probabilities whether our picture goes back to Jesus himself. Lying behind and incorporated into the Gospel of Mark are cycles of miracle stories[2] which give us, at least in broad terms, access to the activity of Jesus. The tradition, including the allusions in Jewish polemical writings, is unanimous that he did perform exorcisms and healings,[3] so that we are obligated to treat this aspect of the primitive picture of Jesus with the same seriousness as we devote to the analysis of his teachings. The Gospel writers have expanded the miracle stories, adapting them to serve their own special purposes, and the oral tradition undoubtedly elaborated and supplemented the wonder-working aspects of Jesus' ministry as well. But certain layers of the miracle tradition can be shown to be very old; in all probability they go back to recollection of Jesus' actual career.

Scholars have often assumed that the story of Jesus' sufferings and death was the first extended narrative unit to appear in the Gospel tradition and that it was the nucleus around which the later tradition gathered, or to change the figure, the climax for which the rest of the tradition was assembled as prelude. The gospels have been called "passion stories with extended introductions."[4] Although this remains a possibility, it seems more likely that the story

---

[2] A recent discussion of these miracle cycles is by Paul J. Achtemeier, "Toward the Isolation of Pre-Marcan Miracle Catenae," Journal of Biblical Literature, LXXXIX (1970), 265–291; "The Origin and Function of the Pre-Marcan Miracle Catenae," Journal of Biblical Literature, XCI (1972), 198–221.

[3] See for example the judgment of Rudolf Bultmann, *Jesus and the Word* (New York: Scribner's, 1934), pp. 27–28. Also in C. E. Braaten and R. A. Harrisville, eds., *Historical Jesus and Kerygmatic Christ* (New York and Nashville: Abingdon, 1964) p. 22.

[4] Martin Kähler, *The So-called Historical Jesus*, tr. C. E. Braaten (Philadelphia: Fortress Press, 1964), p. 80, n. 11.

of the trial and death of Jesus was built up in part out of oral tradition but in large measure out of Christian reading of the Old Testament, by which process it was shown that the Crucifixion was not a betrayal of the disciples' hopes but the unfolding of a divine, predetermined plan.[5] There may once have existed a rudimentary Passion narrative, but it is now thickly overlaid by the theology and apologetics of the Church expressed through proofs from scripture. In the present reconstruction, therefore, we shall confine ourselves to the main outline of the teaching of Jesus, some of the characteristics of his activity, the fact of his death, and the expectation that God would vindicate both Jesus and his disciples in the New Age.

THE KINGDOM OF GOD HAS DRAWN NEAR

At the outset of Jesus' public activity in the Q version (Mt. 3:1–12 = Lk. 3:2–17), he is pictured as associating himself with a movement calling for eschatological repentance led by John the Baptist. The Baptist announced that those who considered themselves to be God's Chosen People were unworthy of that honor, but that they could prepare themselves to participate in the Age to Come if they repented of their sins and showed their concern to be pure by accepting baptism at his hand. To be cleansed by water was now a guarantee of safe passage through the baptism of judgmental fire that was soon to fall on all mankind. It is with this group awaiting and preparing for the New Age that Jesus associated himself by coming to John for baptism.

It was a commonplace of Jewish apocalyptic thinking that God's Rule could not be established until that of his adversary (Satan) had been overthrown. That overthrow was not to occur without a struggle, or without a desperate effort on the part of Satan to thwart God's purpose. The temptation story, told in a fuller version in Q than in Mark (Mt. 4:1–11 = Lk. 4:1–11), depicts graphically the struggle as to whether Jesus will submit to the offer of easy power and quick reward extended by Satan or whether he will stand unswervingly by the will of God. Although the Temptation story is legendary in the form in which Q preserved it, its presence at this point in the tradition points up that what is at stake is not merely Jesus' own vocation but also the fulfillment of God's promise to establish His Kingdom. The Temptation story, therefore, comes appropriately just before the introduction of the theme of Jesus' ministry:

> The time is fulfilled,
> and the Kingdom of God has drawn near
> —MARK 1:15

---

[5] H. C. Kee, "Scriptural Quotations in the Markan Passion Narrative," in *Papers of the Society of Biblical Literature, Atlanta, 1971,* published by SBL at Missoula, Montana, 1972, pp. 475–502.

THE JORDAN VALLEY *at its lower end, near the traditional site of Jesus' baptism, looking toward the hills of Judea.* (Howard C. Kee)

The firm tradition that Jesus did not begin his public preaching until after John the Baptist had been put in prison is probably based on historical fact. Passages in the Gospel of John (1:35–42; 3:22–26; 4:1–2), although somewhat confusing and even contradictory in detail, imply that there was a period in which Jesus and John were first associated in baptizing activity in the Jordan Valley, followed by a period of outright competition (Jn. 4:1), after which Jesus withdrew to Galilee (Jn. 2:12; 4:43). Then when John was in prison, Jesus resumed his preaching. The point at issue can be inferred from the differing accounts of their respective messages: John denounced sinners and called on them to prepare for judgment which was about to fall; Jesus is presented in the tradition as the friend of tax-collectors and sinners (Mk. 2:13–17; Mt. 9:9–13; Lk. 5:27–32). In Mark 2:18–22, where Jesus is reported as defending his work among religious outcasts, the conflict is made explicit between Jesus and the followers of John over whether it was proper to share a meal with those who were ceremonially unclean by Jewish standards. It is probably this controversy which gave rise to the poignant question sent to Jesus by the imprisoned John (Mt. 11:2–6), and to which Jesus replied by pointing concretely to the liberation he was effecting in setting men free from the illnesses that bound them and in extending to them the invitation to share in the New Age ("the poor have good news preached to them").

It was not *good* news to announce merely that judgment was imminent, and it was not *news* to declare that God was going to establish a New Age. The new element in the message of Jesus was that he asserted the New Age to have drawn so near ("the time is fulfilled") that not only could men now prepare to enter it, but also the signs of God's final triumph were already evident to the eyes of faith in the ministry of exorcisms and healing that Jesus was carrying out. His opponents did not deny that he had extraordinary powers, but they credited these powers to the prince of demons (Beelzebub) who, they asserted, was at work through him (Mk. 3:22). His response was to show how foolish it would be for Satan to undermine his own control over

97

THE MOUNT OF TEMPTATION *has been identified by local tradition as the place where Jesus was tempted by Satan. The belt-like monastery on the side of the mountain contains a tiny chapel in a cave, which is supposed to be the place where Jesus spent forty days and nights in prayer.* (Matson Photo Service)

men by accomplishing exorcisms through Jesus; this would lead to the destruction of Satan's rule over the present age (Mk. 3:23–26). At this point the Q version of the tradition adds the telling point that it is by God's power ("the finger of God"—Lk. 11:20) that Jesus is able to expel the demons, and further that in these actions the Rule of God has already begun to impinge on the present situation: "The kingdom of God has come upon you."

As is evident in the later gospel tradition, in Matthew and John but especially in the apocryphal gospels never included in the New Testament canon, the miracles attributed to Jesus were understood in some cases to be manifestations of divine power or even of a divine nature (see, for example, John 2:11; 20:30–31); but in the older tradition, the wonders performed by Jesus are offered as signs that through him the power of Satan over men is being broken. This is clearest in the simple story of the demoniac in the synagogue at Nazareth (Mk. 1:23–27), according to which Jesus' utterance of the "commanding word" (that is the force of the Greek word regularly translated wrongly as "rebuke")[6] results not only in the expulsion of the demon but also in the subjection of the evil spirits more generally. Since demons were regarded in

---

[6]H. C. Kee, "The Terminology of Markan Exorcisms," New Testament Studies, XIV (1968), 232–246.

this time and culture as the agents by which Satan maintained his control over the present age, anyone who could control them was already on the way to wresting from Satan his hold on the present age. Terms with identical connotations are used of Jesus in healings (Mk. 1:43; Lk. 4:39). Among the Dead Sea Scrolls, the Semitic original of these terms is used to announce the situation about to come when Beliar (another name for Satan) is defeated and the Reign of God established. It is significant that in the later, more highly developed miracle stories, including exorcism tales (Mk. 5:1–20), this primitive term does not appear. Jesus' ministry of healing and exorcisms was accordingly seen in the earliest tradition as the first round in the battle that would end in the defeat of God's enemies and the actualization of his Rule.

THE GOD WHOSE KINGDOM IS DRAWING NEAR

Part of the tension between Jesus and John the Baptist concerned the issue of what God was like. John was doubtless influenced by such passages as these:

> The Lord whom you seek will suddenly come into his temple . . . but who can abide the day of his coming, and who can stand when he appears? For he is like a refiner's fire and like fuller's soap; he will sit as a refiner and purifier of silver, and he will purify the sons of Levi [i.e., the priests]. . . .
>
> Behold, I will send Elijah the prophet before the great and terrible day of the Lord comes. And he will turn the hearts of fathers to their children and the hearts of the children to their fathers, lest I come and smite the land with a curse.
>
> —MALACHI 3:1–3, 23–24

Indeed, the tradition later did identify John the Baptist as Elijah (Mt. 17:13), whose coming was widely awaited among Jews in the first-century A.D. But Jesus' expectation of the God whose Kingdom was coming was sharply different. The note of warning in view of the need to repent is there (Lk. 13:1–5): "Unless you repent, you will all likewise perish." But the next line in Luke presents a parable in which the forbearance of God is depicted under the image of a farmer who decides to give an unfruitful tree one more chance.

It is in the material found in Luke and Matthew and to some extent in Q that the clearest representation of God is seen, though a similar view is implied throughout the tradition. In the three adjoining parables of Luke 15:1–32, Jesus' understanding is presented by analogy with three different persons, each of whom has lost a treasured object and takes the initiative to regain it. The Parable of the Rejoicing Shepherd (Luke 15:3–7) points to the joy of God himself ("joy in heaven") over the recovery of one of his creatures who has been estranged from him. Similarly, the Joyous Housewife is an image of God's

joy at regaining what had been lost. Most vivid of all is the double Parable of
the Rejoicing Father and the Peevish Son (Lk. 15:11–24 and 25–32), in which
the aged father's initiative in reconciling to himself the alienated son is resented
by the stay-at-home brother. In each case, it is not that what has been lost
is grudgingly allowed to return to its proper place, but that the shepherd,
the housewife, and the father take the initiative by searching the desert,
sweeping the house, and starting down the road toward the errant son. In
each instance the aim is to restore the object to its intended home. Jesus therefore sees his own ministry of befriending outcasts and, those religiously dis-
approved by his contemporaries as an extension of the nature of God himself.

The direct correspondence between what God is like and how Jesus and his
disciples are to carry out their mission is expressed forcefully in a parable,
The Great Supper, which is preserved in its most original form in Luke
14:15–24. Leaving out of account verses 22–24, which seem to represent the
special interests of Luke (see Chapter Fourteen), the parable describes a
man who plans a feast and sends out a preliminary announcement to a list
of prospective guests. Those invited are so preoccupied with their worldly
affairs—their property, their livestock, or their family obligations—that each
declines the invitation. Luke was probably faithful to the intention of Jesus
when he prefaced the parable with a pronouncement about the coming of
God's eschatological Kingdom (Lk. 14:15), so that the feast is an image of the
eschatological banquet as depicted by Jewish hopes. A meal of this type is
described in one of the Dead Sea Scrolls, The Rule for the Future Community.
The point of Jesus' parable is that men value so highly what they possess in
this age that they deny themselves the opportunity to accept God's gracious
invitation to enter the Age to Come. But God's purpose is not thwarted by the
fact that those originally invited are preoccupied: the invitation now goes out
to those most desperately in need, and therefore most ready to heed: "the
poor, the maimed, the blind, the lame."

In the Gospel tradition we have not so much a picture of who or what
God is, but of how he acts. The disparity between Jesus' understanding of
what God's grace is like and the simpleminded fairness that man expects to
be in effect in God's universe is vividly portrayed in the Parable of the Laborers
(Mt. 20:1–15). The workers who have spent the whole day in the scorching
sun, on learning that those who have worked only a single hour receive a full
day's pay (a denarius), leap to the conclusion that they will receive much
more. But in fact, God gives equally to all, and challenges those who begrudge
him his generosity.[7]

The same point is made in more direct language in Q material included by

[7]Matthew has added a saying at 20:16 that shifts the meaning of the parable: the
Gentiles who enter the community last will end up in the preferred position. This interpretation serves well Matthew's purpose (see Chapter Twelve) but distorts the parable's
original thrust of pointing to the incalculable quality of divine grace.

Matthew in his Sermon on the Mount (Mt. 6:25–34), but it is given in what is more likely the older form in Luke 12:22–31. God's gracious care for his creation is seen in the provision of feed for birds and in the transient beauty of flower-carpeted hillsides. In the face of such divine concern, man should find no place for anxiety about his daily needs nor for avarice about possessing more worldly goods. The highest priority must be given to seeking God's Kingdom, which is God's own goal for his creation. Luke adds at this point the declaration that God is going to give his Kingdom to the "little flock": they are the nucleus of the people of the New Covenant who are prepared to enter the Age to Come.

Jesus' ethical teaching is often based on an appeal that men should act graciously toward their fellow men because that is the way God acts toward his creatures. Matthew's version of the Q saying about loving one's enemies (Mt. 5:43–48) brings this out clearly. By loving enemies and by being concerned for one's persecutors, the member of the new community demonstrates that God is his father, since he allows men to enjoy the cycle of day and night and the indispensable falling of rain regardless of their moral qualities. For Jesus the standard for moral behavior is not a legal code or abstract ethical principles, but the very nature of God as it is evident in his gracious acts toward men (Lk. 6:36). In praying for the coming of God's Kingdom, Jesus enjoins his followers to expect divine forgiveness only if they are willing to forgive others with undischarged obligations toward them (Lk. 11: 4). To pray for the hallowing of God's name is to ask that men acknowledge God for what he is, the sovereign of the universe; when men are prepared to do so, God's reign will become an actuality on earth (Mt. 6:10).

Luke has probably preserved the older form of the Beatitudes (Lk. 6:20–23; cf. Mt. 5:3–12), in which the hearers are addressed directly ("you" rather than the generalized "the poor"); and their present deprivation is contrasted with the Kingdom which they are soon to receive. Their hunger will be replaced by satisfaction in the Age to Come, and their sorrow will be turned into joy. Whatever difficulties or hostility they may experience should not surprise them, since that was the kind of treatment afforded God's messengers in the days of the prophets.[8] The message in the days of the prophets and in the time of Jesus was: Stand faithful to your calling by God, and he will vindicate you before your enemies when his eschatological Rule is established.

The call of the disciples to share in preparing men for the coming of God's Kingdom is directly described in Mark 1:16–20 and 6:6–13, where the twelve are sent out to preach repentance, to heal, and to perform exorcisms. In view of the impending End of the Age, they are to make no provisions for a long-range ministry, but to move quickly from place to place, summoning as many

---

[8]The experiences of Jeremiah when he was threatened with death (Jer. 26), and of Daniel when he was delivered from starvation and from the lions are especially relevant here.

as they can reach with the message of the Kingdom of God. The implication is that Jesus received his calling from God and that he now has passed on to the disciples the authority to carry forward his work (Mk. 6:7). Matthew and Luke have greatly expanded this segment of the tradition, each of them making it serve his own special aims. They are to rely on local hospitality to meet their daily needs. The parables of the Kingdom make a parallel point that the immediate results of the disciples' preaching activity will be mixed (Mk. 4:3–7), but when the New Age arrives—here represented in keeping with the Jewish prophetic tradition of the time of harvest—it will be seen that their activity in behalf of the coming Kingdom has produced astonishing results (Mk. 4:8).[9]

THY WILL BE DONE

Although there are many points at which the ethic of Jesus overlaps or echoes that of the rabbis who were his contemporaries, his approach to the question of obedience to God was in its overall method so radical that it is easy to see how his teaching would have been regarded by the religious authorities as a threat. Although the explicit setting of his interpretation of the divine will over against the Law of Moses ("You have heard it has been said . . . but I say to you") seems to have originated with Matthew, the implied setting aside of the demands of Jewish Law is readily apparent in the older layers of the tradition. This is perhaps clearest in his attitude toward divorce and ceremonial cleanliness. Deuteronomy 24:1 gives direct authorization for a man under certain circumstances to divorce his wife by writing the appropriate certificate. The rabbis argued as to what "some indecency" meant, since this was set forth in Torah as the ground for divorce. Some said infidelity was the sole justification for divorce; others interpreted the term more broadly. Jesus (Mk. 10:1–12) rejects the whole notion of divorce on the ground that marriage was a part of the order of Creation (Gen. 1:27) and that the marriage union is not to be severed.

By seeking out as table companions those who were religiously ostracized by the prevailing Jewish standards of his time, Jesus was undermining the whole notion of the need for the Covenant people to be separate from all others. When challenged on the subject (Mk. 2:16–17), Jesus replied that his mission was to call to repentance those who knew their own need. Although the tradition concerning defilement (Mk. 7:1–23) has been expanded by Mark and the other gospel writers to serve the special needs of the church for which they were writing, the basic point likely goes back to Jesus: overcoming sin and defilement is a matter of inner motivation and personal integrity rather

---

[9]The original force of these parables is evident in the tradition as it stands in Mark 4:3–8, but Mark and the other synoptic writers have shifted the point from the sure results of the sowing to the question of the receptivity of the hearers of the Christian message.

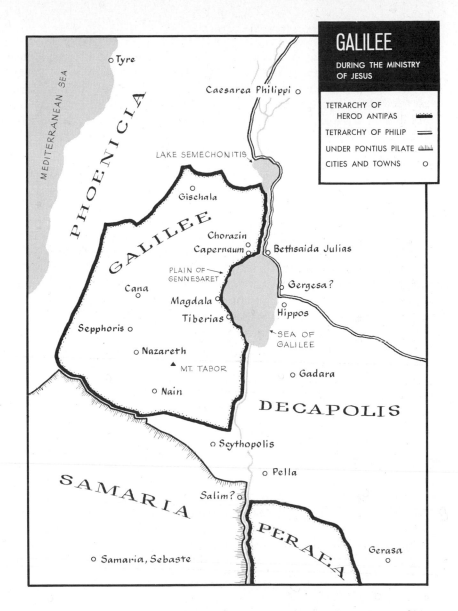

than of mere external contact: "What comes out of a man is what defiles a man" (Mk. 7:20).

Similarly, observance of the Sabbath Law, fundamental to the identity of Jews for millennia, is for Jesus not so important as human need. This is evident in the stories of his defense of the disciples' preparation of food on the Sabbath (Mk. 2:23–27) and of his own act of healing on the Sabbath (3:1–6). The conflict between Jews and Christians—or possibly between Jewish and Gentile Christians within the Church—is the occasion for elaborating this theme in the other gospels, especially in Luke, who reports two incidents in which Jesus is involved in conflict with religious leaders over his having performed a healing on the Sabbath day (Lk. 13:10–17; 14:1–6). But in spite of expansion of the Sabbath controversy as the Church and the synagogue drew ever farther apart in the last third of the first century A.D., it is extremely likely that Jesus considered the prohibition of work on the Sabbath as justifiably set aside when there was opportunity to meet the need of one of his fellow men.

Another of the commandments that Jesus reinterpreted in a radical fashion concerned the love of one's neighbor. Mark reports Jesus as reaffirming the ancient Jewish commandment of love to God and combining it with the commandment to love one's neighbor (Mk. 12:28–34). Similar statements about the central core of the commandments are attributed to rabbis and other ancient religious teachers, so that there is nothing startling in this formulation. When, however, the concept of love of neighbor is extended to include one's enemies as in a Q sayings complex (Lk. 6:27–28, 32–36 = Mt. 5:43–48), a fundamentally different attitude is introduced. Among Jews from very early times, there was an obligation to offer hospitality and the protection of one's home to a wayfarer or stranger in the land, as is evident in the story of the homosexuals who want to rape the visitors in Lot's house in Sodom (Gen. 19:1–11). What Jesus enjoins upon his followers is not merely to protect or to meet the needs of itinerant strangers but to love enemies. This love is not a matter of attitude but of action, as is implied by the phrase "and do good" in parallel with the command to love (Lk. 6:35). Love is not to be practiced in order to convert the enemies into friends, since Jesus adds that the disciples in loving enemies are to "expect nothing in return." As we have already observed, the basis of this moral appeal is the nature of God and his acts of unmerited favor to all men.

Jewish students of the New Testament have often objected justifiably that neither the Old Testament nor the rabbis taught hatred of enemies, as is implied in Matthew's version of the saying (Mt. 5:43). There are, of course, many passages in the Old Testament which express a fierce spirit of vengeance, as in the familiar words of Psalm 137, where the poet is lamenting the fate of the nation Israel in captivity among the Babylonians:

> Happy shall he be who requites you
>   with what you have done to us!
>
> Happy shall he be who takes your little ones
>   and dashes them against the rock!
>   —PSALMS 137:8,9

Among the Dead Sea Scrolls, however, there is a saying that directly calls for hatred of the enemies of God's people.[10] But since the phrase is found in the framework supplied by Matthew ("you have heard . . . but I say") rather than in the Q version itself (it is missing in Luke), the parallel suggests a link between Matthew and Qumran rather than between Jesus and the Dead Sea community.

---

[10]The Dead Sea community's Manual of Discipline enjoins hatred of enemies, I. 4, 10.

Jesus' call to men to give up all that they possess (Mk. 10:17–31) is more than what we would term an extreme act of charity, though giving to the poor is part of the commandment (10:21). It is an appeal to abandon riches, since they become the basis for a man's sense of security. His confidence is in what he has acquired by his own accomplishment or good fortune, not in the God who calls him to discipleship in behalf of the coming Kingdom. Jesus acknowledges that it is as difficult to imagine a rich man divesting himself of his tangible security as it is to envision such an ungainly beast as a camel passing through a needle's eye. That the problem of wealth was not in possessing it but in being possessed by it is evident in the Parable of the Rich Fool, found only in Luke (12:13–21). His folly lay in the false confidence that his future was somehow guaranteed by the fact that he had great and growing wealth. But his life (not "soul" as in most translations) was about to be brought to an end, so that there was no basis for confidence in his amassing of worldly goods.

Granted the authoritative and independent way in which Jesus recast the commandments, it is fully understandable that his opponents questioned the source of his sovereign reinterpretation of the will of God. According to several elements in the gospel tradition, some of his contemporaries asked him to perform a miracle so that they could be sure he really was sent by God and that his teachings were accordingly divinely sanctioned. In the Markan form (Mk. 8:11–12), the request for a sign is simply refused: "No sign shall be given to this generation."

In the Q form of the saying, which is considerably more extended (Lk. 11:29–32 = Mt. 12:38–42), the point is only slightly altered. "The sign of Jonah" is not a sign at all in the sense of a miracle, but is rather the power of the prophetic call to repentance. Even the wicked Gentile city of Nineveh had repented when Jonah preached. Now Jesus has come with a proposition greater than that of Jonah—that is, the announcement of the End of the Age—and yet men are unwilling to repent in response to Jesus' message. The pericope has been modified and expanded, especially in the Matthean version, as we shall observe in later chapters, but in its older form it seems to have asserted that, with the coming of Jesus as messenger of the dawning New Age, something greater had drawn near than either the preaching of Jonah or the wisdom of Solomon had anticipated. Yet the proof of this imminent event was not to be found in wonders that Jesus performed but in the penitence with which his message was received.

THE DAY OF THE SON OF MAN

Before turning to the place of the concept, Son of Man, in the earliest Jesus tradition, it is essential to explore briefly the history of that term in pre-Christian times. The earliest occurrence of the term is in Daniel 7, where the Kingdom of God that comes in replacement for and triumph over all earthly kingdoms is described as "like a son of man"; that is, like a human being, in contrast to the horrendous beasts which Daniel presents as representing the succession of world empires that come to an end with the establishment of God's rule. It seems likely that other apocalyptic writers, following the lead of Daniel, transformed the simile, "like a son of man," into a title for the person—or community—through whom God's Kingdom was to be established on the earth. The Similitudes of Enoch (Chapters 37–71)[11] depict a redemptive figure through whom man's redemption is accomplished and who was called the Son of Man. His coming would bring to an end the present age and inaugurate the Age to Come. In the oldest layers of the Jesus tradition, Jesus spoke of the coming Son of Man. A later stage of the tradition also utilized the phrase to refer to Jesus' role in uttering authoritative words and in performing authoritative acts in his ministry (Forgiving Sins, Setting aside the Sabbath Law; Mk. 2:1–12;[12] 2:23–28). And a still later stage (Mk. 8:31; 9:31; 10:33ff.) links Son of Man with Jesus' suffering. We shall see that this development is probably part of Mark's own contribution to the emerging theology of the Church, especially as it tries to account for the fact that the one acclaimed by his followers as Lord and Messiah had been put to death. Almost certainly the oldest form of Son of Man sayings is that found in Mark 8:38:

> Whoever is ashamed of me and of my words in this adulterous and sinful generation, of him will the Son of Man also be ashamed when he comes in the glory of his father with the holy angels.

Jesus here speaks of himself in the first person, but uses the third person in referring to the Son of Man. The common interpretation of this passage is that Jesus was merely stating indirectly his identity with the coming Son of Man. But what is more likely is that Jesus, in speaking of the coming Son of Man, built on the tradition of Daniel 7 as modified by the notion expressed in the Similitudes of Enoch that the coming agent who would establish the Rule of

---

[11]It is not yet clear whether this section of the Enoch literature is pre-Christian or has itself been fundamentally influenced by Christianity. The probability is that the Ethiopic version, which is the only complete form in which this part of Enoch has been preserved, was itself preserved by Christians, but there is no direct evidence of Christian influence on the substance of the Similitudes in what is the now-lost Aramaic original apart from the term, Son of Man. And already by the second century the term Son of Man was beginning to pass out of use by Christians, who preferred to describe Jesus as Lord or Son of God. It is difficult to explain why Christians would have taken the trouble to create the Similitudes of Enoch, only to leave them devoid of distinctive Christian teaching. Most probable is that a Jewish apocalyptic sect began to use the term, based on Daniel 7, and that it was sufficiently familiar to Jews of the period as to require no explanation.

[12]The older version of the story probably moved directly from Mark 2:5a to 2:11, and contained no mention of the forgiveness of sins, an issue that was important for the early Church but is not likely to have been significant for disciples of Jesus as they were awaiting the End of the Age. If this is an accurate observation, then the Son of Man idea was also introduced into a simple healing story, which indicates that the Son of Man as an authority figure was a later development in the faith of the early Church and not a part of the teaching of Jesus.

God would not merely be "one like a son of man," but would *be* the Son of Man. His reinterpretation of the Law, his appeal to his followers to stand fast in the face of possible persecution, his transmission of secret knowledge about the Age to Come—all these mesh smoothly with the apocalyptic outlook of much of the eschatological literature of Judaism in this period. It was wholly fitting that Jesus would expect the apocalyptic Son of Man to bring about the shift of the ages whereby the Kingdom of God would become an actuality instead of merely a hope. With the rise of faith in Jesus' Resurrection, the Church began to assert that Jesus was himself the Son of Man whose coming they awaited; the tradition was modified accordingly, so that as it now stands Son of Man is used of Jesus as not only the coming one, but as the authoritative figure of his past ministry and the suffering one whose death liberates men from the powers of the Old Age.[13]

The Q source lays stress on the coming Son of Man (and has no mention of Jesus as suffering Son of Man, which is a peculiarity—and probably a theological contribution—of Mark): Mt. 24:26–28 = Lk. 17:23–24; Mt. 24:37–41 = Lk. 17:26–30. Both passages make the point that the time of the coming of the Son of Man is not subject to human calculation. In the first instance, men are so busy trying to determine how and where he will appear that they are unprepared for his unheralded arrival. In the second case, men are so preoccupied with ordinary family social routines that they are unaware that the judgment of God is about to bring to an end the present age through the coming of the Son of Man. The same point is made in the parabolic Q tradition of the householder whose lack of precaution enabled a thief to steal his goods (Mt. 24:43–44 = Lk. 12:39–40). Just as one must be constantly on the alert against thieves breaking in, so one must be ready at any moment for the coming of the Son of Man.

Although Mark 13, with its extended apocalyptic discourse allegedly uttered by Jesus on the occasion of his announcement of the destruction of Jerusalem, is very likely a creation of Mark in its present form,[14] it includes ideas which are congruent with what Jesus is reported as saying elsewhere, especially in the Q tradition. Above all, the basic assumption seems to be well grounded historically: that Jesus did predict the destruction of the Temple and its city. Mark's "prophecy" is written just before or just after the event took place (70 A.D.), and is colored by the historical occurrences connected with the Temple's destruction; but the frequency and diversity of references to the destruction of the Temple at various spots in the Gospel tradition suggest that this is an authentic recollection of Jesus' actual teaching (Mk. 14:58 and par.;

---

[13]On the development of the Son of Man concept, see H.-E. Tödt, *The Son of Man in the Synoptic Tradition* (Philadelphia: Westminster, 1965). Also Frederick Borsch, *The Son of Man in Myth and History* (Philadelphia: Westminster, 1967).

[14]G. R. Beasley-Murray has sought to show that the discourse attributed to Jesus in Mark 13 is a unity and that it originated with Jesus, but the evidence he presents is not convincing. See his *Commentary on Mark 13* (New York: St. Martin's Press, 1957).

John 2:19, in addition to the explicit prediction in Mk. 13:1–2 and par. and the implied analogy with the desecration of the Temple in the days of the Macca-bees in Dan. 9:27; cf. Mk. 13:14). The starting point for the growing tradition about Jesus' role in the destruction of the Temple was probably a simple pre-diction on his part that it would occur.

As we noted in connection with the role of John the Baptist, one of the important preconditions for the coming of the New Age and the reconstitution of the Covenant people was the renovation of the Temple in Jerusalem. Jesus' attention to the Temple included not only the announcement of its destruction but an act of cleansing, carried out according to and justified by appeals to the Jewish scriptures:

> Is it not written, "My house shall be called a house of prayer for all the nations" (Is. 56:7), but you have made it "a den of robbers?" (Jer. 7:11).
>
> —combined and quoted in MARK 11:17

There is no denying that in the eyes of Jewish and Roman officialdom Jesus was an unauthorized person carrying out an unwarranted breach of the peace. The fact that he based his action on an appeal to the sacred scriptures made it only more rather than less reprehensible in their eyes. Some scholars have conjectured that Jesus' arrogation of authority in the temple took place in the autumn months rather than a few days before the Passover, which was a spring festival. This would have allowed a longer time for Jesus' opponents to build up a case against him. Mark 14:49 surely indicates a more extended string of appearances in the Temple courts than the highly condensed account in Mark 11:11 implies.

There was no spot in the world closer to the heart and the purse of official Judaism than the Temple. It was not only justly honored as one of the archi-tectural wonders of the world, but was also the chief source of revenue in Palestine, by virtue of the tithes and offerings presented there as well as through the facilities that the city had to provide to house and feed the thousands of pilgrims who came there to worship throughout the year. As the chief pride of the Jewish people and their main industry, any threat to its existence undermined both the religious identity and the economic stability of the nation. It is not surprising that Jesus' prediction would have aroused such fierce opposition.

Closely related to Jesus' challenge to the Temple was the announcement of the fall of Jerusalem, the earliest form of which may well have been the lament over the city, preserved in Q (Mt. 23:37–39 = Lk. 13:34–35). Implic-itly Jesus is here ranked among the prophets, whose fate he seems destined to share. It is noteworthy that none of the language of the Crucifixion colors this lament, so that we cannot readily assume it was written by the Church after the death of Jesus had already occurred. And even in its reference to the

Coming One, he is not directly identified as being Jesus, nor are any of the distinctively Christian titles assigned to him. All that is promised is that he will be vindicated when the Blessed One arrives who comes in the name of Yahweh, the Lord. The words of the promise were quoted from Psalm 118, which was understood by Jesus' Jewish contemporaries to refer to the eschatological fulfillment when God established his Rule through his chosen agent.

Although the story of the Last Supper is told in Mark in such a way as to link it with the Jewish Passover (Mk. 14:12–16), it is likely that the meal actually took place before the Passover proper began, as John's version of the story clearly states: "Now before the Passover. . . " (Jn. 13:1). The meal which Jesus ate with his disciples came to be understood by the early Church as the Christian equivalent of the Jewish Passover, and with Jesus as the Paschal Lamb (I Cor. 5:7); but its original significance is implied in the words spoken by Jesus in the oldest tradition relating to the shared bread and wine, especially in the version preserved in the oldest and best manuscript copies of Luke:

> "I have earnestly desired to eat this passover with you before I suffer; for I tell you I shall never eat it again until it is fulfilled in the kingdom of God." And he took a cup, and when he had given thanks he said, "Take this, and divide it among yourselves; for I tell you that from now on I shall not drink of the fruit of the vine until the kingdom of God comes."
>
> —LUKE 22:15–18

The implication is that Jesus had hoped to live to celebrate the Passover yet once more with his "family," his disciples, but on the eve of his execution he was aware that this could not be. He was confident, however, that God would vindicate him and his endeavors in behalf of the Kingdom by enabling him and his followers to be reunited in the New Age. From the Qumran community there has been preserved a document which describes the procedure for the community when it is gathered in the presence of the Messiah—actually, there were to be two messiahs at Qumran: an anointed king and an anointed priest—and shares bread and wine in the New Age. It is this form of expectation that lies behind the Last Supper; the Passover imagery is almost certainly secondary, and arose at a time when the Church was trying to offer a scripturally reasonable explanation for the death of Jesus.

The Q document seems to have carried no account of the Crucifixion and no explicit reference to the Resurrection. But since the Q traditions expected that Jesus and his followers would be vindicated by God at the coming of the Son of Man, the Resurrection faith seems to be presupposed or at least implied in passages like these:

> You are those who have continued with me in my trials; as my Father appointed a kingdom for me, so do I appoint for you that you may eat and drink at my table in my kingdom, and sit on thrones judging the twelve tribes of Israel.
>
> —LUKE 22:28–30

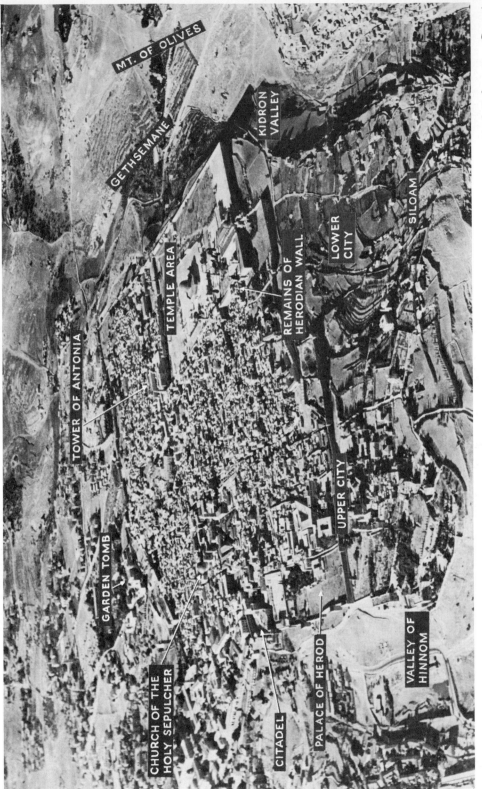

MT. OF OLIVES

KIDRON VALLEY

GETHSEMANE

SILOAM

LOWER CITY

TEMPLE AREA

REMAINS OF HERODIAN WALL

TOWER OF ANTONIA

UPPER CITY

GARDEN TOMB

VALLEY OF HINNOM

CHURCH OF THE HOLY SEPULCHER

CITADEL

PALACE OF HEROD

AIR VIEW OF JERUSALEM

MODEL OF THE JERUSALEM TEMPLE designed by M. Avi-Yonah, showing the colonnade surrounding the sacred precincts and the central structure comprising the Court of the Priests and the Holy of Holies. (Howard C. Kee)

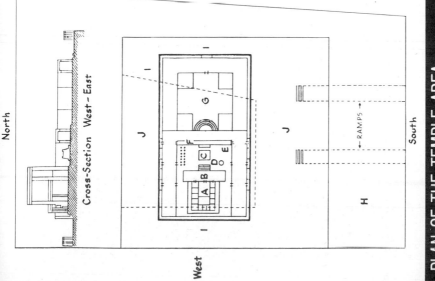

PLAN OF THE TEMPLE AREA IN THE TIME OF JESUS

North

West

East

South

Cross-Section West–East

RAMPS

A. "THE HOUSE"
B. PORCH
C. ALTAR
D. LAVER
E. COURT OF THE PRIESTS

F. COURT OF ISRAEL
G. COURT OF WOMEN
H. ROYAL PORCH
I. SURROUNDING WALL
J. MOUNTAIN OF THE HOUSE

Matthew's equivalent of this pericope includes the third-person reference to the Son of Man sitting on his glorious throne (Mt. 19:28). Which of the two forms of the saying is older is difficult to say, but the basic idea of God vindicating his faithful servants in the New Age is in keeping with other Jewish eschatological views of the period, and is constant with the other Q traditions about God's restoring the fellowship of Jesus with the disciples after his death.[15]

JESUS AND THE ESCHATOLOGICAL PANGS

Birthpangs was an obvious metaphor in the thought of Jewish apocalypticists for the struggles which they believed must take place before the New Age would arrive. In the Q tradition, reference is made to the disciples' fidelity to Jesus as "those who continued with me in my trials" (Lk. 22:28–30). Unlike Mark, the Q tradition does not seem to have gone beyond the general reference to suffering or to have developed a theory to explain why Jesus had to die even though he was the one designated by God to be the agent to establish the New Age. As we shall see in the next chapter, where we deal with the developed thought of the Gospel of Mark, the Church began to construct theories to account for the death of its Messiah; but Q seems to have been content to hint at the sufferings, confident that beyond the impending trials and sufferings God would intervene some day in his behalf, that he would vindicate both him and his followers, and that their fellowship would be restored in the End of the Age.

The Q document gives no hint as to when the End was to be expected. Mark 9:1, on the other hand, states clearly that the vindication of the Son of Man will take place within the lifetime of the first generation of Jesus' disciples. A similar outlook is expressed in other parts of the Jesus tradition; for example, Matthew 10:23 reports Jesus as saying that the disciples will not have completed a preaching tour of Galilee before the Son of Man appears. Similarly, Mark 13:30 expects the end before the passing of the then present generation. The closer in time the emergence of the Q source is to the events it purports to describe, the sooner it expected these predictions to be fulfilled, and consequently the less interest it had in accounting for the death of Jesus. Mark was probably written as that first generation was passing away, so that it is concerned both with the reason for Jesus' Crucifixion and with providing a terminal point for the coming of the Son of Man. For Q, not even the circumstances of the Resurrection are important: the one paramount consideration is the expectation of Jesus' vindication by God, who will very soon reveal Jesus as the exalted Son of Man and establish his Kingdom. Unlike Paul, who reports

---

[15]See H. C. Kee, *Jesus in History* (New York: Harcourt Brace Jovanovich, 1970), pp. 101–102.

appearances of the risen Jesus to himself as well as to the other apostles and to "more than five hundred" of the followers of Jesus (I Cor. 15:4–8), neither Q nor Mark describes a post-Resurrection appearance of Jesus. Mark explicitly predicts that the disciples will see Jesus after his Crucifixion (Mk. 14:28; 16:7), although the actual appearance is not described in Mark.[16] Belief in the Resurrection of Jesus is presupposed by both Mark and Q, however, even though they do not directly describe it. It is because they are convinced that God has raised Jesus from the dead that they are confident that God will soon vindicate him publicly and install him as king in the New Age.

---

[16]On the question of the end of Mark and the expectation that Jesus would be vindicated by God in the future, see H. C. Kee, "The Transfiguration in Mark: Epiphany or Apocalyptic Vision?" in *Understanding the Sacred Text* (Valley Forge, Pa.: Judson Press, 1972), pp. 135–152.

The New Covenant in Word and Act

Mark

CHAPTER FIVE

The Gospel of Mark is the oldest surviving sequential account of the career of Jesus. In all probability, it represents the very first attempt to write a consecutive report of what Jesus said and did, earlier efforts having been limited to records of primarily his teachings, as is the case with Q. By various clues, which we shall assess in a moment, it can be inferred that Mark wrote just before or just after Jerusalem fell to the Roman army in A.D. 70. Why did Jesus' followers, or the Church which they brought into being, wait so long to create this kind of record about his life and teachings?

For nearly a generation, the traditions about Jesus had been transmitted in the churches orally, and that sufficed for both preaching and teaching aims. But two closely related factors demanded that a written account be prepared. The first of these was the apparent threat to the Church's existence with the passing of the original generation of Jesus' followers, who could no longer be regarded as the living voice of the tradition. But the other factor was that the very fact of the passing of the disciples' generation was understood within the Church as marking the outer limit of the epoch of evangelism that was expected to culminate in the appearance of Jesus as exalted Son of Man, the judgment of the world, and the establishment of the New Age. Mark reports Jesus as affirming,

> Truly, I say to you, this generation will not pass away before all these things take place.
>
> —MARK 13:31

The sense of urgency is conveyed by the oft-repeated "immediately" in Mark's narrative—eight times in the first chapter alone! The counsel to be watchful is repeated three times in a single paragraph (13:32–37). The event that will signify the beginning of the end of the present age is the destruction of the Temple (13:2, 4, 14), but the time of stress and tribulation through which the elect community will have to pass before final deliverance comes is of relatively brief but indefinite duration (13:7, 9, 13, 20). In the time that remains between the present and the final deliverance, the Church must carry forth its task of evangelizing the nations (13:10). The immediate aims of Mark, as this sense of urgency implies, are (1) to reassure the doubtful or wavering that their salvation will come in due time, and at the same time (2) to forewarn the indolent or indifferent about the uncertainty of their enduring through the time of persecution that is to fall upon the Church unless they become more faithful hearers of the Church's teachings (4:17).

The more general aim of Mark, however, and the one that has had lasting significance in the subsequent life of the Church was to provide a concrete basis for the three-fold role of Jesus in the faith of the Church: as subject of the preaching, as authority for its teaching, and as mediator of its worship of God. Or to express this view in the technical terms employed by scholars of Christian origins, Mark specifies the ground of Jesus' function in the *kerygma*, the *didache*, and the *cultus* of the Church. Why does the Church await Jesus' vindication by God as triumphant Son of Man? To answer that question requires an accounting for his shameful death, and of the events that led to that condemnation. It demands an explanation for the authority of his reinterpretation of the Law of Moses. It implies an accounting for the stories of healing and exorcisms that are attributed to him. It must show how the New Covenant relates to the Old, and how it is that his followers can claim him to be the fulfillment of the Jewish scriptures. And if his appearance as the vindicated and vindicating Son of Man is to be seen as the climax of God's redemptive plan, then it must be shown how God has prepared the events that lead up to that climax.

Mark approaches these questions with no literary antecedent at hand—no one before him had written a work in the form of what we now call a gospel[1]—but he is not a solitary figure writing in a sociological vacuum. He has access to a reservoir of oral tradition about Jesus; we have no way of knowing what proportion of what was available he actually utilized. He was writing for a Greek-speaking community, though it is possible that some of its members knew Aramaic as well. Mark's use of Aramaic words and phrases followed by translations into Greek, such as in 3:17, 5:41, 7:11, 15:34, could come from a bilingual community, or could merely reflect the fondness for preserving exotic language in a Greek-speaking Christian community.

Although the language context of Mark is Greek, the arena of discussion throughout his gospel is clearly Jewish, whether the issue is the authority of Jesus, the interpretation of the Mosaic Law, or the claim that Jesus is the fulfillment of scripture. Gentile popular interest in stories of miracle-workers probably influenced the details or even the form of some of the narratives about Jesus in Mark, especially the more detailed accounts in Mark 5 and 6, but the major focus is on Jewish questions. The implication is, therefore, that the community for which Mark wrote was a Hellenized, Greek-speaking Jewish Christian group, whose Bible was read and known in Greek (most of the important quotations come from the LXX tradition rather than directly from the Hebrew). Although Mark has obvious interest in the admission of Gentiles to the Covenant community, as we shall detail, the terms of the Covenant are derived from the Jewish Covenantal tradition, and the specifics originate in the early Christian reading and interpretation of the Jewish scriptures. The destruction of the Temple signifies the end of the present age, and the coming of Jesus as Son of Man fulfills the Christian reading of the kingly promises of the Psalms and the apocalyptic visions of Daniel (see especially Mark 14:62, where Ps. 110:1 and Dan. 7:13 are synthesized). It is with the theme of fulfillment of scripture that Mark's story of Jesus opens.

AS IT IS WRITTEN IN THE PROPHETS

After presenting the title of his work, "The beginning of the gospel of Jesus Christ, the Son of God," Mark turns to the scripture, which he believes was fulfilled with the coming of John the Baptist. *Gospel* could be used here to refer to the good news about Jesus, or to the good news which Jesus proclaims, but the net result is much the same: God has begun something for man's redemption, Mark is declaring, yet in its newness it is a reappropriation of the old promise made through the prophets. And for those who see in this message good news, it provides the basis for a New Covenant community.

The scripture reference is said to be from Isaiah; actually it is a combination

---

[1]On the origins of gospel as a literary form, see H. C. Kee in *Jesus in History* (New York: Harcourt Brace Jovanovich, 1970), pp. 116–123.

of a verse from Malachi 3 and one from Isaiah 40 (what scholars call Second Isaiah, since it was written after the exile of the Jews, rather than prior to it, as was most of Isaiah 1–37). Mark, or the source he is quoting, has modified the pronouns of Malachi 3:1 slightly so that they can better serve his purpose. The Hebrew text says that Yahweh is sending a messenger before Him; Mark says the messenger is to prepare "thy" way. Instead of referring to Yahweh, as in the Hebrew original, the texts are used by Mark to point to Jesus, whom the Church acclaims as Lord, and for whose coming John the Baptist is seen to be the preparer of the way. Other changes have been made in the text as well: Isaiah 40 speaks of someone crying, "In the wilderness prepare the way. . . , " but Mark, recalling that John's preaching was carried on in the wilderness, describes him as "crying as in the wilderness." These subtle shifts in the wording of scripture might seem to us tricky or even deceitful, but we know from the Dead Sea Scrolls that similar alterations of scriptural texts were performed at Qumran in order to bring prophecy and fulfillment closer together. And the fact that the sacred texts had such possibilities testified to their divine origin rather than signifying exegetical chicanery. The scriptures were regarded as containing divine wisdom for the redemptive history of the world; it was essential to show that each detail of what the Christian claimed for Jesus was conformable to scripture.

JOHN THE BAPTIZER APPEARED

From Mark we learn much less of Jesus' relationship with John the Baptizer (literally, the John who baptizes, to distinguish him from others of that name) than we do from Q documents and the Gospel of John; but we are told of his calling men to accept baptism as an expression of their penitence, and we have the crude garb and diet of John vividly described to us (1:6). The mightier one who is coming may have meant in John's mind some undefined agent of judgment who would appear at the End of the Age, but Mark wants his readers to understand it as a reference to Jesus, whose "mightier" acts are to be depicted in the miracle stories that characterize Jesus' ministry in Mark's account. Curiously, no mention is made in Mark of the baptism with fire; all that appears is the contrast between the preparatory role of baptism with water at the hand of John and the baptism with the Spirit by which men will be incorporated into the New Covenant people. Among those who came seeking baptism was Jesus of Nazareth (1:9).

A VOICE FROM HEAVEN

Missing from Mark's account of Jesus' baptism are a number of features from the other gospels which readers of the New Testament have come to regard as essential to the picture. But it is important to note what Mark does not report: there is no hint of recognition of or special treatment of Jesus by John. The implication is that Jesus is just one among the crowds streaming to John to receive baptism. The vision of the Spirit descending and the sound of the divine voice seem to be private experiences of Jesus, since the words are addressed to him alone rather than to John or to the crowds around. The voice from heaven is heard in a dual allusion to scripture: "Thou art my son," recalls Psalm 2, where the king is hailed as God's agent ruling on the earth, and therefore as God's son; "with thee I am well-pleased," echoes Isaiah 42:1, where Yahweh is addressing his servant, who in his gentle way is establishing justice on earth. He is enabled to do so by the power, or spirit, which God has granted him: "I have put my spirit upon him. . . " (Isa. 42:1b).

Some interpreters have suggested a link between the voice and the rabbinic notion that God would attest the right interpretation of the Law of Moses by a celestial echo, *bath qol* (meaning "daughter of the voice"), since Jewish piety assumed that the voice of God itself could not be directly heard by men. But a more fitting analogy is to the Old Testament tradition of theophanies and divine auditions by which especially chosen persons received their commissioning from God, as in the case of Moses at Sinai (Ex. 3:4ff.), Elijah on Horeb (I Kings 19:12ff.), or Daniel on the bank of the Tigris (Dan. 10:2ff.). In Jewish usage of the time the term "Son of God" designated a man who had been chosen and empowered by God to do His will, and especially to exercise authority in God's stead. Hence, it was a familiar way of referring to the king, both the historical kings of Israel (Ps. 2, 45, and especially 72), and the idealized ruler whose coming was to usher in the New Age (Is. 9:6, 7). Although it is often asserted to be the case, there is no evidence that the term "Son of God" was used even in pagan Hellenistic circles to refer to a divinized man. From the time of Augustus on, however, the Roman emperors were on occasion described as "son of the divine Caesar." The voice acclaiming Jesus as "Son" is, therefore, to be understood as the agent of his commissioning for the task of establishing God's Rule on earth. What that role involves is clarified in the remainder of the text of Mark.

THE KINGDOM HAS DRAWN NEAR

[MARK 1:14]

Following a brief sketch of the conflict into which Jesus entered on taking up his career in behalf of the Kingdom—tested by Satan and ministered to by the angels—Mark gives a succinct summary of the message of Jesus: the present age, dominated by Satan and his agents, is coming to a close; and the New Age, for which men may now prepare themselves by penitently believing Jesus' announcement of its advent, is about to dawn. The rest of the gospel is occupied with detailing the ways in which the nearness of the Kingdom is evident and the urgent necessity of heeding the summons to prepare for it.

The work of preparing men for the Kingdom is not restricted to Jesus alone, but as with any rabbi or eschatological leader, there is a group of disciples who gather around him to assist in his work and carry forward his program. Choosing initially from a handful of Galilean fishermen, Jesus is said to have designated them at the outset as "fishers of men" (Mk. 1:17). Later on, Mark describes Jesus' sending them out on an extended tour (Mk. 6:7–13). In view of the urgency of their message and the shortness of time before the End of the Age, they are to make no preparations for their daily needs, relying rather on whatever hospitality is offered them from village to village. Their actual work is specifically stated to be an extension of Jesus' ministry in overcoming disease and demonic possession, which is for Mark the chief sign of the nearness of the Kingdom.

HAVE YOU COME TO DESTROY US?

[MARK 1:24]

Significantly, the first act which Mark depicts Jesus as performing is an exorcism carried out in the synagogue at Capernaum, the lakeside village in Galilee to which Jesus seems to have moved (Mk. 2:1) from Nazareth, following his rejection there (Mk. 6:1).[2] By "teaching" Mark means far more than merely the message of Jesus: it encompasses the whole of his public activity. And its chief characteristic is that it is authoritative, not in the sense that it carries the sanctions of the appropriate religious officials, since that is the exact opposite of the case, but that it brings its own conviction. Its warnings are urgent and lead men to repent; its promises of deliverance are effective, as the results show.

In the story of the demoniac in the Capernaum synagogue, even the demons are aware of this efficaciousness. Before Jesus addresses himself to the demoniac's problem, the demons sense that in Jesus they have met one who is not only their conqueror, but indeed also is to be the victor in the cosmic conflict. Jesus' commanding word, with the effective results, shows conclusively that the demons' question implies, "You have come to destroy us, haven't you?"

In keeping with his overall literary approach, Mark does not tell his reader what he wants him to know or merely declare the truth about Jesus. Instead, he proceeds by a series of questions which invite the response that Mark believes is the only proper one. He wants his readers to respond affirmatively

---

[2]This story is rather awkwardly placed at the beginning of Jesus' ministry in Luke 4, but Luke wants to show throughout his gospel that Jews have rejected God's message, while Gentiles have been open to receive it. Cf. Luke 4:25–27, where the receptivity of non-Israelites is depicted.

GERASA
*has been remarkably well pre-
served. The theaters, temples,
and extensive baths of this city
of the Decapolis are evident
among the ruins. Most manuscripts of Mark report that it
was outside the city of Gerasa
that Jesus healed the demoniac.*
(Howard C. Kee)

to the demons' question, just as he wants them to ask themselves what sort of man could possibly possess the insight and authority that Mark attributes to Jesus. The novelty of his teaching lies not in its specific content, but in the effectiveness of his whole ministry, by which the doom of the demons is not merely announced—there would have been nothing novel in that—but effected: "He commands even the unclean spirits and they obey him."

All that follows in the remainder of Mark 1 is an elaboration of this theme: Jesus' authority is portrayed as extending to overcoming fevers, conquering diseases, even leprosy. The tradition here (1:43) links the healing of leprosy with one of the technical terms for the commanding word of Jesus by which

SYNAGOGUE AT CAPERNAUM
*as reconstructed by an artist. The original structure was
built before the time of Jesus, but the present ruins date
from the second century* A.D.

the evil powers are overcome (see pp. 97–98) and the way prepared for the coming of God's Kingdom. Up to this point in his gospel, Mark has limited himself to those traditions that speak of the coming of God's Kingdom largely in terms of the usual language of Jewish apocalyptic literature. From this point on, however, we begin to see how he has introduced his own special views and terms into his portrait of Jesus.

THE SON OF MAN HAS AUTHORITY ON EARTH

[MARK 2:10]

Unlike the apocalyptic writers who developed the term Son of Man as a way of depicting God's agent to bring in the Kingdom (based on Dan. 7), Mark wants to show that even before the Kingdom was consummated Jesus was the authoritative agent of God during his earthly activity, and as such spoke of himself already at that time as Son of Man. In Jewish eschatology, God would pronounce the forgiveness of sins on the Day of Judgment that would bring to an end the present age and bring in the new. By shifting the issue from the paralyzed condition of the man lowered through the roof by his friends to the question of moral responsibility for his ailment, Mark has transformed the tradition from a straightforward healing story into a claim that Jesus already possesses eschatological powers to pronounce the forgiveness of sins.

Some interpreters have pointed out that the Aramaic phrase, *bar nasha* (or in Hebrew, *ben adam*), can mean simply "a human being," as it does in Ezekiel 2:1. Others have conjectured that "Son of Man" was used as a circumlocution for "I," though this remains debatable if not dubious.[3] But as Mark uses the term (Mk. 2), the force is not simply that mankind in general can forgive sins (2:10) or can set aside the ancient Sabbath law (2:27, 28), but that during his ministry Jesus has the authority to act in these ways, so that for Mark he is the eschatological Son of Man even before the New Age has fully come.

Closely grouped with these two stories into which Mark has apparently introduced the Son of Man idea—in both 2:10 and 2:28 the narrative would read more smoothly without this factor—are three other pericopes in which Jesus is represented as setting aside established patterns of Jewish piety and separatism. The first has to do with Jesus' enjoying the hospitality of the religiously unacceptable (2:15–17); the second offers a justification for the failure of Jesus' disciples to fast (2:18–22); the third is another report of a healing performed on the Sabbath day (3:1–5). The second of these stories is particularly revealing about Mark, since in addition to explaining the more libertarian attitudes of Jesus and his followers during his lifetime, it also shows

---

[3]See, however, Geza Vermes in M. Black, *An Aramaic Approach to the Gospels and Acts*, 3rd ed. (Oxford: Clarendon Press, 1967), pp. 310–328.

why the Church after his time did adopt the practice of fasting: because the bridegroom had been taken from them (2:20), an interpretation which is probably added by Mark. The string of sayings (2:21–22) has only a general link with what goes before, although this section as a whole makes the point that the new thing that is happening through Jesus cannot be forced into the structures of the Old Covenant.

More important for Mark's overall aims in this passage is the pair of references to the death of Jesus. The first of these alludes to the taking away of the bridegroom (2:20); the second to the coalition of religious and civil powers to destroy Jesus (3:6). Mark wants his readers to know from an early stage of the narrative that the death of Jesus was in view, although it is an exaggeration to say with Martin Kähler that the gospels are Passion stories with extended introductions.[4] The reader has been forewarned about Jesus' death, however, before the predictions of the Passion begin at 8:31.

BINDING THE STRONG MAN

[MARK 2:27]

The paradox of simultaneously mounting success and opposition is portrayed in 3:7–35. In a summarizing statement, Mark describes the crowds that are flocking to Jesus to be healed as coming not only from his native Galilee, but also from the more distant Jewish territory around Jerusalem and even from the non-Jewish regions of Tyre, Sidon, Idumea, and the region east of the Jordan. They are reported as acclaiming him Son of God, although the significance of the title has not yet been clarified, as it will be by the time the reader reaches the end of Mark's gospel. The command to be silent about his activity (3:12) comes from Mark, and is in keeping with his conviction that there is no direct path to deliverance and triumph that does not pass through suffering.

After another brief mention of the circle of coworkers that Jesus summoned to assist in his work of announcing and evidencing the Kingdom of God (3:13–19), Mark goes on to indicate the various sources of opposition that Jesus encountered. Typical of his literary method, Mark has divided a story in the middle and inserted another incident between the halves. The narrative of the determination by Jesus' family to remove him from the public scene reads smoothly if one passes directly from 3:21 (reading "his family" instead of the unwarranted translation "his friends" as in RSV) to 3:31, where his mother and brothers are directly mentioned. The link between the two stories lies in the supposition in each case that Jesus is the victim of some kind of aberration: his family assumes that he is out of his mind (3:21), while his official opponents

---

[4]See p. 95, note 4.

infer from his success in performing exorcisms that he is in league with the demonic forces (3:23). Employing one of his favorite editorial devices by which he appends to a saying of Jesus an explanation of his somewhat less than self-evident teaching, Mark has Jesus explain "in parables" (by analogy and metaphor) why the prince of demons would not assist Jesus in establishing God's Rule by diminishing the control that demons hold over men. The first figure is that of a dynasty, and the argument runs that Satan is not likely to work toward the destruction of his own "house." But then the figure changes to that of a household which cannot be stripped of its possessions (*i.e.*, Satan's hold over the present age) until the householder (Satan) is deprived of his power. This is what Jesus is accomplishing by the exorcisms.

But then the argument moves on to deal with issues that are not as appropriate to the life of Jesus as to the life of the Church: What sins are forgivable? How does the Church regard someone who attributes to Satan what is in fact the work of the Holy Spirit? (3:28–30). This subject is not unrelated to that of the source of power behind Jesus' exorcisms, but the situation has altered significantly, since Mark is more interested in addressing the needs of the Church in his own time than in historically and accurately reconstructing the circumstances during the lifetime of Jesus. Or more precisely, he believes that the power of Jesus that once was known among his disciples is still evident by the Holy Spirit in the life of the Church. For him, therefore, the transition is obvious and inevitable.

THE SECRET OF THE KINGDOM

[MARK 4:11]

The Parable of the Sower, which was likely intended by Jesus as an encouragement to his followers as they proclaimed the coming Kingdom, becomes in the hands of Mark a kind of riddle (the Semitic word for parable, *mashal*, can mean riddle, enigma, puzzle), the meaning of which can be discerned only by the inner circle of the followers of Jesus (4:11–12). The allegorical explanation of the parable that follows is clearly addressed to the congregation in Mark's day rather than to the disciples of Jesus.

The seed is identified as *the Word*, which is not a general message or sermon subject but the specifically Christian proclamation. The hearers are the various kinds of soil in which the Word is sown, at least in 4:15, where Satan (the birds) snatches away the seed soon after it has been sown. But by 4:16, the allegory becomes inconsistent, and the hearers are now equated with the seed that has been sown on rocky ground—although by the end of that verse, the seed has once more become the Word and the hearers are the unreceptive soil. But in spite of the awkwardness of the allegory, the fault with the members of the community is painfully obvious. When tribulation or persecution on account of the Christian message becomes a real possibility, they fall away from the faith. Others are turned aside by preoccupation with worldly obligations (4:19). The very fact that riches could be an obstacle to faith indicates that the church for which Mark is writing is not a handful of impoverished itinerant preachers, but an organization of the kind that can attract the wealthy and that is faced with the problems of holding on to those whom it has converted.

The final note in the allegorical interpretation is an encouraging one, however, pointing as it does to the enormous effectiveness of the proclamation of the gospel among those who are prepared to hear and respond faithfully. It is followed by a string of sayings, originally independent of each other, which Mark develops to stress the importance of spreading the light of the gospel (4:21, 22) and the fact that refusal to heed the message will deprive men of even the opportunity to hear it (4:25). The section ends with two more parables concerning seed growing unnoticed (4:26–29) and the mustard shrub (4:30–32), both of which point to the contrast between the small beginnings of the gospel and the great results of its proclamation that will become visible only on the Day of Judgment (harvest). Thus the parables have been adapted by Mark to serve the dual purposes of warning the careless and encouraging the faithful. But only those chosen by God are able to discern what is taking place.

WHO IS THIS?

[MARK 4:41]

The older miracle stories of the Gospel tradition point to the significance of Jesus' ministry: the demonic hold on the present age is being broken by Jesus' healings and exorcisms. In the later stories, the focus shifts to the direct question of who Jesus is that he is able to perform these wonders. The issue is not the soteriological factor as to how Jesus can deliver men from the present age but the christological question as to what it implies to call Jesus "the Christ."

The first of the stories in this series depicts Jesus as stilling a storm on the Lake of Galilee (4:35–41). The language includes the technical term for commanding the demons (wrongly translated "rebuke," 4:39), which is here addressed to the wind (in Greek, *pneuma*) rather than to an "unclean spirit" (which would also be *pneuma*). Mark wants his readers to infer from this story that Jesus is the agent of God's Rule over the whole cosmos, not merely over human needs. But his question, "Have you no faith?" is addressed as much to the Church of his time as it is to the disciples in the boat. In the time of impending stress, it was essential that they be reminded that the God who delivered the disciples from a storm through the Word of Jesus was able to save them from whatever fate might threaten.

The miracle stories of Mark 5 are among the most elaborate and detailed in the Gospel tradition. The details of the demoniac's plight and the stages of his release have parallels in Hellenistic exorcism stories of the time, and at the same time the technical terms of the older exorcism accounts are missing.[5] That Mark is more concerned about his own contemporaries than those of Jesus is apparent in the wording of 5:19, "Go home to your friends and tell them how much the Lord has done for you. . . ," where Mark uses the Church's confessional designation for Jesus—Lord—rather than a title such as "rabbi" or "teacher," by which his own disciples might have addressed him.

Mark interrupts the story of the healing of Jairus' daughter (5:22–24, 35–43) by inserting the account of the woman with the hemorrhage (4:25–34). By doing so, the drama of the first story is heightened, especially since the reader is given the impression that the delay may have resulted in the girl's having died (5:39). But perhaps the contrast between death and sleeping is Mark's way of contrasting Christians' attitude toward death, which was in fact referred to as "sleeping" (I Thess. 4:13, 15), and the views held by some Jews and many pagans that death was final. Giving her food is a way of proving that her return to life is a physical reality and not merely an illusion, just as the developing gospel tradition will describe Jesus as eating food following his Resurrection from the dead (Lk. 24:39–42).

The section ends (6:1–3) with a series of questions addressed by Mark to the reader, requiring him to come to some conclusion as to who this person is who is able to exercise such extraordinary powers. Mark places the questions on the lips of Jesus' detractors, and thereby effects a transition from the description of what Jesus has done where he is responded to in faith to the limitations imposed where there is no faith.

A PROPHET WITHOUT HONOR

[MARK 6:4]

In contrast to the estimate of Jesus offered by those who have benefited from his abilities to heal and to release from demonic power is the reaction to him by his fellow villagers from Nazareth. They can see in Jesus only a carpenter, whose rather large family is well-known to them. His words and actions seem to them no more than vain pretensions. In having Jesus refer to himself as a prophet, Mark may well be preserving an authentic tradition, since prophet is a likely role for Jesus to have adopted for himself. Now, Mark tells us, the rejection of his prophetic role is complete: both family and friends deny

---

[5]The older gospel traditions employ a special term, *epitimān*, which translates a Semitic term used in the Hebrew Bible for God's exercising control over the powers that oppose him, and in the Dead Sea Scrolls for a commanding word that brings the demoniac under control. See p. 98, note 6.

that he is sent by God. Their unbelief deprives them of the benefits of his God-given powers; it is not merely that he *will* not, but he *cannot* do his mighty works among them, Mark declares (6:5).

Even as he reports Jesus sending out the disciples on their missionary tour (6:7–13), Mark provides his reader with a none-too-subtle warning about what the fate of a messenger of repentance is likely to be, especially one whose mission is identified in the public mind with that of a prophet (6:15). In vivid detail Mark describes the fate of John the Baptist at the hand of Herod Antipas, son of Herod the Great and tetrarch of Galilee and Perea, the two territories where Jesus and John respectively carried on their major activity. Once again Mark has sounded an ominous note to prepare his reader for the predictions of death that are soon to appear in his narrative.

IT IS I

[MARK 6:30–56]

Mark has bracketed together two stories that attribute cosmic powers to Jesus: feeding the multitude, and walking on the water. These accounts have stimulated the imagination of rationalistic interpreters of Jesus to come up with ingenious explanations (Jesus shamed the crowd into bringing out and sharing the lunches they had concealed in their sleeves; the water was shallow and Jesus was merely wading). But the stories were preserved in the Church because they had become vehicles for describing the community's belief in the continuing spiritual presence of Jesus in their midst. The technical language of the Communion Sacrament has found its way into the narrative: "he blessed . . . he broke . . . he gave. . . . " The Greek phrase that translates "It is I" can also be rendered "I am," and is the way the LXX translated the name of God, Yahweh, that was disclosed to Moses at Sinai (Ex. 3:14). Since the LXX was the Bible of the Greek-speaking church for which Mark was writing, readers would have been familiar with the terminology of the theophany at Sinai, just as they would likely have associated this story with Yahweh's promise of safe deliverance of His people from the threatening waters (Is. 43:2; esp. 43:25, where the Greek phrase is identical with Mark 6:50). The incident concludes with Mark's account of the mounting popular response to Jesus, which contrasts sharply with the coalescing official opposition to him.

WHAT DEFILES A MAN

[MARK 7:20]

One of the major features of both Pharisaic and Essene Judaism in the time of Jesus was the maintenance of ceremonial purity. The Essenes were so obsessed with the question that many of them[6] withdrew from society—even

---

[6]According to Josephus (*Jewish War*, II.124–125), some of the Essenes lived in the towns and cities, unlike those at Qumran who had withdrawn from society.

Jewish society—so that they could pursue the pure life in their desert monastic community. It was for them essential to maintain their purity so as to be ready to enter with the rest of God's elect into the Age to Come, which they believed He was about to establish. Mark depicts Jesus as sharing a concern comparable to that of the Essenes for preparing the elect for the New Age, but he is portrayed as in total disagreement with them about the importance of ceremonial purity. Whether Jesus himself went as far as Mark suggests, that is, to the point of setting aside all regulations about cleanliness (7:19), is doubtful. But for Mark's community the regulations have no positive value at all; rather, what is essential is integrity and inner moral purity. Man is corrupted by his own evil heart (7:21), not by externals with which he comes in contact. It would appear that whatever may have been the original links between Mark's community and Jewish Christianity, the force of the Jewish traditions of separateness have been almost completely abandoned.

CHILDREN'S BREAD FOR DOGS

Although the geographical indications are somewhat confusing, it appears that Mark wants his reader to see the next series of events in the life of Jesus as occurring in a Gentile setting: Tyre, Sidon, Decapolis, Caesarea Philippi. And the point of the stories is that where there is faith among Gentiles, they have as ready access to the elect community as do Jews. The sarcastic words of Jesus questioning the appropriateness of taking what was originally intended for Jews ("children") and giving it to Gentiles ("dogs") is replied to in kind by the quick-witted, determined Syrophoenician woman with the ailing child. And the result is that her daughter was healed. Similar results are reported with the deaf-mute in the Decapolis and the blind man at Beth-saida. The crowd is fed in Gentile territory (8:1–10) just as another crowd had been fed in a Jewish district (6:35ff.). The numbers of baskets of remaining fragments— twelve and seven (8:19-20)—correspond exactly to the number of leaders said to have been chosen by the Jerusalem Church for its Jewish and Gentile missionary enterprises respectively (Acts 6:1–6). Mark wants to be certain that his readers recognize that the Church's mission to the wider Gentile world was not an afterthought or an expedient once the mission to the Jews had failed, but constituted a part of the divine plan from the outset, sanctioned by the example of Jesus himself.

WHO DO YOU SAY I AM?
[MARK 8:29]

Up to this point in his gospel, Mark has been content to raise questions about who Jesus is only editorially or by implication. Now he represents Jesus

as addressing the question of his identity directly to his disciples. The suggestions as to who Jesus is offered by those other than the disciples are inadequate,
but not wide of the mark. His message does resemble that of John; it does
match well the eschatological function of Elijah; he can be compared with the
eschatological prophet whose coming was announced in Deuteronomy 18 and
who was awaited at Qumran. At first Peter seems to have given the correct
answer: "You are the Christ." But the moment that Jesus declares that his
messianic role involves suffering and death, Peter rejects the notion, thereby
showing that he has not understood Jesus' intention. Although some scholars
see in this passage the effort of the historical Jesus to redefine the traditional
messianic conceptions of Judaism—which had no concept of a suffering Messiah
—it is far more likely that this is one of the main aspects of Mark's own theological interpretation of Jesus, one in keeping with the overall apocalyptic
framework in which he has placed his portrait of Jesus. Mark simply asserts
that Jesus must suffer, without indicating how that suffering will contribute
to the coming of the Kingdom of God or to the redemption of men.

Mark 8:31 is the first of three increasingly detailed predictions of the suffering and death and resurrection of Jesus (the others are at 9:31 and 10:33–34),
all of them tied in with the term Son of Man. Although the one "like a son of
man" in Daniel 7 comes in triumph rather than as a sufferer, the elect community to whom the Kingdom is to be given (Dan. 7:22) is promised that God
will deliver them from whatever punishment the worldly authorities may
require them to undergo, whether a starvation diet (Dan. 1:8ff.), exposure to
wild animals (Dan. 6:16ff.), or being burned alive (Dan. 3:19ff.). One of the
frequently recurring images in apocalyptic writings is that of birthpangs,
which must be endured if the New Age is to be born. There is no direct logical
significance assigned by Mark to suffering, as there might be in a doctrine of
vicarious sacrifice, where the victim suffers so much to produce an equivalence
of benefits. Suffering is rather inevitable if the redemptive outcome is to occur.

By refusing to accept these painful dimensions of Jesus' messianic role,
Peter is portrayed as not only denying what is essential to Jesus' function as
Son of Man, but as also rejecting the role of suffering and persecution that is
an inevitable dimension of discipleship; this Mark tells us by appending to the
prediction of the Passion the words about the cost of discipleship (8:34–38).
The clue to Mark's choice of Son of Man as messianic designation for Jesus
becomes clear in 8:38, where those who endure suffering on Jesus' behalf are
promised vindication by Jesus when he appears in triumph at the End of the
Age. Taking as his starting point the authentic Son of Man words that speak
of his future coming, Mark uses the term, Son of Man, to depict both the
authority of Jesus and the necessity of suffering for him and his followers.
That vindication, Mark quotes Jesus as affirming, will come during the lifetime
of the first generation of Jesus' followers—which confirms the other evidence

that Mark was writing about A.D. 70, when the original disciples would be starting to reach the limits of their life expectancy. Indeed, the problem may well have been made the more urgent by the passing of some of the earliest of Jesus' followers.[7]

In addition to the verbal assurance of vindication in the end (9:1), Mark describes an apocalyptic vision granted to the inner circle of Jesus' disciples, Peter, James, and John (9:2–8). Like the theophanies of the Old Testament, the setting for this experience is a remote mountain where Jesus takes his followers and where they are addressed by a heavenly voice. The presence of the two additional eschatological figures, Moses and Elijah (both of whom were expected by Jews of the period to return to earth before the End of the Age), gives the experience significance. The glowing of the garments of Jesus is reminiscent of what happened to Moses, whose face shone after seeing God (Ex. 34:39ff.), and even more precisely of Daniel's vision (Dan. 10:2–14), even to the point that Daniel's disciples could not grasp what was happening and were in any case enjoined to silence about what they had seen (cf. Mk. 9:9). The conversation that Mark places following the vision (9:9–13) confirms the link between the eschatological messenger and suffering. Whatever the tradition may originally have meant, it seems to refer to John the Baptist, who is Jesus' forerunner in both his message and his death.

YOU DO NOT KNOW WHAT YOU ARE ASKING

[MARK 10:38]

The entire section of Mark from 9:14 to 10:45 is occupied with a series of accounts of misunderstandings or misconceptions on the part of the disciples. The inability of the disciples to cure the demon-possessed mute (10:14–29) is seen as evidence of their lack of faith, and contrasts with the availing faith of the father of the demoniac (9:24). The second announcement of the Passion is greeted with fear and incomprehension (9:32). The two appeals by the disciples for places of special privilege (9:33–37; 10:35–45) are met respectively by lessons on the need to be childlike and on the necessity of accepting suffering and death for the sake of the coming Kingdom. Warnings are issued against rejecting anyone who performs good deeds in the name of Jesus, even though he is not a member of the community (9:38–41), and against leading astray any "little children" in the faith by one's insensitive or irresponsible actions (9:42–50). A similar theme is repeated in 10:13–16.

---

[7]No historically reliable accounts of the death of the apostles have been preserved, but some of the traditions and legends surrounding the death of Paul are sketched in Chapter Six, pp. 166–168.

PREPARING FOR LIFE OF THE AGE TO COME

[MARK 10:17]

Two questions which must have been considered important by the community which Mark is addressing, but which are presented as wrongheaded in Mark's form of the Jesus tradition are, (1) Under what conditions are divorce and remarriage permissible? (2) How good does a man have to be in order to be sure of entering the life of the Age to Come? To the first, Mark has Jesus reply that God intended man and woman to be inseparably united, so that divorce is a concession to human weakness, not a divine provision. Mark adds further, using his characteristic literary device of a private explanation following a public pronouncement (10:10), the arguments against man or woman taking the initiative in divorce. Since women lacked this right in Jewish law, Mark has clearly adapted the tradition to the Gentile situation in which the Romans had provided for the rights of women.

The second question becomes the occasion for a denunciation of riches, apparently on the ground that man cannot differentiate between what he has acquired and his own self-esteem. It is not how a man ranks on the achievement scale of the divine commandments or in the acquisition of wealth that is the essential question, but the intensity of his commitment to the work of preparing men for the Kingdom of God (10:17–31). It is possible that Mark has modified the more stringent original declaration of Jesus against possession of wealth by suggesting a three-stage development: (1) initial renunciation of wealth; (2) an intermediate stage of mingled reward and persecution; (3) the ultimate reward of eternal life, or life of the Age to Come.

The third prediction of the Passion (10:32–34) arouses fear and astonishment rather than comprehension. Even the detailed attempt to clarify the difference between the route of power by which the nations exercise authority and the route of service and acceptance of suffering that Jesus and his followers must follow does not penetrate to the disciples. How the roles of Son of Man and Son of God (King) fit together eludes them completely. Ironically, there is one man who can discern who Jesus is: it is the blind Bar-Timaeus, who calls out to Jesus for help as he is passing through Jericho (10:46–52). Addressing Jesus as Son of David, Bar-Timaeus not only affirms thereby Jesus' role as king, but, by associating messiah and Son of David with restoration of sight, implicitly recalls that in the eschatological Kingdom the eyes of the blind will be opened (Is. 35:5; 42:7; 42:16; 43:8), that this promise is given to the city of David (Is. 29:1, 18), and specifically that the power to open blind eyes is assigned to the Anointed (in LXX, *christos*) of Yahweh (Is. 61:1). In sharpest contrast to the disciples, the blind beggar is able to see clearly who Jesus is.

HE WHO COMES IN THE NAME OF THE LORD

[MARK 11:9]

Mark describes Jesus as entering Jerusalem, apparently for the first time, by way of the Mount of Olives, with its spectacular view of the Temple and city spread out below. The old Roman road that came up from Jericho (800 feet below sea level) through the arid wilderness of Judea twelve miles or so to the crest of the ridge (2,800 feet above sea level) led steeply down the western slope of the Mount of Olives, across the dry bed of the Kidron, and up the slope of Zion to the temple mount. As Mark depicts the journey, it is in apparently conscious fulfillment of the prediction of Zechariah 9 that Jerusalem's king would come to her in humility, not on a white horse, but on a lowly donkey. Unlike the later gospels in which Jesus is addressed as king (Mt. 21:9), the crowds acclaim Jesus as one who comes in the Lord's name, referring to Psalms 118:26, which was quoted in Jesus' day as an eschatological hope of the establishment of God's Kingdom, as Mark 11:10 affirms. There is no hint in Mark of any immediate consequences to this act performed by Jesus. Some scholars think that if Jesus had actually entered the city in this way and permitted his acclaim by the crowd, he would have been seized instantly by the authorities as a messianic claimant and therefore as a threat to the political stability of the land. It was as such that he was finally arrested and condemned, though we cannot be certain historically that he provided the occasion for his seizure by this overt act. For Mark, however, it is the appropriate way for the true Son of David to enter the city which is about to reject him.

The hostility of the leaders of the city toward him is symbolized by the strange account of the cursing and the withering of the unproductive fig tree (11:12–14; 20–22), just as the unsuitability of the Temple as a place of approach to God is asserted in Jesus' act of purging the courts (11:15–18). The place where the Gentiles should have been able to worship the God of Israel (11:17, "for all nations") had become a place of greed and commerce. Pressed by the officials for the source of his authority in performing these arrogant actions in the carefully regulated Temple enclosure, Jesus only throws the question back at his interrogators (11:27–33). In an allegory which is itself based on Isaiah's allegory of the faithless nation, Israel (Is. 5:1–7), Mark reports Jesus to have represented his impending rejection and death as the climax of a long series of events in which Israel had rejected the messengers sent by God. The result is that the nation has forfeited its special place as the people of God; Jesus is now to be seen as the founder of the New Covenant people (12:10–11). As such, this people is to be characterized by faithfulness in prayer (11:22–24), by neither arrogance toward nor dependence upon the civil authorities (12:13–

17), by assurance that God will create new conditions of life for his own people in the Age to Come (12:18–27), by obedience to the twin commandments of love to God and neighbor (12:28–34), by acceptance of a worldly position of humility and poverty (12:38–44). Characteristic of this people will be their conviction that Jesus, the true Son of David, is the one acclaimed in the Church as Lord (12:35–37).

END OF THE TEMPLE AND END OF THE AGE

[MARK 13:1–4]

The editorial hand of Mark is once more evident in the shift from the public pronouncement of the Temple's impending destruction (13:1–2) to the private explanation offered to the disciples. Mark has here assembled the longest consecutive string of sayings to be found in his entire Gospel. The sayings are not arranged in a strictly logical order, and some scholars even think that Mark has copied all or part of this material from a written source as the reference to "the reader" in 13:14 implies. The discourse as it stands attempts to balance two viewpoints: (1) the New Covenant people is facing persecution which, if endured faithfully, will not last longer than they can bear; (2) but this people should not be deceived into assuming too quickly that the End of the Age has come or that every claimant to being a messiah is to be credited. The disturbances that will mark the coming of the end are political (13:7, 8), inter-religious (13:9), intercommunal (13:12), and cosmic (13:24–25).

The unambiguous clue to the approaching end will be the desecration of the Temple (13:14), but in the interim the task of evangelism among the Gentiles must be carried out universally (13:10). Although there is no way to determine the precise time of the end, since that is a secret known to God alone (13:32), the New Covenant people can be sure that it will occur within the life of the first generation of its members (13:30). It is the responsibility of the community to be ever faithful and ever watchful (13:35–37).

The language and point of view of the discourse in Mark 13 are heavily dependent on the book of Daniel.[8] The other synoptic writers have expanded considerably this part of Mark, drawing in large measure on Q material. But the basic structure and the place of the discourse within the overall picture of Jesus' career are the contribution of Mark, who wants his reader to see a parallel between the desecration of the Temple in Daniel's (actually, Macca-bean) times and the destruction of the Temple predicted by Jesus. What was expected by Daniel but did not occur—the establishment of the Kingdom of God—is affirmed by Mark as now about to take place. With this assurance in

---

[8]See Lars Hartmann, *Prophecy Reinterpreted: The Formation of Some Jewish Apocalyptic Texts and of the Eschatological Discourse, Mark 13 and par.* (Lund: Gleerup, 1966).

mind, the reader of Mark is prepared to see beyond the sad story of rejection and death to the promised deliverance.

But the prediction of the Temple's destruction provides us with our best clue to the historical circumstances for the writing of Mark. In the decade of the sixties occurred a series of events which profoundly affected the early church: the leading apostles were put to death: Peter and Paul in Rome, and James in Jerusalem; Jerusalem and its temple fell into Roman hands; the Jerusalem church fled from the city. The community for which Mark wrote was gravely concerned over these developments. As we have noted (pp. 114–115), its members needed assurance that the New Age would arrive within the lifetime of at least some of the apostles (Mk. 9:1). The flight of the Jerusalem Christians and the destruction of the city—whether Mark wrote shortly before or just after these events took place we cannot ascertain—had to be explained to the community of Mark in terms which affirmed the power of God to fulfill his promises and to judge those who rejected his messenger, Jesus. Just as the Maccabean crisis in the days of Antiochus IV had led to the writing of Daniel (about 168 B.C.), so the Roman invasion of Palestine and the disruption of the life of the Christians in Jerusalem seem to have been the occasion for the writing of Mark. So significant were these events for the future of the Church that it is essential that we review them here in broad outline.

In the years A.D. 66-70, the position of the Church in Jerusalem had become increasingly difficult as a result of the Jewish revolt against Roman occupation. The cruelty and corruption of the Roman procurators had been increasing. Nero had made important concessions to the Gentiles in Palestine, and they had begun to interfere with Jewish worship in the synagogues. In the year 66, as a reaction against maltreatment at the hands of the Roman administrators, the Jews refused to permit the sacrifices to the emperor to continue, although these sacrifices were required by Roman law throughout the empire. Riots broke out in every city; Gentile towns were burned; the Roman garrisons were attacked in cities where they were weak; and Jews were slaughtered in reprisal in cities where the garrisons were strong. At first, the Jews succeeded in liberating parts of the land from Roman control; the independence of the Jewish nation was declared, and Jewish coinage was issued. But the poorly armed bands of revolutionaries could not withstand the 60,000 seasoned troops that Rome sent in to quell the revolt. By the year 69 all of Palestine, except for Jerusalem and some outlying fortresses near the Dead Sea, was once again under Roman control.

Vespasian, who commanded the Roman troops, could have quickly destroyed all resistance, but his mind was occupied with other matters: the emperor, Nero, had died under mysterious circumstances in 68, and Vespasian's chances of succeeding him were excellent. Accordingly, Vespasian held back from the fighting for a time to see what the outcome of the contest for the imperial throne would be. When it became clear that the army in the East would

VESPASIAN
invaded Palestine in A.D. *67. He left his son Titus to capture Jerusalem while he returned to Rome to be acclaimed emperor in 69.* (Alinari/Art Reference Bureau)

declare for him, he returned to Rome. His rivals faded from the scene, and he became emperor in 69. His son, Titus, who had been left in charge of the troops in Palestine, pressed the siege of Jerusalem.

The Fall of Jerusalem

The city's resistance might have been greater if the people had not been torn by internal dissension. At the start of the revolt there had been two main parties: the peace party, whose members believed God would free the nation from Rome in his own time and by his own methods; and the resistance party, whose adherents were convinced that the time had come for them to take the initiative in driving the Romans out. With the advent of the Roman troops, the peace party was overwhelmed by the rebels, but any prospect of success for the revolt was ended when the rebels began to fight among themselves under rival leaders. The civil strife continued within the city even during the siege. Although the revolutionaries had killed Annas, who had caused James' death, the Christians appear to have been in sympathy with the peace party. They believed that the hope of the nation lay in the return of their

Messiah to establish the reign of God, not in military victory. The siege, which began in April of the year 70, lasted five months, and during this time thousands died of starvation. Then, when the city fell, the Romans laid it waste and demolished the Temple. A generation later, during the reign of Hadrian, the Jews attempted a second revolt (A.D. 132–135), but at the order of Hadrian the city of Jerusalem was leveled and a pagan city called Aelia Capitolina was built on the site.

The Flight of the Christians

Eusebius, the fourth century A.D. church historian, reports that just before the siege began the Christians decided to flee to a place of safety. At first glance, it seems clear that the reason they would have fled was to escape destruction at the hands of the Romans, but Eusebius tells us that they went to the Gentile city of Pella, east of the Jordan in the region of the Decapolis, in response to a divine oracle. If we take his report as historically reliable, certain questions immediately arise: What was the nature of the oracle? Why did it tell them to go to a despised Gentile city like Pella, which had been among those attacked by the Jewish nationalists only a few years earlier? Why

THE ARCH OF TITUS
in Rome contains this bas-relief. The structure was erected to celebrate Titus' triumph over the Jews. The victors are carrying off from the Temple of Jerusalem the seven-branched candelabrum, the sacred trumpets, and the table where the sacred bread was kept. (Alinari/ Art Reference Bureau)

FALLEN STONES FROM
THE JERUSALEM TEMPLE,
*dating from the time of Herod,
lie on the stepped street where
they fell during the destruction
of the Temple in* A.D. *70. The
largest stone measures about 8
by 10 by 6 feet; the slab still in
position along the left is nearly
30 feet long.* (Howard C. Kee)

were the Jewish Christians—traditionally so fastidious about maintaining separateness from Gentiles—willing to seek refuge in a Gentile stronghold? Considering these questions in reverse order, the probability is that the Jerusalem
Christians would have been willing to compromise their religious scruples for
the sake of saving their own necks. The only place of safety in the whole area
for Jews who had opposed the revolt would be a place like Pella, which was
Gentile and hence free of Jewish nationalist feeling. There they would be safe
from the Romans, who might have taken them for rebels in Jerusalem, and
safe from the rebels, who might have killed them as traitors.

Eusebius gives another theory to explain the flight of the Christians from
Jerusalem. He suggests that the Roman emperors, from Vespasian on, sought
out all descendants of David in an effort to exterminate the Jewish hope of a
revival of the Davidic dynasty. Since Jesus was from "the seed of David" (Rom.
1:3), he and his relatives would have been in the royal line, and his brothers
and other surviving relatives would have been the victims of Vespasian if they
had remained within his reach at Jerusalem. On this theory, the flight to Pella
would have been a communal effort to protect Jesus' family, to whom had
passed the leadership of the Jerusalem community. This story of Eusebius bears
the marks of legendary embroidering, and really conveys little more than the
general impression that (1) the Romans did not understand the nature of

Christian messianic beliefs, and mistakenly identified them with the nationalistic hopes of Judaism, and (2) the Jerusalem wing of Christianity had already lapsed into such complete obscurity by the end of the second century that there were no precise recollections of what had happened to it after the city of Jerusalem fell to the Romans.

As for the oracle that instructed the Christians to flee, there is a possibility that it may be imbedded in the apocalyptic section that precedes the Passion story in Mark and the other Synoptic Gospels (Mt. 24; Mk. 13; Lk. 21). The phrase in Mark 13:14, "let the reader understand," is often interpreted as referring to the reader of the oracle, which Eusebius tells us was circulated in Jerusalem at the time of the Roman invasion.[9]

Although we do not know what happened to the Christians after they fled from Jerusalem, we do know that the destruction of Jerusalem by the Romans was interpreted by Christians generally as a divine judgment on Judaism for its rejection of Jesus as the Christ. This conviction is plainly and repeatedly stated in Eusebius, and it is easy to read it between the lines of the gospels. The very fact that the apocalyptic section mentioned above was incorporated into Mark shows that the fall of Jerusalem was considered by its author to be a major event in the unfolding of the purpose that God had begun with the coming of Jesus. The destruction was understood to be the final proof that the Old Dispensation had come to an end; the New Age was already beginning to dawn.

LAST SUPPER AND NEW COVENANT

[MARK 14:24-25]

Although we have noted Jesus' last meal with his disciples was probably an eschatological celebration, as Mark 14:25 clearly implies, it was recalled in the Church's tradition in light of two other factors: (1) an analogy between the Jewish Passover and the death of Jesus, and (2) the concept of Jesus' death as the sacrifice that sealed the New Covenant, promised by Jeremiah (Jer. 31:31). The Passover in Jewish tradition recalled the act of deliverance by which God freed his people from slavery in Egypt and led them into the new land. The death of Christ was itself identified with the Passover in the Pauline churches (I Cor. 5:7); and in Johannine circles, Jesus was regarded as the Lamb of God (Jn. 1:29; Rev. 5). The annual celebration of the Passover as a ceremony of recommitment probably provided a rough parallel for the Christian's periodic celebration of the Eucharist, which was considered in Pauline circles as a covenant renewal ceremony (I Cor. 11:25), where the term *New* Covenant is actually used (as it is in some manuscript copies of Mark at 14:24). Mark's

---

[9]The attempt by G. R. Beasley-Murray to demonstrate the authenticity of the Little Apocalypse of Mark cannot be called successful. See Beasley-Murray's *Commentary on Mark 13* (New York: St. Martin's Press, 1957).

version of the tradition has not fully developed a theological interpretation of the death of Jesus; it declares only that the life he offered up ("blood" was equivalent to life in Hebrew) was linked with the (new) covenant, and was to the benefit of "many" (14:24). The later Church expanded this seminal notion, developing from it doctrines of the Atonement as substitution, as propitiatory, as expiatory. But just as Mark was content to affirm only that the death of Jesus was necessary, without explaining why or how, so he simply states that Jesus' death is in behalf of others. This is what the Church of Mark celebrates in the Communion, while looking forward to the completion of the number of the elect in the New Age.

DENIAL AND BETRAYAL

[MARK 14:26–72]

In a series of vivid narrative passages, Mark depicts the instability of the disciples even as Jesus is seen struggling to carry out his God-assigned destiny. There is no hint of what Judas betrayed, although imaginations, pious and otherwise, have long speculated on the subject. Probably he did no more than to lead the guards at dark outside the city walls to the place of Jesus' rendezvous with his followers, and identify him positively for arrest. Mark suggests vaguely that Judas was offered money to betray Jesus, but Matthew fills out the detail

A SHEKEL OF ISRAEL
as minted by the Jews during the Jewish revolt of A.D. *66–70. The reverse side is inscribed "Jerusalem the Holy."* (James T. Stewart)

to make the incident conform to scriptural prophecy (Mt. 26:14–15; Zech. 11:12). Scholars have suggested that Judas was disappointed because Jesus failed to side with the revolutionaries, but there is no evidence that Judas was himself a zealot. Theories about plots are unfounded guesswork. All we can be sure of is that Jesus was put in the hands of the authorities by one of his own followers. Even Peter when pressed, professed to have had no acquaintance with Jesus.

CONDEMNATION AND DEATH

The stories of the charges brought against Jesus by the authorities and the various hearings where he was called to account are confused in Mark's account, and hence in the other gospel narratives that are dependent on him. In general, however, the issues raised in the presence of the High Priest and the Jewish leaders gathered as the Sanhedrin, or local governing council, are all religious. Chief among the accusations is his threat to the Temple (14:58), although instead of having predicted its destruction he is quoted by his opponents as having vowed to destroy it. The second issue has to do with Jesus' claim to be the Son of God ("Blessed," since Jewish piety avoided pronouncing the name or vocable, God). According to Mark 14:62, Jesus for the first time states unequivocally that he is the Son of God, but goes on to define that title by a combination of scriptural quotations, one of which is a reference to the Davidic king seated at God's right hand, the place of power (Ps. 110:1), and the other a paraphrase of Daniel 7:13, where (one like) the Son of Man comes on the clouds of heaven to assume authority in God's Kingdom. Here we have the central point in Mark's understanding of Jesus as Messiah: he combines the kingly role of the Son of David, with its title, Son of God, and the eschatological role of representative of the "saints of the Most High" in Daniel to whom the Kingdom of God is assigned. Although the High Priest is represented as horrified by this claim, no action is taken by the Sanhedrin, which turns over responsibility for Jesus to the civil powers represented by Pontius Pilate, the Roman procurator, who was resident in Jerusalem at the time of the festival rather than at his official seat in Caesarea.

Pilate's questions concern the matter over which he would have jurisdiction: the possibility that Jesus was a claimant to the Jewish kingship and therefore a potential leader of a political revolt (15:2). Jesus' response is equivocal, and he refuses to offer any word in his own defense. Although the story of the release of a political prisoner, Barabbas, is not documented outside of the Gospels as having been Roman policy in Palestine or the eastern provinces (and is likely to have been created by the Christians), it keeps its focus on what was probably the historical point at issue in the hearing before Pilate: Was Jesus an insurrectionist? The terms used of Barabbas, "rebel . . . who had committed murder in the insurrection" (15:7), fit well with such a situation, as does the form of execution that was finally decided upon, however reluctantly, by Pilate: crucifixion. If Jesus had been executed by the religious authorities, a legal possibility at this time, he would have been stoned to death, but the unanimous evidence that he was crucified points to his having been condemned on a political charge: that he claimed to be the King of the Jews.

He was treated as an insurrectionist by the soldiers who tormented him and

THE VIA DOLOROSA
is the traditional route through which Jesus carried his cross to Golgotha. In the basement of the building on the right are enormous paving stones that are believed to have formed the courtyard of the Roman fortress that adjoined the Temple area. The arch over the street was probably part of a building erected by Hadrian in the second century A.D. (Matson Photo Service)

by those who were crucified with him. The sign placed on the cross (15:26) makes the charge explicit. Even though many of the details of the Crucifixion scene may be legendary elaboration (15:33, 38), based in part on a Christian reading of the scriptures (15:34 is a quotation from Ps. 22, which also lies behind other details of the account such as Jesus' thirst), the general outline of the story is credible, including the faithful watch of the women (15:40–41) at the cross and the hasty burial of the body in a stone-cut tomb (15:45–46) in order to avoid polluting the Sabbath by allowing a dead body to be exposed.

YOU WILL SEE HIM AS HE TOLD YOU

[MARK 16:7]

The women take the first opportunity to prepare the body properly with spices—that is, at daybreak on Sunday morning (16:1–2). Their chief concern is how they will manage to roll back the stone. This wheel-like slab of stone was made to roll down a hewn track by gravity and close over the opening of the tomb, which was a chamber cut out of the rock. To their astonishment, the stone has been rolled back and the body of Jesus is gone. A young man—the later gospel will have angels—is there to reassure them. He asserts that Jesus has risen, that he will fulfill his promise (14:28) of going before the disciples to Galilee, where he will be seen by them (16:7). Instead of the rapturous joy that one might expect at such news, Mark declares that the women were filled with trembling, astonishment, and fear. The three terms used here by Mark are all to be found in the LXX version of Daniel 10:12, where Daniel is responding to an apocalyptical vision of the eschatological king.

The Gospel of Mark comes to an abrupt close. It has been conjectured that the Gospel originally ended with an account of the appearance of Jesus to Peter and the other disciples in Galilee. Many of the later manuscripts of Mark have supplied endings, although they vary among themselves considerably. But the oldest and best manuscripts end at 16:8, and it seems likely that this is where Mark intended to conclude. He has several times over had Jesus instruct the reader what the final outcome will be: the triumphant appearance of Jesus as Son of Man-King, the vindication of the faithful, and the establishment of God's Rule. There are no external guarantees that this will occur; the evidence carries weight only for men of faith. As he has done throughout his gospel, Mark does not coerce faith from his readers; he invites it as a response. In this mood of invitation and eschatological expectancy, he brings to a close his "good news."

PART THREE

THE CHURCH
BECOMES
AN INCLUSIVE
COMMUNITY

Less than a century after the Crucifixion of Jesus, Quadratus, Bishop of Athens, was presenting an apology for Christianity to the Emperor Hadrian, on the occasion of the latter's visit to Athens. Justin, a native of Neapolis in Palestine, was converted to the Christian faith in Ephesus after a period of time spent as an itinerant philosophical seeker, and went on to Rome to become a major apologist for the faith before Hadrian and a martyr under his successor, Antoninus Pius. On the coast of the Black Sea, the Christians were viewed by the Roman authorities as a threat to the peace, and the Emperor Trajan instructed the governor how to suppress the movement. How could such an apparently insignificant movement that began in Palestine within the framework of Judaism have become within a century so significant and wide-ranging a phenomenon as to demand the attention of the imperial leaders?

Unfortunately it is not possible on the basis of available sources to trace these developments in detail. The fourth-century Church historian and court advisor to the Emperor Constantine, Eusebius of Caesarea, has preserved fragments of earlier writings in which are reported traditions about the journeys, activities, and fates of the followers of Jesus, but in very few cases is it possible to check the accuracy of these reports or to distinguish legend from historical recollection. We learn from various sources that Thomas went to India, that Mark went to Alexandria, that Peter went to Rome, that John lived to a great age in Ephesus, and so on. These reports are of varying historical value, but they shed no light at all on the crucial question of the stages by which the Church moved out from its Jewish matrix to become an inclusive, Gentile-dominated movement. Irenaeus and other later writers[1] report the existence of strongly Jewish sects that considered themselves to be Christians but that came to be regarded as heretical by the main body of the Church. But since Gentile Christianity rather rapidly became the leading element in the early Church, it is with its origins that we must be chiefly concerned.

In the Book of Acts there are bits of information about Christian groups in cities of Palestine other than Jerusalem—Azotus (Ashdod), Samaria, Damascus. Indeed, the conversion of Paul is consummated through a leader of the Church in Damascus, according to Acts 9, but of the founding of Christianity in that city we learn nothing at all. Acts reports that two Christians who had been driven out of Rome, Priscilla and Aquila, were in Corinth when Paul arrived there (Acts 18),[2] but offers no hint how the Gospel reached Rome. It is usually assumed that in Suetonius' *Life of Claudius* the reference to the disturbances in the Jewish community at Rome (which were said to have been instigated by "Chrestos")[3] are a garbled recollection of the arrival in the Jewish community of the message about Jesus as "Christos," which would surely have been disruptive. But how the Gospel reached Rome, we have no firm historical clue, only later traditions and legends. According to Acts, the Church was already well established when Paul arrived (Acts 28).

Accordingly, we are almost wholly dependent on the Letters of Paul for our knowledge of the spread of Christianity beyond Jerusalem, and what information he provides—welcome though it is—is limited in scope, since it obviously concentrates on his own experiences and associations. Nevertheless this is the most important historical source we have, and it must be examined with care if we are to understand how the Church grew beyond its Jewish setting to become an inclusive community.

At first glance, the Book of Acts would seem to be our most promising

---

[1] In his *Against all Heresies*; also Epiphanius, Philostratius, and St. Augustine. Simon Magus, who appears briefly in Acts 8, was credited by some of the Church fathers with being the founder of Gnosticism, but the Acts account is too sketchy and unreliable to decide whether he did indeed contribute to the development of Jewish-Christian speculative sects. See also Jean Daniélou, *The Theology of Jewish Christianity* (London: Darton, Longman & Todd, 1964), especially pp. 55–85.

[2] That they were Christians is implied in Acts 18, and may be inferred from I Cor. 16:15, where Paul names his earliest converts in the Corinth-Athens area, but does not mention Priscilla and Aquila.

[3] Suetonius, *Lives of the Twelve Caesars*, "Claudius," 25.4.

resource, since it begins where the Gospel of Luke leaves off. But as careful examination of Luke and Acts shows, this two-volume work is a fine example of theological history[4] and is even a good demonstration of Hellenistic history writing,[5] but it can be used only with caution as a historical document in our modern sense of the term. The author's aim is only partly to recall traditions surrounding the careers of Paul and his fellow apostles; it is much more concerned to show how the divine plan of the ages was being worked out in this period. He writes from the perspective of the generation after Paul, so that the issues which are alive in Paul's Letters are not significant for Acts; and the controversies that raged in the Pauline churches are either given in mild stylized form or simply passed over in silence. Some scholars have adopted the policy of using Acts as a historical source where it is not in conflict with the Letters of Paul, but no one can be sure that a document that has proved to be historically unreliable where it can be checked against Paul's writings is somehow reliable where it cannot be checked. Accordingly in our reconstruction of Paul, we shall draw upon the information of Acts as a possible supplement to what we can infer about Paul from his own Letters. When it comes to the thought of Paul, however, we are entirely reliant on his Letters, since Acts portrays the apostles, including Paul, as preaching very much the same kinds of sermons, even though we know from Paul's writings that there were quite sharp disagreements among the apostles. In our study of Paul, therefore, we must distinguish sharply between Paul's Letters as our primary source and Acts as a secondary source, which tells us less about the historical Paul and more about how Paul was understood in certain quarters of the Church by the end of the first century A.D.

Thirteen of the twenty-seven books of the New Testament are written in his name and another has often been attributed to him: the Letter to the Hebrews. Careful analysis of the language and content of these writings shows, however, that the so-called Pauline writings fall into the following categories: (1) those unquestionably by Paul: Romans, I and II Corinthians, Galatians, Philippians, I Thessalonians, and Philemon; (2) those Letters about which questions have been seriously raised, but which are probably by Paul: II Thessalonians and Colossians; (3) a Letter which is not by Paul, but which has been developed out of his thought: Ephesians; (4) Letters which bear his name, but which clearly come from another time and set of circumstances in the Church: I and II Timothy, Titus (the so-called Pastoral Letters); (5) a Letter which does not bear Paul's name and which evidences a wholly different thought-world and religious vocabulary from that of Paul: the Letter to the Hebrews. It is obvious that our major sources will be those in category (1), with a somewhat

---

[4] See Chapter Fourteen of this book; for fuller treatments of these themes, see Hans Conzelmann, *Theology of St. Luke* (New York: Harper & Row, 1961); H. Flender, *St. Luke: Theologian of Redemptive History* (Philadelphia: Fortress, 1961).

[5] M. Dibelius, *Studies in Acts* (New York: Scribner's, 1956); H. J. Cadbury, *The Making of Luke-Acts*, 2nd ed. (Naperville, Ill.: Allenson, 1958).

more restrained use of (2). The rest will be discussed at a later point in this book as evidence for the developments in the Church after the time of Paul.

Since we lack any chronicle of Paul's life, we are dependent on a hypothetical reconstruction of his career by inference from his Letters. And the evidence is sufficient to provide us a serviceable framework. It is not possible, however, to show the development of his thought in chronological sequence. On the other hand, if we were to attempt to analyze Paul's thought by means of a book-by-book study, the results would be unsystematic and often repetitive. Our procedure will be to move thematically. Chapter Six focuses on the sources for reconstructing Paul's career and presents a probable sequence of events. Chapter Seven concentrates on Paul's call, his apostleship, and the specific ways in which his apostolic authority manifested itself. Wisdom is the theme of Chapter Eight, both the practical wisdom of the Church's teachings and the eschatological wisdom about its future in the divine purpose. In Chapter Nine we shall treat the Church as the People of God, both the qualifications and mode of admission to the Covenant People and the resources and responsibilities for life within that community.

The Career
of Paul
and the Rise
of Gentile Christianity

CHAPTER SIX

Why is it that of all the early leaders of the Church in the generation immediately following the death of Jesus it is only Paul about whom we have anything like full information? No one knows the answer to that question. Much as we might like to know more about the disciples and other Church leaders mentioned in the gospels and Acts, we can be grateful that at least Paul's Letters—or some of them— have been preserved and that they provide us with a framework for reconstructing the main outline of his career. Probably the reason that the Pauline material was so treasured is two-fold: (1) it had the power to speak meaningfully and movingly to those who had never met Paul in person, and has continued so to function in the subsequent life of the Church; (2) Paul, more than any other man, was instrumental in translating the fundamentally Jewish message about Jesus into the language and cultural terms that could communicate with Gentiles, for whom the world of the Hebrew scriptures was wholly unfamiliar.

"MY FORMER LIFE IN JUDAISM"

[GALATIANS 1:13]

Paul made no attempt to tell his readers the story of his life. His Letters are rather occasional writings: they were written to deal with specific situations that developed or threatened to develop in the churches under his charge or founded by him. The single exception is his Letter to the Romans, whose church he had not yet visited at the time of writing (Rom. 1:13). The Letter to the Romans provides some extremely valuable detail for the last years of Paul's life, and it contains the most systematic statement of his understanding of Jesus and of God's purpose through him. The teaching of Romans will be our major source in reconstructing Paul's thought in Chapter Nine. But as we just noted in the introduction to this section, we are dependent on his Letters for our information, though in them there is very little by way of hint about the extent of his career or sequence of events in it. If Acts were wholly reliable as a historical source, we would know a bit more about his life before his conversion and would have some fixed dates around which to organize our reconstruction of his life. We shall refer to these in passing, but they are offered with real reservations and as historical evidence should be accepted accordingly.

Paul's most personal and emotion-laden letter is the one to the Galatians. The name "Galatian" refers to the Gauls who invaded and then settled in the interior of Asia Minor in the third century B.C. They gave their name to a large central region, so that when the Roman province of Galatia was established in 25 B.C., it included many people who were not descendants of the Gauls and much land that they had never controlled. Accordingly, we do not know what cities or what region was addressed by Paul in his Letter to the "Galatians." It is unlikely that the "churches of Galatia" covered the whole of the Roman province; rather they were probably located within a smaller district of the province, where he could have been on as intimate terms with the members as the personal remarks in his letter imply.

The main issue he discusses in Galatians is whether Gentiles who want to be Christians must first become Jews through circumcision and observance of other Jewish laws (2:3; 5:2–3). But before he can address himself to the main question, he feels compelled to demonstrate to his readers that his commissioning came directly from God, so that he was not and is not in any way dependent on the apostles who had been followers of Jesus, such as Peter (= Cephas, "rock") and James. We shall consider this argument later in this chapter, but for the moment what is of importance is to note how, in developing his argument, he provides a sketch of his life just before and just after his conversion (Gal. 1:11–17).

Paul makes clear that he was a zealous, conscientious, respected Jew before he became a Christian (Gal. 1:14). There is no hint that he was dissatisfied, or that he found upholding the religious traditions to be a burden. This same picture emerges from one of the other autobiographical passages in his Letter to the Philippians, where he points with pride to the fact that he had been brought up from birth in conformity to the demands of the Law of Moses— "circumcised on the eighth day" (Phil. 3:5)—as interpreted by the Pharisaic standards—"as to the law, a Pharisee" (3:5b). The Book of Acts adds to this the report that Paul studied the traditions of Judaism at Jerusalem, that he was brought up there, and that his teacher was the noted rabbi, Gamaliel (Acts 22:3). But there is no hint of any of this in his Letters, and the fact that he makes a point of his not being known by sight to the members of the Jerusalem church (Gal. 1:22) raises serious doubt about the information offered in Acts. The only place associated with Paul in his own conversion account is Damascus, to which he says he returned again (Gal. 1:17) following a sojourn in Arabia.

What he had been doing in Damascus is nowhere stated in his Letters; but since it is implied that there was some link between his being in Damascus and his persecution of the "church of God" (Gal. 1:13), it is possible that the gospel had spread to that city, that a congregation of believers had sprung up there, and that Paul was trying to suppress it. Whether there is any historical basis to the more detailed account of Paul's activities in Damascus in Acts 9 we cannot determine, although it seems unlikely that the High Priest in

DAMASCUS
*is believed by some historians to be the oldest continu-
ously inhabited city in the world. A few traces of Roman
times remain in the old covered markets, but most of the
city presents the modern appearance pictured here.* (Arab
Information Center)

Jerusalem would have been permitted by the Romans to exercise his authority in a city so far outside of Judea (9:1–2). Certainly Paul is much less interested in the details of his confrontation scene with the risen Christ (Gal. 1:16) than is the author of Acts, who tells the story three times over (Acts 9, 22, 26). It is only in the Acts accounts that we hear of the blinding light, the heavenly voice, and of Paul's recovery of sight through Ananias (9:10–19). All that can be inferred from the account in Galatians is that Paul was in Damascus or in its vicinity when the revelation occurred.

The significance of the revelatory experience was absolutely central for Paul's subsequent life. In Galatians he writes simply, "[God] was pleased to reveal his Son to me" (Gal. 1:16). Elsewhere, he writes that he has "seen the Lord" (I Cor. 9:1), and connects this privilege directly with the fact that he has been designated an apostle. The same link between seeing the Lord and apostleship is made in a more extended statement in I Corinthians 15:3–9, where Paul reports that he was the last in the series of persons to whom was granted a revelation of Jesus risen from the dead. Although the implied significance of this series of revelations is not altogether clear in I Corinthians—it is not likely that the "more than 500 brethren" (I Cor. 15:6) were all considered to be apostles—Paul dates his apostleship from the time of the revelation of the risen Christ. The term *apostle* is a Greek verbal noun meaning "one who has been sent or commissioned." It is probably a translation of the Aramaic term for the royal emissaries who were instructed by the Persian monarch to investigate and resolve problems in various parts of the vast empire of the Achemaenid Dynasty (sixth to fourth centuries B.C.).[1] Paul and the other leaders who believed that God had revealed to them Jesus risen from the dead were convinced that through this revelation they had been commissioned by the King of the universe to carry out His will. This was the basis of their authority in preaching as well as in their decisions concerning the common life within the local churches. Although the Book of Acts declares explicitly that a qualification for apostleship was that one had been a follower of Jesus from the time of his baptism on (Acts 1:21–22), Paul asserts that to have "seen the Lord" was the only requirement, and certainly it was the one requisite that he could have met.

Paul's embarrassment and guilt about the peculiar nature of his apostleship lay not in his failure to have been a disciple from the outset of Jesus' ministry, but rather in his having been a persecutor of the Church (I Cor. 15:9; Gal. 1:13; Phil. 3:6) prior to his conversion. In the Galatians passage he says that he persecuted the Church "violently" and that he "tried to destroy it." The reason he offers for his earlier hostility to the Church was his great zeal for "the

---

[1]Attempts to credit the Gnostics with creating the term, as by W. Schmithals in *The Office of Apostle* (New York and Nashville: Abingdon, 1969), falter on the fact that all the evidence adduced is from the time of Paul, or even as late as the Islamic period (sixth century A.D.).

traditions of the fathers" (Gal. 1:14). Most likely he saw in the claims that Christians made for Jesus and in the nature of the Christian community a threat to the identity and continuity of the Jewish community. Since the Christians were claiming that the promises God had made to Israel in the scriptures were fulfilled through Jesus, the issue came down to choosing between two different readings and interpretations of the same set of sacred writings. His devotion to the scriptural "traditions of the fathers" took a new and revolutionary turn when he "saw the Lord [Jesus]," and came to believe that God's raising him from the dead was "according to the scriptures" (I Cor. 15:4). The revelation of the risen Christ transformed Paul from persecutor of the Church into propagator of the gospel.

Attempts have been made to explain on psychological grounds Paul's about-face on the Christian claims for Jesus. Interpreters have pointed to Romans 7, where Paul described his inner moral conflict, torn as he was between what he wanted to do and what the Law of God demanded of him (Rom. 7:7–23), and have inferred from this account of struggle that prior to his conversion Paul was not really at peace within, even though he was so zealous to perform what the Law required. But there is really no evidence that he was anything but content with his way of life under the Jewish commandments: ". . . as to righteousness under the law blameless" he described himself (Phil. 3:6). His awareness of the inadequacy of his former way of life did not come until after he had entered the new life in Christ: "Whatever gain I had, I counted as loss for the sake of Christ" (Phil. 3:7). We are therefore in no position to conjecture what influences prepared Paul for his great change. All he tells us is that the transformation occurred, that its timing was in the providence of God (Gal. 1:15), and that the occasion for the conversion was the vision of the risen Christ (I Cor. 15:8).

"WHEN GOD WAS PLEASED TO REVEAL HIS SON TO ME"

[GALATIANS 1:15]

So completely convincing was the conversion experience that Paul felt no need to consult any human authority in order to confirm the validity of the vision, even though his commissioning seems to have been from the outset to preach the gospel among Gentiles, in contrast to the apostles in Jerusalem, whose activities were limited (at least in the early years of the Church's existence) to evangelism among fellow Jews. Unlike Acts, which reports that Paul made contact with an existing church in Damascus and carried on a program of evangelism among the Jews in that city (Acts 9:10–22), Paul himself states simply that he "went away into Arabia" and later "returned to Damascus." The Romans differentiated three parts of Arabia: the northwestern strip that is rocky, fertile, and sufficiently well watered to produce crops of grain (*Arabia Petraea*, modern Jordan); the main part of the peninsula (*Arabia Deserta*);

and the southern strip, which served as a shipping point from India and the Spice Islands (*Arabia Felix*). Probably Paul went to the first of these. It was, like Damascus itself, under the control of the Nabatean Arabs, whose capital was the fabulous rock-hewn city of Petra. Aretas IV, king of the Nabateans, tried unsuccessfully to seize Paul in Damascus on one occasion (II Cor. 11:32), when friends presumably lowered him over the city wall in a basket and enabled him to escape. Christianity spread very early to the cities east of the Jordan and northeast of the Sea of Galilee, so that it is conceivable that Paul made contact immediately following his conversion with Christians in the strip of land that stretches southward from Damascus. He offers no hint, however, as to how long he remained there, where he went specifically, what he did while there, or why he returned. Even the mention of a three-year interval in Galatians 1:18 is ambiguous, since we do not know for certain whether the period began with his conversion or his return.

"THAT WE SHOULD GO TO THE GENTILES"

[GALATIANS 2:9]

It was probably three years after the revelatory experience that Paul determined to go to Jerusalem to visit the other apostles, among whom his reputation as a persecutor of the Church and his subsequent conversion were matters of common knowledge (Gal. 1:22–23). His visit to Jerusalem was limited to two weeks, and his associations with Christians there were restricted to Cephas, or Peter (respectively the Aramaic and Greek versions of his nickname,[2] meaning "Rock"), and to James, the brother of Jesus, who had risen to the position of head of the church in Jerusalem (Gal. 2:9, 12). If we give credence to the account in Acts 12, James, son of Zebedee and brother of John—both brothers were among the original disciples of Jesus—had been a leader or perhaps the leader in Jerusalem until he was executed by Herod Agrippa I. Herod had originally controlled only the territory of Philip northeast of Galilee, but in A.D. 44, under Claudius, he was made king of the whole of Palestine. Later Acts reports (15:13) that another James, the brother of Jesus, was head of the Jerusalem church, a detail that fits precisely with the evidence from Paul's Letters. The only hint of the outcome of the first encounter between Paul and the Jerusalem leaders is his statement (Gal. 1:24) that "they glorified God because of me." Whether it was merely the fact of his conversion that pleased them or his evangelism "among the Gentiles" (Gal. 1:16; 2:2) as well, we have no way of determining.

Certainly by the time of Paul's next visit to them, the Jerusalem leaders had received fuller reports of Paul's evangelizing work among the Gentiles in the Roman provinces of Syria and Cilicia over a period of more than a decade (Gal. 2:1). His companions were a Jewish Christian and a Gentile Christian,

---

[2]His given name was Simeon, or Simon.

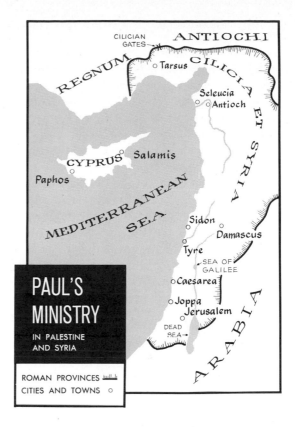

PAUL'S
MINISTRY

IN PALESTINE
AND SYRIA

ROMAN PROVINCES
CITIES AND TOWNS o

Barnabas and Titus, respectively. Barnabas' Semitic name, coupled with the fact that his presence in the Jerusalem church caused no problem, suggests that he was of Jewish background. This inference from Galatians 2 is in general compatible with the reports in Acts that Barnabas was the first to befriend Paul on his initial visit to Jerusalem (9:26ff.),[3] that Barnabas was despatched to Tarsus to persuade Paul to assume leadership in the newly founded Gentile-Christian community in Antioch (11:19–26), and that together Paul and Barnabas went to Jerusalem (11:30), returning to Antioch after they had delivered to the church in Jerusalem a contribution toward a famine relief fund (12:25). But the issue that arose on the occasion of Paul's second visit to Jerusalem as described by him in Galatians 2—whether Gentile converts had to be circumcised (Gal. 2:3)—sounds much more like the controversy that arose on Paul's visit as reported in Acts 15. This would have been Paul's third journey to Jerusalem according to Acts.

Apparently, the author of Acts is more concerned to give a dramatic account

---

[3]The disparity between the accounts in Acts and those in Paul's Letters concerning his visits to Jerusalem have been analyzed critically by John Knox in *Chapters in the Life of Paul* (New York and Nashville: Abingdon, 1950). An attempt to reconcile the two sources is offered by G. H. C. Macgregor in *The Interpreter's Bible*, IX (New York and Nashville: Abingdon, 1954), 198–201.

of Paul's relationships with Jerusalem and to demonstrate that the outcome
of the discussions was one of peaceful agreement (Acts 15:19–21) than to portray
the precise course of events. Paul's whole case for his independence from the
Jerusalem leaders rests on his claim to have visited them only twice and to
have come away with their approval, however reluctant, of his Gentile evangelism. If anyone had been able to show that Paul had in fact been in Jerusalem
to check matters out with the apostles there on more than the two occasions
that he acknowledges, Paul's entire case would have been undermined. His
dependence for his apostolic authority upon the other apostles would have been
clear, and he would rightly have been demoted to a second-rate apostle. The
repeated sarcastic asides about the apostles "who thought they were something"
(Gal. 2:2, 6, 9) shows that the issue of his apostolic authority really troubled
him deeply. This theme we shall explore in Chapter Seven.

The main issue disturbing Paul as he wrote to the Galatians, however, was
the requirements for admission to the Christian community. In giving his view
of the problem, Paul provides us with further autobiographical detail. Titus
was not required to be circumcised, and thereby became the precedent for
all subsequent converts to Christianity from among non-Jews: no one was
required to become a Jew—by circumcision—in order to become a Christian.
Judaism was not a religious vestibule through which the prospective adherent
of Christianity must pass in order to enter the community. The channel led
directly from paganism to the Christian faith; by accepting Titus, the Jerusalem leaders gave approval to Paul's principle that faith was the only requisite
for becoming a Christian. It was agreed, however, that Peter and James would
devote their energies to converting Jews, while Paul and his coworkers would
concentrate exclusively on Gentiles (Gal. 2:7–9). As a visible sign of the unity
of the Christian community, Paul agreed that the churches in his charge would
contribute to "the poor" in Jerusalem (2:10). The term may imply nothing more
than that the church there was in economic straits; Acts 11:29 explains the
poverty as resulting from a widespread famine. It is more likely, however,
that "the poor" was a self-designation of the community, borrowing a term
that occurs frequently in the Psalms (Ps. 9:18; 10:8, 9; 12:5; 34:6; 41:1). In the
second and later centuries, we hear of a Jewish Christian sect known as the
Ebionites (meaning the poor). Attempts to link the Ebionites with the Qumran
community have been unconvincing,[4] but it is possible that the former were
the survivors of the Jerusalem church, which is reported to have fled the city
on the eve of the destruction of the Temple by the Romans in A.D. 70 and to
have taken refuge in the Gentile city of Pella, on the east side of the Jordan.[5]
Paul lived up to his agreement to "remember the poor" and delayed his journey
to Rome in order to accompany the representatives of the Gentile churches

---

[4]See J. A. Fitzmyer, "The Qumran Scrolls, the Ebionites and Their Literature," in
K. Stendahl, ed., *The Scrolls and the New Testament* (New York: Harper & Row, 1957),
pp. 208–231.

[5]Eusebius of Caesarea, *Ecclesiastical History*, III.5.3.

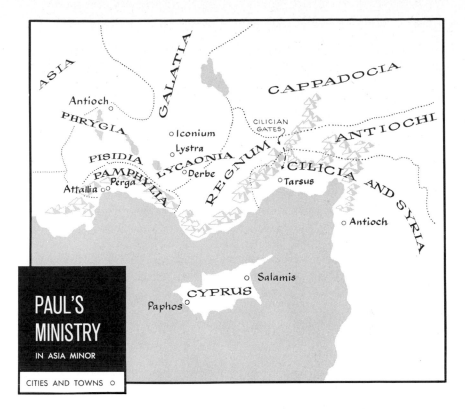

PAUL'S
MINISTRY
IN ASIA MINOR

CITIES AND TOWNS o

founded by him who were taking the contribution for the Jerusalem "saints" (Rom. 15:23–26; I Cor. 16:1–8).

On Paul's return to Antioch, the issue arose again, however. Peter (Cephas) visited the church in Antioch and was happy to enter fully into its fellowship, including sharing meals with Gentiles there. But when certain men from Jerusalem who were closely identified with James also arrived in Antioch, Peter was embarrassed by his own earlier liberal attitude and behavior toward Gentiles, and reverted to the strict separatist policy that prevailed in Jerusalem (Gal. 2:11–13). So effectively did the exclusivists make their point that even Barnabas shifted ground, siding with those who insisted that Christians must observe certain minimal Jewish regulations, presumably on circumcision and the dietary laws (or at least eating with Jews only).

From Paul's Letters alone we have little evidence for the sequence of events in his life beyond this point until we come to the later stages of his activity in which he announced his intention to leave off evangelism in the eastern Mediterranean area and move westward through Rome to Spain (Rom. 15:18–24). Acts, on the other hand, gives fairly detailed accounts of a series of missionary circuits traveled by Paul: the first began at Antioch, moved to Cyprus, returned to the mainland of Asia Minor, moved eastward to the cities of the Anatolian plateau before sailing back to Antioch (Acts 13–14); the second journey took Paul through the inland Asia Minor territories of Phrygia and

Galatia down to the Ionian coast, from which he and his companions crossed the Aegean to Macedonia, where his first convert was a businesswoman named Lydia, a dye seller working in Philippi. They then moved south and westward through Thessalonica, Beroea, and Athens to Corinth (Acts 16–18).

It is on this journey that we begin to have a few points of contact between Acts and the Letters of Paul. Acts provides vivid stories and descriptive detail about the cities Paul visited and his experiences in them. Some of the detail shows accurate knowledge of local conditions and customs, while other aspects of the narrative are of dubious historical value. In any case, we are dependent on Paul's sketchy autobiographical references for sure information, and it is often too fragmentary to do more than prick our imaginations. What does he mean when he speaks of the "bodily ailment" that occasioned his first preaching among the Galatians (Gal. 4:13)?[1] And why was it a trial to the Christians there? What does he imply in reminding them that "Jesus Christ was publicly portrayed before [their] eyes as crucified" (Gal. 3:1)?

"YOU TURNED TO GOD FROM IDOLS"

[I THESSALONIANS 1:9]

We are quite as much in the dark about how Paul carried out his evangelism among the Galatians as we are about what specifically caused the disruption that provoked him to write his sharp, sarcastic letter to them. His stress on their having received the Spirit by faith alone (Gal. 3:2–5) suggests that they were Gentiles who knew nothing of the Jewish Law, but who were appealed to by the power of the preaching, the Spirit, and the miracles performed in their midst. It may be conjectured that there were Jewish Christians who declared that Paul had not given them the fullness of their heritage, and that they should enter into the privileges and benefits that came through obeying the Law of Moses. Their freedom from domination by the demonic powers (Gal. 4:8) had been achieved by the power of faith; in subjecting themselves to religious regulations, they were allowing themselves to be enslaved to a new kind of master: the tyranny of ritual laws and requirements. Since Paul devotes a large section of the Letter to a warning against libertinism (5:13–6:10), it has been argued that the troublemakers among the Galatian Christians could not have been Jewish legalists. But it is easy to imagine that the Judaizers caricatured Paul's position by declaring that if one followed him to the logical conclusion, the result would be a morally irresponsible way of life. But Paul argued that the freedom of which he speaks and into which Christians enter is one where the Spirit produces within man the virtues that the law requires. The relation between faith and works is developed much more fully and precisely in Paul's Letter to the Romans, which we shall examine in detail in Chapter Nine.

[1]See p. 184.

The next point of contact between Acts and Paul is in the First Letter to the Thessalonians. Although Paul makes no mention of a stay in jail at Philippi or of the miracle by which he and his companion, Silas, were set free (Acts 16:16–34), he does write to the Thessalonians concerning the "suffering and shameful treatment" that he had received in Philippi (I Thess. 2:2). Chief city of Macedonia, Philippi had been founded by the father of Alexander the Great, Philip of Macedon, but had remained a small settlement until Mark Antony and Octavian (Augustus) defeated Brutus and Cassius near the city and renamed it Colonia Julia Philipensis. Together with its port city of Neapolis (modern Kavalla), it served as the eastern terminus of the Via Egnatia, which crossed from the Aegean at this point westward to the Adriatic, from which an easy crossing could be made to Brundisium, the southern terminus of the Appian Way. These highways thus provided the major land route between Rome and the East. Lydia, the dye seller who was Paul's first convert in Europe (according to Acts 16:14–15), does not appear in the lists of personal names in Paul's Letters, but the kind of international trade in which she is said to have been engaged (her home was said to be in the Ionian city of Thyatira) is fully plausible at Philippi. Paul notes in his Letter to this church (Phil. 4:14–19) that from the very beginning of his work on the European mainland, the church at Philippi had been faithful in sending him contributions so that his work could be carried out in cities that were reluctant to provide him the basic support he needed. Judging by his Letter to the Philippians, Paul had a uniquely affectionate relationship with the members of the church there.

From Philippi, Paul passed on from his difficult experiences to Thessalonica, where, as I Thessalonians shows, his preaching was effective in converting Gentiles from paganism to Christianity (1:9). The resulting church there was so strong that it not only resisted opposition (1:6), but it also became a model of fidelity and courage throughout the Greek cities from Macedonia in the north to Corinth in the south. The persecution that the Thessalonian Christians experienced was as severe as that endured by the churches of Judea at the hands of the Jewish leaders; however, it was instigated by fellow Gentiles (2:14–16). Paul had developed a great affection and concern for the Thessalonians, and was so troubled about the difficulties they were experiencing that he remained alone at Athens and sent off his companion Timothy to learn of the outcome of the struggle in Thessalonica and report to him in Athens before they continued their journey, presumably to Corinth (3:1–5). The Thessalonians had remained steadfast in the faith in spite of persecution, and Paul's letter (I Thess.) expressed his joy and satisfaction at their perseverance.

In contrast to the Acts 17 account of Paul's dramatic confrontation with and poetic-philosophical appeal to the intellectual leaders of Athens gathered at the Areopagus, the meeting place for the arbiters of the city's moral and cultural issues, Paul himself makes no mention of Athens, except as the place where he awaited Timothy's return (I Thess. 3). There is no indication in Paul's Letters of his having carried out evangelistic work there, much less of his having founded a church there. Indeed, there is a clear indication that if he tried to make converts in Athens he was unsuccessful, since he specifically declares (I Cor. 16:15) that members of a Corinthian family (the household of Stephanas) were the first to be converted in Achaia, the Roman province that included both Athens and Corinth. It is significant for the evangelistic methods of Paul, as well as for the strongly corporate sense of identity of the period, that the Church grew by the conversion of households and not simply by the decisions of individuals.

Paul discloses little about the beginnings of his work in the great commercial city of Corinth. Favorably situated on the western side of the isthmus that connects the main part of Greece with the Peloponnesus, Corinth had not only its own port of Lechaeum, but also a port on the east side of the isthmus, Cenchrae. In order to avoid the treacherous currents and winds that plagued ships sailing below the Peloponnesus, ships put into one of the ports of Corinth, and the goods were transported across the narrow neck of land to a ship at the other port. Traces have been found of a specially grooved road for hauling the loaded ships themselves on wagons across the isthmus. In classical times a temple of Astarte, a Syrian fertility goddess identified by the Greeks with Aphrodite, was located on Acrocorinth, the spectacular mound of rock that rises sharply behind the city to a height of nearly 2,000 feet above the sea. Even though the temple had probably fallen into ruins when the Romans sacked the city in B.C. 146 and its thousand cult prostitutes had disappeared, Corinth was in Paul's day a city famous for its wealth, sensuality, and pleasure-seeking, as the Roman proverb attests: "It does not fall to everyone's lot to go to Corinth."

Acts 18 describes Paul's arrival in Corinth and the beginning of his work there. Several of the persons mentioned in Acts also appear in the lists of those to be greeted included in Paul's Letters to or from Corinth, so that the Acts account is not without historical basis. More significant than the lists of names is the mention of two events which—if authentic or based on historical recollections—provide us for the first time with a pair of relatively fixed chronological points for Paul's career. The first is that Aquila and Priscilla, recently arrived in Corinth from Rome, were among those expelled from the city by Emperor Claudius (Suetonius: *Lives of the Twelve Caesars*, 25.4). On the basis of similar references in later historians, it is likely that the Jews were driven out in 49 or 50 A.D.[6] If the conjecture is correct that "Christos," which would have been an unfamiliar term, was mistaken by Suetonius for "Chrestos" (a common name, meaning "good" or "kind"), then the troubles may have begun when Christian evangelists began working among Jews in Rome. Since Aquila and Priscilla were already converted when Paul arrived, they were likely persuaded to adopt the new faith while still in Rome, to which city they apparently

[6]A full discussion of this historical problem is offered in F. J. Foakes-Jackson and K. Lake, *The Beginnings of Christianity*, V (London: Macmillan, 1933) pp. 445–473.

CLAUDIUS
as pictured on a coin of his reign (A.D. 41–54). He was the emperor who drove the Jews from Rome about the year 50. Some of the exiles found their way to Corinth and became Paul's aides. (James T. Stewart)

returned later when a new emperor reigned who was better disposed toward the Jews. Paul sends greeting to them in Rome in Romans 16:3–4.

The second datable epoch in Paul's career as presented in Acts is the period of the governorship of Gallio (Acts 18:12ff.), brother of the more famous Seneca, philosopher-royal and court advisor in Rome until he fell into disfavor with the irresponsible Emperor Nero. An inscription found at Delphi (across the Gulf of Corinth), fixes the date of Gallio's coming as governor of Achaia at 52–53 A.D. or perhaps a year earlier. On this evidence, it was in the first half of the sixth decade that Paul arrived in Corinth. Among the structures that may be identified with Paul's stay in Corinth are the public rostrum, or *bēma*, where according to Acts 18:12ff. Paul offered his defense before Gallio, the governor. Also discovered by excavators at Corinth was a lintel on which were crudely inscribed the words, "Synagogue of the Hebrews," which may have come from the synagogue mentioned in Acts 18:4ff.

The only hints that Paul offers in his Letters about his experience in Corinth are that he did not approach the Corinthians through proclaiming lofty philosophical notions (I Cor. 2:1) and that the core of the church there consisted of persons who were socially, economically, and intellectually of a lower order

THE BEMA AT CORINTH
(the public rostrum), with the Acrocorinth in the background. Paul was accorded a hearing on this platform before Gallio, the Roman governor, according to Acts 18:2. (American School of Classical Studies, Athens)

(I Cor. 1:26). Corinth never did have a reputation as a center of learning, and this lack seems to have been reflected in the church there as well. As we shall see in Chapter Eight, however, there were Corinthians who had pretensions about wisdom, and Paul had to set them straight as to what true wisdom was.

VISITS TO CORINTH, PAINFUL AND OTHERWISE
[II CORINTHIANS 2:1]

When Paul wrote I Corinthians, he was planning to visit the city once more, as we can infer from I Corinthians 16:5ff. In II Corinthians 2:1 reference is made to a "painful visit," at a time and under circumstances unspecified; and II Corinthians 13:1 speaks of his coming for a third time, though we cannot be sure whether he means coming to visit or coming to them by letter. In any case, the correspondence with the Corinthians shows continuing concern and extended contacts between Paul wherever he was and what seems to have been at once his favorite and his most problem-ridden church. How deeply Paul was concerned for the spiritual welfare of the Corinthians is evident in the extended account of his having sent Titus to Corinth to bring him a firsthand report of affairs there (II Cor. 7:5–16), and in his anxiety on failing to find Titus at the appointed meeting place, Troas. Paul hurried across the Aegean to Philippi to meet Titus at the earliest possible moment with his report on the Corinthian church; happily, at Philippi he did meet Titus, who brought back a reassuring account.

Paul was not above playing one church off against the other. He warns the Corinthians that when next he visits them it will be to complete arrangements for the offering that the Gentile churches were to make for the benefit of the church in Jerusalem. This will, indeed, be the main occasion for his announced visit (I Cor. 16:5ff.). Apparently that plan was delayed, and the Corinthians suspected some sinister motives on his part for not having come. Although the timing of that visit was now changed, and perhaps even the itinerary—he mentions in II Cor. 1:16 going directly (from Ephesus?) to Corinth and then back to Macedonia—but the intention is to pick up the collection together with the official representatives of the Gentile churches and go with them and the offering to Jerusalem.

At the time of writing I Corinthians, Paul was in Ephesus, the major city of Asia Minor at the time, and an obvious center for evangelism of both the Ionian coast and the inland cities, which could be reached easily by highways leading east from Ephesus. Although Paul acknowledged in I Cor. 16:9 that he had "many adversaries" in Ephesus, the intensity of their opposition became almost more than he could bear (II Cor. 1:8). Scholars have conjectured that he was imprisoned there, and that he wrote the Letter to the Philippians from prison there (Phil. 1:14) and, if genuine, the Letters to the Colossians and

Philemon as well. Since the cities of Colossae and Philippi were easily accessible to Ephesus, this would seem to be plausible, but there is no reason that Paul could not have written to those churches from a prison in Rome, since travel and mail service were so dependable in these early years of the Roman empire. Philemon is the only purely personal letter of Paul that has survived. The recipient seems to have been a wealthy Christian resident in Colossae; though the city is not mentioned, the many points of contact between this letter and the Letter to the Colossians make that destination for Philemon virtually certain. But Paul could have encountered the runaway slave Onesimus as well in Rome as in nearby Ephesus (Phmn. 10–17).[7]

In spite of the commercial decline of Ephesus that resulted from the silting up of its harbor, it continued to be a place of wealth, largely from the visitors who streamed there from all over the Mediterranean world to see the meteorite that was worshipped as Artemis and the great temple that had been constructed to honor this "goddess fallen from the sky" (Acts 19:35). Although she was identified with the Greek Artemis, her worship more closely resembled that of Astarte of the Canaanites or the Great Mother of the Phrygians, in that both male and female prostitutes were attached to the Ephesian temple in order to serve the orgiastic cult requirements of the virgin fertility goddess. The main structure of the temple was considerably larger than a present-day football field, and stood on a huge platform that measured more than 200 by 400 feet. The net effect of the imposing proportions, the massive columns more than fifty feet high, together with the elaborate exterior decoration of gold and sculptured marble, must have been extremely impressive. The image of the goddess, by contrast, was quite simple, as we can judge from representations of it on coins of the era. Copies of the sanctuary made and sold by artisans in Paul's day (Acts 19:23ff.) were models of more primitive shrines antedating the magnificent temple that was standing in the first century A.D. According to Acts 19, it was the success of Paul's evangelistic activity that threatened the pilgrim and souvenir trade. Paul, however, describes the difficulties he experienced there in very general terms, even while conveying the deep anxiety that his sufferings had brought him:

> For we do not want you to be ignorant, brethren, of the affliction we experienced in Asia; for we were so utterly, unbearably crushed that we despaired of life itself. Why, we felt that we had received the sentence of death; but that was to make us rely on God who raises the dead; he delivered us from so deadly a peril, and he will deliver us; on him we have set our hope that he will deliver us again.
> —II CORINTHIANS 1:8–10

---

[7]Other scholars have conjectured that the so-called prison letters were written from Caesarea on the Palestinian coast, where Paul was incarcerated for more than two years, according to Acts 24:27. But there is a more plausible case for either Ephesus or Rome as the place of imprisonment. For Ephesus, see G. S. Duncan, *St. Paul's Ephesian Ministry* (London: Hodder and Stoughton, 1929).

By the time Paul wrote his second letter (which is preserved) to the Corinthians, the Corinthians had long since completed their collection for the church in Judea, and Paul boasted about their generosity in speaking or writing to the churches of Macedonia (II Cor. 9:1–5). So eager had the Corinthians been to have their gift on its way that Paul had sent Titus to them as an advance man to make preparations for the collection (II Cor. 8:16–24). Paul counted on them to deliver as promised. Each church was to put aside a certain amount each week, on the first day—our earliest reference to the Christian equivalent of the Jewish Sabbath—with the amount to accumulate in each city until the persons accredited by each participating congregation actually set out with the aggregate collection on their way to Jerusalem (I Cor. 16:1–4).

Paul had apparently been under attack on the ground that his refusal to accept financial support for his work among the Corinthians was in some way self-seeking or even sinister (II Cor. 11:7–11). His support had come from the churches in Macedonia, but other itinerant preachers who had come to Corinth and had accepted compensation for their work there insinuated that if Paul had been dealing squarely with the Corinthians he would have done the same. With bitter irony, Paul replied to those who impugned his integrity and boasted of their own exploits. In doing so, he offered the fullest listing of the experiences that he had undergone in carrying out his apostolic role; contrasting his own devotion to that of his critics, he wrote:

> Are they servants of Christ? I am a better one—I am talking like a madman—with far greater labors, far more imprisonments, with countless beatings, and often near death. Five times I have received at the hands of the Jews forty lashes less one. Three times I have been beaten with rods; once I was stoned. Three times I have been shipwrecked; a night and a day I have been adrift at sea; on frequent journeys, in danger from rivers, danger from robbers, danger from my own people, danger from Gentiles, danger in the city, danger in the wilderness, danger at sea, danger from false brethren; in toil and hardship, through many a sleepless night, in hunger and thirst, often without food, in cold and exposure. And, apart from other things, there is the daily pressure of my anxiety for all the churches.
>
> —II CORINTHIANS 11:23–28

Probably it was not long after Paul dispatched the letter in defense of his apostolic role—a letter that we know as II Corinthians[8]—that he made the pro-

---

[8]It is likely that what we now know as II Corinthians consists of parts of several letters, some of which are fragmentary and out of their original order. As evidence for this literary chaos one may point to the seeming change in the tone of the Letter between Chaps. 1–9 and 10–13, and to the apparent interruption in the flow of thought represented by 6:14–7:1, which when removed allows a smooth transition from 6:13 to 7:2. But since we do not know the precise situations to which Paul was addressing himself in II Corinthians (or for that matter, in any of his Letters), we cannot be certain that different sections of the Letter do in fact presuppose different circumstances and that they therefore must have been written at various times. There may have been some displacement, and we do know in any case that some of the correspondence between Paul and the church at Corinth has been lost (Cf. I Cor. 5:9). But it is not certainly demonstrable that our II Corinthians is a composite document.

jected journey across to Macedonia and southward to Corinth. His Letter to the Romans was apparently written from there, and gives every indication that all was in order with the collection for Jerusalem, in the churches of Achaia as well as in those in Macedonia. Following the final visit to Corinth, therefore, Paul purposed to take the collection to Jerusalem, along with the approved representatives of the churches, and then to leave the eastern Mediterranean for Rome and beyond to Spain (Rom. 15:24–29). The circuit that began at Jerusalem had ended at Illyricum, which lay to the north and west of Corinth. We have no account in Paul's Letters or in the Book of Acts about his work there, but he implied that he had evangelized that area as well, so that the whole northeastern quadrant of the Mediterranean area had been reached by him with the gospel. As a pioneer, however, he could not be content to preach in territory where either he or others had already worked. He had to press on to untouched areas. Hence his stay in Rome was to be brief; after that, it was on to the virgin lands of the west.

ARREST IN JERUSALEM

From Paul we learn nothing of the journey to Jerusalem, or of the reception of the gift by the church there, or of his seizure by the Roman authorities. Acts 20 to 26 gives quite full details of the return trip through Macedonia and the Ionian coast, especially of the touching farewell scene between Paul and the elders from the church at Ephesus. Acts forewarns the reader of the certainty of Paul's death at the hands of the authorities (20:17–37). The specifics of the itinerary are given in Acts 21, including the visits to the various churches en route: Tyre, Ptolemais (modern Acco on the Palestinian coast), and Caesarea, the Roman capital of the province of Judea. The words attributed by the author of Acts to a Christian prophet at Caesarea concerning Paul's death provide yet another reminder of the impending martyrdom of the apostle to the Gentiles (Acts 21:10–14).

The reception of Paul by the Jerusalem Christians was cordial enough, according to Acts, although they failed to come to his support when he was seized by the Roman authorities, and there is no indication in Acts of further association of Paul with the church there. In a series of public addresses, Acts provides Paul the opportunity to describe his conversion, to show his fidelity to the Jewish scriptures (Acts 24:14–16), to demonstrate that none of the religious or civil rulers was able to bring a valid charge against him. Agrippa is made to sum up the point of the author's argument: "This man is doing nothing to deserve death or imprisonment" (26:31).

Mention of these political figures is important to the overall aims of the author of Acts; and even though the details may be unreliable or even fictitious, there is some value in their appearance in the narrative, since they furnish us with approximate dates for the events described. And since Acts does have the right men in the proper chronological order and relationships, we cannot dismiss the historical evidence as worthless. Felix became governor in Palestine about 52 A.D., and was replaced by Porcius Festus sometime between 55 and 60 A.D. Herod Agrippa II, puppet king of Batanea, Gaulanitis, and Trachonitis, arid regions north and east of the Sea of Galilee, had succeeded his father after the latter's death in 44 A.D. and continued to reign until his death in 100. However, his incestuous relationship with his sister Berenice and his collaboration with the Romans during the Jewish revolt of 66–70 A.D. reduced his authority to nearly nothing. In any case, the allusions in Acts to these authorities do not fix the dates for Paul's arrest in Jerusalem, but they suggest that it occurred sometime between 55 and 60. Exercising his right as a Roman citizen to appeal to Caesar, Paul was shipped off to Rome under guard. He did in fact reach Rome, but under circumstances very different from what he had anticipated when writing to the church there.

IMPRISONMENT AND DEATH IN ROME

From this point on, we have no certain information from Paul, unless we assume that the Letter to the Philippians was written from prison in Rome. Scholars have debated its place of origin. Since Paul mentioned in writing to the Philippian church that, as a result of his being arrested and put in prison, the gospel had become known throughout the whole of the praetorian guard (literally, "in the whole praetorium"); and since these were the elite troops who guarded the person of the emperor, the most natural assumption is that Paul was in prison in Rome, adjacent to the imperial residence. There were, however, units of the praetorian guard stationed in other important cities of the empire as well, where they served as visible, though ceremonial, reminders of the imperial authority. It is difficult to square Paul's mention of returning to visit the church at Philippi with his clearly announced intention in the Letter to the Romans (15:28–29) to go on beyond Rome to Spain. As we noted, a likely place from which Philippians may have been written is Ephesus. The implied proximity to his readers fits well, and Paul's mentioning in I Corinthians 15:32 of fighting wild beasts at Ephesus is probably a metaphor for his having been faced with the possibility of execution there.

More significant than its time or place of origin, however, is the outlook on death that Paul reveals in Philippians. In some of his letters—notably I Corinthians and I Thessalonians—Paul writes as though he expected to be alive at the End of the Age, when God would reveal Jesus to the world as exalted Lord (I Cor. 15:51ff.; I Thess. 4:13). In Philippians 1:19ff.; he states that he would in some ways prefer to be delivered from prison and death so that he might continue his work among the churches. But in other ways, he preferred to die, since he thought that death would lead him directly into the presence of the Lord, and this he felt to be far better than earthly life. In spite of his personal preference, he was eager to honor God "whether by life or by death." There is no reason to doubt that Paul maintained the same attitude toward death to the end, whether these views were written from a prison in Ephesus or Rome or in some other city unknown to us.

The Book of Acts, however, gives us extensive detail about the later events of Paul's life, including a vivid narrative of his journey from Caesarea to Rome (Acts 27–28). The specifics of the route—winds, navigational methods, and hazards—all show a precise knowledge of nautical ways in the Mediterranean in the first century.[9] It is likely that the author of Acts had access to an actual travel account of Paul, although he may have embellished it at points with miraculous details. The report of Paul's stay in Rome, on the other hand, is puzzling and inconclusive. He is said to have been living under house arrest (Acts 28:30), after his initially cordial reception by the Jews there had turned into a hostile relationship (Acts 28:25–28). Beyond the predictions of his death uttered on the occasion of his farewell to the elders from Ephesus (Acts 20), the book ends with no account of the trial or hearing before the emperor and no direct report of his death.

Those who regard the Letters to Timothy and Titus as authentic assume that Paul was released and traveled to Spain as he had planned, that he later returned to the eastern Mediterranean, and that he was once again imprisoned in Rome and this time was executed. II Timothy, then, would embody his valedictory words:

> For I am already on the point of being sacrificed; the time of my departure has come. I have fought the good fight, I have finished the race, I have kept the faith. Henceforth there is laid up for me the crown of life, which the Lord, the righteous judge, will award me on that Day. . . .
>
> —II TIMOTHY 4:6–8

Careful study of the style and vocabulary of the Pastoral Letters shows, however, that they come from a considerably later time, perhaps as late as the middle of the second century.[10]

Extra-Biblical tradition supplies other accounts of the ministry of Paul, of which the apocryphal Acts of Paul is the most extensive and most romantic source. Although it could scarcely be considered unorthodox in its representation of Paul, it is highly fanciful in its expansion and supplementation of the narrative of Acts and the autobiographical notes included by Paul in his Letters. Best known of these imaginative additions to the Pauline story is the series of incidents that associate him with a woman named Thecla, who was converted by him in Iconium and who is reported to have become a faithful

---

[9]On navigational methods and hazards in the Mediterranean in this period, see H. J. Cadbury in Foakes-Jackson and Lake, *Beginnings*, IV (Commentary on Acts), 324–340; and V (Added Notes), 345–353.

[10]For a full discussion, see W. G. Kümmel, *Introduction to the New Testament* (New York and Nashville: Abingdon, 1966), pp. 258–272.

helper and faithful witness in the cities of Asia Minor. Two apocalypses of Paul are known: one which has long been known in various versions, and which purports to describe the experiences of Paul when he was caught up to the "third heaven" (II Cor. 12) and met Moses, Elijah, and other worthies of Israel's past; the second is a completely different apocalypse in the name of Paul, found among the Gnostic documents at Nag Hammadi in Egypt in 1945. All these documents are fanciful, even the Acts of Paul, which were highly regarded and widely read in the Church as early as the second century.[11] Often-quoted from the Acts of Paul is the sole physical description of him that has survived from antiquity, though we have no way of knowing whether it is accurate: "A man small in stature, bald and bow-legged, with eyebrows that meet and a somewhat prominent nose, yet full of grace."

In the late second century, Tertullian, a leading theologian of the Latin-speaking Church, reported that Paul was executed by the Roman authorities at a certain spot on the Via Ostiense. Two sites are identified as the place of his martyrdom: one is the Church of St. Paul at the Three Fountains, but the structure there is late and the location is unlikely to be authentic; the other is the Church of St. Paul Outside the Walls, which was built at an unprepossessing spot outside the city, as its name implies. This site was in all likelihood chosen because of the persistent memory preserved among Roman Christians that here was in fact the place where Paul died. The original church was built by the Emperor Constantine (completed by his son), but in the later fourth century streets were cleared away to make room for a more imposing memorial to Paul's martyrdom. Although this magnificent basilica was destroyed by fire in the early nineteenth century, it was rebuilt along nearly identical lines and with great splendor. Under the high altar may still be seen the inscription that dates back almost certainly to the time of Constantine:

PAULO APOSTOLO MARTYRI.

---

[11]Translations with excellent introductions to all these pseudo-Pauline writings are to be found in E. Hennecke and W. Schneemelcher (ed. R. McL. Wilson), *New Testament Apocrypha*, Vol. II (Philadelphia: Westminster, 1964).

Paul
among the Apostles

CHAPTER SEVEN

In most of the Letters of Paul, he identifies himself to his readers as "Paul, an apostle. . . . " (See Rom. 1:1; I Cor. 1:1; II Cor. 1:1; Gal. 1:1; Col. 1:1. The term, though not the concept, is lacking in the other Letters.) He felt no need to define the term, even though it was not in wide use among Greek-speaking people of his time, and there was not a current, fixed meaning for it. As is true of several important words that Paul uses, "apostle" had connotations in both the Gentile and the Jewish communities that Paul could draw upon, or that the Church before Paul had already drawn upon, which served well as a designation for the apostolic role as it developed very early in the churches.

Among the Cynic-Stoic philosophers of the period, the designation *apostolos* was used by the teachers to support their claim to being the bearers of divine truth. Since they lacked any definite conception of God, however, they thought of themselves as partners with divine reality in the spreading of wisdom about the true nature of things. In the Jewish community, on the other hand, the term equivalent to *apostolos* was *shaliach;* it was applied to persons commissioned by God (as in the case of the prophets, for example Isaiah: "I heard the voice of the Lord saying, 'Whom shall I send, and who will go for us'" [Is. 6:8] or to those assigned tasks by the Jewish community to be carried out in behalf of others. Examples mentioned in the rabbinic sources are conducting business, obtaining a divorce by proxy, or offering a sacrifice for the benefit of someone other than the *shaliach* himself.

Paul uses the term in a way which both resembles and differs from either the pagan or Jewish meanings. He obviously did not invent the term or give it private meaning, since he is at such pains to show that he belongs to an already existing circle of apostles (I Cor. 9:1; 15:3–9; II Cor. 11:5; Gal. 1:1, 15–17).

SET APART FROM THE WOMB TO BE AN APOSTLE

[GALATIANS 1:15]

Like Jeremiah, who came to believe that God had chosen him to be a prophet to the nations "before I formed you in the womb" (Jer. 1:5), Paul was convinced that he had been ordained by God for the special mission of carrying the Gospel of Jesus to the Gentile nations. He saw in himself no special merit for the task, although the historian looking back from a modern vantage point can see significant features of Paul's background and training that fitted him especially well for his apostolic role to the Gentiles. He was bilingual, and he seems to have known the scriptures in both the Semitic original and in the Greek translation, so that he had no difficulty in interpreting the texts to non-Jewish hearers. He was devoted to the traditions of Judaism, but reared as he was in a thriving, cosmopolitan Gentile city, he not only recognized the values of certain aspects of Hellenistic culture but also incorporated some features of its language and concepts into his own religious views. As a result, he was well-equipped to serve as the preeminent person through whom the essentially Jewish message of Christianity was transmitted comprehensibly and attractively to Greek-speaking Gentiles.

Paul, however, seems consciously to have attached no significance to his experience prior to his conversion. Indeed, he states directly: "Whatever gain I had, I counted as loss for the sake of Christ" (Phil. 3:7). The new "gain" which led him to count "everything as loss" was "the surpassing worth of knowing Christ Jesus" as Lord (Phil. 3:8). It was from his encounter with the risen Christ that Paul's life had its new beginning as an apostle.

Although Acts suggests that Paul's regular strategy was to begin preaching in the synagogues and to continue evangelizing among Jews until he was forced to leave, his own Letters give the impression that his energies were devoted to preaching the Gospel to Gentiles from the outset. The function of apostle was readily recognizable—Paul was never challenged in Jerusalem as

ANTIOCH-ON-THE-ORONTES *with Mt. Silpius in the background. Located near the Mediterranean Sea, it was an early seat of Paul's operations and one of the most important centers of Christianity in the first three centuries* A.D. (Matson Photo Service)

to whether he was an apostle so far as we can tell from Galatians 1 and 2—and he was treated by the Jerusalem apostles as one who differed from them only with respect to the subjects with whom he worked: Gentiles, as contrasted with their Jewish Christians. Perplexing as it is for us to understand what an apostle did, he and his detractors seem to have been in complete agreement on what apostleship constituted. Even when his enemies attacked him, it was on the ground that he was not fulfilling faithfully the apostolic role in the churches under his care rather than on the basis of a disagreement over what an apostle was. A few scholars have suggested that *apostle* was an office developed by pre-Christian Gnosticism, which Paul introduced into the Church.[1] But all the evidence indicates that Paul was a newcomer in an existing circle of Jewish-Christian apostles, as Galatians 1:17 clearly states.

Initially (Gal. 1:18–2:10), the Jerusalem apostles agreed to Paul's evangelism among Gentiles, and on that point they did not go back on their compact with him. The conflict arose on the issues about requiring Gentiles to be circumcised and the propriety of Jewish Christians eating with uncircumcised

---

[1]See note 1, p. 152, on the attempt to credit Gnostiss with originating the term, apostle.

Gentiles. Apparently the Jerusalem-centered apostles thought it quite proper for Paul to convert Gentiles, so long as they then went on to observe some of the basic principles of Jewish identity: circumcision and the dietary laws. On his fidelity to his part of the agreement—apostleship among the Gentiles—he could not be and indeed was not faulted.

The essence of the apostolic role for Paul, as is evident from the introductory words of his Letter to the Romans—one of the last of his preserved writings, if not the very last—was to preach the Gospel. In words that recall his sense of having been divinely chosen for his work, he wrote:

> Paul, a servant of Jesus Christ, called to be an apostle, set apart for the gospel of God, which he promised beforehand through his prophets in the holy scriptures, the gospel concerning his Son, who was descended from David according to the flesh and designated Son of God according to the Spirit of Holiness by his resurrection from the dead, Jesus Christ our Lord, through whom we have received grace and apostleship to bring about obedience to the faith for the sake of his name among all nations. . . .
>
> —ROMANS 1:1–5

The major themes of Paul's apostleship are all in this preamble to his Letter: the demonstration from scripture that what happened to and through Jesus fulfilled the divine plan as laid down in the law and the prophets; the centrality of the Resurrection to prove that Jesus is the Son of God, as Paul had himself experienced it in his encounter with the risen Lord; the divine gift and commissioning of Paul to call Gentiles to believe the "good news" about Jesus.

I AM EAGER TO PREACH THE GOSPEL

[ROMANS 1:15]

Fortunately, the Letters of Paul supply the modern reader with enough evidence to reconstruct how he went about preaching the gospel in Gentile cities and districts. Often this information may be derived from passages in which he is recalling what he did or said when he first came among them. By this method it is possible to determine what he preached, why he went to some places rather than others, what his evangelistic strategy was, and how he was able to maintain himself during the pioneer stages of his work.

What he preached is summarized for us in I Corinthians 15:1–8: Jesus' death, burial, and resurrection were in accordance with the scriptures. In the summary he states merely that "Christ died for our sins" without explaining how his death provides benefits for "us." Yet clearly this was the central theme of his preaching, since he reminds the Corinthians that when he first came among them he knew "nothing but Christ Jesus and him crucified" (I Cor. 2:2). This emphasis in early Christian preaching was not invented by Paul, but, according to Paul (I Cor. 15:3), had been passed on to him so that he in turn passed it on to his hearers in Corinth and elsewhere. This is the force of the Greek words that are rather blandly translated as "delivered" and "received," but which connote, to use coined verbs, that Paul *transdelivered* what he had *transreceived*. Before the conversion of Paul, therefore, the earliest Christians were convinced not only that the death of Jesus had itself been in fulfillment of the Jewish scriptures, but also that his death was in some way the potential instrument of man's redemption.

How the Cross brought about redemption is nowhere in Paul developed fully into a theological theory, but it is repeatedly and simply stated, often in connection with a vivid image or model. We shall sketch here the main outlines of these models to indicate the range and freely imaginative nature of Paul's thought on the subject of the death of Jesus. The first of these models is that of the obedient man from heaven. It is to be found in a hymn incorporated by Paul into his Letter to the Philippians (2:6–11), which he may have found circulating in the Church or which he may have penned prior to writing this Letter.[2] The point of the hymn is that Jesus did not seek equality with

[2] A third possibility, that Paul has adapted a pagan hymn of the Gnostic Redeemer, is claimed by Rudolf Bultmann, in *Theology of the New Testament*, Vol. II (New York: Scribner's, 1955), pp. 11–14.

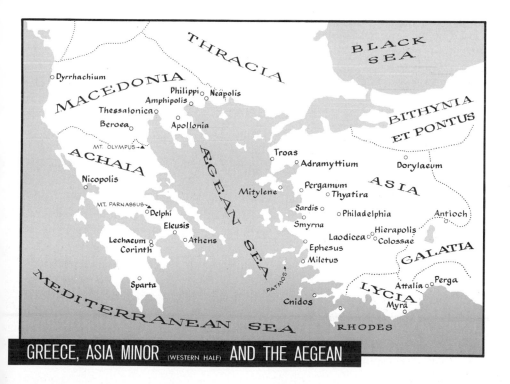

GREECE, ASIA MINOR (WESTERN HALF) AND THE AEGEAN

PHILIPPI
*was the eastern terminus of the Via Egnatia, which led
across from the Adriatic to the northern Aegean Sea.
Paving stones of the ancient road are visible at this excavated point where the Via passed through the agora
of Philippi.* (Darryl Jones)

God, but became totally obedient to God to the extent of accepting fully the
limitations of humanity even to the acceptance of his death. In the Philippian
Letter, Paul uses the hymn to appeal for humble obedience on the part of his
readers; but the concluding lines of the hymn, by their prediction of Christ's
exaltation over all the Creation, suggest that the chief benefit of Jesus' death
is that his act of obedience leads on to the consummation of the divine purpose
in the Creation. In other words, the climax of the hymn is in its portrayal of
the Resurrection of Jesus as his exaltation, the effect of which will become
fully evident when all Creation is subjected to him. This theme will concern
us in Chapter Eight, where we consider Paul's message of wisdom. But the
death itself is here represented in an unexplained way as in accord with God's
will, which therefore had to be accepted by Jesus in humble obedience.
Through that acceptance have come and are yet to come redemptive benefits
for the whole Creation.

A second model for understanding the death of Jesus as Paul viewed it is
that of liberation from slavery. This Paul sets forth in Galatians 3–5. He
pictures all mankind as enslaved to the rules and regulations of legalistic
religious systems. This is the case among the Jews especially, Paul writes (Gal.
3:10–13), who insisted on demonstrating their acceptability to God by obeying
the Laws set forth in the Mosaic Code. They should have known that the only
way to find acceptance with God was by faith, for this had been true of

Abraham, the progenitor of the nation of Israel (Gal. 3:6–9), who had received a son and heir, Isaac, as a gift from God when his own capacities and those of his barren wife, Sarah, were inadequate to supply the need. Because Abraham had trusted confidently that God would fulfill his promise, even against all human possibilities, God accepted him—or he was "justified," to use the familiar translation. The Law of Moses was given by God (Gal. 3:15–18) more than four centuries after the time of Abraham, but it did not abrogate the prior principle that man's relationship with God is established by faith, not by keeping the commandments of a moral code. The Law of Moses had a useful function, however, because it served to keep man under moral restraint during the period of his immaturity, just as in the Hellenistic world, a tutor was assigned the task of guiding and rearing a child until he reached the age when he could assume full adult responsibilities as son and heir. Without clarifying the logic of his argument, Paul declares that the curse that falls on all who try in vain to approach God by strictly obeying the Law actually fell on Jesus, who was ironically the only one who fully obeyed it. As a result of his "being hanged on a tree," liberation is available for all who will come to God by the route that Abraham exemplified and that Jesus has once again opened: the way of faith.

Liberation from a religion of rules is equally as important for Gentiles as for Jews, Paul declares (Gal. 4:1–11), since the demonic powers of the universe work through the ritual requirements of pagan religions as well as those of Judaism to create the false notion that keeping such rules makes men more acceptable before God, or conversely that if they fail to keep the rules, God will abandon them. Paul declares that Christ sets men free from this deluded atmosphere of mingled pride and guilt which characterizes "formal" religion.

A third image of redemption employed by Paul is the overcoming of alienation. The motif is enunciated in II Cor. 5:16ff., where Paul depicts the body of Christians as a "new creation" which God has "reconciled to himself" through Christ. The notion of Christians as a "body" will be explored more fully in the next chapter, but here it is sufficient to point out the significance for Paul of the restoration of the Creation to its proper, divinely designed relationship to God as the central reality in his doctrine of reconciliation. What that implies is portrayed in much fuller detail in the first three chapters of the Letter to the Romans. There Paul declares that all mankind can infer from the splendor and order of the created world the deity and power of God, and that accordingly they should acknowledge him as their creator and sovereign (1:19–20). But instead of thus honoring God, they turn to worshipping things they themselves have made and which are therefore subject to man's control (1:21–23). It is a variant of the Creation story of Genesis, in which the tempter convinces Adam and Eve that if they partake of the forbidden fruit, they will be like God (Gen. 3:5)—that is, they will be in control of their own life and destiny. As a consequence of man's refusal to accept his proper role in relation to God as obedient creature who rules over the creation in God's stead (Gen.

1:28)³— that is, because man distorted the creature–Creator relationship—every other relationship of man is similarly distorted. The long catalog of human vices in Romans 1:24–32 is the evidence of man's alienation from his Creator, not the cause of it. In more elaborate form than in the Letter to the Galatians, Paul in Romans 2 and 3 shows that man cannot attain the "glory of God" (Rom. 3:23)—that is, the glorious estate as divine agent ruling obediently over the Creation—that God intended for him (Ps. 8, especially 8:5) by conforming to any set of moral commandments, whether they be the best that pagan ethics has to offer (Rom. 2:14) or the Law of Moses (Rom. 3:1–4). Man's problem is not that he must close the gap between his moral performance and the moral demands of God, but that his arrogance and rejection of God as his sovereign has disoriented him toward the whole of life and, most seriously, has estranged him from God. The death of Jesus is for Paul the instrument by which God bridges the gulf between Him and alienated man, removing the barrier of man's guilt, and demonstrating concretely that it is God's nature to take the initiative in setting man in right relationship to Himself (Rom. 3:21–26). This motif and its implications are discussed at greater length in Chapter Nine.

In speaking of Gentiles enslaved to the worship of idols and to religious regulations associated with that worship, Paul in Galatians 4:8–9 describes such persons as "in bondage to beings that by nature are no gods" and as turning back again "to the weak and beggarly elemental spirits, whose slaves you want once more to be." The implication is that Christ is the instrument through whom man is freed not only from his existential guilt, but from his enslavement to the demonic powers of the universe. The same motif is present in the expression of hope voiced in I Corinthians 15:24ff. that at the End of the Age Christ will deliver the Kingdom to God the Father after destroying every rule and every authority and power: "For he must continue to exercise his rule until he has brought all his enemies under his feet." Sharing with the culture of his time the belief that the cosmos is dominated by hostile, threatening spirits and demons, Paul is convinced that the establishment of the reign of God must be preceded by the overcoming of the rule of Satan and his hosts. If the powers of this age had known that the Cross of Christ was to be the instrument of their defeat, "they would not have crucified the Lord of glory" (I Cor. 2:8). Indeed, Paul depicts in Romans 8:19ff. the cosmos itself as groaning in travail until the liberation of the "sons of God" is complete, which event will be accompanied by the liberation of the cosmos itself.

The most elaborate statement of Christ's role as cosmic redeemer is in the Letter to the Colossians, where he is presented as the instrument of the creation of the world (Col. 1:15–17), of the reconciliation of all earthly and heavenly beings to God (1:19–20), and of the defeat through the Cross of the principalities and powers (2:15). Some scholars consider the cosmic dimensions

---

³Obviously Paul made no distinction between the highly structured priestly account of the Creation in Genesis 1 and the more existential account in Genesis 2–3, as modern literary critics do.

of the role of Christ in Colossians to be too elaborate to have been written by Paul. They assume, rather, that it was produced by a follower of Paul who was under Gnostic influence.[4] We shall consider this possibility in more detail in the next chapter, but it is important to note here that many of the elements of the cosmic redemption described in Colossians are already present in the undeniably Pauline corpus itself. It was surely an important dimension of the effectiveness of Paul's preaching of the gospel that he could present Christ as one through whom the whole range of human needs and anxieties could be met, from the guilt of unfulfilled religious obligations, through the sense of estrangement from the Creator, to the threat of domination by hostile spiritual powers.

"THE DAILY PRESSURE OF MY ANXIETY FOR ALL THE CHURCHES"

[II CORINTHIANS 11:28]

Once converts had been made in any given place, it fell to Paul as apostle to the Gentiles to organize the community for the twin purposes of self-preservation and self-propagation. The leadership in each local church seems to have been of two types: (1) those charged with overall administrative and regulatory responsibility for the congregation, designated as "bishops" (Phil. 1:1) or overseers. This term may be a translation into Greek of a term for administrators used in Jewish communities, as attested from Qumran.[5] (2) The second type of leader was the *diakonos*, transliterated as "deacon," meaning one who serves. It may be that the division between these two classes of leadership was not so sharp as is implied by Acts 6, where one type preaches and the others (deacons) "serve tables," but clearly the deacons had a more menial and practical role in the churches than that of the overseers.

We have already noted that the first to be converted in the central district of Greece known as Achaia—specifically at Corinth (I Cor. 16:15)—was the household of Stephanas. Paul reminds the congregation at Corinth of this family's priority among the members of the church there, and pleads for the church to be subject to them since they have devoted themselves to its service (*diakonia*). In spite of their service role, therefore, the deacons were in positions of leadership, as Paul felt obligated to remind the members.

In addition to the official ranks, the churches required a series of functions to be fulfilled by various persons. All these capabilities were regarded as gifts of the Spirit, as I Cor. 12:4–11 shows. There was an inevitable tendency for those who possessed one gift to think it more important than another's gift, with the result that pride and rivalry even over spiritual gifts divided the

---

[4]E. Käsemann, *Essays on New Testament Themes* (Naperville, Ill.: Allenson, 1964), pp. 149–168.

[5]In the Qumran Rule of the Community, the administrator is known as *mebaqqer*, which is the equivalent of the Greek *episkopos*, "overseer," often rendered as "bishop."

Church. Paul's apostolic authority had to be exercised to put these people in their places—that is, to show them that the welfare of the whole body depended on the proper function of each member. After enumerating the gifts and declaring them all to be important, Paul nevertheless lists them in order of significance (I Cor. 12:28):

> And God has appointed in the church first apostles, second prophets, third teachers, then workers of miracles, then healers, helpers, administrators, speakers in various kinds of tongues.

As we have observed, the apostolic group was relatively small, although its numerical size can no longer be determined; it consisted of those who were believed to have been specially commissioned by the risen Lord (I Cor. 9:1; 15:7, 8). The prophets were those through whom the Spirit guided the Church in the new situations that it constantly faced. Prophecy was the living voice of God in the midst of his people. The prophets might speak through the interpretation of scripture, or they might utter oracles concerning the future, as Acts 21:10ff. suggests. The specific content of the prophecies is implied in I Cor. 13:2, where Paul says prophetic powers enable one to "understand all mysteries and all knowledge." It is likely that Paul is exercising his own prophetic function when he hands down a ruling about marital relationships within the Christian community (I Cor. 7:8–16). In the case of a married person who is considering divorcing his or her spouse, Paul can quote a saying of Jesus ("the Lord"). But where there is no dominical saying, he gives his own word, which carries equal authority, since Paul is convinced that his decisions are given to him by the Spirit of God (I Cor. 7:40).

The whole of I Corinthians is taken up with Paul's responses to questions that have been addressed to him in a letter or letters from the Corinthians (I Cor. 7:1) or that he has heard by indirect report (I Cor. 5:1). But to both kinds of intelligence he reacts as an apostle, deciding hard questions for the corporate health of the Christian community. In most instances the problems that have arisen originated within the community itself but have grave import for the attitude of the outsiders toward the gospel. These include the partisan conflicts within the Church resulting from personal loyalties to one or another of the apostles (I Cor. 1:10ff.), the appeal to civil courts to settle disputes within the Church (I Cor. 6:1ff.), the sensual and emotional excesses that characterize the Church's worship, especially in connection with the eucharistic meal (I Cor. 11:20ff.), and speaking in tongues (I Cor. 14:23), which may lead outsiders to think that the Christians are mad.

Most serious of all, however, was the Corinthian church's condoning of incest among its members (I Cor. 5:1–2), which had brought opprobrium on the name of Christ from pagan outsiders. In this situation, Paul acted *in absentia* as an apostle, pronouncing judgment on the culprit, ordering his expulsion from the community, and his consequent exposure to the attacks of Satan from which his membership in the Church had up to this point afforded protection (I Cor. 5:3–5). The solemn convocation that was to effect this judgment would be acting in concert with Paul's spirit and on the authority given him "in the name of the Lord Jesus." Here we see apostolic authority in one of its most dramatic and mysterious manifestations.

An obvious issue on which Paul's apostolic judgment was sought by the Corinthians was sex. He was asked if Christians should have sexual relations at all, if they should separate from unconverted spouses, if children born to a couple only one of whom was converted were in some way unholy (I Cor. 7:1–16). On most of these issues there was no "word from the Lord," but he felt justified in ruling on the issues by the power of the Spirit. In keeping with the basically positive attitude toward sex and family that characterizes the Jewish scriptures as well as later Jewish tradition, Paul does not consider sexual relations to be in any way sinful (7:28, 36). His sole reservation about Christians marrying is that they will be distracted from their churchly responsibilities by family obligations (7:32). Although the phrase is somewhat ambiguous, the mention in I Corinthians 7:25 of "the impending distress" as a reason for abstaining from marriage is probably a reference to the coming End of the Age, which Paul expected to occur speedily and which was to be preceded by a time of unprecedented difficulty for the elect community. This was a part of the dogma of apocalyptic writers that Paul and the early Christians shared, and was for him sufficient reason to remain single during the brief interim before the End of the Age would arrive. Far from laying down ascetic rules for an ongoing institution, Paul was offering practical suggestions for the immediate future on how the Lord's work could most expeditiously be accomplished. For those who could endure celibacy, as he himself could (7:7), that was the most efficient way to carry out evangelism. But for those who were preoccupied by sexual drives, it was better to marry (7:9). Paul would prefer a married man who, however great were the demands of his wife and family on his time, could at least turn his undivided attention to the Church, rather than a single man constantly distracted by sexual urges.

From the frequent allusions to women in his Letters, it is apparent that women were important workers in the Pauline churches (I Cor. 16:19; Rom. 16:1–16).[6] Acts so depicts them, including the story of Paul's first convert in Europe: Lydia, the dye seller (Acts 16:14). And of course Priscilla and Aquila were Paul's main coworkers in Corinth, according to Acts 18. Nevertheless

---

[6]Probably Romans 16 was originally part of an otherwise lost Letter, possibly to the Ephesians. It is unlikely that Paul would have known so many persons in Rome by name as he greets in Romans 16, though it is not impossible. And the oldest manuscripts of the Letter to the Romans indicate that the Letter originally ended with the doxology of 15:33.

Paul assigned a subordinate role to women in the Church (I Cor. 11:2–15) and kept the principle, apparently in effect in synagogue worship, that women were not to be heard either by way of question or comment (I Cor. 14:33–35). While it is not fair or accurate to say that Paul was a misogynist, he did not go beyond the limits that his age placed on women, even though in his theory of the unity of the Church he declares:

> [In Christ] there is neither Jew nor Greek, there is neither slave nor free, *there is neither male nor female,* for you are all one in Christ Jesus.
>
> —GALATIANS 3:28

Judging by the evidence we have of his practice in the churches, Paul seems to have given women a more significant role than his principle of silence suggests, and yet the very fact that he laid down that principle shows that he did not develop the implications of his own concept of eliminating all barriers—racial, economic, and sexual—in the body of Christ.

In II Corinthians, especially, we can sense the strong emotional ties that existed between Paul and the churches he had founded. "Open your hearts to us; we have wronged no one," Paul pleads in II Corinthians 7:2. He identifies fully with Corinthian Christians when he writes, "If we are afflicted, it is for your comfort and salvation; and if we are comforted, it is for your comfort, which you experience when you patiently endure the same sufferings that we suffer" (II Cor. 1:6). We noted earlier how upset he was when he failed to find Titus at an appointed meeting place in Troas (II Cor. 2:12–13) and then how relieved he was to meet him at Philippi in Macedonia, especially since he brought a favorable report about the Corinthians and their regard for Paul (II Cor. 7:5–7). His ability to accept setbacks, rebuffs, or even actual physical suffering is reflected in the string of paradoxes in II Corinthians 6:8–10:

> . . . In honor and dishonor, in ill repute and good repute. We are treated as impostors and yet are true; as unknown, and yet well known; as dying, and behold we live; as punished, and yet not killed; as sorrowful, yet always rejoicing; as poor, yet making many rich; as having nothing, and yet possessing everything.

Perhaps the boldest image Paul uses to portray his attitude toward those under his charge is in Galatians 4:19, where—by means of a mixed metaphor—he describes himself as in birth pangs over their spiritual rebirth, and then refers to Christ being formed in them, as though they were the womb in which the gestation of the new people of God was taking place:

> My little children, with whom I am again in travail until Christ be formed in you!

NOT IN THE LEAST INFERIOR TO THESE SUPERLATIVE APOSTLES!

[II CORINTHIANS 11:5]

Apart from the central issue that divided Paul and the other apostles—whether Gentiles were to be required to observe the Law of Moses—the chief sources of conflict among the apostles were personalities and money. The Corinthian church was split into factions by the affection that various segments of the community there had developed toward one or another of the leaders: some preferred Paul, others Cephas (Peter), and still others Apollos. According to Acts 18:24ff., Apollos was an Alexandrine Jew, eloquent and versed in the scriptures. It is tempting to assume that Paul's striking out against human wisdom in I Corinthians 1 and 2 is a veiled attack against the learned Apollos, but we have no way of checking the accuracy of the Acts account; and in I Corinthians 3, Paul's point is that the contributions that he and Apollos have made to the upbuilding of the Corinthian church are complementary and essential to their sound spiritual growth.

On the issue of money, Paul was in trouble all around. In some quarters he was under attack because he did not earn his own support, but was dependent on the churches to supply his material needs. The other apostles were accompanied by their wives and received support (I Cor. 9:5), and no one seemed to raise any objections. Yet when Paul and Barnabas, who were unmarried, depended on contributions for "food and drink" (9:4), their enemies accused them of sponging from others. By means of an allegorical interpretation of a humane law (Deut. 25:4), Paul grounds in scripture his right to be supported by the churches:

> . . . The Lord commanded that those who proclaim the gospel should get their living by the gospel.
>
> —I CORINTHIANS 9:14

But after having made the case for his right to claim support, Paul goes on to show that in fact he did not take advantage of his right, but endured deprivation in order that no one could charge him with making his living by preaching the death of Christ. It is only in II Corinthians 11 that we learn how to explain this seeming contradiction. There Paul states that he did not want to give anyone at Corinth the opportunity to accuse him of exploiting his apostolic role for personal gain, so he continued to accept support from churches elsewhere, especially from those in Macedonia (II Cor. 11:8–11).

The depth of gratitude that Paul felt for the Macedonian churches, and particularly the church at Philippi, is expressed movingly in Philippians 1:3–11; 4:10–20, where he speaks of their gift as "a fragrant offering, a sacrifice acceptable and pleasing to God." Or again he writes, ". . . It was kind of you

THE ACROPOLIS AT ATHENS *with the hill of Areopagus in the foreground. According to Acts 17, Paul defended himself and his message before the court that traditionally met on the Areopagus.* (Darryl Jones)

to share my trouble" (4:14). For Paul the contributions from the churches were not a necessary burden that they had to bear, but a concrete way of sharing in the apostolic work that Paul believed he had been commissioned to perform.

The strongest evidence for Paul's conviction about the close connection between devotion and contributing lies in his careful plans and intensive efforts to gather the funds for the church in Jerusalem. It was a major administrative and diplomatic undertaking to convince the Gentile churches that they should collect the money and see that the appointed representatives were ready to leave together with the others on the way to Jerusalem (I Cor. 16:1–4). Each church was to accredit its delegates "by letter" so that there would be no question that they were in fact the duly chosen persons assigned to accompany the gift to its destination.

Although Paul declares that "it is superfluous" for him to remind the Corinthians about having the money ready at the appointed time (II Cor. 9:1ff.), he not only does remind them but indicates how embarrassed he will be if they are not prepared with their share of the offering when he arrives. Indeed he is so lacking in confidence in them that he has sent some of his associates on ahead to guarantee that everything will be ready when he arrives. He assures them that not only will God reward them for their generosity, but also their reputation will be enhanced among the other Gentile churches (II Cor. 9:11–15).

So important for Paul was his fulfillment of the obligation worked out with the Jerusalem leadership to "remember the poor" (Gal. 2:10), that he delayed his long-awaited journey to Rome and Spain in order to accompany the delegates and the gift back to Jerusalem before setting out for the western shores of the Mediterranean (Rom. 15:22–29). It was the discharge of this commitment—partly spiritual and partly administrative—that led him into the hands of the Roman authorities in Jerusalem and resulted in his death. His prayer for deliverance "from unbelievers in Judea" was not to be answered as he expected, since from there he was led off to Rome for trial and execution.

In addition to the conflicts that arose over money, the modern cliché "controversial person" seems to fit Paul well. There was not only the problem of personal preferences for one or another of the apostles at Corinth, but also Paul seems to have drawn to himself bitter criticism on the ground that he was ineffective in personal dealings. He describes himself—apparently quoting some of his detractors—as one whose "bodily presence is weak" and whose "speech is of no consequence" (II Cor. 10:10). In the same context he pictures himself as "meek when face to face" (10:1), and then goes on to remind his readers that he carries on his battles by means other than those employed in ordinary human controversies,[7] the sort of thing that might be called today "throwing his weight around." Paul as a person lacked "weight"; what was weighty about him was the power of his letters (10:10).

His opponents accused him of vacillating, so that the early part of II Corinthians is devoted to answering that charge (1:12–2:4). He takes care to explain why he was unable to come as he had originally planned, and then goes on to say that it was better for the Corinthians that he did not come at the agreed-upon time, since it would have been a "painful visit" (2:1) on account of the unresolved conflicts between them. Paul's "Yes" is "Yes" and

---

[7]The Greek word *sarx*, literally "flesh," is translated in the RSV as "worldly," but its basic meaning is simply "human." Paul's strength lies in spiritual power, not in such human resources as a forceful personality, which for him would be "flesh."

THE STOA OF ATTALOS *has been reconstructed at the foot of the Acropolis. The original was built as a public portico by Attalos II, King of Pergamum, and the marble for the reconstruction was taken from the same quarry that he used in the middle of the second century* B.C. *(American School of Classical Studies, Athens)*

his "No" is "No." He has been commissioned by God and does not deviate from that commitment.

In writing to the Galatians Paul alludes to the circumstances connected with his first visit to them (Gal. 4:13–15). He states that his bodily condition was the occasion for his first preaching in their area, and that his ailment was such as might have led them to scorn or despise him. But instead of disdaining him, they were filled with compassion and would have plucked out their eyes and given them to him. Does this mean that he was afflicted with a disgusting disease of the eyes? Some literal-minded scholars have suggested that he was subject to epilepsy and that his visions were the consequence of epileptic seizures. Whatever his problem was, it was sufficiently distinctive and perhaps offensive that Paul could never forget the generosity of the Galatians in accepting him and his gospel in spite of his wretched condition. It is possible that the affliction was temporary; or perhaps the repeated references in his letters to his weak appearance may allude to some permanent handicap that made him strikingly unattractive. Whatever his problem was, it could not have given him a weak physique; no one who was physically puny could have endured the harassments and punishments that Paul describes in II Corinthians 11:23–28. Paul speaks in bitter irony when he asks, "Who is weak and I am not weak?" (II Cor. 11:29). It is perhaps this "weakness" to which Paul refers in II Corinthians 12:7 when he writes,

> To keep me from being too elated by an abundance of revelations, a thorn in the flesh was given to me, a messenger of Satan to harass me, to keep me from being too elated. Three times I besought the Lord about this, that it should leave me; but he said to me, "My grace is sufficient for you, for my power is made perfect in weakness." I will all the more gladly boast of my weaknesses, that the power of Christ may rest upon me.
>
> —II CORINTHIANS 12:7–9

HIS LETTERS ARE WEIGHTY AND STRONG
[II CORINTHIANS 10:10]

Criticism of Paul often played on the contrast between his weak appearance and the power of his letters. It was the letters which served as the main channel for communicating his apostolic authority to the churches that he had founded. If Colossians is an authentic Letter of Paul, then it was he who introduced and encouraged the practice of circulating the letters among churches other than those to whom they had originally been addressed:

> And when this letter has been read among you, have it read also in the church of Laodicea and see that you read also the letter from Laodicea.
>
> —COLOSSIANS 4:16

The Letters of Paul are precisely that: letters rather than epistles. In the Graeco-Roman world there was a widespread custom of addressing communications to distant persons or even nearby persons to inform them or disabuse them of some notions or convictions. These discourses in the external form of a letter are what we properly call *epistles*. In contrast to an epistle is a genuine letter, written by a known person to a known recipient or group of recipients, in which the writer deals with specific matters of common interest. The letter is an occasional writing—that is, there is a specific occasion or set of circumstances which the sender and the receiver have as a part of their common experience and concerning which communication must take place. These generalizations apply to all the authentic Letters of Paul, even the Letter to the Romans. This was addressed to a group who had not yet met him, but who surely had heard of him and among whom he may already have been a controversial figure. He had common interests with them in spite of whatever differences there may have been between their traditions and his.

The form of a letter was quite firmly fixed in Paul's day. The pattern is as follows:

> Identification of the sender, and his associates, if any.
> Identification of the receiver, with formal greetings.
> Expression of pious sentiments and wishes for good health and prosperity.
> The main subject matter of the letter.
> Pious exhortations.
> Concluding personal comments.
> Concluding salutation.

Among the thousands of commonplace documents written on papyrus that were found in Egypt in the decades around the turn of the twentieth century were hundreds of letters from ordinary people: a homesick son writing to his parents; a runaway son seeking reconciliation with his estranged father; reports of miraculous healing by one of the gods; parents' counsel to their children. From these it is possible to observe how Paul used the existing conventions of letter writing, but modified them in ways that made the form better serve his ends in exercising apostolic authority at a distance.

Some of the changes reflect his own bilingual and bicultural background. For example, instead of the ordinary Greek greeting *chairete* ("May you be well") or the traditional Hebrew *shalom* ("peace"), Paul writes, "Grace (*charis*) to you and peace." Similarly, his expressions of thanks and concern for his readers' welfare are not uttered merely in the name of "God," but also include a reference to "the Lord Jesus Christ," through whom the grace of God has been made available for faith. In the hortatory sections at the close of his letters—for example, Romans 12–14; Galatians 5–6; Philippians 4—Paul's moral appeals are based in part on allusions to the Jewish scriptures, but also directly incorporate pagan virtues, especially the Stoic ideal of self-control (Gal. 5:24; I Cor. 9:25).

It is in the body of the Letters, however, that both the distinctive style and the unusual power of his written communication come through to the reader even today. His method of asking questions that his opponents would likely pose, as in Romans 6 or I Corinthians 9, shows the influence of the rhetorical style known as the *diatribe* and widely used among the Cynic and Stoic philosopher-teachers. Some of his metaphors are commonplace, such as the athlete striving for the prize (I Cor. 9:25), but this is followed immediately by a more original analogy with a boxer beating his own body into submission (9:26). His attempts at allegory are distinctly unsuccessful, as demonstrated by the awkwardness of the Law/Grace = Sarah/Hagar = Jerusalem/Sinai passage in Galatians 4:21ff. Yet even beyond the familiar passages—I Corinthians 13, with its poem about love, comes to mind instantly—the enduring qualities of Paul's Letters are attested by the fact of their survival, by the early practice of distributing them among churches other than the intended recipient, and by the widespread imitation of them, some written in his name and some in the name of one of the other apostles. It is due to Paul more than to any other that as the Christian scriptures began to develop and accumulate, the Letter genre was firmly placed alongside the gospel.

SO ALSO OUR BELOVED BROTHER PAUL WROTE TO YOU

[II PETER 3:15]

It is surely a tribute to Paul and to the power of his letters that Christian writers after his death began to produce writings in his name.[8] In keeping with the literary traditions of the ancient world, their aim was not to deceive the reader into thinking that yet another authentic work of Paul had been found, but rather to honor and in part to borrow from the veneration in which he was held by the Gentile churches. Even though the authority of Peter was central to the ecclesiastical leadership in Rome, the main body of the Christian scriptures was linked with Paul by reason of the apostolic authority of his name.

The *authority* of Paul the apostle is evident not merely in the fact that his name is invoked, but even more in the issues under discussion that Paul's weighty opinions are intended to resolve. These include the problem of submission to the authority of leaders in the Church, and the mounting battle over what is to be considered the true faith as distinguished from error. These questions are treated at length in Chapter Ten. But it is significant that when

---

[8]The writings attributed to Paul, but written pseudonymously, are called Deutero-Pauline, and include I and II Timothy, Titus, and Ephesians; some scholars would list Colossians as well.

later generations wanted to present a decisive word in the midst of a conflict, they appealed to the name of Paul. Later Christian writers may have had difficulty comprehending Paul's Letters, as the author of II Peter testifies (3:16): "There are some things in them hard to understand. . . ." But there was no doubt about the weight of his judgments or of his authority within the churches and among the apostles.

Paul's Understanding of Wisdom

CHAPTER EIGHT

Up to this point, our study of Paul has been largely thematic, moving back and forth throughout the Pauline corpus in order to reconstruct his life (Chapter Six) and his role as an apostle (Chapter Seven). In this chapter and the next, however, we shall approach Paul by analyzing two of his major Letters: here we examine I Corinthians, treating it as a statement concerning true wisdom; in the next chapter we analyze the Letter to the Romans as a comprehensive statement of the nature, resources, and responsibilities of the Church as the people of God.

Although Paul's ethics show the influence of Stoicism, as we have noted (p. 186), his Letters indicate no other links with Greek or Roman philosophical modes of thinking. None of the traditional questions about physical or metaphysical reality appears in his writings. Beginning in the second century, the Christian apologists, notably Justin Martyr, sought to develop a synthesis of Christian revelation and the Greek philosophical tradition, as Philo of Alexandria did with his allegorical interpretation of scripture in the first century. But when Paul ventures into allegorical interpretation, as he does in I Corinthians 10, it is to issue a moral warning to the elect community, which will be punished for complaining against God even though it has been baptized (passing through the Red Sea and under the cloud of the divine presence are presented as a symbolic baptism of the people of Israel [Ex. 14:22; 16:10]). There is in his work no hint of metaphysical speculation, which indicates that he had no interest in engaging the attention of philosophers of the period or of developing a critical or comparative approach to philosophical questions from the side of Christian truth.

Yet Paul is clearly disturbed by the charge made by his detractors that his Christian preaching and teaching were lacking in wisdom. His annoyance was of two kinds: first, he did not intend to compete with the purveyors of wisdom who were highly esteemed by many in his day; second, his gospel did contain a kind of wisdom, though not of the rational or merely intuitive variety taught by philosophers.

What was the "wisdom" that Paul's detractors or competitors were propagating? As we observed in Chapter One, some scholars have suggested that a primitive kind of Gnosticism was widespread in the Hellenistic-Roman world and threatened to distort the Christian gospel; it was this perversion of the truth that Paul was combatting in I Corinthians. If we adopt a very broad definition of Gnosticism, then perhaps this thesis is correct. But apart from the implication that the source of man's conflict in the world is unseen spiritual beings and that the knowledge as to how they are to be overcome is reserved for an inner group of spiritual persons, none of the features of later Gnostic mythology is mentioned in Paul's polemics against his opponents. And few if any of the religious elements that have been said[1] to be the recurrent images used by Gnostics have any significant role in I Corinthians; certainly the Gnostics had no monopoly on concerns about light-darkness or death-life, nor were they the only group to speak of a "world beyond."[2] Perhaps the most we can say is that Paul was under attack in Corinth by representatives of a religious movement that claimed that the secret knowledge it possessed provided the sole means of man's salvation and that Paul's message lacked the requisite knowledge. Certain aspects of the teachings of his opposition were taken up by the movement we know in the second century and later as Gnosticism. It was this esoteric, religious type of wisdom that Paul contrasted with the gospel rather than philosophical wisdom in the traditional Greek sense.

FOOLISH WISDOM

Paul leads in the main theme of wisdom following his denunciation of the cult of personality that had divided the church at Corinth (1:10–17). Appar-

[1]For example by Hans Jonas in characterizing the religious mood of the first century A.D., in *The Gnostic Religion* (Boston: Beacon Press, 1958), pp. 48ff.
[2]Jonas, *Gnostic Religion*, pp. 51, 57–58.

THE TEMPLE OF APOLLO
*at Corinth, with the Gulf of
Corinth beyond.* (American
School of Classical Studies,
Athens)

ently some of the Corinthians had been priding themselves that they had been baptized by their favorite apostle or leader. Paul rejoices that he is not and never was in the competition for the most baptismal candidates, and neither was he an entry in an apostolic oratorical contest:

> For Christ did not send me to baptize but to preach the gospel, and not with eloquent wisdom, lest the cross of Christ be emptied of its power. For the message of the cross is foolishness to those who are perishing, but to us who are being saved it is the power of God.
> —I CORINTHIANS 1:17–18

It is possible that the negative remark about eloquence is an oblique thrust at Apollos, who is mentioned among the competitors in 1:12, and whose fame in rhetorical skill is described in Acts 18:24. As we have seen, Paul did use the rhetorical forms of his time, but only to make his point more effectively and not to entice hearers who might otherwise have been put off by the lack of intellectual stimulus in his message.

Paul thought he understood what people wanted. His Jewish audience was interested in "signs," overt demonstrations of divine approval for Paul's work in the form of miraculous manifestations. There were miracle workers among those specially endowed by the Spirit (I Cor. 12:28), but Paul wanted the healings and other "signs" to be the evidence of the Spirit's work within the Church rather than an advertising inducement to lure people into the Church.

The other kind of appeal, which Paul spends most of I Corinthians setting in proper perspective, was calculated to interest the Greeks: wisdom (I Cor. 1:22). To be candid about it, there were not many—perhaps Paul really meant not *any*, but was too polite to say so—Corinthians who were sufficiently learned to have understood the gospel if it were presented in philosophical terms. But in any case, God chose to reveal the truth through a message that is devoid of wisdom as measured by human standards (I Cor. 1:26).

Unlike a philosopher's persuasive rational arguments, Paul's message centers on the symbol of human weakness: the Cross. From the human perspective, there is only evidence of weakness and failure in the death of Jesus. Jesus and his followers were unable to outwit, much less overcome, the power of the Roman governor, and the consequence of their incapacity was his death. If the Corinthian Christians had had access to the Passion story later incorporated in the Gospels, with the account of Jesus' refusal even to defend himself in the hearings before the civil and religious authorities, the evidence for the charge of weakness would have been even greater. And rationally, it is completely contradictory to claim, as Paul did in his Gospel, that the means by which the divine will would accomplish its ends was the death of a man who was rejected by his own people and abandoned by his own followers. If he was unable to defeat his earthly foes, how could he be the instrument of eschatological victory, as Paul claimed? Furthermore, the fact that Jesus had died by being suspended from a wooden cross—"Hanged on a tree" (Gal 3:13)—placed him under a curse, in accord with Jewish law (Deut. 21:23). It is not an overstatement to say that for Jews, the notion of a crucified Messiah was a stumblingblock (I Cor. 1:23) to their acceptance.

Paul insists, however, that God uses the message of the Cross for man's redemption because of its stress on weakness. Indeed, this is the way God works in fulfilling his aim of calling together a New Covenant people. He chose one who was obedient unto death (Phil. 2:8), allowed him to be executed as a criminal (Gal. 3:13), chose a humanly weak person, Paul, to be his chief messenger to the Gentiles, and reached through Paul the people of this world who by human standards were of lesser worth:

> For consider your call, brethren; not many of you were wise according to worldly standards, not many were powerful, not many were of noble birth.
> —I CORINTHIANS 1:26

God chose the weak, not because he had no other means, but because he did not want the redemption of man to rest in any way on human strengths or virtues. Only in this way would arrogant man be brought to acknowledge his dependence on God:

> But God chose what is foolish in the world to shame the wise,
> God chose what is weak in the world to shame the strong,
> God chose what is low and despised in the world,
>   even the things that are not,
>   to bring to nothing the things that are,
> so that no human being might boast in the presence of God.
> —I CORINTHIANS 1:27–29

In this poetic and paradoxical speech, Paul shows how essential it is that the message of the Cross should be, humanly speaking, foolishness.

WISDOM FOR THE MATURE

After summarizing the positive role of weakness both in the gospel itself and in him as its messenger (I Cor. 2:1–5), Paul's argument takes a new tack: he asserts that there is for Christians a hidden wisdom, but it is not available either for outsiders or for the immature among those within the community. Furthermore, it is hidden from the powers that control the present age,[3] since if they had been aware of the power of the Cross as God's instrument in conquering them, they would not have unwittingly contributed to their own defeat by crucifying Jesus.

The wisdom for the mature is not perceptible to human eyes or ears, nor is it conceivable to the mind of man. It is accessible to man only as a gift of the Spirit of God. Man may probe the depths of his own being, but only the Spirit can perceive the depths of God's being. By his own native capacities man cannot enter into these mysterious truths. It is important to note that the terms Paul uses to describe the man incapable of discerning the divine truth are (1) *psychikos*, "natural," and (2) *sarkikos*, literally, "fleshy": both connote the merely human, unaided by the divine Spirit. He never uses *hylikos*, "material," though that would have been important for Gnostics, since they saw the realm of spirit and the realm of matter as basically opposed. Paul did not share the Gnostic view that the material world was inherently evil, but instead believed that when man was redeemed, the whole creation would be redeemed as well (Rom. 8:19–23). As a faithful reader of the Law of Moses, including the Genesis account of Creation, he could not believe that the world was created by any agency other than God, or that it was anything but good (Gen. 1:31): "And God saw all that he had made, and behold it was very good." For Paul it was God's own Spirit which communicated to man knowledge of the divine purposes (I Cor. 2:11).

The true sign of maturity, which man could achieve only by being under control of the Spirit, was enjoyment of the common life in the Christian community. Those who claimed to be superspiritual, but whose lives were filled with jealousy and divisiveness, showed that they were not living by the Spirit at all, but by their own self-seeking motives (I Cor. 3:1–4). True spirituality would manifest itself in a concern to build up the Church, which Paul compares to a growing crop and a building under construction (3:5–9). The material that one brings to this building process will be tested by the fires of judgment in

---

[3]Scholars have disputed whether the "rulers" (in Greek, *archontes*) referred to in I Cor. 2:6 are conceived by Paul to be the actual authorities who put Jesus to death—Pilate, with the support of the high priest, Herod Antipas—or the unseen demonic powers which have wrested from God control over the present age. The latter seems more likely, in view of Paul's words about the spiritual warfare in II Cor. 10:3–5; but even if this is the case, the spiritual powers work through the visible authorities, so that the two sets of *archontes* are closely related.

the end; only the truly worthy will survive the test. With a slight shift of metaphor, Paul then declares that the real building is the temple, where God dwells in the midst of his people. Tearing down the church is the same as destroying the sanctuary where God dwells by his Spirit (3:16–17). There is no ground for boasting in one's accomplishments in behalf of the church, just as there is no basis for choosing one leader for another, as though his role were in some way the most essential for the common life. All are needed; each task is essential for the welfare of the whole; and all the gifts by which the work is carried on are gifts of the Spirit (3:18–23). All that any of them possesses he owes to Christ.

Those who have been making accusations against Paul will be either vindicated or—as Paul is confident—exposed on the Day of Judgment. Far from feeling guilty about his errors or misdeeds, he is so bold as to set himself up as an example for others to emulate. In the vivid translation of the Today's English Version, he lashes out in bitter sarcasm:

> For Christ's sake we are fools, but you are wise in Christ!
> We are weak, but you are strong!
> We are despised, but you are honored!
> To this very hour we go hungry and thirsty; we are clothed in rags;
> we are beaten; we wander from place to place;
> we work hard to support ourselves.
> When we are cursed we bless;
> When we are persecuted, we endure;
> When we are insulted, we answer back with kind words.
> We are no more than this world's trash;
> We are the scum of the earth to this very hour.
> —I CORINTHIANS 4:10–13

Then he goes beyond this ironical poem to make an appeal:

> I do not write this to make you ashamed, but to admonish you as my beloved children. For though you have countless guides in Christ, you do not have many fathers. For I became your father in Christ Jesus through the gospel. I urge you, then, be imitators of me.
> —I CORINTHIANS 4:14–16

In what follows, however, Paul turns from exhortation to rebuke as he warns that as a father he will come and take them to task for their irresponsible behavior:

> Shall I come to you with a rod, or with love in a spirit of gentleness?
> —I CORINTHIANS 4:21

The wisdom which Paul imparts, or which he believes God imparts through His Spirit, is not merely concerned with the otherworldly. It has, rather, direct bearing on such practical affairs of this world as personal morality, marriage, legal disputes, earning a living, eating dinner with unconverted friends, complaining about one's lot, getting drunk at community gatherings. It is on these specific matters that Paul utters the wisdom granted him for the benefit of the churches under his charge.

The first issue on which Paul gives his authoritative opinion is whether it is permitted to liberated Christians for a man to take his father's former wife (presumably his own stepmother) as his own. Apparently the Corinthian Christians not only condoned such behavior, but actually boasted of their moral liberation in countenancing this marital arrangement. Among Greeks, as the Oedipus story shows, incest was a most heinous violation of the divine will. Here were Christians who felt themselves so superior to the pagans around them that they could flaunt this elemental moral principle and take pride in doing so. Paul sees in this sanction of an immoral act the opening wedge of a force that would corrupt the Church, just as "a little leaven ferments the whole lump" (I Cor. 5:6). As a Jew, this image reminded him of the Feast of Unleavened Bread, of the Passover, but for Paul as a Christian it is linked with the sacrifices of Christ. He is the Paschal Lamb for Christians, Paul writes (5:7). Just as Jews make a fresh start as symbolized by the unleavened bread, so the Christians must have a new moral beginning in Christ (I Cor. 5:8).

Foolish Christians, unable to settle disputes among themselves, have been turning to the evil courts to adjudicate their conflicts. Paul tells them that they are ignorant of the role that they are yet to fulfill as participants in the final judgment at the End of the Age (6:3). If this is indeed to be their eschatological privilege, how stupid it is of them to appeal to pagan judges in this age!

Others, glorying in their new-found freedom in Christ, are performing all sorts of outlandish deeds in order to demonstrate how free they are. One person is presumably indulging himself by overeating (6:13); another has married a prostitute (6:15). But Paul reminds his readers that they as Christians are no longer independent individuals, and that every action they take directly affects the other members of the body of Christ; since the Church is God's dwelling place by His Spirit (6:19), such immoral actions desecrate His sanctuary.

The same theme occurs in I Corinthians 8 and 10, where Paul inveighs against those who are so freed from religious involvement with pagan worship that they can go with friends to take part in a meal at a pagan temple (10:14–21) or buy food that had originally been offered to idols (8:4). This meat was allowed to remain before the idol for a brief time, as though it were symbolically consumed by the god which the idol represented; the priests would then sell the meat for a reduced price, as only slightly used. Christians were taking advantage of the bargain and boasting that of course their act had no religious significance, because they knew that the idols had no real existence. Paul agrees with their superior "Knowledge" (8:1), but reminds them that their actions are being misunderstood by new converts and others with less of a grasp on Christian freedom. These new members of the church apparently think that those who eat the sacrificial meat are either hypocritical or frivolous in religious matters. Paul's wisdom leads them to see that such careless involvement with idolatrous practices not only upsets the newly converted, but actually exposes the members of the Church to demonic powers at work in pagan religions: "You cannot partake of the table of the Lord and the table of demons" (10:21).

As we observed in our study of Paul's apostolic office, he is free to make pronouncements concerning marital matters in full confidence that his word as apostle is as much the work of the Spirit of God as is the word of the Lord (Jesus): "To the rest I say, not the Lord" (7:12). But at the same time he can offer his own opinions on issues (7:25), while remaining certain that the Spirit of God is with him in rendering these judgments (7:40).

Paul employed the same procedure of offering practical wisdom for settling issues and regularizing life within the Christian community in I Corinthians 11–14. Here he discusses the role of women (11:3, 10–16; 14:34–35), the variety of spiritual gifts (12:4ff.) and their relative values for the Church as a whole (12:27–31; 14:1–30), and—most impressive of all—the factor of love which is the source of renewal and mutuality within the Church (13:1–13). Some scholars think Paul had written this hymn to love prior to this Letter and merely incorporated it at this point. But whether he had composed it in advance or wrote it spontaneously as he was dictating the Letter, it remains one of the greatest literary creations of the New Testament and even of the literature of the entire period. Yet even as Paul writes in praise of love, he reminds his readers that self-seeking is a sign of immaturity and that only the mature (13:11) live the life of love. The concluding lines of the hymn remind us of the source to which Paul attributed all the wisdom that he and the churches possessed: the revelatory vision of God (13:12). That final vision of God was yet to come, when the work of redemption was complete.

The initial vision of God through which Paul had received knowledge of the Gospel was in the revelation of the risen Christ (Gal. 1:12, 16). But the mystical vision of God is continued, Paul asserts (II Cor. 3:4–18), through the work of the Spirit. Paul builds his imagery in II Corinthians 3 on the story of Moses' vision of God on Mt. Sinai told in Exodus 34:29–35. When Moses returned to the people at the foot of the mountain after communing with God, his face shone with the reflected glory of God. The divine radiance is described as literally having rubbed off on Moses, who had to veil his face so that the people would not be filled with awe by the divine glory. Paul offers a different explanation for the face-veiling, however: he declares that Moses was embarrassed by the fact that the glory was fading and so covered his face to conceal the declining radiance from the people. That decline, Paul states, is what has happened to the Old Covenant, of which Moses was the chief agent. But in the New Covenant, the glory increases and the faces of those transformed by that glory are not veiled. The divine radiance is now to be seen in the change that is taking place in the faithful as they take on more and more of the divine likeness in which they were created. This renewal of the creation among men of faith is in process (3:18), so that the purpose of God in creating man in His image is now being accomplished. The close connection between the Creation story and the transformation of believers is shown explicitly by Paul:

> It is the God who said "Let light shine out of darkness" who has shown in our hearts to give the light of the knowledge of the glory of God in the face of Jesus Christ.
>
> —II CORINTHIANS 4:6

The light of revelation in Jesus Christ had set Paul on the way of faith, and it was continuing to exercise its power on him, changing him more and more into the divine image. But it was not an everlasting process: its goal is "Becoming like him" in his death and Resurrection (Phil. 3:10), an objective which will be achieved only at the End of the Age when the Resurrection of the Dead takes place (Phil. 3:11), or what Paul calls "the prize of the upward call of God in Christ Jesus" (Phil. 3:14). This transforming knowledge that Paul is striving for is not knowing *about* Jesus Christ, but knowing *him* (Phil. 3:8), which for Paul has "surpassing worth." What he seeks is direct mystical experience, not merely intellectual information about Jesus, and through him of God. The change that is taking place in Paul will not be complete until the End of the Age. He cannot regard himself as perfect, as having fully attained his own potential. Even though he knows that he cannot arrive at full apprehension in this age, he nonetheless presses on "to make it my own, because Christ Jesus has made me his own" (Phil. 3:12). In offering wisdom to the mature, Paul is himself on the way to maturity.

BEHOLD, I SHOW YOU A MYSTERY

[I CORINTHIANS 15:51]

Although for Paul wisdom is not so much a matter of information as of mystical insight and illumination, there are nevertheless certain important items of knowledge that are available only to men of faith. Significant among these is the disclosure of the details of the circumstances that will lead to the consummation of God's purpose at the End of the Age.

The foundation of Paul's eschatological "mystery" is the experience that he shared with the other apostles and many of the earliest Christians: Jesus appeared to them risen from the dead, or rather, raised from the dead by God. It was for Paul not a timeless mystical vision, but an event that could be dated to the third day after the Crucifixion (I Cor. 15:4). Since days were computed from sundown to sundown, and each part of a day counted as a whole, the period from Friday afternoon to early Sunday morning was counted as three days. The fact that Paul instructed the church at Corinth to set aside the money for the collection on "the first day of the week" (I Cor. 16:2) suggests that from the outset, the churches—or at least the Pauline churches—held their main meeting for worship on the first day rather than the seventh, as in the Jewish tradition. It was the day of Resurrection, or as the Revelation of John was later to put it, "the Lord's day" (Rev. 1:10). The Resurrection faith was the basis for an early, radical break between the Jewish and the Christian communities: the Christian setting aside of the Sabbath Law, one of the most distinctive features of Judaism.

So fundamental was this belief in the Resurrection that Paul could not stand by quietly and allow its validity to be questioned at Corinth. His line of attack on those who deny the Resurrection shows how thoroughly he was imbued with both the teachings of the Pharisees and the basic assumptions of popular Hellenistic philosophy. As a Pharisee, he believed in the Resurrection before he became a Christian. Although the concept of resurrection cannot be documented in Jewish scriptures, except for a passing reference in Daniel 12:2, the Pharisees asserted that at the end of the present age, God would raise up all the dead, reward the righteous, and punish the wicked. In some forms of this expectation, the messianic king would also appear at the end-time and establish God's Rule on the earth. Paul by no means repudiated this notion when he was converted; instead, he modified and elaborated on it in the light of his own religious experience of the risen Lord.

His argument in support of the Resurrection begins with the Corinthians' own experience: they had heard the message of the Cross and the Resurrection, and in response to it they had become members of the Church. Now they were so foolish as to be taken in by persons skeptical that the Resurrection of the Dead would or could occur. If there is no such thing as resurrection, then there is no such thing as the Resurrection of Jesus, and their faith rests on a misrepresentation. Paul and the others have deceived the Corinthians about God by claiming that he raised Jesus from the dead, when in fact no such event took place. In that case, they have not received the forgiveness of sins, as they claimed, and their faith rests on a vain hope that does not extend beyond the limits of life as they now know it (I Cor. 15:12–19). Their confidence is totally misplaced, and they are pitiable wretches.

Then the argument shifts from logic to direct experience. Paul *knows* God raised Jesus from the dead, because he *saw* him. The Pharisaic hope of Paul for the future has been radically modified by the experience in the recent past. The Resurrection is not a concept, Paul is persuaded, but a part of his own religious experience. The hope he once held as a Pharisaic Jew is grounded in first-hand observation. Now he is confident that the Resurrection of Jesus is the first instance of what will occur generally, as he had long expected, but without confirmatory evidence. The evidence he has himself witnessed, however, and he knows that the Resurrection of Jesus is only the beginning—or as he says in the metaphor of Old Testament agricultural language, "the first fruits" (I Cor. 15:20) of the Resurrection that is yet to be. Just as Torah (Deut. 26:1–2) required every farmer to take the first crops produced by his lands and present them to God as a sign that all that the farmer possessed was a gift from his Lord, so Christ, "the first fruits," has gone to present himself to God. Thereby he has become the archetype of the new humanity, the people of the Resurrection. The old humanity, as embodied in Adam, is characterized by disobedience, estrangement, and death; the New Man exemplifies obedience, reconciliation, and life. But the fullness of Christian life is not communicated automatically by ritual or magical means, as with the mystery religions. Being made alive in Christ is for Paul something that is yet to occur in the future, even though the basic event which has created the Resurrection faith in him has already taken place in his own past.

The great event that lies in the future is the completion of what Christ's Resurrection has now guaranteed. At his "coming" (15:23), the rest of his own people will be united with him in the Resurrection life. The word translated "coming" is *parousia*, which means "presence, being there," and was used in connection with the imperial presence. It could refer to an actual visit made by the emperor to a province, where he appeared as the living embodiment of the power of the Roman state, or it could be his symbolic or representative presence, as personified by a governor or plenipotentiary sent by the emperor to carry out his work. The most important connotation of *parousia* is not the act of coming or route of arriving, but the potency of the kingly presence. The term was appropriate, therefore, for the triumphant Christ at the End of the Age. He will embody the power of the New Humanity, and will represent the authority of God, ruling as God's agent over the whole of the Creation. Indeed, that kingly authority is even now being exercised, although invisibly, and that Rule must continue to be extended until all the unseen forces of the universe, including the demonic powers, are brought under Christ's control (15:24–25). All God's enemies will go down in defeat at the hand of Christ. Here Paul is simply presenting in Christianized form what may be found, with some changes of detail, in Jewish apocalyptic writings of this era. Paul makes specific reference to Psalm 8, where it is stated that God established man to rule over the Creation in his stead. Now, Paul says, that design is being achieved, but not through just any man: it is being accomplished through the Last Adam, the Man, Jesus Christ. When that work of bringing all things under subjection to the divine will is complete, Christ will himself take a subject role (15:27–28).

Paul shifts the argument briefly (15:29–34) from describing the events of the eschatological fulfillment to return to the evidence for believing in the Resurrection. He reminds his readers of two kinds of experience that would be pointless if there were no such thing as a Resurrection. The first is the curious practice of being baptized for the dead. We do not know precisely why or how this was performed, but it seems to have been an act of piety for a Christian to accept baptism repeatedly for the benefit of one who had died.

EPHESUS *today: the ruins. In Paul's day, Ephesus was one of the great cities of the eastern Mediterranean, but the silting up of its harbor rendered it useless as a port and caused it to be abandoned.* (Darryl Jones)

Paul does not comment on the practice or condone it, but seems rather to accept it as a custom already established among the Christians in Corinth. They are wasting their time, he says, if there is no Age of Resurrection in which the vicarious benefits can be experienced by the dead.

The other factor to which he points in his argument is his and others' willingness to risk their lives for the sake of the gospel. Even though the mention of fighting with wild beasts (15:32) at Ephesus may be metaphorical, it was nonetheless true that he did have to face up to the possibility of his own martyrdom. If this life in this age is all that there is for man, then why run the risk? Why not adopt the hedonist's creed of good food, good drink, and a good time? What delivers man from this sensualist, cynical view, Paul declares, is that death is not the end. It is only a stage on the way to the Resurrection.

Paul's contemporaries would have had as much difficulty—perhaps even more—conceiving the Resurrection than our contemporaries. There was no tradition in the Hellenistic world for such an idea, because it was assumed that only the soul of man could survive death. Certain especially endowed men might after death be raised to the rank of heroes and live among the gods, but there was no expectation that the bodies of the great mass of humanity had any other prospect than death and decay. Even in those philosophies and religious systems that believed in the transmigration of souls from one body to another, in each case the body was of no enduring significance and returned to the earth following death, freeing the soul to enter a new body about to be

199

born. In none of these systems of belief was there any place for the idea of bodily resurrection. However we may evaluate the historical reliability of Acts 17 in its account of Paul's preaching to the Athenians about the Resurrection, the scornful response attributed to his hearers in the Anthenian *agora,* "What is this babbler trying to say?", is precisely the kind of reaction one might expect from first-century Greeks or Romans.

Using the method of argumentation common to the Stoic preachers of his day, Paul anticipates for his Corinthian readers their objections to the notion of the Resurrection. Seizing on the ambiguity of the word "body"—in Greek as well as in English—Paul argues that one cannot assume that a Resurrection body will be identical with a body of a presently living human being. It is essential to bear in mind that for Paul *body* does not mean primarily a tangible, physical substance, but an identifiable object, or in the case of a personal being, a self—what distinguishes one individual from another. He draws an analogy between a "self" that dies, is buried, and is to be raised from the dead and a seed that is sown in the soil, decays, but brings forth new life. The body is not lost but is exchanged (15:35–39). And bodies differ not merely in a general way, but in glory, as exemplified by the way that the glory of the sun differs from the glory of the moon or the stars (15:41).

The body of man as he will be raised from the dead—and of course Paul is reasoning throughout his argument on the basis of his own vision of the resurrected Jesus—is not dishonored by death and decay, but is made glorious, in that it represents what God intended for man when he created him as a "living being" (Gen. 2:7) and "crowned him with glory and honor" (Ps. 8:6). What characterizes the Resurrection body is imperishability, power, and glory (15:42–43). The body placed in the grave is physical; the body that comes forth in the Resurrection is spiritual (15:44). Paul does not tell us what a spiritual body is, though he does state flatly that it does not consist of "flesh and blood" (15:50) and is therefore not subject to the limitations of bodily existence as humanity knows it. He launches rather into a series of contrasts between the bodily existence that is typical of Adam and the new bodily existence that Christ's Resurrection makes possible (15:45–50).

In the process of contrasting the First and Last Adams, Paul makes two remarkable statements about Jesus as the Christ. First, he calls him a "life-giving spirit"; second, he calls him "the man from heaven." The implication of both these terms is that Paul has little interest in the earthly origins of Jesus. He did mention in his Letter to the Galatians (4:4) that Jesus had been born of a woman and was therefore truly human. But in I Corinthians 15 he stresses Christ's redemptive function as conveyed by the spiritual power which he embodies and as represented by his coming from or even perhaps originating in heaven. The term "man from heaven" (15:47) recalls for many Pauline interpreters the concept first documented in Iranian religion and later prominent in Gnosticism that the Redeemer of mankind is himself the archetypal man, whose origin is in heaven and who is able to take the faithful with him to the heavenly realms.[4] It seems strange to speak of Jesus as a heavenly man while asserting (Rom. 1:3) that he was descended from David according to human lineage. The most plausible explanation for the seeming conflict between the earthly and the heavenly lineage of Jesus in the thought of Paul lies in assuming that Paul thinks of Jesus in much the same way that Jewish eschatological tradition came to think of Moses, Enoch, and Elijah. That is, it was taken for granted that they had all lived on earth, indeed had been born under wholly human circumstances, but that following their death they had been taken up into the presence of God, and that God's task for them would be completed only when they came back to earth in the end-time to defeat God's enemies and vindicate the faithful elect of His Covenant people. This is the point of view offered in Malachi 3:1ff; 4:5, where the return of Elijah is awaited at the End of the Age. It was a living expectation at Qumran among the members of the Dead Sea community that a prophet like Moses, or perhaps even Moses himself, would reappear on the earth in the last days in fulfillment of the promise of Deuteronomy 18:18.[5]

In harmony with this eschatological view, therefore, Jesus was now in heaven and would reappear when his redemptive work was about to be completed. The details of this expectation are provided by Paul in I Thessalonians 4:13–17, where he offers words of reassurance to those Christians who are disturbed by the fact that some of their members have died before the *parousia* of Christ has occurred and therefore may not be able to take part in the Age to Come. Paul believed he had a prophetic revelation ("by the word of the Lord") on the subject (I Thess. 4:15). The Christians were not to mourn for their departed fellow-believers as though they would never see them again, or as though they would not share in the Kingdom of God because they had died before its consummation. God will bring along those who have "fallen asleep"— the Christian euphemism for dying—when the *parousia* takes place. Indeed, they will have precedence over those living at the time of the end, and Paul writes in the second-person plural in full expectation that he will be among those who will live to witness the *parousia*. That event will consist in the Lord's appearing from heaven, accompanied by a commanding cry, an archangel's call, and a celestial trumpet's sound. These features represent the defeat of the evil powers, as suggested by the military imagery of the word of command and the trumpet call to the troops. Then all the faithful, both those who have been raised from the dead and those who never died, will be joined with the

---

[4]See C. H. Kraeling, *Anthropos—Son of Man* (New York: Columbia University Press, 1927); more recently, Frederick Borsch, *Son of Man in Myth and History* (Philadelphia: Westminster Press, 1967).

[5]The vitality of this hope is attested at Qumran, where the expected deliverer was called "the Prophet" (*Manual of Discipline*, ix, 11), and in the Psalms of Joshua, where Deut. 18:18 is quoted directly.

Lord forever. The meeting in the air (I Thess. 4:17) may be to accompany him to heaven, and it is so represented in popular Christian piety; but it is more likely an allusion to the figure of Daniel 7, where "one like the Son of Man" appears on the clouds of heaven on his way to earth to receive authority over God's Kingdom. The saints of I Thessalonians 4 are therefore the hosts who accompany the eschatological King to earth to receive his Kingdom.

Although the details are not repeated in I Corinthians 15, the possibility that some of the faithful will survive until the eschatological trumpet sounds (15:51–52) shows that the same event is in mind. And in I Corinthians 15:51, the information concerning this event is called a "mystery," the details and significance of which are apparently available only to the elect. There is no indication, on the other hand, that the Christian belief in the *parousia* at the End of the Age was an esoteric bit of knowledge. Rather, it can be called a mystery because the certainty of it and the actual course of eschatological events have been revealed to Paul and, through him, to the community. These events will culminate in the final defeat of God's enemies, including death itself.

On two counts, however, the hope of the Resurrection had direct bearing on the quality of life in the Church during the interim before the *parousia*. First, it gave meaning and encouragement to the work that the members carried out in extending the gospel and in strengthening the converts. If their hope was limited to this life only, it would be easy to become discouraged with a lack of immediate results. But since the enterprise in which they were engaged was to reach its glorious climax in the Resurrection, they could go about their tasks confident that they and their works would be vindicated when the King assumed his throne in the New Age (I Cor. 15:58).

The second factor is one we have already considered. Paul declared to the Philippians (3:10–14) that his present manner of life would have a direct bearing on his participation in the Resurrection event: ". . . that if possible I may attain the resurrection of the dead." The Resurrection hope thus served both as reminder of the shortcomings that he could observe in his own present way of life and as a future goal of what he might yet become. With this prospect before him, he was striving for ever-increasing maturity in the faith.

"THE MYSTERY OF LAWLESSNESS IS ALREADY AT WORK"

[II THESSALONIANS 2:7]

Paul had written to the Thessalonian Christians that the *parousia* would take place like the coming of a thief in the night—*i.e.*, without warning (I Thess. 5:2)—from which some enthusiasts in Thessalonica concluded that the day of the Lord had already occurred. And in order to lend credence and authority to their view, they circulated a letter purporting to be from Paul to that effect (II Thess. 2:2). Very soon after he had sent off what we know as I Thessalonians, therefore, he had to follow it with a second letter, perhaps within a space of a few weeks. Now he must warn the church that, while the end will come soon, there are certain events which must take place in the closing days before the *parousia* actually occurs. Because of the apparent contradiction between saying the end will come with no warning and saying that certain events must intervene, some scholars have denied that the same man could have written both letters, and incline to regard II Thessalonians as a forgery written in the style of Paul.

There is no need for such a radical conclusion, however, since in both Letters Paul is drawing on the ample fund of apocalyptic imagery and expectation. The picture presented in II Thessalonians 2 of an arrogant ruler who defiles the temple of God by asserting his own authority there is strongly reminiscent of Daniel, the apocalyptic sections of Mark, and the other Synoptic Gospels. Efforts to identify the "man of lawlessness" and the restraining force (2:7) are probably idle, since these are more or less stock characters in the apocalyptic dramas. Even the picture of the evil one being destroyed by the Word of the Lord (2:8) is a part of the traditional picture of the final conflict between God and his enemies. The sufferings of the faithful are to be understood in this context as well. The unbelievers will become more and more hostile, since in the last days Satan's power to persuade them to believe his lies will be greater (2:9–11). These warnings are wholly in keeping with the apocalyptic traditions about the *parousia* of the eschatological King that Paul had described in his first Letter to the church at Thessalonica. Then the issue had been a different one: How could the Christians who had died share in the End of the Age? Now the question was whether the *parousia* had already occurred. While the questions are related, they are sufficiently different as to require separate answers. It is for this reason that I and II Thessalonians differ. But in both cases, Paul was drawing consciously on the special knowledge that had been granted him in revelations and through the prophetic gift; but unconsciously he was utilizing the great store of apocalyptic imagery and expectations that was a part of his heritage as a Pharisaic Jew. Paul therefore did not think of these hopes of final redemption as offering him a private and individualistic salvation; rather, he believed that by faith he had become part of the people of the New Covenant, and it was for their corporate history that God was primarily concerned. What he looked forward to was not simply to "be with Christ" (Phil. 1:23), but to be united in triumph forever with all the saints: "And so shall we always be with the Lord" (I Thess. 4:17).

From this vantage point, it was possible for Paul to accept the most severe sufferings with equanimity. He did not deny that pain really happened, or accept suffering as an inevitable part of an impersonal, fate-bound universe, as did the Epicureans, but he believed that the trials were necessary of the Age to Come. He could endure the rage and buffetings brought about by the "man of lawlessness," since he was convinced that, "we suffer with Christ in order that we may be glorified with him" (Rom. 8:17). But even the sufferings themselves, no matter how severe, took on lesser importance when compared with the prospect that, he was convinced, lay ahead for him and the new community:

> I consider that the sufferings of this present time are not worth comparing with the glory that is to be revealed to us.
>
> —ROMANS 8:18

When he wrote to the Philippians concerning the "fellowship of sufferings" (3:10), it was this mystical union with Christ and his people that Paul had in mind, a union now in suffering and service, and a triumphant union yet to come in the New Age.

Paul's Understanding
of the
People of God

CHAPTER NINE

Toward the end of his career Paul wrote from Corinth to
the church at Rome, a congregation which he had not
founded and which seems to have had little if any previous
direct association with him. It is possible that Priscilla and
Aquila (mentioned as having been driven out of Rome in
Acts 18:1–2) returned there after their period of association
with Paul in Corinth and Ephesus (I Cor. 16:19), but there
is no indication that the apostle (Peter?) who founded the
church at Rome was of the same persuasion as Paul concerning the gospel or the nature of the Christian community. Paul wrote, therefore, to announce his intended visit,
to make his views known to the church there, and to indicate
that he was coming in a spirit of mutuality (Rom. 1:12),
rather than to correct their ideas of Christian truth. As a
result of these circumstances, his Letter is the most systematic of all that have been preserved, and perhaps the
most systematic that he ever wrote. Coming as it did late in
his life—it is perhaps the latest of his preserved Letters—
it summed up both his understanding of the gospel and his
assessment of the work that he had carried out. Using

Romans as the basis for our reconstruction, we shall consider seven of the main themes of Paul's thought, concentrating on his arguments as developed in this Letter, but drawing where necessary or useful on the other Letters as well.

ALL HAVE SINNED AND FALL SHORT

[ROMANS 3:23]

In the Jewish world-view, which was a part of Paul's heritage and by which the early Church was guided, morality was not a matter of living up to ideals, but of obedience to a living, personal God. It is true that in Torah there were many specific precepts by which Israel was expected to live, but these were thought of as concrete expressions of the will of God, rather than as abstract ethical principles. Immoral action, therefore, could be traced to two major causes: (1) rebellion against God's will, and (2) subjection to a power that was opposed to God rather than subjection to God himself. This might be a voluntary subjection to the forces of evil, or it might result from a divine judgment by which God permitted the evil power to possess a person, or it might be a wholly involuntary seizure by an unusually potent demonic power. The one general term to describe a man's condition when he is outside an obedient relationship to God is *sin*. The acts that a man performs as a result of this broken relationship to God and the consequent lack of proper direction in his life are *sins*. Paul devotes the opening section of his Letter to the Romans to a development of the theme of the sinfulness of man.

HARBOR OF CAMPANIA
probably Puteoli, where Paul landed in Italy according to Acts 28:13. Here represented in a mural, the painting was on the wall of a house that was destroyed by the eruption of Vesuvius in A.D. *79.* (Museo Nazionale, Naples)

Since the time of the Protestant Reformation, many within and without the Christian Church have thought of sin and redemption in purely or largely individualistic terms. A sin is a wrong committed by a person. If he seeks forgiveness, it is as a private matter between himself and God. This attitude has been sharpened in America where so much is said and written about the rights of the individual. Every man is expected to be able to determine his own destiny by making up his own mind. Even though sociologists and social psychologists have shown how powerful the group is in shaping decisions and influencing behavior, the notion of individual autonomy persists. For those who share this view of human existence as a solitary matter, it is difficult to sense the import of the picture of man that is assumed by the New Testament writers, who in turn draw on the image of man found in the Old Testament.

For Paul, together with the other writers in the early Church, man is inevitably part of a human *community*. The Biblical writers conceive of man as bound by birth to his nation, his tribe, his family. But above all, man is bound to the human race as a whole in its seeking to be independent of God. The story of Adam, with its report of Adam's longing to be like God (Gen. 3:5), is the story of every man. It is not something that happened "way back then"; it is an insight into an attitude of self-seeking autonomy that characterizes the whole human race in every age. Is there a remedy for such a predicament?

Paul shares with the Old Testament writers the belief that there is a remedy. Out of the race of disobedient mankind, God called into being a new people— a People of God—who would obey and serve him. This was the nation Israel, which was designed by God to be his own People in a special way, as we can infer from the words addressed to Israel at Sinai:

> Now therefore, if you will obey my voice and keep my covenant, you shall be my own possession among all peoples; for all the earth is mine, and you shall be a kingdom of priests and a holy nation.
> —EXODUS 19:5, 6

In words apparently addressed to the nation, depicted by the prophet as the Lords' servant, II Isaiah wrote:

> I am the Lord, I have called you in righteousness,
>   I have taken you by the hand and kept you;
> I have given you as a covenant to the people,
>   a light to the nations,
> To open the eyes that are blind,
> To bring out the prisoners from the dungeon,
> From the prison those who sit in darkness.
> —ISAIAH 42:6, 7

The mission of the People of God, therefore, was to be a holy nation and thereby to serve as a light to bring the knowledge of God to the Gentiles, who sit imprisoned and in darkness. In the judgment of Paul—and his view is shared by the other New Testament writers—this mission had not been fulfilled. God was accordingly bringing into being through Jesus Christ a New People of God, in whom these unfulfilled objectives would be achieved. The concept of the New Covenant had been set forth by Jeremiah:

> Behold the days are coming, says the Lord, when I will make a new covenant with the house of Israel and the house of Judah, not like the covenant which I made with their fathers . . . which they broke. . . . I will put my law within them, and I will write it upon their hearts; and I will be their God and they shall be my people.
>
> —JEREMIAH 31:31–33

This New Covenant, Paul is convinced (I Cor. 11:25), had been brought into being by the sacrificial death of Jesus Christ. Other New Testament writers shared his view (Lk. 22:20;[1] Heb. 9:15ff.; 10:16ff.) that the New Covenant people consist not of those obedient persons descended biologically from Israel and Judah, but of those persons of whatever race or national origin who respond in faith and obedience to the God of Israel who has addressed all mankind in Jesus Christ.

The question, therefore, is not, "How will individuals believe and be saved?" but, "How in the midst of disobedient humanity is God calling into being his New People?" The familiar Pauline theme—justification by faith—is therefore not the major theme of the Letter to the Romans, nor is the defense of his Gentile mission Paul's main concern. Both these themes are part of the larger objective: to show how God is establishing his People.

After a brief introduction, in which Paul outlines the Gospel and explains his

---

[1]A number of important Greek manuscripts of Matthew add "new" before "covenant" at Mt. 26:28; a somewhat less impressive group add "new" at Mk. 14:24.

THE APPIAN WAY
just south of Rome, with the arches of the Claudian aqueduct in the background. Paul traveled this road on his way to Rome. (Alinari/Art Reference Bureau)

delay in visiting the community in Rome (Rom. 1:1–15), he plunges into the argument that occupies most of the remainder of the Letter. It is clear from the outset that, although he thinks of himself as commissioned to preach primarily to the Gentiles, he is gravely concerned for the Jews and for their status— now apparently forfeited—as the People of God. He believes that both Jew and Greek (*i.e.,* Gentile) are to share in God's salvation—that is, the deliverance of man and the universe from the power of evil, and the fulfillment of God's purpose for man and all creation. The direction that the argument will take is set in the key phrase: "The righteousness of God revealed through faith" (1:17). But before Paul can state what righteousness involves, he must show how it has been revealed and why it can be known only through faith.

The knowledge that God exists, and that he is the power behind the universe, is not the property of any favorite group of men to whom alone it has been revealed; rather, it is an inescapable inference from the majestic order of the natural world. Man, when he ignores the Creator and chooses to worship instead some created thing, is guilty of willful defiance of God. Paul paints a fearful picture of the moral degradation that results from man's alienation from his Creator (1:18–32). Even though the Jews were given a more direct revelation through Torah, or perhaps *because* they had this unique opportunity of knowing God's will, they are the more reprehensible for failing to fulfill his demands. Their moral shortcomings are symptoms of the fact that they, like the unenlightened Gentiles, are alienated from God, and hence "under the power of sin" (2:1–3:9). The condemnation under which the human race stands is sweeping, and man cannot possibly escape from it by striving to be better. Torah itself serves only to remind man of his failure, and thus to increase his sense of guilt.

Into this apparently hopeless situation, God himself has come in the person of Jesus Christ. (The relationship between God and Jesus will be considered below.) Through Christ, the enmity of man toward God is overcome, the alienated are reconciled, man's sense of guilt is removed, and he stands delivered from the powers of evil that have kept him enslaved. Once he has been liberated from his condition "under the power of *sin,*" man can then turn his attention to the matter of *sins* and ethical demands. Until he is liberated, it is useless to talk to him about ridding himself of any particular sins, since these are only symptoms of his real problem.

Man's failure to gain divine approval is not the result of occasional or even perennial moral lapses: he is simply manifesting his oneness with the entire human race, which has lost the splendor of the image of God in which man was created (3:23). The reference here is to the account of Creation in Genesis 1, where man and woman are said to have been created in God's image. That Paul accepts this as the true account of the origin of man and the character God intended him to possess is evident from the description of man as the "image and Glory of God" in I Corinthians 11:7. We have seen that Paul

believed that all mankind shared in the responsibility for Adam's sin of disobedience to God (Gen. 3) and that all men justly suffer under the judgment
resulting from that sin. The conviction was a part of the traditional Hebrew
belief in the solidarity and inner unity of the nation. In ancient times, all Israel
suffered when David, their king, sinned by taking a census. Presumably, the
number of God's People was supposed to be a divine secret into which no man
could inquire; hence, the judgment fell on David—and on all Israel—for his
wicked act.

Since all men stand under condemnation because of their share in Adam's
sin, the hope of redemption must involve the creation of a new race. The old
race is characterized by Adam's disobedience; the new race will be characterized by the complete obedience of Jesus to the will of God. Simply to tell men
they ought to be better is useless; unaided by divine grace, men cannot be
good. Conversely, merely to trim off a man's imperfections is not to solve his
basic moral problem. A complete reorientation to God and an inner transformation are the prerequisites of goodness.

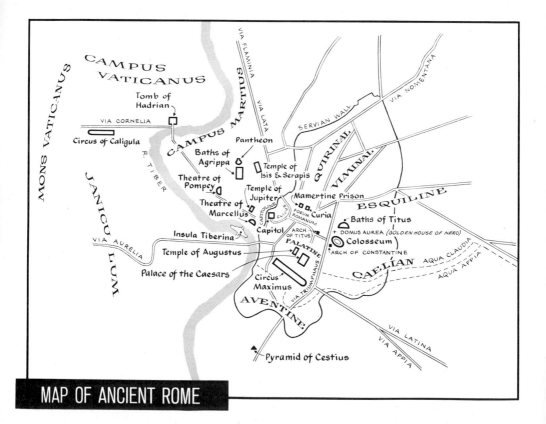

MAP OF ANCIENT ROME

A MAN IS JUSTIFIED BY FAITH

[ROMANS 3:28]

Justification by Good Works

Paul had respect for the terminology and even the precepts of the moral philosophies of his Greek contemporaries. But he was convinced that to talk ethics to a man bound to a morally impotent race was not only a waste of time, but grossly misleading. Such an approach to righteousness suggested that if man only tried hard enough, he could arrive at the state in which God would be obligated to accept him. Paul, as we have seen, was convinced that the finest moral injunctions that he knew (those embodied in Torah) only frustrated man by reminding him of his shortcomings. The real hindrances to obedience—a sense of estrangement from God, and the lack of inner motivation to do what was right—were aspects of the problem that remained untouched by mere moral appeal. Laws do not make men good; they only remind men of what is wrong (Rom. 3:20).

Justification by Faith

Now, however, God has begun to work on an entirely new basis: justification by faith. This possibility for man has been declared with fresh clarity and with finality through Jesus Christ, but it was the basis for the relationship that had existed between God and men of faith as far back as the time of Abraham (Rom. 4), as we have already seen in Paul's Letter to the Galatians (p. 175). The good news of salvation that has come by Jesus Christ is not, therefore, a radical break with the past. It is not as though God had dealt in a legalistic way with Israel, and then had set up faith as a basis for dealing with the Church. Throughout Torah it is clear that what God desired was the devotion of his People, not the performance of empty ceremonies or the scrupulous observance of regulations out of a sense of obligation. The burden of the prophets of Israel was to protest against formalism and to issue a summons to loving, obedient trust in God. The essence of Paul's gospel, as stated succinctly in Rom. 3:21–26, is that God has acted decisively through Jesus Christ to free men from bondage to sin and the evil forces that held them captive (redemption), to remove the barrier of guilt that kept men from God's presence (expiation), and to restore men to a right relationship with God in spite of their sins (justification). Since this statement is so compact, and since the way of thinking that it represents is so strange, let us examine in some detail the meaning of these words.

The word "righteousness" in English usage usually means a moral quality of uprightness and justice; as such, it could be ascribed either to God or to man. "To justify," which is the cognate verb, would signify "to make right" or "to declare right." To justify God would be to demonstrate his righteousness; and to justify man would be either to declare him to be morally right or to make him right. In any case, righteousness would be regarded as a moral attribute.

In the thought of the Hebrews, however, the concept is quite different. The word that we usually translate as "righteousness" is not primarily a quality, but an activity. When a judge in ancient Israel "justified" a man who had been wronged, he did not instill a quality of uprightness, nor did he publish a decree that the man was innocent of wrong; rather, he rectified the situation, and thus restored the wronged man to his rightful place. In a psalm included in one of the Dead Sea Scrolls, dating from the beginning of the Christian Era, there is a passage in which both "justification" and "righteousness" are used in the sense of what God does for those who trust in him:

> For as for me, my justification belongs to God;
> And in His hand is the perfection of my way,
> Together with the uprightness of my heart.
> Through His righteousness my transgression shall be blotted out. . . .[2]

The emphasis here clearly falls on God's work, by which the oppressed are vindicated; the uprightness of the heart is regarded as a by-product of God's justifying, or vindicating, act. Similarly, when Paul speaks of "the righteousness of God" (Rom. 3:25), he is not merely describing the character of God, nor is he suggesting that God infuses his own qualities into certain persons. He is declaring that God has taken the initiative in restoring man to his proper relation to God and man.

The earlier part of the Letter has shown the degradation that man suffers when he is apart from God, and the hopelessness of man's attempts to deliver himself from alienation from God and from enslavement to sin. Now, we see that being set right in relation to God is not a condition that man is called on to strive for, but that right relationship results from an action that God has performed in Jesus Christ, the benefits of which are offered as a gift, to be received by faith (Rom. 3:24). God's work of vindication is not dependent upon man's fulfillment of Law, although Torah and the writings of the prophets bear witness that God's nature is such that he does vindicate the oppressed (Rom. 3:21).

The Ground of Justification by Faith

God's justifying activity is focused in the death of Jesus on the Cross. That death is looked upon by Paul, as it was reported to be by Jesus himself

---

[2]Quoted from *The Manual of Discipline*, or *Rule of the Community*, the translation by W. H. Brownlee in *Bulletin of the American Schools of Oriental Research*, Supplementary Studies, Nos. 10–12, "The Dead Sea Manual of Discipline" (New Haven, 1951), pp. 42, 43.

(Mk. 10:45), as a ransom. The ransom was thought of as a means of release for one in bondage, not as a price to buy off the captor. The conviction that the death of Jesus was the means for freeing men from subjection to the evil powers is elaborated in the Letter to the Colossians (2:13–15). There, in words that are reminiscent of Jesus' allusion to pillaging Satan's household, Paul declares that in the Cross man's bondage to law was broken and the powers that oppress man in this age were decisively defeated. If these powers had realized that the seeming tragedy of the Cross would be the means of God's triumph over them, they would not have instigated his crucifixion. (The early Church was convinced that behind every temporal authority was an unseen spiritual power, and that it was these invisible powers that plotted against the purposes of God. See Chapter Fifteen.) Later in the Letter to the Romans (6:20), Paul describes the former condition of the Roman Christians as "slaves of sin"; here in a single phrase he proclaims that God has acted to free men from such bondage.

The agent through whom God's justifying act was achieved is Jesus, whom God ordained for this role. When Paul speaks of Jesus as "an expiation by his blood" (Rom. 3:25), it sounds as though God were a vengeful deity whose wrath could be appeased only by the slaughter of a bloody victim. The term "propitiation," which is used in the King James Version to translate the Greek word that is here rendered "expiation," heightens the picture of a God of wrath. Actually, the term in question is used in the Septuagint to describe the removal of the guilt that stands as a barrier between man and God. If guilt is removed by man's action, the proper rendering is "expiation"; if it is simply a matter of God's gracious removal of the barrier, "forgiveness" is the appropriate translation.[3] As we saw earlier, in Hebrew usage blood means life. The point of Paul's phrase, then, is this: Through Jesus' offering up his life to God, obedient unto death, the barrier of guilt that separated man from God has been removed.

The idea that the obedience of Jesus removes the guilt is explicitly stated in Romans 5:19 and is reaffirmed in Philippians 2:8. But the logic of the idea is not clear to a modern mind unaccustomed to thinking of religion in terms of sacrifice. From the gospel records it is clear that the major reason for the determination of Jesus' enemies to have him executed was their belief that he was undermining the moral standards and the institutional structures of their religion. He refused to abide by the regulations that required him to keep separate from defiled people; he persisted in befriending religious outcasts; he would not condemn sinful people; he enjoyed deflating those who, according to accepted standards, excelled in piety. His parables told of a God of grace and forgiveness. So it is not surprising that he was regarded as a religious subversive. It was in large measure because he was the friend of "tax collectors and sinners" (Lk. 7:34) that he was put to death. In spite of the growing opposition to his ministry, Jesus continued to challenge the religious institu-

---

[3]For a full discussion of the key words in this passage, see C. H. Dodd, *The Epistle to the Romans* (New York: Harper & Row, 1932), pp. 48–61.

tions and to proclaim the grace of God, because he believed it was God's will for him to live and teach in this way. Paul was not drawing on his imagination when he said that Jesus was "obedient unto death," or when he connected Jesus' death with the forgiveness of sin; it was part of the tradition he had received.

The initiative of God in bringing men into the right relationship with himself has been fully and finally made known in Jesus Christ (Rom. 3:25, 26). Up until the time of Jesus' coming, God has been forgiving toward man, and forbearing towards man's sins, but man's sense of guilt and spiritual blindness kept him from understanding the true nature of God. Weighed down by guilt, man fled from God's presence and sought peace and safety in the worship of false gods. But now Jesus has come, completely dedicated to God, even to the extremity of death. Thus he has demonstrated once and for all that God is One who vindicates the oppressed, removes the barriers that separate man from him, and brings man into relationship with himself. In response to what God has done, man is expected to trust God and to rely for his salvation on God's justifying act in Christ.

Jew and Gentile

There is no place in such a scheme for human pride, since a man is accepted before God not on the basis of what he does, but on the strength of what God has done for him in Christ (Rom. 3:27, 28). So there is no place for any distinction between Jew and Gentile, since both must come to God on the same basis: faith. Even circumcision, which the Judaizers had been insisting on as a requisite for admission to the Christian community, was not required of Abraham until after he had trusted God, and had been accepted by him. There is, therefore, neither reason nor precedent for demanding that the Gentiles be circumcised in order to enjoy salvation. The fulfillment of the promise to Abraham rested solely on faith (Rom. 4:13ff.).

We might conclude from this line of argument that a man who has faith can live as he pleases. Paul puts the issue in an exaggerated form: If our sins cause God to display his gracious forgiveness, we should sin more so that more grace might be available (Rom. 6:1ff.). But the answer to such a suggestion is an emphatic no. The believer who is convinced that God has revealed himself in Jesus Christ, and that God has taken the initiative in removing the barrier that separates man from God, comes under the control of an influence which is strong, yet unlike the burdensome necessity of keeping the Law. The new influence is the love of God, as the believer has experienced it in Christ (II Cor. 5:14, 15). Man is free either to respond to God's love or to ignore it. But when he does respond in faith, he feels himself overmastered by Christ's love, which was demonstrated by his willingness to die in order that all men might be reconciled to God. The force, then, which compels the believer to do the will of God is not a sense of obligation, but an overwhelming feeling of gratitude for what God has done for man in Christ.

GOD WAS IN CHRIST

[II CORINTHIANS 5:19]

So far in what we have said about Paul's formulation of the Gospel, we have referred only in passing to the relationship between Jesus and God. Actually, Paul never defines this relationship, although he gives considerable attention in his Letters to what God has done through Jesus. It is important to remind ourselves that the Hebrew mind does not express itself in abstract concepts, but in terms of action and concrete events. Ancient Israel did not construct a set of ideas or theories about God; she gloried in what God had done for Israel and how he had made himself known in her historic experiences. Similarly, when Jesus was asked to define "neighbor," he did not launch into a lengthy discourse on neighborliness, or on the ideal qualifications of being a neighbor; rather, he told the unforgettable story of the Good Samaritan, who demonstrated what a neighbor was by what he did (Lk. 10:29–37). It is this action thinking, rather than the conceptual or theoretical type, that must be foremost in our minds if we are to understand Paul's belief about the nature of Jesus' relation to God. Before attempting to trace out what it was that Paul believed God to have done in Christ, let us look briefly at the titles that Paul gives to Jesus in his redemptive role.

Jesus as Lord

Paul never says that Jesus is God. He does, however, so closely identify Jesus and God that it is sometimes difficult to tell to which one he is referring—as in his many references to "the Lord," for example. This title for God, which is *kurios* in Greek, was the one used by the translators of the Septuagint when they found in the Hebrew text "YHWH," the unpronounceable name of God. It was Jewish practice to read this "YHWH" as though it were the Hebrew word, *adonai*, which means "Lord." The Greek translators translated the substitute word, *adonai*, rather than the original Hebrew, YHWH, the meaning of which was no longer known. Therefore to any reader of the Septuagint—and of course every Dispersion Jew was familiar with it—*kurios* was the most common name for God.

As it happened, the term *kurios* was also widely used by the pagans, particularly by the devotees of the mystery cults. In the worship of Osiris or Dionysus, for example, *kurios* was the common designation for the savior-god. Paul acknowledged in writing to the Corinthians (I Cor. 8:5) that in the Roman world there were many competing "lords" or *kurioi*. The earliest Christian preachers had affirmed that God had made Jesus "Lord" (Acts 2:36); Paul echoes this conviction in his words to the Philippians (Phil. 2:9–11). The affirmation "Jesus is Lord" is the earliest form of Christian confession (cf. Rom. 10:9, 10).

Because this term *kurios* is first widely used in the New Testament by Paul, we must not infer that Paul invented the idea of calling Jesus *kurios* in order to put him into competition with other Hellenistic saviors. Paul's quotation (in I Cor. 16:22) of the Aramaic phrase, *Maranatha*, which means, "Our Lord, come!", shows that Jesus was called "Lord" by the earliest Christian community in Palestine; Paul simply adopted the practice from them, translating it into Greek, the language that was meaningful to those among whom he was working. Later theological elaborations of the nature of Jesus were aided by the connotations of the word *kurios* among both Jews and Greeks of the day. But the term was a part of the earliest Christian tradition and was not introduced as part of a process of deifying the man Jesus. Paul goes so far as to apply to Jesus passages from the Old Testament that referred in their original context to the God of Israel. A prime instance of this occurs in the Letter to the Romans, where Paul quotes the promise of the prophet Joel that "everyone that calls upon the name of the Lord will be saved." Here the title "Lord" is clearly taken to mean Jesus (Rom. 10:9–13).

Jesus as Son of God

Another of Paul's favorite designations for Christ is "Son of God." In the usage of ancient Israel, this phrase was applied to the ideal king, who, because he had been designated by God to reign over God's People, was called the "Son of God" (Ps. 2:7). The term continued to be used throughout Israel's history, although later it was not applied to a historical personage, but rather to the king who would one day come and establish the reign of God over creation. The belief in Jesus as the one anointed to bring in God's reign was clearly in the back of Paul's mind when he applied the title to Jesus. But Paul added to this traditional meaning for "Son of God" the conviction that there was an intimate relationship between Jesus and God which gave Jesus a unique claim to the title (Col. 1:13), even though the term was commonly applied to the saviors of the Hellenistic religions. Furthermore, the character of Jesus was such that his concerns for mankind and his selfless attitudes were identified by Paul as divine qualities. He described the death of Jesus in behalf of sinners as "God showing his love" (Rom. 5:8). The fluid way in which Paul shifted from speaking of Jesus to speaking of God is puzzling grammatically, but it is thoroughly compatible with Paul's conviction that Jesus' relation to God was unique.

Paul rarely referred to Jesus as simply "Jesus." He preferred such expressions as "Jesus Christ," or "Christ Jesus," or "the Lord Jesus Christ." The title "Christ," as we have seen, is simply the Greek form of the Hebrew word "Messiah," meaning "anointed." It was often used in referring to the king, as one anointed to rule for God, but it could be used of any man who had a special role to play in the purpose of God. It was used of Cyrus, the Persian ruler who gave orders for the nation Judah to return to Palestine from captivity in Babylon (Is. 45:1). It is applied to the Servant of God through whom the coming of the day of Israel's redemption is announced (Is. 61). When Paul called Jesus "Christ," he meant that Jesus was the one through whom God was working to defeat the forces of evil and to restore man to a right relationship with God.

Jesus as Redeemer

In later centuries, after Christianity had become the official religion of the Roman Empire, theologians devoted a great deal of discussion to questions about the relation of the human to the divine elements in the person of Jesus. They tried to decide whether Jesus had a divine will *and* a human will, or simply one *composite* will; whether he had a divine *and* a human nature, or just *one*. They struggled with the problem of what happened to the divine characteristics (for example, omniscience, omnipresence) during the time that Jesus was on earth and was subject to the human limitations of localization, hunger, thirst, and incomplete knowledge (Mk. 13:32). Paul, however, had no such interest in theorizing; for him the important fact was that God had acted decisively in Christ for the redemption of his Creation. Paul had himself experienced this deliverance, and had taken his stand within the community that had similarly come to a new understanding of God's nature and purpose and that felt a new sense of kinship with him. Paul's task in his Letters, therefore, was to inform the members of the community about what God has done through Christ, and what the implications of this work of redemption were for the life and faith of the community.

Paul's classic statement of what God did through Christ is found in the Second Letter to the Corinthians (5:19): "God was in Christ, reconciling the world to himself. . . ." The meaning of these words is developed more fully in the fifth chapter of Romans, where Paul describes the whole human race as alienated from God, and actually at enmity with him. Man, conscious of his disobedience and burdened with a sense of guilt, had fled from God's presence as Adam had in the Genesis story. In his estranged state, man's resentment against God had mounted to the point where man became an enemy of his Creator. It was in this spiritually helpless condition that man had languished prior to the coming of Christ. In the obedient life of Jesus, man could see in concrete form what complete dedication to the will of God meant. Even though Jesus' life had ended in seeming defeat, God had vindicated him by raising him from the dead and exalting him at his right hand. There could be no doubt that God in Christ was victor over both sin and death. But in the extremity to which God went to achieve his redemptive purpose, the depth of God's love was made known. There was no limit to the grace of God, since he was willing to "put forward" (Rom. 3:25) his Son to die in order that men might understand his love and be reconciled to him.

When men responded in faith to God's redeeming act in Jesus Christ, they realized that Jesus, by his "obedience unto death" (Phil. 2:8), had removed the barrier of guilt that separated man from God, and had defeated the powers of evil who had sought to destroy him. The new relationship with God that results from his work in reconciliation in Christ is contrasted in detail with the results of Adam's disobedience (Rom. 5:12–21). Adam, the man who typi-fied the Old Creation, had violated the will of God, and had brought con-demnation and death on all humanity as a result. Christ's justifying act will result in the transformation of men from sinners into righteous, obedient People of God.

As the rest of the Letter to the Romans shows, this transformation is not merely a matter of juggling the records, as though God arbitrarily listed as righteous those who believed what he said. Paul makes clear that what God did in Christ was to remove the barriers that stood between man and himself, but that until man responds in faith to God's offer of reconciliation the work of redemption will have no effect on him. When man comes to a realization of what God has done, and responds in grateful trust, God's Spirit will begin to work in his heart, transforming and shaping his desires and aspirations in order to conform them to God's will. (This aspect of Paul's teaching about redemption will be treated more fully below.)

Christ as Preexistent

Paul did not feel that the importance of Jesus began with Jesus' birth, nor that it was confined to the promise of salvation to all mankind. Paul be-lieved that Jesus had existed before his birth, and that he was God's agent in creating the world. Furthermore, the program of redemption would not be complete until all Creation was restored to the condition that God had intended for it when he brought it into being. The idea of preexistence was a common one in the Judaism of Paul's day. In the Book of Psalms (139:13–16), the belief is expressed that a man's form and the whole pattern of his life are in existence in the plan of God before man is born. The claim to preexistence would not, therefore, in itself be unique. The uniqueness of Jesus lies in the creative role that he is described as having fulfilled before his incarnation—that is, before he assumed human form.

In the Wisdom Literature of Judaism, of which the Book of Proverbs is the most important representative in the Hebrew canon, there is the conviction that God is too sublime and exalted to have been involved in the business of creating the universe, and that this work was done through an intermediary. Usually, the intermediary is Wisdom, personified; at other times, Torah is described in personal terms as the creative agent. Paul adopted this concept of the intermediary through whom the Creation was accomplished, and modified it for his own purposes. Jesus Christ was the one in whom "all things were created, in heaven and earth . . . all things were created through him and for him" (Col. 1:16, 17). When the New Age has fully come, the whole of Creation will share in the benefits of redemption. The powers of evil that have held the created world in subjection will be overcome, and Creation will enter a new era of freedom comparable to the freedom that men of faith experience in the new life into which they enter through Jesus Christ (Rom. 8:18–23). Just as believers are called on to suffer in this life so that they may partake of glory in the Age to Come, so Creation itself groans like a woman in childbirth until the day of its deliverance from the powers of evil.

In barest outline, these are the chief meanings behind Paul's phrase, "God was in Christ." Although Paul refrains from saying that Jesus was God, he comes within a hair's breadth of doing so. He speaks of Jesus as "in the form of God" and as refusing to grasp at equality with God (Phil. 2:6). He ascribes to him the qualities and functions of God, as we have seen. He turns with ease from speaking of the grace of God to mention "the grace of our Lord Jesus Christ." Later New Testament writers define the relationship between Jesus and God in terms of virgin birth (Matthew and Luke), or develop the idea that Jesus was the preexistent Logos of God (Jn. I). Paul introduces his convictions about the nature of Jesus Christ only incidentally, when they help to drive home a practical point that has arisen in connection with the life of one of his churches. For example, the magnificent passage on Jesus' taking human form appears in Philippians 2 as an encouragement to the Christians to be humble.[4] The description in Colossians 1:15–20 is built up to pave the way for Paul's attack on a serious error that has developed in the Colossian church. Paul's chief concern in all that he wrote about the significance of Christ was to inform his readers of what God had done for them, and to relate to them his own liberating, transforming experience of the Christ who had appeared to him risen from the dead.

---

[4] R. Bultmann has declared that Paul is here drawing on a pre-Christian Gnostic's redeemer myth, which he has adopted and christianized. E. Käsemann has elaborated on this theory in *Exegetische Versuche und Besinnungen* (Tübingen: J. C. B. Mohr, 1962), pp. 51–95. Although it is generally agreed that Paul is using a pre-Pauline hymn at this point in Phil. 2, and although it might be conjectured that oriental syncretism of some sort may have affected the viewpoint and terminology of the hymn, there is as yet no clear evidence that in pre-Christian times Gnosticism had developed into a recognizable movement. (See pp. 28–33.)

IF ANY MAN BE IN CHRIST

[II CORINTHIANS 5:17]

The man who by faith in Jesus Christ had experienced reconciliation to God, Paul believed, was part of a whole new order of being. He was not just a reformed sinner; he was part of the "New Creation" to which everyone belonged who trusted Christ to bring him into right relationship with God. The new sphere of existence that was constituted by Christ's renewal of the Creation Paul identified by the simple phrase "in Christ" (Rom. 6).

All believers who have been baptized have, by participation in that rite, attested to their identification with Christ in his death, burial, and resurrection, which the rite symbolizes. Since they share with him by faith in his obedience unto death, they also now share with him in the new life that is brought into being by the Resurrection. Here is a form of human existence that is not subject to death, and that is triumphant over sin and the powers of evil which held the old life in subjection. Paul states the concept of the New Creation succinctly in writing to the Corinthians (I Cor. 15:22): "As in Adam all die, even so in Christ shall all be made alive." Again, we see the Hebrew conviction of the solidarity of God's People expressing itself in the inclusion of all humanity under two heads: Adam and Christ.

The fact that a man is "in Christ" does not free him from responsibility for his actions. His life should correspond to his spiritual status in the New Creation. Even though from the divine perspective the final outcome of the whole scheme of redemption is foreseen, it is man's responsibility to guide his actions and order his life in a manner befitting a Christian. So long as man is in his physical body, temptations to sin will always be present and the possibility of his yielding to the pull of the old life will continue to be very real. Nothing in his new status before God makes it impossible for him to allow sin to control his body. But Paul appeals to those who have discovered the potential for new life in Christ to avail themselves of their spiritual resources, and to allow God to use them for his purposes. We shall see later on that the service of God was a corporate rather than an individual matter, but each member was to see to it that the controlling influence of his life was obedience to God and not a yielding to sinful impulses. To sharpen the issue, Paul speaks as though there were no halfway house between the life of obedience and the life of sin. Either a man devoted himself to the service of God or he became the servant of sin, in spite of his having been set free from the power of sin. If he chose voluntarily to return to his former enslaved condition, God would permit him to exercise his own will in the matter.

But we must not infer from this passage in the Letter to the Romans that Paul thought a man must be either sinlessly perfect or hopelessly sinful. He makes this clear in writing to the Philippians (Phil. 3), when he tells them that he is himself bending every effort to increase in righteousness and to become more like Christ in his unconditional obedience to God's will. But he also warns them that he has not achieved perfection. Although failures have plagued him, he tries to leave them behind, pressing on to the prize that awaits the obedient. Yet the compelling force behind Paul's earnest striving was not "the prize," but an eagerness to express gratitude and devotion for the redemption that he and the whole community had experienced "in Christ."

WE WERE ALL BAPTIZED INTO ONE BODY

[I CORINTHIANS 12:13]

Paul's favorite metaphor to describe the community is "the body." This is a highly useful figure, since it is obviously familiar to everyone, and since it is capable of being developed in several ways to illustrate various aspects of the corporate life of the community.

The Unity of the Body

The first of these aspects—the unity of the body—we have already considered in Paul's dealing with the problem of the schisms that marred the unity of the Church at Corinth. But for Paul, the unity of the Church was not merely a feeling of togetherness but a belief in a mystical oneness "in Christ," with whom the Church was identified in death and resurrection. Developing the figure of "the body" in connection with another illustration, Paul demonstrates that the Christian, because he is a member of the Body of Christ, is free from obligation to the Law, just as a widow has no legal obligation to her husband after he has died (Rom. 7:1-6). And just as she is free to remarry, so the believer is now free to be joined in mystical union with Christ. The marital relationship as an illustration of religious experience is common in the Old Testament (cf. Hosea, Isaiah), but it was also widely used among devotees of the popular religions and mystery cults. Gentiles, then, would find this analogy familiar, even though they were not familiar with Torah.

Diversity within the Body

In Romans 12, Paul speaks of the need for the Church to recognize the diversity that must exist within the unity of the body. The one Spirit that came upon all believers in baptism is now at work in their midst to perform through them the various functions that are needed to carry on the work of God. The "gifts"—that is, the duties bestowed or the qualities granted by the Spirit to believers—include both participation in the active ministry of the

Church (prophecy, exhortation, teaching) and simple good works (contributions, acts of mercy). The body cannot function when every member wants to do the same job, or when any member thinks the others are negligent or unspiritual because their share in the work of the Church does not correspond to his. The Spirit is the one who operates within the members to show them their appointed tasks; the diversity of ways in which the Spirit manifests itself must never obscure the fact that there is just one Spirit behind all these differing functions.

The life of the community, like the life of the human body, is dependent on certain central organs. No member of a human body can live independently, although the body can continue to function even after some members have been removed. For Paul the central organ in a human body was the head, which he regarded as the seat of life. Analogously, the life of "members" in the Body of Christ was dependent upon the "Head" (Col. 2:18, 19)—that is, Christ. The head is not only the source of life for the entire body; it also determines the form of the body's growth and integrates the life of the whole body. The theme of the oneness of the body and its dependence on the head is developed much more elaborately in the Letter to the Ephesians, which, though it parallels Paul's thought, was probably not written by him (see p. 186).

The community, therefore, cannot consider itself as autonomous. It depends for its existence and for its continuance on Jesus Christ, who called the community into being, who died to seal the Covenant on which the community is founded, and who has sent the Spirit to guide and empower its corporate life.

WALK ACCORDING TO THE SPIRIT

[ROMANS 8:4]

The Spirit as Power

In the thinking of the Gentiles to whom Paul sought to interpret the Christian message, the existence of spirits and their power over human life were among the accepted facts of life. The phenomenon of demonic possession was a commonplace: the spirit that took control of a man might be beneficent, as in the case of the inspired prophetess of Apollo as the Delphic Oracle, or it might have a ruinous effect on a man's life and personality. The Greek word *pneuma*, like the Hebrew word *ruach*, meant "breath" or "wind" as well as "spirit"; so the evanescent, intangible quality of spirit was emphasized in the word itself. When Paul spoke of "the Spirit," however, he did not mean a generalized, immaterial force. In the thinking of the Stoic philosophers of Paul's day, even *pneuma* was a material substance, though a highly refined one. For Paul, "the Spirit" was the pervasive power of God through which his purposes were fulfilled. It is not surprising, therefore, that in Paul's Letters the person of Jesus and the Holy Spirit are very closely related. Occasionally, Paul will shift from one to the other without warning, as for example in Romans 8:10, 11, where he speaks of "Christ . . . in you" and, in the next breath, of "the Spirit . . . in you." It is as though the character and personality of God's continuing work of redemption were demonstrated in the person of Jesus, but as though the unseen yet efficacious power behind the work were defined as the Holy Spirit. In keeping with this relation between Christ and the Spirit, Paul describes the life "in Christ" as a life lived "according to the Spirit."

The Flesh against the Spirit

It has sometimes been supposed that it was frustration over his own inability to keep the Law that drove Paul into the Christian faith. If one were to read Romans 7:7–25 as a straightforward autobiographical account, then perhaps this understanding of Paul's alleged moral impotence would be justified. Probably, however, Paul is describing in this passage what he believed to be the struggle of every man in his own moral consciousness, as he was confronted on the one hand by what he acknowledged to be just moral requirements and on the other hand by his inner compulsion to ignore or defy those moral demands. Paul tells us in Philippians 3:4–6 that, so far as righteousness could be gauged by the Law, he was "blameless." What troubled him was not his inability to be law-abiding, but the unsatisfactory nature of his relationship to God in spite of his outward conformity to the demands of the Law.

The injunctions of Torah had proved to be a stimulus to disobedience rather than a means of moral achievement (Rom. 7:5–25). Now that he found himself liberated from the Law, and free to serve God through the new power that the Spirit had brought into his life, he characterized the life of defeat that he had previously experienced as life "in the flesh." By "flesh" Paul does not mean simply "the material body." Rather, "flesh" is the quality of being human, with such inevitable limitations as transitoriness, apprehension, and weakness. The flesh relies on insecure foundations in its misguided effort to stabilize life. It judges by appearances and fails to understand the nature of reality. It mistakes the worldly standards of wealth, force, and social approval for the real values in life. It was through these susceptibilities in man that the tempter in Eden was able to lead man to disobey God, by arousing his pride and by promising power that was supposed to come through increased knowledge. It is these ethical and religious considerations that Paul has in mind when he contrasts the life "in the flesh" with the life "in the Spirit." He is not identifying "flesh" with matter and then simply echoing the dualistic belief that matter is inherently evil and that only spirit is good.

All humanity, or, to translate literally, "all flesh" (Rom. 3:20), stood under condemnation and moral helplessness because of the inability of man to do the will of God even with the aid of Torah, the classic statement of God's purpose for his people. Undeterred by the ineffectiveness of Torah to bring man into right relationship with God, God sent his son, who was identified with humanity in every way, except that he was wholly obedient. Thus the hold which sin maintained upon humanity, through the weakness of the flesh, was broken; or, as Paul phrases it "[Christ] condemned sin *in the flesh*" (Rom. 8:3). Now, those who are in Christ measure up to the requirements of the Law; but they do so, not by moral striving, but through the power of the Spirit at work within their lives. Men of faith, therefore, "walk, not according to the flesh, but according to the Spirit" (Rom. 8:1–11).

In the life according to the Spirit, Paul testifies that he found peace and a sense of kinship with God that striving to obey the Law had never brought. That feeling of intimacy with God is epitomized in the term of address that Paul uses in prayer: "Abba" (Rom. 8:15), a word that is commonly used by Aramaic-speaking people when talking to their fathers. For Paul, therefore, the working of the Spirit was not some vague, impersonal force, but an intimate experience of closeness to God that his former life in Judaism had never made possible.

Life "in the Spirit" was not, however, free from difficulty or conflict. Paul was able to endure the difficulties that overtook him because he was convinced that they were the prelude to a New Age of Righteousness that was to come. Here, too, the role of the Spirit was an important one: the presence of the Spirit was an anticipation of the new situation that would obtain throughout Creation when the will of God triumphed over all opposition (Rom. 8:23). As he phrased it in writing to the Corinthians (II Cor. 1:22), the Spirit that dwelt within him was a guarantee or a kind of "down payment" on the time of consummation that lay in the future. Until that time came, however, the Spirit was at hand to give guidance to the man of faith in praying to God (Rom. 8:26–27). In the midst of trials, men of faith could look forward to the day when God's purpose for Creation would be fulfilled, confident that God was even now at work shaping events to his ends (Rom. 8:28ff.). But until the time of total victory came, the man of faith might live his life free from guilt and fear, conscious that nothing could separate him from God's love (Rom. 8:31–39).

The Commands of the Spirit

Paul recognized, as Jesus had earlier, that it was not enough to tell a man that he should obey God; some specific indications of attitude and actions were needed. As real as Paul felt the power of the Spirit to be, he was careful in his Letters to include a set of detailed, practical instructions by which the communities could regulate their corporate and personal lives. "What is good and acceptable and perfect" (Rom. 12:2) had to be spelled out in unmistakable terms. In the concrete ethical injunctions that are given in Rom. 12, 13, and 15, there are a few instances in which Paul's language parallels that of the Greek ethical systems of his day, but the whole orientation of Paul's ethics is much more Hebraic than Greek. His appeal rests on love and gratitude to God, rather than on the essential logic of his ethic. He does not discuss the abstract principle of the "good," nor does he even ask what the duty of man is. Rather, the life of service and dedication to which man is called is simply a response to "the mercies of God" that believers have experienced in Jesus Christ.

The nearest that Paul comes to a formal set of ethical precepts is the list of instructions in the Letter to the Colossians. There (Col. 3:5–4:6), Paul gives advice to the various members of the Christian families to guide them in their mutual relations. A similar, though longer, list is found in the post-Pauline Letter to the Ephesians (4:25–6:20). Yet even in didactic passages such as these, Paul is not merely telling men that they should be better. The whole appeal is set in the context of the forgiveness of God in Christ, the operation of the Spirit in the lives of the faithful, the love of Christ for the Church, the need of the Church for maintaining the respect of those who are not members. For Paul, the ideal was not conformity to a standard of virtue, but the dedication of oneself to God—that is, sanctification. It was the holy character of God with whom man had, through Christ, been brought into a relationship that required purity of life on the part of man; it was not merely that goodness was reasonable, or "according to nature," as the Stoics phrased it. Man's nature led him away from the will of God, but the Spirit of God at work within him both aroused the urge to do right and gave man the moral strength to achieve the right. To experience this inner transformation was to "walk according to the Spirit."

WE SHALL ALL BE CHANGED

[I CORINTHIANS 15:51]

As we have observed (p. 220), Christianity cannot be appropriately described as the religion of individualism, even though Protestant Christianity has, in fact, stressed individual freedom throughout its history. From the beginning, the Christian faith affirmed that God's purpose was to create a *community* of the obedient, not merely to snatch isolated individuals from destruction. We have seen that Paul was concerned with the establishment of the New People of God, a group that he believed to be already in the process of formation but that would come to its fullness at some time in the future.

Has God Turned from the Jews?

This conviction raised for Paul an acute problem, which he dealt with at length in the Letter to the Romans (Rom. 9–11)—namely, the relation of the former People, Israel, to the New People, the Church. In this extended passage he acknowledges the place of peculiar favor that Israel enjoyed because the earlier covenant was established with her, the prophets spoke through her, and the promises of future blessings for creation were given to her. But just as God acted in sovereign choice among various descendants of Abraham, choosing some for honor and passing others by, so God has now chosen to pass Israel by temporarily in order to have his message of redemption proclaimed to the Gentiles. Since God is the sovereign Creator of his universe, man is in no position to dispute the wisdom or justice of his actions (Rom. 9:14–24). Israel will share ultimately in the blessings that are now being enjoyed by faith among those who, whether Jew or Gentile, respond in faith to the gospel. The tragic mistake of Israel has been her effort to gain standing before God by her own efforts in obedience to Torah (Rom. 9:24–10:4). At this point (Rom. 10:5ff.), Paul uses a method of interpreting the Old Testament that seems strange to modern readers, but that was an accepted practice among the rabbis of his day. He takes a few phrases from the Book of Deuteronomy (30:12–14) which declare in a vivid way how the word of God has been made readily accessible to man in Torah; he then interprets these phrases as referring to the word of the gospel, which has now been proclaimed to all men, whether Jew or Gentile. The one response demanded of man is that he confess "Jesus is Lord." His lips and his heart are to give outward expression to his inner trust.

If men are to be brought into the fellowship of the People of God by response to the *kerygma*, someone will have to serve as a proclaimer of the Good News. Faith can arise only when men have heard (Rom. 10:14ff.). Israel has heard and has not responded in faith, however, because God's purpose is that the Gentiles should be saved as a result of Israel's failure. Israel's rejection of the Messiah made redemption possible; her rejection of the message about the Messiah had led the Christian preachers to turn to the Gentiles with it (Rom. 10:18–11:12). But Paul is convinced that Israel will not persist in her unbelief indefinitely; she will return to God. And when she does, the blessings that will follow for all the world will be immeasurably greater than before she turned away in disobedience.

Paul develops an extended allegory of the grafting of branches onto an olive tree. The allegory is difficult from the standpoint of logic as well as of horticulture (Rom. 11:13–24). But the point is clear: God still will have a purpose for Israel when his work of summoning the Gentiles to obedient trust has been completed. A divinely determined number of Gentiles must come into the fellowship of God's People, and the New Age will not come in its fullness until that number has been reached (Rom. 11:25ff.). The argument in verses 28 to 32 is not clear, and it involves Paul in a series of contrasts that are perhaps overdrawn. But the passage ends in a majestic hymn of praise to God, whose wisdom transcends man's capacity to comprehend. Man may rest assured that God's purpose is effectively at work throughout his creation. From his poetic outburst of praise to God, Paul turns to practical considerations (Rom. 11:33–36).

In contrast to the inconclusiveness of the discussion about the place of the Jews in God's plan, Paul was certain of two things: that he had reason to be proud of his heritage of Jewish faith and piety, and that God had called him to turn from the Jew to the Gentile as the major target of his evangelizing. The passage from Romans 9, 10, and 11 summarized in the preceding pages gives evidence of the importance Paul attached to the whole question of the relation between the community of the Old Covenant in which Paul had been reared, and the community of the New Covenant in which he was now at work in the service of God. He was convinced that "in Christ" there was no place for racial distinction (I Cor. 12:13), and yet he believed that the promises made by God to Israel were not simply abrogated by Israel's unbelief. The Jewish hope of the coming Kingdom of God was a strong element in Paul's thinking (I Cor. 15:24ff.), and, as a result, he made no attempt to legislate for a Christian society or to give instructions for the establishment of a new social order. At "the end," God would restore Israel to favor and to faith, and would defeat his enemies, thereby establishing his rule over Creation. Paul longed for the day of peace and deliverance, and labored for its coming. It was not his task to bring in the Kingdom; he was charged with the mission of preaching the Good News, and thus preparing men for the Kingdom that God was about to establish.

What Will Eternal Life Be Like?

Although one of Paul's major concerns was for the future of the community, he did have words of comfort and admonition about the future for individuals as well (p. 200). It is impossible to reconstruct a neat system out of Paul's thoughts on the theme of the future life even though he dealt at length with the subject in I Corinthians 15. At times, he writes as though he expected to be transported immediately to the presence of Christ when he died (Phil. 1:23). At other times, he speaks of those who have died as being asleep, awaiting the trumpet call at the Day of Resurrection (I Cor. 15:51; I Thess. 4:13). In one famous passage, he describes a "body" in which the believer is "clothed" at death, when he is transported into the presence of the Lord (II Cor. 5:1–4). In I Cor. 15, however, Paul speaks of the "spiritual body" as though it were bestowed at the time of the Resurrection, rather than immediately upon death. Efforts have been made to reconcile these two aspects of Paul's thought by assuming that in II Corinthians 5 Paul was describing an intermediate state. A similar diversity of detail we have already noted (p. 203) is to be seen in a comparison of I Thess. 4 and II Thess. 2. In the first passage, the return of Christ is expected with little delay, since Paul's hope was to see that event; in the second passage, Paul explains what must happen in the interim before Christ's return. But what is most important is that Paul was not interested in developing a systematic theology; he was living in a time of crisis, during which his job was to preach, to exhort, to instruct, to prepare men for the coming of the New Age.

PART FOUR

THE COMMUNITY
CONFRONTS
THE WORLD

For the later generations of Gentile Christians Paul became the symbol of the all-important step which moved beyond the confines of the Jewish community. In fact, the historical importance of Paul's work for the expansion of the Christian mission can hardly be overestimated, even though he remained a controversial figure in early Christian circles and was admittedly only one among a large number of missionaries who carried the message into the scattered regions of the empire during the latter half of the first century.

Luke's account of the Christian beginnings gives an impression of the high esteem in which the apostle was held by early generations. He not only parallels Paul's role with that of Peter, the leader of the Twelve, but implies that it was primarily through Paul that God carried out his purpose beyond the limited beginnings of the "ends of the earth" (Acts 1:8). Numerous legends about the person of the apostle were soon in circulation, celebrating him as a unique hero in the cause of God.

As in the case of other apostles, we have extensive fragments of so-called "Acts of Paul" which in popular fashion tell of the adventures of the apostle on his journeys, using the itinerary of the canonical Acts as a basis, and filling in with fabulous details and legendary stories.[1] A central part is the romantic account of Paul and the noblewoman Thecla with its focus on the standard themes of Paul preaching the Resurrection and the need for continence. The book ends with a fictitious "Martyrdom of Paul," according to which Paul was beheaded in Rome, but after his death appeared to the frightened emperor (Nero) prophesying to him God's punishment for his wickedness.

More problematic was the apparent use of Paul as the favorite authority in certain heretical movements. Ascetic as well as antinomian and even libertine tendencies were justified by an appeal to his position, and Gnostics seem to have written the earliest commentaries on the Pauline Letters in order to prove their esoteric speculations. Marcion (see pp. 4, 256–257) reveals his intention of merely drawing out the implications of Paul's theology by giving ten Letters of Paul (Galatians, I and II Corinthians, Romans, I and II Thessalonians, Ephesians [here called Laodiceans], Colossians, Philippians, Philemon) the prominent place in his canon. This trend caused considerable embarrassment in the Church, which continued to revere Paul as one of its founding heroes. The latest book of the New Testament, the so-called Second Letter of Peter, contains a remark illustrating this uneasiness. The author who presumably is fighting libertine Gnostics and defending the Christian hope of the Second Coming against doubts arising from its long delay, connects his final appeal with a reference to the "misuse" of Paul:

> So also our beloved brother Paul wrote to you according to the wisdom given him, speaking of this as he does in all his letters. There are some things in them hard to understand, which the ignorant and unstable twist to their own destruction, as they do the other scriptures.
> —II PETER 3:15–16

The passage, in the first place, witnesses to the unquestioned authority of Paul in the Church of this time. A collection of Paul's Letters is already Christian literature of equal standing with "the other scriptures"—i.e., the Old Testament. They are regarded as a common possession and therefore as being addressed to every Christian generation. But the author also issues a warning. In the new situation of his time, the "wisdom" given to the great apostle may have its limitations and therefore stands in need of supplementation and interpretation—just as the other scriptures do (cf. II Pet. 1:20ff.). The polemic obviously is directed against false teaching that claims to stand in the Pauline tradition.

The figure of the great apostle proved to be even more of a stumbling block in another context. It seems that the opposition of a strict Jewish-Christian wing against Paul's doctrine of freedom from the Law did not subside, and

---

[1]See texts and introduction in E. Hennecke and W. Schneemelcher, *New Testament Apocrypha*, II, ed. R. McL. Wilson (Philadelphia: Westminster, 1965), 322–390.

even found literary expression. Under the name of Clement of Rome, we have preserved for us a rather sentimental Christian novel, perhaps the first one of its kind. It tells the story of the reunification of Clement's family, which through various misfortunes had been dispersed all over the world. Instrumental in the happy reunion is the apostle Peter, the true hero of the story. Presented as a traveling missionary and philosopher, Peter is involved in a fierce battle with the "sorcerer" Simon (cf. Acts 8:9ff.), following him through various cities along the Palestinian-Syrian coast and refuting his teachings in lengthy sermons until he finally convicts him publicly in a debate at Laodicea. The writing, known as the "pseudo-Clementine novel," has come to us in two different recensions, the "Homilies" and the "Recognitions," both of which seem to go back to an earlier version, perhaps written in Syria early in the third century and now lost.[2] Obviously, various sources have been used in the composition of the prototype, among them the "Preachings of Peter," a Gnosticizing Jewish-Christian document which many scholars assume to go back as far as the beginning of the second century A.D. In this document, Paul and his "lawless" teaching were the target of most violent attacks, which in the later orthodox recension of the novel had to be eliminated; this was done simply by substituting the figure of the arch-heretic Simon, who now displayed the same features used to characterize Paul in the original document.

Quite apart from these problems with the great apostle, one thing is clear. Paul's vision of Christianity, and his deliberate mission outside the limits of Judaism were bound to lead to more difficulties both with the Jewish community which, toward the end of the century, underwent a series of profound trials, and with the authorities of the Roman world into which the Church was quickly moving. We will have to discuss the development of both conflicts before we come back to the post-Pauline Letters of the New Testament.

THE CONFLICT OF CHURCH AND JUDAISM

The fact that after the close of the apostolic age leadership in the Church passed from Christians brought up in a Jewish religious tradition and converted as adults, to Christians brought into the faith from paganism and nurtured in it by non-Jewish parents, did not lessen the tension between Jew and Christian. On the contrary, as long as there was a strong group of loyal Jewish Christians in the Palestinian heartland, they felt most keenly the mounting antagonism as they became more and more identified by their Jewish compatriots as an apostate sect dominated by non-Jews. The Jerusalem church itself was subjected to an unprecedented persecution by Jewish author-

---

[2]A full translation of both recensions is found in Volume VIII of *The Ante-Nicene Fathers* (reprint, Grand Rapids, Mich.: Eerdmans, n.d.), pp. 73ff. The English text of a reconstruction of the *Kerygmata Petrou* by G. Strecker is in Hennecke-Schneemelcher, *op. cit.*, pp. 111–127.

ities in the years immediately following the death of Paul. The events surrounding the fall of Jerusalem to the Roman army in A.D. 70 gave the final direction for future relations. It meant the complete withdrawal of Jewish Christianity from the tragic fate of Judaism, and at the same time the surviving Jewish community's final rejection of Christianity as an intra-Jewish option. In the wake of the national disaster, disappointed Jews still turned in fair numbers to the new messianic faith in the various provinces of the Empire; but with the consolidation of Judaism under the rabbis toward the end of the century, which was a necessary act of self-defense, this choice was rapidly becoming a choice between Jew *or* Christian.

Evidence of mounting hostility between Jew and Christian in the later first century is found in both Jewish and Christian sources. The rabbinic traditions that have been preserved from this period refer to Christians as *minim* (heretics) and reflect growing fears about the divisive consequences of the new faith for Jewish identity. The story that Jesus was the illegitimate son of Mary by a Roman soldier appears to have originated with Jewish polemicists of the time.[3] Concurrently, the Christians were modifying the Gospel stories to intensify feelings against the Jewish leaders by portraying them as having assumed full blame for the death of Jesus. Matthew quotes the Jews as saying at Jesus' trial, "His blood be on us and our children" (Mt. 27:25). The fact that these words link the sad fate of the Jews with their alleged guilt in such strong terms, coupled with the fact that they are found in none of the other Gospel accounts of Jesus' trial, suggests that they were added as a polemic against the Jews at or shortly before the time Matthew wrote his Gospel.

Similarly, the harsh treatment that Jewish converts to Christianity received at the hands of Jewish authorities and synagogue leaders during this period is reflected in the New Testament writings in various ways. Evidence of Jewish-Christian tensions appears in the heightening of the element of conflict in the gospel accounts of Jesus' encounters with the Pharisees; it is included in the predictions of persecution for faithful disciples in the apocalyptic section of Mark (Mk. 13:5ff.), and in the stories of Jesus sending the disciples out to preach (Mt. 10:17–25; cf. Lk. 12:4–12; 21:12–19). These specific warnings of Jewish opposition were probably added by the early Church to Jesus' predictions of the general resistance that preachers of the Gospel would meet, and the additions were probably made just when Jewish hostility to Christianity was mounting everywhere. In three different passages, the Gospel of John speaks of the practice of putting a man out of the synagogue if he confesses that Jesus is the Christ (9:22; 12:42; 16:2), and we know that Christian congregations in Asia Minor called the local synagogue "synagogues of Satan" (Rev. 2:9ff.; 3:8ff.) because they were permanently kept out of them.

The full extent of animosity between Christian and Jew during the later

---

[3]For a survey of anti-Christian elements in the rabbinic tradition, see J. Klausner, *Jesus of Nazareth* (New York: Macmillan, 1926), pp. 18–54.

decades of the century is reflected in the Gospel of John, especially in the story of the Passion. The whole movement of the trial scenes in John points up the belief that Pilate could find no cause for condemning Jesus, but that he yielded to the pressure of "the Jews." The very phrase, "the Jews," quite apart from its Johannine use as shorthand for "unbelievers," demonstrates that for the audience of the Gospel, the wide differences between Jewish sects that prevailed in Jesus' day no longer existed, so that all opposition from Jewish quarters could be lumped together as traceable to "the Jews." The author does have a high regard for the Jewish roots of Christianity as the true Israel, and for Jesus' own mission among his fellow Jews (4:22; 19:19). But even Jesus himself is now quoted as putting the major blame on his own people: "He who has delivered me to you has the greater sin" (19:11)—that is, the Jews are really responsible for his death. Further evidence of conflict between Jew and Christian in the time when John's gospel was written is to be found in the questions that appear throughout the book, always on the lips of the Jewish antagonists: "Is not this Jesus, the son of Joseph, whose father and mother we know?" (6:42); "How can this man give us his flesh to eat?" (6:52); "Are you greater than our father, Abraham?" (8:53). From the words of the prologue, "His people received him not" (1:11), throughout the book the theme recurs that "the Jews" were obstinate and blind in their failure to accept Jesus as the Christ.

The mutual ill will between Christian and Jew that developed at this time is apparent not only in the literature of the period, but also in direct reports of specific incidents from Christian and non-Christian sources. Luke says that Herod Agrippa "pleased the Jews" by executing James (and possibly his brother John, see p. 240), though it seems unlikely that the idea of persecuting the Christians originated with Herod. At any rate, he continued the persecution in Jerusalem by arresting Peter who, however, escaped and left (Acts 12:2–19). With Peter, James, and John removed as leaders of the Jerusalem community (about A.D. 44), the tensions between Christians and Jews relaxed for a while. When James, Jesus' brother, took over as head of the church in Jerusalem (cf. Acts 12:17; Gal. 1:19; 2:9), he was eager to maintain good relations with the Jewish leaders, especially since his own convictions and practices were quite traditional. It was he who took the initiative in demanding that Gentile Christians respect certain aspects of Jewish legal regulations (Acts 15:13ff.; 21:25; see p. 391), and who was most embarrassed by Paul's presence in Jerusalem, since Paul was notorious for his contacts with Gentiles and for his concessions to their way of life (Acts 21:20–24). The Jerusalem Christians, at least until A.D. 62, were zealous to demonstrate their loyalty to Judaism by participating in the Temple worship and strictly observing the Law. Even the riot stirred up by Paul in A.D. 55 does not appear to have resulted in immediate unfavorable reactions against the Jerusalem Christians. In any case, they remained aloof from the incident and made no effort to come to Paul's aid. According to one theory, Paul's removal was in fact such a boost to the Jerusalem leadership of the entire Church that Christianity could have developed again into a Jewish sectarian movement.[4]

However, two incidents ended this peace and sharpened the conflict. In A.D. 62, James, the brother of Jesus, was put to death by order of the High Priest. There are two independent—and probably irreconcilable—accounts of the execution of James.[5] Josephus, the Jewish historian of the period, tells in his *Antiquities* that Annas, the High Priest, sentenced James to death on an alleged violation of Jewish Law. The sentence was passed and the execution performed during the interim between the death of Festus (A.D. 62) and the arrival of Albinus, his successor; so the absence of a Roman governor provided Annas with an opportunity to act independently. Probably Annas wanted to destroy James out of resentment for his popularity with the people, who seem to have admired James' piety. Since James was famous for his fidelity to the Law, the charge brought against him by Annas was almost certainly false. There was a strong reaction to Annas' plot, both from the Jewish officials, who sought to have Annas deposed, and from the procurator himself, who did in fact remove Annas from the high priesthood.

The other account of the death of James comes to us in two forms from Eusebius, who quotes from two of the Church Fathers, Clement of Alexandria (around A.D. 200) and Hegesippus (around A.D. 180). According to these stories, James was first thrown down from a pinnacle of the Temple and then beaten on the head by a workman with a club until he died. The details of the story are what we would expect to find in a legend of the death of a martyr. Although Josephus' more sober version is to be preferred to the accounts in Eusebius, the stories agree that James was executed by an official Jewish action in spite of, and in part because of, his popularity with the people of Jerusalem.

The climax of the conflict came with the events of the Jewish revolt against Roman occupation in the years A.D. 66–70. At first, the Jews succeeded in liberating parts of the land from Roman control; the independence of the Jewish nation was declared, and Jewish coinage was issued. But the poorly armed bands of revolutionaries could not withstand the 60,000 seasoned troops that Rome sent in to quell the revolt. By the year 69 all of Palestine, except for Jerusalem and some outlying fortresses near the Dead Sea, was once again under Roman control.

Vespasian, who commanded the Roman troops, could have quickly destroyed all resistance, but his mind was occupied with other matters: the Emperor Nero had died under mysterious circumstances in 68, and Vespasian's chances of succeeding him were excellent. Accordingly, Vespasian held back from the

---

[4]This is part of the thesis of S. G. F. Brandon, *The Fall of Jerusalem and the Christian Church: A Study of the Effects of the Jewish Overthrow of A.D. 70 on Christianity*, 2nd ed. (London: S.P.C.K., 1957).

[5]These accounts are quoted and analyzed in detail by M. Goguel, *The Birth of Christianity* (New York: Macmillan, 1954), pp. 124–132.

fighting for a time to see what the outcome of the contest for the imperial throne would be. When it became clear that the army in the East would declare for him, he returned to Rome. His rivals faded from the scene, and he became emperor in 69. His son, Titus, who had been left in charge of the troops in Palestine, now pressed the siege of Jerusalem.

The city's resistance might have been greater if the people had not been torn by internal dissension. At the start of the revolt there had been two parties: the peace party, whose members believed God would free the nation from Rome in his own time and by his own methods; and the resistance party, whose adherents were convinced that the time had come for them to take the initiative in driving the Romans out. With the advent of the Roman troops, the peace party was overwhelmed by the rebels, but any prospect of success for the revolt was ended when the rebels began to fight among themselves under rival leaders. The civil strife continued within the city even during the siege. Although the revolutionaries had killed Annas, who had caused James' death, the Christians appear to have been in sympathy with the peace party. They believed that the hope of the nation lay in the return of their Messiah to establish the reign of God, not in military victory. The siege, which began in April of the year 70, lasted five months, and during this time thousands died of starvation. Then, when the city fell, the Romans laid waste to it and demolished the Temple.

THE FATE OF THE JERUSALEM CHURCH

Presumably it was just before the siege began that the Jerusalem Christians decided to flee to a place of safety. At first glance, it seems clear that the reason they fled was to escape destruction at the hands of the Romans, but Eusebius tells us that they went to the Gentile city of Pella, east of the Jordan in the region of the Decapolis, in response to a divine oracle.[6] Certain questions immediately arise: What was the nature of the oracle? Why did it tell them to go to a despised Gentile town like Pella, which had been among those attacked by the Jewish nationalists only a few years earlier? Why were the Jewish Christians—traditionally so fastidious about maintaining separateness from Gentiles—willing to seek refuge in a Gentile stronghold? Considering these questions in reverse order, the probability is that the Jerusalem Christians were willing to compromise their religious scruples for the sake of saving their own necks. The only place of safety for Jews who had opposed the revolt would be a place like Pella, which was predominantly Gentile and hence free of Jewish nationalist feeling. There they would be safe from the Romans, who might have taken them for rebels in Jerusalem, and safe from the rebels, who might have treated them as traitors.

Eusebius gives another theory to explain the flight of the Christians from

---

[6]Eusebius, *Ecclesiastical History*, III.5.3.

Jerusalem. He suggests that the Roman emperors, from Vespasian on, sought out all descendants of David in an effort to exterminate the Jewish hope of a revival of the Davidic Dynasty. Since Jesus was from "the seed of David" (Rom. 1:4), he and his relatives would have been in a royal line, and his brothers and other surviving relatives would have been the victims of Vespasian had they remained within his reach at Jerusalem. On this theory, the flight to Pella would have been a communal effort to protect Jesus' family, to whom had passed the leadership of the Jerusalem community.[7] This story of Eusebius, like the ones about James mentioned above, bears the marks of legendary embroidering, and really conveys little more than the general impression that (1) the Romans did not understand the nature of Christian messianic beliefs, and mistakenly identified them with the nationalistic hopes of Judaism, and (2) the former Jerusalem wing of Christianity had already lapsed into such complete obscurity by the end of the second century that there were no precise recollections of what had happened to it after the city of Jerusalem fell to the Romans.

As for the oracle that instructed the Christians to flee, there is a possibility that it may be imbedded in the apocalyptic section that precedes the Passion story in each of the synoptic gospels (Mt. 24; Mk. 13; Lk. 21). The phrase in Mark 13:14: "let the reader understand," is often interpreted as referring to the reader of the oracle, which Eusebius tells us was circulated in Jerusalem at the time of the Roman invasion.

Although we do not know exactly what happened to the Christians after they fled from Jerusalem, we do know that the destruction of Jerusalem by the Romans was interpreted by Christians generally as a divine judgment on Judaism for its rejection of Jesus as the Christ. This conviction is plainly and repeatedly stated in Eusebius, and it is easy to read between the lines of the gospels. The very fact that the apocalyptic section mentioned above was incorporated into the synoptics shows that the fall of Jerusalem was considered a major event in the unfolding of the purpose which God had begun with the coming of Jesus. The destruction was understood as the final proof that the Old Dispensation had come to an end, and that a New Israel had taken the place of the old.

On the other hand, the catastrophe of A.D. 70 was for the remnant of faithful Jews the signal to draw even more closely together in order to save the paternal heritage and at least a remnant of national identity. School differences and religious quarrels became less important in the face of the threat to sheer survival. The last decades of the first century saw the emergence of Pharisaism as the one and only "normative" religious trend in Palestine that greatly helped to keep something like a Jewish identity. It is in connection with this process that the Jews themselves were pressing for a sharper separation from the Christians. When during the reign of Hadrian, the Jews attempted a second

---

[7]Eusebius, *ibid.*

revolt (A.D. 132–135) which eventually led to the total destruction of the city of Jerusalem and the erection of a pagan city, Aelia Capitolina, on the site, the military leader of their guerrilla army, Simon Bar Kokhba (Bar Koseba) is said to have persecuted the Christians who would not join the revolt.[8] The wiping out of the last rebels spelled the end of a Palestinian center of Judaism and Christianity for some time to come. The conflict between Jew and Christian moved into the arena of contacts between local synagogues and gentile Christian churches in the various provinces of the empire.

Yet the distinctive Jewish Christian heritage was not completely lost. Writers in the second century, and again in the fourth, tell of various groups living east of the Jordan, some of whom may have been the survivors of Jewish Christianity. One of these sects, known as the Ebionites (meaning "poor"), appears to have been directly related to the Jerusalem community, which also called itself "the poor" (Gal. 2:10; Rom. 15:26; cf. Lk. 6:20).[9] The Ebionites are reported to have regarded Jewish Law and tradition as the basis for their outlook and practices. From all the Christian writings, they accepted as scripture only the Gospel of Matthew, although they denied the virgin birth of Jesus. Judged by the standards of Pauline Christianity or by the growing orthodoxy of the Fathers of the second century, the Ebionites seem scarcely to be Christian at all.

None of these Jewish-Christian groups east of the Jordan retained the Jerusalem type of Christianity unchanged; under the influence of the unorthodox Jewish sects in the Jordan region, they engaged in fantastic elaborations of the faith. Early in the second century there appeared a prophet named Elxai (Alexis in Greek), who insisted on the observance of the full Jewish ritual, but who recognized Christ as Son of God. Elxai had first-hand knowledge of Christ, since he had seen him in a vision in which Christ appeared as a mountain ninety-six miles high!

Fortunately for the subsequent history of Christianity, this type of bizarre speculation never became a dominant factor in the Church. Like the rivers of Damascus, it flowed out to the edge of the desert and vanished. The church buildings that have survived in this territory east of the Jordan date from the time of Constantine (fourth century) or later, and demonstrate by their form and decoration that the orthodox type of Christianity eventually prevailed here as elsewhere. Jewish Christianity as a distinct phenomenon died out.

THE FATE OF THE APOSTLES

The later fate of most of the original Jerusalem apostles is unknown to us. The death of James, the brother of the Lord, has been discussed in connection

---

[8]On the episode in the light of recent discoveries, see J. A. Fitzmyer, "The Bar-Cochba Period," in *The Bible in Current Catholic Thought*, J. L. McKenzie, ed. (New York: Herder & Herder, 1962), pp. 133–168.

[9]See the discussion of the poor on p. 156.

with the fall of Jerusalem. Jude, in the letter that bears his name, is depicted as calling himself "Jude, the brother of James." About Jude we know nothing else, although there was a person of this name among the brothers of Jesus (Mk. 6:3; Mt. 13:55). He would have been dead at the time of Domitian when his grandsons were investigated by the future emperor as being descendants of David and therefore possible pretenders to the Jewish throne.[9]

As to the fate of James and John, the sons of Zebedee (Mk. 1:19; 10:35), we have very little to go on. James was the first victim of Herod Agrippa (Acts 12:2; see above, p. 235); later tradition supports the suggestion that his brother John died with him in A.D. 44. Irenaeus in the late second century speaks of the residence in Ephesus of the venerable John, "a disciple of the Lord," for which report he is probably relying on the earlier witness of Papias. Papias' own account seems to have differentiated between John the Elder (to whom Irenaeus probably is referring) and John the son of Zebedee. It is possible that the John of Ephesus (John the Elder) was one who had become a follower of Jesus during his lifetime, and who had subsequently become a leader of the church in the vicinity of Ephesus following his migration there from Palestine. The remark by bishop Polycrates of Ephesus (mid-second century) that John of Ephesus was a priest, would fit with this conjecture. Significantly, in these early patristic references, John of Ephesus is described as a "disciple," not as an "apostle." Thus, the tradition that connects the Johannine Gospel and Letters (and the Revelation) with John of Ephesus does not claim that these works were written by the apostle John, the son of Zebedee, who probably was long dead by this time.

The Acts of the Apostles report the departure of Peter from Jerusalem at

---

[9]Eusebius, *Ecclesiastical History*, III.20.6.

OBELISK
in St. Peter's Square, brought to Rome from Egypt by the emperor Caligula. The obelisk was placed by Nero in the pleasure gardens that he built between the low hills of the Vatican. (Alinari/Art Reference Bureau)

the time of the persecution under Herod Agrippa, but give us no information as to where he went (Acts 12:17). He reappears briefly in Acts 15 at the time of the so-called Jerusalem Council, though he is called "Symeon" on that occasion (Acts 15:14). There is strong support for the theory that he spent much time on extended missionary journeys. Later Church tradition claims that Peter went to Rome and that he became the first bishop of the church there. There is considerable plausibility in the report that he was martyred in Rome under Nero (A.D. 64) in the same year that Paul was executed. Since

THE MARTYRION
was a simple shrine erected over the probable burial place of Peter. The remains of this shrine, which date back to the beginning of the second century, were discovered directly below the high altar of St. Peter's Church in Rome. The fact that the shrine is in the midst of pagan tombs tends to confirm its authenticity, since it is unlikely that Christians would have invented a burial place for Peter on unholy ground. The martyrdom of Peter is reported to have occurred in the reign of Nero in the gardens between the Vatican hills.

Peter was not a Roman citizen, he could have been crucified, as tradition reports he was. The site of his execution and burial is thought to have been in the gardens of Nero, which lay across the Tiber from the main part of Rome. It is in this area that archeologists have uncovered a pagan cemetery, in the midst of which is a memorial thought to have been erected in honor of Peter by early Roman Christians. Over this spot was built the Church of St. Peter in the time of Constantine, which was replaced in the sixth century by the great Renaissance Basilica of St. Peter.[10]

We have only traces or pious legends about the fate of some other apostles. Thomas is said to have gone to India, where the Mar Thoma Church preserves his name. Andrew, the brother of Peter, may have preached in Northern Greece and Scythia. He is reported to have been crucified at Patras, Greece. The most

---

[10]For a full discussion, see Daniel W. O'Connor, *Peter in Rome: The Literary, Liturgical and Archeological Evidence* (New York: Columbia University Press, 1969). A comprehensive investigation of the Peter question is O. Cullmann, *Peter: Disciple, Apostle, Martyr,* rev. ed. (Philadelphia: Westminster, 1963).

significant monument of all that the Jerusalem apostles left was their living witness to Jesus, the risen Christ, and to the power of the Spirit by which the Church believed God was guiding it in the changing situations that it confronted as the first Christian century ended.

THE GROWING CONFLICT WITH ROME

With the missionary effort of Paul and his fellow workers the Christian message had moved rapidly into the wide world of the Roman Empire. The success of the movement in some areas, *e.g.*, Asia Minor, must have been astonishing. For the post-Pauline churches, the political and religious situation in their particular corner and the reaction of the Roman authorities to their faith was soon more important than the continuing conflict with the Jews. The new conflict, which eventually led to the persecution of Christian minorities by the civil authorities, was not deliberately sought by the Christians, neither was it precipitated by deliberate action of the state. It was an almost inevitable consequence of the rapid growth of the Christian community and of the peculiar convictions of its members which distinguished them from other groups, even from Judaism. When the Pharisees and the Herodians questioned Jesus about paying taxes to Rome, Jesus is reported to have said: "Render to Caesar the things that are Caesar's and to God the things that are God's" (Mk. 12:17). Thus he had taken the moderate line of those Jews who refused to revolt

242

against Rome and urged loyalty as long as it was made clear that there was no ultimate authority invested in the transitory institution of the state.

The same attitude prevailed in Paul. His appeal to the Roman Christians to accept the governing authorities as the gift of God (Rom. 13:1) has sometimes been interpreted as a demand that the Christian submit totally to every state "as having authority over him." This is a misinterpretation. Paul put the will of God above the will of the state, which is an institution of "this passing age" destined to secure law and order in subjection to God's plan, though he had no quarrel with the claim of the Roman state to the loyalty of its citizens. Nevertheless, both Jesus and Paul seem to have been executed by the Roman authorities on political grounds. The state quite obviously was not concerned with the content of their teaching, but with its effects. Groupings and movements which were likely to disturb the established order, the "peace" (*pax Romana*) based on wide tolerance in religious matters, created a situation which for the sake of law and order Rome was unwilling to tolerate. It was a matter of political expediency, not of religious intolerance, that there were early Christian martyrs.

Actually, we have little precise knowledge of the various stages in the conflict between Christianity and the Roman state. The first clear evidence of a serious encounter comes from the time of the Emperor Nero (A.D. 54–68) and concerns exclusively the Christians of Rome. In the summer of A.D. 64, a fierce fire raged through Rome for more than six days, devastating large areas of

NERO
was emperor of the Roman Empire when the first persecutions of Christians in Rome began.
(Musei Capitolini, Rome)

the city, especially west of the Tiber. According to the Roman historian Tacitus, there was a persistent rumor that Nero himself was responsible for the conflagration. In order to counter this suspicion, Nero laid the blame on "those who were hated on account of their viciousness by the people and were called Christians." He first had some of them arrested and confessions extracted:

> Then, on their information, large numbers of others were condemned —not so much for incendiarism as for their anti-social tendencies. Their deaths were made farcical. Dressed in wild animal skins, they were torn to pieces by dogs, or crucified, or made into torches to be ignited after dark as substitutes for daylight.[11]

There are several important points in this information. One is that at that time in Rome, Christians were already recognizable as a group even by the civil authorities; they were no longer simply identified with the Jews. Moreover, in blaming the Christians, Nero seems to have capitalized on a general hostility toward the Christians among the population. Tacitus, some forty years later, still shared this feeling in spite of his disapproval of Nero's action, and recognized the validity of the conviction on the ground of a "sullen hatred of the human race" (*odium generis humani*). His contemporary, Suetonius, mentions among Nero's "good and reasonable" measures the execution of Christians, who are "advocates of a new superstition, dangerous for society,"[12] without mentioning the context. There is ample evidence for this general hostility in the Christian writings of the New Testament as well as of the entire second century.

It is difficult for us to understand the point of this widespread and universal feeling; but at that time, the civil life of the whole empire was so inextricably bound up with the state cult in its polytheistic religious formulations, which had intruded so thoroughly into every activity of civil life, that the Christians with their rigorous monotheism, their eschatological fanaticism, and their clannish separatism had cut themselves off from much of the daily routine of the average Roman citizen. It was this separation from society (Greek: *amixia*), this "withdrawal" from public life, that made the Christians appear a threat to society. An especially grave problem seems to have been created by the frequent conversion of only one member of a family, and the ensuing tensions that resulted. In a frequently recurring motif of apocryphal literature, the martyrdom of a Christian apostle or evangelist is credited to the effects of his preaching on wives of influential citizens. These wives, following the ascetical preaching of the Christian hero, would refuse themselves to their husbands —and thus would start the deadly process that culminated in the hero's martyrdom.

To some extent, Christians shared this fate with the Jews, who, because of

---

[11]Tacitus, *Annals*, XV.40, 44. Translated by Michael Grant, *Tacitus: The Annals of Imperial Rome* (Baltimore: Penguin, 1956), p. 354.
[12]Suetonius, *Life of Nero*, Chapter 16.

their struggle for national and religious identity in spite of their dispersion, did not fit the framework of the Roman system, and therefore were widely regarded with suspicion, even contempt. However, they enjoyed the status of a privileged cult. Hence the Roman officials very probably looked upon the Christians as a Jewish sect, and indeed first treated them in this category. If arrests, imprisonments, or expulsions occurred, then this was on civil, not religious, charges. However, as soon as the break between Jews and Christians came to be recognized, which was especially the case after the revolt of A.D. 66–70, the question of Christianity's legal status in the empire was bound to arise.

The Neronian persecution, though it did not extend beyond the limits of Rome, must have been a catastrophe for the Roman congregation. If Tacitus is right in saying that the executions involved "large numbers," then perhaps only very few of the Church members remained. That the members of the congregation came mainly from the lower social strata is indicated by the extremely shameful methods of execution. It is all the more astonishing that the event has left barely a trace in the Christian literature of the time. Not even the strong tradition that both Peter and Paul met death during that period has an unassailable basis in the earlier texts. We have here a striking example of the insufficiency of our sources. On the basis of the surviving Christian literature, we could hardly surmise the importance and the dimensions of this persecution.

THE ROMAN FORUM
and the Arch of Septimius Severus from the Palatine Hill. The plain, squarish building across the Forum is the Curia, where the Senate convened. At the lower right are the steps and column bases of the Basilica Julia, one of the colonnaded porticos used for transacting business in ancient Rome. Behind the arch appears the flat roof of a small church that was built over the ruins of the Mamertine Prison, where, according to tradition, Peter and Paul were imprisoned. (Trans-World Airlines)

Among Nero's successors, it seems to have been Domitian (81–96) under whom new troubles arose for the Christians.[13] He was the first of the Roman emperors to claim for his own person divine honors which hitherto had been granted to deceased sovereigns only, and to apply the title "Lord and God" *(Dominus et Deus)* openly to himself. This meant that whoever refused to perform religious ceremonies honoring the emperor along with the state gods could be found guilty not only on civil grounds *(crimen laesae majestatis)* but even on religious grounds. We hear that in the year 95, Domitian accused many persons of "godlessness" and of loyalty to Jewish customs. The Roman consul Flavius Clemens was executed, and his wife, Flavia Domitilla, who was Domitian's niece, was ordered into exile. The discovery of an early Christian cemetery in Rome that was the gift of a Flavia Domitilla, according to the inscriptions, has led some to believe that Clemens and Domitilla themselves were Christians. It may well be that the "sudden and repeated misfortunes" that are mentioned in I Clement 1:2 refer to these events, and we can say with reasonable assurance that the Book of Revelation with its vision of threatening persecutions was written about the same time.

Apart from the rather dark allusions in the Revelation of John, we would know nothing about the situation in the provinces, were it not for the preservation of two pieces of correspondence between the Emperor Trajan (98–117) and Pliny the Younger, who was Trajan's imperial legate in the province of Pontus-Bithynia in Asia Minor around A.D. 110.[14] Pliny came into conflict with the Christians because Trajan had forbidden secret meetings of unapproved societies. The reason for this ban is clear: Rome was threatened with invasion from Parthia to the east, and Trajan could not have Asia Minor riddled with secret societies that might become cells of political disruption.

Pliny, who had no experience with this sort of thing, wrote to Trajan for information about how to examine and punish the Christians. By way of report, he outlined the procedure he had been following so far: first, he asked the accused if they were Christians. If they said yes, he asked a second and a third time, threatening them each time with punishment. If they persisted, he executed them. In dealing with those who had been accused of being Christians by the townspeople, sometimes anonymously, he again asked whether the accusation was true. If the accused denied it, he demanded that they invoke the state gods and worship the emperor's statue with incense and wine, and then curse Christ. Some of the accused said that though they had been Christians in the past, they were not any longer. But they claimed that even when they were Christians, they had done nothing more than meet together, sing hymns to Christ as to a god *(carmen dicere Christo)*, bind themselves by an

---

[13]See the excellent discussion in E. Stauffer, *Christ and the Caesars*, tr. K. and R. Gregor Smith (Philadelphia: Westminster, 1955), pp. 147–191.

[14]The texts are quoted in J. Stevenson, *A New Eusebius: Documents Illustrative of the Church to* A.D. *337* (London: S.P.C.K., 1957), pp. 13–16.

oath not to commit theft or robbery or adultery, not to break their word, and not to refuse to pay a debt. Beyond that, they had simply participated in eating a harmless meal of harmless food.

Trajan replied that Pliny had taken the right course, and that no general rule or fixed form of action could be laid down. Christians were not to be sought out, but if they were accused, they would have to be punished. If anyone denied that he was a Christian and agreed to worship the gods, he was to be pardoned, even if he had been under suspicion. And certainly no one was to be charged anonymously.

According to Trajan's decision (which incidentally makes no reference to a precedent), it is clear that Christianity was to be regarded as an illegal religion. The "name as such" (*nomen ipsum*) was to be punished. To the average Roman citizen, including the governor, the Christian viewpoint seemed to be a "depraved and extravagant superstition." As a tolerant and enlightened polytheist, he could not see how the recognition of the state gods in any way threatened individual religious loyalty. Even with this clarification, however, no general persecution was envisaged. In fact, we hear only of individual martyrdoms under Trajan and his immediate successors, not of a general action against the Christians. Ignatius, Bishop of Antioch, met his death in Rome on these terms; Symeon, son of Klopas and cousin of Jesus, was executed in Palestine. One of the earliest reliable reports of a Christian martyrdom, that of Bishop Polycarp of Smyrna (155–56) illustrates most vividly the practice in Asia Minor based on the principles of the Pliny-Trajan correspondence.[15] It was thus in an atmosphere of increasing visibility and mounting hostility that the Church found itself in the decades at the end of the first and the opening of the second Christian centuries—a very different state of affairs from the numerically insignificant movement that began with Jesus, or even from the apparently intra-Jewish tensions that characterized the launching of the Gentile mission under Paul. Now the Church could no longer avoid taking a stand in relation to the politics and culture of the rest of the world, just as in response to contemporary challenges it had to define its concepts and organization.

---

[15]See text and notes in *Martyrdom of Polycarp, Fragments of Papias*, tr. W. R. Schoedel, in *The Apostolic Fathers: A New Translation and Commentary*, ed. R. M. Grant (Camden, N.J.: Nelson, 1967), pp. 47–83. On the entire question consult the book by W. H. C. Frend, *Martyrdom and Persecution in the Early Church: A Study of a Conflict from the Maccabees to Donatus* (Oxford: Blackwell, 1965).

Toward Institutionalizing the Church

Ephesians; The Pastorals;
I, II, III John; Jude; II Peter

CHAPTER TEN

At the same time that the exterior conflicts with the Jews and the Roman officials grew in intensity and helped the Christian movement to find a distinctive identity of its own, the Christians' contact with both worlds, the Jewish and the Roman, resulted in interior problems which were perhaps even more serious than the danger of dissolution into a Jewish sect or of being wiped out by action of the state. One of these problems was the conflict over false teaching, the other the problem of adapting a hitherto rather free-wheeling movement to the pressures of institutionalization.

THE MOVEMENT TOWARD ORTHODOXY

Everywhere in the later books of the New Testament these problems have left more noticeable traces than the parallel conflicts with the Jews and the Roman government. This fact does not mean that the exterior conflicts were un-important. It may suggest, however, that the conflict over false teaching, over heresy,[1] was more dangerous in terms of the inner development of the Church. In the conflict with the Jews, the dissociation from the self-conscious remnant of the Jewish nation proved in the long run advantageous for the Christian missionary enterprise, especially after the catastrophic events of A.D. 70 and A.D. 132–135. Christians soon started to capitalize on the Jewish national tragedy, explaining it not only as a fulfillment of ancient prophecy, but also as God's final punishment. On the other hand, the lines in the conflict with the Roman state were quite clearly drawn. The Christians made up a minority group, highly vulnerable to social ostracism and political disfavor, and therefore anyone who chose to join the Christian community was aware that he could find himself under suspicion at every moment and that he might have to suffer for the "name." Obviously, the death of Christ could not become an abstraction to people who were faced with the possibility of dying in his behalf. Thus, wherever the threat of persecution became apparent, it served, instead of curbing the movement, to deepen and strengthen the faith; it helped in bringing together the members of the community into a more closely knit group; and it taught Christians the patience to take upon themselves suffering and hardship, which was a major factor in the final victory of the expanding movement.

The lines were not so clear in the conflict over false teaching. The trouble here lay in the fact that the Church of the postapostolic age did not enter this battle as a well-ordered organization with a well-defined doctrinal tradition and a well-prepared ethical code. It was still in search of ecclesiastical forms, and therefore open to all kinds of influences that promised assistance in working out the statement of faith, the norms of conduct, and the forms of organization that were needed. Judaism was no longer the only storehouse from which materials were drawn; with the opening of the door toward the Gentiles, the whole religious world of the empire, with its manifold concepts and ideas, stood ready to be used. A process of adaptation was under way, unplanned and unforeseen, but coming rapidly upon the Church.

In this situation the conflict over false teaching proved to be a tremendous catalyst. By working at this problem, the Church slowly learned to draw lines between "right" and "false" teaching.[2] The chances which this conflict provided may not have been seized upon in a really fruitful way by all the writers of the epoch. We should not be surprised to find that occasionally, in

---

[1] The word is derived from Greek *hairesis*, meaning a school, or party (cf. Acts 5:17; 15:5). The negative connotation of "sect" or "sectarian (false) doctrine" must have developed as early as the postapostolic period (cf. II Pet. 2:1).

[2] See the classical study by W. Bauer, *Orthodoxy and Heresy in Earliest Christianity*, ed. R. A. Kraft and G. Krodel (Philadelphia: Fortress, 1971); critical of Bauer is H. E. W. Turner, *The Pattern of Christian Truth: A Study in the Relation Between Orthodoxy and Heresy in the Early Church* (London: Mowbray, 1954).

the process of definition and adaptation, the *kerygma* itself appears to have exchanged its missionary bent for a rather defensive orthodoxy, or even that the center of the original message has become obscured.

The problem of sources for this conflict proves to be an even greater handicap than in the case of the conflict with the state or with the Jews. This is not due to the scantiness of information. Actually, there is perhaps no area in the history of postapostolic times about which our sources contain so much detailed material. But the picture is so bewildering that once more we are unable to piece the details together into a coherent whole.

One thing is obvious. Gnosticism,[3] which in many regions may first have appeared as a friend, helping with the formulation of Christian doctrine, soon was recognized as enemy number one. It would not be difficult to trace the struggle of the Church to free itself from Gnosticism, if we could use the approach of the early Christian heresiologists. One of them, the Church Father Irenaeus, demonstrates by the very title of his antiheretical work *(Detection and Overthrow of Gnosis Falsely So-Called)* that he regards Gnosticism as *the* heresy *par excellence.* According to him, the "father of all heresies" was Simon Magnus, the Samaritan "sorcerer" whose conversion and subsequent expulsion from the Christian community is told in legendary style in Acts 8:9–24. The sect that gathered around him became, as Irenaeus thinks, the cradle for the whole plague of the Gnostic religion. A certain Menander, he says, was Simon's successor; and in the next generation, with Satornilus of Antioch and Basilides of Alexandria, the "systems" of the Gnostic type spread all over the empire.

On the basis of the sources, there can be no doubt that Simon was indeed a more important figure than the account in Acts suggests. He seems to have founded a sect which at the time of Justin Martyr (mid-second century) had tremendous success in Syria[4] and may have been the starting point for other Gnostic-syncretistic groups. But Irenaeus' fundamental statement that "from the sect of Simon all heresies [he means Gnosticism in its various forms] took their origin" oversimplifies the complex issue. It starts from the assumption that true Christianity was earlier than the distortion which appears in Simon's doctrine. But if Simon, according to Acts 8:9ff., had carried on his Gnostic preaching already before he was attracted to Christianity, the implication is that Gnosticism as such existed and developed in the pre- and non-Christian world. The picture modern research has been able to trace of Gnosticism reveals a wide range of "sources," influences, and motifs that have shaped this religious mood which was so readily adaptable to most any form of faith, but was to unfold into clearly organized forms mainly under the impact of the Christian movement.

Another point in Irenaeus' account needs modification: In his identification of Gnosticism as *the* heresy, he seems to subsume everything he regarded as

---

[3] See pp. 28–30.
[4] Justin Martyr, *Apology* I.26 and 56; II.15; *Dialogue with Trypho,* 120.

heretical under the term "Gnostic." Thus, the Nicolaitans (Rev. 2:6), the Marcionites, even the Ebionites—all fall under this category. Again, this is an oversimplification. To be sure, modern historical research has vindicated Irenaeus' statement to the extent that groups like the Marcionites or the Ebionites exhibit trends in their teaching which are akin to the cosmological, anthropological, and soteriological speculations known to us from Gnostic sources. But this does not automatically make them "Gnostic schools," as Irenaeus describes them. The picture, indeed, is much more complicated, and the interaction between Christianity and Gnosticism much more delicate. For the post-Pauline New Testament literature, this means that we cannot presuppose a clearly defined and organized "Gnosticism" as the enemy, although Gnostic trends may be present in the doctrine of many false teachers we encounter. In trying to describe the false teachers, we have to take each case, each local situation, by itself.

Most important for our image of the emerging postapostolic Church is the polemical method and the argumentation of the ecclesiastical writers themselves and their own definition of what is "Christian." Again, we cannot expect to find a unified pattern, but our attempt to understand how various writers dealt with the danger of false teaching will lead us deeply into some of the most controversial problems of the postapostolic period: the development of "tradition," of an organized ministry, of the notion of "apostolic succession." They all reflect a changing self-consciousness of the new Christian generation.

We must realize that much of this change was simply due to the fact of ongoing time. Christians originally had not reckoned with this possibilty. Their hope was that within their lifetime the End of the Age would come. But by A.D. 70, the Twelve and Paul were probably all dead, and the intense expectation of the imminent Coming of the Lord was diminishing. To be sure, in situations of stress and suffering like the period during which the Book of Revelation was written, the coals of expectancy would be fanned to white heat here and there. But there was a growing feeling that things were probably going to continue pretty much as they were, at least for a time. The Church now had to take seriously the realities and demands of an *extended,* perhaps *very* extended, intermediate period. It began to see that being chosen as God's people of the end-time meant being sent on a long and hard pilgrimage—a pilgrimage of people who were aliens and strangers in this world, yet had to walk through it in order to reach their goal.

ONE HOLY, APOSTOLIC CHURCH

[EPHESIANS AND THE PASTORALS]

The dominant themes in the literature of the postapostolic period give us a clue for the understanding of the changing situation. There is, first, the theme of *unity.* From the very start, the Christian community had taken its unity for granted. Those who entered the Church believed that they were becoming members of a new community which God had called into being through the Messiah, Jesus, and together they awaited Christ's coming and the consummation of God's purpose. They felt that they had a sure sign that they were the People of God—the presence of the Holy Spirit or the spirit of Jesus Christ in their midst. However, as time went on, this feeling of unity became problematical. Of course, from the beginning, unity in the Christian Church did not exclude variety, even tension, among those who worshipped Christ as Lord. The sources of Acts as well as the Pauline Letters constantly remind us of this fact. But variety and tension were never felt to endanger the unity in Christ as long as the Spirit was at work and drove Christians to seek means of expressing their unity in acts of solidarity. In the postapostolic period, this Spirit seemed to be no longer a standard by which unity could be determined. In the growing Church herself, the gift of the Spirit no longer manifested itself as intensely as it used to; too many "Spirits" were claiming to speak in the name of Christ. The Church had to raise the question of the marks of her unity; moreover, this unity itself had now to be defined in terms of its ground, its practical possibilities, and its limits.

Another theme is *holiness.* Christians of the earlier days called themselves "the saints," a title which probably is derived from the self-designation of esoteric Jewish groups. It expressed the conviction of being elected by God, made holy in order to fulfill the mission of the holy remnant in the world. It obviously included the expectation that with the God-given new life, sin would cease to dominate this group in which the Kingdom of God had already broken in upon the world. Again, this concept of holiness was rendered problematical as time went on. Of course, there had never been a really sinless period in the Church. But the expectation of the imminent End of the Age had made it easier to deal with the problem of sin in a spontaneous way. Open sinners were simply excluded from the community of saints. In the postapostolic period, this was no longer a sufficient answer to the problem. Sin proved to be a constant reality, not only outside the Church, but within as well. Facing its long pilgrimage, the Church had to find ways of living with this reality. It had to redefine what it meant by speaking of itself as "holy" and had to help Christians to distinguish between "holy" and "unholy" by developing an ethical code.

A third theme is *apostolicity.* The earliest Church of course was "apostolic" inasmuch as its leadership was in the hands of the apostles, who represented the authentic continuation of Jesus' own authority. So long as they were living, they provided a ready court of appeal for all problems confronting the Church. With the passing of that generation, the meaning of the Church's apostolicity necessarily became a problem. Where could the true apostolic tradition be found? The difficulty in answering this question became clear when Gnostic teachers claimed that they possessed "secret teachings" of the apostles. How was the Church to show that this claim was false? It had to develop standards by which the true apostolic tradition could be distinguished from false teaching. This is the context in which a new concept of tradition and its guarantee—a regular, organized ministry—emerged. It is also the background for much of the pseudonymous writing in the early Church.

Modern scholarship recognizes that numerous writings in the New Testament are "pseudonymous" (Greek for "written under false name"). For us, this practice seems to be fraud. We connect every work of literature immediately with the personality of the author, and conversely the author enjoys public protection for his intellectual production. This was not so in antiquity. Pseudonymous writing was practiced for a wide variety of reasons.[5] What Tertullian says concerning the apocryphal "Acts of Paul"[6]—namely, that they were admittedly written by a presbyter in Asia Minor "out of love for the Apostle" in an attempt to "enhance Paul's reputation by adding to it something of his own"—is probably a good explanation for much of the later pseudonymous writing under the name of an apostle. We have a fictitious exchange of letters between Paul and the Corinthians, known as "III Corinthians," a pseudo-Pauline letter to the Laodiceans, and even a correspondence between Paul and the Roman philosopher Seneca that tries to show how much the two men admired each other.[7] The fact is that Paul, through his letter writing which was so readily imitated, exerted an enormous influence upon the literature of the postapostolic period. But there were more serious reasons for imitating him than this. The anonymous authors who put their writings under the authority of an apostle usually did not intend to deceive or simply to entertain their readers; in some cases the addressees may even have known their true identity. Their only intention often was to preserve the *true* apostolic tradition in a time of confusion, and for this purpose they used a literary device that enabled them to give their message a strong backing. They were convinced that they wrote in the way the apostle himself would have written had he been in their place, since a clearer word on the issues of right doctrine and conduct seemed to be needed than what was found in the existing letters. To be sure, the Church did not consciously encourage such pseudonymous writing. But by accepting these specific books into its "apostolic" canon, she endorsed them as representative of the true apostolic tradition, and therefore as part of the standard in the fight against false doctrine. That its decision was no guarantee against historical error about the actual authorship of a particular writing is a truth which the Church of all times has humbly to acknowledge.

Within the New Testament corpus of Pauline Letters, Ephesians and the

---

[5]See the survey of the question and the literature in B. M. Metzger's article, "Literary Forgeries and Canonical Pseudepigrapha," *Journal of Biblical Literature*, XCI (1972), 3–24.
[6]Tertullian, *On Baptism*, 17.
[7]Translations of these writings may be conveniently found in M. R. James, *The Apocryphal New Testament*, corr. ed. (Oxford: Clarendon, 1960), pp. 288ff. and 479ff.

three Pastoral Letters are widely regarded as pseudonymous. By the same token, the so-called "Catholic Epistles" (James; I and II Peter; I, II, II John; Jude) probably all belong in the same category. It is perhaps Ephesians that stands out most clearly as a witness for the new self-understanding of the postapostolic Church and its implications. The writing purports to be a Letter of Paul, and its emphases on justification by faith, the in-dwelling of Christ, and the Spirit, are highly reminiscent of Paul. However, careful study shows that the total style is post-Pauline,[8] that words are used with different shades of meaning from what they have in the genuine Letters of Paul. Ephesians, for example, refers to the "holy apostles" (3:5), a phrase that would be almost inconceivable for Paul to use in referring to his own kind. And more important, the conflict with Judaism lies in the past, whereas in the Pauline Letters, it is still a burning issue.

Unlike the genuine Pauline Letters that were written to specific churches to deal with specific problems, Ephesians appears to have been written for general reading by a number of churches. Even the phrase "in Ephesus" is missing from the address in several of the oldest manuscripts (1:1). According to one theory,[9] the author put together the first collection of Paul's Letters and appended his own writing as a general introduction. Since Ephesians shows clear literary dependence on Paul's Letter to the Colossians, it has been suggested that the author was very familiar with it and used it as his model.

Two great themes dominate the thought of Ephesians: *the unity of all things in Christ,* and *the Church as the symbol and agent of that unity.* They are introduced in an unusually long, hymnic benediction (1:3–23) which praises the Christian's redemption in a language saturated with baptismal imagery. Since the Letter contains more such hymnic passages (2:4–7; 2:14–16; 5:14) all of which allude to baptismal themes, the suggestion has been made that the author used liturgical material connected with baptism in the composition of his work. In baptism, the Christian is united with Christ through the seal of the Spirit (1:13). Sin and death have lost their power over his life (2:1–5). But the author immediately extends this theme of unity in Christ far beyond the individual horizon into the proclamation of a unity "of all things in heaven and on earth" (1:10). His image of Christ is that of a "cosmic Christ," who, according to God's eternal plan, through his Resurrection has gained control over all powers in the universe, evil or good, so that now and forever everything may be subject to him (1:20–22). God gave him his throne as He has also given seats "in the heavenly places" to those whom he has saved (2:4–6). The message is not that the triumphal event will occur in the future, as part of some apocalyptic drama. Futuristic eschatology plays only a very minor role

---

[8]The best study is C. L. Mitton, *The Epistle to the Ephesians: Its Authorship, Origin, and Purpose* (Oxford: Clarendon, 1951).

[9]First advanced by E. J. Goodspeed, *The Meaning of Ephesians: A Study of the Origin of the Epistle* (Chicago: University of Chicago Press, 1933). Goodspeed thought of Onesimus as the possible author.

in Ephesians. Rather, the cosmic victory *has* been won, the fullness of time *has* been reached, and the unity of all things under Christ's dominion is a fact. What is left is that this "mystery," this plan of God which was hidden for ages, must now be announced, disclosed, proclaimed by those whom God has elected. As in Colossians, we feel a certain closeness to Gnostic language when we listen to this exuberant celebration of the Christian's present salvation.

The difference from Colossians appears in the role assigned to the Church. For the author of Ephesians, the Church is the visible symbol of the cosmic unity which God has brought about through Christ. Her membership of Jews (and now mainly Gentiles) witnesses to the fact that with Christ's victory even mankind's divisions have been healed, that the "dividing wall of hostility" has been torn down (2:13–19). Thus, one new people of God has been created, a people which possesses the distinctive marks of unity: one Lord, one faith, one baptism (4:5). But this Church is more than a visible symbol. Drawing on the Pauline images of head and body, bride and groom, the author describes her as the living extension of the cosmic Christ. Christ is the heavenly Head, the Church his heavenly Body (1:22), united with him in a mysterious union (5:22). She is herself a cosmic reality through which the mystery of God's purpose "might be made known to the principalities and powers in the heavenly places" (3:10). This bold vision of the Church as a cosmic organism "growing" into the stature of the fullness of Christ (4:13), and thus into its true mission, makes it possible to proclaim the Church's essential unity regardless of her actual difficulties and divisions.

But the difficulties remain. There is the danger of doctrinal insecurity, of immaturity in the new faith (4:14), of deceit and relapse (5:6–8). Against these dangers, the author stresses the Church's apostolicity. The Church is "built upon the foundation of the apostles and prophets" (2:20). Paul himself appears as a prime witness to the basic apostolic revelation (3:1–6), and "his" Church in Ephesians knows a hierarchy in which apostles definitely rank before the Christian prophets, the evangelists, pastors, and teachers (4:11). In this Church, the daily struggle for more evidence of the new life in Christ has a prominent place. A long concluding section deals with the renewal of ethics (4:17–6:20). It contains quite specific rules for wives and husbands, children and parents, slaves and masters (5:21ff.), and ends with the plea to put on the "whole armour of God" in the ongoing fight with sin and temptation (6:11–17). The reality of the cosmic victory must remain in tension with the realities of the continuing life of the postapostolic community in the world.

The other group of pseudonymous documents in the New Testament written under Paul's name, the three Pastoral Letters, are dominated by the conflict over false teaching to such an extent that the fight against it appears to be their only immediate goal. Their author, if he is not Paul, probably speaks as a member of that generation of Church leaders which Titus is thought to have appointed (Tit. 1:5). I Timothy seems to have best preserved the form of Church order. II Timothy suggests a kind of last will or testament of the apostle (cf. 4:6ff.). Titus centers around personal instruction. Despite the numerous personal allusions and possible fragments of authentic Pauline writings, all espistles deal with the same subject matter of rules for the churches and their leaders in a dangerous situation. The danger is described with the colors of an apocalyptic evil in II Timothy 4:3ff.:

> For the time is coming when people will not endure sound teaching, but having itching ears, they will accumulate for themselves teachers to suit their own likings and will turn away from listening to the truth and wander into myths.

The author clearly speaks of a danger from within, not from outside. The "people" of whom he is talking are Christians; and "truth"—*i.e.*, the "sound teaching" (cf. I Tim. 1:10; 6:3; Tit. 1:9; 2:1; II Tim. 1:13)—is the sum of Christianity as he tends to see it. To follow it is, in fact, the only way to hold the three ideal themes of earlier Christianity together: unity, holiness, apostolicity.

GUARDING THE TRUE FAITH

Who are these "false teachers," and what are their arguments? The polemic of the Pastoral Letters furnishes us with numerous details which at first glance seem to provide a rather full picture, including even names (I Tim. 1:20; II Tim. 1:15; 2:17). But it is almost impossible to combine all these indications into one coherent picture.

I Timothy 6:20 has often been taken as the key in establishing the identity of the false teachers:

> O Timothy, guard what has been entrusted to you. Avoid the godless chatter and the contradictions of what is falsely called knowledge, for by professing it some have missed the mark as regards the faith.

A reading of the Greek text reveals better than the English translation the importance of this sentence. The word for "knowledge" is *gnosis,* and the combination (literally) "pseudonymous gnosis" is the very term which Irenaeus took over to characterize the whole Gnostic movement. Thus, it appears likely that the "false teaching" the Pastoral Letters have in mind is some form of Gnosticism. To some scholars it seems likely that the verse yields evidence for an even more exact identification. The Greek word for "contradictions" is *antitheses;* and we know, particularly from the detailed refutation by Tertullian, that Marcion had written a work with this title. It was an exegetical treatise contrasting texts from the "Law" (Old Testament) with the "Gospel" (Marcion accepted only an expurgated version of Luke's gospel and ten Pauline Letters), and was written in support of Marcion's dualistic theology. If we could follow this theory, then the author of I Timothy would issue an official warning against this dangerous book, and the fact that he writes under the name of Paul would indicate the attempt to reclaim the authority of the apostle for the teaching of his Church against the false claims of the Marcionites.[10] The Pastoral Letters would then have to be dated rather late—Marcion's *Antitheses* appeared around 140 A.D.—and even then the ingenious proposal to regard Polycarp of Smyrna as their author would not meet with insurmountable difficulties.[11]

Part of the difficulty in identifying the opponents stems from the polemical method applied. Paul, in his Letters, usually gives at least fragmentary hints of his opponents' positions. In the Pastorals, however, the enemies are no longer opposed by argument. On the contrary, the author gives the advice not to engage in controversy (II Tim. 2:23; cf. I Tim. 4:7; Tit. 3:9). The young leader must avoid the contact with this type of teaching and its representatives (I Tim. 6:20; II Tim. 2:16; 3:5). In spite of the rhetorical challenge to "fight the good fight of faith," one senses behind these injunctions a certain insecurity: the danger obviously was serious. On the one hand, the enemies are dismissed as only "some" (I Tim. 4:1; 5:15; 6:10), or "certain individuals" (I Tim. 1:3, 19). However, they are not only upsetting the faith of a few (II Tim. 2:18) but of whole families (Tit. 1:11), and the author sees the false doctrine spread like gangrene (II Tim. 2:17). His anticipation is that the situation will become still worse (II Tim. 3:12f.).

For his evaluation of heresy, the image of gangrene is revealing. False teaching appears as a creeping disease, an "unhealthy" matter in contrast to the "healthy" doctrine. Thus, his advice of cutting off the relationship to the "sick" members is a radical but necessary cure to protect the health of a developing orthodoxy. Here we see that argument has been replaced by a formal pattern of antiheretical terminology. Developed as a means of defense, this pattern certainly cannot claim objectivity in its description of the enemy. We notice that false teaching is always dealt with in a most summary fashion that leaves no room for individual differentiation: "If anyone teaches otherwise and does not agree with the sound words of our Lord Jesus Christ and the teaching which accords with godliness, he is . . ." (I Tim. 6:3ff.). There follows a spell of highly abusive terms, accusing the "heretics" of every vile and evil quality. A similar list appears in II Timothy 3:2ff. It is placed in the framework of a general apocalyptic warning, but the context (verses 5b, 6) again shows that the author really has the false teachers in mind. A third list in I Timothy 1:9f. seems to enumerate the categories of serious criminals for whose restriction the law is given. Nevertheless, the summary in verse 10 makes it clear that the author even here thinks of the heretics he is fighting. Rather than

---

[10]This explanation has been cautiously adopted by F. D. Gealy in his introduction to the Pastoral Letters in *The Interpreter's Bible*, XI (Nashville: Abingdon, 1955), 358ff.

[11]The reference is to Hans von Campenhausen, "Polykarp von Smyrna und die Pastoralbriefe," in *Sitzungsberichte der Heidelberger Akademie der Wissenschaften*, No. 2 (Heidelberg: Winter, 1951–52).

dealing with the opponents on their terms, the author is using prefabricated "catalogues of vices," similar to those in Galatians 5:19–21, or Romans 13:13. Recent research has shown that such catalogues have their origin in Hellenistic-Jewish moral tradition; beyond this, they draw from a rich background of oriental forms.[12] This insight is fundamental. The pattern of antiheretical language is rarely formed *ad hoc*, but uses a standard stock of phrases and motifs. In the Pastoral Letters we can watch this phenomenon in its formative stage.

Part of the pattern is the connection of "heresy" and "immorality." On the assumption that heresy is a disease, it was easy to think of it in moral terms: false doctrine equals immoral life. The heretic is *per se* an immoral person. As a pattern, however, this "dogma" is not restricted to Christians. After all, Christians themselves experienced the hatred of others in the form of the accusation of "godlessness" coupled with moral turpitude.

Some features of this pattern in the Pastorals may have a more real background; for example, the charge that the heretics used their preaching "as a means of gain" (I Tim. 6:5; Tit. 1:11). The Acts account concerning Simon Magus (Acts 8) charges that love of money was the motive out of which he sought to become part of the Christian community. There may be reason to believe that Gnostic teachers actually had considerable financial success. Yet the charge of mendicancy could hardly be avoided by any group who had to make a living by itinerant evangelism. Even Paul was no exception (cf. I Thess. 2:5; I Cor. 9:6ff.). The Pastoral Letters themselves tell of a regularly paid local ministry (I Tim. 5:17f.). We may have to translate the Greek word *timē* (honor) in the technical sense of "honorarium" so that the verse would recommend higher pay for good presbyters. Occasional suspicion against the paid clergy must have arisen, and was perhaps nourished by unfortunate experiences. Our texts often emphasize that a minister of the Gospel should not be a "lover of money" (I Tim. 3:3; I Pet. 5:2). The danger on this point was probably as great in the Church of the Pastorals as it was in the circle of the opponents. The problem certainly cannot be solved by contrasting the "good conscience" on one's own side (I Tim. 1:5, 19; 3:9; II Tim. 1:3) with a "bad conscience" on the other (I Tim. 4:2; Tit. 1:15), thus implying ill will and deliberate self-deceit on the part of the heretics. This reproach again is stock, and the "false teachers" were probably as convinced as our author that they represented the true Church. This is the dilemma faced by an orthodoxy which was just starting to develop its own standards.

Concerning these standards, the Pastoral Letters are a most important witness of two positive ways in which the postapostolic Church tried to find her own identity over against the false teaching: the appeal to a new concept of *tradition*, and the development of an established *ministry*.

---

[12]See S. Wibbing, *Die Tugend- und Lasterkataloge im Neuen Testament*, Beihefte zur Zeitschrift für die neutestamentliche Wissenschaft, XXV (Berlin: Töpelmann, 1959).

In the Pastoral Letters, Paul's rather free-wheeling concept of tradition was not felt to be safe enough from tampering. Thus, the Pauline term *paradosis* (tradition) is now replaced by *parathēkē* (deposit; I Tim. 6:20; II Tim. 1:12–14; cf. I Tim. 1:18; II Tim. 2:2). The term belongs in the legal sphere where it emphasizes the integrity of a given definition. Tradition according to this understanding is a fixed deposit, something which has "once" been laid down and now can only be "guarded." With Paul, the author still calls it "gospel," but other terms seem to be much more appropriate. In the first place, tradition now is "doctrine" (the word occurs fifteen times in the Pastoral Letters), and this doctrine is distinguished from false teaching by the adjective "sound" ("sound doctrine"—II Tim. 4:3; Tit. 1:9; 2:1; "sound words"—I Tim. 6:3; II Tim. 1:13; Tit. 2:8). Another important shift is noticeable when we consider the relationship of the apostle, in whose name the author is writing, to this tradition. He is no longer seen as one link in the chain of those who are "entrusted with the Gospel," receiving it as well as handing it on, but as the beginning of it, the depositor of the gospel which the later generations have to keep intact (I Tim. 1:11f.; 6:14; II Tim. 1:13; 2:8; 3:14; Tit. 1:3). Tradition has become a body of fixed doctrine guaranteed by the authority of the apostle. In this form, the Pastorals even equate it with "faith." In Paul, faith was primarily trust in, and commitment to, God in response to the Gospel; it could not really be measured and manipulated. To be sure, this nuance of trust is not absent from the Pastorals. However, it seems that faith now *can* be measured and "handled" (II Tim. 2:15)—namely, by its congruence with the deposited body of correct doctrine. Faith still is the essence of the Christian's life (faith = Christianity: I Tim. 5:8; Tit. 1:13), but it is a faith of fixed and final content, identical with the "sound word," the healthy doctrine. This faith can be "kept" (II Tim 4:7). It can be "disowned" (I Tim. 5:8), missed (I Tim. 6:21), departed from (I Tim. 4:1), denied (I Tim. 5:8; 4:1)—all of these being equivalents for "heresy." Faith has become the formal criterion for being a Christian.

The content of this faith is not presented systematically. The author simply presupposes it and occasionally quotes it in the form of traditional statements that have a flavor of venerable age. They seem to come mostly from liturgical or credal tradition (I Tim. 1:15, 17; 3:16; 6:13–16; II Tim. 1:9f.; 2:11f.; Tit. 2:11ff.). In the apparent allusions to a formulated creed (cf. I Tim. 6:12) one notes that the polemic against false doctrine has already become a normal ingredient of the creed. Statements like I Timothy 2:4–5 are in all probability formulated in antithesis to false doctrine: God's will is that *all* men shall be saved—not just a selected group of Gnostics; there is *one* God and *one* mediator between God and man—not several gods and a plurality of intermediaries; Jesus Christ, the *man*—not an incorporeal divine being. In the history of the early Christian Church, this development culminated in the formulation of the Nicene Creed with its specific refutation of Arian doctrine.

Yet in spite of all his dependence upon traditional Christian formulations, including Paul's, and his declared intention not to add anything, the author often presents his "sound doctrine" in a language borrowed from popular Hellenistic-Jewish religiosity. He does not hesitate to call his faith "religion" (I Tim. 2:10; 4:7f.) and use Hellenistic epithets for his Lord: Christ is "God" (Tit. 2:13), "Savior" (II Tim. 1:10; Tit. 1:4; 3:6); his appearance among men is an "Epiphany" (II Tim. 1:10; Tit. 2:11; 3:4) like the epiphany of a Hellenistic god or of the emperor-god. Our Letters give impressive evidence of the extent to which the beginning orthodoxy of the postapostolic age felt free to assimilate concepts of its religious surroundings—not *in spite of*, but *because of* its new understanding of tradition as a fixed deposit.[13]

MINISTERS AS INSTRUMENTS OF ORDER

According to the Pastoral Letters, the preservation and correct transmission of the true faith is a task of the *ministry* of the Church. The Pastorals are the only writings in the New Testament that deal specifically with the ministry, and it is significant that this is done in the context of the conflict over false teaching. The Church as the "pillar and bulwark of truth" (I Tim. 3:15) could fulfill its role only through an organized and legitimized ecclsiastical office.

The historical development of the Christian ministry during the postapostolic period is still a field of many open questions. In our sources, the basic ideas for its functioning are presupposed rather than spelled out; and where ecclesiastical offices are mentioned, the terminology is often confusing, indicating at least that things were in great flux. The major handicap is the scantiness of information about the general constitutional development in the early Church. The Church was not planned as an institution with a projected long-range future. We must remember this simple fact.

What we can safely say about the ministry in the postapostolic period is perhaps this:

1. There is a definite development from a rather loose organization to a more structured form of ecclesiastical order in which a hierarchy of offices emerged with a single "bishop" as head of the local congregation ("monarchical episcopacy").

2. The tendency toward more structured patterns of organization was at least enforced, if not initiated, by the needs of the conflict with heresy. The ministry in the Church became, in the first place, the guardian of tradition, legitimized by a special ordination, and thus acknowledged as a guarantee of the effectiveness of all salutary activity in the Church, especially the sacraments.

3. The various stages of this development were not reached everywhere at

---

[13]For this aspect see especially the commentary by H. Conzelmann, *Die Pastoralbriefe*, Handbuch zum Neuen Testament, XIII, 3rd ed. (Tübingen: Mohr, 1955).

the same time. Local differences, therefore, have to be taken into account. While in one church or one area the development toward a monarchical episcopacy seems to have made rapid advance, other churches still preserved more archaic forms of church government for a long time.

Although the Pastoral Letters do not develop a "doctrine" of the ministry, the author is laying down fundamental rules in the light of his specific situation. The image of the apostle Paul serves as the basic point of reference. He offers himself as the true model for the ministry of the Church at all times.

Paul's life first illustrates the basis on which all Christian ministry is carried out: God's grace for sinners. He is the great example of the Christian experience of conversion. Once an ardent foe of Christianity, the "foremost of sinners" (I Tim. 1:15), he now is the living witness to God's life-changing power. God's mercy, not his own merit, made his appointment to the "service of Christ" possible (I Tim. 1:12). What is this service, this *diakonia*? It is the ministry of the Gospel—a Gospel that leads into suffering (II Tim. 1:11–12; 2:10). Again, Paul's whole life is witness to this fact that every Christian minister must face: hardship and persecution are his share (II Tim. 3:10–12). But he is not fighting for a private cause. The Lord stands behind him watching over the precious deposit which he has left in the apostle's hand so that it may accomplish its goal of being heard (II Tim. 4:17; cf. 1:12). The summary of Paul's life in II Timothy 4:7 characterizes the goal set before every good minister: "I have fought the good fight, I have finished the race, I have kept the faith." One may find in this bold statement traces of the veneration of the great apostle by a later generation which already sees him crowned with the "crown of righteousness" (II Tim. 4:8) and tries to excuse his former life in retrospect as "ignorance" (I Tim. 1:13).

At two points, Paul's ministry is defined by the terms preacher, apostle, teacher (I Tim. 2:7; II Tim. 1:11). It is striking that the title of apostle is mentioned only in second place. For our author, Paul is first of all preacher, *keryx*. The Greek word naturally suggests the connection with the term *kerygma*. However, since our author interprets the *kerygma* as implying a static concept of tradition, it would seem that all three terms really point in the same direction. Paul's function is the proclamation *and* the codification of the true apostolic tradition, of the right teaching. His deposition of the apostolic *kerygma* has set the standard for all Christian ministry after him.

If the image of Paul is the basic point of orientation, Timothy and Titus are the more immediate models for a Church leader, as our author has him in mind. Young, as he presents them (I Tim. 4:12; 5:11; II Tim. 2:22; Tit. 2:6f.), they are the prototypes of the younger generation which needs help and guidance and for which his Church order is intended. The Church itself is like a small social organism, a family in which the minister must recognize fathers and mothers, brothers and sisters beside him (I Tim. 5:1f.). What distinguishes him is his public role, which lays upon him a great responsibility.

His life must show to everyone what it means to be a Christian, to have been converted from impurity to purity. He must renounce "youthful passions" and must set his mind on the true aims of righteousness, love, and especially peace in order to be a "vessel for noble use" (II Tim. 2:20ff.). He must set the example of the integrity which Christians are to demonstrate in word and action so that no criticism can be leveled against them from outside (Tit. 2:7ff.). Or course, he is not yet perfect, but he will make progress. For this, "soundness" and common sense are important qualities. There is no need for special ascetic exercises (I Tim. 4:8). But hard work in the assigned duties is necessary—strict devotion, self-discipline, and willingness to suffer.

What are the minister's duties? What is the function of his ministry? Again, preaching is given a prominent place (II Tim. 4:1–2). Timothy's ministry can be defined as that of an "evangelist" (II Tim. 4:5). But just as the *kerygma* has become doctrine, the evangelist actually is a teacher. His preaching has to do with the handing on of correct doctrine and of the corresponding moral code. He is to instruct Christians in the face of threatening heresy (I Tim. 1:3; Tit. 1:5ff.). But the conflict with false teaching in which he has to carry the main burden, calls for a man who really has *all* areas of Church life and Church order under his control. Especially the image of Timothy contains evidence for administrative functions of the ministry. The long instruction concerning widows (I Tim. 5:3–16) presupposes that the Church is engaged in organized charity.[14] Widows without family are supported by the Church, and it is the task of the ministry to watch over the correct "enrollment" (I Tim. 5:9) so that the congregation is not unduly burdened. The minister also acts as a disciplinary authority watching over the right procedure in disciplinary cases. He is not to show partiality and has to make sure that only well-founded complaints are brought against honorable elders (I Tim. 5:19ff.). He has to rebuke the sinner (including the heretic), admonishing him once or twice; if this has no effect, he has to draw the line and expel the "factious" person (Tit. 3:10; cf. I Tim. 1:20). There is a third area in which the ideal minister has to take leadership: the worship life of the congregation. According to I Timothy 4:13, he is not to neglect the public reading of scripture, or preaching and teaching. Some of the practical problems connected with worship—as, for example, the question of prayer—are dealt with in I Timothy 2. We will discuss this aspect in our next chapter.

From the Pastoral Letters we learn that the postapostolic Church knew a distinctive, public act of ordination for the ministry at which the charge to "guard" the deposit, and the spiritual authority for this office was conferred. In Judaism, the tradition of the commissioning of Joshua by Moses (Num. 27:21–23) had served as the model for the ordination which the student of the

---

[14]For a full discussion of the charity of the early Church, see A. Harnack, *The Mission and Expansion of Christianity in the First Three Centuries*, tr. J. Moffat, I (New York: Putnam's, 1908), 147–198; republished in the Harper Torchbook series, 1964.

Torah received from his teacher and which conferred the authority of exercising all the functions of a rabbi. The main rite was "the laying on of hands." In Acts we hear of the installation of the Seven with prayer and laying on of hands (6:6) and of the commissioning of Paul and Barnabas by the Antiochene church with the same rite (Acts 13:3). Elsewhere in Acts the laying on of hands is connected with the gift of the Spirit, which poses difficult problems because the relation to baptism is not entirely clear (cf. Acts 8:17; 19:6). Behind all these instances stands the general idea of a transmission of charismatic power or blessing by the laying on of hands (cf. Acts 9:12, 17; 28:8).

In the Pastorals the term "laying on of hands" refers to the ordination rite (I Tim. 4:14; II Tim. 1:6; cf. I Tim 5:22), but a connection with the gift of the Spirit is indicated ("the gift which is within you"). Although it is now the appointment to a regular office in the Church, the ministry is still regarded as a charisma; the reference to "prophetic voices" from the congregation that designated Timothy before or when he was commissioned (I Tim. 1:18; 4:14) implies just this. It is in the last instance the Spirit that guarantees the authority of the ministry. But the conflict with false teaching has made it necessary to bind this gift, once it is recognized in a person, to a regular ministry in order to make sure that the *right* Spirit remains at work. The close interrelation of office and charisma, Spirit and tradition, is quite characteristic of the situation. For our author, it is more important than the question of who ordains: in I Timothy 4:14 it is the presbytery, in II Timothy 1:6 the apostle himself. This seeming contradiction is resolved once we remember that he constantly projects the situation of his time back into the apostolic frame of the Letters. For him, the ordination by the elders of his time *is* the legitimation by apostolic authority, the outward insurance of a proper "apostolic succession" in the preservation of the deposit of faith.

The confounding of apostle and presbytery may also point to another dimension. In practice, the problem of the true apostolic succession in the ministry was that of local situations, not that of the Church at large. The author has tried to give his approach a global flavor. He presents Paul as a kind of central authority in the Gentile Church, Timothy and Titus as his assistants whose task it is to supervise and establish the ministry in churches of a vast geographical area. Many scholars have inferred from this scheme that Timothy and Titus represent some early form of archbishops or metropolitans as the later Church knew them. However, there is no clear evidence for either a centralized authority in the postapostolic Church, nor for the existence of such regional authorities. For all practical purposes both Timothy and Titus were conceived from a local viewpoint, the only immediate battleground in any conflict with heresy. They are the projected *ideal* of a more or less centralized local ministry which in this form is at best just starting to be organized. This is the reason why it is also quite difficult to identify them simply as "bishops" of unknown local congregations. For the projected ideal, the title of bishop in the sense of the monarchical episcopacy may be appropriate. But the glimpses of the actual situation which we seem to catch in the Church order show that, with the Pastoral Letters, we are still in the middle of the transition, even though the later outcome may already be in sight.

THE MOVEMENT TOWARD A HIERARCHY

The tension between the ideal projection and the actual situation makes it difficult to explain the various technical designations used for the Christian ministry in the postapostolic literature. To be sure, we no longer have the free variety of Pauline times, when every Christian, as a vessel of the Spirit, had a function, and when Paul could mention apostles, prophets, teachers, healers, miracle-workers, believers, leaders, administrators, and givers all in one breath. The Pastorals speak of specific "offices" with technical titles: bishop, deacon (perhaps deaconess), presbyter; even the "widows" seem to form a distinct group of functionaries.

The word "bishop," which comes from the Greek *episcopos*, means primarily "overseer." It was used as the title of an administrative officer in civic and cultic societies in the Hellenistic world, but it also appears in the Septuagint as the description of various jobs of supervision (Judg. 9:28; Num. 31:14; II Kings 12:11; Neh. 11:9; 14:23). As we noted in connection with Paul's apostolic leadership in the churches, the Qumran community knew the office of *mebaqqer*, an elected member of the group who administered the property of the community and may well have been called *episcopos* in Greek. It is impossible to decide where Christianity found the precise antecedent for its own use of the title. The analysis suggests in any event, that it was originally connected with the administration of local congregations and that the number of bishops in one place was not restricted to one. Paul, who is the first to mention the title in a Christian context (Phil. 1:1), probably understood it in this sense.

The combination "bishops and deacons" which is used in Paul, points in the same direction. The word "deacon" comes from the Greek *diakonos* and means "servant." Paul uses it often in a general sense: every preacher "serving" through the Word, and also every Christian who "serves" his brother following the example of Christ, may be called a *diakonos*. In Philippians 1:1, however, it is clearly the title for a specific function in the Church. Acts 6, the appointment of the Seven, in which the verb *diakonein* (to serve) is used, would indicate that its origin was in the ministry to the outward needs of the Church. The combination "bishop and deacon" has never ceased to exist in the terminology of the Christian ministry. It is usually taken to imply a hierarchical subordination: the deacon "assists" the bishop in his functions. When Paul speak of Epaphras, Tychicus, or Timothy as his "deacons" (Col. 1:7; 4:7; I Thess. 3:2), the notion of "assistants" certainly is in the foreground. To what extent such subordination is implied in Philippians 1:1, remains unclear.

"Elders" (Greek: *presbuteroi*, presbyters) may simply designate a respected group of older members in a given community. In Jewish congregations, such a body of "elders" was usually in charge of the administration. Luke speaks of a group of elders in the Jerusalem church (Acts 15; 21:18) and in other churches at Antioch (11:30) and Ephesus (20:17). However, the distinction between general and technical use is often hard to make. In many cases where the term occurs in the postapostolic literature we cannot decide with certainty which one is meant.[15] Whenever it is clear that "elders" is a title for Church leaders, however, the question arises how this office is related to that of bishop. After Paul, the duties of bishops were probably quickly growing beyond pure administrative functions. In the Didache, for example, the church in the province is being encouraged to elect local bishops and deacons to take the place of migrant charismatics, especially with regard to worship (Did. 15:1f.). The Didache does not mention presbyters. Conversely, other writings such as James, I Peter, and Revelation mention only presbyters, but not bishops. In many books we find both terms (Luke-Acts, I Clement, Ignatius, Pastoral Letters, Polycarp, Hermas). For Luke, the existence of the two titles side by side is simply a terminological problem: "bishops" and "presbyters" are two designations for the same office (see Acts 20:17, 28).[16] But when he maintains that Paul and Barnabas appointed "elders" in the churches of Asia Minor (Acts 14:23), while Paul himself in his Letters never mentions them, it becomes clear that Luke's solution is too easy. For the historian it would seem that the patriarchal institution of elders as Church leaders first developed independently of the administrative offices of bishops and deacons, and that the two forms eventually merged—a process which is reflected in our sources in a variety of "types."[17]

The most advanced type in terms of the future development may be found in the Letters of Ignatius. Here, a clear hierarchy of the local ministry is presupposed, consisting of bishop, presbyters, deacons—the so-called "three-fold ministry" (Magnesians 2; 6:1; Trallians 3:1; 7:2; Eph. 2:2; Philadelphians, Preface, etc.).[18] Deacons are clearly subordinated to bishops and presbyters alike (Magnesians 2). They "serve" everybody (Trallians 2:3), and three of them accompany Ignatius as servants on his voyage to martyrdom. The role of the presbyters is not sharply defined. As the bishop's "synhedrium" (Philadelphians

---

[15]For example, I Clem. 44:5; 47:6; 54:2; 57:1; I Pet. 5:1,5; Jas. 5:14; and from the Apostolic Fathers, Polycarp: Phil. 6:1; 11:1; Hermas: Vision II.4.2f; III.1.8.

[16]In modern times, the theory of an original office of presbyter-bishops has found a widespread following ever since J. B. Lightfoot's classical essay, "The Christian Ministry," in *Saint Paul's Epistle to the Philippians*, rev. ed. (London: Macmillan, 1890), pp. 181–269. See also B. H. Streeter, *The Primitive Church* (New York: Macmillan, 1929).

[17]This is the thesis of Hans von Campenhausen, *Ecclesiastical Authority and Spiritual Power in the Church of the First Three Centuries*, tr. J. A. Baker (Stanford: Stanford University Press, 1969).

[18]The Letters of Ignatius, like the Letters of Paul, are known by the names of the churches addressed, e.g., the Letter to the church at Magnesia is referred to simply as Magnesians. The extant letters together with a preface by Ignatius are collected under his name as a part of the early Christian (second century A.D.) Apostolic Fathers.

8:1) they are connected with him; they surround him as the apostles surround Christ (Trallians 2:1f.) and produce with him a harmony like the strings of a harp (Eph. 4:1). But it is quite clear that their share in active leadership is insignificant. The true congregational leader is the one bishop. As the guardian of the true apostolic tradition and the center of unity around whom Christians gather at the altar of the Eucharist, he is the God-given bulwark in the fight against heresy. In his high vision of this office which he himself held in Antioch, Ignatius may be somewhat ahead of the reality, but he can already address other monarchical bishops by name in some of the churches of Asia Minor: Damas in Magnesia, Polybius in Tralles, Polycarp in Smyrna, Onesimus in Ephesus. He implies that there is a bishop in Philadelphia, but fails to mention the bishop in either Rome or Philippi. This omission probably means that the monarchical episcopacy had not yet emerged in those two cities at this time. For Corinth, I Clement implies presbyterial leadership, even though the author seems to indicate that leaders in Rome are called bishops and deacons.

It is impossible to explain how the monarchical episcopacy emerged. Bishop Polycarp, in writing a letter to the church in Philippi, introduces himself as a *member* of the presbytery. This suggests one explanation: out of a college of presbyters, one man rose to the position of president and was distinguished by the title "bishop." Another explanation would be that in a given situation, the number of bishops was gradually reduced until a one-man office resulted.

Compared with Ignatius, the situation in the Pastoral Letters remains ambiguous. Very little is said about the range of duties for bishops, deacons, presbyters, widows, and about their relationship to each other. The Church order only lists the prerequisites (I Tim. 3:1ff.: bishop; 3:8ff.: deacons [and deaconesses?]; Tit. 1:5ff.: elders and bishop). The moral standards are generally stock: a good reputation, married only once, temperate, managing his household well, not loving money. Special features include the warning not to appoint a recent convert as bishop (I Tim. 3:6), and the requirement that the bishop be well thought of by outsiders (I Tim. 3:7). According to the quote in I Timothy 3:1, the office of bishop is regarded as "old," and the sequence in the chapter may imply superiority over the deacon. That the bishop's role, like that of Timothy and Titus, figures primarily in the fight against heresy, must be concluded from Titus 1:9. But his relationship to the presbytery is not clear. Sometimes bishops and presbyters seem to be identified (Tit. 1:5, 7). But the bishop always appears in the singular and is never mentioned together with the presbyters. Furthermore, the presbyters are clearly treated as a special group of regular officers (I Tim. 5:17f.) who among other things preach and teach. At any rate, in the projected ideal situation, presbyters do not have a leading function but at best an assisting role. The actual situation may have been similar to that in Smyrna: the bishop was a member of the presbytery which, as a patriarchal body, was composed of an honored group of older Christians *and* of others who, regardless of age, were honored on account of their office.

Whatever the title of the regular leaders in a local congregation may have been, they carried an immense responsibility. We have no evidence that many of them were profound thinkers, but they were loyal to Christ and to what they believed was the tradition of the apostles. They were the men who helped forge a strong community when the first enthusiasm of the primitive Church (and with it the effectiveness of the charismatic leadership) was fading. They sought to make the teachings of the Church and the Christian way of life relevant in a world that seemed less likely to come to an end soon than it had a few decades earlier.

THE JOHANNINE LETTERS WARN AGAINST ERROR

Among the Catholic Letters it is the Johannine Letters that are dominated by the conflict with false teaching. Here, however, we enter a completely different world of antiheretical argument. As to form, the category of "letter" does not really apply to all three writings. III John is a genuine private letter, addressed to a private individual. In II John, the address "To the elect lady and her children whom I love in truth" could refer to an individual Christian woman and her family, but since no name is mentioned and the admonitions seem to be directed to a Christian congregation, it may be a figurative expression for a particular church or for the Church at large. I John, though written with literary intentions ("I write to you"), is rather a tract or sermon without an epistolary frame.

To form an exact idea of the false teaching that the letters are opposing is not easy. The Johannine style abounds in allusions and often veils what it has to say in somewhat mystical language. However, the main features appear with reasonable clarity. Again the danger comes from within the Church. The false teachers were originally members of the Christian community where they went unnoticed until by open separation—maybe by founding a separatist assembly—they revealed their true identity (2:19). They are "false prophets" (I Jn. 4:1), "antichrists" (2:18). The language pattern of this description has its roots in apocalypticism. Jewish apocalypticism, and especially the apocalyptic literature of Qumran, considered the figure of Belial as the personification of the hellish powers of the End of the Age. The expectation of a powerful antimessianic figure had also become part of the Christian expectation from early times on (cf. II Cor. 6:14f.; II Thess. 2:3–4; Mk. 13:14; the "beast" of Revelation). As the allusions in Revelation show, Christians were tempted to connect this figure with contemporary phenomena and thus to understand their historic hour as the time immediately preceding the End. In this context, the message of I John: "The antichrist is in the world already" (4:3), being therefore the "last hour" (2:18), may not have been surprising. What is surprising is the widening of the concept to a plural, "many antichrists" (2:18), and its identification with the heretics. The problem of heresy for our author obviously has dimensions which can only be accounted for as manifestations of the apocalyptic End. For him, the dangerous nature of the antichrist is that he comes in disguise and is not easily recognized. Thus the aim of the Letters is to "unveil" his incognito by pointing to the marks which identify him. Recurring phrases like "if we say. . . ," or, "whoever says. . . ," introduce such statements which should help the reader to distinguish between "true" and "false."

The first and most prominent mark of these heretics is in the doctrinal field of Christology. They deny that "Jesus is the Christ" (2:22). This sounds like a Jewish denial of Jesus' messiahship, but another passage points in a different direction. What they deny is that "Jesus Christ has come in the flesh" (I Jn. 4:2; cf. II Jn. 7). It seems that Ignatius in his Letters confronts a similar heresy. He denounces in strong terms people who do not confess Jesus Christ to have been a "fleshbearer" (Smyrneans 5:2f.). For them Jesus' entire life was only appearance. He was not really born. He did not really grow. Ignatius' zeal for martyrdom makes him particularly alert against the implication that Jesus did not really suffer, but only appeared to. Against such "docetism" (from *dokein*, to appear), he quotes the Christian *kerygma*, emphasizing the reality of all events of Jesus' life. According to the antiheretical literature of the early Church, there were indeed certain Gnostics who pretended that Jesus Christ had been a "bodiless phantom."[19] Like Ignatius, the author of I John appeals to the kerygmatic tradition: against any heretical denial of Christ, the Christian "confesses" that Jesus has come in the flesh. The word "confess" (I Jn. 1:9; 2:23; 4:2f.; 4:15; II Jn. 7) suggests that the appeal is based on credal formulations, and it is precisely the center of the creed—Christ's death for us, *i.e.*, the "expiation for our sins" (2:2; cf. 1:7)—that is endangered by a docetic Christology.

The false teachers boastfully claim to have the Spirit, to be pneumatics (4:1ff.) and therefore to be "without sin" (1:8, 10). We cannot tell what consequences this conviction had in their case. But we know from other sources that the Gnostic feeling of superiority not only led to ascetic renunciation, but was sometimes carried to the other extreme of antinomianism and moral libertinism, especially with regard to sex. "To a king, they say, there is no law prescribed."[20] The heretics in the Johannine Letters are not accused of sexual license. But one consequence of their spiritual self-assurance seems to be that they look down upon the nonspiritual Christians in the Church. Again and again our author lashes out against the lack of brotherly love on the part of these separatists. One cannot love God and at the same time hate the brother (4:20). Lack of brotherly love simply indicates the denial of Christianity. The Church was always suspicious of Christians whose alleged superior knowledge separated them from fellowship with other Christians. Love of self instead of love of brother was not what God commanded. But we must admit that the definition of "brother" often tended to restrict the term to the narrow confines

---

[19]Pseudo-Justin, *About the Resurrection*, 2; Irenaeus, *Against Heresies*, I.24.2; Hippolytus, *Refutation*, VII.31.
[20]Clement of Alexandria, *Miscellanies*, III.30.

of the community, and that the conflict with heresy saw the Church itself in danger of becoming "sectarian." The Johannine Letters do strike the note of a universal Gospel (I Jn. 2:2, 29). But they also illustrate the peculiar dilemma of a Church that had only limited criteria to ward off false teaching.

Unlike the writer of the Pastorals, the Johannine author does not appeal to the fixed norms of a deposited faith and to an authoritative ministry. His authority is the appeal to the Holy Spirit, the Spirit of God, together with the reminder that his readers, too, have been "anointed" so that they are taught about everything (2:20, 27). Even the ambiguous witness with eye and hand to which he appeals in the famous opening of I John (1:1–3), and which may indicate his intention to put his writing under the authority of the apostle John, ought perhaps to be understood in terms of the general Christian claim to having the "right" spirit. The "we" is more than a reference to the Twelve. It includes all Christians who, through the gift of the Spirit, have "eternal life" already. In their spiritual unity with the Lord, they all witness to what they "have seen and heard" (1:3), what "was in the beginning" (1:1; cf. Jn. 1:1)—to the Word of life.

In the conflict over heresy, this spiritual claim had its weakness as well as its strength. The author of our Letters calls himself "the Elder." Scholars agree that this title probably points to some kind of spiritual authority rather than to a jurisdictional office, and III John may be taken as an illustration of the dilemma arising therefrom.[21] The Elder seems to be in close contact with the church in which Gaius, the addressee, is to be located (III Jn. 1). Some brethren —probably itinerant evangelists (verse 7)—have been visiting there recently (verse 3), and Gaius is commended for his hospitality (verse 5f.). The missionaries are now on their way to visit the church again, and the letter urges Gaius to help them once more "as befits God's service" (verse 6). But then, the Elder complains about a certain Diotrephes who does not "accept" him and his circle (verse 9). Diotrephes refuses to receive the missionaries and even "excommunicates" those who are willing to receive them. It has often been suspected that, as in I and II John, some kind of heresy is involved here. But there is no indication that Diotrephes is a heretic. The charge against him is that he "likes to put himself first" (verse 9), and that he—successfully—breaks off communion with the circle of the Elder, who seems very eager to see the situation corrected (verses 10, 13). Rather, this would suggest a strong leader of a local congregation, perhaps a "bishop," who wants to protect his flock from uncontrolled wandering "heretics."

With this evaluation of the emissaries of the Elder, Diotrephes has no doubt overshot the mark. But his opposition shows that the Johannine spirituality could easily be misunderstood as "Gnosticism" in a situation where the local leader, determined to keep the ship of orthodoxy afloat, would throw out everything that even smacked of Gnosis. We will see in a later chapter that the

---

[21] For the following, see E. Käsemann, "Ketzer und Zeuge," *Zeitschrift für Theologie und Kirche*, XLVIII (Tübingen: Mohr, 1951), 292–311.

Gospel of John makes use of Gnostic terminology in its interpretation of the Jesus tradition. It is the same in I John. Dualistic terminology abounds (light-darkness, truth-lie, God-the Evil One, love-hate, life-death). The "world" is not only regarded as passing away (2:15–17), but as the domain of the Evil One (5:19). The sinlessness of those who "know" is stressed emphatically (3:4ff.). However, at this last point, the evaluation of sin, the Johannine flavor becomes evident. The author says both: the Christian cannot sin, and: it is wrong to say we have no sin. The tension between the gift bestowed and the responsibility to make it real in action day by day does not leave room for resignation before a paradox (2:1f.). It is in the daily prayer for forgiveness that the Christian experiences what freedom from sin really means.

"John" is no Gnostic, even though he may have used Gnostic sources.[22] But the Johannine question reveals how difficult it was to draw the line between orthodox and heretical. On the one hand, the Church had to strive for a clearer, handier formulation of the *kerygma;* it had to develop a regular, authoritative ministry. Measured by these standards, the weapons "John" was using in his antiheretical fight were insufficient. But his call for "distinguishing the spirits" reminds us that in the last instance the effectiveness of any weapon rested in the one element which even the Church cannot "handle": The Spirit who makes alive.

JUDE AND II PETER LASH OUT AGAINST ERROR

How serious, if not actually desperate, the problem of false teaching became for the Church, and how grave the danger of losing its own identity became in the battle against heresy, may be gleaned from the brief letters called Jude and II Peter. It is generally assumed today that both are rather late and must be dated around the middle of the second century. To be sure, the author of II Peter wants to present a kind of last will of the apostle Peter (1:13–15), who is consistently presupposed as speaking. But it is easy to demonstrate the artificial character of his frame: (1) He refers to a rather complete New Testament canon (Synoptic Gospels: 1:16ff.; 3:10; Pauline Letters: 3:16; I Peter: 3:1). (2) He borrows extensively from Jude who in turn depicts the apostolic generation as being no less remote from the present than are the Old Testament prophets (verse 17). Actually, out of the twenty-five verses of Jude, no less than nineteen appear in one form or another in II Peter. (3) His letter implies a rather developed stage of the conflict with heresy.

The heresy against which both writings warn has certainly to do with Gnosis. A new aspect seems to be introduced by the attack on "authorities and excellencies," *i.e.*, higher angels who must have played a role in "Jude's"

---

[22]The assumption of a Gnosticizing source which was noted by the Johannine author is the basis of R. Bultmann's important commentary, *Die drei Johannesbriefe* (Göttingen: Vandenhoeck, 1967).

cosmological system (Jude 8ff.). Much of the material, however, repeats the general stock of antiheretical jargon (Jude 12–13; 16; II Pet. 2:12ff.; charge of immorality: Jude 7; II Pet. 2:14; love of money: Jude 11; II Pet. 2:3, 14). The reality behind this stylized picture seems to be much more alarming, however. In the church to which Jude is writing, the heretics are not even separated from the Christian congregation. Jude finds it painful to see them participate in the sacred meals, the love feasts (he speaks of their "carousing," Jude 12; cf. II Pet. 2:13). One would expect him to advise drawing the line and throwing out these men. But the Letter contains no such proposal. It offers only the hope that the faithful may "convince some who doubt," and "save some by snatching them out of the fire" (Jude 23). A possible explanation is that the heretics were in the majority, and Jude had only a small remnant of faithful Christians to write to.

The reaction to this situation on the part of "Jude" and "Peter" is deplorably weak. Of course, appeal is made to the Christian tradition, the "faith once for all delivered to the saints" (Jude 3). But the major traditional pattern to which both authors appeal is apocalypticism. As in I John, we find the image of the heretics who, being predestined "long ago" for their condemnation, have entered the Christian Church in disguise (Jude 3). Their appearance is the fulfillment of old prophecy—"Jude" refers to the apocryphal Book of Enoch (14ff.) as well as to the predictions of "the apostles of our Lord Jesus Christ" (17). The Christian can only preserve the faith, pray, and wait patiently, knowing that the punishment of the heretics is under way (20f.). Obviously, this latter point was crucial in the dangerous situation. "Jude" goes to great pains illustrating its truth by a catalogue of Old Testament examples that depict the destruction of the wicked: the unbelieving wilderness generation (verse 5); the fallen angels of Genesis 6 (verse 6); the immoral cities of Sodom and Gomorrah (verse 7); Cain, Balaam, and Korah (verse 11). The author of II Peter repeats this apocalyptic argument. As in Jude, the major point is that the destruction of heretics is near. They are kept "under punishment until the day of judgment" (2:9), or, using the venerable term of ancient Christian eschatology, until "the Coming of the Lord" (1:16).

Again, all this seems to be no longer self-evident. There are "scoffers" who raise doubts about this Coming and the reality of the Judgment (3:3ff.). Their argument is that even after the death of the previous generation ("the fathers"), which had every reason to believe that the End would come upon them, nothing has happened. Everything remained as it was from the beginning of Creation, and probably will so continue. The author seems to recognize the seriousness of this argument, because for himself the delay of the expected *parousia* is a problem. In his answer he first refutes the notion that the course of the world has remained unchanged ever since Creation. Once already, in the Great Flood, the created cosmos was destroyed; thus, "the heaven and the earth that now exist" will suffer similar destruction—this time by fire (3:5–7). However, the question of the exact time of the catastrophe must remain unresolved. God's chronology is different from ours (3:8). If the time seems somewhat long, there is still no reason for criticizing God's slowness, but rather for praising his forbearance which gives the sinner a chance to repent (3:10). Obviously, several apologetic arguments have been combined here in an attempt to explain the delay of the *parousia*. They are not all equally convincing. It is their application that really counts: the catastrophe is coming, only the date is uncertain.

II Peter has been called an "apologia for primitive Christian eschatology."[23] This certainly is true in a formal sense. But there is one important difference. The apostolic Church waited for the Coming of the Lord as the revelation of Christ's dominion over all the world. "Peter" is waiting for the Judgment that will finally wipe out the ungodly and vindicate the righteous. When he waits for a "new heaven and a new earth in which righteousness dwells" (3:13), he is longing for a world in which Christians finally will be at rest from their enemies. It is the whole misery of a hard-pressed Christian generation that appears in this transformation. We may feel sympathy with its troubles. But there can be no doubt: the more the Church allows the pressures and troubles of the present to dominate its faith and hope, the more difficulty it has in preserving its own identity. The author of II Peter is certainly unaware how close he himself has come to a "heretical" interpretation of Christianity. When he describes it as the goal of faithful life that the Christian "may escape from the corruption that is in the world because of passion and become partaker of the divine nature" (1:4), he has gone over the brink into pagan notions of apotheosis which are foreign to the *kerygma* that he wants to preserve.

The Church in the postapostolic period shows the marks of the bitter conflict with forces from outside and inside that threatened to submerge the Gospel under a general Hellenistic syncretism. It was the experience of these battles and the need to adjust to the fact of ongoing history that forced the direction of further development. There was an urgent need to fix the content of "faith" into a manageable tradition because it had come to this generation in a form insufficient to combat the ever-new countenance of false teaching. But what emerged as "orthodox" faith proved by no means a guarantee against error. The danger of losing contact with the Gospel remained an ever-present possibility. There was also the necessity of developing an institutionalized ministry because the freedom of the Spirit, in which authority rested pretty much on the persuasiveness of each preacher, proved ineffective in fighting the claims of false teachers. But again, this ministry was no guarantee against error. The Church leaders often lacked the competence to draw correct lines. Nevertheless, the Church had to take risks for the sake of the Gospel that was to speak to a new generation. It had to leave behind the innocence of its early days in order to grow to maturity.

23E. Käsemann, "An Apologia for Primitive Christian Eschatology," in *Essays on New Testament Themes*, tr. W. J. Montague, *Studies in Biblical Theology*, XLI (London: S. C. M. Press, 1964), 169–195.

Toward Stabilizing Worship and Ethics

I Peter, James, Hebrews

CHAPTER ELEVEN

We have seen to what extent the history of the Church in the postapostolic period was shaped by outside and inside conflicts. It would be a mistake, however, to reduce the determinative forces for the Church's development to mere defensive reactions. The substance of the Christian message from the beginning centered around the positive call to a new life in a new community and in the situations of everyday ethical decisions. The eschatological expectation of the early generation did not stifle, but rather enhanced the urgency of the appeal. The apostle Paul was convinced that the worship life of his congregations and the shape of their ethical conduct were the most important self-expression of the new Christian spirit. All his Letters were probably meant to be read out to the addressees when they were assembled for worship. They all contained important sections explaining how the *kerygma* can be applied to ethical situations of immediate concern. With the trend toward institutionalizing the Church in the postapostolic period, much of the spontaneous immediacy in worship and ethical instruction may have begun to wane. Regulated forms of worship became the norm, with the emerging ministry taking a more prominent part, and the frame for a fixed ethical code soon developed as part of the new concept of tradition. Yet there still was variety of self-expression in worship as converts from all kinds of backgrounds joined the Christian community, and the formation of a generally accepted ethical code remained a continuing problem as the issues to be solved were changing. The later Letters of the New Testament illustrate these developments in a fascinating way.

THE CENTRALITY OF WORSHIP

Any experience of conversion in the classical world led to new experiences of worship. The Christian convert joined a community whose eschatological self-consciousness shaped its worship in a rather unique way. Christians everywhere had a particular center of their celebration: God's act in Jesus Christ whom He had raised from the dead. Their celebration and worship life always reflected this basic fact of the Easter faith. Even the organization of their weekly calendar was an expression of it.

The prophet John in the Book of Revelation says that his first vision came to him on the "Lord's Day" (Rev. 1:10). In the time of Paul, Christians regularly assembled "on the first day of the week" (I Cor. 16:2). There are references to the "Lord's Day" in the Didache (14:1) and in Ignatius (Magnesians 9:1), and Barnabas mentions a meeting on the "eighth day" (15:9). The first day of the new week was the day after the Jewish Sabbath, the eighth day if one counted from the first day of the previous Jewish week. Justin Martyr, whose description of Christian worship is the single most important source from the second century, uses the pagan name, the "day of the sun."[1] According to the Easter tradition, Sunday was the day of Christ's Resurrection and therefore, from earliest times on, had become the main occasion for all Christians to gather together wherever they might be. Long before there was an annual celebration of Christ's Resurrection on Easter, the Church celebrated the Resurrection every week, on Sunday.

As far as we can tell, the elements of the Sunday worship service were pretty much the same as they had been in apostolic times: prayers, readings, preaching, instruction, and the singing of hymns and psalms.[2] It is easy to show that, formally, all of these had their antecedents in the worship service of the Jewish synagogue.[3] The Old Testament was read as a regular part of

---

[1]Justin Martyr, *Apology*, I.67. See also F. A. Reagan, *Dies Dominica and Dies Solis: The Beginnings of the Lord's Day in Christian Antiquity* (Washington, D.C.: Catholic University of America Press, 1961); W. Rordorf, *Sunday*, tr. A. A. K. Graham (Philadelphia: Westminster, 1968).

[2]For a more detailed discussion, see G. Delling, *Worship in the New Testament*, tr. P. Scott (Philadelphia: Westminster, 1962).

[3]See W. O. E. Oesterley, *The Jewish Background of the Christian Liturgy* (Oxford: Clarendon, 1925); C. W. Dugmore, *The Influence of the Synagogue Upon the Divine Office* (Oxford: Oxford University Press, 1944).

the service. This reading aloud was for many the only way to become familiar with the scriptures. No doubt the reading was often lengthy; Justin Martyr says that it went on "as long as there was time." We do not know whether there was any particular order in the readings from the Old Testament. In the service of the Jewish synagogue, from the third century A.D. on, the reading of the Law and the prophets was planned in such a way that the entire Old Testament was covered in one year. Moreover, the lectionary was coordinated with important religious festivals. Many scholars believe that this practice was much older; if so, it is possible that some such arrangement was practiced in the Christian Church as well, perhaps under the direct influence of the synagogue.[4]

In addition to the Old Testament, other writings were read in the church service. Later, Revelation was composed to be read in the churches of Asia Minor; I Clement to be read in Corinth; the Shepherd of Hermas in Rome, and so on. In recent years some scholars have theorized that the literary structure of the Gospels of Matthew, Mark, and John suggests that they were composed for liturgical reading. Whether or not we accept this thesis, it is likely that the gospels *were* read in the churches. Some churches may have preferred one gospel over another. Justin Martyr probably refers to gospel readings when he says that "the memoirs of the Apostles" were read regularly along with the Old Testament.

The reading of the scriptures was followed by preaching, teaching, and exhortation. This combination again seems to be Jewish heritage. The so-called Second Epistle of Clement, which in reality is a sermon, alludes to it (II Clem. 19:1f.); and Justin Martyr tells us that after the lesson, the leader would give a sermon explaining and applying the passage read.

Prayer was also an important element in the service. As we have seen, spontaneous and free prayers were common in the Pauline churches, especially among the Christian prophets. Under the influence of the synagogue and Jewish Christianity, however, the formulated corporate prayer took precedence over spontaneous prayer. In I Timothy it is urged that "supplications, prayers, intercessions, and thanksgivings be made for all men" (I Tim. 2:1). This indicates some of the regular elements of prayer in the community. Fortunately, one of these liturgical prayers that was used in the church of Rome has survived and is found in I Clement 59–61. It is a good illustration of how prayers that were undoubtedly used in the Hellenistic synagogues of the Diaspora were adapted to Christian usage. The main features are clearly visible: the invocation with an elaborate kerygmatic predication of God; the general prayer of intercession, including a prayer for peace and welfare and a prayer for the government; and the final doxology. Of particular importance was the Lord's Prayer, which in the Gospel of Matthew is already presented as the one

---

[4] A. Guilding, *The Fourth Gospel and Jewish Worship: A Study of the Relation of St. John's Gospel to the Ancient Jewish Lectionary System* (1960), tries to show that the structure of the fourth Gospel follows the order of a synagogue lectionary.

prayer which Jesus taught his disciples. It must have been in general use in the worship of the Church at an early date. The Didache instructs Christians to say the Lord's Prayer and adds: "Pray thus three times a day" (8:3), an indication that it was not only used as part of corporate worship but as a personal prayer as well.

Finally, part of the worship service was given over to psalms and hymns. In several places Paul mentions the use of hymns among Christians (I Cor. 14:26; Col. 3:16). Most of the psalms were taken from the Old Testament, but other kinds of hymns and songs were used, too. It is recognized today that many books of the New Testament make use of Christian hymnic traditions. In some cases it is relatively easy to recognize hymns or hymnic fragments which, by virtue of their rhythmic structure, stand out from the context: the three hymns in Luke 1–2, known as the *Magnificat* (1:46–55), the *Benedictus* (1:68–79), and the *Nunc Dimittis* (2:29–32); the hymns in Revelation (4:8, 11, 11:17f; 12:10ff.; 15:3f.; 19:1–8); the fragments in I Timothy 3;16 and Ephesians 5:14, and others. A hymnic background has been suggested for numerous New Testament passages (e.g., Phil. 2:5–11; Jn. 1:1ff.). In their use of hymns, Christians seem to have been heavily indebted to the Jewish synagogue; but like the Jewish heterodox movements, they also created new hymns, often in competition with Gnostic circles. The discovery of the *Odes of Solomon,* a second-century Christian Gnostic book of hymns to Christ and to the Christian virtues, is a good illustration.

The worship service also included doxologies or brief acclamations of praise to God, some of which are already found in the Pauline Letters (*e.g.,* Rom. 9:5; 11:36; 16:25–27). The later writings of the New Testament abound with both doxologies and benedictions. Often we are unable to establish their precise liturgical function. However, many seem to have been connected with the fellowship meal which during our period gained more and more importance and formed the climax of the regular Christian service.

We still have a variety of designations for the meal which Christians apparently were celebrating in every congregation. The Didache calls it "breaking of bread," a term that had been used from earliest times (Acts 2:42; 20:7). Ignatius and the Letter of Jude (verse 12) speak of *agapē*–a Greek word meaning "love," or in this connection, "love feast." Both terms suggest a special rite related to the fellowship meals. But a new term gained increasing prominence during the postapostolic era: *eucharist*–a Greek world meaning "thanksgiving." It is derived not only from the thanksgiving characteristic of the prayers used in the rite, but also from the character of the rite itself as a "sacrifice of thanksgiving" to God for his gift of salvation in Jesus Christ. As in the earlier period, however, the primary meaning of the meal was Christ's presence in the midst of those who ate together, and the hope it engendered in his final Coming.

There is some difference of opinion among scholars as to whether a special rite of the Lord's Supper (Eucharist) was ever observed *apart from* the fellow-ship meal in the first century A.D. It is perfectly clear from the Didache and Ignatius that the fellowship meal had not completely disappeared at the beginning of the second century, and we have further evidence to this effect in the letter of Pliny mentioned earlier (p. 246). The first certain proof we have for the separation of the two comes from Justin Martyr (*Apology* I. 65 and 67) who speaks of the Eucharist only and does not mention the fellowship meal. What probably happened was that this separation came with the growing importance of sacramentalism and took place gradually in different churches during the late first and early second centuries.

By the end of the first century A.D. certain liturgical forms for the Eucharist had developed. The Didache instructs Christians to come together on the Lord's Day, break bread, and hold the Eucharist "after you have confessed your transgressions" (Did. 14). This is an indication that a prayer of confession was already in use. Concerning the cup, the following words are to be repeated (9:1–2):

> We give thanks to thee, our Father, for the holy vine of David, thy child, which thou didst make known to us through Jesus, thy child. To thee be glory forever.

And concerning the bread (9:3–4):

> We give thanks, our Father, for the light and knowledge which thou didst make known to us through Jesus, thy child. To thee be glory forever. As this broken bread was scattered upon the mountains, but was brought together and became one, so let thy Church be gathered together from the ends of the earth into thy kingdom, for thine is the glory and the power through Jesus Christ forever.

Furthermore, the rule is urged that only baptized members be allowed to eat and to drink of the elements (9:5; cf. Justin, *Apology* I. 66.1). Then the author gives a final prayer for the Eucharist (10:25) which, as the other two, shows strong resemblance to Jewish prayer style. There is also a short responsive fragment which probably was arranged in the following way (10:6):

> LITURGIST: Let the grace come and let this world pass away!
> CONGREGATION: Hosannah to the Son of David!
> LITURGIST: If any man be holy, let him come! If any man be not,
>   let him repent! Maranatha!
> CONGREGATION: Amen.[5]

---

[5]See H. Lietzmann, *Mass and Lord's Supper: A Study in the History of Liturgy*, tr. with appendices by D. Reeves; introduction and supplementary essay by R. D. Richardson (Leiden: Brill [fasc.4], 1955), p. 193.

We cannot say how representative these prayers were. Even the Didache, after quoting the final liturgical prayer, adds: "But suffer the prophets to give thanks as they will" (Did. 10:7). This is an acknowledgment of the prophet's right to engage in free and spontaneous prayer. The difficulty was that prophets were not always available, and it seems that it is for this reason that the author offers a formulary that could be used as a regular substitute.

The tendency toward a more formal liturgical setting for the Eucharist certainly had been enforced by the Church in its battle against false teaching. In his Letters, Ignatius repeatedly insists that the Eucharist can be held only where bishop, presbyters, and deacons are present. Ignatius knew that in some churches members were celebrating the Eucharist isolated from the main body of Christians. Others were refusing to participate at all. He sensed a real danger here, for once the rite stopped being shared by all Christians, their unity would be threatened. So Ignatius attacked misconceptions about the Eucharist and insisted that there was only one Eucharist—the one shared by the whole Church and interpreted by its recognized leaders. His own interpretation gave the Eucharist special theological importance because here, in the immediate communion with the flesh and blood of the Lord, the Christian already can find the goal of his salvation: the "life that triumphs over death." Thus, the one bread in its identity with Christ's body and blood, acquires almost magical powers. Ignatius calls it "medicine of immortality," or "antidote against death" (Eph. 20:2) in order to indicate the reality of the new life which the Christian experiences in this celebration.

It is clear that for Ignatius the bishop, who alone guarantees the effective distribution of the sacramental food, has a priestly function. The equation, "with the bishop = in the realm of the altar" (Eph. 5:2; Trallians 7:2) indicates this fact. With the idea of the priestly bishop acting at the altar, the Christian ministry took on a new significance. Soon his priestly mediation was to become the center of the Christian understanding of the ministry.

However, for the postapostolic period, this development was still far overshadowed by the importance of one worship experience in which the Church, together with the crowds of new converts, celebrated in a most solemn way the triumphal consequences of Christ's Easter victory: the rite of baptism. There can be no doubt that the old form of baptism, as the initiation of the individual into the community of the God-given new life, took on tremendous significance in the Gentile churches. The "rebirth" (I Pet. 1:3, 23; Jn. 3:3), the "illumination" (Heb. 6:4; Eph. 5:14), or "sealing" (Eph. 1:13f.; 4:13; Hermas, Similitudes IX.16.4), as it is variously described, mediated a new life affecting *all* phases of the existence: forgiveness of past sins, strength and direction for right conduct in the present, and the gift of the Spirit which "sealed" the Christian for eternal life in the New Age. We do not know much about the form in which baptism was administered, although the picture presented by

Justin Martyr later in the second century may give us an idea.[6] Acts, like Eph. 1:13f., stresses the general sequence of hearing the word, believing, and being baptized. When the head of a household took this step, other members probably simply followed along (Acts 2:39; 2:41; 8:12; 9:18; 10:47f.; 16:33). But children are not mentioned in this connection.[7] Luke presupposes that the rite originally was rather informal and spontaneous (Acts 2:41; 8:36–37). There is, however, reason to believe that in his reports of baptisms he occasionally slips into formulas of the baptismal liturgy of his own time (cf. Acts 16:30f.; 8:37; see p. 289).

We have clear evidence of a concern for the proper form of the rite in the instruction contained in the Didache (Chapter 7):

> Concerning baptism, baptize thus: Having first rehearsed all these things, baptize in the name of the Father, and of the Son, and of the Holy Spirit, in running water; but if thou hast no running water, baptize in other water, and if thou canst not in cold, then in warm. But if thou hast neither, pour water three times on the head in the name of the Father, Son, and Holy Spirit. And before the baptism let the baptizer and him who is to be baptized fast, and any others who are able. And thou shalt bid him who is to be baptized to fast one or two days before.

The most important feature here is that the solemn rite (which presupposes a trinitarian formula!) is connected with a time of preparation marked by a fast. "Preparation" for baptism seems also to include some kind of formal instruction. The phrase, "having rehearsed all these things," refers to the first six chapters in which the conduct in the "way of life" is contrasted to that in the "way of death." A very similar pattern of ethical instruction is found in the Letter of Barnabas (Chapters 18–20). It is quite probable that this "catechism of the two ways," which may have roots in the proselyte instruction of the synagogue, was part of the baptismal instruction in the community where the writings originated.[8] Just how long the Church had been giving formal instruction in connection with baptism we cannot tell. But scholars today are inclined to trace a fair amount of the didactic materials in the New Testament to the situation of "catechesis," i.e., to baptismal instruction. It must have been one of the most important opportunities not only to explain the basic structure of

---

[6]Justin Martyr, *Apology*, I.61ff. See the translation in *Early Christian Fathers*, Cyril C. Richardson, ed., The Library of Christian Classics, I (Philadelphia: Westminster, 1953), 282ff.

[7]For the debate concerning infant baptism, see the (positive) study by J. Jeremias, *Infant Baptism in the First Four Centuries*, The Library of History and Doctrine (Philadelphia: Westminster, 1960); and the (critical) answer by K. Aland, *Did the Early Church Baptize Infants?*, tr. with an introduction by G. R. Beasley-Murray, preface by J. F. Jansen (Philadelphia: Westminster, 1963).

[8]On the divergent views concerning the origin of this catechism, see the introduction in J. P. Audet, *La Didaché: Instructions des apôtres* (Paris: Gabalda, 1958), pp. 122ff.

THE OLDEST BAPISTRY (reconstruction) *ever found was in a tiny chapel at Dura Europos, on the Euphrates River in northeastern Syria. The walls of the chapel, which was destroyed in* A.D. *258, were covered with paintings of Biblical scenes, traces of which are still visible. The person to be baptized stood in the shallow pool and had water poured over his head.* (Yale University Art Gallery)

the *kerygma,* the message about Jesus Christ, but also to lay a sound basis for the convert's ethical life in a future which no longer seemed likely to end soon.

I PETER AS A WORSHIP DOCUMENT

Among the writings of the New Testament, the so-called First Letter of Peter is the most important document from the postapostolic period in which the liturgical frame of the baptismal celebration is as much present as the element of catechetical instruction, and thus the teaching of the Christian ethical code. Worship and daily life are not separated for this generation. On the contrary, one lives from the other.

I Peter reflects the normal frame of the Gentile Christian experience in this period as we have characterized it earlier. To become a Christian, to be baptized, meant first of all to meet the threat of misunderstanding, of suspicion, of persecution from one's surroundings. It is astonishing how well the situation to which the author addresses himself, fits in with the circumstances known to us from the Pliny-Trajan correspondence (see pp. 246–247). On the basis of the mention of "Babylon" (5:13), which probably is a cryptic designation for Rome (cf. Rev. 14:8; 18:2), and of the tradition that associates Mark with Peter in Rome, the Letter is believed to have been written from Rome. No better alternative has been proposed. It is directed to Christians in Asia Minor. The list of five provinces (Pontus, Galatia, Cappadocia, Asia, Bithynia) includes the areas of Pliny's actions. Allusions to the addressees' "former ways" make it quite clear that they are former Gentiles (1:14, 18, 21; 2:9f.; 3:6; 4:2ff.). The people in their environment react with surprise and open hostility to the Christian's withdrawal from the activities and pleasures of ordinary life which the author paints appropriately in the colors of vices (4:3f.). The new faith even splits families. Christian wives are urged to refrain from open attempts at converting their husbands, but rather to win them by their conduct as good wives (3:1f.). Christians are being accused as "criminals" (2:12; 4:14ff.), and there seems to be no way of appealing such an accusation. Only by his correct behavior can the Christian show his innocence. For the rest, if he has a good conscience, he must be prepared to "suffer for righteousness' sake."

The word "suffer" dominates much of I Peter. Suffering here probably means more than just bearing the general hostility of one's neighbors.[9] If it is "suffering as Christian" for the "name" (4:16), then the threat of the "fiery ordeal" (4:12) must be the type of persecution Christians were facing under the rules laid down in the Pliny correspondence.[10] The Christian is advised not to act provocatively ("in your hearts reverence Christ as Lord"). However, when he is called to account, he should with a clear conscience affirm his allegiance and take the consequences (3:13ff.). The author's insistence on blameless conduct is aimed at keeping the issues clear. Christians were accused of civil crimes such as murder, theft, "wrong-doing," "mischief-making" (4:15), and later Church Fathers refer to even more atrocious popular charges.[11] In the face of such charges, the great danger for the new Christian was to yield to pressure and become apostate: "Your adversary the Devil prowls around like a roaring lion, seeking someone to devour. Resist him, firm in your faith. . . ." (5:8f.).

At several points in the Letter, the dangers of the present are placed in a wider context. The sufferings which the Christian has to endure are a necessary episode and test faith like fire that purges dross and exposes the true gold (1:7); it is a signal that the great Judgment, which begins with the Church (4:17), is coming upon Christians throughout the world (5:10). In spite of this apocalyptic horizon, the author has not yet drawn the conclusion of Revela-

---

[9]The latter is the interpretation of W. C. Van Unnik, who consequently denies any reference to persecution in the Letter: "Christianity According to First Peter," *Expository Times*, LXVIII (London, 1956), 79–83; "Peter, First Letter of," in *The Interpreter's Dictionary of the Bible*, III (Nashville: Abingdon, 1962), 762.

[10]See the commentary by F. W. Beare, *The First Epistle of Peter*, 2nd ed. (Oxford: Blackwell, 1958).

[11]See especially Origen, *Against Celsus*, VI.27, 40; and Tertullian's *Apology*.

tion—namely, that his generation is witnessing the final battle in which, under the cover of the Roman state, the powers of hell are fighting against God and his People. Although he warns that those who persecute will also be subject to judgment (4:17), he urges Christians to recognize the emperor and his officials as the powers of order (2:13; 2:17). In the face of the tests and troubles of the End of Time, the Christian entrusts himself humbly into the hands of the True Judge, waiting for the day when he will rejoice in glory. This attitude of loyalty and moderation toward Rome in fact characterizes the second-century Church, where the prayer for the emperor was part of the liturgy,[12] and where the attempt was made to work out a way of coexistence with the empire.

There can be little doubt that the main body of I Peter must in some way be connected with the rite of baptism. The author addresses himself to new converts (1:12ff.; 2:2; 4:3ff.); and if we can take our clue from later baptismal liturgies or sermons it seems obvious that baptismal terminology abounds throughout the Letter (e.g., 1:23; 2:2; 3:21). Of special interest are the exodus typology (1:2; 2:9f.), and the reference to Noah and the Flood (3:20). Arguing from these facts, the suggestion has been made that I Peter preserves the liturgical formulary of a full baptismal service in the early Church,[13] including first an initial prayer psalm (1:3–12) and a brief instruction (1:3–21) which immediately preceded the act of baptism (after 1:21). Then came a short exhortation (1:22–25), a hymn (2:1–10), a longer sermon (2:11–3:12), an apocalyptic address (3:13–4:7a), and finally the concluding prayer (here changed to an exhortation) ending with the doxology (4:7b–11c). According to this interpretation, the prayers and exhortations in 4:12–5:11 (which is generally acknowledged to be independent of the major section) would reflect a brief concluding service involving the whole congregation.

I PETER AS A MANUAL OF ETHICS

Such an analysis may be too bold. But there is good reason to believe that the material in 1:3–4:11 was meant to be delivered in connection with a baptismal service. For converted Gentiles, the ethical implications of entering the new life *were* a serious matter. They had to renounce all the ways of their past (4:3). If baptism had freed them from sin, they needed advice how to keep

---

[12]I Clement 61; Polycarp: Letter to the Philippians 12:3; Justin Martyr, *Apology*, I.17.3; Tertullian, *Apology*, 30.

[13]The following analysis is that of H. Preisker in the Appendix to the commentary by H. Windisch, *Die Katholischen Briefe*, 2nd ed., Handbuch zum Neuen Testament, XV (Tübingen: Mohr, 1951), 156–160. F. L. Cross, *I Peter: A Paschal Liturgy* (London: Mowbray, 1954), even suggests that I Peter constitutes the celebrant's part in the liturgy of a baptismal service on Easter Eve. See, however, the criticism of C. F. D. Moule in *New Testament Studies*, III (Cambridge: Cambridge University Press, 1956–57), 1–11.

their new status undefiled. Ethical instruction was a necessary part of the Word, the "good news" which preceded their baptism (1:12; 1:23; 2:8; 3:1). The Church did not weave its norms of conduct out of thin air. Today we can distinguish a wide range of influences under which the Church, though often quite unconsciously and spontaneously, worked out the details. There are five main sources: first, there was the Old Testament, which Christians accepted as their sacred scripture. Second, there was the ethical tradition of various apocalyptic sects in Judaism which depended on the Biblical tradition, although in a peculiar form. The Dead Sea Scrolls have shed much light on the whole movement. Third, there were the teachings of Jesus, preserved by oral tradition and finally written into the Gospels. But since Jesus had not tried to give a systematic code of ethics, later Christians, especially in a Gentile environment, were confronted by many ethical decisions for which they had no ready answer from the tradition about his teachings. Evidences of reinterpretation reflecting the need to adapt this teaching to a new environment are already found in the Gospels themselves. A fourth source of ethical standards was the instruction used in the Hellenistic synagogues for the training of proselytes. Hellenistic Judaism was indebted not only to the Jewish tradition, but also to the ethical teaching of Hellenistic philosophy, the influence of which is evident throughout the New Testament. A fifth source was the common store of Hellenistic moral instruction, as it is represented by the preaching of the wandering stoic and cynic moralists, although in many cases it may be difficult to ascertain whether the borrowing was direct or mediated through the Hellenistic synagogue. In the Christian catechetical context, the details may have varied, but, being structured after the pattern of the *kerygma,* the emerging norms of conduct gave a concrete expression to the common faith and began to identify the Church as a cohesive social organism in the Roman world. I Peter is so valuable for our study of the Church's ethical teaching because it provides an actual example of content and form of this teaching as it was used in preparing converted Gentiles for baptism.

The author of I Peter prefaces his instructions with a statement on the substance, source, and aim of the faith that lies at the heart of all ethical action (1:3–12). In baptism, Christians enter a *radically* new life, they are "born anew." What is the source and substance of this new life? The source is God himself, the Father of Jesus Christ—of the Lord to whom the Christian has committed himself. Its substance is a living "hope"—a word which the author uses almost interchangeably with faith (*e.g.,* 3:15). This hope is a gift, made possible when God raised Jesus Christ from the dead and thereby revealed that men will obtain salvation. Since faith and hope are the source of the Christian's joy (1:6), Christians will not sidestep ethical decisions that bring them trials and hardship; their actions are not directed toward temporal ends, but toward proving their faithfulness to God (1:6–7). This then is the foundation which the author lays for his ethical instruction—a sure knowledge that the new life is not to be measured primarily by what the Christian does, but by what he hopes and believes.

The Christian's primary concern with faith, however, does not free him from responsibility for his actions. He must be capable of making sober judgments in his daily life if he is not to betray the hope he has (1:13). This means that Christians can no longer follow their desires as they did before they knew God as revealed through Jesus Christ (1:14). The central demand is that they conform in their conduct to the fact that he is holy (1:16); he is the judge of all men, and he judges them according to their deeds (1:17). Through Jesus Christ, God has ransomed them from their bondage to pagan idolatries and from the futile dissipation of the way of life they had inherited from their fathers (1:18). But this means that they have really become exiles in the world (1:17). God's holiness has revealed the futility of any way of life except that lived in faith and hope in the God who raised Jesus Christ from the dead. Christians can no longer be at home with the world's ways.

What is the way of holiness? It is the way of love. Christians who have obediently responded to God's act of love have been purified and have been given a new birth in a new community of love. This community's life is born out of and sustained by one thing: the active power of God's saving Word disclosed in the Gospel. All other grounds of life are transient. The substance of the new life in the new community is the sincere love of the members for one another (1:22–25).

Notice how logically the author has proceeded through this opening discussion. First, he announced that the new life is grounded in faith (1:3–12). Then, he emphasized that faith inevitably demands holiness (1:13–21). And now he concludes that faith and the new life it brings are the foundations of a new community (1:22–25). This community is called "a chosen race, a royal priesthood, a holy nation, God's own people" (2:9). All of these are titles of honor which, in the Old Testament, explained Israel's role as the instrument of God's plan of salvation for all men. The early Christians held that by rejecting Jesus, the People of Israel had forfeited this role. Through the death and resurrection of Jesus, God was finally calling his People together in a new way, fulfilling his promises to them through the coming of the Holy Spirit and using those who "were no people," the despised Gentiles, as his "New Israel." As a holy nation, then, the Church takes over the role of Israel. She is in exile in the world and Christians are aliens (2:11). And as long as the community lives in this world, its one authority for action is God's holy will, as revealed through Jesus Christ. This meant that the most the Church could do before the final salvation was to adjust herself to the world for the time being. Political, social, economic institutions, and the temporal purposes for which they were set up, were all part of a life that would soon pass away. Consequently, the Church worked out no program of social or political reform. She accepted the social order as it was, although its acceptance did not imply absolute approval. The primary obligation of the Church was to live in and to bear witness to the world according to the will of God. Sometimes this meant separating herself completely from the practices of the world—as she did on matters involving pagan worship and the loose attitude toward sex. But on other points, the Church accommodated herself—as in her relation to government and to social institutions like slavery.

The ethical instruction in I Peter reflects the teaching of the early Church on these matters. Beginning with 2:1, and continuing through 4:11, we have a series of exhortations. Study of the Greek text shows that each instruction begins with a technical phrase derived from a Hebrew formula.[14] This phrase is used elsewhere in the New Testament, especially in Colossians and Romans, I Thessalonians, Ephesians, and throughout the Pastoral Letters. In fact, all these passages, including those in I Peter, show similarity of content as well. In Colossians (3:8–4:12) we find a series of exhortations to put off certain vices, worship God, submit to certain people, and be watchful. In Ephesians (4:22–6:20) there are similar exhortations regarding putting off sins, worshiping, submitting, and watching. And I Peter has instructions to put away insincerity (2:1), to worship (2:4–5), to abstain (2:11), to be subject (2:13), to submit (2:18; 3:1; 3:7), and to watch (keep sane and sober because the end of all things is at hand)—(4:7). Each of these epistles contains a brief statement about the new life of the Christian in terms of the New Creation (Col. 3:10ff.; Eph. 4:24), and the same reference appears in I Peter in terms of regeneration (1:3). Apparently, there is embedded in all these Letters a pattern of instruction defining the nature of the new life given in baptism and governing the conduct of Christians in the world.[15] Each teacher would use the basic pattern, but adapt the materials to the local situation.

According to I Peter, the one law that determines the life of the Christian community is the law of love. But this is not a vague or sentimental quality; basically, it is love for Christ as Lord (1:8). And to love Christ means to love what he loved—hence, Christians are to love one another. Now the author goes on to spell out in greater detail just what is meant by love. Since love is always concerned with the welfare of the brother, any words or deeds that harm him must be put aside (2:1). Like newborn babes, Christians should long for the holy life of love (spiritual milk) in order to be nurtured in preparation for their coming salvation. Obviously, since it was within this community that "the kindness of the Lord" (2:3) was known, it is here and not in any other community of the world that the life of love can be nurtured.

---

[14]D. Daube, *The New Testament and Rabbinic Judaism* (London: Athlone, 1956), pp. 90–105.

[15]See P. Carrington, *The Primitive Christian Catechism* (Cambridge, England: Cambridge University Press, 1940).

Christian Action in a Non-Christian World

Having dealt with the new life as the basis of ethical action, and with the new community as the place in which the new life is nurtured, we shall now consider the relationship between Christians and the pagan world. The instruction takes the form of a catechism dealing with various relationships: *government, slavery, marriage and the family.* The formula and content of the various duties prescribed in I Peter and in other Letters of the New Testament (Col. 3:18ff.; Eph. 5:22ff.; I Tim. 2:8ff.; 6:1f.; Tit. 2:1ff.) show a dependence on pre-Christian codes of ethical action.[16] These codes are commonly referred to as "household tables," because they describe the duties of the average person in his relationship at home and in the world. The foremost source from which these materials are borrowed is the Hellenistic synagogue which had already been influenced by the ethical teaching of Hellenistic philosophies.

GOVERNMENT.   The first specific instruction deals with the Christian's relation to the Roman government. We have already dealt with this aspect. The Christians' respect for the law and for the officials who enforced it did not stem from political convictions. They were simply accommodating themselves to the times, although their decision to do so was based on what they believed to be the will of God—that is, to do no moral evil. Ultimately, the Christian was a servant, not of the emperor, but of God. The instruction in I Peter says, "Honor the emperor"—only God is to be feared.

SLAVERY.   This same principle came into play when the Christian community tried to work out the relationship between slaves and masters. This was an acute problem, for there were many slaves in the Christian community.[17] The fact that the instruction in I Peter, contrary to Ephesians and Colossians, makes no mention of the masters' obligations to their slaves may mean that this instruction was intended mainly for slaves. Paul had already defined the relation of slaves and masters in the Church. There was no distinction among those who were in Christ (Gal. 3:28). But this freedom was a gift of God and not of the world. The Roman world had its own definite laws regarding free men and slaves; and Christians, who were subject to the Roman state, might possess slaves. Paul even wrote a letter (Philemon) to a fellow Christian, urging him to permit a runaway slave to return without punishment.

So the instruction reads, "Servants, be submissive to your masters with all respect, not only to the kind and gentle, but also to the overbearing"—(2:18).

---

[16]See the discussion in E. G. Selwyn, *The First Epistle of St. Peter,* 2nd ed. (New York: St. Martin's Press, 1958), pp. 194ff.

[17]See P. Allard, *Les Esclaves chrétiens depuis les premiers temps de l'Eglise jusqu'à la fin de la domination romaine en occident,* 5th ed. (Paris: Lecoffre, 1914).

Yet, from the standpoint of the Christian faith, slavery was just as transient an institution as the Roman government itself. Consequently, the government's approach to the relationship between slaves and masters was different from the Christian approach. According to Roman law, the slave was a chattel in the hands of his master. He had no civil rights and his master could punish him as he pleased. The instruction here obviously implies that the slave should fulfill his obligations to his master in accordance with customary practice, and that he should be a good slave (cf. Col. 3:22ff.; Eph. 6:5ff.; I Tim. 6:1f.; Tit. 2:9f.; Didache 4:11). The slave must even go beyond what is expected of him and be kind and gentle to a master who may abuse him, for he is ultimately obligated to the will of God. The pattern for his conduct is none other than Christ himself: "When he was reviled, he did not revile in return; when he suffered, he did not threaten; but he trusted to him who judges justly"—(2:23).

Here we see how Christians conformed to convention while searching for an ethical code. While the slave fulfills his obligations to his master, his conduct is not governed primarily by law, but by the spirit of Christ. It is not surprising that many masters were led into the Church through the example of their Christian slaves.

Unfortunately, this early Christian instruction was to be used centuries later as a justification for slavery. In America, during the early nineteenth century, many sermons were preached on this very text to justify slavery as a divine institution established by God's will as revealed in the New Testament. Nothing could have been further from the mind of the early Church. Slavery, like every human institution, existed by God's sufferance as long as this world order continued. Christians made no effort to justify slavery on the grounds of philosophical or social theory, for they did not expect the present order to last much longer. They did not try to defend it as a divine institution; they merely asked themselves the question: Given this relationship between Christians and the world, how can we act to bear witness to God's will?

MARRIAGE AND THE FAMILY.   The instruction in I Peter next deals with marriage (3:1–7). The requirement that the Christian wife "be submissive" to her husband was in no sense peculiar to the Christian community (cf. Eph. 5:22ff.; I Tim. 2:9–15; I Clement 1:3; Polycarp 4:2). Both Jewish and Gentile teachers pictured the ideal wife as faithful and obedient. But again, we find the ideal interpreted in a peculiarly Christian way. The instruction implies that the wives who are being addressed are married to non-Christian husbands. According to the Hellenistic philosopher Plutarch, the ideal wife should accept her husband's religion. But for a Christian wife to renounce her faith would be to act contrary to the will of God. And yet, she was not to withdraw from the relationship altogether. In all other respects she was to live up to the common ideal of the good wife in simplicity and with a "gentle and quiet spirit."

Here again we see how the Christian, though following a pattern of conduct not peculiarly Christian, in a relationship also not peculiarly Christian, is to act in such a way as to transform the whole relationship. When we recall the common hostility against the Christians, we can imagine how little peace there must have been in homes where Christian wives were regarded as insubordinate by their non-Christian husbands. But through the manifestation of the new life into which she had entered, she was to give new meaning to marriage so that her husband might be won to Christ, and the ultimate sanction for her fulfilling the role of wife was not to satisfy convention, but that she "do right" in the sight of God (3:6).

The instruction to husbands again brings up what was regarded as the proper conduct of husband toward wife (3:7). The Christian husband is to live "considerately with his wife." The translation does not quite do justice to the original Greek, which literally reads "live with her according to knowledge." The phrase refers to the "knowledge" that the husband has been granted through his new faith: "You are joint heirs of the grace of life." Although the husband is to maintain his traditional authority, through his faith he is to regard his wife as a joint partner in eternal hope and life. In the future world, there will be no difference (Mk. 12:25). He is no longer to think of her as simply the woman who bears his children or who acts as steward in the household. Their life together is to be transformed into a Christian relationship within the context of an institution that was in no sense peculiarly Christian.

THE AUTHOR'S APPEAL TO THE JESUS TRADITION.   The instruction concerning ethical action in relation to the world ends with a plea for "unity of spirit, sympathy, love of the brethren, a tender heart and a humble mind" (3:8). It brings together two qualities of the new life that are most difficult to hold in balance: humility on the one hand, and acting in accordance with the will of God on the other (3:8–21). True humility means that Christians must return a blessing when they are reviled (3:9). It means defending their faith, not in arrogance, but in gentleness (3:13–15). Christians are to conduct themselves in such a way that their accusers will be shamed. And the pattern for humility is to be found in the example of Jesus Christ, who himself stood before the Roman procurator, Pilate, and then suffered on the Cross (3:17–4:1).

This is already the second instance in the course of his ethical exhortations where the author makes an elaborate appeal to the Jesus tradition. In 2:21ff. he had based the rule that the Christian slave should submit patiently even to punishment for doing right, on the example of the patient suffering of Jesus Christ. The same argument is used here when he stresses the suffering of the "righteous for the unrighteous" (3:18). However, the rest of the long kerygmatic digression does not seem to be to the point. In the next verse, mention is made of Christ's having "preached to the spirits in prison" who are identified as the unbelieving contemporaries of Noah who perished in the Flood (3:20). In the context of the exhortations, this reference may be intended as an encouragement for Christians not to shy away from bearing witness to unbelievers, just as Christ preached to the disobedient spirits.[18] But the quick transition from the "water" of the Flood to the "water" of baptism (3:21) and Christ's resurrection indicates that the author does not simply offer illustrations for his ethical teaching. He rather quotes (and adapts) preformed kerygmatic materials which only partly suit his aim. Most scholars think this represents a kind of credal statement.

It is no surprise to find credal materials in a baptismal context. As we have seen, baptismal instruction included both the formal contents of faith and the ethical rules derived therefrom. We can infer from the later development that the act of baptism presented perhaps not the only, but the most important, opportunity for a recital of the creed.[19] The Church Father Irenaeus (*Against Heresies* I.9.4) speaks of the "rule of truth" being received in baptism. And the two major creeds still in use in our churches, namely the Apostles' Creed and the Nicene Creed, have a long history as baptismal confessions—a history which reaches back as far as we can trace their origins.

Some of the older credal formulae may have been rather brief. They could contain a reference to God the Father, but at least those connected with baptism always centered around the essence of the *kerygma*, i.e., the person and work of Jesus Christ. Traces of such short formulae are found in many New Testament books; Eph. 4:5f.; Acts 16:31 (Western text), 16:3 among others, leave no doubt about a baptismal context. The earliest clear traces of a trinitarian affirmation (Didache 7:3; Mt. 28:19; cf. I Pet. 1:2f) also appear in the context of baptism.

The rich kerygmatic material in I Peter seems to imply a well-developed form of the Christological creed. It contains many elements which we know from pre-Pauline or Pauline tradition. Christ "was destined before the foundation of the world and manifested at the end of the time" (1:20; cf. Phil. 2:6; I Cor. 8:6; I Tim. 3:16). He died "for sins once for all" (3:18; cf. 1:18f.; 2:24f.). His "resurrection from the dead" (1:3) is described as the basis of our "dying to sin and living to righteousness" (2:24)—a term clearly connected with baptism (cf. Rom. 6:1–11). He is "sitting at the right hand of the Father," i.e., all "angels, authorities, and powers" are subject to him (3:22; cf. Phil. 2:11; I Cor. 15:24ff.), and he will be "revealed" in glory (1:7). But there is evidence that we have moved to a more developed stage. To the traditional images for the death of Christ (his blood, his wounds, the lamb without blemish) is added the designation of the Cross as the "tree" (2:14) which had only a tentative fore-

---

[18]This is the interpretation given by Bo Reicke in his comprehensive book, *The Disobedient Spirits and Christian Baptism*, Acta Seminarii Neotestamentici Upsaliensis, XIII (Copenhagen: Munksgaard, 1946).

[19]About the various occasions which led to the formulation of a creed, see O. Cullmann, *The Earliest Christian Confessions*, tr. J. K. S. Reid (London: Lutterworth, 1949).

runner in Paul (Gal. 3:13), but became very popular in the postapostolic period (Acts 5:30; 10:40; 13:29; Barnabas 5:13; Polycarp 8:1). As in the old formula of Rom. 1:4, the Resurrection is connected with the "Spirit" (3:19), but it seems to be distinguished from the Ascension (3:22). Among the gospel writers, only Luke seems to have knowledge of this latter tradition (Lk. 24:15f.; Acts 1:2; 1:9–11). Furthermore, Christ's "ascent" is paralleled by the idea of his "descent" into hell or limbo (3:19f.)[20] which probably is rooted in ancient mythical traditions, but is evident as part of the Christian *kerygma* only in later strata of the tradition (Eph. 4:9; Rev. 1:18; Gospel of Peter; Ignatius, Magnesians 9:2f.).

On the other hand, a more developed stage is indicated by the lack of interest in the notion of scriptural fulfillment which had been essential in the earliest formulations of the *kerygma* (cf. I Cor. 15:3). To be sure, most of the credal elements are linked to their Old Testament background. "Messianic" texts such as Isaiah 53 or Psalms 110 are presupposed in statements like I Peter 2:24f. and 3:22. The reference to Christ as the stone rejected by men but chosen and precious in the sight of God even contains a full scriptural "testimony" (2:4ff.). But for the Gentile Christians, scriptural proof was less important than the application of the *kerygma* to their new life. This does not mean that the Old Testament had become unimportant. Rather, the Old Testament was so completely absorbed by the Christian frame of mind that the average believer simply assumed it was a Christian book to begin with. The prophets have already fully announced what the Christian preacher says; they knew that they were addressing the Christian generation (I Pet. 1:10–12). The Book of James and especially the Letter of Barnabas demonstrate how even the Old Testament Law was Christianized by reducing it to its "moral essence" and eliminating the ceremonial law by "spiritual" exegesis.

Kerygma and ethical code are intimately connected in I Peter. But it is not so much of details of the Jesus tradition to which the author appeals. It is the general structure of the *kerygma* in terms of Jesus' "suffering and his subsequent glory," of humiliation and exaltation, which he uses in impressing the implications of the new life upon Gentile Christians. Here, the basic paradox of God's salvation has become manifest: God has chosen what is low and humble in the world, not what is high and exalted (5:5). In baptism, the young Christians have taken the first step toward conforming to this pattern. With Christ, they "died to sin and were raised to righteousness" (2:24). Now they have to be told how their whole lives should manifest this fact. They must be reminded that by joining this group of "exiles," rather than having entered into glory, they are thrown into an arena of fierce fight, of temptation and suffering. The basic rule of conforming to the pattern which dominates the last part of I Peter (4:12–5:11) is summed up in 5:6: "Humble yourselves therefore under the mighty hand of God, that in due time he may exalt you."—(cf. 4:13; 5:1; 5:10).

---

[20]See J. M. Robinson, "Descent into Hades," in *The Interpreter's Dictionary of the Bible*, I (Nashville: Abingdon, 1962), 826–828.

This "due time" is not far off any more (4:7). The author again and again says that only a little while, a short span, separates this time of exile from the final glory (1:6; 1:17; 4:17; 5:10). In accordance with Jewish and Christian tradition, he thinks of this "end" as judgment. But for the Christian, this judgment is as little frightening as are the trials of the present. The very fact of his suffering indicates that the judgment is already under way, and he knows that in the end it will be the occasion when his sharing in Christ's glory will become manifest.

Thus, it is the expectation of the final manifestation of God's righteousness that shapes the last contours of the ethical code. In formulating this code, Christians were not only looking back to the example of Jesus as they saw him through the medium of tradition. They were also looking forward to his Coming at the End of the Age. All actions of the Christian appear *sub specie aeternitatis*, "in the light of eternity."

Early Christian ethics have sometimes been called "interim ethics." This term would be inappropriate if it implied that ethical decisions were rather haphazard and casual because Christians were preoccupied with the shape of the world to come rather than with the shape of this world. To be sure, they knew that the shape of this world would pass away, that they were strangers and exiles. But they also knew that during this "interim" all their activity in the world was a witness to the message which they were commissioned to proclaim. It was their constant hope that through their conduct, other men might be led to glorify God. Thus, their ethical code, worked out only for a "temporary" situation, was nevertheless firmly and universally grounded in the structure of the message out of which it grew.

FAITH AND WORKS ACCORDING TO JAMES

When we turn to the Letter of James, it is evident how necessary it was to give concrete directions for the new life in the everyday situation of the average Christian and the average congregation. The whole Letter is concerned with one simple truth: It is not enough to "be" a Christian, if this fact does not show in one's conduct. The author sees the basic danger of the Christian message in its being misunderstood as merely intellectual doctrine. "James" vigorously denounces every attempt to restrict the new life to the realm of theory and mere talk instead of letting it have its effect on Christian action. Thus, his concern is not so much the formulation of the ethical code, but its application. The Church, which accepted the Letter into its canon, always saw the author as the representative of an activist trend in early Christianity, as a warning voice that Christianity is an eminently practical religion.

For us, the Book of James is important because it gives some idea of how Christians faced the worldliness in their own midst. For the Christian, as we have seen, sin was thought to have been dealt with basically in baptism. The new life meant forgiveness of past sins and included the expectation that, with the help of the Holy Spirit, the Christian henceforth would walk toward the goal of perfection, still involved in a daily fight with sin, but certainly without committing any major sin. Practice, however, revealed that this principle did not square with reality. "Sin," even grave sin, remained a phenomenon within the communities, and had to be dealt with.

James does not seem to have a very sophisticated attitude toward the problem of sin. He simply assumes that "we all make many mistakes" (3:2). There are no special distinctions. Sin for him is basically action, wrong action, although he occasionally refers to the older idea of sin as a demonic power which stems from the root of concupiscence and causes death and sickness (1:15; 5:15f.). In the case of "sickness," the mention of "sins" as being connected with it may be an echo of the healing stories of the Jesus tradition. However, it also could stem from popular beliefs, like those behind the exorcistic ritual of healing a sick person by the "prayer of faith," as it is described in 5:14:

> Is anyone among you sick? Let him call for the elders of the church and let them pray over him, anointing him with oil in the name of the Lord; and the prayer of faith will save the sick man, and the Lord will raise him up.

Sin has to be met by active repentance, by a return to the pattern of the new life, and by doing the "works" which in the Judgment will outweigh the "multitude of sins." We shall see how important the idea of the Judgment is for James' whole ethical orientation.

Again, we must realize that whatever insight we gain from James is but an isolated glimpse of a wide landscape. We do not really know where the Letter belongs in the overall picture, and thus even the most elementary questions must still remain unanswered. Is it really a letter as is suggested by the epistolary address? Even if the writing was meant for "general" circulation, the abrupt ending without any epistolary salutation would be puzzling. Or was it a sermon? The frequent use of "my brethren" as an address, and a rich rhetorical imagery, would speak for this possibility. But no formal plan or governing theme is recognizable. Pieces of sometimes more general, sometimes rather specific exhortation seem to be strung together, often simply by means of catch-word connection. This does not mean, however, that we would find no coherence at all. In fact, some of the themes occur several times (trial and temptation: 1:2f.; 1:12ff.; steadfastness: 1:2f.; 5:10f.; rich and poor: 1:9–11; 2:5–7; 5:1–6), and others are alluded to or taken up again in a different context (prayer without doubt: 1:5ff.; cf. 4:3 and the "prayer of faith" in 5:16; quick to hear, slow to speak: 1:19, cf. the passages about the tongue and the necessity of bridling it: 1:26; 3:2–12, cf. 4:11ff., evil talk against each other; doers and hearers of the word: 1:22ff., cf. the discussion about faith and works in 2:14–26). In this sense, at least, a certain unity seems to emerge.

This loose structure, as well as the presentation with its skillful rhetoric, would suggest something like a treatise, originally destined for public reading in congregations of a certain area. We remember that it was not unusual in Christian churches to read edifying letters in the worship service. This may account for the rudiments of the epistolary form as well as for the sermonic flavor.

What kind of person would have written such a treatise? The later tradition, which claims the apostle James as its author, has little to commend itself. Only the name James is mentioned in the address. The treatise itself does not identify this James with the apostle, and its outlook as well as the Greek style are anything but what we would expect of an Aramaic-speaking Palestinian Jew.

There is a passage in 3:1 that may give us some clue. The author warns the brethren not to let too many become "teachers." "You know," he continues, "that we who teach shall be judged with greater strictness." James obviously regards himself as belonging to that special group of teachers. Paul's list of charismatic offices in the Church mentions "teachers" along with "prophets and apostles" (I Cor. 12:28f.); there can be little doubt that the origin of this function had to be linked with the Jewish "teacher," the rabbi.

The post-Pauline Church continued to count the teacher among the charismatic leaders and to honor him accordingly (cf. Eph. 4:11). Acts 13:1 represents the leading group in Antioch in terms of "prophets and teachers." The Didache furnishes most valuable evidence that in rural areas the charismatic offices of "prophet and teacher" were still held in high esteem. They had an active and privileged part in the worship life (15:1) and were to be supported by the local congregation if they stayed and settled down. In general, however, they seem to have migrated from place to place, very much like the migrating philosophers of Hellenism. This system had its weakness. For the congregations, it must have been difficult to separate the chaff from the wheat and to know the true charismatic from the false. The Didache gives some rules: if a prophet stays more than three days, if he asks for money or other things in his prophecy, then he is a false prophet. That his "teaching" had to do with the catechetical (baptismal) instruction seems to be presupposed by Hermas, in Mandates IV.3.1. In this situation, the "teaching" would embrace not only the contents of faith, but also the ethical code. We may assume that, depending on the local situation and the background of the teacher, this latter aspect often dominated the instruction, sometimes even to the point of a flat moralism. The "teaching" referred to in Didache 11 is certainly the *Catechism of the Two Ways* with all its ethical rules. And another "teacher," the author of the Letter of Barnabas, shows the same ethical preoccupation. He is the one who defines Christianity as "the new law of our Lord Jesus Christ which is not a yoke of compulsion" (Barnabas 2:6). His letter is addressed to a congregation where he had taught before (1:3–5). It is very likely that we have to think of the author of James in the same general terms. As the example of Barnabas shows, the literary form of a treatise styled as a letter which could be read publicly in worship, is nothing unusual for a teacher; and the heavy emphasis on ethical questions would be expected of him.

Even the obvious dependence of James on both Jewish and Greek moral teaching seems to be typical for a man of his profession. As a matter of fact, for almost every single exhortation, illustration, and particular doctrine, parallels may be found in either Jewish or Hellenistic literature, often in both.[21] It is especially the literature and tradition of Hellenistic Judaism (Old Testament apocrypha, Philo of Alexandria) that seem to have served as a model for the form, and partly for the content, of his treatise. In order to give his exhortations the desired literary touch, he borrows freely from many sources: scripture, especially the Psalms; the poets; the philosophers; the rhetorical school tradition; and the store of popular wisdom. He likes the parabolic comparison (the rich man is like grass that withers 1:11, 13–14; the tongue is like a little fire that sets ablaze a whole forest, 3:6); he uses the commonplaces of popular philosophy (the image of the mirror, 1:23f.; the wheel of existence, 3:6; the taming of all animals by humankind, 3:7), he takes over theological concepts (God as the unchanging Father of light, 1:17).

The thoroughly Jewish flavor has led repeatedly to attempts to explain the whole Letter as a Jewish document which has been reworked only slightly. The most interesting theory took its clue from the enigmatic address: "James, a servant of God and of the Lord Jesus Christ to the twelve tribes in the dispersion."[22] It claimed that the original writing used the literary fiction of a "Testament" (Letter) of the patriarch Jacob (James) to his twelve sons (twelve tribes) as the frame of a grandiose allegory in which every son represented a specific ethical theme. Jewish tradition in fact knows such writings (cf. the apocryphal Testaments of the Twelve Patriarchs) as well as the motif of allegorizing the twelve tribes, and the title "Servant of the Lord" is frequently applied to Jacob in the Old Testament. However, there are too many difficulties with this theory, and scholars generally have abandoned it. According to the most likely interpretation, the term "twelve tribes in the dispersion" would mean *all* Christians living in the world as strangers and exiles.

Apart from an occasional echo of baptismal language (1:18; 1:21), there is no direct reference to baptism in our treatise. As in the Letter of Barnabas, the situation is not that of catechesis. But it would be inappropriate to think of the "teacher" in his capacity as catechist only. As a charismatic leader, he would speak up, instructing the Church whenever he found it necessary. The author of Barnabas, for example, regards it as sufficient justification for his writing to say that he wants to "communicate something of that which I have received . . . in order that your knowledge may be perfected along with your

---

[21]For this material see the excellent commentary of M. Dibelius, *Der Jakobusbrief* (Göttingen: Vandenhoeck, 1921; re-edited with a supplement by H. Greeven, 1956).

[22]The reference is to Arnold Meyer, *Das Rätsel des Jakobusbriefs*, Beihefte zur Zeitschrift für die neutestamentliche Wissenschaft, X (Berlin: Töpelmann, 1930).

faith" (Barnabas 1:5). Unfortunately, we have no way of telling when or where James wrote. Those who do not retain the idea of James the Apostle as author usually date it in the time between A.D. 70 and 130. Even the situation to which the Letter speaks is far from being clear. Most of the warnings—to the rich, to the self-indulgent, the complaining, the deceitful, the talkative, the proud— seem to be very general. But there are some references which suddenly open up an alarming picture of the inner difficulties which a church of those days was facing and which actually are reflected in all the details of the Letter.

It is especially the little dissertation about the tongue, that "restless evil, full of poison" (3:1–12) which at closer scrutiny reveals a very real background. It leads directly up to a sharp attack against the evil of "jealousy and selfish am- bition," against "boasting" of a wisdom which is "earthly, unspiritual, devilish" and results in "disorder and every vile practice" (3:13ff.). Here the readers are directly addressed: These things happen in your midst! The problem seems to be quite similar to that which Paul had to fight in Corinth (I Cor. 3:3; 14:33; II Cor. 12:20f.) and which Clement of Rome tried to set straight in his Letter to the Corinthian church some forty years after Paul (I Clement 1:1; 3:2f.): trouble stirred up by a group or factions within the Church and leading to rivalry, strife, and worse evils (cf. 1:5ff.; 1:21). The "tongue" is involved not only by its sinful boasting, but also by the fact that Christians defame each other (4:11). True wisdom is characterized by peace (3:17). But instead of peace and a meek spirit, there are wars and fightings going on among Christians (4:1).

When the author asks why this is so, his answer first follows the pattern of popular philosophy: It is the "passions" of the human flesh that evoke fight and envy. Apatheia, the freedom from the passions of the material world, was the ideal of the Stoic wise men. But James goes beyond this preliminary answer. The Greek word used in the beginning of 4:4 is difficult to understand. It is derived from the word for fornication, which from the time of the prophets on had been an image for Israel's apostasy from God. Thus, for James the boastful mood among Christians and its atrocious consequences are outright apostasy. Friendship with the world means enmity with God. But all is not lost yet. God gives "more grace"—even after baptism—if the sinner submits to God, resists the Devil, and cleanses his hand and heart (4:7–8). This appeal is based on a quotation from Proverbs 3:34 ("God opposes the proud but gives grace to the humble."). It is the same quote which appears in I Peter 5:5, where it describes the basic paradox of God's salvation. Peter's summary of the ethical code is almost identical with James'; "Humble yourselves before the Lord and he will exalt you" (Jas. 4:10). Even if James knew I Peter, or is drawing upon the same tradition, it is clear that in doing so he links his ethical appeal to the structure of the kerygma.

This can be shown at another important point of James' teaching: his dealing with the question of rich and poor. Verses 2–7 of Chapter 2 present a hypothetical scene which the author obviously regarded as a true story.

Two visitors—he thinks of non-Christian sympathizers—appear at the regular assembly of a Christian congregation, one of them well-to-do and well dressed, the other "a poor man in shabby clothing." The rich man is treated with great courtesy and attention while the poor man is not given any consideration at all. The point James wants to illustrate is the warning against "partiality" (Jas. 2:1). But he himself is far from being impartial. In his comment on the story, he does not hide a strong antipathy against "the rich." It is possible, though unlikely (cf. 5:4ff.), that he tries to blame a group of rich people for an actual persecution of Christians when he says that they oppress Christians, drag them into court, and deride the "name." Most important, however, is the reason he gives for his siding with the poor. It is again that paradox of God's salvation: "Has not God chosen those who are poor in the world to be rich in faith and heirs of the kingdom?" (2:5).

A similar view of rich and poor is apparent in Luke. Here, too, the motif of the exaltation of the poor and the humiliation of the rich is an example for the paradox of God's salvation (Lk. 1:51–53; 6:20ff.; 12:16ff.; 16:19ff.). In this predilection for the poor, an important religious heritage becomes visible. Jewish tradition had long known the equation "poor = pious" (Ps. 86:1f.; 132:15f.), and particularly the Wisdom Literature speaks of the great reversal of the relationship that is to come. Apocalyptic circles and esoteric groups like the Qumran community seem to have characterized themselves as "the poor" (anawim, ebionim)—this is, as God's elect, the holy remnant of the End of the Age. This tradition seems to have found its continuation in the early Jerusalem church; Paul, in his references to "the poor of the saints" in Jerusalem (Rom. 15:26; cf. Gal 2:10) seems to imply actual poverty, but the Jewish Christians who after their exodus from Jerusalem in A.D. 66–67 settled east of the Jordan, retained this designation as their title of honor (Ebionites).

For James, although he must be seen in the light of this tradition, it is the practical relationship between rich and poor which informs his stand. The message that God accepts the lowly and rejects the proud only supports his conviction that, in social terms, "Christian" means "poor," and "rich" per se means "wicked" and doomed. In vivid colors he describes the miserable fate which awaits the rich (1:10–11; 5:1ff.). In these texts, a strong apocalyptic flavor is noticeable. The change from exaltation to humiliation and vice versa (1:9) is not visible yet, but the Coming of the Lord is at hand (5:8). James no doubt has a very realistic imminent expectation; behind his pleas for patience we feel his own anxiousness to see the day when the rich will fall and the poor will be exalted in glory. He checks his own impatience by saying that what he is waiting for comes almost as a natural process. The day will come, as certain as the rain comes to the land in due season (cf. I Clem. 23:4f.).

Unlike the author of I Peter, James does not himself draw lines from the ethical code to the Jesus tradition. This lack has always puzzled the interpreters. At one point, he appears to allude to Gospel tradition (5:12), but only twice (1:1; 2:1) does he even mention the name of Jesus Christ; the references to the "Lord" can apply to God as well. And while a Christian (cf. I Peter) naturally quotes Christ as the example of steadfastness, James speaks of the prophets and of James (5:10, 11). The "end" of which the Christian message speaks is for him in the first place the Judgment which will destroy the wicked and vindicate the righteous, not the revelation of Christ's victory (cf. 5:9).

In fact, the threat of Judgment seems to be the orientation point for the author's whole understanding of Christianity. Whether a man's "religion" is right or wrong is a matter of how it will stand God's Judgment in the light of the standards that are being applied there (1:26f.). James' use of important theological concepts finds its framework here. Take, for example, the *law:* for James the law is not the dead-end street of salvation which is superseded by the Gospel. It is God's standard in the Judgment, and therefore retains utmost importance for the Christian. The judge, who can "save and destroy," has laid down his rules so that they are known (4:12). Of course, this law does not include the ceremonial code of Judaism; its basic content is the rule of love (2:8), which is interpreted by such moral laws as "Do not commit adultery," "Do not kill" (2:11), "Do not speak evil against one another" (4:11). In this reduced form, however, it is as strict in its demand as was the old Jewish code: to break one of these rules means to break the whole law (2:10–11). This law is the "perfect," the "royal" law, the "law of liberty" (1:25; 2:8, 2:12) and as such really identical with the saving Gospel (the Word—1:21). "Doer of the word" (1:23) and "doer of the law" (4:11) are synonymous. With this equation of law and Gospel, James shares a tendency of the postapostolic age, which not only characterizes Jewish-Christian thinking, but the general Christian approach as well (cf. Barnabas 2:6; Hermas, Similitudes V.6.3; Ignatius, Magnesians 2). Or take *righteousness:* righteousness is not a gift bestowed by God, but a claim which God acknowledges in his Judgment; man must "work" toward it by taking notice of God's standards and heeding them (1:20f.). Thus, to be justified is not the sinner's being declared righteous but one's classification as righteous in the Last Judgment by virtue of one's approved actions (2:21; 23, 24).

The verses last quoted form part of the famous passage of faith and works (2:14–26) which has caused theologians like Martin Luther to regret that the Letter of James was ever included in the canon. The author, indeed, seems to reject flatly the idea of justification by faith. Faith alone is inadequate to render a man acceptable to God. In a passage that seems to be a direct criticism of Romans 3:28, the author sternly opposes the claim that faith alone can save: "You see that a man is justified by works and not by faith alone." As we shall see, however, the real quarrel is not with Paul, but with a misuse of Pauline formulae which the author, in his concern for the ethical code, regarded as a danger.

The argument is presented in the form of a "diatribe," a dialogical style very popular with the philosophical moralists who knew how to attract the attention of an audience in the street. James uses the same tricks here: the rhetorical question in the beginning (14), the grossly exaggerated example (15–17), the fictitious interjection (18) which starts a dialogue with argument and counter-argument, the surprise exegesis of the opponent's major proof texts (21–25), and finally, a catching slogan as conclusion (26). Again, the whole point cannot be understood apart from the dominating concept of Judgment. The preceding passage (2:8–13) had closed with the clear statement that the standard of the Judgment is nothing else but the "law of liberty," the Christian law of love—or, as verse 13 puts it, of "mercy": "Judgment is without mercy to one who has shown no mercy; yet mercy triumphs over judgment."

The following verses stress that there is simply no way around this requirement. Nobody will pass judgment (be saved) just by *saying* "I have faith." Faith in the sense of mere words, as a recital of a formula—even if it were the most correct one (19)—does not substitute for the required acts of mercy (15–16). If the Christian message is not just theoretical doctrine, but also ethical code, then no "faith" without "works" of mercy will do.

This all would be nothing new for Paul, who never thought of faith other than as a "faith active in love," and for whom, therefore, "works of love" were the immediate fruit of faith. But the author has Christians in mind who would recite Christian creed and yet would live as though his "faith" did not include the structure for a new life. We may recall the troublemakers of 3:13ff. In James' eyes, what is lacking there is not right doctrine, but commitment to the ethical code *which is part of it*. For him, this latter aspect is more important than all sophisticated talk about "faith." Let these people talk about the "law of freedom"; let them invoke Paul for their doctrine of faith alone; let them adduce scriptural examples of justification by faith alone (the case of the harlot Rahab must have been particularly impressive). Their *whole* talk about faith is out of gear. If it really came down to an alternative—faith *or* works—then the solution is completely clear: in God's judgment it was the acts of mercy and obedience that "justified" Abraham and Rahab, not the recital of a "faith."

We hear the serious warning behind all of the argumentation: Do not deceive yourselves (1:22)! In the Judgment, God does not accept "faith" in the form of mere words, correct as they may be. He demands active conformity to the rule of love. The emphasis seemed to be quite legitimate at a time when the trend was to identify "faith" more and more with a body of correct doctrinal beliefs. There may be reason to believe that the teacher James was not really up to the task of arguing with the "sophisticated" standpoint of his opponents on a doctrinal basis, and that he therefore led the discussion on a level where he was at home and could really make his point. At any rate, he made clear that the Christian's new life initiated in baptism can never remain in the lofty sphere of arguments. It must be lived. It has to develop, to grow; it must be nurtured and corrected, in order that the goal be attained which God himself has placed before the Christian. With this understanding of the ethical code, James is perhaps closer to Paul than we are sometimes willing to admit.

THE TRUE WORSHIP OF GOD IN HEBREWS

Not everywhere was the development and application of the ethical code and its connection with the worship life of the community, especially baptism, so much in the foreground. Indeed, we have in the New Testament more speculative writings from the hands of Christian "teachers" who, like James and the author of I Peter, presuppose a pattern of worship and work with it as a self-understood reality.

Sometime in the latter part of the first century such a teacher wrote what he called a "word of exhortation" to a congregation or group of Christians in an unknown place. His writing later came to be called "To the Hebrews" and was eventually accepted into the New Testament canon as a Letter of Paul. Since there is no claim to Pauline authorship in the text, and since language as well as theology differ markedly from the apostle's authentic writings, doubts about the authorship were raised from the earliest centuries on, especially in the West. Luther and Calvin regarded Hebrews as non-Pauline, and so do almost all scholars today. Numerous other authors have been suggested (Luke, Barnabas, Silas, Apollos, Aquila or Priscilla, Clement of Rome), but the question of who wrote it remains one of the unsolved riddles of the New Testament.

The language, style, and form of the Letter to the Hebrews indicate that the author had been educated in the Hellenistic tradition. He was at home in the Greek language, and his vocabulary and style compare favorably with the good literary prose of the period. He uses terminology and concepts that show some familiarity with Platonic thought, as in his tendency to see earthly phenomena in contrast to heavenly and eternal realities. In this he shows affinity to the writings of Philo, and some scholars have argued that the writing originated in Alexandria, Philo's home city. The author also resembles Philo in his allegorical method of interpreting scripture, in his dependence on Jewish Wisdom Literature, and in his interest in etymology. On the other hand, he also seems familiar with rabbinical principles of interpreting scripture. We should assume that he had come to know Christianity as it was interpreted under the influence of Hellenistic Judaism.

The author says himself that he belongs to the postapostolic generation (2:3). Since he refers to the threat of persecution in the past and in the present, and since I Clement 36 shows acquaintance with the beginning of the Letter, a date between A.D. 70 and 90 seems plausible as the time of composition. The only clue to the actual destination is found in 13:24: "Those who come from Italy send their greetings." This phrase has generally been interpreted to mean that the addressees are located in Rome, and that there were Roman Christians with the author in his (Eastern?) exile (13:19) who sent greetings to their friends back home. Even if the phrase is a later addition, it attests the early connection of Hebrews with Rome.

As an experienced "teacher," the author is naturally concerned with the ethical code. Chapter 13:1–17 contains a series of specific admonitions on the treatment of fellow Christians, on marriage, money, respect for leaders, as well as general exhortations very much in the style of the Christian parenetic tradition of the postapostolic time which we have discussed already. Although there is an occasional warning against "diverse and strange teachings" (13:9), the fight against heresy is not a prominent feature. Rather, the somber context of all admonitions in the Letter's second part (10:19ff.) seems to be the threat of renewed persecution and the very real danger of apostasy among the frightened Christian flock (10:32ff.). With great seriousness, the author warns that such a deliberate and grave sin, if committed after baptism, cannot be forgiven (10:26ff.; 6:4–8). But the tenor of his exhortation on the whole is not so much the threat of the Judgment. He rather sees it as his task to strengthen the weakening faith and to help his fellow Christians stand firm in the trials of their time. This sounds rather general, but the temptations to which the author has to address himself contain an ingredient we have not met yet and that is worth noting.

It is very clear from several passages that the author of Hebrews presupposes the connection of the ethical code with baptismal instruction. He even complains that what his addressees in their present state of mind really need is a return to those "first principles," to the "milk" they were fed as children in the faith (5:12–14). But he promises to leave this elementary stage behind and encourages them to go on to true maturity, to the "solid food" that seems to be his true concern (6:1–3).

The reason he sets aside the need for a reminder of their baptismal instruction may be that the relation between worship and ethical code for them has its problem at a peculiarly different point. Like so many other Gentiles in the postapostolic Church, they seem to be fascinated by the ritual aspects of the Jewish religion, their beauty, their symbolism, their potential importance for the approach to God. The entire doctrinal part of the Letter (chapter 1:1–10:18) could be seen as arguing against Christian tendencies to make the Jewish sacrificial cult respectable again as a tool to gain access to God in the wake of the new interest in cult, liturgy, sacrament, and effective forms of worship. Since it was old and full of mysterious ceremony and symbolic meaning, its attraction in non-Jewish circles was indeed considerable. Perhaps we ought to think of it not so much as a crude re-judaizing tendency to reinstate the entire Temple ritual as part of true Christian worship (after all, the Temple was destroyed), but rather as a highly sophisticated adaptation of the symbols of Jewish ritual through allegorizing interpretation. At any rate, our author is determined to show that the entire worship system of the Jewish priestly sacrifices, including the venerable institution of the Levitical priesthood, or its allegorization as angelic powers that serve as priests on man's behalf, is obsolete; it has been replaced by God's deed in Jesus Christ and by the celebration in the liturgy of the Christian life, the life of true faith.

In the magnificent prologue, the author proclaims the finality of God's revelation in Jesus Christ (1:1–4). In ages past, God had revealed himself through the prophets, but now in the "last days" he has given his full revelation in his Son. The Son is the "heir of all things"; all God's promises to man are being realized through Christ (6:12, 17). Philo had referred to the *logos* as the "heir"—the divine, immanent principle that guides the world to its appointed ends. Our author, like Paul and John, is clearly influenced by the wisdom and *logos* speculation of Hellenistic Judaism when he attributes to Christ preexistence and a mediating role in Creation (Heb. 1:2). But his major concern is not with cosmological speculation, but with God's purposes in Creation as they are revealed in the salvation accomplished through the Son: *The end of Creation is redemption.*

He speaks of the finality of God's revelation in two senses: First, in the eschatological sense that with the coming of the Son the "last days" of this Age have been entered. And second, in the more philosophical sense that the Son has fully revealed the nature of God. To the Hellenistic mind, the very title "Son of God" would have suggested a unique relation of oneness with God. But our author is very explicit on this point. Christ *reflects* the glory of God, and bears the very stamp of God's divine nature. The Greek word translated as "reflects" is a Hellenistic term that was borrowed both by Philo and by the Jewish Wisdom Literature. A favorite analogy to explain how the transcendent God could manifest himself in the world was that of the sun and its rays. As the sun's rays (reflections) participated in the very essence of the sun's light, yet without diminishing that essence, so the divine life was mediated in the world without diminishing or disturbing the source from which it came.

The author comes to the crucial point of God's revelation in Christ when he refers to "purification for sins" and Christ's having "sat down at the right hand of the Majesty on high" (1:3). Here he turns to God's act of salvation in the historical death of the Son through which purification was accomplished, and to its consummation in the Son's exaltation to heaven. These are to be the subjects of the main section of his writing. The reference to the historical work of the Son, standing as it does in the midst of quasi-philosophical terminology, clearly relates God's final revelation to the historical person Jesus. In the death and exaltation of this historical person, God's salvation has been accomplished and Jesus' unique relation as Son has been revealed.

The author now elaborates on Christ's superiority to all other beings; he considers angels first (1:5–2:9), using Old Testament passages to support his thesis. Like other Christians of his day, our author regards the Old Testament writings as prophecies looking forward to Christ. Turning to a passage from the Psalms (Ps. 2:7) and to a passage from II Samuel, he points out that Christ has been called "Son" by God (1:5), whereas the angels have not. On the contrary, angels have been commanded by God to worship the Son (1:6), and according to Psalm 45 the Son has been anointed by God as the righteous ruler of God's kingdom (1:8–9). The author interprets Psalm 45, which was originally an enthronement psalm written to celebrate the anointing of a Jewish king, as a reference to God's appointment of Christ as the Messiah-King. This same theme of the victorious rule of the Messiah-King is also found in his next statement—namely, that God has promised that all the enemies of righteousness will be put in subjection to the Son (1:13); in contrast to Christ, angels are not to be served, but rather are to act as ministering servants to those who are to obtain salvation (1:14; 1:7).

But what point are the readers of the Letter to gather from this discussion of Christ's superiority to the angels? This is just what the author tries to make clear in the first of his series of exhortations to his readers (2:1–4). Since their salvation is given only through the Son himself, who is superior to all heavenly beings, he asks them how they can escape judgment if they neglect "such a great salvation."

In developing this argument, the author is making use of a rabbinic principle of interpretation called *a minore ad majus* ("from the lesser to the greater"). If breaking the Torah that was given by lesser beings (according to Jewish tradition God had given the Torah through angels) brought judgment, a far worse judgment will result from disobeying the word of the Son of God, who is far superior. Later on in his writing, the author uses this same principle repeatedly.

Now the author quotes from another psalm, which he interprets as God's promise that in the Age to Come (the New Age) all things will be put in subjection to man, and not to angels (2:5–8). But anyone can see that all things are not yet subject to man; in particular, our author has in mind the power that death still seems to hold over man. The author calls upon his readers to fix their gaze on Jesus (2:9–18), who has suffered death but who has been exalted and crowned with honor and glory. It is to Christ that they must look for evidence of the New Age and of man's victory over death. Jesus has tasted death for every man. The author believes that the promises God gave to man have been fulfilled in the man Jesus, who through his suffering became the pioneer of salvation to many "sons" who share in his "sonship" and in the promises. This fulfillment was made possible because Jesus was a man ("partook of the same nature") and through his death destroyed the Devil, who holds man in the power of death.

The author does not say just how this victory has been won. Later on, he speaks of Jesus' being "made perfect" through obedience (5:8–9), and we may assume that it was in Jesus' perfect obedience to God's will that he overcame the power of evil and the death that is the inevitable consequence of sin. But this mode of thinking about the meaning of Jesus' death is not central to the author's argument, for his major concern is not the destruction of the Devil but the expiation of sins by Christ acting as a faithful High Priest (2:17). Although the term "High Priest" is injected here, its meaning is not discussed until we come to the main theological argument of the writing (4:14–10:25).

Next, the author shows the superiority of Christ to Moses (3:1–4:13). Christians share in a "heavenly call" given by Jesus, who is the "apostle" and High Priest. This is the only place in the New Testament where Jesus is called "apostle." The term here has its usual technical meaning of one sent with the commission and authority of the sender (God).[23] But notice that it appears side by side with the term "High Priest," a fact that may give added meaning. According to rabbinic tradition, on the Day of Atonement the High Priest entered the Holy of Holies as the apostle of the people and represented them before God. Since the author later pictures Christ in these very terms (9:24), he may purposely be using the word "apostle" in an ambiguous way here.

In contrast to Christ's call, Moses had called the House of Israel into being. But Moses, as the representative of the House of Israel, was merely a servant; the author believes that what Moses said and did merely testified to, or foreshadowed, what Christ was to say and do (3:5). Since the true household that Christ built was merely foreshadowed by Moses and Israel, the author argues that Christ is far superior to Moses.

Again the author exhorts his readers to hold fast to their confidence in Christ, through whom the true household of God (the Church) has been built in order that they may remain members of that household (3:6–4:13). Quoting Psalm 95, he calls to his readers' mind the story of how Israel disobeyed Moses in the wilderness when they doubted God's promises that he would lead them to a new land (Num. 12:7ff.). From the Psalm, he recalls how Moses warned them that unless they refrained from rebellion "today" they would not enter into God's "rest." Then he interprets the word "today" as actually foreshadowing the day in which Christ has called the true household into being. The author uses the term "today" in an eschatological sense to refer to "these last days" (1:2) when the Messiah, the Son of God, has come to lead God's People to God's "rest."

The "rest" that was promised to the Israelites was entrance into the Promised Land. But here again the author uses a term to foreshadow something that came later—the "rest" foreshadows the better promise that the author refers to variously as entrance into the heavenly sanctuary (10:19), into the city of the living God (12:22), or simply salvation (2:3). He is depending here on Jewish speculation about the statement in Genesis (2:2ff.) that when God had finished the Creation he rested. But it was inconceivable to the Jews that God had ceased his divine activity after Creation. Philo, for example, insisted that the "rest" merely referred to God's continuing work; since it was of the very nature of God to create, this rest was a symbol of his effortless, unhindered, divine activity. One rabbinic interpretation was that the rest referred to God's completion of his work in judgment and salvation. All these interpretations were related to the meaning of the Sabbath, which commemorated the Creation. And the author of Hebrews says there remains "a sabbath rest for the

---

[23]For a discussion of the term see pp. 169–171.

people of God" (4:9). This is the true rest, the heavenly sanctuary, into which Jesus Christ, having been perfected through suffering, has already entered. It is the rest into which the People of God will enter if they are obedient and hold fast their confession of faith (4:11–14). To fall short of that "rest" is to come under the judgment of God, who discerns the inward thoughts of men (4:12–13).

Christ, the True High Priest—Hebrews 4:14–7:28

The author now turns to his central teaching about Christ, in which he compares and contrasts Christ's work with that of the Levitical priesthood. Throughout the early stages of the argument he emphasizes two points: First, because Christ was a man, and therefore was tempted as all men are, he can sympathize with men's weakness and give help in time of need (4:14–16). This point would be particularly meaningful to his readers, who were facing a threatening situation. In one of the few references to the historical ministry of Jesus found outside the gospels, the author recalls the synoptic story of Jesus' agony in the Garden of Gethsemane (5:7–9): "In the days of his flesh, Jesus offered up prayers and supplications, with loud cries and tears, to him who was able to save him from death, and he was heard for his godly fear." The second point is that through Christ's obedience to God even unto death he fulfilled his own destiny as Son by becoming the source of eternal salvation to all who obey him (5:8).

Like the Levitical priests, Jesus is human, and so he can understand and sympathize with human weakness. This is a truth that must not be lost in face of the belief that he is a great High Priest who "has passed through the heavens, Jesus, the Son of God" (4:14). And just as the High Priest in the Levitical line is appointed by God to act on behalf of men in their relations to God, offering gifts and sacrifices for sins, so Christ is appointed by God and offers a sacrifice (5:1). But there is a difference: The Levitical High Priest is beset by human weakness and has sinned, and he must offer sacrifices for himself as well as for the people (5:2–3). Christ, though a man, is without sin (4:15), and so does not need to offer sacrifices for himself.

There is also a difference in the way in which Christ was called to his ministry. Just as Aaron and his descendants in the Levitical line of priests were appointed by God and not self-appointed, so Christ was appointed by God (5:5–6). But Christ was called to his ministry as Son (5:5). The author again quotes Psalm 2, which he, along with other Christians, believed was a prophecy of Jesus' appointment as Messiah. This is an important point, for it shows that it is *as Messiah* that Jesus exercises his priestly role. But the author also quotes Psalm 110:4, "Thou are a priest forever after the order of Melchizedek," which he also interprets as a reference to Christ. Now the first verse of this Psalm, "The Lord says to my Lord: sit at my right hand, till I make your enemies your footstool," was commonly interpreted by Christians as referring to Christ's exaltation to heaven as Messiah (Mt. 22:44; Mk. 12:36; Acts 2:34; I Cor. 15:25; Eph. 1:20). But our author is the only New Testament writer to use the reference to the order of Melchizedek. What he intends to do is to show the superiority of Christ's order of priesthood (Heb. 7) to the Levitical order; but before he does that he again exhorts his readers (5:11–6:12).

He reprimands them for their dullness of hearing (5:11) and for their sluggishness in faith and conduct (6:11–12). He is not referring simply to his readers' understanding of doctrine. The meaning of "dullness' depends upon the meaning of the word "mature," which is a translation of the Greek word meaning "perfect." As used in the mystery cults, this term referred to the state of those who had been initiated. In Gnostic circles, it referred to those who were in possession of the secret knowledge whereby the Gnostic was guaranteed salvation from the material world. Paul uses the term to refer to Christians who through the Spirit have come to know the wisdom of God revealed in Christ (I Cor. 2:6–10).

In Hebrews, "perfection" has a somewhat different connotation. Essentially, it refers to the status of one whose sins have been forgiven through the sacrificial death of Christ (9:26). "For by a single offering he has *perfected* for all time those who are sanctified" (10:14). The author stresses that as a consequence of this forgiveness the believer has had his conscience purified (9:14; 10:22). What is "hard to explain" because they are "dull of hearing" is the truth that having been forgiven they must maintain moral purity of life or they will forfeit their salvation. This is implied by the author's statement that those who live on milk are "unskilled in the word of righteousness" (5:13), whereas solid food is for those who have been trained "by practice to distinguish good from evil" (5:14).

In Chapter 7, the author turns to his interpretation of Christ's work in terms of priesthood. Although Hebrews is the only New Testament writing to speak of Christ's work in these terms, the author may not have been the first to do so. Jewish speculation had already proposed that the Messiah would come from a priestly line. We find evidence of this in *The Testament of the Twelve Patriarchs*, and in the Dead Sea Scrolls a Messiah from the line of Aaron is expected.[24]

The thesis of Christ's priesthood is developed in relation to the mysterious Old Testament personage, Melchizedek (Heb. 7), who is mentioned in two Old Testament passages, Genesis 14:17–20 and Psalm 110:4ff. According to the account in Genesis, Melchizedek, king of Salem and priest of the Most High

---

[24]The stress on the superior priesthood of Christ parallels the claim at Qumran that theirs was the true priesthood, in contrast to the "wicked" priests in Jerusalem. But the theory of Y. Yadin which attributes Hebrews to the Dead Sea community has not found wide acceptance. See Y. Yadin, "The Dead Sea Scrolls and the Epistle to the Hebrews," in *Aspects of the Dead Sea Scrolls, Scripta Hierosolymitana*, IV (Jerusalem, Israel: Hebrew University Press, 1957), 36–55.

God, had met Abraham returning from his battle to release Lot from captivity. Melchizedek blessed Abraham and took from him a tenth of all he had.

By a method of interpretation common in the author's day, though it seems far-fetched today, he seeks to establish the superiority of Melchizedek over both Abraham and the Levitical priesthood descended from Abraham. This superiority clearly shows, he argues, that perfection was not attainable through the Levitical line; otherwise the other order of priesthood through Melchizedek would not have been necessary (7:11). The point of the author's involved interpretation is to show that it is in the priesthood of Melchizedek alone that the priesthood of Christ is foreshadowed. Melchizedek was not from the tribe of Levi, nor was Christ (7:13). Melchizedek was made a High Priest forever, and so was Christ (7:3, 7:24). Christ's priesthood was not validated by his being in the line of Levi but by his "indestructible life" (7:16). The Lord, as the scripture testifies, swore that Christ was a High Priest forever (7:21).[25]

There is one other important line in the author's argument. If Jesus, in the order of Melchizedek, represents a priesthood that supersedes the Levitical priesthood, then the Law that established that priesthood is superseded (7:12), and a former commandment is set aside (7:18). The author, like Paul, believes that with the coming of Christ the Law has been set aside. But there is a difference in the two views. Paul thought of the Law in terms of its unrealizable ethical demands, and so the Law held him in bondage to sin and death. With the coming of Christ, the power of the Law was broken, for man is justified by faith and not by works of the Law. The author of Hebrews thinks of the Law in terms of the cultus, with its priesthood, sacrifices, and sanctuary, none of which he believes can provide forgiveness of sins. But with the coming of Christ, the true priesthood, sacrifice, and sanctuary are revealed. With Christ a new covenant is given that is superior to the old one that established the cultus (7:22). And a better hope grounded in better promises is given whereby man is able to draw near to God (Heb. 7:19, 25). It is to establish the superiority of the new priesthood, sacrifice, sanctuary, covenant, promises, and hope that the author now compares Christ and the Levitical priesthood.

The Heavenly Sanctuary—Hebrews 8:1–10:18

Having established Christ as a priest after the order of Melchizedek (Heb. 7), the author mentions Melchizedek no more. His purpose has been served, for he has shown that in Christ a priesthood that supersedes the Levitical priesthood has found its fulfillment. The author now turns to the climax

---

[25]For a discussion of the complicated problems raised by the author's reference to Melchizedek and of previous speculation about this figure, see Alexander C. Purdy and J. Harry Cotton, "The Epistle to the Hebrews," *The Interpreter's Bible*, XI (New York: Abingdon, 1955), 660.

of his theological argument, in which he explains how Christ's priesthood is superior to the Levitical priesthood.

The author draws his comparison in terms of a High Priest in a heavenly sanctuary built by God (8:1–2), and in terms of the setting up of an earthly priesthood and the building of an earthly sanctuary according to the Law revealed to Moses on Mt. Sinai (8:5). Here the author alludes to the instructions regarding the tent (tabernacle) in the Book of Exodus (24–27). According to this account, Moses was to "make everything according to the pattern which was shown you in the mountain" (Ex. 25:40). Throughout his discussion, the author has in mind this tent that was set up in the wilderness, rather than the Temple at Jerusalem, which he had probably never seen. His description of the sanctuary is clearly drawn from the Biblical account.

There had been a good bit of speculation among the Jews about this statement to Moses. The word "pattern" had led them to the conclusion that the earthly Temple was a copy of an invisible heavenly sanctuary in which angels continually interceded for the sins of men. The author of Hebrews was undoubtedly influenced by such speculation. But he was also influenced by Hellenistic dualism, which tended to think of earthly phenomena as copies or shadows of heavenly realities. He uses the words "copy" (8:5; 9:23, 24) and "shadow" (8:5; 10:1) in contrast to the "true" (8:2; 9:24; 10:1), the "perfect" (9:11), "the real" (10:1). Philo spoke of the Temple as a symbol of the true temple, the invisible world of ideal forms whose Holy of Holies is the heaven, and whose High Priest is the *logos* who leads men to understand that the material world is patterned after the immaterial world.[26]

And yet the author of Hebrews is not primarily interested in the cosmos or a replica of the tent in the heavens, but rather in the revelation of the true priest Jesus Christ and the heavenly sanctuary that God has made through him. Not only has Christ obtained a priesthood that is more excellent than the old; he has also mediated a covenant that is better. The author finds his authority for this New Covenant in a prophecy of Jeremiah (8:8–12). From the beginning, Christians had believed that this promise of a New Covenant prophesied by Jeremiah had been fulfilled in Christ (Mt. 2:18; 26:28; Mk. 14:24; Lk. 22:20).

He describes the earthly sanctuary with its ineffectual priesthood and sacrifices (9:1–14). Here he is dependent on the Exodus account (Ex. 25ff.). Obviously he was not aware that his description (9:1–5) derives from an idealized account by priestly scribes who wrote long after Moses' time. Nor was he apparently aware of certain discrepancies between his own description and that in the Exodus account.[27] But, as he himself says, he is not concerned with details (9:5). The major features for his interpretation are the two inner tents.

---

[26]See E. R. Goodenough, *By Light, Light* (New Haven: Yale University Press, 1935), pp. 108ff., 116ff.

[27]For these discrepancies, see Purdy and Cotton, "The Epistle to the Hebrews," *Interpreter's Bible*, XI (New York: Abingdon, 1955), 685–687.

The outer of the two, known as the Holy Place, was open to all classes of priests, though not to the people; in this area the daily sacrifices were offered. The inner tent, the Holy of Holies, only the High Priest was allowed to enter, once a year on the Day of Atonement (9:7). This great occasion, described in Leviticus 16, preoccupies our author and he deals with it as representative of the whole Levitical system of sacrifices. On that occasion the High Priest entered through the curtain to sprinkle sacrificial blood upon the mercy seat. The author argues that these animal sacrifices could only guarantee ritual cleansing after some infractions of the laws dealing with ritual purity (9:10), such as those found in Leviticus 11. But he contends that none of these sacrifices could perfect the conscience (9:9).

Now the author explains that the outer tent is actually a symbol of the present age, and that as long as it stands it is impossible to enter into the inner sanctuary—the heavenly sanctuary (9:8–9). He seems to mean that until the "New Age" came, no matter how often the High Priest entered the Holy of Holies, he never actually entered into the presence of God. But with the exaltation of Christ to the right hand of God (8:1), the New Age has come (9:26) and the true High Priest has entered the heavenly sanctuary, into the presence of God himself (Heb. 9:24). And in entering that sanctuary he offered himself and not the blood of goats and bulls (9:11–12).

The superiority of Christ's offering of his life is that it purifies the conscience from dead works through forgiveness of sin. His offering of a life without blemish (sin), through the Spirit, was able to purify men from all sins (9:14; 2:9–18) and so perfect those who were consecrated by that offering (10:14; 10:29). The superiority of Christ's sacrifice is also substantiated by the fact that it was a single sacrifice that could never be repeated (7:27; 9:25–26; 10:10, 12, 14), whereas in the tent sacrifices had to be continually offered, showing that the conscience was never purified from sin. By implication, this single offering was sufficient for all time. It marked the end of the Old Age of sin and the beginning of the New Age in which sin and death were overcome by Christ, who was now seated at the right hand of God (10:12–13; 2:9–15). Interpreting words from Psalm 40 as words of Christ, the author can say that Christ himself came to do away with all other kinds of sacrifice (10:5–7) by doing the "will of God," and in his death he consecrated once and for all those who believe.

Christ's sacrifice was superior in yet another sense, for through his sacrificial death he had become the mediator of the New Covenant. Alluding to his earlier statement that through Christ the believers are led into God's "rest" (3:7–4:10), the author now declares that the promises of the New Covenant are better than those of the Old, for those whose sins are forgiven will receive the promised eternal inheritance; they will enter into the heavenly sanctuary with Jesus Christ (9:15, 19). As the former covenants were ratified by the sprinkling of blood (9:15–22), so Christ, through his death, has ratified the New Covenant; those who are consecrated by Christ's offering of himself in perfect obedience to God's will are heirs of the better promises.

The author concludes this section with an exhortation (10:19–39) in which he shows the implications of Christ's priesthood for the reader. Although in the Jewish cultus only the High Priest was allowed to enter the Holy of Holies, Christ's "brethren" have confidence that they may enter into the heavenly sanctuary (10:19)—that is, into the heavenly presence of God himself. This is the climax of the author's argument, and he urges his readers to hold fast their confession of Christ and to remain faithful. They must continue steadfast in good works and in confidence lest they lose their reward (Heb. 10: 23–25, 35–36).

No matter how elegant this rhetorical argument may have seemed to the first century, to the modern reader it inevitably sounds rather strange. But the author's basic conviction is remarkably clear: Because man is sinful, his relationship to God is broken, and man himself cannot restore the relationship. Jesus Christ, through his sacrificial death, accomplished what no man could do for himself: he made forgiveness of sins possible and opened the doorway to a new relationship with God through the promise of salvation.

Our author never explicitly explains why a sacrificial death was necessary. There is certainly nothing in the writing that suggests the concept of an angry God who must be appeased. Nor is there any explicit suggestion, as in John and Paul, that it is through Christ's death that God's love is revealed and the believer is made a new creature or is born again.

Two questions stand unanswered: (1) Why was the sacrifice necessary? (2) How did it benefit man? In answer to the first question, the most we can say with certainty is this: The author of Hebrews seems to accept the Old Testament principle that in the relationship God had established with his People (through covenants) and in the Peoples' continuing effort to maintain that relationship (through worship) sacrifice was of primary importance. What was true of the Old Covenant foreshadowed the situation under the New Covenant established through Jesus Christ.

It is equally difficult to decide just how man is to benefit from Christ's sacrifice. The author seems to presuppose that his readers will accept the crucial significance of sacrifice for establishing relations with God. On the basis of this presupposition, he is content to argue the finality of Christ's sacrifice and to summon them to faith that through his sacrificial death their sins are forgiven. The primary benefit seems to be found in the assurance that the believers experience through this acceptance of the effectiveness of Christ's death and the power this faith gives them to endure temptations and to maintain a pure conscience.

The Way of Faith—Hebrews 11:1–13:21

Chapter 11 is one of the best-known passages in Hebrews. It is a roll call of the heroes of the Old Testament who followed the way of faith. The author hopes to strengthen his readers by reminding them that they are not alone in their struggles, and to inspire them to faithfulness by recalling the example of their forebears in the faith.

In his opening lines he gives the only explicit definition of faith that appears in the New Testament (11:1–4). When he says that faith is the "conviction of things not seen," and that through faith we know the world is made out of things that do not appear, he is speaking in language that was common in Hellenistic philosophical thought. The heavenly world of reality is what is in the author's mind when he says it was through faith that Abraham looked forward to "the city which has foundations, whose builder and maker is God" (11:10). So he pictures the great Old Testament heroes of faith as "strangers and exiles on the earth" (the material world) looking for a "homeland," "a better country, that is, a heavenly one" (11:13–16). It is into this heavenly world that Christ had gone when he "passed through the heavens" (4:14).

Our author says that it is through *faith* that we understand the existence of such a world. A philosopher like Philo would have said it was through the mind (*nous*) or *logos* (reason) that man knew of its existence. Nevertheless, he clearly reflects the concern of Hellenistic philosophy for a rationally acceptable interpretation of reality understood in terms of a transcendent order beyond this world of time and space.

But when our author calls the Old Testament roll of those who have been approved by God for their faith, he stresses another aspect of the meaning of faith: the more familiar Biblical concept of faith as that immediate, trusting response to the word of God and to the promises substantiated by that word. Abel, Enoch, Noah, Sarah, and especially Abraham are examples of this faith. Abraham responded obediently to God's call and journeyed into a strange country, trusting only in God's promise that he would lead him to a new land. The author comments that all these heroes were really seeking for something far more than the partial fulfillment of the promise, such as Abraham's arrival in Canaan. It was really the City of God toward which they journeyed, though they did not know the way. Here the author uses faith very nearly in the sense of hope, since in his mind the entrance into the city of God had to await the fulfillment of the promise in Christ.

In the last list of persons (11:23–38), faith has the meaning of patient endurance, a meaning that we have frequently met earlier in the epistle. In this list, which covers the period from Moses to the Maccabeans, he recalls men and women who risked their lives, suffered, or died a martyr's death in obedient response to God's word. All these, though faithful, did not receive what was promised (11:39–40). This was because God intended for them the promise that was revealed and fullfilled only through Jesus Christ.

The author summons up this host of witnesses before his readers in order to encourage them (12:1). Having given them grounds for faith, he now gives them living examples of faith. And in the center once more he places Jesus Christ, the pioneer and perfecter of faith. Like the faithful in all ages, Jesus suffered; but by his suffering and elevation to the right hand of God he has revealed the true substance and meaning of faith.

Now the author calls his readers to recognize that, in view of the suffering of the faithful people of the Old Covenant and of Christ himself, they must expect to undergo the discipline of suffering in resisting sin and abuse (12:5–11). The Greek word for discipline literally means "education" (*paideia*). The author develops the thesis, found frequently in Jewish Wisdom Literature, that it is through the discipline of suffering that God educates his people in righteousness. The Stoics had also emphasized that a man must endure suffering as part of his education into true manhood. This was in contrast to the classical Greek concept of *paideia*, which was concerned more with the full-rounded education of the mind, body, and soul according to the ideal of the true, the good, and the beautiful. Quoting from Proverbs (3:11–12), the author says it is through endurance that Christians realize their sonship to God even as Christ did (5:8). If Christians endure present pain, they will share in God's holiness when they reach the heavenly city. For they do not have to do with the covenant of Moses delivered on Sinai (12:18–21), awesome as that event was; they have to do with the covenant mediated by Jesus Christ (12:22–24), and with those of all ages who have been faithful to the promises, and with God who is the judge of all men. If those did not escape who failed to obey Moses, who was merely a man, what chance of escape do they have who reject God, who speaks from heaven through his own Son, Jesus Christ (12:25–29)? For what they confront is not the lightning and thunder on Mt. Sinai, but rather the shaking of the foundations of the heavens and the earth in judgment; in this finale only those who have received God's unshakable Kingdom will not be consumed. In thankfulness for such a Kingdom, Christians are to offer acceptable worship to God with awe and reverence (12:28–29). The author refers not only to worship in the formal sense, but to worship of God through good deeds (13:15).

Once more the bridge appears that has occupied our thoughts throughout this chapter: the bridge between worship and ethics. For early Christianity, there never was a gap between the two. Christian worship in all its varied forms was the act of celebrating God's final deed of reconciliation with man in Jesus Christ, in his death and Resurrection. But this reconciliation could not have any reality if it was not celebrated as much in the daily lives of Christians as it was in the worship of the community—the Sunday assembly, the joyful meal, the baptismal liturgy. The need for stabilizing the code of Christian conduct in view of the Church's ever-lengthening pilgrimage through a hostile world may have led to some rather dull moralizing on the part of many "teachers," who no longer acted in the context of the original enthusiasm. But the author of the Letter to the Hebrews shows that not all teachers were of this kind. Whatever the actual background of his polemic against the rehabilitation of the Jewish cult may have been, his fascinating Christian speculation about the Christ event as the center of both cultic worship and ethics stands as a reminder of the truly creative forces in the Christian community at the postapostolic period.

The Church
as the True Israel

Matthew

CHAPTER TWELVE

From the second century down to the present, the Gospel of Matthew has been considered the first gospel, not only in the list of the New Testament books, but in importance as well. Its place at the beginning of the canon means, of course, that it is probably the most frequently read of all the New Testament writings. But more significant than its location is the fact that the words of Matthew's gospel are among the most familiar of all New Testament themes. The coming of the Wise Men, the Sermon on the Mount, the familiar form of the Lord's Prayer, the Coin in the Fish's Mouth, the Parable of the Sheep and the Goats are found only in Matthew. Only in this gospel does Jesus address Peter as the Rock on which the Church will be built. There can be no question why Matthew has taken and held the prime place among the gospels in the esteem of the Church.

Papias, bishop of the Hierapolis in Asia Minor in the early second century, stated that Matthew was the compiler of the sayings (in Greek, *logia*) of the Lord in Hebrew, and that every man interpreted or translated them as he was able. This testimony of Papias (written presumably about

A.D. 140) has usually been understood to refer to the Gospel of Matthew, and therefore to affirm that that gospel was originally written in Hebrew.

There are many difficulties with Papias' testimony. First of all, we cannot be at all sure that he was talking about our Gospel of Matthew when he spoke of the "logia" of Jesus. If logia means "sayings," as it sometimes does, then we note immediately that Matthew's gospel contains far more than merely sayings; it is a careful blend of narrative and discourse material. In any case, Papias could not be referring to Matthew as we know it.

It has been suggested that *logia* was a term used in the early Church for collections of Old Testament texts, used by the Church to prove that Jesus was the fulfillment of the Hebrew prophecies. Among the manuscripts found at Qumran was a sheet of Old Testament passages which may have served to provide a ready list of messianic proof texts among the Essenes of the Dead Sea community. But Matthew, while attaching great importance to the fulfillment of the Old Testament, has far wider interests, and includes much more than scripture quotations in his gospel.

Papias has further been charged with error in his claim that the *logia* were in Hebrew, since the language in common use in Palestine in the first century was Aramaic, a Semitic dialect closely related to Hebrew. But the discovery of the Dead Sea Scrolls, most of which are in Hebrew rather than Aramaic, has weakened the force of this argument, since it is now evident that Jews in first-century Palestine were using Hebrew as the official tongue of their religious communities. But whether Papias meant Hebrew or Aramaic, he can scarcely have been referring to the original of the Gospel of Matthew, since it was clearly written first in Greek, and dependent on Greek sources.

At an early period in the Church's life, however, there were those who claimed to have found the Hebrew original of the first gospel. In the fifth century, Jerome (famous for his translation of the Bible into Latin, known as the Vulgate, the official Roman Catholic version) announced that he had discovered and translated the "original Hebrew" form of the Gospel of Matthew. What he actually found was a paraphrase in Aramaic of the Greek Gospel of Matthew.[1] The paraphrase was known as the Gospel of the Nazarenes, a Jewish-Christian group that flourished in that part of Syria through which the Euphrates flows. Other fathers of the Church mistook other books—some of them heretical—to be the Hebrew original of Matthew's gospel. The fact is, however, that our Gospel of Matthew is based on the Greek Gospel of Mark, although of course the oral tradition drawn upon by Mark, as well as the

---

[1] B. W. Bacon has denounced Jerome's claims of discovery as fraudulent; see his *Studies in Matthew* (New York: Holt, 1930), pp. 478–481. This Gospel is also discussed in Hennecke-Schneemelcher, *New Testament Apocrypha*, I (Philadelphia: Westminster, 1963), 139–146.

tradition embodied in Matthew's other written sources, go back ultimately to the Semitic speech spoken by Jesus and his contemporaries in Palestine.[2]

There is no need to repeat here the evidence that Matthew had Mark before him, as well as a document (now known as Q) consisting mostly of sayings of Jesus (see pp. 78–81). What should be noted here, however, is the great skill with which Matthew has reworked and edited his material, supplementing it here, abridging it there.[3] Throughout, he has handled his materials in such a masterful way that both the overall structure and the development of details contribute effectively to his major theological and polemical aims in writing his gospel. Before turning to an analysis of Matthew's aims, however, we direct our attention to the question of the probable time and place of writing of this influential document.

WHEN AND WHERE WAS MATTHEW WRITTEN?

Allusions to the Gospel of Matthew in the writings of Ignatius of Antioch (*ca.* 115) provide us the latest date to which the writing of this gospel can be assigned. That Ignatius quotes it as authoritative suggests that it had been in circulation for some time, perhaps since at least A.D. 100. On the other hand, Matthew's dependence on Mark as one of his sources proves that the gospel could not have appeared earlier than A.D. 70. This supposition of a post-70 date is confirmed by the direct mention in Matthew 22:7 of the fall of Jerusalem and the burning of the city which took place in the year 70. A likely date for the writing of Matthew would be, therefore, about 80 to 85.

To settle on so late a date as this virtually excludes the disciple Matthew from consideration as the author. We shall see that on other grounds it is not likely that this book was written by a disciple of Jesus, since a person so closely connected with Jesus would not have had to depend as a literary source on Mark, who at best was reporting at second hand the recollections of an apostle. Indeed, the Gospel of Matthew itself makes no claim to have been written by an eyewitness, much less by one named Matthew. It is true that only in Matthew is the tax-collector who became a follower of Jesus (Mk. 2:13–14) called Matthew (Mt. 9:9; 10:3), but there is no hint of a connection between this man and the authorship of the gospel. The divergences among the lists

---

[2]A comprehensive and judicious assessment of the Semitic element in the language of the Gospels is presented by M. Black, *An Aramaic Approach to the Gospels and Acts* (Oxford: Clarendon Press, 1954).

[3]For a concise summary of the modification that Matthew has made in the Markan material, see R. Bultmann, *History of the Synoptic Tradition* (New York: Harper & Row, 1963), pp. 350–358; also H. C. Kee, *Jesus in History* (New York: Harcourt Brace Jovanovich, 1970), pp. 148–164.

of disciples found in the three Synoptic Gospels are such as to warn us against basing historical judgments on variations in the name. We must confess that, as with the other three gospels, we do not know who the author of Matthew was. For the sake of convenience, however, we shall continue to refer to him as "Matthew."

The author's use of a Greek source makes it obvious that the gospel was originally written in Greek, as we have noted. This conclusion is strengthened by the fact that a number of the quotations from the Old Testament are taken, not from the Hebrew text, but from the Septuagint, the widely used Greek translation of the Old Testament that had been prepared in the third and second centuries B.C. for the use of Jews scattered throughout the Hellenistic world who no longer readily understood Hebrew. We look, then, for a city or region where there were Greek-speaking Christians of Jewish origin as the likely place where Matthew was written. Alexandria has been proposed, but there is no evidence to connect Matthew with that city. Caesarea has been suggested, but largely on the basis that Peter, who is given a place of special importance in Matthew (especially 16:16–19), was the one through whom the Church was established in Caesarea, according to Acts 10. But the story of Peter at Caesarea serves the author of Acts as a stylized account of the transition from Jewish to Gentile evangelism rather than as a straightforward historical report. Antioch is the city where the first echoes of Matthew are heard in the form of quotations and allusions in the writings of Ignatius. The dominant view among Biblical scholars has been that Antioch is in fact that place where Matthew was written,[4] although it is more probable that the gospel originated in a community in the area to the east of Antioch near the Euphrates Valley. We know of the existence of strong Jewish communities in Aleppo, Edessa, and Apamea[5] in this period, and that Christian communities flourished there in the second century. The interest in the Magi and the miraculous star are fitting in such an environment, although astrological speculation had pervaded the whole of the empire by this time.

At best we can only conjecture, on the basis of hints from within the work itself, about the specific type of community in which the Gospel of Matthew might have arisen. It was, as we have seen, a Greek-speaking group, but one which was strongly influenced by Jewish perspectives and aspirations. As we shall see in our subsequent analysis of Matthean themes, there is on the part of the author of this gospel a paradoxical attitude toward Judaism. On the one hand he is deeply sympathetic with Judaism, especially its Law and the moral demands contained therein. But on the other hand, he is profoundly, at times bitterly, critical of Judaism, especially of its leaders, whom he regards as hyp-

---

[4]The classic statement of this position is given by B. H. Streeter, in *The Four Gospels* (London: Macmillan, 1924). Streeter connects each of the gospels with one of the four great centers of Christianity.

[5]See the discussion of the possibility of this area as the place of origin of Matthew by B. W. Bacon, *Studies in Matthew* (New York: Holt, 1930) pp. 24–36.

ocrites (Mt. 23:1–36, especially vv. 13, 15, 16, 23, 25, 27, 29). The reader senses that Matthew has the mind and attitude of a convert from Judaism, who loves its institutions and shares many of its convictions, but who is profoundly troubled by what he considers to be its inability to grasp the fuller truth which God has now revealed in Jesus Christ. This truth is not antithetical to the faith of Judaism, but it is more than a mere supplement. Christianity is for Matthew the divinely disclosed fulfillment of the Law and of Jewish hopes; he cannot comprehend that those who stand in the tradition of the Law could fail to discern the truth as it is in Jesus. In presenting his gospel, therefore, Matthew meets his Jewish opponents on their own ground, arguing from scripture and employing typically Jewish methods of debate. Although the Gospel of Matthew contains polemics against Judaism, it is not written primarily as a polemical document; rather, it is a book of instruction for those living in a situation of tension with Jews. The author does not refute the claims of the Jewish scriptures; he claims instead that the Church is the true Israel,[6] while the people that calls itself "Israel" has actually forfeited that claim by its failure to recognize Jesus as God's Messiah.

The theory has been advanced that the primary aim of Matthew in writing his gospel was "to supply, from the treasure of the past, material for the homiletical and liturgical use of the Gospel in the future."[7] But apart from the traces of liturgical phraseology that have been introduced into the material included by Matthew in the Sermon on the Mount,[8] there seems to be no greater interest in worship here than in any of the other gospels. A more fitting characterization of the book is a manual of Church instruction and administration, perhaps comparable to the Dead Sea community's so-called Manual of Discipline.[9] In our examination of the themes and motifs that characterize the Gospel of Matthew, we shall see how devoted the author is to the matter of maintaining order in the Church.

STRUCTURE IN MATTHEW'S GOSPEL

Many interpreters of Matthew have drawn attention to the fondness for structure which is evident throughout the book. In the genealogy which opens the book, the author has arranged the generations in sets of 14, even though

---

[6]This understanding of the Church by Matthew has been convincingly developed by W. Trilling, *Das Wahre Israel* (Leipzig: St. Benno-Verlag, 1959).

[7]Thus G. D. Kilpatrick, *The Origins of the Gospel According to St. Matthew* (Oxford: Clarendon Press, 1946), p. 99.

[8]For example, the Beatitudes and the Lord's Prayer are both given by Luke in simpler form than by Matthew. Luke has Jesus pray simply, "Father"; Matthew has the more elaborate form suited for liturgical use: "Our Father who art in heaven." Luke presents the Beatitudes as direct address ("Blessed are *you* poor . . ."), while Matthew reproduces them as more general statements ("Blessed are *the* poor in spirit").

[9]This theory was developed by K. Stendahl, in his *The School of St. Matthew* (Uppsala: C. W. K. Gleerup, 1954; rev. ed., Philadelphia: Fortress Press, 1968).

this process obviously requires the omission of several links in the genealogical sequence (Mt. 1:2–17). But the most striking instance of Matthew's having structured his material is in the main body of the gospel, which he has divided into five sections, each of which concludes with some such phrase as, "When Jesus had finished these sayings . . ." (cf. Mt. 7:28; 11:1; 13:53; 19:1; 26:1). Each of the sections begins with a series of narratives concerning the activities of Jesus, and each concludes with an extended discourse. Preceding the first such section is the story of the birth and infancy of Jesus; following the fifth discourse is the account of the Passion and Resurrection. The opening and closing parts of the gospel are, however, far more than mere prologue and epilogue; they are essential elements of the story as a whole. The structure of the Gospel of Matthew can be viewed schematically as shown below.

I. The Coming of Jesus as God's Messiah—Chapters 1 and 2

II. The Ministry of the Messiah—Chapters 3 through 25

    (1) Preparation and Program of the Ministry—Chapters 3–7
        Narrative: Baptism, Temptation, and Call of Disciples—3:1–4:25
        Discourse: Sermon on the Mount—Chapters 5–7

    (2) The Authority of Jesus—Chapters 8 through 10
        Narrative: Healing and Forgiveness of Sins—8:1–9:38
        Discourse: Sending of the Twelve Disciples—10:1–42

    (3) The Kingdom and Its Coming—Chapters 11–13
        Narrative: Controversy Resulting from Men's Inability To Discern the Kingdom's In-breaking—11:1–12:50
        Discourse: The Parables of the Kingdom—13:1–58

    (4) Life of the New Community—Chapters 14–18
        Narrative: Anticipations of Hostility toward and Common Life within the New Community—14:1–17:27
        Discourse: Regulations for the Common Life—18:1–35

    (5) The Consumation of the Age—Chapters 19–25
        Narrative: Intensified Conflict between Jesus and Judaism—19:1–24:2

        Discourse: The End of the Age (Synoptic Apocalypse)—24:3–25:46

III. The Humiliation and Exaltation of the Messiah—Chapters 26–28
    The Passion and the Resurrection Stories; The Final Commissioning of the Disciples for the World Mission

A careful reading of the gospel following this outline will disclose that Matthew has not followed through his scheme with complete consistency. In Section II (4), for example, it is difficult to differentiate between narrative and discourse.

In Sections II (1) and II (2), however, there is no mistaking the division, since the narrative portion in each case closes with a summarizing account of Jesus' public ministry. Thus Matthew 4:23 reads:

> And he went about all Galilee, teaching in their synagogues and preaching the gospel of the kingdom and healing every disease and every infirmity among the people.

And Matthew 9:35 reads similarly:

> And Jesus went about all the cities and villages, teaching in their synagogues and preaching the gospel of the kingdom, and healing every disease and every infirmity.

The other subsections of Section II are *not* thus marked off by summarizing statements.[10]

Some interpreters have suggested that the fivefold structure of Matthew's central section is a conscious imitation of the fivefold Torah. Thus Jesus would be giving the New Law on the mountain in Galilee as Moses had given the original Law on the mountain in Sinai. But this proposal has several weaknesses. First, there is no real development in Matthew of the image of Jesus as a second Moses,[11] although Moses is depicted as appearing to him on the Mount of the Transfiguration (Mt. 17:3f.), as is the case in the other synoptic accounts. More significantly, one of the main arguments of Matthew is that it is precisely the Law (*sc.*, of Moses) and the prophets that have their fulfillment in Jesus (Mt. 5:17). In addition to this explicit reference to the fulfillment of the Law, the book is marked from beginning to end by the claim that what God has done in Jesus Christ has been to effect the fulfillment of the scriptures. This leads us to an examination of the main themes developed by Matthew.

GOD'S MIGHTY WORKS

Although all the gospel writers present a picture of Jesus that is marked by marvelous powers on his part and by miraculous events that accompany his ministry, Matthew lays greater stress on this than do the other evangelists. The birth story consists almost entirely of divine disclosures through dreams and miraculous occurrences, chief among which is the supernatural conception of Jesus in the virgin's womb. Only slightly less wonderful is the guiding star that

---

[10]This and other inconsistencies in the structural arrangement of Matthew have been noted by F. V. Filson in his article, "Broken Patterns in the Gospel of Matthew," *Journal of Biblical Literature*, LXXV (1956), 17ff.

[11]See the treatment of the theme, "New Exodus and New Moses," in W. D. Davies, *The Setting of the Sermon on the Mount* (Cambridge: Cambridge University Press, 1964), especially pp. 92, 93.

led the Magi to the birthplace. All these miracles are told in distinctive Matthean passages.

Matthew reproduced nearly all the miracle stories found in his sources, Mark and Q. At times he has abridged them; at other times he has expanded them. On occasion his modification has had the effect of heightening the miraculous element, such as when the ruler's daughter is not merely at the point of death, but dead (cf. Mk. 5:23 with Mt. 9:18), and when the blind man at Jericho in Mark 10:46 becomes two men (Mt. 20:30). But for the most part, Matthew's changes in the miracle stories serve his theological objectives, by concentrating on the faith of the persons healed, or on the authority of Jesus, or on the demands of discipleship.[12]

The sheer joy in the miraculous, however, comes out most clearly in Matthew's account of the empty tomb. Mark soberly describes the stone as already rolled back, and a young man present who announces that Jesus has been raised from the dead. Matthew on the other hand reports a great earthquake, an angel descending from heaven, the terror that strikes down the guards. At the death of Jesus, according to Matthew alone, there had been an earthquake and the bodies of many saints were raised even before the resurrection of Jesus took place (27:52). The intention of all this is not simply to impress the reader with miraculous detail, but to demonstrate that God was at work throughout the whole of the earthly life of Jesus, and that his (God's) action had culminated in the greatest of all miracles, the Resurrection.

---

[12]The way in which Matthew has brought out these motifs in the miracle stories, partly by expansion of his sources and partly by condensing them, is set forth in detail by H. J. Held in his long essay, "Matthew as Interpreter of the Miracle Stories," in *Tradition and Interpretation in Matthew*, by G. Bornkamm, G. Barth, and H. J. Held (Philadelphia: Westminster, 1963), pp. 164–299.

THE GARDEN TOMB *outside the wall of the Old City of Jerusalem. Though it probably dates from the late first or early second century* A.D., *it is thought by some to have been the tomb in which Jesus was laid.* (Matson Photo Service)

THE SCRIPTURES ARE FULFILLED

God's action in Jesus' behalf was not to be thought of as arbitrary or random; rather, it was the unfolding of a divine plan which the eye of faith could see as having been given beforehand in the Hebrew scriptures.

The Fulfillment of "Prophecy"

The foretelling of Jesus' ministry was not limited to the obviously prophetic sections of the Old Testament, but included passages which did not appear to be predictive at all, or which to an outsider might not even seem to apply. At least one scripture quoted by Matthew cannot be found in the text of the Hebrew Bible as we know it; there is nothing in the Old Testament that corresponds to the words that purport to be a quotation from the prophets: "He shall be called a Nazarene" (Mt. 2:23). Possibly the Old Testament reference that the writer had in mind was Judges 13:5; or Isaiah 11:1; or a combination of the two. In the first of these passages, a person who in a special way is dedicated wholly to God is called a Nazirite; in the second, the coming Messiah of the Davidic line is called (in Hebrew) *nezer* (meaning "a shoot which springs from a cut-down stump"). The meaning is that, although the royal line that began with David is apparently dead, there will yet come one from that family who will be the ideal king. Since the Jews believed that the consonants (which alone were written in the original text of the Hebrew Bible) were sacred, and that they were capable of several meanings, depending on what vowels were supplied to fill out the words, perhaps Matthew recognized

NAZARETH
in Galilee. An insignificant village in Jesus' day, it was expanded by the Crusaders and given the appearance of a provincial town of northern Italy.
(Israel Information Service)

that a different set of vowels used with *nezer* would provide scriptural confirmation for Jesus' association with Nazareth.

A distinctive feature of Matthew's quotations from scripture is an introductory formula which he uses eleven times: 1:22; 2:5; 2:15; 2:17; 2:23; 4:14; 8:17; 12:17; 13:35; 21:4; 27:9–10. With variations, the formula runs: "This was done to fulfill what was spoken by the Lord through the prophet. . . ." It must be acknowledged that, by current standards of Biblical interpretation, none of these prophecies means in its original context what Matthew had made it mean in his setting. For example, "Out of Egypt have I called my son" is in Hosea a reference to the exodus of the nation Israel from its bondage in Egypt; here it is a prediction of God's calling Jesus back from his temporary residence in Egypt after the death of Herod, who had threatened his life. In at least one instance, Matthew seems to have created a story (Mt. 27:3–10) to fit his combination of two or three prophecies (Zech. 11:12–13; Jer. 32:6–15; 18:2–3). The actions of the prophets in neither of these passages has reference to the betrayal of the Messiah or to money received as a bribe. None of the other gospels reports this incident at all, so that it would appear to be a product of Matthew's concern to demonstrate how God's purpose revealed in scripture was fulfilled even in Jesus' betrayal by one of his own followers.

Although the prophecy of the king coming on an ass seems to lie behind the Markan version of Jesus' entry into Jerusalem, Matthew makes the allusion to Zechariah 9 explicit. In doing so, however, he shows that he does not understand the nature of Hebrew poetic form in which the prophecy is set forth. Hebrew poetry is characterized by parallelism, in which the meaning of the first line is echoed or amplified in the second:

> The earth is the Lord's, and the fulness thereof,
> The world and those who dwell therein.
>
> —PSALM 24:1

When Zechariah wrote of Israel's king coming "on an ass, and on a colt the foal of an ass" (Zech. 9:9, as rendered literally from the Hebrew in the *King James Version*), he had in mind only one animal, as the other evangelists have recognized. Matthew, on the other hand, finding mention of two animals in the text, reports Jesus as giving orders to procure for his entry "an ass . . . and a colt."

Although it may not be warranted to speak of a school of interpretation standing behind these formula quotations,[13] there is a parallel between the method of applying the scriptures freely to the present situation, as was done at Qumran, and Matthew's procedure. In both instances, it was assumed that the group interpreting the scripture was an eschatological community awaiting

---

[13]This is the view of K. Stendahl, *The School of St. Matthew* (Uppsala: C. W. K. Gleerup, 1954), especially pp. 20–35.

the last days and the consummation of God's purpose. To them had been granted special insight into the future by means of the unlocking of scriptural mysteries. Therefore, even though—or perhaps more precisely *because*—the surface meaning of a passage of scripture did not seem to apply to the present, the inspired interpreter could see in these writings, out of an ancient setting, a clue to the divine purpose at work in the present historical circumstances.

The Fulfillment of the Law

The scriptures were also understood by Matthew to be fulfilled in another than the prophetic sense: that is, in fulfillment of the ethical demand contained in the Law and the Prophets. This claim is set forth in the opening section of the Sermon on the Mount (Mt. 5–7). Although Luke has also reproduced a "sermon" (Lk. 6:20–49) that shares some features in common with Matthew's better-known Sermon—both evangelists apparently drawing on Q— Matthew has given distinctive qualities to his version, and has included far more than has Luke. The Beatitudes which open the Sermon show that Matthew does not regard ethics as a matter of mere conformity to legal standards; membership in the People of God cannot be attained by meeting legalistic requirements. Rather, God's People are those who have received as a gift of his grace all that they have. By this world's standards they are the poor, the bereaved, the despised, the persecuted; but in the Age to Come, it will be evident that they are the special beneficiaries of divine favor: theirs is the kingdom, they shall inherit the earth, they shall see God (Mt. 5:3–8). They are the salt of the earth, the light of the world: let them perform now their proper functions in doing good works, that men may glorify their heavenly Father (Mt. 5:13–16).

The heart of Matthew's attitude toward the Law, however, is disclosed in two passages: the general statements about the Law (Mt. 5:17–20) and the series of antitheses ("You have heard that it was said to the men of old . . . but I say to you. . . ."—Mt. 5:21–48). Since these statements are found only in Matthew in this form, it is likely that they originated with him, or at least that they have been shaped by him to suit his purposes. Let us examine this passage in three parts:

> (1) Think not that I have come to abolish the law and the prophets;
>   I have come not to abolish them but to fulfill them.
> —MATTHEW 5:17

The first part of the verse implies that the charge has been leveled against Jesus (or against the Church which honors him) that Christianity seeks the destruction of the Jewish Law. This accusation is denied, countered by the claim that Jesus intends to *fulfill* the Law and the Prophets. "Fulfill" cannot mean in this context what it meant in the formula quotations discussed above; instead, it means that Jesus has come to accomplish what the Law promised, to actualize in human existence the will of God which the Law summons man to obey. That the weight falls on the ethical demand is obvious from the third general statement in verses 19 and 20.

> (2) For truly, I say to you, till heaven and earth pass away, not an iota, not a dot, will pass from the law until all is accomplished.
> —MATTHEW 5:18

A parallel to this statement appears in Luke 16:17, where it is apparently ironical; that is, Jesus mocks the Pharisees who would rather have the whole Creation pass away than for a single stroke or dot of the Written Law to be changed. As Matthew reproduces the saying, however, it is not ironical but affirms the unchangeability of the Law with an absoluteness that even some of the rabbinic interpreters did not enjoin. Matthew is convinced that what has been wrong with the nation that called itself Israel is that it has not in the proper and complete way expected the Law to be fulfilled; now the new community for which he is the spokesman looks forward to the true and total accomplishment of everything promised and commanded in the Law. Although this principle is not carried out with complete consistency in the interpretation of the Law that Matthew gives in the antitheses, the point of view expressed there is a full, radical affirmation of the Law. There is no hint of reducing the Law to a single principle, such as the law of love, nor is the Law presented as an instrument that will drive men to despair of their own moral abilities and thereby throw them back in repentance upon the grace of God. Interpreters of Jesus have read these passages in this way, but without warrant from the texts themselves.

> (3) Whoever then relaxes one of the least of these commandments and teaches men so, shall be called least in the kingdom of heaven; but he who does them and teaches them shall be called great in the kingdom of heaven. For I tell you, unless your righteousness exceeds that of the scribes and Pharisees, you will never enter the kingdom of heaven.
> —MATTHEW 5:19–20

Several features of this astonishing passage must be noted. First, the role of the member of the community is twofold: doing and teaching. Unlike the Pharisees, whose teaching may conform to the Law but whose way of life does not (see Mt. 23:3), the true child of the Kingdom teaches rightly and lives rightly. The person who aspires to leadership by assuming a teaching role in the community takes upon himself a serious and solemn responsibility.

The second part of this passage, rather than denouncing the Pharisees as immoral persons, calls for the member of the true Israel to go beyond them in obedience to the Law. The popular caricature of the Pharisee is that of a pedant, a prude, a prig—and a hypocrite. While denouncing the hypocrisy of the Pharisees (especially in chapter 23), Matthew has no quarrel with the moral demands that they make; his complaint is that they do not live up to their own standards. The New People of God should not only live up to pharisaic standards, but should go beyond them in the stringency of their interpretation of and conformity to the Law. The Law, therefore, is understood to be binding in a most radical way.[14]

JESUS' ATTITUDE TOWARD THE LAW.   In the Synoptic tradition as a whole, Jesus is represented as at times setting aside what is explicitly permitted or prohibited in the Law, and at other times as going beyond the statement of the Law to a more profound demand. Of the first type is the teaching about divorce, a practice which was explicitly permitted in Deuteronomy 24:1. The rabbis of the first century disagreed as to the conditions implied in the specification of adequate grounds for divorce ("because he has found some indecency in her"), some interpreting the phrase strictly to apply only to adultery, others interpreting "indecency" more broadly. According to the version of Jesus' word on divorce in Mark 10:11–12, there were to be *no* conditions under which divorce and remarriage were to be permitted. In Matthew's versions of this saying (he reproduces the word twice: Mt. 5:31–32 and 19:9), there is provision for divorce in case of "unchastity." In this passage, Matthew therefore depicts Jesus as less radical than he actually seems to have been, according to the older form of the tradition preserved in Mark.

On the other hand, the radical nature of obedience is powerfully set forth in the words of Jesus on murder (Mt. 5:21–26), on adultery (5:27–30), on retaliation (5:38–42), and especially on love of enemies (5:43–48). In each instance the moral issue is moved clear out of the realm where one can calculate what is legally permissible and what is not. Not the overt act of murder, but hatred of one's brother is forbidden. Not extramarital intercourse, but lusting after a woman who is not one's wife is condemned. Not acquiescence in performing a burdensome duty, but willing cooperation in demands and obligations is enjoined. One is not to have love only for those who are friendly and close at hand, but for one's enemies as well.

These commandments are radical, not merely in the sense that they are stringent and demanding, but because they get at the root of man's relation-

---

[14] A detailed analysis of the radical reinterpretation of the Law in the Synoptic tradition and especially in Matthew is presented by H. Braun, *Spätjüdisch-häretischer und frühchristlicher Radikalismus*, 2 vols. (Tübingen: J. C. B. Mohr, 1957), especially II, 34–61.

See also in this connection the essay of G. Barth, "Matthew's Understanding of the Law," in G. Bornkamm, G. Barth, and H. J. Held, *Tradition and Interpretation in Matthew* (Philadelphia: Westminster, 1963), pp. 85–105; also H. C. Kee, Introduction and Commentary on Matthew, in *Interpreter's Commentary* (New York and Nashville: Abingdon, 1970).

ships with his fellow man, rather than dealing with the externals of those relationships. It is too simple to say that Jesus is here pictured as concerned with the spirit rather than the letter; he is concerned about the letter of the Law as well, as we see from his appeal, in defense of his position on divorce, to the prior principle of God's intention in instituting marriage: "[So] God created man . . . male and female" . . . "and they became one flesh." "What therefore God has joined together, let not man put asunder"—(Mk. 10:6–9; Mt. 19:4–6—cf. Gen. 1:27; 2:24).

The basic appeal of the ethics of Jesus as shown in Matthew is to the nature and purpose of God himself:

> But I say to you, love your enemies and pray for those who persecute you, *so that you may be sons of your Father who is in heaven*; for he makes his sun rise on the evil and on the good, and sends rain on the just and on the unjust. . . . You, therefore, must be perfect, as your heavenly Father is perfect.
>
> —MATTHEW 5:44, 45, 48

The term "perfect" here does not mean simply absence of moral imperfection, but the wholeness and singlemindedness by which God goes about fulfilling his purposes and by which standard man is called to obey him.[15] Luke has toned down the force of this demand in his parallel form of this saying by substituting the word "merciful" (Lk. 6:36), but Matthew is closer to what was likely the original intent of Jesus' word.

Obedience to the Law, as Matthew describes it, was not confined to *ethical* performance, however: it included participation in such typical Jewish acts of piety as prayer (Mt. 6:5–8), giving of alms (6:1–4), fasting (6:16–18), and apparently offering the appropriate sacrifices as prescribed by the Temple regulations in the Law. These may have been empty requirements by Matthew's time, since the Temple was no longer standing,[16] but they show that in principle Matthew did not make our modern distinction between the ceremonial Law (as not binding on Christians) and the moral Law (as valid).

THE WAY OF RIGHTEOUSNESS

A characteristic term of Matthew's is "righteousness." He has introduced incidents into his account where the term is used, and inserted it in accounts where he is paralleling Luke. (An example of the latter is Mt. 6:33: while Luke 12:31 reads "seek first his kingdom," Matthew adds "and his righteousness.")

---

[15]See the discussion of this term by G. Barth, *op. cit.*, pp. 97–103.

[16]K. W. Clark has sought to show that, even after the destruction of the Temple in A.D. 70, the sacrificial worship was continued, presumably in the ruins. This would account for mention of bringing sacrifices to the altar (*e.g.*, in Mt. 5:23), as well as the reference to the Temple cultus as continuing, in Heb. 8:4, 5. See "Worship in the Jerusalem Temple after A.D. 70," *New Testament Studies*, VI (July 1960), 269ff.

The theme of righteousness is laid down at the very beginning of Jesus' ministry in Matthew's account (3:15). At this point in the narrative of the baptism of Jesus, John protests that he is inferior to Jesus and needs to be baptized by him. Jesus, however, insists that "it is fitting for us to *fulfill all righteousness*." Each of these italicized words is important. The demands of God's will are to be *fully* met. Even Jesus—nay, Jesus most of all—is under divine obligation to meet these demands. Righteousness is to be complied with in its *totality;* partial obedience will not suffice. Although the context in Matthew 3 does not tell us precisely what "righteousness" implies, we can see from the evangelist's use of the term throughout the gospel what it involves, and how Jesus is presented as the embodiment of righteousness. But that the term does not mean only ethical performance according to the will of God is made clear from Matthew 21:32, which speaks of John the Baptist as having come "in the way of righteousness."

There is an eschatological dimension to righteousness which is important for Matthew. This aspect is implied in Matthew 6:33, where "kingdom" and "righteousness" are linked. That is, the will of God is not fully achieved by the obedience of individuals; the whole sweep of human history is involved in the unfolding of God's purpose. Only when his goals are fulfilled in history—when his kingdom has come in its fullness—will the "way of righteousness" reach its divinely determined end. One aspect of that goal is set forth graphically by Matthew 25:31–46, in the Parable of the Last Judgment. Strictly speaking, this is not a parable, but a highly stylized picture of the end of history, when all men—Jew and Gentile—are brought to account before God. In it we can sense Matthew's blending of eschatology and ethics: human behavior is the prime criterion in God's action to effect the consummation of history.

The specifics of the ethical demand are spelled out in the Sermon on the Mount as a whole, though especially in the antitheses, in which Jesus reportedly contrasts his interpretation of what the Law requires with the way it was understood by his Jewish contemporaries. Apart from one instance in which "righteousness" is used as a term for the alms given by the pious (Mt. 6:1), the word itself occurs in the Sermon in more general statements. That it has been introduced into the tradition by Matthew is evident from the comparison with the Lukan version of the same passages. Luke reads: "Blessed are you that hunger now" (Lk. 6:21); Matthew reads, "Blessed are those who hunger and thirst *for righteousness*" (Mt. 5:6). In contrast to Luke, who simply reports the blessedness of those whose names will be reviled on account of the Son of Man (Lk. 6:22), Matthew has a unique passage in which he declares blessed those who are persecuted "for righteousness' sake." It is not only for confession of the name of Christ ("on my account," Mt. 5:11), but for following the way of life called forth by Jesus' interpretation of the will of God. Matthew does not stop with the general appeal to do "good works" (Mt. 5:16); in the Parable of the Last Judgment he gives concrete examples: feeding the hungry, clothing the naked, visiting the imprisoned, welcoming strangers into one's home.

Conversely, to fail to perform these acts of mercy is to invite condemnation in the Day of Judgment. Yet the parable does not imply that works of kindness are to be done *in order to* achieve a reward. On the contrary, those who (according to the parable) performed them did so solely on the grounds that they had encountered another human being who was in need. They are represented as wholly astonished that they have done anything worthy of reward: "Lord, when did we see thee hungry. . . ?"

The way of righteousness, therefore, is not a path of legalism, by which the commandments are obeyed in order to "keep the rules." It is a way of life according to which the commandment to love is put into concrete action. It is not the one who says "Lord, Lord," but the one who does the Father's will who enters the kingdom (Mt. 7:21); it is not the one who *hears* Jesus' words, but the one who *does* them whose work endures (Mt. 7:26). It is to such, Matthew tells us (25:34), that the King will say at the Judgment: "Come, O blessed of my Father, inherit the kingdom prepared for you from the foundation of the world." It is they who are in truth "the righteous" (25:37).

Righteousness: a Community Responsibility

The way of righteousness is more than a matter of individual behavior; for Matthew it involves the life of the individual in the corporate experience of the community as well. In Matthew 18, the gospel writer has reworked synoptic material in such a way as to lay stress on community responsibility within the Church. Mark's account of the dispute of the disciples among themselves, as to which was greatest, is modified by Matthew (18:1–5) to a general statement that becoming humble like a little child is the way to greatness in the kingdom. Further, every true disciple is to be ever concerned for the welfare of the weaker members of the community. He is to exercise great care lest he offend one of the "little ones" (18:6–9). The Parable of the Lost Sheep, which in Luke (15:3–7) depicts the joy of God at the recovery of one of his lost creatures, has become in Matthew a warning to the Church to guard with care even the lowliest of its members from harm. In a uniquely Matthean verse (18:14), the point is made that God will hold the Church responsible for the loss of even "one of these little ones."

In 18:15–35, Matthew has brought together material from several sources to stress the obligation the Christian has for trying to restore an erring brother and to forgive one who has offended. Not seven times, but seventy times seven, the true follower of Jesus must be willing to forgive. A parable which must originally have carried the point that one dare not take advantage of God's forgiveness, lest it be withheld in the Judgment,[17] has been attached by Mat-

---

[17] J. Jeremias, *Parables of Jesus*, rev. ed. (New York: Scribner's, 1963), pp. 210–214.

thew to the appeal that the Christian be willing to forgive his brother repeatedly. While the parable does not intend to depict God as in every way like the
king—complete with his own official torturers (18:34, where "jailers" should be
translated "torturers"), he does want to impress his reader with the seriousness
of the command of Jesus for Christian brothers to forgive one another.

GOOD AND BAD IN THE CHURCH

While Matthew, as we have seen, sets before the Church the goal of perfection, he is fully aware that the Church, like any other human institution, will
have obedient members and disobedient ones, and that the leadership must be
prepared to deal with disobedience. The mixed nature of the Christian community is clearly pictured in Matthew's versions of the Parables of the Kingdom,
together with the interpretation of these parables which he offers. In addition
to the general terms "kingdom" and "kingdom of heaven" (Kingdom of God),
Matthew speaks of the "kingdom of the Son of Man" and the "kingdom of
the Father." The former refers to the Church in the present age in its mixed
form, including good and bad. The kingdom of the Father is the Age beyond
the Consummation, when only the faithful are present among the People of
God.

In the Parable of the Weeds, which is found only in Matthew (13:24–30),
and in the interpretation of it that is given (Mt. 13:36–40), we have two
different points that are being made. In the original form of the parable, the
point was that the messenger of the Gospel should go about his work without
stopping to evaluate the outcome or to remedy unwanted results. The focus
of the parable is on the eschatological Judgment, portrayed under the figure
of the harvest. God will evaluate in that day; man's task is to sow, leaving the
results to God. Matthew, in the interpretation attributed to Jesus, has transformed this story into an allegory, warning members of the Church that some
of them are worthy and some are not. The latter will be cast into the furnace
of fire, where men weep and gnash their teeth (13:42). The task of sorting out
in the Day of Judgment will be handled by the Son of Man, whose angels will
gather "out of *his* kingdom" (the Kingdom of the Son of Man) the causes of
sin and the evildoers. But the righteous "will shine like the sun in the *kingdom
of the Father.*"

The Parable of the Net (Mt. 13:47–50), which originally was addressed to
the messengers of the good news, encouraging them to leave to God the esti-
mation of the results, is likewise made into an allegory warning men that they
should not be "bad fish" whose destiny is to be thrown into the furnace. What we
see at work in Matthew's modification of this parabolic tradition is concern
about the mixed state of affairs in the Church. He is here warning the members

to examine themselves, to see whether they will find their lot with the good or the bad in the Day of Judgment.[18]

Although there is no contrast between the Kingdom of the Son of Man and the Kingdom of the Father in Matthew's addition to the Parable of the Feast (Mt. 22:1–14; compare Lk. 14:16–24), the lesson is once more that the People of God are a mixed group. Luke's version of the parable stresses that the religious outcasts have responded to the Gospel invitation and are now certain of a place in the eschatological community. Matthew reshaped the parable so that those who have finally come to the feast are "both good and bad" (Mt. 22:10). Among them is one man who lacks the appropriate garb. He is cast out into outer darkness. Presumably the garment is the cloak of righteousness, which conforms to what we have already seen to be a dominant theme in Matthew.

The Church cannot wait, however, until the eschatological Judgment to settle matters of good and evil within its own group. There must be some system of adjudicating disputes and some structure of authority. Matthew alone among the gospels makes provision for this need. The story of Peter's confession of Jesus as the Christ is expanded by Matthew (16:17–19) to include the designation by Jesus of Peter as the rock on which the Church will be built. This passage cannot be original, since Mark, whose interest in Peter is great and obvious, would scarcely have omitted it from his account. Although "Church" would not here mean institution but eschatological community,[19] it is probably anachronistic to attribute such a statement to Jesus.[20] For Matthew, however, Peter's central role is not that of broad ecclesiastical administration but the exercise of authority in regulating the inner life of the community. The binding and loosing mentioned here are repeated in Matthew 18:18, and echoed in John 20:22–23. One of the functions of the rabbis, referred to in Jewish tradition as "binding and loosing," was the formulation of interpretations of the legal parts of the Old Testament in order to determine the situations in which a given law was or was not applicable. Matthew has obvious interest in and respect for rabbinic practices. In Matthew 13:52, Jesus is quoted as comparing a "scribe who has been trained for the kingdom of heaven" with "a householder who brings out of his treasure what is new and what is old." The leadership role in

---

[18]A detailed analysis of these parables is given by J. Jeremias in *The Parables of Jesus*, rev. ed. (New York: Scribner's, 1963), pp. 81–85, 224–227. Jeremias shows that on the grounds of vocabulary alone, the interpretations of these parables cannot be regarded as coming from the tradition; they originate with Matthew.

[19]For a defense of the authenticity of these words, see K. L. Schmidt, "The Church," in *Bible Key Words*, J. R. Coates, ed. (New York: Harper & Row, 1951), pp. 35–50; also translated by G. W. Bromiley, in *Theological Dictionary of the New Testament*, Vol. 3 (Grand Rapids: Eerdman, 1965), pp. 501–536.

[20]O. Cullmann in the revised edition of his *Peter: Disciple, Apostle, Martyr* (Philadelphia: Westminster, 1962), argues that the words were spoken in a post-Resurrection appearance, rather than at Caesarea-Philippi (pp. 161–217).

the Church, therefore, includes the task of interpreting the Law—whether old or new—in relation to the daily needs of the Church's life.

The strange and difficult Parable of the Laborers in the Vineyard, found only in Matthew (20:1–16) was originally a vindication of Jesus' Gospel against his critics.[21] God's nature is to be merciful toward all; he does not match his grace to man's performance. By adding the free-floating saying, "So the last will be first, and the first last," Matthew has shifted the meaning, so that the parable is in his setting a defense of the fact that the late-arriving Gentiles gain priority over God's People, the Jews, who were there from the beginning. As was the case with Paul in his struggle over the place of Israel in the purpose of God, Matthew here suggests that they have lost their place of special favor in God's sight. Whether this implication was intended by Matthew in 20:1–16 or not, it is clearly his meaning in his addition to the Parable of the Wicked Tenants in 21:33–46. Verse 43 reads:

> Therefore I tell you, the kingdom of God will be taken away from you and given to a nation producing the fruits of it.

Lest the reader be in any doubt as to the force of these words, he continues:

> When the chief priests and the Pharisees heard his parables, they perceived that he was speaking about them.

The most interesting feature of this prediction that the Kingdom of God will be given to others is the use of the term "nation" to refer to the Church. The true nation, i.e., Israel, is no longer the Jewish people, Matthew declares: it is the Church.

What of the fate of Old Israel? In one of the bitterest passages in all the New Testament, Matthew describes the Jewish leaders as inviting upon themselves full responsibility for the death of Jesus: "His blood be on us and our children!"—(Mt. 27:25). Regrettably, this bit of Matthean polemic has been seized upon by anti-Semites ever since. But Matthew did not stop there: in 23:32–36 he went on to bring down on the heads of the Jewish leadership the guilt for the murder of all God's messengers, from the days of Cain and Abel to the present. Israel has, as Matthew sees it, forfeited its right to be called the People of God; that privilege has been granted the Church.

EXPECTATION OF THE END

The theme of the nearness of the Kingdom of God (literally, of the heavens) is sounded by John the Baptist, according to Matthew alone. The other gospels

---

[21]See J. Jeremias, *The Parables of Jesus*, pp. 33–40.

speak only of his preaching of repentance. Drawing on Markan and Q material, Matthew builds up a vivid picture of John as announcing the coming of the Kingdom, and as the instrument by which Jesus inaugurates the way of righteousness (Mt. 3:14). Only in Matthew, among the Synoptic writers, is John aware of Jesus' sonship at the moment of his baptism (Mt. 3:16). Jesus is represented as taking up John's message when, in Matthew 4:17, he begins his public ministry. The eschatological nature of the Kingdom is emphatically stressed in Matthew's account of Jesus and John.

The summarizing statements in Matthew 4:23 and 9:35 concerning Jesus' ministry both use the peculiar phrase "the gospel of the kingdom," thereby pointing to the eschatological nature of his message. The signs which point to the inbreaking of the Kingdom are evident in the works of healing and the exorcisms which Jesus performs. Similarly, the discourse on the sending of the Twelve (Mt. 10) instructs the messengers that they are to preach the nearness of the Kingdom (10:7) and to manifest the signs of its coming. The eschatological dimension of their work is heightened by the inclusion in the mission discourse of Markan material that is found in the Synoptic Apocalypse (cf. Mt. 10:17–25 with Mk. 13:9–13), and which is obviously tied in with the judgment that Matthew believes fell when Jerusalem was destroyed; the Markan passage (Mk. 13:9–13), which Matthew has lifted out of its context and inserted in his mission discourse, leads directly into the prediction of the destruction of Jerusalem (Mk. 13:14ff. = Mt. 24:15ff.).

From various parts of Mark and Q, Matthew has brought together a series of sayings which he has modified in order to point up one of his major concerns, the Coming (parousia) of the Son of Man: Matthew 24:3 (where mention of the Consummation is also added to the Markan form of the word); 24:27, where a Q word mentioning the Son of Man "in his day" is converted into an explicit prediction of the parousia; 24:29–31, where the Markan prediction of the Coming of the Son of Man is expanded; 24:37, 39, where the Q expression "days of the Son of Man" becomes a direct reference to the parousia; 24:42, where Matthew introduces a distinctive word about watching, lest the Lord come on a day when he is not expected.

In three parables included by Matthew in his version of the apocalyptic discourse, the point is in each case the need for watchfulness in view of the delayed parousia. The Parable of the Faithful and Wise Servant (Mt. 24:45-51) furnishes both encouragement for those who remain faithful and ready in spite of the delay ("My Lord delays his coming"—Mt. 24:48), and a solemn warning of the judgment that will fall on those who are not watching at the time of his Coming. It reinforces the point we noted earlier, that the Church of Matthew is composed of worthy and unworthy, watchful and indifferent. In the Parable of the Ten Maidens (Mt. 25:1-13) the point is once more that when the parousia occurs, some will be ready and some will not. "No one knows the day nor the hour—watch, therefore." The Parable of the Talents, which like that of the Wise Servant comes from Q, calls for faithful stewardship of one's gifts during the interval before the Coming of the Master. That the interval is protracted in Matthew's view is evident from his adding the phrase (25:19): "after a long period of time" the Lord came again. Twice Matthew underscores the catastrophic consequences of failure to be ready, by appending his gloomy warning: there will be weeping and gnashing of teeth (24:51; 25:30).

There are hints in Matthew, however, that the interval between the First Coming of Christ and his *parousia* in glory is not to be viewed as an insignificant period of waiting. Rather, a new responsibility and a new reality have come into being as a consequence of the Resurrection. The new responsibility is the obligation of the followers of Jesus to preach the Gospel and to instruct in his teachings among all the people of the world. In contrast to the universal outreach commanded in the post-Resurrection words of Jesus in Matthew 28:19, 20, the mission discourse specifically instructs the disciples to limit their evangelism to the "lost sheep of the house of Israel" (Mt. 10:5, 6), by which is meant, not that all Israel is lost, but that the abandoned ones—the outcasts— from within Israel are to bear the good news. We shall see in the next chapter that this theme is greatly developed by Luke. Nevertheless, the mission is to the Jews. The mission to the Gentiles has been anticipated, however, in the opening words of Matthew describing Jesus' public ministry (4:12ff., especially v. 15), where Galilee is mentioned as "Galilee of the Gentiles [or nations]." The fact that there will—indeed must—be a mission to the whole world before the Consummation can occur is explicitly affirmed in Matthew's apocalyptic discourse, 24:14:

> This gospel . . . will be preached throughout the whole world [Greek, *oikoumene*], as a testimony to all nations, and then the end will come.

It is a fitting climax to this development, therefore, when the risen Christ commissions his followers to launch this world mission in 28:19, 20.

The new reality referred to above is the Church itself, composed not only of good and bad, but of Jew and Gentile. We have noted that the Church is represented by Matthew as a new nation, which will produce the fruits of righteousness that the People Israel have failed to do (Mt. 21:43). Upon Israel within the then-present generation will fall the doom appropriate to her guilt (Mt. 23:32ff.):

> Fill up, then, the measure of your fathers. You serpents, you brood of vipers, how are you to escape being sentenced to hell? Therefore I send you prophets and wise men and scribes, some of whom you will kill and crucify, and some you will scourge in your synagogues and persecute from town to town, that upon you may come all the

righteous blood shed on earth from the blood of innocent Abel to the blood of Zechariah the son of Barachiah,[22] whom you murdered between the sanctuary and the altar. Truly I say to you, all this will come upon this generation.

This fearful and vindictive indictment is surely written out of a situation of direct conflict between the growing church of Matthew and the Jewish community, torn as it was both with conflict with Rome and with the Church. Although the prediction of doom is addressed against the Pharisees (Mt. 23:13ff.), it reads as a denunciation of the whole Jewish nation. These passages tell us a great deal about Matthew and his attitudes; they tell us nothing about Jesus. It is simply not possible to square this cruel invocation of wrath with the command of Jesus—ironically, also reproduced by Matthew (5:44)—to love one's enemies. The supreme irony in Matthew's viewpoint, however, is not that he denounces the Jews, but that he expects the Church to take over so much of Jewish institutions and practices: scribal interpretations, ceremonial requirements, alms, fasting, and so on. He is able to view the Church in this way because, as we have already noted, the Church is for him the true Israel which takes the place of the nation which did not see in Jesus God's Messiah.

In the interval before the return of the triumphant Son of Man, the new community is to continue to confess him before men; if they fail to do so, they will not be vindicated by him at his *parousia* (Mt. 10:33). This Markan word (Mk. 8:38) has been placed by Matthew in the midst of instructions to the messengers of the Gospel. In fulfilling their work as witnesses, they function under the authority of this risen Christ: "All authority in heaven and on earth has been given to me"—(Mt. 28:18). It is by this power that they are to carry on their ministry, the specific tasks of which correspond precisely to the ministry that Jesus himself performed: healing, exorcisms, preaching the Gospel (Mt. 10:7, 8). But in addition, they are now to perform baptisms, and to do so in the trinitarian name of God. This is one of the few instances in the entire New Testament canon of an explicitly trinitarian formula; elsewhere, there are usually only implications of the Trinity (*e.g.*, II Cor. 13:14).[23] Their lives are to be characterized by complete obedience to the commandments which he has given them during the period of his ministry among them; they are not only to teach these commandments, but to see that they are observed. They may rest assured that, though their Lord is not visibly present, he is nonetheless among them: "Lo, I am with you always, to the close of the age"—(Mt. 28:20). In this way, Matthew alleviates the problem created by the nonfulfillment of the *parousia* expectation. On the one hand, the passage of time must not

---

[22]Abel is the first one murdered in the first book of the Bible; Zechariah is the last one to be murdered in the last historical book, II Chronicles. Matthew has, however, confused his Zechariahs, since the son of Barachiah was not a priest, but a prophet (Zech. 1:1) and was not murdered, so far as is known.

[23]See p. 289.

permit the members of the community to grow lax or to lose their zeal, since the return of the Son of Man is certain; on the other hand, to consider him as absent is to misunderstand the facts, since he has promised his continuing presence in their midst until God's purpose through him is consummated and the Old Age has given way to the Kingdom of the Father.

The Community
of New Life

John

CHAPTER THIRTEEN

It is a striking fact that the Gospel of John, one of the most profound and distinctive writings in the New Testament, poses more enigmatic problems than any other gospel writing. Even the sequence of the text raises baffling questions. The gospel seems to reach a satisfactory conclusion at 20:31, but then another chapter follows. Chapter 21 serves principally to enhance the status of Peter and predict his death (21:15–19); it also corrects a mistaken notion on the part of some that "the disciple whom Jesus loved," an enigmatic figure who is mentioned but not named in the gospel, was not going to die until Christ's return (21:20–23). It appears that the last chapter also serves to identify this figure as the author of the gospel, which is one reason many believe that Chapter 21 is the addition of a later hand. Its presence has expanded the search for evidences of an editorial hand. The strange fact that certain sections of the gospel seem out of place—for example, Chapter 5 ends with Jesus in Jerusalem, while at the beginning of Chapter 6 he crosses the Sea of Galilee—has led to theories of editorial rearrangement. Numerous dislocations of the text and editorial touches have been proposed, but the wide divergence of reconstructions testifies to their uncertainty. This is but an example of the many problems that have been collectively called "the Johannine Problem." While we cannot discuss them all, we will consider several of the most important issues.[1]

THE PROBLEM OF SOURCES

One baffling problem concerns the relation of John to the three Synoptic Gospels: there are such obvious similarities and startling differences. In agreement with the Synoptics, John introduces the ministry of Jesus with an account of John the Baptist. The gospel contains familiar stories found in one or more of the Synoptics: these include the Cleansing of the Temple, the Feeding of the 5,000, the Stilling of the Storm, the Anointing of Jesus, the Last Supper, the Triumphal Entry into Jerusalem, the Hearings before the Jewish religious authorities and Pilate, the Crucifixion. In addition to these specific parallels there are numerous passages containing possible allusions to the Synoptics.

But the differences between John and the Synoptics are more striking than the similarities. In the first place, even where John presents parallel material his version shows marked verbal variations. John sometimes has a different chronology of events. For example, the Cleansing of the Temple comes at the beginning of Jesus' ministry rather than toward the close, where the Synoptics place it. He has both the Last Supper and the death of Jesus take place a day earlier than in the Synoptics. In John the ministry of Jesus lasts about three years rather than the one year implied in the Synoptics. John also locates Jesus' ministry mainly in Jerusalem and Judea, as over against its Galilean orientation in the Synoptics.

There are notable differences in the form and content of Jesus' words. The parables, similes, and crisp sayings so characteristic of the Synoptics are missing; in their place are long discourses and dialogues on recurring themes. These are not the familiar themes of the Synoptics: righteousness, forgiveness, the coming of the Kingdom, the apocalyptic Coming of the Son of Man, urgent calls to preparation and watchfulness. John pursues such themes as eternal life, light, darkness, blindness, sight, glory, truth. He prefers symbolical language, and often gives words and events a double meaning. In two series of sayings, one introduced by the words "I am," and the other by the words, "Verily, verily, I say unto you," Jesus makes striking pronouncements about himself and his mission. He explicitly affirms he is the Son of God in terms strange to the Synoptics. The greater part of John has no parallels in the Synoptics.

In explaining these similarities and differences contemporary scholarship is in sharp disagreement. Some scholars account for the similarities on the basis

---

[1]For a thorough discussion of these problems, see Raymond E. Brown, *The Gospel According to St. John*, The Anchor Bible, Vol. 29 (New York: Doubleday, 1966), xxi–cxlvi.

of the author's knowledge of the Synoptics—primarily Mark and Luke—in written form. Others believe he was not acquainted with written gospels but did have access to certain oral traditions which later found their way into the written Synoptic Gospels. However, in recent years, in view of John's decided differences from the Synoptics, it has been argued that John did not use them; rather, he was dependent on sources totally independent from those of the Synoptic Gospels, sources now usually referred to as the "Johannine tradition."[2] In contemporary Johannine studies no task is receiving more attention than that of identifying and reconstructing these sources.

No single book has been more influential in stimulating research into this problem than the commentary of John written by Bultmann.[3] It was the first full-scale effort to systematically reconstruct the sources behind John's gospel. According to Bultmann's reconstruction, the evangelist made use of three principal sources: (1) a source containing the Prologue and a large part of the discourse material that Bultmann designated "revelation discourses"; (2) a source containing much of the narrative and particularly the miracles in Chapters 1–12, which he calls the "sign source"; (3) a source that underlies John's version of the Passion Narrative. There has been little agreement among scholars regarding Bultmann's detailed reconstruction of his sources;[4] however, his hypothesis regarding the existence of a discourse source and a sign source has played a major role in acknowledging the existence of an independent Johannine tradition.

Two serious problems confront the discussion of sources in John. In the first place, it is generally agreed that there is a common language, style, and theology throughout the gospel. If the author has utilized sources, they now bear the marks of the author's interpretative language and thought in varying degrees. Because of this it is possible to speak of the unity of the gospel as a whole. Just how John utilized his sources remains highly debatable. This leads to the second and closely related problem: determining the extent to which the content of John is to be accounted for by his own creative theological imagination. Before the current interest in the discovery of Johannine sources, it was common for critical scholars to assume that those passages in John not dependent on Synoptic tradition were largely products of his own originality and creativity. While most scholars would be disinclined today to attribute so

---

[2]A thesis first developed by P. Gardner Smith, *Saint John and the Synoptic Gospels* (Cambridge: Cambridge University Press, 1938). See also the thorough study by C. H. Dodd, *Historical Tradition in the Fourth Gospel* (Cambridge: Cambridge University Press, 1963).

[3]Rudolf K. Bultmann, *The Gospel of John*, tr. G. R. Beasley-Murray (Philadelphia: Westminster Press, 1971).

[4]For a detailed analysis and critical evaluation, see Dwight Moody Smith, Jr., *The Composition and Order of the Fourth Gospel: Bultmann's Literary Theory*, Yale Publications in Religion, No. 10 (New Haven: Yale University Press, 1965).

much to John, nevertheless, the acknowledged evidence of his interpretation throughout the writing poses very difficult problems for those who seek to reconstruct his sources. Redaction criticism is confronted with far greater difficulties here than with Matthew, Mark, and Luke.

PROBLEM OF THE BACKGROUND OF JOHN'S RELIGIOUS THOUGHT

The question of the background of John's religious thought has also prompted divergent opinions. In the late nineteenth and early twentieth centuries, it was quite common to stress the strong influence of the Hellenistic mystery religions on John. His language of union with Christ, the centrality of eternal life and rebirth, and his sacramental teaching—all were believed to have derived from this source. Later, a Gnostic environment was emphasized. For example, in his important commentary, Bultmann proposed that portions of the "revelation discourses" were derived from Gnostic circles, although the author of the gospel Christianized their meaning when he incorporated them. Integral to Bultmann's interpretation is the hypothesis that John was also influenced by a Gnostic myth of a divine redeemer who came from heaven to reveal the way of salvation to man. The major sources for this reconstruction are the writings of the Mandaeans (see p. 31).[5] While the earliest sections of the literature in its present form date from the seventh or eighth century A.D., it is dependent on traditions that emerged as early as the first century. The major debate centers on the nature of these earlier traditions, and particularly on whether or not there existed a pre-Christian redeemer myth of the alleged type. Other scholars have preferred to find the Gnostic-like background of John in the religious thought of the Hermetic literature.[6] This literature dates from the third or fourth century A.D. and derives from earlier traditions in Egypt. While the question of influence is contested, one of the striking features of both the Mandaean and Hermetic literatures is the similarity in the style of discourse and sayings with portions of John. One of Bultmann's important contributions was his meticulous study of this style in John's discourses and sayings. It seems necessary to assume that John was influenced by a style common to his Hellenistic environment, whatever is said regarding his use of Gnostic sources and their influence on his religious thought.

Other scholars have stressed the importance of the Jewish background for understanding John. His knowledge of the Old Testament is evident in his allusions as well as his quotations. A strong case can be made both for his dependence on Jewish apocryphal literature and for his knowledge of rab-

---

[5]For a discussion of this sect, see C. H. Dodd, *The Interpretation of the Fourth Gospel* (Cambridge: Cambridge University Press, 1953), pp. 115–130.

[6]*Ibid.*, pp. 10–53, for a discussion of the Hermetic literature.

binical modes of interpretation. Interest in the Jewish background has received a new impetus with the discovery of the Qumran (Dead Sea) Scrolls.[7] At an early stage in the study of the Scrolls attention was called to striking phrases that were found in John: "spirit of truth," "sons of light," "do the truth." There was also a common dualistic language, such as the contrast between light and darkness, truth and falsehood. It has pointed out that John's dualistic view is much closer to the eschatological dualism of the Qumran sect than to the metaphysical dualism of Hellenistic thought, especially Gnostic thought in some of its varieties. There is no question but that the discovery of the Qumran Scrolls has strengthened the case for the strong Jewish influence on John's thought.

ASSUMPTIONS CONCERNING THE AUTHOR AND HIS GOSPEL

The question of the authorship of John is sharply debated, although as early as the second century A.D. the writing was attributed to the apostle John, the son of Zebedee. An equally ancient tradition designates Ephesus, where

---

[7]There is now a large body of literature on the subject. For example, see Raymond E. Brown, "The Qumran Scrolls and the Johannine Gospel and Epistles," in *The Scrolls and the New Testament*, ed. Krister Stendahl (New York: Harper & Row, 1957), pp. 183–207. Also R. E. Brown, *The Gospel of John*, op. cit., pp. lxii–lxiv.

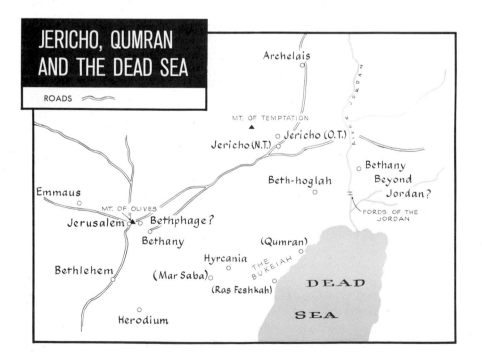

JERICHO, QUMRAN AND THE DEAD SEA

ROADS

Archelais

MT. OF TEMPTATION

Jericho (O.T.)

Jericho (N.T.)

Bethany Beyond Jordan?

Beth-hoglah

FORDS OF THE JORDAN

Emmaus

MT. OF OLIVES

Jerusalem   Bethphage?

Bethany

(Qumran)

Hyrcania

THE BUKEIAH

Bethlehem

(Mar Saba)

(Ras Feshkah)

DEAD

Herodium

SEA

John was supposed to have lived to an advanced age, to be its place of origin. This has also been challenged, and alternative cases have been made for Alexandria and Syria. In critical scholarship, decisions regarding the questions of authorship, date, and place of writing have always been related to conclusions concerning the religious background and purpose in writing. Scholars who have stressed the Hellenistic influence have tended to date the writing toward the end of the first century A.D. and to deny apostolic authorship; they have seen it as a missionary effort to communicate the Christian message to Gentiles in language and thought-forms familiar to the Hellenistic world. Others have seen it as a defense against Gnostic distortions of the Christian faith. More recently, on the basis of similarities between John and the Qumran Scrolls, some have argued for both a much earlier date and for Palestine as the place of writing. Furthermore, attention has been called to the Judean or southern Palestinian orientation of portions of the gospel. This has been seen as evidence that a significant portion of the peculiar Johannine tradition derived from southern Palestine. This emphasis on an earlier date and a Palestinian origin has in some instances been accompanied by a revival of the traditional view that the apostle John was the author, or at least a primary source of the traditions used by the author.

Two of the problems confronting those who argue for an early date—for example, before the Gospel of Mark—have been, first, providing a convincing purpose for which the author wrote, and second, accounting for his use of the gospel as a literary form. Although efforts have been made to deal with these two problems, none of the solutions has been persuasive enough to attract substantial support. The burden of proof seems to rest with those who would argue that the Johannine tradition took its final literary form as a gospel in total independence from one or more of the Synoptic Gospels.

Whatever position is taken on the nature of John's sources, the extent of his creative contribution, and the background, date, and purpose of his writing, it must recognize the diversity of opinion in contemporary studies. It seems necessary to assume, in the present state of research, that John had some knowledge of the Synoptic tradition, written or oral (the present authors assume John did not independently originate the literary form of gospel) and also of non-Synoptic tradition. While his thought is deeply rooted in the Jewish and Christian traditions, Hellenistic influences (even Gnostic influences) cannot be denied; they probably have been mediated through the author's Hellenistic Jewish environment. It seems certain that he was a Jew nurtured in the Judaism of the Diaspora synagogue; the case for identifying him with the apostle John remains dubious. It is probable that the type of thought reflected in the Qumran Scrolls had influenced this environment. But there is no certain basis for claiming direct borrowing. There are more differences than likenesses between John and the Scrolls.

There is one aspect of John's thought which may provide a clue to both his date and his purpose in writing. One of the principal features of the gospel is its stress on the presence of Christ and eternal life to and for the community of believers. In his obvious emphasis on these truths, the expectation of the Coming of Christ and the Consummation of the Kingdom appear subordinate. It may be that John, like Matthew and Luke, spoke to that problem which confronted the Christian community when the expected Coming of Christ failed to find fulfillment in the apocalyptic sense. At least, the burden of proof rests upon those who would find in the period before A.D. 70 a place for such a radical modification of the apocalyptic language and hopes of the Christian community. In stating his purpose John writes, ". . . but these are written that you may believe that Jesus is the Christ, the Son of God, and that believing you may have life in his name"—(20:31).

It has normally been argued that the words in the first part of the statement necessitate the assumption that John wrote mainly for nonbelievers. However, in one sense all the gospels were written to the Church to strengthen its belief in, and understanding of, Jesus as Christ and Son of God. Perhaps not enough attention has been given to the last phrase, "you may have life in his name." If equal stress is given to these words, then John would have written to the Christian community for the purpose of stressing that to believe in Jesus Christ means having life *now*. On the basis of an interpretation that differed from Matthew and Luke, like them he sought to lead Christians to an understanding of their relation to Christ and the world at a time when the failure of Christ's expected return constituted a major problem for faith. Such a time would certainly have been after the fall of Jerusalem in the period A.D. 75–100.

This later date would also be supported by John's attitude toward the Jews. It has long been argued that his attitude reflects the hostility between Christianity and the synagogue after A.D. 70. The fact that the argument over the Law has been largely superseded by the conflict over the person of Jesus, especially his relation to God (or the divinity of Jesus), likewise suits the later period. Like Matthew and Luke, John may also be dealing with the problem of the relation of Christianity to Judaism. With them he acknowledges the Jewish roots of Jesus and the Church ("salvation is from the Jews"—4:22), but he goes much further in stressing the intensity of the Jewish rejection, and the contrast between the old and the new. Writing from the standpoint of one who had seen the Gentiles acknowledge the truth which the Jews had rejected, he interpreted the story of Jesus as the revelation of the "Savior of the world" (4:42) whose coming marked the end of the old and the beginning of the new.

However, John undoubtedly had more than one or two purposes in writing. Not least, he wanted to write a theological interpretation of the life, death, and resurrection of Jesus. Though he makes use of the gospel as a literary form, his main concern is not to repeat the story of the ministry of Jesus as found in the Synoptics or any other traditions he might have passed. He aims to *reinterpret* the ministry in the light of his faith that Jesus was the eternal Son of God. And so it is that Jesus speaks and acts as the divine Son of God throughout the gospel. John assumes that his readers are familiar with the ministry of Jesus, and then proceeds to reinterpret the words and deeds of Jesus as remembered in the traditions, in order to discover their deeper meaning. This is an important point for the modern reader to keep in mind, for at first glance John's use of the gospel form suggests that he meant simply to record events, rather than to present an interpretation of those events.

THE PROLOGUE OF THE GOSPEL OF JOHN

John begins with a Prologue that sets forth the subject of his gospel (1:1–18) —namely, the Word of God (1:1–5). This is the Word that was with God from the beginning and through which all things were created and life was given to man. And this life, in turn, is the light that alone dispels the darkness of the world, the light to which John the Baptist had borne witness. But when the light of God came to "his own" (the Jews), many of them rejected him (1:10). Yet some of them received him and believed in him; to these Jews was given the power to become children of God (1:12). It was not, however, because they were earthly descendants of the Jewish people that they became children of God; rather, it was by an act of God's will. And God's will was accomplished when his Word became flesh and lived as a man among men (1:14), thereby revealing the "only Son" from the Father. Everyone who shared the "fullness" of Jesus' Sonship with those who believed in him also became children of God. Moses had given the Law, but it is only through the Son, Jesus Christ, that God's grace and truth are revealed. Since only the Son had seen the Father, only he can reveal the grace and truth through which men become children of God.

In short, then, John announces in his Prologue that he is going to tell his readers how God brought into being a new community through his only Son, Jesus Christ, through whom his life-saving Word was revealed. And he is also going to explain how the Jews' rejection of Christ was paralleled by the Gentiles' acceptance of Christ.

The terminology of the Prologue reveals how close John's religious thought was to that of the Hellenistic world in which he lived. For example, he describes the world as a place of darkness into which men are born and from which they can escape only by being born anew by one who brings light and truth from the divine world (Jn. 3). Immediately we are reminded of the Hellenistic practice of dividing reality into two realms of existence—the divine realm of light, truth, and life, and the lower world of darkness, falsehood, and death. Apart from the language of rebirth, and the "only Son," it also bears resemblance to the dualistic language of the Qumran Scrolls, as we have already noted.

And yet John differs from Hellenistic religious thought in important respects. In the first place, he modifies the absolute distinction between the realm of light and the realm of darkness by affirming that God, through his Word, had actually created the lower world. Moreover, he asserts that the divine Son of God "became flesh"—that is, he dwelt as a man among men. Clearly, then, if the divine Son himself was clothed in a material body, there could be no absolute distinction between the realm of spirit and the realm of flesh. And John is emphatic on this point, for he affirms Christ's true manhood (2:3; 4:6–7; 11:35; 19:26–27), refers to Jesus' "flesh and blood" (6:53–55), and vividly describes his death as a human being by referring to the blood that poured forth on the cross (19:34). There is no doubt that in emphasizing Jesus' humanity John was combating a view of Jesus that tended to neglect or deny his humanity while stressing his divinity. This conception of Jesus, called *docetism* (from the Greek word "seem" or "appear"—he *seemed* to be a man), was fostered by Gnostic elements in the Church. This particular aspect of Gnostic thought is also opposed in I and II John, which clearly originated in the same milieu as the Gospel of John. John was as eager as the docetists to acknowledge that Christ was a divine being, but he vigorously rejected any refusal to acknowledge that the divine Christ was also the man Jesus of Nazareth.

No term in John's Prologue is more pregnant with meaning or richer in religious association than the term *logos* (Word). This term had many shades of meaning in the Hellenistic world. The Stoics, for example, had popularized the *logos* as the rational principle that pervaded and constituted and ordered the universe. In the religious philosophy of the Hermetic literature, *logos* designates, among other things, a divine power enabling men to know God and themselves. And the term had come to have a particular religious significance to Greek-speaking Jews who read their scriptures in the Greek translation (Septuagint), for here *logos* was used to refer to the creative Word of God through which he had created the universe. The account in Genesis (1:3ff.) records that the Creation came into being when God *spoke*, and as time passed men decided that it was by God's *logos* that he had brought forth his creation

Logos took on additional meaning in connection with the development of another concept in Judaism: wisdom. The Wisdom Literature of the Old Testament and the Apocrypha shows a growing interest in the place of wisdom in the Creation of the world. There was even a tendency to personify wisdom, although the rigorous monotheism of the Jews kept them from suggesting that wisdom could exist independently. Later, however, under the influence of Greek speculation, *logos* was sometimes identified with wisdom as God's agent in Creation. And, since the Law (Torah) was the embodiment of God's wisdom and his Word, there was also a tendency to ascribe to the Law all the attributes of Wisdom and Word.

In the Old Testament, the Word of God appears not only as the means by which God created the world, but also as the vehicle by which God revealed his purposes for Israel and the world. The Old Testament prophets, for instance, often preface their prophecies with the phrase, "The Word of the Lord." Here the revelation consisted not merely of what the prophets had to say, but in the series of events that was set in motion by the prophets' words and actions. This use of *logos* as a vehicle of revelation was also common in popular Hellenistic philosophy and religion. Philo, for example, sees the *logos* as the divine instrument whereby is revealed the knowledge of God, and in Hellenistic religious thought it is through the *logos* that salvation is disclosed to man.

But what does all this have to do with John's use of *logos* in the Prologue to his gospel? Simply that he was using a term that had broad associations in the Hellenistic world among both Jews and non-Jews. Many efforts have been made to explain John's usage in terms of his dependence on either the Jewish or Hellenistic usage, but it would be more historically correct to recognize a common influence.

There is one sense, however, in which John's use of *logos* is unique, for when he says, "the Word became flesh," he *identifies* the *logos* with Jesus Christ. This means that John conceived of the *logos* primarily in personal and historical terms rather than in mythological or cosmological terms. His understanding of the *logos* is determined by his understanding of the life and work of Jesus. True, John opens his gospel by naming the *logos* as the agent of creation, a reference that would be familiar to both Jews and non-Jews. But he quickly turns to the *logos* as the personal revealer of God, the One through whom salvation is revealed and given. And in the rest of the gospel, though the word rarely occurs, John retains this emphasis on its religious significance.

THE REVELATION IN THE WORLD

After the Prologue, the content of the Gospel seems to fall into two major divisions according to subject matter. The first twelve chapters deal with Jesus' public ministry, the story of the Word's revelation in the world, which reaches its climax when certain Greeks come to Christ (12:20–21). Beginning with Chapter 13, John portrays the final period, during which Jesus privately converses with the twelve disciples (13–17); this section, concluding with the Passion Narrative and Resurrection story (18–20), reaches its climax with the Coming of the Spirit (20:21–23). Like the Synoptists, John begins his story of the ministry of Jesus with an account of John the Baptist (1:19–34), though he completely subordinates the Baptist's role to that of Jesus. In several passages he depreciates John the Baptist's mission (1:6–8; 1:35–37; 3:25–30; 10:40–42), and from the very beginning ascribes words to him to indicate that the Baptist himself was aware of his subordination to Christ (1:15). John's account of Jesus' baptism completely omits the Baptist's message, and leaves him simply to proclaim Jesus as the "Lamb of God, who takes away the sin of the world" (1:29–34) and as the Son of God. In the Synoptics (except for Matthew) John does not recognize Jesus, but in the Gospel of John God reveals Jesus' identity to

THE WILDERNESS OF JUDEA
through which passes the modern road from Jericho to Jerusalem. In the background are the Dead Sea and the delta of the Jordan River. (Matson Photo Service)

the Baptist through the Spirit. It is Jesus, upon whom the Spirit comes and permanently abides, who will baptize with the Spirit. In interpreting Jesus' relation to John the Baptist, John is utilizing a theological principle that he will develop more fully in the rest of the gospel—namely, that knowledge of Jesus' identity is revealed by God through the Spirit only to those who believe. Although John is deeply concerned with the historical foundation of Jesus' ministry ("the Word became flesh"), his primary interest is in reinterpreting that ministry in the light of the theological truth it has revealed.

On the basis of Josephus' brief report of the activities of John (Antiquities XVIII. 116–117) and from later evidence of baptizing sects in Syria, scholars have inferred the existence in the first century of a sect which revered John the Baptist. In playing down the role of John the Baptist, John was possibly hitting out at his rival sect in Asia Minor made up of the Baptist's followers. But quite apart from this motive, John's subordination of the Baptist was consistent with his tendency to treat everyone in his gospel as lesser actors in a drama that was played out for only one purpose: to reveal to the world the central figure, Jesus Christ. The Baptist speaks for every character in the gospel when he says: "He must increase, but I must decrease" (3:30). It is the emphasis that helps account for the artificiality of the dialogues between Jesus and the rest of the *dramatis personae* throughout the gospel; the others are important only in providing a setting for Jesus' words and deeds. This approach contrasts with that of the Synoptics, where hints of the historical tensions of the times often break through.

With the Baptist's proclamation that Jesus is the "Lamb of God," John introduces a subject that he later develops in interpreting the death of Jesus as the sacrificial lamb. Here at the very beginning, he alludes to the death as crucial to an understanding of the revelation and the mission of Jesus, the one who alone baptizes in the Spirit. While in the Prologue Jesus' divine Sonship was affirmed on the basis of his having been with God from the beginning and having seen God (1:1, 15–18), here his Sonship is affirmed on the basis of the fact that he will baptize through the Spirit. As John proceeds, he will disclose how the Sonship of Jesus was revealed in history and how the Spirit was imparted to men through Jesus Christ.

In John's version of the call of the disciples, he differs decidedly from the Synoptics (1:35–51), for here Jesus is recognized as the Messiah from the beginning. And Peter is named "the Rock" (Cephas) at his call rather than later in the ministry (Mt. 16:18). The climax is the story of Nathaniel's call. This is the first of a series of dialogues between Jesus and certain persons who take on symbolical significance. Nathaniel, the Jew "without guile," finds no basis in Jewish tradition for believing that Jesus is the Messiah ("Can anything good come out of Nazareth?"). But in spite of his doubt, he is willing to "come and see." For John, this is the essence of faith: the openness of mind that leads a man, in spite of doubt, to approach Christ to be shown. When Nathaniel approaches Christ, he is amazed by a knowledge that he cannot account for in human terms (1:47–48), and on the basis of this experience he believes. Christ responds by promising Nathaniel that a day will come when his belief will be founded on something far more profound than Christ's superhuman knowledge —the day when he will see "heaven opened, and the angels of God ascending and descending upon the Son of man." This is John's way of saying that a greater revelation will come to Nathaniel when he realizes that it is Jesus Christ through whom God has access to man on earth and through whom man has access to God in heaven. John is referring here to the death and Resurrection of Christ, the moment in which this full revelation will be given. Nathaniel stands in vivid contrast to the unbelieving Jews who are later pictured as unwilling to open their eyes to the possibility that in the words and works of Jesus God is revealed (Jn. 7–9).

The New Life Given by Christ

In the first twelve chapters, John reconstructs the story of Jesus' public ministry around the framework of seven miracle stories and a series of discourses and dialogues, and several trips to Jerusalem at festival seasons. The first of the miracles sets the theme for the entire ministry of Christ (2:1–11). During a wedding feast attended by Jesus in Cana, a village in Galilee, the wine is depleted. At his mother's request, Jesus provides a superabundant supply. He takes six large vessels normally used for Jewish purificatory rites and has them filled with water, which he then miraculously changes into wine. This miracle, which is found only in John's gospel, may derive from an independent tradition. Indeed, some interpreters believe John had access to a collection of miracle stories—a "Book of Signs," as some label them.

But John's interest is not primarily in the physical miracles as such, and, in contrast to the Synoptic Gospels, he uses the term "signs" in referring to them. To John, Jesus' signs are manifestations of the power of God, which brings salvation to those who believe. In this sense, the miracle itself, met by faith, discloses the glory of God to the disciples (2:11). In John, the symbolic term "glory" refers not only to the transcendence and ineffable power of God, as in Hellenistic religious thought, but also to the power revealed in Jesus Christ (1:14, "We have beheld his glory")—the power that brings salvation. In the seven signs, Christ reveals God's power by doing God's works (5:36; 9:3). But the full manifestation of God's glory must include the death and resurrection of Jesus, and for John this is the greatest of all the signs, the one through which the meaning of all the others is revealed.

The word "sign" carries a second meaning in John's gospel, for each of the physical miracles serves as the vehicle for an unobservable truth. To put it another way: The signs are manifestations to the naked eye of God's power, but at the same time they are symbols of truth that cannot be observed directly. In the miracle at Cana, for example, the wine that Christ miraculously produces from the water is symbolic of the new life that he brings to mankind. It is the new life of the Christian community as contrasted to the old life of Judaism, symbolized by the water jars intended to be used for the ritual purifications required by Jewish Law. What the miracle really says is that Jesus is already engaged in the work through which man is purified and is thereby given access to salvation. Here, as in each of the succeeding six signs, we find a double meaning, for the observable deed carries with it a symbolic meaning.

In referring to the miracles as "signs," John differs from the Synoptic Gospels, in which the term "signs" generally refers to the apocalyptic events that were to mark the final Coming of the Kingdom. But since it is a basic theological belief for John that in Jesus Christ the true life of the Kingdom was already revealed, he readily refers to the works of Jesus as manifestations of that life in history. This underlying belief also accounts for John's symbolical use of the term "hour." At Cana, for example, he tells his mother, "My hour has not yet come" (2:4). This is the hour of death and resurrection when God's revelation will be fully consummated (12:23–25), and when Christ will accomplish all that his signs foretell. But for John, who stands beyond that event in time, the term "hour" refers to that moment in history when the Eternal Word was made incarnate in Jesus Christ—that is, the time of Jesus' ministry. Since it was only with his death and resurrection that the meaning of all Jesus' words and deeds was finally revealed, John here refers to that last event as the "hour." But insofar as the coming of Christ into the world is the beginning of that hour, John can also say that the hour "now is" (4:23).

The miracle at Cana is followed by the Cleansing of the Temple (2:13–22). Here again John differs from the Synoptic Gospels, which place this event in the final days of Jesus' ministry. It is generally agreed that John put the Cleansing of the Temple where he did because the change of order served his theological purpose. By placing it at the opening of the ministry, John emphasizes that the Spirit that was bringing into being a new community of worshipers was present in Jesus Christ from the very outset, but that the full coming of the community had to await the Resurrection and the consequent Coming of the Spirit.

The climax of the story comes in Jesus' words: "Destroy this temple, and in three days I will raise it up" (2:19). John explains this saying symbolically: Jesus is really prophesying his resurrection, when the risen Christ will replace the Temple as the place where man finds God. Those who worship in his Spirit are the true worshipers (Jn. 4). As the changing of the water into wine symbolizes the new life that Christ gives, so the cleansing of the Temple symbolizes the spiritual worship of the new community of Christ that is brought into being through faith in the risen Lord.

This act, which heralds the day when the Temple worship will be superseded, fits into the overall scheme of John's gospel. John builds the chronology of Jesus' ministry around a series of Jewish festivals, beginning with the Cleansing of the Temple at Passover (2:13), and closing with the Crucifixion at Passover (19:14). Between these events, Jesus makes significant pronouncements in or near Jerusalem at other festival seasons. It is probable that John has constructed this chronology in order to show that Jesus has supplanted all the old festivals of Judaism. He has revealed a new way to worship God, a way open to all men.

The New Birth

John 3, which purports to be a conversation between Jesus and a prominent Pharisee, Nicodemus, may be John's reinterpretation of Jesus' conversation with the Rich Young Man (Mk. 10:17–22). Here, however, the dialogue runs off into a discourse (3:16–21), which is obviously John's commentary on the conversation. The subject, entrance into the Kingdom, is reminiscent of Jesus' teaching in the Synoptic Gospels. But when Jesus begins to discuss *how* one enters into the Kingdom, he uses language peculiar to John's gospel. To enter into the Kingdom one must be "born anew" (3:3, 7). The Greek phrase that is translated "born anew" can also be translated "born from above," and John undoubtedly intended that the phrase should convey this double meaning. To be born anew is to be born of the Spirit (3:6). All men are born of the flesh in their physical birth, but only those who are born anew by the Spirit enter the Kingdom. Since the Spirit comes from "above," those who are born anew are also "born from above." This new birth has been made possible by the Son of Man, who has descended from heaven and ascended again (3:13). Those who believe in him "have eternal life" (3:15). This passage could readily be taken for a commentary on the statement in the Prologue: "But to all who received him, who believed in his name, he gave power to become children of

God; who were born, not of blood nor of the will of the flesh nor of the will of man but of God" (1:12–13).

The entire dialogue with Nicodemus presupposes not only the earthly ministry but the death and resurrection of Jesus, and the faith of the Church. This is evident in the shift from the first person singular to the first person plural in the words, "we speak what we know, and bear witness to what we have seen; but you do not receive our testimony" (3:11). Here we have the Christian Church speaking through John; the birth through "water and the Spirit" (3:5) clearly refers to Christian baptism, which John considered the sacramental rite in which rebirth was consummated. Furthermore, the death and Resurrection are presupposed when John says that the Son of Man has descended and ascended again, making this rebirth possible (3:13). John contrasts the Old Testament story of Moses, in which a bronze serpent is set up so that Israelites who were bitten by snakes could be restored to physical health (Num. 21:4–9), with the lifting up of the Son of Man "that whoever believes in him may have eternal life" (3:14). The words "lifted up" in John are symbolical, for they refer both to the elevation of Christ on the Cross (death) and to the elevation of Christ to heaven (resurrection).

In the discourse that follows, John gives the purpose of Christ's mission to the world (3:16–17). It is because God "so loved" the world that he sent his only Son, and the ultimate purpose of that love is that the world might be saved through the gift of eternal life. But Christ's coming has brought judgment as well as salvation, for those who do not believe in him are already condemned. The judgment is this: the light (Christ) has come into the world and men have preferred darkness to the light because their deeds are evil (3:18–20). In their blindness they bring judgment on themselves.

For John, the great sin is unbelief, a logical outgrowth of his conviction that in Jesus Christ, God's truth ("I am the way, the truth, and the life") has been revealed. Unless a man knows the true way of life as revealed in Jesus Christ, he will inevitably walk the way of darkness or sin. In part, then, faith is belief in the proposition that Jesus is truly the Son of God. But John does not make faith simply an intellectual matter. He insists that the knowledge that Jesus is the Son of God cannot be verified by reason alone; it is revealed through the Spirit. This revelation is possible only when men open their minds and hearts (as Nathaniel did) to Jesus Christ. Involved here is an act of trust and commitment to the possibility that God was revealing himself through Christ. In short, faith means not just accepting certain propositional truths about Christ; it means entering into a personal relationship with Christ in which trust and obedience become the controlling factors in a man's life, thought, and action.

In the discourse with Nicodemus, we have an example of how John transformed the eschatological teachings of Jesus and of the early Christian community. For John, life in the Kingdom is presented primarily as a *present reality* rather than a *future expectation*, since eternal life has already entered into history with the coming of Jesus Christ. Baptism is not a baptism of repentance in expectation of the Coming of the Kingdom; it is being born anew as a child of the heavenly world of the Spirit.

Further, although John uses the title "Son of Man" to designate Jesus Christ, he no longer pictures an apocalyptic figure coming on the clouds of heaven to effect final judgment. The final judgment has already begun with the coming of the Son of Man; it is an event that is now occurring in history as a result of the coming of Jesus Christ. The Jewish and early Christian apocalyptic concept of the Son of Man has been appreciably modified in John by his concepts of the heavenly Son of God and the preexistent *logos*. It is debated whether or not John's concept of the Son of Man was also influenced by Jewish speculation concerning Adam, or oriental speculation about a "primal man." Whatever influences might have been at work, John's central meaning has been shaped by his understanding of the work and words, death and resurrection of Jesus Christ.

The Savior of the World

In the dialogue with the Samaritan woman (Jn. 4), John develops the theme of the new life bestowed by Christ. When Jesus asks for a drink from Jacob's well, the woman is puzzled not only by the fact that a Jew would ask a Samaritan for a drink (John explains that the Samaritans and Jews were not on the best of terms), but also by Jesus' statement that he gives "living water" that becomes a "spring of water welling up to eternal life" (4:14). The water metaphor appears frequently in the Old Testament as a symbol of God's activity in giving life to men. In an eschatological passage in Zechariah, for example, it is prophesied that when the "day of the Lord" comes, "living waters" will

AGORA AT SAMARIA, *the Roman Forum and part of a temple at Sebaste, the Greek-style city of Samaria built by Herod the Great and named in honor of Augustus—"Sebaste" in Greek.* (Howard C. Kee)

flow out of Jerusalem and the Lord will become king over all the earth (Zech. 14:8–9). In rabbinic usage water was often used as a symbol for the Law. But John uses water as a metaphor for the Spirit, as he explicitly says (7:38–39). With the Coming of Jesus the Messiah, all the expectations of the final "day of the Lord" are being realized; not the least of them is the coming of the Spirit and the life it brings.

When Jesus discloses intimate details of the Samaritan woman's past life, she calls him a prophet and asks him to answer the question that has divided the Jews and the Samaritans for centuries: Where is the proper place of worship—the Temple in Jerusalem, or Mt. Gerizim in Samaria, where the Samaritans worshiped (4:20)? Jesus answers that true worship occurs neither in Jerusalem nor on Mt. Gerizim, for the "hour is coming and now is" when worship "in Spirit and truth" shall prevail. The woman realizes that this answer is more than a prophecy, and replies that only the Messiah could possibly "show us all things" (4:25). Then, in response to her dawning faith, Jesus tells her, "I who speak to you am he" (4:26). This characterization of Jesus as the revealer of all things has associations both with Jewish speculation about the Messiah and with the Gnostic concept of a divine revealer who leads men into knowledge of truth. It is significant, however, that John never uses the noun *knowledge* (*gnosis*), though he frequently uses the verb *know*. Perhaps this reflects a conscious effort to avoid a term which might be misinterpreted.

In this dialogue between Jesus and the Samaritan woman, John explicitly links together the new life and the new worship that he has already alluded to in the sign at Cana and the Cleansing of the Temple. It is no accident that the setting for this dialogue is Samaria, for the coming of the Samaritans (4:39–42) demonstrates the universal nature of eternal life and true worship. The disciples would postpone the true and universal worship of God until the Coming of the Kingdom (four months until the harvest, 4:35); but Jesus declares that the hour has already come when the true God is being worshiped universally. While salvation is from the Messiah of the Jews (4:22), Jesus, who is that Messiah, has proved to be the universal savior of all men. So the Samaritan friends of the woman confess "this is indeed the Savior of the world" (4:42). In calling Jesus "Savior," John is using a term that would have greater religious significance to Gentiles than the strictly Jewish term "Messiah" would have. Jesus has come to accomplish God's work (4:34), and that work is no less than the salvation of the world.

In the second of Jesus' signs, which follows immediately after the dialogue with the Samaritan woman, John illustrates the work that God has sent Christ to perform (4:46–54). Jesus heals a Roman official's son who is at the brink of death, and by so doing elicits the faith of the Roman official and his entire household. The fact that the man is a Roman emphasizes again the universal scope of the salvation Jesus brings. The sign points to the ultimate work of Christ —the healing of men at the brink of spiritual death through his life-giving word and through faith in its power. In the very hour that Jesus utters his healing word (4:53), the official's son recovers from his illness. But just as Christ's word restores physical life, so also is his word the source of eternal life to all who believe—Jew, Samaritan, or Roman.

The Work of the Father and the Son

The third of Jesus' signs, the healing of the man in Jerusalem at the sheep-gate pool (5:2–18), seems to be a reinterpretation of one of the Synoptic healings (Mk. 2:11; Mt. 9:6; Lk. 5:24). In the Synoptic account, however, it is Jesus' forgiveness of the man's sins that arouses a dispute with his Jewish opponents, whereas in John it is the fact that he makes himself "equal with God" by calling God "Father." Even the argument over his performing the miracle on the sabbath is subordinated to this central difficulty.

In the long discourse that follows the miracle (5:16–47), the true meaning of the sign is given. Jesus heals the man according to the Father's will, not his own; and the sign points to the final work of the Father, which is raising the dead and giving eternal life (5:20–21). Since the Father loves the Son and has sent him to accomplish his work, whoever hears the Son's word and believes God who sent him has eternal life, does not come into judgment, and has already passed from death to life (5:24).

In the fifth chapter, John develops several themes that he is to elaborate further in the rest of the gospel. Earlier, he had used mythological language in commending Christ's authority and power. Christ is the unique Son of God who has come from heaven (1:14; 3:13, 17, 31, etc.). Though John continues this theme, he speaks more and more of Christ's Sonship in terms of his doing the work of the Father. The Father has sent the Son to give eternal life to the world (3:16; 5:21, 26), but the Son's coming also involves judgment (3:17–21; 5:22–23). Those who believe the Son have eternal life; those who do not, stand under judgment. While John lays stress on the present reality of judgment and life, he frequently alludes to a future resurrection and judgment (5:28–29; 6:39, 40, 44, 54; 11:24; 12:48). Some interpreters believe such references contradict the author's point of view, and have assigned them to a later editor. But there is no textual evidence for this. It is more likely that John retains the traditional resurrection hope, though his major emphasis is upon the reality of Christ's presence now as both judge and source of eternal life. The crucial point of later discussions is whether or not Jesus was "sent" from God.

The Greek word that John uses for "sent" is significant. In the Old Testament, it was used to refer to the office and work of a prophet or any other man who was believed to have been commissioned by God to speak or act in his name. One who was "sent" by God bore the authority and represented the power of the sender, and it is in this sense that the word is used elsewhere in the New Testament. The noun "apostle" comes from the same root, and means "one sent with a commission from God to speak and act on his behalf." This use of the term was also familiar to Hellenistic religious thought—in Gnosticism, for example. But John claims that Jesus, being the Son, not merely represents the authority of God and speaks the word of God, but actually bears *in himself* that authority and power. The words he speaks *are* God's, and the works he does *are* the work of God. This is because he is himself God's Word.

This identity of Christ's work, authority, and will with God's leads to increasing conflict with the Jews. They continue (5:39) to seek for eternal life through their scriptures (Torah), while all the time the living Word is in their midst. John argues that if the Jews understood their scriptures, they would recognize Christ as the one prophesied by Moses (5:45–47). Their failure to understand their own scriptures, in which Moses himself wrote of Christ (5:46–47), is proof that they do not understand who Christ is.

The fourth (6:1–14) and fifth (6:16–21) signs, also reinterpretations of Synoptic miracles (Mk. 6:34–44, 45–52), further emphasize the divine power manifested in Christ's work. The fourth sign is John's version of the Feeding of the 5,000. When Jesus has finished feeding them, the people declare that he is "the prophet who is to come into the world" (6:14), and they wish "by force to make him king." The crowds do not understand the true meaning of the sign—they do not realize the nature of the one with whom they deal, and hence they fail to recognize that his kingship is "not of this world" (18:36).

The fifth sign is Jesus' walking on the water, and the climax comes in his words to the disciples, "It is I" (6:20). The English translation of these words does not convey the full significance of the Greek *ego eimi*, which literally means "I am." This was a technical phrase that had already been used as a name for God in the Greek translation of the prophet Isaiah. John uses it to signify the presence of God himself in the person of Jesus. Although the crowds saw in the miracle of the Feeding the power of an earthly king, here, in the words "I am," Jesus discloses to the disciples that God himself is with them. But even the disciples do not fully understand.

In the lengthy discourse that follows (6:25–65), John tries to explain the meaning of the Feeding of the 5,000. The crowds have seen it only as a miraculous work that reveals Christ's power to establish an earthly kingdom (6:26–27). But Jesus tells them that the Son of Man has not come to supply material needs but to give food that is the source of eternal life. The contrast between Moses and Jesus, already suggested earlier by John (1:17; 5:46), is further drawn when Jesus recalls that Moses miraculously gave the Israelites manna to sustain them in the wilderness, and yet they all died (6:49). Now Christ does what Moses could never do; he gives the "true bread from Heaven" which affords eternal life to the world.

In answer to the request that he produce some of this bread, Jesus says, "I am the bread of life; he who comes to me shall not hunger, and he who believes

THE LAKE OF GALILEE
and its shores were the setting for many of the events in Jesus' career according to the gospel tradition. Lying more than 600 feet below sea level, its waters come largely from Mt. Hermon, whose snowy slopes rise to the north. (Israel Information Service)

in me shall never thirst" (6:35). This is the first of a series of sayings that are prefaced with the words "I am," and are followed by a phrase with symbolic meaning, such as "bread of life," "the light" (8:12), "the door" (10:7), "the good shepherd" (10:11), "the resurrection and the life" (11:25), "the true vine" (15:1), "the way, the truth, and the life" (14:6). Although this form of pronouncement is not found in the Synoptic Gospels, it had been used from ancient times in the Orient as a mode of speech for a divine being. According to one Jewish view, when the Messiah came the heavenly manna would again descend from heaven as it had in Moses' day and would provide food for the faithful. According to another view, the manna was a symbol for the Law that was given through Moses. But in John the heavenly food has a unique meaning, for here Jesus Christ is the "true bread." Just as he gives the living water (Jn. 4) that brings eternal life, so he offers the food that gives "life to the world." He accomplishes this by doing the will of the Father (6:38), by giving his flesh for the world. When John identifies the true bread with the "flesh" of Jesus, he emphasizes that it is through the words and deeds of the historical person Jesus Christ that God has given man eternal life.

This discourse on the true bread is followed by a dispute among the Jews, who ask how Jesus can give his flesh to be eaten (6:52). Jesus replies, "He who eats my flesh and drinks my blood has eternal life, and I will raise him at the

355

last day. For my flesh is food indeed, and my blood is drink indeed." This answer seems to confirm the Jews' misunderstanding rather than to resolve it. But to his disciples Jesus explains that the flesh avails nothing; it is the "Spirit that gives life" (6:63). Only when they have seen the Son of Man "ascending where he was before" will they be given this food. In speaking of the ascent of the Son of Man, John refers once again to the Resurrection of Jesus, which is necessary before the Spirit is sent; the Spirit alone reveals the truth of Christ's words and deeds and is the source of eternal life to those who believe.

John's account of the Feeding of the 5,000, and the discourse that follows, obviously reflect the eucharistic teaching of the early Church. As the community ate the bread and drank the wine, it was conscious of the fact that Jesus, the Son of God, the Messiah who had lived as a man among men, now shared his life through the gift of the Spirit. Although the Son truly revealed himself in the flesh, the full revelation came only when he sent the Spirit after the Resurrection. For John, the ultimate meaning of the sign of the Feeding of the 5,000 was the death and Resurrection of Jesus Christ, through which eternal life was given to the world. And John interprets the feeding as the sign in Jesus' ministry of the eucharistic meal of the early Church. Through participation in the meal, the believers shared in the spiritual life bestowed by the risen Son of God.

John's language here is close to that of certain Hellenistic religious cults, which believed that through a sacred meal they entered into the life of the deity (see Chapter One). Jesus says, "He who eats my flesh and drinks my blood abides in me, and I in him" (6:56), and the phrase "abide in" occurs with increasing frequency in the latter part of the gospel. John uses this term to express the mystical union between Christ and the believer, in a sense that is close to Paul's concept of being "in Christ." John explicitly interprets the Eucharist through this concept of mystical union. When John later deals more extensively with what he means by mystical union (Jn. 14–17), the difference between his understanding of the concept and the notions popular in his day become obvious. In John, the man is not absorbed by the deity, nor is there any deification of the man in which the distinction between man and God is broken down. And in his teaching about the Eucharist he avoids identifying the bread and wine as the body and blood in a way that would suggest they had some magical power when consumed ("The flesh is of no avail," 6:63). The words and the spirit are the source of life.

The Children of God and the Children of the Devil

John 7 and 8 are concerned largely with the controversy between Jesus and the Jews, especially the Pharisees. Actually, the controversy reflects the later antagonism between the synagogue and the Church, though ostensibly it is over the Law (7:24) in general and the Sabbath observance in particular (and to this extent recalls the Synoptic reports of the actual conflict during Jesus' ministry). But the real issue is over Jesus' messiahship (7:40–52) and unique Sonship (Jn. 8). In his second "I am" saying, Jesus declares: "I am the light of the world; he who follows me will not walk in darkness, but will have the light of life" (8:12). The Pharisees charge Jesus with bearing witness to himself (8:13); and they insist that his testimony is invalid in the light of the Old Testament requirement that more than one witness is needed to establish a case (Num. 35:30; Deut. 17:6). But Jesus claims that the Father also bears witness to him. The very fact that the Jews do not recognize Jesus' claim is proof that they do not know the Father, since Jesus has come from the Father (8:14), and all he declares is what he has heard from the Father (8:26). Contrary to the Jews' claim, they are neither children of Abraham nor children of God, for they seek to kill Jesus (8:39–43); rather, their unbelief and hatred show that they are children of the Devil. They do not hear the words of God spoken by Jesus because they "are not of God" (8:47). Consequently, they are slaves of sin (8:34ff.) and will die in their sins (8:24).

As John develops this conflict between Jesus and the Jews, he seems to build up a rigid determinism—for example, in such sayings as "no one can come to me unless it is granted him by the Father" (6:65; cf. 6:44). John seems to say that God has predetermined who can and will believe in Christ. John's determinism springs, not from any tendency to indulge in speculation about man, but rather from his firmly held concepts of faith and revelation. For John, faith is that trusting response to God's Word and action that is the only means of arriving at knowledge of and communion with God. John clearly understands that faith depends on both God's act *and* man's response. But throughout his gospel he emphasizes the divine side of the relationship: God's revelatory act in Christ. Unless God acts, man cannot know him. It is this emphasis that accounts for the many references to the fact that no one comes to God except he lead them, and except they be his children. Since John believed God's complete revelation was in Christ, God's true children are those who believe in Christ.

Conversely, John says that those who do not respond to Christ are not children of God but children of the Devil. Their actions reveal not the truth of God, but the lies of the Devil, who is the "father of lies" (8:44). John gives two reasons for the Jews' failure to believe in Christ, and thus for their subservience to the lies of the Devil. First, they judge by "appearances" rather than by right judgment (7:24); John means they place their traditional beliefs —that is, what *appears* believable to them—above God's revelation in Christ. Second, they seek "their own glory" (5:44; 7:17; 12:43)—that is, they take more delight in the pride that comes from being Abraham's children, the Chosen of God, than in the glory revealed in Christ, through whom Abraham's hope that all men become God's children by faith was fulfilled. Men become children of the Devil because their desires are his desires (8:44ff.): they seek their own glory and close their eyes to the revelation of God's truth.

In spite of John's apparent determinism, it is evident that all men, without distinction, are potentially children of God. Though all are born in sin (Jn. 9) and must be born again (Jn. 3), God sent his Son to be the savior of the whole world. But only those who in faith are "taught by God" will recognize him as savior (6:45).

In the sixth sign (Jn. 9), John deals with the cardinal sin of unbelief. The occasion is the miraculous restoration of sight to a man who had been born blind. In the extended controversy with the Pharisees that ensues, two themes are dominant. On the one hand, there is the Pharisees' blindness to the possibility that Jesus' healing act can be in God's power, since Jesus is a sinner who has broken the Sabbath laws. On the other hand, there is the blind man's confidence; his recovery is evidence enough that Jesus is from God and has acted according to God's will.

As with the other signs, however, it is only when we grasp the symbolism of this sign that we can understand its ultimate meaning. The clue is found in the man's confession that Jesus is the Son of Man whom he worships (9:38). The true miracle is not the man's recovery of his physical sight, but rather the opening of his "spiritual eyes" when Jesus reveals in faith that he is the Son of Man. John uses physical sight as a metaphor for the faith whereby man sees God in Christ (14:8–11). With the other signs, this sign anticipates the death and Resurrection; it was only the risen Lord who fully opened men's eyes and was worshiped by them.

In contrast to the healed man's faith and sight stands the blindness of the Pharisees. To them Jesus says: "For judgment I came into this world, that those who do not see may see, and that those who see may become blind" (9:39). What does John mean by this cryptic statement? He is saying that in reality all men are blind from birth, not physically but spiritually. The man who was born blind is a symbol of all men, for no man has the power within himself to penetrate the darkness in which he walks. He knows not where he goes, because he knows not where his true life is to be found (8:12). Only God's light can dispel the darkness and reveal the true life, for it is only in God that men have life. But only those who acknowledge their blindness can have their spiritual eyes opened; this acknowledgment is the beginning of faith and sight. On the other hand, those who claim that they see do not know they are blind. They walk in the light of their own knowledge, believing it to be the true light. This is the sin of the Pharisees: Christ cannot open their eyes to who he is because they already claim to know who he is—a demon-possessed man (8:48). Their judgment derives from their own preconceptions of what the Messiah will do and say. It is their claim to sight (their own understanding of how God will reveal himself) that brings judgment upon them. The Pharisees are symbolic of the children of the Devil who walk in darkness; the man born blind is symbolic of the children of God who walk in the light. For

Christ is the "light of the world" (8:12ff.), without which men do not know whence they go.

In contrast to the Pharisees, who are blind leaders of the blind (as evidenced by their maltreatment of the blind man), Jesus is portrayed in the tenth chapter of John as the "good shepherd" who cares for the sheep. This shepherd-sheep metaphor is commonly used in the Old Testament, where God frequently is called the shepherd of his people (Psalm 23; Is. 40:11). King David, the ideal ruler, is also described as a shepherd (Ps. 78:70; Ezek. 37:24). And in Ezekiel 34 the prophet utters God's promise that he will give his people a shepherd in the Davidic line who will lead them to salvation from the false rulers who are destroying them. Here the shepherd is a messianic figure. John was clearly influenced by the Old Testament in his use of the shepherd-sheep metaphor.

But the metaphor was also common in the non-Jewish world, for it had been used as a divine title in the religions of Egypt, Babylonia, and Persia. It also appears in the Hermetic literature, where one book is entitled *Poimandres,* a Greek word meaning "shepherd of mankind." The shepherd is *nous* (personification of mind), who reveals all truth to mankind. So the metaphor had associations for Jew and non-Jew alike.

Jesus, however, is the "good shepherd," the *true* shepherd of the sheep. All who came before him are robbers who would lead the sheep astray (10:8). He alone gives life to the sheep, through laying down his life (the Crucifixion) and taking it up again (the Resurrection). His sheep include not only the Jewish disciples who first believed, but others who are not of this fold (10:16). John refers here to the Gentiles who accepted Christ when the Jews rejected him, and who made up most of the early communities. These sheep know the Father and the shepherd, since the Father and the shepherd are one (10:29). It is ultimately God who calls the sheep through Jesus to the eternal life that no one can take from them, for he is the source of all life (10:25–30).

The Last Sign—Resurrection and Life

John brings Jesus' public ministry to its close with the seventh sign, the raising of Lazarus from the dead (Jn. 11). This is clearly intended to be a climactic finale, the greatest of the signs. Each of the preceding six signs points to this seventh, in which Jesus actually restores life to a dead man in the most dramatic demonstration of his divine power. As with the other signs, this miracle is seen as a manifestation of the glory of God (11:4) and the glorification of the Son.

This miracle is found only in John, and there are obvious problems over the historicity of the event. If this striking miracle was known to the other gospel writers, it is very difficult to explain why they omitted it; only two other accounts of raising the dead are reported, and the early Church would hardly have overlooked this one. As it stands, the story is typical of John's language and theology. Furthermore, it is not incidental to the public ministry but actually serves as the climax. The most that can be said is that John was working with traditional materials, on the basis of which he presented Jesus as the giver of eternal life. One explanation suggests that John is reinterpreting as a literal event the Parable of the Rich Man and Lazarus (Lk. 16:19–31), where the point is made that the Jews would not be persuaded even if someone returned from the dead to tell them the truth that Moses and the prophets had spoken. And indeed the raising of Lazarus does not convince the Jews that Jesus is the expected Messiah; rather it leads to the final conflict.[8] Whatever its background in tradition, it is the *symbolic* meaning of this miracle that is important to John.

Lazarus and his two sisters, who live in Bethany, are pictured as close friends of Jesus (11:3, 5). When Jesus receives word that Lazarus is ill, he says that it is not an "illness unto death" and delays two days before going to his friend. Only when it is certain that Lazarus is dead does Jesus go to Bethany with his disciples (11:14–15). As he approaches Bethany, Martha greets him with the pitiful words that Lazarus would not have died had Jesus been there sooner. When Jesus assures Martha that Lazarus will rise again, Martha shows her belief in the traditional Jewish view of a future resurrection, saying that she knows Lazarus will "rise again in the resurrection at the last day" (11:24). But Jesus corrects this misunderstanding with his reply: "I am the resurrection and the life; he who believes in me, though he die, yet shall he live, and whoever lives and believes in me shall never die" (11:26). This saying summarizes the view of eternal life that has been evident throughout the gospel. Jesus gives eternal life *now* to those who believe in him; those who believe, though they suffer physical death, will never lose the eternal life already bestowed by Christ. When Jesus asks Martha if she believes this, she replies, "Yes, Lord; I believe that you are the Christ, the Son of God, he who is coming into the world." To believe that Christ is the Resurrection and the life is to believe that he is the Christ, the Son of God.

The "I am" saying of Jesus, followed by Martha's confession, forms the climax of the story and provides a clue to the symbolical meaning of the sign. For the glory of God that is revealed in the restoration of Lazarus to physical life is but a partial manifestation of the glory that is disclosed in God's gift of eternal life through Christ. The ultimate revelation of this life is to be given only in the death and Resurrection, not of Lazarus, but of Jesus. Lazarus is the symbol of all men: apart from Christ, they are already dead; through him, even in this world, they share in eternal life. John now has the High Priest unwittingly prophesy the gathering together of the true children of God through the death and Resurrection of Christ: "You do not understand that it is expedient for you that one man should die for the people and that the

---

[8]For an excellent discussion, see Alan Richardson, *The Miracle-Stories of the Gospels* (London: SCM Press, 1941), pp. 120ff.

whole nation should not perish" (11:50). Not only the Jews who believe, but also the Gentiles (the children of God scattered abroad), are to be gathered into one community (11:51–52) of life.

THE FULFILLMENT OF CHRIST'S HOUR

The events following the raising of Lazarus take place under the shadow of the imminent death of Christ. John concludes his account of the ministry of Jesus with a series of brief semipublic incidents. As in the Synoptic Gospels, the action occurs during the Passover season (12:1). In the home of Mary and Martha in Bethany, Jesus is anointed by Mary. But John, unlike Mark, has the anointing take place immediately before the Triumphal Entry (12:12ff.; cf. Mk. 11:7–10). Whereas in Mark the anointing is interpreted as preparation for burial, in John the event symbolizes Jesus' anointment to kingship. After the anointing, Jesus enters Jerusalem and the people proclaim him "King of Israel" (12:13). Neither the crowd nor the disciples understand Jesus' kingship (12:16); it is only after his Resurrection that they understand ("when Jesus was glorified"). He dies as the king of the Jews (19:12); but again the terminology is symbolic, for his kingship is "not of this world" (18:36).

In consternation, the Pharisees cry: "Look, the world has gone after him" (12:19). Again John places an unwitting prophecy on the lips of the Pharisees, for John writes from the vantage point of one who has seen men from all over the world, mostly Gentiles, enter into the Church. The coming of the Greeks to "see Jesus" (12:21) is John's dramatic way of announcing that Christ's death is near. With their coming, "the hour" in which the Son of Man will be fully glorified is near. The hour of Christ's death is the hour of judgment on this world whose ruler (the Devil) is cast out (12:31), and the death is the doorway to the Resurrection in which the victory over death and darkness (the realm over which the devil presides) is completely manifested. The world is judged for its unbelief; by their rejection of Christ, the Jews have shown themselves sons of the Devil (the ruler of this world, 8:44). At the same time, the "hour" of Christ's glorification is the moment when "all men" will be drawn unto him (12:32)—that is, when the whole world will acknowledge him as the *logos* who came to "his own" but was rejected (1:11). Christ is glorified by God because through him the whole world is given a share in the life of the Father.

The Meaning of Discipleship

After the Triumphal Entry, Jesus withdraws for a period of intimate association with his disciples (13:1ff.). The evening meal is clearly John's version of the Last Supper recorded in the Synoptics, but John has it take place the day before the Passover eve. Whether or not John's dating is more correct than that of the Synoptic Gospels is not of great importance, for John was not primarily concerned with historical accuracy. By placing the meal the day before Passover eve, he has synchronized the Crucifixion of Jesus with the traditional slaying of the lamb on the day of the Passover. John the Baptist had announced Christ to be the "Lamb of God who takes away the sin of the world" (1:29). Now as the Lamb of God Christ dies in fulfillment of John's proclamation. His bones are not broken on the Cross (19:36), just as scripture had enjoined that the Paschal Lamb's bones not be broken (Ex. 12:46; Num. 9:12). In contrast to the Passover, which celebrates God's leading of the Israelites safely out of their Egyptian bondage, John sees the death of Christ as the event through which God leads all men out of death and darkness into eternal life.

John, like the Synoptics, includes in his narrative of the last meal a reference to Judas' betrayal and the prediction of Peter's denial. But unlike them he omits any account of how the Lord's Supper was instituted.[9] In place of the account of the Last Supper, John substitutes the narrative of the Foot-Washing (13:2–20). The clue to the meaning of this act lies in the introductory words, "Having loved his own who were in the world, he loved them to the end" (13:1). The phrase "the end" may mean either "completely" or "to the point of death." John undoubtedly intends both meanings. The Foot-Washing must be understood against the background of Jesus' death, in which he completely revealed his love. In washing the disciples' feet, Jesus was performing a menial task that was usually the duty of the Jewish slave in the household. This act of humility surprised Peter, who wanted to stop Jesus from performing it. Peter's reaction is reminiscent of his rebuke to Jesus for announcing his coming death, as recorded in the Synoptics (Mk. 8:32ff.). Peter is told that he does not know what Jesus is doing but that someday he will (13:7). Jesus' words to Peter, "If I do not wash you, you have no part in me" (13:8), are a symbolical reference to Christ's death, for it is through Jesus' death, Resurrection, and the gift of the Spirit that Christians are washed and have a part in Christ.

John's account of the Foot-Washing recalls the image of Jesus as the Suffering Servant that is so vivid in the Synoptic Gospels. John's interest in presenting Christ as the divine Son has led him to a portrayal that conveys the heavenly glory of Christ, but only at the expense of the profound human emotions and sympathy with which Jesus entered into the sorrows and afflictions of a troubled people. And yet in this brief episode John makes it perfectly clear that the divine Son is none other than the Suffering Servant. In this one dramatic moment John recalls the lowly path trod by Jesus, a path that John has all but obliterated in his desire to show that Jesus has revealed the glory of God.

---

[9]For a discussion of this omission, see A. J. B. Higgins, *The Lord's Supper in the New Testament* (Chicago: Regnery, 1952), pp. 75–78.

It is significant that when John refers to the humble servant he turns his attention momentarily from Christ to the disciples. He speaks of discipleship in the terms of a lowly servant, and points out that there are implications for the disciples in the Foot-Washing. For to call Jesus teacher and Lord means that the disciples must follow the example of Jesus, since "he who is sent [the disciple] is not greater than he who sent him [Jesus]." The true disciple is recognized not only by his faith in the divine Son but also by his following the path of love and humble service trod by the historical Jesus; the disciples must love one another (13:35) even though this means death (15:13), as it did for Jesus. Again we see that although John often used the language of mythology, his divine redeemer is no mythological figure who inhabits the heavens. Rather, he is the historical person, Jesus, who saved men by entering into history. And eternal life is not a victorious journey through heavenly space; rather, it is a journey, here and now, along the path that Jesus has trod.

John sets up a vivid contrast between this description of the true disciple and his portrait of Judas, the false disciple. Judas is present through it all, already planning the betrayal. Paradoxically, he will help bring about Jesus' death, through which all men are washed clean, but he himself will not be made clean (13:11). That is why John remarks, "It was night," when Judas leaves (13:30). He is referring not to physical darkness but to the darkness of unbelief of one who fails to see that in Jesus is to be found light and life.

Judas' departure marks the first in the final sequence of events leading to Jesus' death, the moment of the glorification of the Son of Man and God himself. For by his death the Son of Man reveals the love of God for man. In anticipation of his death, Jesus leaves his disciples with one commandment: "That you love one another" (13:34). This is not a "new commandment," except in the sense that the love enjoined is for the first time revealed in Jesus Christ. The disciples are to love "as I loved you" (13:34), a love that is revealed in the life of humble service dramatized by the Foot-Washing and the death that it symbolically anticipated. Although there were tendencies in the early Church to interpret Jesus as a new lawgiver (see pp. 323–328), John presents Jesus as the giver of eternal life that may be shared by entering into union with him. Like Paul, John believes that the ethical life is the "fruit of the Spirit," not the product of rigid adherence to legal prescriptions.

The Farewell Discourses

The last meal provides the setting for a series of long discourses (Jn. 14–16) and a lengthy prayer (Jn. 17). There is some question about whether we have these chapters in their proper sequence, since the words at the close of Chapter 14 suggest a departure from the meeting ("Rise, let us go hence"). Yet it is clear that Chapters 14–17 stand in close relationship and must be read and interpreted as a unit. These discourses deal with Christ's departure from his disciples and his coming again. Although there is nothing comparable to them in the Synoptic Gospels, they undoubtedly represent John's interpretation of several Synoptic passages. Chief among these is the apocalyptic discourse in Mark 13, which speaks of the Coming of the Son of Man in the clouds of heaven. John's farewell discourses represent his interpretation of these expectations.

In John's gospel, the discourses are delivered to the original disciples on the last night of Jesus' life. There can be no doubt, however, that it is the risen Lord who is speaking and that the hearers are Christians living in John's own day. All that is said presupposes the death and Resurrection of Jesus, the coming of the Spirit, and the Christian community's long history of experience. True, Jesus' words often seem to refer to the future, but this is because John continues to write within the dramatic framework of this historic ministry.

Several themes recur throughout the discourses. Chief among these is the relationship between Jesus and God, the Father. Jesus enjoys a mystical union with the Father, for he is "in the Father" and the Father is in him; the Father dwells in Jesus (14:11), and is with him in his hour of death (16:32). But this union of Jesus with the Father is not a mystical absorption in which the identity of either is lost. As he has throughout the gospel, John continues to recognize the distinction between Father and Son: the Father is greater than Christ (14:28). Rather, it is a union grounded in the love of the Father for Christ and Christ's love for the Father; the love of the Father is manifested in his faithfulness to the Son to the end (16:32); Christ's love is manifested in his perfect obedience to the Father's will (14:31; 15:10), finally sealed by his death. And so the words Christ speaks and the works he performs are not his alone but the Father's (14:10–11). John has continually emphasized that in Christ's words and works he was saying and doing his Father's will. But now it is the Father's last work, the death of Christ, that is on John's mind. The seven "signs" were mighty manifestations of power, but the death is to all outward appearances only a show of weakness. And yet, only those who see it as the perfect revelation of God's love can understand the true meaning of the signs and the words that Christ spoke.

This revelation is possible, however, only if Christ goes to the Father. And so Jesus repeatedly refers to his going to the Father (14:28; 16:7, 17, 28), in reference to both the death and the Resurrection. For John, Christ's going is important as the event by which Christ sends the Spirit. After his death there will be momentary sadness. But then there will be joy (16:16–24), for when the Spirit comes he will reveal the truth of life, death, and resurrection.

Jesus promises to come again. Though it is a point of controversy among interpreters, John seems to allude to a final Coming of Christ when he speaks of his going to prepare a place, and returning to take the believers with him (14:2–3). This aspect of the Coming should be related to the several references to the future Resurrection already mentioned. But this Coming is overshadowed by another mode of Christ's Coming on the basis of which John seeks to understand any Coming in the future. Unlike those Christians who thought of the Coming largely in terms of some future event, John stresses Jesus' coming in the Spirit to the community. In several passages Jesus promises that he will send the Spirit. When the world is no longer able to see Jesus because he is not physically present, the Christian community will see him in the coming of the Spirit (14:18). The Spirit, being the Spirit of truth, will bear witness to the truth about Christ (15:26). He will reveal all the truths that the disciples could not "bear" (understand) during Jesus' ministry (16:12). Christ will speak to the community through the Spirit, because the Spirit will faithfully declare Christ's words; and, because these are also God's words, they will be true (16:14–15). Since it is only with the coming of the Spirit that all truth is revealed, it is only the Spirit who can reveal that Jesus is "the way, the truth, and the life" and that "no one comes to the Father" except through Christ (14:6). Only those who possess the Spirit will understand that to know and see Christ is to know and see God (14:7–9).

Clearly, it would be impossible to overemphasize the significance that the concept of the Holy Spirit had for John. Like Paul, John thought of the Spirit in terms of God's pervasive power through which God carried out his purposes in the world. It is as Spirit that God is present in the world. But since God fully revealed himself in Christ, it was in Christ that the meaning of Spirit was revealed. John speaks of the Spirit as *parakletos* (our anglicized equivalent is *paraclete*). In Greek usage this term regularly means "advocate," one who pleads a cause in the legal sense. The term is not found elsewhere in the New Testament and John's usage has unique features in contrast to normal Greek usage. On one occasion he seems to use the term meaning advocate, but as one who convicts or convinces (16:8–11) the world; elsewhere the *paraclete* leads to truth (16:12–13; 14:26), witnesses to Christ (15:26), and even consoles (14:15–18). In the latter passages perhaps *counselor* is the best translation. Whatever influences were at work in John's use of the word (and the issue is unsettled), John by his own theological understanding gives it a new force in his gospel.

Apart from the Spirit, there could have been no community, for it is through the Spirit that the community knows that Christ lives and that the community itself lives by sharing in his life (14:19). And it is through the Spirit that the community knows that it shares in the union of Christ with the Father. But, as Christ's union with the Father is grounded in mutual love, so must be the union of the community with Christ and the Father. It is by loving Christ and by keeping his commandment of love for the brethren that the community comes to know the love of the Father. Where such love is present, Jesus and the Father come to make their home (14:21–24). This is eternal life as John sees it: life motivated and sustained by trust in the love of God revealed in Christ.

In the discourse on the vine, John allegorizes the union of Christ and the

Church (15:1–17). Christ is the vine, and Christians are the branches that depend on the vine for life. This allegory is meant to help the Church understand the meaning of the union, for if the branches do not bear fruit they are cast forth. To "bear fruit" has a double meaning: in the first place, the Church must obey Christ's commandment of love in order that God may be glorified. In this the fruits of discipleship of the Church are demonstrated (15:8). But in the second place, it is through this love that the Church witnesses God's love to the world, with the result that other disciples are led to God (fruits). As the Great Prayer of Jesus (Jn. 17) reveals, the only reason for the Church's existence is to bear witness to the Father's love in word and deed. The Church realizes its union with the Father as it bears witness to that love through the Spirit given by Christ.

The Church can expect persecution in the world (15:18–22), because the world does not know the Spirit and does not receive it (14:17). The Spirit passes judgment on the world's sin (hatred) in the light of God's righteousness (love); insofar as the world does not desire forgiveness for its sins it turns away from God (16:7–11; 3:19–21). The sin (hatred) of the world, manifested in rejection of Christ's words and love and its persecution of him (15:18–24), has come under God's judgment. But as Christ loves to the end, so the Church, even though persecuted, must continue to manifest Christ's loving Spirit so that all the world may believe (17:20).

The Great Prayer

The farewell discourses conclude with a long prayer, purportedly by Jesus. But the language and thought are typically John's, and at one point John even has Jesus refer to himself in the third person (17:3). The prayer is a résumé of what John believes Jesus had actually done for the Church through his life, death, and Resurrection and through the gift of the Spirit. John formulates all this as a great petitionary prayer to God on behalf of man. In the deepest sense, the prayer was not an invention of John, for it was inspired by what Christ had accomplished in obedience to the Father's will. Just what did John consider Christ's accomplishments to have been?

In his "hour" of death, Christ had glorified God by revealing God's love to man (17:1). By dying in obedience to God's will, Christ had finished his work; and when he was raised up into the presence of the Father, he had revealed through his Spirit that to know the only true God was to have eternal life (17:2–5). He had manifested God's name—that is, he had revealed the will, purposes, and love of God to the Church, and the Church had treasured and proclaimed this revelation (17:6). The Christian community knew that everything Christ said and did was a revelation of God, for it believed he had been sent with the commission and authority of God (17:7–8). Through the continuing presence of the Spirit, the community knew that it was under God's watchful care, and this knowledge was a source of joy (17:11–13). Because of its faithfulness to God's Word revealed in Christ, the community had been separated from the world and had come to know its hatred (17:14). Yet, confident of God's victory over the world and its evil, the community had been kept from the grasp of evil power (17:15). Instead of being removed from the world, the community had actually been sent by Christ into the world to proclaim the truth that he himself had revealed (17:17–19). The community of disciples had, through their proclamation of the Word, led many new believers into the community of Christ, and there they had come to know the love of God, which is eternal (17:20–24). They believed that Christ would continue to reveal this love throughout all the future (17:26).

This prayer has sometimes been called Christ's "High Priestly Prayer," a term that indicates what John seems to imply—namely, that in the prayer Christ consecrated the Church to its life and task in the world. But John clearly shows that it was not through any single word or prayer of the historical Jesus that this consecration took place, but rather through his *total life*. And the consecration did not cease with Jesus' death; rather, it continues to be consecrated through the Spirit throughout the life and history of the Church.

The Coming of the Spirit

This prayer is the climax of John's gospel. The speaker is Jesus, the Word of God, who is known not only through the words and deeds of his historical ministry, but also as the living Christ who is present in the community and who leads it to understand the meaning of his ministry for the world. It is through the inspiration and revelation of this Spirit that John has seen Christ's life as a prayer for his people, and it is this Christ whom John has been portraying throughout the gospel. The ultimate truth about Christ and his works does not spring from a recounting of the literal words he spoke or of the literal works he performed; the truth is disclosed only by interpreting the historic ministry in the light of the meaning that the living Christ continued to reveal to the community in the days beyond the Resurrection right up to the time John wrote. We can now understand why John's portrait of Christ differs so decidedly from that of the Synoptics. Even the portrait in the Synoptics reflects the theological interpretation of the early community, but John has carried the interpretation much further. It is as though John had said: Let us retell the story of the life and work of Jesus on the basis of the meaning that has been revealed to the present day. Let him speak in language that will be meaningful to us. And let us reinterpret the events of his ministry from the standpoint of later happenings that have unfolded new meaning.

It has been said that John gave his gospel to all the ages—that is, he freed the life and ministry of Jesus from its narrow Jewish setting and presented him as the savior of the world in language that would be familiar to non-Jews. But there is a more profound sense in which John gave Christ to the ages. By implication, John says that the historical Jesus is meaningful to men only when he is known as the Christ who lives in all ages, revealing himself and the Father to the Church.

This does not mean that John fails to affirm the significance of the Word become flesh, the historical ministry of Jesus. As we suggested earlier, he constantly presupposes the memory of the apostles as recorded in the Synoptic tradition. Nowhere is this more clear than in John's Passion Narrative (Jn. 18–20), which agrees with the Synoptic record on point after point. In fact, John may even include invaluable historical data that are not found in the Synoptics. But here again John's interpretative mind is at work. He uses Jesus' trial before Pilate as an occasion for the pronouncement, "My kingship is not of this world" (18:36). And on the Cross the last words are "It is finished" (19:30), words that have John's typical double meaning: it is not so much that Jesus' life is ended as that his work as Incarnate Word has been accomplished. And the accomplishment is not marked by the death on the Cross, though that is the conclusion of the earthly ministry. It is the gift of the Spirit that marks the accomplishment, as is indicated in John's final comment, "and he . . . gave up his spirit" (19:30). Here John refers not only to Christ's death but also to his giving of his spirit to the world (7:38–39). John's version of Pentecost is intimately related to Jesus' death and the Resurrection appearances of Jesus, the time at which the disciples receive the Spirit (20:19–23).

And the last word of John is consistent with his position throughout the gospel: "Blessed are those who have not seen and yet believe." These words are intended for the readers of John's own day. It is not those Jewish disciples who saw Jesus in the days of his flesh who are blessed, nor even those who experienced the post-Resurrection appearances; blessed are those in all places and all ages who through their faith know Christ as present in the Spirit in the community of believers—the community of the New Life.

The Church's Place
in World History

Luke-Acts

CHAPTER FOURTEEN

Matthew was concerned to move beyond Mark's rather simple assumption that the End would come after a period of Gentile evangelism had been completed (Mk. 13:10). He felt it was important to provide for an understanding of the Church's existence, and did so by depicting it as the true Israel, in contrast to the historic Israel that had forfeited its right to that title. He had indicated the ground of the Church's authority in the apostolic designation of Peter (Mt. 16:18–20), and had sketched out the basis for the maintenance of discipline within the Christian community (Mt. 18:15–20). Nonetheless, he did not set forth a theory of the whole sweep of history by which the Church could understand itself and its reason for existence in the interim before the coming of the End of the Age. It was Luke who took on the task of developing an encompassing view in which the place of the Church in God's overall purpose would be depicted. His story of Jesus and the Church in the perspective of God's historical purpose is set forth in the twofold work—unfortunately divided in our New Testament—known as Luke (Part I) and Acts (Part II).

Ancient tradition, quoted by Eusebius of Caesarea in his *Ecclesiastical History*, affirmed that the third gospel was written by Luke, a physician and companion of Paul (Col. 4:14; II Tim. 4:11). Scholars were at one time inclined to think that this was a reliable account of the author, since he was supposed to have had a special knowledge of medical terms and to have shared the universalistic outlook of Paul. Closer study, however, has shown that his allegedly superior medical knowledge is no greater than might be expected of any well-educated Greek-speaking Gentile of his time, and his theological outlook turns out to be distinctively different from that of Paul. He acknowledges in the preface to his gospel (Lk. 1:2) that his information about Jesus derives from others who were eyewitnesses, and there is no reason to suppose that he had any more direct access to the career of Paul. Some scholars have inferred from the sections where the narrative is reported in the first-person plural (*e.g.*, Acts 16:10ff.) that the author was a companion of Paul for parts of his journeys; but the shift back and forth from first- to third-person narratives has parallels in the Hellenistic literature of the period. All that can be said with assurance is that the author of Acts utilized as one of his sources a travel account concerning Paul, and that this document was more reliable in topographical and local detail than in its historical account of the career of Paul as a whole.[1]

WHY AND HOW
A CHRISTIAN HISTORY SHOULD BE WRITTEN

It is difficult for anyone who looks back over the history of Christianity from the vantage point of nearly 2,000 years to comprehend the seriousness of the question that must have confronted the Christians of the first century: Why should there be a Church? If the End of the Age was to be the next act in the redemptive drama of God, what meaning could be found for the Church as an ongoing institution? To provide a satisfactory answer to this kind of question, one would have to discover some positive significance in the situation before the End, rather than looking only to the End itself to provide meaning for human life.

There have, of course, been those in every century of the Church's existence who have looked on life in this age as merely transitional, and who claim to see no positive worth in anything that this age has to offer. Everything they want will become theirs in the sweet bye-and-bye. Luke was not content with this viewpoint, and instead set about describing the redemptive purpose of God in such a way as to show the essential role of the Church in the achievement

---

[1]On the question of the authorship of Acts and the use of sources, see the full and judicious discussion in W. G. Kümmel, *Introduction to the New Testament* (New York and Nashville: Abingdon, 1966) pp. 123–132.

of that purpose. In his view, the establishment of the Church was as much a part of the fulfillment of the divine plan as the act of Consummation itself. Indeed, the act of the drama in which the Church has the center of the stage is an indispensable antecedent of the End of the Age. The Age of the Church is the midpoint in the whole drama, as Luke sees it.[2]

Luke's Historical Method

Luke's scheme can be discerned not only from direct statements, but from the ways—at times subtle, at times more obvious—in which he modifies the tradition as he received it. The modifications are most clear, of course, where we have parallels from Mark and Matthew with which to compare Luke's handling of the material. But the special interests and even the distinctive vocabulary of Luke can be detected in material which he alone among the evangelists records. He was peculiarly well fitted for this task by his apparent knowledge of historical and literary methods of the cultured world of his own time, as well as by his thorough familiarity with the language of the Greek Old Testament. As a result of those two streams of literary influence, his work serves admirably as a bridge from the Jewish setting in which the Gospel arose to the Gentile world to which the message was to be interpreted. Luke is equally at home with the Semitic-sounding hymns of the infancy stories ("My soul magnifies the Lord"—Lk. 1:46) and the philosophical platitudes of the Hellenistic world ("In him we live and move and have our being"—Acts 17:28).

Luke's knowledge of his world extends beyond the literary to include precise political and historical information, as well. For example, in Acts 17:6 the city officials in Thessalonica are referred to as "politarchs." The term is used without explanation and occurs nowhere else in the New Testament. Inscriptions found in the region, however, confirm that the title was in use there and suggest that it was not used elsewhere. The accuracy of Luke's designation of the rulers of the city is thereby confirmed.

One of the few relatively fixed points of chronology in the whole of the New Testament is the stay of Paul in Corinth (Acts 18:12ff.). Luke reports that the Roman governor in Corinth at the time of Paul's sojourn there was Gallio. From an inscription found across the Gulf of Corinth at Delphi it is possible to determine that Gallio began his term as governor in the first half of A.D. 51. This confirmation of Luke's account receives further support from the mention in Acts 18:1ff. that two Jews who had recently arrived in Corinth and who later helped Paul in his work there had fled from Rome following a decree of the Emperor Claudius against the Jews in the imperial city. The date of

---

[2]The basic work on Luke-Acts in which the redemptive periods are traced out is *The Theology of St. Luke*, by Hans Conzelmann (New York: Harper & Row, 1960). This study is translated from the original German, which is titled appropriately, *Die Mitte der Zeit—* that is, *The Mid-Point of Time*. For details of this scheme, the reader is referred to Conzelmann's work, which is here presupposed.

that decree, as can be inferred from Suetonius' *Life of Claudius,* is approximately A.D. 49, which of course fits in precisely with Luke's account. In short, Luke has access to accurate information and uses it effectively in setting forth his story of the spread of the Gospel from Galilee to Jerusalem and on to Rome.

EVALUATING LUKE AS HISTORIAN.   It would be unreasonable, however, to expect Luke to measure up to modern standards of historical reliability, much less objectivity. He compares favorably with his contemporary historians, and indeed uses many of their methods and literary conventions.[3] One sees this from the outset in the formal literary prefaces with which he has prefixed both volumes of his twofold work:

> Inasmuch as many have undertaken to compile a narrative of the things which have been accomplished among us, just as they were delivered to us by those who from the beginning were eyewitnesses and ministers of the word, it seemed good to us also, having followed all things closely for some time past, to write you an orderly account, most excellent Theophilus, that you may know the truth concerning the things of which you have been informed.
>
> —LUKE 1:1–4

And the second recalls the first:

> In the first book, O Theophilus, I have dealt with all that Jesus began to do and teach. . . .
>
> —ACTS 1:1

The complexity of the sentences, the acknowledgment of predecessors in the field, the expression of purpose by the writer, and the address to the patron are all part of the literary conventions of the time. Luke is making a bid to have his books regarded seriously by the literarily, perhaps even the intellectually, sophisticated of his day.

It is easier to assess Luke's place among the historians of his time than it is to evaluate his work as a historian for the modern man who seeks historical knowledge of the beginnings of Christianity. On the one hand, Luke uses his sources in much the same way as his contemporary historians, although the evangelistic purpose which lies behind his work gives his books a special quality that the other historical writings lack. On the other hand, he raises problems for the modern man in search of "historicity" by adopting the first-century custom of inventing speeches or modifying the accounts of events. This was done even when the historian was an eyewitness, since his aim was not ver-

---

[3]For an appreciative study of Luke's literary and historical methods in comparison with those of other Hellenistic historians, see H. J. Cadbury, *The Making of Luke-Acts* (London: S.P.C.K., 1961), pp. 113–212.

batim reporting but portraying what was characteristic or what he thought was significant in the incidents which he was reporting. The late interpreter and historian of early Christianity, Martin Dibelius, has said:

> The ancient historian does not wish to present life with photographic accuracy, but rather to portray and illuminate what is typical, and his practice of aiming at what is typical and important allows the author of Acts partly to omit, change or generalize what really occurred. So it is that, where he sometimes appears to us today to be idealizing, and describing what was typical, he was really trying to discharge his obligations as an historian. Thus, through the literary methods of the historian, he was able to discharge his other obligation of being a preacher of faith in Christ.[4]

Basic for the work of an historian today is a chronological sequence of the events with which he is dealing; none such was available to Luke, however. In all probability, Luke had only an itinerary of Paul to follow for the sequence of events he depicts in Acts. Even there, his other objectives lead him to halt the course of his account of Paul to introduce other interests or to insert speeches attributed to Paul. This is especially evident in the famous sermon on the Areopagus in Acts 17. In preparing the Gospel of Luke, there was likely no chronology or sequence of events available, except for Mark's. Luke follows Mark's sequence in a general way, but feels free to depart widely at the beginning and the end, and to make considerable modifications in the middle, since his avowed purpose of setting forth "an orderly account" seems to refer not so much to chronological order but to logical or even theological order. As we shall see, it is to his purpose to have the story of Jesus' rejection at Nazareth come right at the outset of his public ministry (Lk. 4), even though Mark locates it at the end of a period of successful activity in Galilee (Mk. 6). It is important, therefore, to try to discover what the pattern or "order" was which guided Luke in the arrangement of his material for the first Christian history.

A Christian Perspective
on the Whole Scope of History

Luke's undertaking is an ambitious one: he wants to place the ministry of Jesus and the work of the Church in the context of the universal purpose of God. Although the actual chronological scope of the events directly reported runs only from the birth of John the Baptist to the imprisonment of Paul in Rome, there are many pointers in both volumes which look backward to the story of ancient Israel and forward to the consummation of the Ages.

---

[4]M. Dibelius, in "The First Christian Historian," from *Studies in the Acts of the Apostles* (London: SCM Press, 1956), pp. 136, 137.

THE FIRST EPOCH: FROM ANCIENT ISRAEL TO JOHN THE BAPTIST. The best clue to the way that Luke regards history as divided into periods is Luke 16:16. In Matthew 11:12–13, the more original version of the saying reads:

> From the days of John the Baptist until now, the kingdom of heaven has been suffering violence, and men of violence are seizing it. For all the prophets and the law prophesied until John; and if you are willing to receive it, he is Elijah who is going to come.

Luke has greatly reduced this saying (or this cluster of sayings) and has omitted the reference to John the Baptist as Elijah. But more important than these changes is the attitude implied toward John the Baptist: for Matthew, John marks the beginning of the new era of violence that presages the Coming of the Kingdom. For Luke, John marks the *end* of the epoch of the Law and the Prophets:

> The law and the prophets were until John; since then the good news of the kingdom of God is preached, and every one enters it violently.
> —LUKE 16:16

In Luke's view, John the Baptist brings to a close the old era of the Law and the Prophets, during which the promises of redemption were given, but in which the promised deliverance did not occur. It is the period of the ministry of Jesus that brings about the fulfillment of the promise. Luke tells us this in a unique passage (4:16–30). He describes Jesus preaching in the synagogue at Nazareth. After reading the words of promised redemption ("good news to the poor, release to the captives, deliverance for the oppressed"), Jesus declares forthrightly:

> Today this scripture has been fulfilled in your hearing.
> —LUKE 4:21

Although he does not carry the theme of fulfillment to the extreme of Matthew, Luke is careful throughout his account of the ministry of Jesus to show how what Jesus did was the fulfillment of scripture. Before considering the subject of fulfillment in Luke in detail, we must identify the end of this period in Luke's scheme and the beginning of the next.

THE SECOND EPOCH: THE EARTHLY MINISTRY OF JESUS. The period of Jesus' ministry is the second great epoch, and is itself divided into three phases. The first opens with the launching of the ministry with the programmatic sermon already referred to above. By the time Luke reaches the point in his narrative that corresponds to Mark 9:38–41 (*i.e.*, Lk. 9:50), we should expect the ministry to be nearing its close, as is the case with Mark's report. Instead, the ministry is now ready to go into its next phase: the preaching of the Gospel outside the land of Galilee, as 9:52 shows. The significance of the first phase is the gathering of the witnesses in Galilee, as is shown by the special attention and miraculous circumstances surrounding their call into his service (Lk. 5:1–11). The importance of these eyewitnesses has been anticipated in Luke's preface (1:2); it is confirmed by the special Lukan word to his followers on the eve of the Crucifixion, in which he addresses them as "you who have continued with me in my trials" (22:28), as well as by the choice of a replacement for the traitorous Judas from among those "who have accompanied us during all the time that the Lord Jesus went in and out among us, beginning from the baptism of John until the day that he was taken up from us. . . ." (Acts 1:21, 22).

According to Luke 4, the rejection of Jesus by his fellow countrymen is expected from the outset. He must, therefore, turn to others in seeking a response of faith wherever it may be found. It is appropriate that Luke closes off the first phase of Jesus' ministry with the story of the strange exorcist, according to which Jesus rebukes the disciples for their exclusivism and encourages them to welcome support from whatever source (9:49–50): "Whoever is not against us is for us."

Although Jesus "must" now leave Galilee, he does not set out aimlessly: the clear goal that he has in view is Jerusalem, where his final rejection is to occur (9:51). Appropriately, this phase of his work is preceded by the sending of seventy evangelists to call men to repent and to announce the nearness of the Kingdom of God (10:1–16, especially v. 11). The number seventy seems to be here (as is often the case in Jewish tradition) symbolic of the seventy nations into which it was believed the human race was divided. Luke is here preparing for the mission to the Gentiles that is to be the theme of volume two of his work.

The event which signals the right time for the new phase is not simply the negative factor of the rejection in Galilee. Indeed, Luke reports widespread response to Jesus from Galilee, Judea, and Gentile regions beyond (e.g., 6:17–19). The factor which brings about the change of locale and hence the change of procedure is the announcement by Jesus of his impending suffering and death (9:18–22). In Luke's version of the Transfiguration which follows the first prediction of the Passion, an incident occurs which he alone reports: the conversation of Jesus with Moses and Elijah ("the law and the prophets") concerning his "departure which he was about to fulfill in Jerusalem" (9:31). This theme is sounded again when Jesus' final departure from Galilee is recounted in 13:31–33. The immediate occasion for Jesus' statement is a report to him by Pharisees that Herod (Antipas, the tetrarch of Galilee) is seeking to destroy him:

> Go and tell that fox, "Behold, I cast out demons and perform cures today and tomorrow, and on the third day I finish my course. Nevertheless I must go on my way today and tomorrow and the day following; for it cannot be that a prophet should perish away from Jerusalem."

The first "journey" of Jesus and the Seventy begins after the fact of his suffering has been disclosed, but before its significance is understood.[5] The final journey begins (13:33) when the suffering is about to be undergone. Luke moves up to this point his version of Jesus' lament over Jerusalem, in contrast to Mark (followed by Matthew), who assigns it to the last days of Jesus in Jerusalem. For Luke it serves as a symbolic indication that Jesus' rejection in Jerusalem and the subsequent judgment of God on the city are necessary elements in the outworking of the divine redemptive plan. The destruction of Jerusalem is mentioned unambiguously by Luke (21:20), whereas in Mark (13:14) and even in Matthew (24:15) the desecration of the Temple and the fall of the city are alluded to or described only in veiled language. It is also in Jerusalem that the triumphant Christ is to be revealed as judge at the Consummation of the Age (Acts 1:8). Jerusalem, then, is central to the whole redemptive purpose of God in Luke's understanding, and it is to Jerusalem that Jesus *must* go.

The third phase of the activity of Jesus takes place in Jerusalem, beginning with the approach to the city by way of Jericho and reaching its climax in his rejection and crucifixion there. The nucleus of the new eschatological community is present at the Last Supper, according to a tradition found only in Luke (22:15–30).[6] The post-Resurrection appearances of Jesus occur in Jerusalem or in that vicinity, in Luke's account. On the other hand, Matthew reports them as taking place in Galilee; and Mark, who does not describe any appearances, nevertheless expects them to occur in Galilee. According to Luke, it is from Jerusalem that the world mission of the Church is to begin (Lk. 24:47), and it is there that the community will receive the gift of the Holy Spirit to empower it to fulfill its divinely appointed task (Acts 1:8).

THE THIRD EPOCH: FROM THE ASCENSION TO THE RETURN OF CHRIST.   The ascension of Jesus Christ—reported only in Luke—marks the transition to the third major epoch in Luke's scheme of the Ages: the Age of the Church's mission to the world. During this period, Christ is seated at God's right hand (Acts 2:33; 3:20, 21). Having poured out the Spirit upon the Church, his next great work will be that of Judge of all men at the End of the Age (Acts 10:42; 17:31). God's work is, in the present epoch, being achieved by the power of the Spirit at work through the Church. It began with those who were eyewitnesses of Jesus' own activity (Acts 1:21–22) and is continued by those who succeeded them in the community of faith. It does not matter, therefore, how long the Last Day may be delayed: the ground of the redemptive activity has

---

[5]Cf. Conzelmann, *op. cit.*, p. 65.

[6]The account of the Supper is found, of course, in the other gospels, but the emphasis on the eschatological nature of the meal (22:16) and the words addressed to the disciples as the beginnings of a new community (22:28ff.) are distinctively Lukan. If one assumes that the so-called Western text of the Greek New Testament is the original, and omits 22:19b–20, the eschatological nature of the Supper is all the more striking.

THE JERICHO ROAD,
little used now, led in Roman times past the fortress-palace of Herod before entering the Judean hills to begin its climb of more than 3,000 feet up to Jerusalem. Ruins of Herod's palace lie beneath the mound in the lower left of the picture.
(Howard C. Kee)

been laid in the work of Jesus Christ in fulfillment of the Law and the Prophets. The power of God is at work in the Church as it was in the ministry of Jesus. All is leading to the promised day, whose coming is now made certain by God's provision of the Messiah, by his triumph over death, by the power of the Spirit, and by the activity of the Church in fulfilling its mission.

ALL THINGS WRITTEN IN THE LAW
ARE NOW FULFILLED

Luke's conviction that the Law and the Prophets are fulfilled in Jesus Christ is far more pervasively present in both volumes of his work than the direct references to the fulfillment of scripture might indicate. We have already noted the explicit claim attributed to Jesus in his sermon at Nazareth that on that day the scripture was fulfilled in the hearing of those present (Lk. 4:16–30). Luke's gospel concludes on the same note; the doubting disciples are told:

> These are my words which I spoke to you while I was yet with you, that everything written about me in the law of Moses and the prophets and the psalms must be fulfilled.
>
> —LUKE 24:44

The sermons of Acts are full of allusions to the Old Testament and of the claim that the promises made to the Fathers (*i.e.*, the Fathers in Israel) have been fulfilled now in Jesus Christ (Acts 2:16, 30; 3:18; 4:11, 4:25; 7:52; 8:35; 10:43; 13:32). But to note the direct claims and specific promises which are believed to have been fulfilled is only part of the picture.

377

THE JUDEAN DESERT
and the villages of Bethphage and Bethany, as seen from the crest of the Mount of Olives, where, according to Luke-Acts, Jesus was taken up to heaven. (Matson Photo Service)

John the Baptist and the Old Testament

The stage is set for the development of this theme in the opening verses of Luke, following the formal preface (1:1–4). The birth of John the Baptist is described in its priestly environment and in an atmosphere of pious obedience to the Jewish Law. The miraculous circumstances surrounding John's conception and birth are reminiscent of the birth of Samuel (I Sam. 1, 2). He comes in the spirit of Elijah and his ministry will have its effect upon "the sons of Israel" (1:16, 17). The hymns of praise and gratitude uttered by the angels, by Mary, by Zechariah, and by the aged Simeon in the Temple (2:29–32) are written with the cadences, the vocabulary, the imagery of Old Testament poetry. So strong is the Semitic flavoring of the language in these passages, that some scholars think that the hymns have been translated from Hebrew or Aramaic originals. The same could be said, indeed, of the narrative context in which Luke has placed them. It is possible that there were Semitic originals, but it is perhaps even more likely that Luke, with his great literary skill, has written the narrative in the style of the Semitic-flavored Septuagint with which he was familiar and from which he regularly quotes. It would have sounded to him like Biblical language in much the same way that the language of the King James Version sounds "like the Bible" to us today.

The hymns may have originated in pre-Christian times and may have been adapted by Luke for his own purposes. It has been conjectured that they originally belonged to a sect that honored the Baptist as the eschatological prophet. Traces of such a sect may be discerned beneath the surface of John 3 and 4, as well as in Acts 18:24ff. A sect that honors John the Baptist as redeemer survives to the present day in Iraq.[7] Some ancient Biblical manuscripts of Luke attribute the so-called Magnificat (1:46ff.) to Elizabeth rather than to Mary, in which case the savior would be John and not Jesus. In any case, the continuity between the Covenant People of Israel and the new thing God is doing is vigorously set forth in the opening chapters of Luke. The venerable worshipers, Simeon and Anna, both of whom are looking "for the consolation of Israel" (2:25, 38), with true prophetic insight recognize in the infant Jesus the realization of their hopes.

Jesus' Ancestry as a Link to the Old Testament

The directness of the continuity between Jesus and Israel's hopes is affirmed in the genealogy of Jesus, which differs significantly from Matthew's (cf. Lk. 3:23–38 with Mt. 1:1–17). Matthew traces Jesus' ancestry back to Abraham; Luke traces it back to Adam. When linked with the expansion of John's quotation from Isaiah 40 to include the words "all flesh shall see the salvation of our God" (Lk. 3:6), it is obvious that Luke wants his readers to know that Jesus Christ is the *world's* redeemer, not merely the deliverer of Israel. Although we can recognize the artificiality of the genealogy, and although it is impossible to harmonize it with Matthew's, Luke's "historical" purpose still stands clear: God's guiding hand is to be seen throughout the whole range of history, culminating in the history of Jesus and the redemption of the world that is made possible through him.

Israel's Misunderstanding of the Prophecies

Even while affirming the hand of God at work in the history of his People, Luke asserts that the nation Israel has come under judgment because it has failed to comprehend the will of God through the prophets. The speech of Stephen in Acts 7 is the fullest and most vivid evidence of this, with its climactic accusation:

> You stiff-necked people, uncircumcised in heart and ears, you always resist the Holy Spirit. As your fathers did, so do you. Which of the prophets did not your fathers persecute? And they killed those who

---

[7]See the works cited on p. 32, note 9 and p. 339, note 5.

> announced beforehand the coming of the Righteous One, whom you
> have now betrayed and murdered, you who received the law as de-
> livered by angels and did not keep it.
>
> —ACTS 7:51–53

The fault lies not with the Law or the promises contained in it, but with the people who have failed to hear in it God's Word for them. Yet even their rejection of his Word has been turned by God to good purpose. The Crucifixion itself, though accomplished "by the hands of lawless men," was nonetheless "according to the definite plan and foreknowledge of God" (Acts 2:23). Or in the words that Luke attributes to the risen Christ, "Was it not necessary that the Christ should suffer these things and enter into his glory?" And Luke goes on to say:

> And beginning with Moses and all the prophets he [Jesus] interpreted
> to them in all the scriptures the things concerning himself.
>
> —LUKE 24:27

THE SPIRIT POURED OUT ON ALL FLESH

The effective agent in the accomplishment of God's purpose in the epoch of preparation through the prophets, the epoch of Jesus' ministry, and the epoch of the Church's mission, is the Holy Spirit. Thus David's prophecy about the Messiah and the demonic opposition he would encounter were uttered "by the Holy Spirit" (Acts 4:25). Israel's resistance to the Word of God proclaimed by the prophets was, according to Stephen's speech, "resisting the Holy Spirit" (Acts 7:51).

The Spirit Commissions Jesus

Similarly, the Spirit is operative in the preparations for the coming of Jesus Christ in the infancy stories of Luke 1 and 2: John the Baptist will be filled with the Holy Spirit; the Spirit will come upon Mary so that she may conceive and bear a son; Elizabeth is filled with the Spirit when she greets Mary; Zechariah prophesies by the Holy Spirit, as does Simeon. Luke alone depicts the coming of the Spirit upon Jesus at baptism as being "in *bodily* form, as a dove" (Lk. 3:22). The anointing by the Spirit characterizes Jesus' ministry from the outset, both in the initial return from the Jordan to the desert (4:1) and from the desert to Galilee (4:14), and in the sermon based on Isaiah 61, which Jesus claims to be now fulfilled in him.

The Spirit Empowers the Church

The coming of the Spirit on the Day of Pentecost (Acts 2) is for Luke the sign that the promise made through Joel is being fulfilled: God's Spirit will be poured out on all flesh (*i.e.*, on all humanity) and whoever (*i.e.*, whether

Jew or Gentile) will call on the Lord's name will be saved. The day of universal salvation, or universal opportunity for salvation, is here. The miracle of simultaneous translation described by Luke (Acts 2:5–11) is told in a manner which parallels the Jewish tradition about the marvelous manifestations of divine power that accompanied the giving of the Law at Sinai. According to this Jewish legend, there were seventy tongues of fire on the mountain, representing the seventy languages of the seventy nations of the earth. The Law, however, remained largely the private possession of Israel, its light rarely reaching to the Gentiles. Now at the End of the Age, Luke is telling his reader, the goal is achieved: all men come under the power of the Spirit of God. And furthermore, the divine judgment at the Tower of Babel is reversed: mankind, who was then divided by language barriers into many hostile peoples, is now brought into one by the power of the Spirit in order to prepare all men to hear the one Gospel that can redeem the race.[8]

The Spirit is the effective power in enabling the ministry of the community to perform its work. The disciples, forbidden by the religious officials in Jerusalem to speak the message of God, are given courage through the Holy Spirit to defy the authorities and to speak the Word (Acts 5:9). The criteria for selection of the "deacons" to assist in the ministry of the community include that they must be "full of the Spirit" (6:3). Stephen is given strength to go to a martyr's death faithful in his witness by the power of the Holy Spirit (7:55). The validity of the evangelistic work done among Samaritans (8:19) and Gentiles (10:44) is confirmed by the fact that those who hear the Gospel in faith receive the Holy Spirit. It is the gift of bestowal of the Spirit that the mercenary Simon Magus tries to purchase (8:18). The seal of Saul's conversion is the reception of the Spirit (9:17). The Spirit leads the community and its ministry in selecting persons for special tasks (13:2), in shaping the itinerary of the traveling evangelists (13:4; 16:7; 19:21), and in the supervisory roles within the community itself (20:28). Angels at times lend assistance, according to Luke (e.g., Acts 8:26; 10:3; 12:7; 27:23), but it is the Spirit who is the chief agent of the achievement of God's purpose in this age.

THE MISSION OF THE CHURCH
TO THE WHOLE WORLD

The first clear indication that Luke gives us of his concern for the universal benefits that are to come through Christ appears in the words of the aged holy man, Simeon, whose utterance now forms an important part in the liturgy of the Church:

> Lord, now lettest thy servant depart in peace,
>   according to thy word;

---

[8]See the discussion of this difficult passage in E. Haenchen, *Acts of the Apostles* (Philadelphia: Westminster, 1971), pp. 166–175.

> for mine eyes have seen thy salvation
>> which thou hast prepared in the presence of all peoples,
> *a light for revelation to the Gentiles,*
>> and for glory to thy people Israel.
>
> —LUKE 2:29, 30

The Light for the Gentiles

There is ample precedent in the Old Testament for the thesis that Israel's mission is to be a light to the Gentiles (Is. 42:6; 49:6), but Simeon as he beholds the infant Jesus affirms that it is through this child that the promise is to be fulfilled. We have already noted that Luke quotes a more extended passage from Isaiah 40 in connection with the ministry of John the Baptist, with the result that the savior for whose Coming John prepares the way is the savior of "all flesh" (Lk. 3:4-6). Even before Jesus launches his public ministry, Luke is letting his reader know that in the purpose of God the benefits which Jesus brings are to be extended to all humanity, and are not to be the exclusive privilege of the Jewish nation. In this way Judaism is not excluded from the grace of God, but the scope in which the grace of God is at work is extended beyond any ethnic bounds. In the words of the angels' song:

> Glory to God in the highest, and on earth peace among men with whom he is pleased.
>
> —LUKE 2:14

Peace is for all who respond in faith, rather than the prerogative of a chosen few.

The occupations of the two groups of persons who are reported by Luke to have repented at John's preaching are such as to exclude them automatically from religious acceptability judged by Jewish standards. A tax-collector was considered a traitor to Judaism because of his collaboration with the hated Roman overlords and the dishonest dealings which seem to have been characteristic of his trade. Soldiers, who were always subject to duty on the Sabbath or any other day, could not possibly keep the Jewish laws against work on the Sabbath. Jews were excused from military service by Roman law; if a Jew chose a military career, he virtually forfeited his claim to participation in the life of the Covenant People. Luke tells us, however, that it was persons of this sort— that is, religious outcasts, when judged by Jewish standards—who heard John's message and repented. Even before Jesus appears, then, Luke is preparing us for the fuller story of the God who in Jesus Christ seeks the outcasts and accepts those who know their need and acknowledge it.

The Good News for the Outsiders

The converse of this concern for the outcasts is the constant attack on the rich. The theme is also sounded in the hymns of the infancy stories:

He has scattered the proud in the imagination of their hearts,
> he has put down the mighty from their thrones,
> and exalted those of low degree;

He has filled the hungry with good things,
> and the rich he has sent empty away.

—LUKE 1:51, 52

The opening theme of the programmatic sermon at Nazareth is the claim that "The Spirit of the Lord . . . has anointed me to preach good news to the poor." The word "poor" resounds throughout the Gospel of Luke. Instead of the religious designation in the Beatitude recorded by Matthew, "Blessed are the poor in Spirit," Luke has simply, "Blessed are you poor" (6:20). Only in Luke's version of the Parable of the Great Supper is it explicitly stated that those who are brought into the feast after the group originally invited has declined are the "poor and maimed and blind and lame" (Lk. 14:21). The invitation is symbolic of the Gospel invitation to share in the joys of the Age to Come. The Jews to whom the invitation was originally extended have refused to come; the offer now goes out to the outcasts. Only in Luke do we hear of the rich Fool whose wealth is his sole ground of security (12:13–21) and of the wretched Lazarus, who enters the realm of the blessed while the rich man lingers in torment (16:19–31).

Although Luke shares with Matthew the tradition about the questioners who come from John the Baptist, in which Jesus points to the works of healing and the proclamation of good news to the poor as evidence of his mission (Mt. 11:5; Lk. 7:22), Luke alone develops the theme widely. At times this motif appears in the form of a modification of material used by the other evangelists. For example, Matthew and Mark report at the end of Jesus' public ministry the story of the woman who anointed him for burial. In Matthew 26:8 and Mark 14:4, the disciples complain about the waste of money, which might better have been given to the poor. Jesus' famous reply is that the poor are always on hand, but that he will not be on hand for long. In Luke's version, however, the story has become an account of the pronouncement of forgiveness to an outcast, a woman who is a "sinner." She comes to him in a spirit of devotion, seeking nothing. He offers her forgiveness and salvation (Lk. 7:36–50, see especially 48, 50). No mention is made of anointing for burial, and the whole point of the incident centers on the forgiveness of sin even to the one who most obviously violates the moral and ceremonial laws of Judaism. Luke underscores this by locating the incident immediately following the report of the contrast between Jesus and John the Baptist, in which Jesus quotes his critics as calling him, "A glutton and a drunkard, a friend of tax-collectors and sinners" (7:34).

The same note is sounded in the story, reported only by Luke, concerning Zacchaeus, the tax-collector (Lk. 19:1–10). Once more, Jesus violates the Jewish laws of ceremonial purity by not merely having contact with a tax-collector, but actually inviting himself to his house for a meal. As in the case of the woman who anointed him, Jesus announces that "salvation has this day come to his house." The story is rounded off by a saying in which Jesus epitomizes his redemptive program: "The Son of man has come to seek and to save that which is lost."

God Takes the Initiative toward the Outcasts

In these narratives, Luke is telling us that not only is God willing to *accept* those who are estranged from him and to forgive those who are grievous sinners, but that he is actively *seeking out* those who are far from him, whether Jews who were excluded from the life of the Covenant People or Gentiles who never had a part in the Covenant. Luke underscores this conviction in both narrative and discourse material. Nowhere has he set this forth more powerfully than in the three parables which he presents in sequence: the Lost Sheep, the Lost Coin, and the Lost Son (Lk. 15:1–32). The last two of these are found only in Luke, and the first appears in an expanded version (cf. Mt. 18:12–14). In each case, the title of the parable might well be changed to lay the stress on the joy of the one who has recovered what has been lost, thereby making the point of the parable the nature of God rather than the condition of the one who is lost. Accordingly, the parables would become the Joyous Shepherd, the Joyous Housewife, and the Joyous Father. The story of the rejoicing father is actually in two parts, with the second focused on the disgruntled older brother who refuses to welcome back his wayward brother. He will not even acknowledge him as his brother, preferring rather to refer to him as "that son of yours." Luke (or Jesus?) is here striking out against the critics of his message of God's grace by comparing them with the self-centered, unforgiving, graceless brother, just as Jesus rebukes those who condemn him for his forgiving attitude toward the sinful woman. Luke views Jesus as the foe of prideful moralism and as the spokesman for God, whose grace flows out to all who will acknowledge their need and receive that grace by faith.

The Outcasts Are Ready To Respond

The readiness of the Gentiles to accept the grace of God is indicated by the two illustrations that bring to a close Jesus' sermon in the synagogue at Nazareth. The only person who was miraculously fed during the famine in the time of Elijah was a Sidonian woman—that is, a Gentile. Similarly, only the Gentile leper, Naaman, was healed in the time of Elisha. The implication is that others do not benefit from the divine redemption available to them because they are not ready to receive it. If God's grace can evoke no response of faith in Israel, it will turn to the Gentiles.

As we noted earlier in this chapter, Luke anticipates the Gentile mission when he depicts Jesus as sending out the Seventy. This mission of the Seventy is in addition to the sending of the Twelve that Luke has taken over from his

Markan source (9:1; cf. Mk. 6:7ff.), and which Matthew has greatly expanded in his account of the mission of the disciples (Mt. 9:35–10:16). Perhaps Luke intends the sending of the Twelve to symbolize the initial mission of the Gospel to Israel, and the sending of the Seventy to represent the subsequent turning of the messengers of the Gospel to the nations of the world. The shift of attention from the mission to Israel to the world mission is specifically pronounced in Acts. In Antioch of Pisidia, where Paul and Barnabas have been evangelizing, the success of their efforts has aroused violent hostility from the Jewish community. The apostles' reaction to their attack is a turning point in Luke's description of the apostolic mission.

> And Paul and Barnabas spoke boldly and said: "It was necessary that the word of God should be spoken first to you. Since you thrust it from you, and judge yourselves unworthy of eternal life, behold, we turn to the Gentiles. For so the Lord has commended us saying, 'I have set you to be a light to the Gentiles, that you may bring salvation to the uttermost parts of the earth.'"
>
> —ACTS 13:46, 47

The belief that the Gospel was to be heard first by the Jews and then by Gentiles is not peculiar to Luke (cf. Rom. 1:16), but it is declared by him with unique clarity and persistence.

Going into All the World

Just as Luke's gospel begins with a sermonic program outlining the ministry of Jesus, so the Book of Acts begins with a program laid down by the risen Christ to be effected by the power of the Holy Spirit through the Church. The disciples—now to be styled *apostles*, or *sent ones*—are to bear witness to the Gospel of Jesus Christ; first in Jerusalem, then in all Judea, then in Samaria, and then to the end of the earth (Acts 1:8). It is appropriate that the witness begins in Jerusalem, since, as we have seen, Jerusalem is for Luke the place of revelation *par excellence*. The proclamation of the Gospel in Judea brings the message to the Jews, in keeping with the divinely ordained order ("the Jew first"). The shift to Samaria brings the opportunity to hear the good news of Jesus Christ to those who are alienated from Israel but who share a common heritage. [The Samaritans were a Semitic people who shared with Judaism the belief that the Law of Moses was the Word of God, although their version of it differed slightly from the accepted Jewish version. But their chief point of disagreement was on the place of worship (Mount Gerizim rather than Jerusalem), where they had their own priesthood distinct from the Jerusalem priesthood. Samaria was a kind of enclave within predominantly Jewish territory.] Once the preaching of the Gospel moved beyond the borders of Palestine, it would know no bounds until it reached the ends of the earth.

Luke does not merely set out the program, however: he describes the progress of the Gospel as it moves on toward what is at least a symbolic achievement of its goal. The first seven chapters of Acts depict the efforts of the apostles to proclaim the good news in Jerusalem. Their work met with considerable success (". . . and there were added that day [of Pentecost] about three thousand souls."—2:41), as well as with violent opposition. As a result, the disciples were imprisoned, interrogated, warned (4:17–22), beaten, and forbidden to speak in the name of Jesus Christ (5:40). The threats and punishments were ineffective, however, and the work of evangelism in Jerusalem is described by Luke as continuing until, following the belligerent speech of Stephen, the Jewish leadership had little choice but to launch a counterattack. In that speech Stephen denounced the nation as having never been ready to hear God's messengers when they came (7:51–53), including Jesus, whom they have murdered. In response, the authorities turn on the infant community; as a result of the great persecution which follows, the friends and coworkers of Stephen flee (8:1b).

That this scattering is symbolic of the spread of the Gospel rather than an historical occurrence in which the Jerusalem community was wholly dispersed is evident from Luke's own account, since he reports continuing activities of the apostles in Jerusalem down to the time of the arrest of Paul there (21:17ff.). Jerusalem continues to be the base of operations for the evangelists even in this same chapter of Acts (8:14, 25). The victims of the persecution and the subsequent scattering seem to have been, not the original circle of twelve disciples, but men whom Luke refers to as "Hellenists" (6:1), all of whom bear Greek names. Their assigned role in the Church is that of "deacon," which means "servant" or "assistant" (6:2, 3). Although their original assignment is reported by Luke as caring for "tables" (that is, taking care of the menial and more secular aspects of the community's life), they very soon are engaged in preaching the Word of God. This is most obvious in the case of Stephen (Chapters 6, 7) and Philip (Chapter 8).

It would appear that Luke has reworked some traditional material in such a way as to document several convictions: (1) that the division in the Church between Jewish Christians and Gentile Christians was by agreement and divine intention rather than a result of conflict; (2) that the proclamation of the Gospel to non-Jews carried the full sanction of the Jerusalem community; and (3) that the death of Stephen was the divinely planned occasion for drawing Saul (Paul) under the influence of the Gospel, thus preparing him for the distinctive role he was to play in the spread of the Gospel to the Gentiles. There is a splendid irony in the fact that it is Paul who leads the very persecution that results in launching the Gentile mission of the Church (8:3). Apart from a general description of himself as a persecutor of the Church (Gal. 1:13), we have no word of this from Paul, so that we cannot determine whether or not it may rest on historical fact. But it is used here by Luke in a fitting way to show how the work of God's Spirit proceeds not only in spite of, but by means of, human opposition (8:4).

The Progress of the Gospel

The spread of the Gospel to the end of the earth has been anticipated by Luke in his description of the Day of Pentecost. This is the case, not only in the symbolic significance of the tongues of fire, but in the enumeration of the widely scattered lands from which the dispersion Jews have come (2:9, 10). Luke goes so far as to say that they were present "from every nation under heaven" (2:5). Luke depicts them as including (1) Jews who had moved to these lands and were returning for the feast; (2) Gentiles who, by accepting baptism and circumcision, had become proselytes, members of the Covenant community; and (3) devout Gentiles who had come to participate in the Jewish festival. But here for Luke they represent the whole of humanity. All mankind will soon have opportunity to hear the Gospel, Luke is telling his reader; from the outset these representatives had opportunity to witness the power with which the Gospel goes forth. The miracle of simultaneous translation was itself enough to fill them with awe and to foreshadow the coming of the Gospel to every nation:

> "We hear them telling in our own tongues the mighty works of God."
> And all were amazed and perplexed, saying to one another, "What does this mean?"
>
> —ACTS 2:11, 12

Luke is not content, however, merely to anticipate the world mission of the Church: he depicts each stage of its development. The first is of course the preaching to the crowds in Jerusalem, and especially in the Temple itself, the religious center of Judaism (3:11–26), and before the Sanhedrin, Judaism's chief governing body (5:27–32). Following the first persecution (8:1ff.), the next stage is launched when Philip preaches the Gospel in Samaria with impressive results, Luke reports (8:4–8). Soon thereafter the Gospel moves to a wider circle when Acts recounts the conversion of an Ethiopian eunuch (8:26–40). According to the Mosaic Law, a eunuch could not have participated in the Covenant worship (Deut. 23:2), but the term "eunuch" is often used of a powerful court figure, without any of the usual connotations of the word. The story is filled with miraculous movements and coincidences. That the Ethiopian official was prepared in advance to hear the Gospel is evidenced by his reading from the Jewish scriptures the Suffering Servant text from Isaiah 53, which Philip immediately interprets for him as a prophecy of Jesus Christ (8:33–35). This story must have originated in Hellenistic circles, perhaps connected with Philip the evangelist, whose daughters joined him in his work (21:9), but it has been worked over by Luke to serve the overall objectives of his work. Here it paves the way for the Gentile mission, which begins in full force with the conversion of Cornelius (10:1–48).

The importance of this story for Luke is emphasized by the fact that it is first told (Chapter 10) and then retold (Chapter 11). What is significant is not only that the Gospel was heard and received by a non-Jew, but that God had placed his stamp of approval on this by sending his Spirit on the new believers (10:44). The point is reaffirmed (10:45), and then put in question form by Luke (through Peter) to any potential critic of the practice of evangelizing Gentiles: "Can anyone forbid water for baptizing these people who have received the Holy Spirit just as we have?" (10:47). The apostolic circle in Jerusalem, Luke reports, approved the evangelism and gave its sanction to the results (11:18): "Then to the Gentiles also God has granted repentance unto life."

Opening the Door of Faith to the Gentiles

For a century and a half, critical study of the New Testament has debated the question as to why Acts depicts Peter as the one through whom the Gentile mission is launched, while the Letters of Paul give one the impression that he was the pioneer in this field. An ingenious solution which still exerts wide influence originated with the so-called Tübingen School of interpretation, which was under the domination of Hegel's philosophy of history. According to Hegel's theory, all history moves by the emergence of an idea (*thesis*) which evokes its opposite (*antithesis*); the conflict between the two continues until there emerges a third possibility (*synthesis*). By this view of history, Peter's Jewish-legal understanding of Christianity is the thesis, and Paul's Law-free Gospel is the antithesis: from it emerges the universal synthesis of catholic Christianity, of which Acts is a chief document.[9]

It is possible that at the basis of Luke's story is an historical tradition of an encounter of Peter with a Roman officer who became a Christian. It is difficult, however, to square the story as it is told, including all the divine sanctions for the conversion, with Peter's refusal to have table fellowship with Gentiles as reported in Galatians 2. Luke, however, lays heavy stress on the reluctance of Peter to go along with the Gentile mission and on the necessity of repeated divine intervention in order to convince Peter to visit Cornelius; thereby Luke demonstrates to his reader that the decision to open the common life of the Church to all without forcing submission to the Jewish Law was not Peter's idea, nor Paul's, but God's.[10]

In the chapter following Peter's report to the apostolic circle, Luke describes another period of persecution—this time by the civil authority, Herod Agrippa I —and after a brief term of imprisonment, from which he is miraculously de-

---

[9]For a summary of the view of the Tübingen School, see A. Schweitzer on F. C. Baur, in *Paul and His Interpreters* (London: A. and C. Black, 1912), pp. 12–21. For a critique of the view, see J. Munck, *Paul and the Salvation of Mankind* (Richmond, Va.: John Knox Press, 1960), pp. 69–86.

[10]So Martin Dibelius, in *Studies in the Acts of the Apostles* (London: SCM Press, 1956), p. 122.

livered, Peter disappears from Jerusalem and from the narrative of Acts. A possible exception is the inclusion of "Symeon" (Peter?) in the Apostolic Council detailed in Acts 15. But Peter's main mission is fulfilled for Luke when he has broken down barriers and become the first agent of Gentile evangelism.

Meanwhile, the apostolic circle had commissioned a man named Barnabas to exercise authority in Antioch, which was becoming a center for a newly founded Christian community (11:19–26). As his coworker, he chose Saul of Tarsus, whose conversion had proved something of an embarrassment to the Jerusalem church (9:1–30). After effective evangelism in Antioch, Paul and Barnabas went on an evangelistic tour of Cyprus and southern and central Asia Minor (Chapters 13 and 14). Their procedure in each town was to preach first among the Jews, and then, when opposition was encountered, to turn to the Gentiles (14:27).

But not everyone at Antioch was pleased with the results of Paul's work, Luke tells us. Certain persons from Jerusalem (whether official inspectors or self-appointed busybodies is not stated) came to Antioch insisting that obedience to the precepts of Mosaic Law was necessary for participation in the life

TEMPLE AREA FROM THE MOUNT OF OLIVES
The Mount of Olives stands out in the background above the eastern hill of Jerusalem. The domed structure is the Dome of the Rock—a Muslim shrine erected in the seventh century A.D.—which stands on the site of the altar of sacrifice of the Jewish Temple. (Arab Information Center)

of the Christian community. Superficially, at least, this sounds like the situation of which Paul writes in Galatians 1 and 2. According to Acts 15 and Galatians, it was decided to have Paul and Barnabas go to Jerusalem to work out a settlement of a disagreement over the proper basis for admitting Gentiles to the Church. Closer examination, however, shows that the consultation in Acts 15 and the one described by Paul in Galatians can scarcely be the same. In Acts, the meeting in Jerusalem is a kind of public hearing, at which the entire community (15:12) is present and listens to the verdicts handed down by the leaders of the apostolic circle. Paul makes a point in Galatians 2:2 that the conversation was a private one, with "those who were of repute." Titus is present in Paul's account; he is not mentioned in Acts. Even more striking is the difference between the agreement reached according to Acts and the one referred to by Paul in Galatians 2:10. According to Paul, it was agreed that he and his associates would carry on the evangelism of the Gentiles, while the Jerusalem group would restrict itself to work among Jews. The only further requirement was that Paul, and presumably the churches established by him, were to "remember the poor." This seems to be a reference to the practice attested to in the two preserved Letters to the Corinthians by which the Gentile churches collected and submitted an offering to the Jerusalem church.

THE "APOSTOLIC DECREES."   In Acts, however, Paul agrees to communicate to the Gentile churches the so-called "apostolic decrees." These were four: (1) abstinence from idolatry; (2) abstinence from blood—that is, from food containing blood and therefore unclean by Jewish dietary rules; (3) abstinence from eating animals that had been killed by strangling, again in accord with Jewish food laws; (4) abstinence from unchastity. In one group of New Testament manuscripts known as the Western text the words "and from things strangled" are omitted while others add a form of the Golden Rule. This allows for an interpretation of the three remaining requirements as strictly moral rather than cultic or dietary. "Blood" would be interpreted as a decree against committing murder. This would ease the problem somewhat by saving us from having to assume that Paul agreed to certain legalistic food laws as being prerequisite to acceptance into the family of faith. But even with the three rules, we are left with the sense that Paul must have compromised his teaching of justification by faith if he agreed to these laws for admission to Church membership. Although he would not have condoned such practices as were here forbidden in the churches under his care, it would have clouded the issue of faith to have held these particular rules up as prerequisite to accepting the Gospel of grace. Some scholars have conjectured that Paul agreed to these rules, but never sought to enforce them among the Gentile Christians; others have proposed that he made the simpler agreement reported in Galatians first and then accepted the more stringent rules later.

THE "NOAHIC" LAWS.   It would appear that Acts 15 and Galatians are simply incompatible, so that Paul could not have accepted two such contradictory sets of regulations. Perhaps the clue to this difficulty is to be found in the correspondence between the fourfold requirement of Acts (in the non-Western text) and the way in which Jerusalem understood the force of the decrees connected with the Covenant of Noah in Genesis 9:1ff. These Noahic laws were considered by first-century Judaism to be binding on all humanity, rather than as especially enjoined on Israel alone. The regulations of Acts 15 would be one version of the minimal requirements for Gentiles if they were to remain in God's good favor. Some scholars think they find a further trace of these "decrees" in Revelation 2:20–23. But it appears that Luke has included them here because he thought they were appropriate, not because he found them in a document reporting the decision reached at any Apostolic Council. The actual decision between Paul and the Jerusalem church was the one reported by Paul in Galatians 2; the decisions described in Acts 15 were written at a time when the tensions between Jewish and Gentile Christians had subsided—and, one might conjecture, after the full force of Paul's doctrine of justification by faith had been eclipsed by an end-of-the-first-century surge of moralistic Christianity, such as we see in James and other late New Testament books. For Luke, this council marks an important turning point in his story: the leadership of the Jerusalem church has passed from the apostles to the elders. Probably "Symeon" is Peter, but he is no longer the leader of the group; that role has been assumed by James, the brother of Jesus. Luke is showing that there was a common agreement and a unified set of ground rules by which the Church everywhere would from that time on operate. But already the center of attention for Luke has shifted from the historical and eschatological center in Jerusalem to the spread of the Gospel among the Gentile cities, culminating in Rome.[11]

THE CENTER OF ACTS.   The story of the conversion of Cornelius marks the center of the book, both in the aim of the author and in amount of material.[12] From that point on, Luke is interested in showing how the Gospel evoked faith among the Gentiles, first in the cities of Asia Minor, then on the mainland of Europe (Acts 16). Each step along the way is taken by divine hindrance (16:7) or divine call (16:9). None of the many civil authorities before whom Paul and his associates are brought can find anything worthy of punishment. The movement, Luke is telling his readers, is the work of God and is not in conflict with the laws of man. Whether it be in a jail (16:24ff.),

---

[11]A full statement on the details of Acts 15, on the history of its interpretation and critical judgments concerning the historical elements in Luke's account, are to be found in E. Haenchen's *The Acts of the Apostles* (Philadelphia: Westminster, 1971), pp. 440–472.
    [12]*Ibid.*, pp. 305–308.

before the venerable Athenian court of manners and morals known as the Areopagus,[13] or at a public hearing before a Roman proconsul (18:12ff.), Paul has an appropriate word from God. There are none, of whatever origin or station in life, who are to be denied an opportunity to hear the Gospel. And from every stratum there is a faithful response, whether from a jailer (16:34) or an Areopagite (17:34). Paul's preaching is varied in approach, ranging from capitalizing on the jailer's terror to quoting Greek poets before the members of the Areopagus. Paul's faithfulness in his mission provides him with opportunities to preach the Word before the rulers of the Greek cities, the territories of Palestine, the Jewish authorities, and finally in the city of Rome itself. In capsule form, the whole sweep of the world mission of the Church is discernible in the work of Paul and his aides. Its symbolic consummation is represented in his stay in Rome, where he is able to proclaim the Gospel of the Kingdom, preaching about Jesus Christ without restraint (Acts 28:31). It is on this joyous note that the twofold work of Luke-Acts ends, even though Luke has given us full notice of the impending death of Paul (Acts 20:17–38).

---

[13]Meaning "Hill of Mars." Originally the court met on this hill, overlooking the agora or market place. Later it met in its own building, though we cannot tell where Luke understood it to have met on the occasion he describes.

THE EPHESUS THEATER
was, according to Acts 19, the scene of a public assembly to protest the effects that Paul and his co-workers were having on the city, and especially on the economy connected with its temple of Artemis. (Darryl Jones)

Before turning to consider the value of Acts for our knowledge of Paul, let us examine more fully the content of the early Christian preaching as we see it reproduced in Acts. Does it give us direct access to the way that the very first apostles preached?

EARLY CHRISTIAN PREACHING
ACCORDING TO ACTS

Even a casual reading of the brief sermon summaries that Luke has included in the Book of Acts will show the reader how different they are in theological perspective from Paul or even Mark. Although both Paul and Mark have their own distinctive features, they join in stressing the importance of the death of Jesus. For Paul, the death on the Cross is the central theme of his message, even though it is always closely linked with the Resurrection. The kerygmatic summary in I Corinthians 15:3–6, or the hymn of Philippians 2, will show this clearly enough. But both the theological emphases and the terminology of the sermons in Acts are decidedly non-Pauline—even in the case of the sermons attributed to Paul (Acts 13:16–41; 14:15–18; 17:22–31). Furthermore, there is no real difference between the sermons of Peter and the sermons of Paul in Acts, in spite of Paul's acknowledgment in Galatians 1 and 2 of the great tensions and disagreements between them. Two questions confront us: What is the unity which links these sermons? And to what source should this unity be traced?

The following themes appear in the sermon summaries of Acts:

(1) Jesus is from the posterity of David.
(2) Jesus' ministry was approved by God, as may be inferred from the mighty acts which Jesus performed through the Holy Spirit.
(3) The Jews put Jesus to death, and, without realizing it, thus fulfilled the scriptures which point to his suffering.
(4) Gentiles ought to recognize God's concern for them in that his divine provisions for their needs are everywhere apparent.
(5) God has placed his stamp of approval on Jesus by raising him from the dead on the third day after his burial. Now God has exalted him and through him has sent the Holy Spirit.
(6) All men are called to repent and to receive salvation through the name of Jesus, who is destined to be the Judge of mankind.

The Acts Sermons and the Pauline Kerygma

While not all these themes appear in all the sermons, and other themes are to be found that have not been listed here, these are the recurrent motifs that Luke has reported in his accounts of the early Christian preaching. A most significant omission from this list is the interpretation of the death of Christ as somehow related to the forgiveness of sins. Nowhere does Peter or Paul say in Acts: Christ died *for our sins.* Yet this is paramount in Pauline theology. Attempts have been made by New Testament scholars to find a substratum of common affirmation behind the Acts sermons on the one hand and Paul on the other.[14] Except for the importance of the Resurrection as God's demonstration of his approval of the humiliated and crucified Jesus, there is no real identity. And even the Resurrection receives a different interpretation in Paul from the one given it in these sermons. For Paul it is the ground of man's justification as well as the basis of his hope of participation in the Age to Come (Rom. 4:25; I Cor. 15:20–22), whereas in Acts the Resurrection is the exaltation of the rejected Christ, by which he remains at God's right hand until the time has come for his work as Judge of all humanity.

The appearance in these sermons of certain unusual terms, such as the reference to Jesus in Acts 4:30 as "thy Holy Child," has led some interpreters to assume that we have archaic theological language, antedating the more sophisticated terminology, for example, of Paul. Luke's use of rather awkward turns of expression in his otherwise smooth Greek narrative, especially in these early chapters of Acts, led others to the conclusion that Luke was utilizing an Aramaic source, which he had rendered into Greek.[15] But as we have already remarked, the language of Luke-Acts is influenced by that of the Septuagint, which was of course the Bible of the Greek-speaking early Church for which Luke was writing and in which he was likely reared. As for the archaic theological terms, H. J. Cadbury has warned us:

> There is danger of arguing in a circle, since our ideas of early Christianity, with which the speeches in Acts are said to conform so exactly, are derived in large part from those very speeches.[16]

The sermons in Acts, it would appear, are not to be considered as evidence for the earliest Christian preaching, though one cannot exclude the possibility that there are some reflections of older kerygmatic tradition included in them. Rather, they are to be regarded as having been composed in the same manner used by historians roughly contemporary with Luke, who attributed speeches

---

[14]The classic statement of the position that finds in Paul and the Acts sermons evidence for a pre-Pauline common *kerygma* is given by C. H. Dodd, in *The Apostolic Preaching and its Development in the New Testament* (New York: Harper & Row, 1951). A vigorous critique of this theory is given by C. F. Evans, in "The Kerygma," *Journal of Theological Studies,* N.S., VII (1956), 25–41.

[15]This theory was propounded by C. C. Torrey in *The Composition and Date of Acts* (Cambridge: Harvard University Press, 1916). A more cautious assessment of the evidence is to be found in M. Black, *An Aramaic Approach to the Gospels and Acts* (Oxford: Clarendon Press, 1954).

[16]H. J. Cadbury, *The Beginnings of Christianity,* V, ed. F. J. Foakes-Jackson and K. Lake (London: Macmillan, 1933), 416.

to various figures in their historical narrative. Whether the historian wrote about his own contemporaries or whether he wrote of a distant past to which he no longer had direct access, much less reliable documents, he saw his task as composing the speeches in such a way as to serve the overall purpose of his book. There was an obligation to write the speeches so as to convey what the author deemed appropriate to the occasion he was describing.[17] What the author considered fitting was determined not by "what really happened," as a naive modern student of history might put it, but by what he thought the events meant. The fact that the speeches attributed to Paul do not correspond with the vocabulary and theological perspectives that we find in Paul's own Letters would not in itself mean that Luke was not the companion of Paul and did not have access to Pauline material. It would signify only that Luke's purpose in setting forth his grand design of the divine plan of salvation, working out in history under the guidance of the Spirit, was better served by what Luke wrote for Paul than it would have been by direct quotations from Paul himself. The content and the unity of the speeches is to be derived from Luke's consistent point of view set forth in both volumes of his work, and not from his faithful reproduction of a peculiar way of proclaiming the *kerygma* that was shared by all the apostles. Even if there were such uniformity among the apostles, we should not be warranted in inferring it from the reports of the sermons in Acts. Luke's skillful literary method would have smoothed over the differences in serving his wider objective. The Acts sermons show us, therefore, not necessarily what the apostles preached, but what Luke thought they ought to have preached. The question remains, however: If Luke was so free in creating speeches for Paul and the other apostles, how much credence can we place in his account of Paul's travels and ministry?

ACTS AS A SOURCE FOR THE LIFE OF PAUL

We have already seen that both in regard to his speeches and to the Apostolic Council in Jerusalem, Luke has created material that serves his purpose rather than limiting himself to repeating whatever authentic information was available to him. Does this mean that Acts is worthless as an historical source? It does mean that for many of the historical questions to which we should like answers, Acts provides no information. But, in keeping with the conventions of the time, Luke does provide us in both Luke and Acts with references to contemporary incidents or persons by which we can ascertain the relative time of the events he is describing. This is most notably the case in the famous

---

[17]See the discussion of the style of speech writing among Hellenistic and Roman historians in H. J. Cadbury, *The Making of Luke-Acts* (London: S.P.C.K., 1961), pp. 184ff. Also see the chapter on "The Speeches in Acts and Ancient Historiography" in M. Dibelius, *Studies in the Acts of the Apostles* (London: SCM Press, 1956), pp. 138–185.

synchronism of 3:1, 2, where Luke ties in the beginning of the ministry of John the Baptist with the reigns of various rulers in the eastern end of the empire. There are some historical difficulties involved in it,[18] but it does provide us a useful basis for establishing a relative chronology of the life of Jesus. That is, according to this chronology, Jesus would have begun his ministry in the year A.D. 26–27 or 27–28. Similarly, the references to pagan rulers in Acts have given us a fixed point: the accession to the governorship of Gallio, the Roman pro-consul of Corinth in A.D. 52.

Paul's Itinerary and the Sources of Acts

It would appear further that Luke had access to a travel itinerary of Paul which he used as the basis for the Pauline section of Acts. It has been proposed that those sections of Acts in which Luke shifts from the customary third-person plural to the first-person plural of the narrative indicate the author's use of a travel diary. The account begins, "They went down to Troas" (Acts 16:8); but while referring to the same group, the writer without warning changes person to include himself: "We sought to go on to Macedonia" in 16:10. Some have thought that Luke joined Paul at this point, especially since the "we" passages are resumed when Paul returns to Troas on a later journey (20:5). There is no difference in literary style or in vocabulary between the "we" sec-tion and the rest of Acts, so that we can be sure the author has reworked the whole carefully to suit his purposes. But the feeling that the events are being reported by an eyewitness is surely heightened by the "we" sections; further, there is no compelling reason to deny that a companion of Paul—perhaps Luke[19] —composed the whole, utilizing his own notes.

Although it has been proposed that Acts ends inconclusively because it was written before Paul's trial was over,[20] it is more likely that it ends as it does because the Gospel has by Acts 28 achieved the goal of being freely proclaimed in Rome, the capital of the Gentile world. The author of Acts does not leave us in any uncertainty as to the ultimate fate of Paul, however; the touching story of Paul's farewell to the elders from the church at Ephesus (20:17–38) makes it clear that Paul is to die for his testimony to the faith. The language of the valedictory speech of Paul uses terms and envisages situations in the Church which correspond to the post-Pauline era and which have their closest parallel in such deutero-Pauline writings as the Pastorals. This is especially noticeable in 20:28–30. Accordingly, we may infer that Luke has written the history of Paul and the beginnings of the Church at some time after the events

---

[18]See the discussion in H. J. Cadbury, *The Making of Luke-Acts* (London: S.P.C.K., 1961), pp. 204–209. The difficulties are treated more fully by J. M. Creed in *The Gospel According to St. Luke* (London: Macmillan, 1930), pp. 48–50.

[19]So M. Dibelius, *Studies* (London: SCM Press, 1956), p. 104.

[20]According to A. Harnack, *Neue Untersuchungen zur Apostelgeschichte und zur Abfassungszeit der synoptischen Evangelien* (Leipzig: J. G. Hinrichs, 1911), pp. 63–114.

MILETUS
was the ancient port city where, according to Acts 20, Paul bade farewell to the elders from the church at Ephesus on his way to Jerusalem for the last time. (Darryl Jones)

which he is describing. The changed situation in which he finds himself is reflected in the way he depicts the earlier state of affairs, but it also provides perspective on the meaning of what has occurred. If we assume, as it appears we must, that he is writing after the apostolic generation has passed, we can understand why the eschatological note, which is so dominant in Paul's Letters, is muted here in Acts. What Luke has done, then, is not consciously to distort the history of Paul, but to place it in a wider setting of the overarching redemptive purpose of God, which is the main concern of his entire work.

THE ENDURING CONTRIBUTION OF LUKE

We are now in a position to evaluate what Luke has done. It is true that he has given us nearly all the information we have about the historical beginnings of the Church, even though we should like to have more details and to have them placed in a framework more suitable for modern historical inquiry. Specifically he has given us some additional information about Paul which we could not infer from Paul's Letters and which we cannot evaluate historically: *e.g.*, his residence in Tarsus, his education under Gamaliel. But Luke's chief contribution is a theological one: he provided a perspective of meaning for the Church and its mission which enabled the Christian community to survive what might have been a fatal crisis in the nonfulfillment of the expectation of the *parousia*.

Paul has reckoned with a delay in the *parousia* (Phil. 1:23ff.; II Thess. 2:3ff.). Matthew's gospel had provided regulations for the Church's life (Mt. 5–7, 18), but there was no broad framework for comprehending the meaning of the Church in the long-range purpose of God. It was this need that Luke so brilliantly filled, by showing that the redemptive work promised in the holy scriptures and begun by the earthly Jesus was to be carried out under the power of the Holy Spirit through the Church. The *parousia* was still to come, and the judgment that would occur then was a solemn matter for all mankind. But its urgency was not so great, since the groundwork of redemption was already accomplished by the One who was seated at God's right hand. The carrying forth of the Gospel and the manifestation of redemptive power was the task of the Church, but God had already acted through the apostles to see that work to completion in principle, with the progress of the Gospel from Jerusalem to Rome. Even now his Spirit was at work in the Church to bring it to consummation throughout the world.

There are a number of questions which Acts hints at, but does not really formulate, much less answer. We feel as we read this book that there must have been a tension between the young Church and the Roman State, and that the author is trying to speak to that problem at least indirectly. He takes care to show that every time Jesus or his later followers were brought before civil authorities, there was no charge that could be made to stick against them. The tensions between Judaism and Christianity, of which we learn from Church historians and which are reflected in the oral traditions from this period later included in the rabbinic writings, are hinted at but not directly depicted. Luke is content to lay stress on the shift of focus of the Gospel from the Jew to the Gentile. One suspects, however, that the issue of the theological and institutional relationships between Judaism and Christianity was still a live one in the time that Acts was being written. Most clearly of all, the Church in Luke's day seems to have been struggling with the problem of changing from a free-moving evangelistic enterprise to a settled institution. Some scholars have seen in Acts a giant step in the direction of catholic or universal Christianity, as over against the local areas of the Church which continued to honor the apostle who had founded work there, and which followed the lead of his interests and emphases. Acts is surely concerned to stress the oneness of the Church and the common Gospel that is and ought everywhere to be proclaimed.

The Church
and the
End of the Age

Revelation

CHAPTER FIFTEEN

From its very beginning, the Christian community had looked forward eagerly to the time when God would complete the work of transforming his Creation. This mood of hopefulness and expectancy had been strong in the Hebrew prophetic tradition, from which Christianity had inherited so much. Jesus had appeared on the scene of his public ministry announcing, "The kingdom of God is at hand." His works were pointed to by him as signs of the nearness of the Kingdom. The apostles, together with the Aramaic-speaking Church of the first generation, prayed "Maranatha" (meaning "Our Lord, come!"). The prevailing atmosphere, therefore, was one of waiting for God to establish his new order.

The New Testament writers were agreed *that* God would established the New Age; as to *when, where,* and *how,* there was not such unanimity. There is some evidence that single individuals—notably Paul—may have changed their views on this subject with the changing situations. Although we cannot be certain of the order of his Letters, it appears that in I Thessalonians (which is usually thought to be among his earliest Letters), he expected the coming of Christ to take place soon, and surely within his own lifetime (I Thess. 4:13–17). By the time he wrote Philippians, however, he thought he might not live to see the return of Christ (Phil. 1:19–25). His expectation of deliverance was not limited to his own future, but included the "eagerly awaited" redemption of the whole creation (Rom. 8:18–25).[1]

The writers of the gospels modified Jesus' own views of the Coming of the Kingdom of God in various ways. Although Jesus's message about the Kingdom was basically apocalyptic, he did not engage in the bizarre speculations and doleful predictions about the events at the End of the Age, such as we read in Daniel or the Book of Enoch. The Synoptic Apocalypse, however, both in its older Markan form (Mk. 13:5–37) and in its greatly extended Matthean form (Mt. 24:4–25:46), has elaborated on the signs of the End and predictions of doom. We have already seen how Matthew has modified the eschatological message of Jesus by differentiating between the kingdom of the Son of Man (the present, mixed form of the Church, with good and evil within) and the Kingdom of the Father (from which all evil will be purged).[2] Luke has eased the sense of urgency about the Coming of Christ by depicting him as already ruling at the right hand of God, while the Church extends the redemptive mission which he had launched.[3]

In the Gospel of John, the weight of attention has been shifted from the future fulfillment to the present availability of the life of the Age to Come. The effect of this shift is to lead Christians to look within the realm of their own experience for the realization of God's redemptive promise rather than to the future or to the Creation as a whole.[4]

In some of the later books of the New Testament, the hope of redemption has been modified in still other ways. In the Pastorals, for instance, it survives in largely formal expressions, such as "that Day" (II Tim. 4:8), by which the writer refers to the Day of Judgment. The author of II Peter tries to resolve the problem of the nonfulfillment of the Lord's Coming by suggesting that God's mode of calculating time is different from man's, so that the time which has elapsed since the promise of his Coming was uttered is not very great (II Pet. 3:8–10).

---

[1]On the possibility that Paul's views of the future changed, see C. H. Dodd, *New Testament Studies* (New York: Scribner's, 1954), pp. 108–118.

[2]For a fuller discussion, see pp. 329–331.

[3]For a development of this view see pp. 376–377.

[4]This theme is treated throughout Chapter Thirteen. The tendency to treat the inner life of the individual as the place where God is fulfilling his "historical" purpose is most evident in the work of R. Bultmann. See his *Theology of the New Testament*, II (New York: Scribner's, 1955) and *History and Eschatology* (Edinburgh: University of Edinburgh Press, 1957).

THE REVELATION OF THE NEW JERUSALEM

There was one circle in which were seen clearly the implications of the growing struggle between the City of Earth (Rome) and the coming City of God. This was the Christian group in Asia Minor that produced the prophet, John, the author of the Book of Revelation. Tradition has identified this prophet with John the Apostle, and has ascribed to him the authorship of the Gospel of John, the Letters of John, and the Book of Revelation. If this tradition were reliable, it would mean that we have an extended body of literature that comes to us from the hand of one of Jesus' most intimate followers and that might be presumed therefore to represent a point of view very close to Jesus' own.

In fact, however, there are serious difficulties connected with the theory that John the Apostle wrote the books with which he has been credited. Since he was a Galilean fisherman, uneducated and perhaps even illiterate (Acts 4:13), it is most unlikely that he could have written—in Greek—a work of the theological subtlety of the Gospel of John. Efforts to demonstrate that the Gospel of John was originally written in Aramaic have not been particularly convincing to most scholars. The skill of the apologetic that the Gospel of John contains suggests that it was written by a man who had had protracted contact with and intimate knowledge of the Greek world. It has been argued that the Gospel and the Letters of John, which both language and theological content show came from the same circles, were written by John when he was very old and had had a lifetime in which to theologize. Even if this proposal were to be considered plausible, there is some evidence in the New Testament[6] that the disciple John was martyred at the same time as his brother James—i.e., A.D. 44. If this evidence is valid, then none of the books bearing the name of John could have been written by John, the son of Zebedee, the disciple of Jesus. It would have been a simple matter for the early traditions of the Church to confuse a notable leader named John from the church in Ephesus, or from some other city of Asia Minor, with the disciple of the same name.

The Book of Revelation, which is the only book in the New Testament that claims to have been written by John, differs radically in style and perspective from the Gospel and Letters of John. In the gospel, the emphasis falls on the spiritual life of the Church as an ongoing fact, free from time-bound considerations. In Revelation, the author is gravely concerned to stress the crisis that is now impending. For him there is no indefinite or unlimited period of time stretching out into the future, but rather a conviction that very soon the conflict of the powers of evil against God and his people will reach its climax. We might

---

[6]For example, Mk 10:39, where "cup" and "baptism" symbolize death, can be understood as referring to the martyrdom of James and John.

conclude from this that Revelation was written by a disciple, since this understanding of God's purpose would be likely to exist among the followers of Jesus. But John the Prophet also looks backward with veneration to the times of "the twelve apostles of the Lamb" (Rev. 21:14)—a phrase more appropriate to one who, with awe and reverence, has heard about the apostolic leaders than to one who was himself a member of the Twelve.

Purpose of the Book of Revelation

The book was written at a time when efforts were being made to cripple the Church. The community was ill prepared to meet the crisis precipitated by the Christians' refusal to participate in emperor worship, for it had become half-hearted in matters of Christian faith and life. "Because you are lukewarm, and neither cold nor hot, I will spew you out of my mouth," John reports Christ as saying to one of the Asian churches (Rev. 3:16). The genius of John the Prophet, as the author of Revelation may fittingly be called, was not primarily foresight, but insight into the real nature of the problems confronting the Christian community. He saw with clarity the issues on which the Christians must make decisions, and the far-reaching consequences of those issues. John's ultimate concern, therefore, was not for a solution to the immediate problem of the empire's demand that Christians worship the emperor. Rather, he viewed the immediate crisis as a crucial stage in the final conflict between God and the evil powers. Steadfastness in this crisis would lead the community on to complete victory, in which God's purpose for His Creation would be achieved. We must examine the Book of Revelation with the aim of understanding how through this conflict the community saw the fulfillment of its hope.

Promises and Predictions

After a brief but impressive introduction (Rev. 1:1–8), John addresses in turn seven of the churches of Asia Minor, pointing up in each case its weaknesses, strengths, and prospects. Some had been lulled to sleep and needed to be aroused; some had flirted with paganism and needed to be warned in the strongest terms of the consequences of such behavior. John himself had been exiled to the tiny, barren isle of Patmos as a result of his courageous testimony to the faith, and the faithful Christians in the churches addressed could expect the same fate or worse.

THE LETTERS TO THE CHURCHES.   The words addressed to the individual churches are not merely general comments; in each case, the remarks are peculiarly appropriate. For example, Pergamum is warned about Satan's throne, an apparent reference to the fact that the emperor was worshiped as divine in Pergamum long before the emperor cult was begun in Rome. Pergamum had been from the beginning the setting for "Satan's throne"—*i.e.*, the seat of imperial worship in the East. To Sardis, John wrote a warning of the coming of the Lord "like a thief," an unmistakable reference to a famous incident in which the seemingly impregnable city of Sardis had been captured by the Persians, who entered the acropolis through a tiny crevice while the fabulous King Croesus sat in complete confidence in his splendid palace. The spiritual blindness of Laodicea is stressed because, ironically, it took pride in its great hospital dedicated to Aesclepius, the god of healing, and in its famed eye salve, which was supposed to cure blindness. It is fitting for John to heap scorn on this city for its pride of riches, since at a time of earthquake when other cities had had to ask for financial assistance from the empire, Laodicea had, in proud self-sufficiency, announced that she had ample resources to meet the emergency.[7] In spite of these words of warning to the churches of Asia Minor, and in spite of the troubles that were soon to fall upon these churches, the Christians were to remain confident in God's love for them, and in the fulfillment of his purpose through these difficulties. The New Age could not come without these birthpangs, and the people of God must meet them informed and confident.

---

[7]Tacitus, *Annals*, 14:27.

PERGAMUM
ruins of a street. The most spectacular of all the Hellenistic cities of Asia Minor, Pergamum was a center of the cult of divine kings and later of the Cult of the Roman Emperor. (Darryl Jones)

THE GREAT ALTAR OF ZEUS
at Pergamum: a reconstruction. With its grand propor-
tions and its magnificent sculpture, this was one of the
wonders of the ancient world. The allusion to Satan's
throne in the letter to the church at Pergamum (Rev.
2:13) may have been a reference to this colossal architec-
tural monument.

THE VISIONS.   The ingenuity of the writer is nowhere more apparent than in the series of apocalyptic visions that occupy the rest of the book (Rev. 4:1–22:19). The recurrence of the number seven is one of the most striking features of this section: there are seven seals (6:1–8:1), seven trumpets (8:2–11:15), seven visions of the kingdom of the dragon (11:16–13:18), seven visions of the coming of the Son of Man (14:1–20), seven bowls (15:1–16:21), seven visions of the fall of Babylon (17:1–19:10), and seven visions of the End (19:11–21:4).[8] Perhaps the greatest difficulty in interpreting this book has resulted from the effort to discover a chronological sequence in this series of visions. This method of interpretation has appeared in two forms: the futuristic, which sees in these visions pictures of the successive situations that will arise in the last days; and the historical, which relates the visions to the ongoing history of the Church, and identifies the symbolic figures of the book with historical personages. The futuristic method ignores the clear historical allusions of the writing. And the historical method must constantly be revised with the passage of time, since as historical crises pass it becomes clear that there was no basis for seeing in them the fulfillment of John's prophecies. There is scarcely a demagogue of international fame who has not been identified by interpreters of prophecy as the beast of Revelation 13. Napoleon and Hitler were awarded this label, to name only two. In the 1930s Biblical literalists opposed to President Roosevelt's New Deal even claimed that the Blue Eagle which all merchants were required under the terms of the National Recovery Act to display was "the mark of the beast" (Rev. 13:17)!

---

[8] Based on Ernst Lohmeyer's outline.

The most plausible approach to the apocalyptic section, and hence to the entire book, requires (1) an awareness of the historical crisis—actual or impending—that was the immediate provocation for the book, and (2) a recognition of the cyclical structure of the writing. The historical situation that gave rise to the book was the empire's opposition to Christianity. The Christians of Asia Minor had come under suspicion of subversion because of their refusal to join in the worship of the emperor. On the eastern edge of Asia Minor were located the Parthians, a warlike people who remained a constant threat to the peace of Rome, and whose border was the one perennially unsettled boundary of the entire empire. There can be no doubt that any show of disloyalty to the emperor in the region of Asia Minor would be viewed with special suspicion, since it might indicate collusion with those perennial toublemakers, the Parthians. The involved and highly figurative language of a book like Revelation would serve to communicate a message of resistance to those who understood the imagery, but would at the same time conceal the message from eyes for which it was not intended. Since this kind of writing had become common in late Judaism, neither the form nor even some of the specific images had to be invented. The author simply had to rework these well-known materials in terms of the new crisis of faith that he saw looming on the horizon.

It is misleading to suppose that the series of visions of the end is intended to describe a sequence of events in strict chronological fashion. Rather, the images and prophecies are presented in cyclical form in order to bring out the full implications of the end in a manner in which a single set of visions could not. It is as though the author were saying to the reader: "I have described the end under the figure of the trumpets; now, lest you have missed something of the fullness of meaning, I shall go back over the same territory, but this time I shall use the figure of the kingdom of the dragon."

The apocalyptic section begins with a magnificent vision of the throne of God (Rev. 4). With typical Jewish reluctance to picture God, only the throne and its surroundings are described (4:2). But this description conveys a sense of the awesome majesty of God, surrounded by the symbols of his universal authority. Clearly, however, God's authority is not limited to heaven, since John outlines the things which, it has been revealed to him, "must take place after this" (4:1). There can be no mistaking that the author shares the apocalyptic viewpoint which is characteristically deterministic: these things *must* take place. But the author is not a fatalist. He regards the history of the world as moving by divine will and in fulfillment of a wise and gracious purpose, and not as proceeding by chance. The ultimate outcome of this determined course of history will be the achievement of God's program of redemption for His Creation. Unlike Paul, however, John does not expect the redemption of all things; he looks forward to the unending punishment of the wicked spirits and of the dragon, their leader.

For his imagery in the description of the divine throne, John draws heavily on Old Testament resources. The living creatures resemble the cherubim, which are designated as the guardians of God's throne both in the historical shrines of ancient Israel (Ex. 25:18ff.; I Kings 6:23) and in the prophetic visions (Ezek. 1:5ff.). The twenty-four elders seem to represent the People of God of every generation, who fall in adoration before him. The prose descriptions break over periodically into poetry, as in the ascription of praise with which Revelation 4 closes:

> Worthy art thou, our Lord and God,
> To receive glory and honor and power,
>   for thou didst create all things,
>   and by thy will they existed and were created.

THE VICTOR.   At the opening of Revelation 5 there appears a figure, both majestic and humble, both conquering and submissive, who dominates the Apocalypse, and, according to John's conviction, dominates the unfolding of God's purpose. Although this figure is not named, the opening words of the book make it clear that it is Jesus Christ, who is both Lion (5:5) and Lamb (5:6). He comes in humility, yet he is the one through whom victory over the powers opposed to God will be won. He is the only one worthy to unroll the seven-sealed scroll, which is a symbol for the unfolding purpose of God (5:2). What follows in the rest of the book is an elaboration through complicated symbolism of what will be achieved according to God's plan. Fearful conditions will arise on earth: war (6:2, the white horse), civil strife (6:3–4, the red horse), famine (6:5–6, the black horse), and plagues (6:8, the pale horse). There will be astronomical disturbances (6:12–17)—reminders that, as the New Testament writers understand it, the fate of the whole universe is involved in the fulfillment of man's destiny.

In the midst of this destruction and misery, however, God is at work bringing together his faithful witnesses. They look forward with eagerness to the final deliverance of the Creation from its subjection to the control of the evil powers (6:9–11), even though they know that their fidelity to God will bring about their martyrdom. The word "martyr" is simply a transliteration of a Greek word meaning "witness"; the implication is that the Christian who is faithful in his witness to what he believes to be the truth will meet a martyr's death. These witnesses are considered by John to be the special objects of God's loving care; they are granted the privilege of everlasting shelter in the presence of God. It is at moments like this that the prophet shifts over to poetry:

> Therefore are they before the throne of God,
>   and serve him day and night within his temple;
>   and he who sits upon the throne will shelter them with his
>   presence.
> . . . The Lamb in the midst of the throne will be their shepherd,
>   and he will guide them to springs of living water;
> and God will wipe away every tear from their eyes.
>   —REVELATION 7:15, 17

Terrifying as some of John's visions are, there can be no doubt that the primary intent of his book was not to frighten but to comfort the Christians living under the shadow of persecution. No matter how oppressive the situation might become, they were to have confidence that beyond tribulation lay peace and God's victory.

THE VANQUISHED.   New pictures of the struggles with the evil powers are presented under the figure of the seven angels with the trumpets (Rev. 8:1–2). The angels announce the scourges that are to come upon the earth, and release fearful, fantastic creatures that spread death and destruction on the idolaters of the world. As numerous as locusts, and more horrible than dragons, these creatures torture with their scorpionlike stings, and kill with sulphurous fumes and fire (Rev. 8 and 9). Even though a third of mankind is slaughtered, the suffering is still not at an end (9:18). The Holy City itself is to be visited with judgment, and the prophets of God bring drought upon the surrounding land (Rev. 11). The wicked try in vain to destroy the witnesses, just as the dragon (Satan) tries to destroy the child who is destined to rule over the earth (Rev. 12). In cunning fashion, the dragon gives supernatural powers to "the beast" (Rev. 13), who is a symbol of the emperor, with his demands for divine honors. The special powers are designed to lure the unwary into worshiping him, on the supposition that he is divine.

The prophet reveals the beast's identity by a cryptic number, 666. This figure must have had meaning for John's original readers, but now we can only guess at what it meant. Probably the number was arrived at by adding the numerical values of the letters in the emperor's name. This would be an obvious kind of cryptogram, since in Greek and Hebrew the letters of the alphabet also served as numbers (alpha was 1; beta 2; iota was 9; and so on). Since the number of combinations to give the sum of 666 is almost infinite, it is impossible to determine with certainty which emperor the author had in mind. One likely conjecture is Nero: the letters of Nero Caesar add up to 666, if spelled in Hebrew. The fact that Domitian was probably emperor at the time of John's writing raises no serious problem, since it was customary for apocalypticists to reuse materials from earlier times without recasting them and bringing them up to date. Although the identity of the figure hidden behind the number cannot be known, certainly the intent of the symbol is unmistakable: it is a veiled allusion to an emperor claiming divine honors—in all probability, Domitian.

In contrast to all these demonic figures, John now turns to a sevenfold picture of Christ, through whom the promise of victory is fulfilled. He is portrayed as the Lamb in its purity (14:1–5), as the herald of the Gospel throughout the earth (14:6–7), as the herald of doom for the emperor-worshipers (14:8–11), as the Son of Man who both announces the judgment (14:14–16) and executes it. In vivid imagery based on Isaiah 63, he is pictured as trampling out the grapes of God's wrath just as the ancients pressed out the wine from the grapes with their feet in the winepresses. His feet and garments are spattered with the blood of the fallen as a man in a winepress would be stained with the juice from the grapes (14:17–20; cf. Isa. 63; 3, 4).

Following a magnificent hymn of praise to God for his might and majesty ("Great and wonderful are thy deeds, O Lord God the Almighty!"–15:3), John introduces two new series of seven woes each: one series is to fall on all the earth, in a vain effort to bring it to repentance (Rev. 15–16); the other is to fall on Babylon–that is, Rome–the scourge of God's People in John's day as Babylon was in the days of the ancient prophets (Rev. 17). The proud splendor and moral corruption of Rome are described under the unforgettable figure of a harlot, gorgeously clad in scarlet, trying to entice all the world to engage in emperor worship. John, like the Hebrew prophets, looks upon idolatry as closely related to adultery. The harlot was seated on seven hills (Rev. 17:9), which are the seven hills of Rome.

THE COLOSSEUM
Built by Vespasian and Titus as an arena for great public spectacles, it seated more than 50,000 people. In the later years of the empire, many Christians were slain here by Roman gladiators and wild animals. (Lufthansa Airlines)

THE MAUSOLEUM OF HADRIAN *on the west bank of the Tiber River, with the dome of St. Peter's in the background. It is ironical that the Mausoleum, one of ancient Rome's grandest monuments, should have become a Christian shrine, the Castello Sant' Angelo, and that the city should be dominated by a church honoring Simon Peter.* (Pan American Airways)

The seven heads of the beasts are almost certainly seven emperors, but which seven are meant is difficult to determine. Since three emperors sat on the throne in a single year (Otho, Vitellius, and Galba, in 68–69), it is impossible to tell whether or not the writer included all three in his computation. Estimates are further affected by the weight we attach to the theory that the king who "was and is not" (17:11) is the same as the one who was earlier pictured as mortally wounded and healed (13:3). Perhaps both these references are allusions to the belief prevalent in the first century that Nero would come back from the dead to lead Rome's traditional enemies on the eastern border, the Parthians, against Rome. Since Nero died under mysterious circumstances, reportedly by suicide, there was much speculation about his death. The rumor spread that perhaps he was not really dead, but would return. Finally, the theory arose and became widespread that he would be raised from the dead to lead the attack on Rome. If Nero is the man behind John's symbol here, we have additional evidence of the prophetic insight that saw in the purely local persecution of Christians under Nero the first rumblings of a tremendous conflict that was later to develop between the Church and the empire. The completeness of the destruction of the city of seven hills (Rev. 17:9) is celebrated in an awesome dirge (Rev. 18):

> Fallen, fallen is Babylon the great!
> It has become a dwelling place of demons,
>   a haunt of every foul spirit,
>   a haunt of every foul and hateful bird;
>   for all nations have drunk the wine of her impure passion. . . .

> Alas, alas, for the great city
>> that was clothed in fine linen, in purple and scarlet,
>> bedecked with gold, with jewels, and with pearls!
> In one hour all this wealth has been laid waste.
>
> —REVELATION 18:2, 3, 16, 17

THE FINAL VICTORY.   The final chapters of the Revelation portray in majestic fashion the finale of the present age and opening of the new. Conflict and judgment are at an end; the adversary and his demonic aides are banished and enchained forever; the hostile nations are destroyed in the great battle of Armageddon, after which the birds of prey swarm over the field of the fallen warriors to gorge themselves on their flesh (Rev. 19). Then begins the period of 1,000 years (Rev. 20), which is an initial stage of the reign of God over His Creation. But even under these ideal conditions, man continues to disobey God. The period ends in a final Judgment of man, the destruction of death itself, and the renewal of the entire Creation (Rev. 21). The book closes with a description of the serenity and plenty that come upon God's Creation when, at last, it is subject to his will:

> Then I saw a new heaven and a new earth; for the
> first heaven and the first earth had passed away.
> . . . And I heard a great voice from the throne
> saying, "Behold, the dwelling of God is with men.
> He will dwell with them and they shall be his people."

> Then he showed me the river of the water of life,
> bright as crystal, flowing from the throne of God
> and of the Lamb . . . ; also, . . . the tree of life with
> its twelve kinds of fruit, yielding its fruit each
> month, and the leaves of the tree were for the healing
> of the nations.

> And night shall be no more; they need no light of
> lamp or sun, for the Lord God will be their light, and
> they shall reign for ever and ever.
>
> —REVELATION 21:1, 3; 22:1, 2, 5

Suggestions for Additional Reading

The most complete survey of the critical study of the New Testament, especially in the period from the eighteenth century to the present, W. C. Kümmel's *The New Testament: The History of the Investigation of Its Problems*. The latest edition of Kümmel's *Introduction to the New Testament*, with comprehensive discussion of the origins of the individual books of the New Testament and of questions relating to the text and canon, translated by H. C. Kee from the 17th German edition, is to be published in 1974 by Abingdon Press, New York and Nashville. Other excellent introductions include: R. M. Grant, *A Historical Introduction of the New Testament* (New York: Harper & Row, 1963); a Roman Catholic study by Alfred Wikenhauser, *New Testament Introduction* (New York: Herder & Herder, 1963); and an imaginative introduction that stresses worship in the early church, Charles F. D. Moule, *The Birth of the New Testament* (New York: Harper & Row, 1962). For the historical development of the early church through and beyond the New Testament period, highly readable and perceptive is Henry Chadwick, *The Early Church* (Baltimore: Penguin Books, 1967). An original and provocative study of the development of New Testament thought is Rudolf Bultmann, *Theology of the New Testament*, 2 vols. (New York: Scribner's, 1951 and 1955). Information on details of places and things mentioned in the New Testament, as well as brief analyses of the books and accounts of persons, are available in *Interpreter's Dictionary of the Bible*, 4 vols. (New York and Nashville: Abingdon, 1962). Translations of writings and documents contemporary with the New Testament are available in H. C. Kee, *The Origins of Christianity: Sources and Documents* (Englewood Cliffs, N.J.: Prentice-Hall, 1973).

CHAPTER ONE

QUESTS FOR COMMUNITY AND IDENTITY IN THE EARLY ROMAN EMPIRE

Two classic treatments of the history of this period are *Cambridge Ancient History*, vol. 11, The Augustan Age, and M. Rostovtseff, *The Social and Economic History of the Roman Empire* (Oxford: Clarendon Press, repr. 1966). Accurate sketches of the history of the period with special reference to Palestine are to be found in R. H. Pfeiffer, *History of New Testament Times* (New York: Harper & Row, 1949) and in F. C. Grant, *Roman Hellenism and the New Testament* (New York: Scribner's, 1962). The religious developments of the period are described illuminatingly in A. D. Nock, *Conversion* (New York: Oxford University Press, 1961), in H. R. Willoughby, *Pagan Regeneration* (Chicago: University of Chicago Press, 1929) and in S. Angus, *Religious Quests of the Graeco-Roman World* (New York: Scribner's, 1929). The effects of eastern religions on the religions of the Roman empire are described graphically in Franz Cumont, *Oriental Religions in Roman Paganism* (New York: Dover, repr. 1956).

CHAPTER TWO

THE PEOPLE OF THE BOOK AND THEIR DESTINY

A thorough study of the period is found in Werner Foerster, *From the Exile to Christ: A Historical Introduction to Palestinian Judaism*, trans. Gordon E. Harris (Philadelphia: Fortress Press, 1964). A significant technical study of the economic and social conditions in Jerusalem during New Testament times is found in Joachim Jeremias, *Jerusalem in the Time of Jesus*, trans. F. H. and C. H. Cave (London: SCM Press, 1969). Two brief, popular studies of intertestamental history and thought are Lawrence E. Toombs, *The Threshold of Christianity* (Philadelphia: Westminster Press, 1960) and D. S. Russell, *Between the Testaments* (Philadelphia: Muhlenberg Press, 1960). For a comprehensive survey of the Dead Sea Scrolls and their significance, see F. M. Cross, *The Ancient Library of Qumran*, rev. ed. (New York:

Doubleday, 1961). A translation of the scrolls is found in G. Vermes, *The Dead Sea Scrolls in English* (Middlesex, England: Penguin Books, 1962). Two excellent studies with a primary interest in the religious practices and thought of the Qumran sect are Helmer Ringgren, *The Faith of Qumran* (Philadelphia: Fortress Press, 1961) and A. R. C. Leaney, *The Rule of Qumran and Its Meaning* (Philadelphia: Westminster Press, 1966).

CHAPTER THREE

THE GOSPEL AND THE GOSPELS

Two general introductions to the gospels are Vincent Taylor, *The Gospels: A Short Introduction,* 7th ed. (London: Epworth Press, 1952) and Frederick C. Grant, *The Gospels: Their Origin and Their Growth* (New York: Harper & Row, 1957). An excellent, brief, non-technical commentary on the synoptic gospels, employing methods of source criticism and form criticism, is Francis W. Beare, *The Earliest Records of Jesus* (New York: Abingdon, 1962). Two classic studies of form criticism of the gospels are Rudolf Bultmann, *History of the Synoptic Tradition,* trans. John Marsh (New York: Harper & Row, 1963) and Martin Dibelius, *From Tradition to Gospel,* trans. Bertram L. Woolf (New York: Scribner's, 1935). The best general introduction to form criticism is Vincent Taylor, *The Formation of the Gospel Tradition* (New York: St. Martin's Press, 1953). For an introduction to the methods and problems of redaction criticism, see Norman Perrin, *What Is Redaction Criticism?* (Philadelphia: Fortress Press, 1969).

CHAPTER FOUR

JESUS, PROPHET OF THE NEW AGE

Two classic reconstructions of the message of Jesus—and to a lesser extent, of his activity—are R. Bultmann, *Jesus and the Word* (New York: Scribner's, 1958) and M. Dibelius, *Jesus* (Philadelphia: Westminster, 1949). Among the most effective recent attempts at reconstruction are Gunther Bornkamm, *Jesus of Nazareth* (New York: Harper & Row, 1960) and E. Schweizer, *Jesus* (Richmond: John Knox Press, 1971). A probing essay concerning the necessity for historical reconstruction of the career of Jesus is by Ernst Kaesemann, "The Problem of the Historical Jesus" in *Essays on New Testament Themes* (Naperville, Ill.: Allenson, 1964); a sequel in which Kaesemann takes on his critics is "Blind Alley in the 'Jesus of History' Controversy" in *New Testament Questions of Today* (Philadelphia: Fortress Press, 1969).

CHAPTER FIVE

THE NEW COVENANT IN WORD AND ACT [MARK]

The best of recent commentaries on Mark is D. E. Nineham, *St. Mark*, Pelican Gospel Commentaries (Baltimore: Penguin Books, 1963). Also useful is S. E. Johnson, *The Gospel According to St. Mark* (New York: Harper & Row, 1960). For a technical study of the origin and development of Jesus' teaching, see Norman Perrin, *Rediscovering the Teaching of Jesus* (New York: Harper & Row, 1967). Special studies of Markan thought are by W. Marxsen, *Mark the Evangelist* (New York and Nashville: Abingdon, 1969) and T. A. Burkill, *Mysterious Revelation* (Ithaca, N.Y.: Cornell University Press, 1963). See also H. C. Kee, *Jesus in History* (New York: Harcourt Brace Jovanovich, 1970), pp. 104–147 for a sketch of Mark's literary method and theological aims. On the development of the Son of Man tradition, see H. E. Toedt, *The Son of Man in the Synoptic Tradition* (Philadelphia: Westminster, 1965).

CHAPTER SIX

THE CAREER OF PAUL

Valuable reconstructions of the life of Paul are those of M. Dibelius and W. G. Kümmel, *Paul* (Philadelphia: Westminster, 1953), A. D. Nock, *St. Paul* (New York: Oxford University Press, 1953), and John Knox, *Chapters in the Life of Paul* (New York and Nashville: Abingdon, 1950). Older, classical studies of Paul include Albert Schweitzer, *The Mysticism of Paul the Apostle* (London: A. & C. Black, 1931), Adolf Deissmann, *Paul: A Study in Social and Religious History* (New York: Harper Torchbook, repr. 1957), and Jas. S. Stewart, *A Man in Christ* (New York: Harper, n.d.). For detailed historical studies of the setting for Paul's activities, see F. J. Foakes-Jackson and K. Lake, *The Beginnings of Christianity*, vol. 5, Additional Notes (Grand Rapids, Mich.: Baker, repr. 1966).

CHAPTERS SEVEN, EIGHT, NINE

[ON PAUL]

Excellent studies of Paul's thought are Rudolf Bultmann, *Theology of the New Testament*, vol. 1 (New York: Scribner's, 1951), and Victor Furnish, *Theology and Ethics in Paul* (New York and Nashville: Abingdon, 1968). A technical treatment of the life of Paul with special attention to the Corinthian church and Paul's associations with it is John C. Hurd, *The Origins of I Corinthians*

(London: S.P.C.K., 1965). A superb comprehensive treatment of Paul is Günther Bornkamm's *Paul*, trans. D. M. Stalker (New York: Harper & Row, 1971). Fine commentaries on Paul's Letter to the Romans are by C. K. Barrett (New York: Harper & Row, 1957), C. H. Dodd (New York: Harper, n.d.), and F. J. Leenhardt (Cleveland: World Publishing Co., 1957). For studies of the concept of "church" in the New Testament, see E. Schweizer, *Church Order in the New Testament* (Naperville, Ill.: Allenson, 1961) and R. Schnackenburg, *The Church in the New Testament* (New York: Herder & Herder, 1965).

CHAPTER TEN

TOWARD INSTITUTIONALIZING THE CHURCH
[EPHESIANS; THE PASTORIALS; I, II, III JOHN; JUDE; II PETER]

A good popular introduction to the epistles is J. C. Beker, *The Church Faces the World: Late New Testament Writings* (Philadelphia: Westminster, 1960). For introduction and commentary on individual books, see F. W. Beare, *Ephesians*, Interpreter's Bible, vol. 10 (New York and Nashville: Abingdon, 1953); C. K. Barrett, *The Pastoral Epistles in the New English Bible* (Oxford: Clarendon Press, 1963); J. N. D. Kelly, *The Pastoral Epistles* (New York: Harper & Row, 1963); C. H. Dodd, *The Johannine Epistles* (New York: Harper, 1946); Bo Reicke, *The Epistles of James, Peter and Jude*, The Anchor Bible, vol. 37 (Garden City, N.Y.: Doubleday, 1964). On the development in theology and church organization, see Maurice Goguel, *The Primitive Church* (New York: Macmillan, 1964) and R. Bultmann, *Theology of the New Testament*, trans. K. Grobel (New York: Scribner's, 1955), I, pp. 133–152; II, pp. 95–126; 231–236. An illuminating discussion of the development of organization in the early church is J. Knox, *The Early Church and the Coming Great Church* (New York: Abingdon, 1955). An interesting discussion of "false teaching" confronting the early church, in general, is found in M. Goguel, *The Birth of Christianity*, trans. H. C. Snape (New York: Macmillan, 1954), pp. 393–435, and with reference to the Pastorals, in particular, in F. D. Gealy, *I and II Timothy and Titus*, Interpreter's Bible, vol. 11 (New York: Abingdon, 1955), pp. 350–360. For a study of the development of the ministry, see appropriate sections in Eduard Schweizer, *Church Order in the New Testament*, Studies in Biblical Theology, No. 32 (Naperville, Ill.: Allenson, 1961). Two excellent introductions to New Testament worship are Gerhard Delling, *Worship in the New Testament*, trans. P. Scott (Philadelphia: Westminster Press, 1962) and C. F. D. Moule, *Worship in the New Testament* (Richmond, Va.: John Knox Press, 1961). Regarding baptism, see G. R. Beaseley-Murray, *Baptism in the New Testament* (New York: St. Martin's Press,

1962), and on the subject of Eucharist, see A. J. B. Higgins, *The Lord's Supper in the New Testament*, Studies in Biblical Theology, No. 6 (Naperville, Ill.: Allenson, 1952). For a thorough study of the development of the Church in relation to its environment, see A. Harnack, *The Mission and Expansion of Christianity in the First Three Centuries*, trans. J. Moffatt (New York: Harper & Row, 1961).

CHAPTER ELEVEN

TOWARD STABILIZING WORSHIP AND ETHICS
[I PETER, JAMES, HEBREWS]

For a discussion of the historical problems connected with I Peter, see F. W. Beare, *The First Epistle of Peter* (Oxford: Blackwell, 1947), pp. 1–41. An excellent popular commentary on I Peter and James is Bo Reicke, *The Epistles of James, Peter and Jude*, The Anchor Bible, vol. 37 (Garden City, N.Y.: Doubleday, 1964). An important article dealing with the ethical teaching of I Peter is W. C. van Unnik, "The Teaching of Good Works in I Peter," *New Testament Studies*, I, No. 2 (Nov. 1954), pp. 92–110. An excellent brief introduction to the book of James is given in M. Goguel, *The Birth of Christianity* (New York: Macmillan, 1954), Part IV, Chapter 6, and a helpful commentary is James Moffatt, *The General Epistles* (New York: Harper & Row, n.d.). Two commentaries on the book of Hebrews, written from somewhat different perspectives, the first being less technical, are W. Neil, *The Epistle to the Hebrews* (London: SCM Press, 1955) and Jean Héring, *The Epistle to the Hebrews*, trans. A. W. Heathcote and P. J. Allock (London: Epworth Press, 1970). For a theological interpretation of the development of ethical teaching, see R. Bultmann, *Theology of the New Testament*, trans. K. Grobel (New York: Scribner's, 1955), II, pp. 203–231, and W. Beach and H. R. Niebuhr, *Christian Ethics* (New York: Ronald Press, 1955), pp. 46–57. For a helpful, brief discussion of New Testament ethics, see W. D. Davies, "Ethics in the New Testament," article in the *Interpreter's Dictionary of the Bible* (New York and Nashville: Abingdon, 1962), vol. E-J, pp. 167–176.

CHAPTER TWELVE

THE CHURCH AS THE TRUE ISRAEL [MATTHEW]

See Edward P. Blair, *Jesus in the Gospel of St. Matthew* (New York: Abingdon, 1960); G. Bornkamm, *et al.*, *Tradition and Interpretation in Matthew's Gospel* (Philadelphia: Westminster, 1963); K. Stendahl, Exposition of Matthew in *Peake's Commentary on the Bible,* ed. M. Black and H. H. Rowley (London and New York: Nelson, 1962); and H. C. Kee on Matthew in *Interpreter's One-Volume Commentary on the Bible* (New York and Nashville: Abingdon, 1971). An excellent popular commentary on this gospel is *St. Matthew,* by J. C. Fenton in the Pelican Gospel Commentaries (Baltimore: Penguin Books, 1963). A fine study of the Sermon on the Mount in the context of the first century is W. D. Davies, *The Setting of the Sermon on the Mount* (Cambridge: The University Press, 1964). For analysis of the content of the Sermon see M. Dibelius, *The Sermon on the Mount* (New York: Scribner's, 1940); T. W. Manson, *The Sayings of Jesus* (London: SCM Press, 1949). On the method of interpretation of scripture used in Matthew, see K. Stendahl, *The School of St. Matthew* (Philadelphia: Fortress Press, 1968) and Barnabas Lindars, *New Testament Apologetic: The Doctrinal Significance of the Old Testament Quotations* (London: SCM Press, 1961).

CHAPTER THIRTEEN

THE COMMUNITY OF NEW LIFE [JOHN]

For the most thorough survey of the historical, literary and theological problems, and the most comprehensive commentary on the text of John, see Raymond E. Brown, *The Gospel According to John,* The Anchor Bible, vols. 29 and 29a (Garden City, N.Y.: Doubleday, 1966 and 1967). An important source for the study of the background of John's thought is C. H. Dodd, *The Interpretation of the Fourth Gospel* (Cambridge: Cambridge University Press, 1953). Significant for their study of John's sources, as well as interpretation, are Rudolf K. Bultmann, *The Gospel of John,* trans. G. R. Beasley-Murray (Philadelphia: Westminster Press, 1971) and C. H. Dodd, *Historical Tradition in the Fourth Gospel* (Cambridge: Cambridge University Press, 1963). The major exposition and critique of Bultmann's book is Dwight Moody Smith, Jr., *The Composition and Order of the Fourth Gospel: Bultmann's Literary Theory,* Yale Publications in Religion, No. 10 (New Haven: Yale University Press, 1965). A provocative effort to deal with the setting, purpose, and religious thought of John is James L. Martyn, *History and Theology in the Fourth Gospel* (New York: Harper & Row, 1968). For a study of the much discussed relation between John and the Qumran sect, see the series of essays in James H. Charlesworth, ed., *John and Qumran* (London: Geoffrey Chapman, 1972). A brief and suggestive effort to provide guidance on the theological perspective and literary method of John is found in A. Wilder, *New Testament Faith for Today* (New York: Harper & Row, 1955), pp. 142–164.

CHAPTER FOURTEEN

THE CHURCH'S PLACE IN WORLD HISTORY [LUKE-ACTS]

A fundamental study of the aim of Luke-Acts is Hans Conzelmann, *The Theology of St. Luke* (New York: Harper & Row, 1960). A perceptive study of the literary background and origins of Luke's work is H. J. Cadbury, *The Making of Luke-Acts* (London: S.P.C.K., 1961). A massive study of the setting of Acts and a detailed analysis of its contents is F. J. Foakes-Jackson and K. Lake, *The Beginnings of Christianity*, repr. in 5 vols. (Grand Rapids: Baker, 1965–66). The most complete recent commentary on Acts is E. Haenchen, *The Acts of the Apostles* trans. H. Anderson (Philadelphia: Westminster, 1971). Other useful commentaries are by E. E. Ellis in the Century Bible Series (Camden, N.J.: Nelson, 1966), A. R. C. Leaney in the Harper Commentary Series (New York: Harper & Row, 1958), and G. B. Caird in Pelican Commentary (Baltimore: Penguin Books, 1963). Important studies of Luke are H. Flender, *St. Luke: Theologian of Redemptive History* (Philadelphia: Fortress, 1967) and L. E. Keck and J. L. Martyn, eds., *Studies in Luke-Acts* (New York and Nashville: Abingdon, 1966).

CHAPTER FIFTEEN

THE CHURCH AND THE END OF THE AGE [REVELATION]

The most complete survey of the historical setting of the Book of Revelation is that of W. Ramsay, in *The Letters to the Seven Churches* (New York: Armstrong, 1905). An excellent commentary on Revelation is *The Revelation of St. John*, by M. Kiddle (New York: Harper & Row, 1940). The fullest technical analysis of Revelation is *The Revelation of St. John*, by R. H. Charles (New York: Scribner's, 1920). For an illuminating survey of the changing interpretations of New Testament eschatology in the present century, see Chapters 1–3 of A. N. Wilder, *Eschatology and Ethics in the Teaching of Jesus*, rev. ed. (New York: Harper & Row, 1950). Three popular interpretations of Revelation are John W. Bowman, *The Drama of the Book of Revelation* (Philadelphia: Westminster, 1955); Hans Lilje, *The Last Book of the Bible* (Philadelphia: Muhlenberg Press, 1957); and Thomas Kepler, *The Book of Revelation* (New York: Oxford University Press, 1957). An excellent treatment of the relation of the Church and the Roman government is O. Cullmann, *The State in the New Testament* (New York: Scribner's, 1956). A similar study, though dealing more extensively with non-Christian sources and covering a period up to the beginning of the fourth century, is R. Grant, *The Sword and the Cross* (New York: Macmillan, 1955). A series of historical essays dealing largely with various Roman emperors up to the fourth century is Ethelbert Stauffer, *Christ and the Caesars*, trans. K. and R. Smith (Philadelphia: Westminster 1955). For a brief analysis of the development of eschatology in the New Testament, see H. A. Guy, *The New Testament Doctrine of the Last Things* (London and New York: Oxford University Press, 1948). An existentialist interpretation of eschatology is offered by R. Bultmann, in *The Presence of Eternity* (New York: Harper & Row, 1957).

Appendixes

I. ABBREVIATIONS

The following abbreviations are widely used to identify books of the Bible. In this book, these abbreviations are used only when followed by a chapter (or chapter-and-verse) number; where no chapter or verse is cited, and with extracted material, the names of the books are spelled out.

OLD TESTAMENT ABBREVIATIONS

Gen.	Genesis	I Kings	I Kings	Eccles.	Ecclesiastes
Ex.	Exodus	II Kings	II Kings	Song	Song of Solomon
Lev.	Leviticus	I Chron.	I Chronicles	Is.	Isaiah
Num.	Numbers	II Chron.	II Chronicles	Jer.	Jeremiah
Deut.	Deuteronomy	Ezra	Ezra	Lam.	Lamentations
Josh.	Joshua	Neh.	Nehemiah	Ezek.	Ezekiel
Judg.	Judges	Esther	Esther	Dan.	Daniel
Ruth	Ruth	Job	Job	Hos.	Hosea
I Sam.	I Samuel	Ps.	Psalms	Joel	Joel
II Sam.	II Samuel	Prov.	Proverbs	Amos	Amos

Abbreviations (cont'd)

Obad.	Obadiah	Nahum	Nahum	Hag.	Haggai
Jon.	Jonah	Hab.	Habakkuk	Zech.	Zechariah
Mic.	Micah	Zeph.	Zephaniah	Mal.	Malachi

NEW TESTAMENT ABBREVIATIONS

Mt.	Matthew	Eph.	Ephesians	Heb.	Hebrews
Mk.	Mark	Phil.	Philippians	Jas.	James
Lk.	Luke	Col.	Colossians	I Pet.	I Peter
Jn.	John	I Thess.	I Thessalonians	II Pet.	II Peter
Acts	Acts	II Thess.	II Thessalonians	I Jn.	I John
Rom.	Romans	I Tim.	I Timothy	II Jn.	II John
I Cor.	I Corinthians	II Tim.	II Timothy	III Jn.	III John
II Cor.	II Corinthians	Tit.	Titus	Jude	Jude
Gal.	Galatians	Phm.	Philemon	Rev.	Revelations

II. A RECONSTRUCTION OF Q

The following reconstruction of the hypothetical Q document was prepared by Frederick C. Grant for *Harper's Annotated Bible* (New York: Harper & Row, 1955), and is used by permission. Scarcely two scholars agree in every detail on what to include as Q material, but here one may see the major themes of Q and gain an impression as to how extensively Matthew and Luke have relied on this source.

The Contents of Q

The ministry and message of John the Baptizer
    Luke 3: [2b], 3a, 7b-9 John's preaching of repentance (cf. Mt. 3:1-10)
    3:16, 17 John's prediction of the coming Judge (cf. Mt. 3:11, 12)
The ordeal of the Messiah
    4:1b-12 The Temptation (cf. Mt. 4:1-11)
Jesus' public teaching
    6:20-49 The Sermon on the Plain (or Mountain; cf. Mt. 5:3-12, 39-48; 7:12, 1-5, 16-27; 10:24, 25; 12:33-35; 15:14)
The response to Jesus' preaching
    7:2, 6b-10 The centurion's faith (cf. Mt. 8:5-13)
    7:18b, 19, 22-28, 31-35 John's emissaries; Jesus' words about John (cf. Mt. 11:2-6, 7-19)
    9:57b-60, 61, 62 Various followers (cf. Mt. 8:19-22)
The mission of the Twelve
    10:2-16 The mission of the disciples (cf. Mt. 9:37, 38; 10:7-16, 40; 11:21-23)
    [10:17b-20 The return of the Twelve]
    10:21b-24 The rejoicing of Jesus (cf. Mt. 11:25-27; 13:16, 17)

Jesus' teaching about prayer
    11:2-4 The Lord's Prayer (cf. Mt. 6:9-13)
    [11:5-8 The parable of the friend at midnight]
        11:9-13 Constancy in prayer (cf. Mt. 7:7-11)
The controversy with the scribes and Pharisees
    11:14-22 The charge of collusion with Beelzebul (cf. Mt. 12:22-30)
    11:23-26 The story of the unclean spirit (cf. Mt. 12:43-45)
    11:29b-32 The warning contained in the "sign of Jonah" (cf. Mt. 12:38-42)
    11:33-36 Jesus' sayings about light (cf. Mt. 5:15; 6:22, 23)
    11:39b, 42, 43, 46-52 The controversy with the scribes and Pharisees (cf. Mt. 23:4-36)
Jesus' teaching about discipleship: the duties of disciples when persecuted
    12:2-12 The testimony of disciples amid adversaries (cf. Mt. 10:26-33; 12:32; 10:19, 20)
    12:22-31 On Freedom from care (cf. Mt. 6:25-33)
    12:33b-34 On treasure (cf. Mt. 6:19-21)
    12:39, 40, 42-46 Three parables on watchfulness (cf. Mt. 24:43-51a)
    12:49-53 Messianic divisions (cf. Mt. 10:34-36)
    [12:54-56 Signs of the times (cf. Mt. 16:2, 3)]
    12:57-59 The duty of speedy reconciliation (cf. Mt. 5:25, 26)
    13:18-21 The parables of the mustard seed and the leaven: the steady growth of the kingdom despite opposition (cf. Mt. 13:31-33)
    13:24-29 The narrow way (cf. Mt. 7:13, 14; 7:22, 23; 8:11, 12)
    13:34, 35 The fate of Jerusalem (cf. Mt. 23: 37-39)
    14:11 = 18:14 On self-exaltation (cf. Mt. 18:4; 23:12)
    14:16-23 The parable of the great supper (cf. Mt. 22:1-10)
    14:26, 27 On hating one's next of kin, and on bearing the cross (cf. Mt. 10:37, 38)
    14:34, 35 The saying on salt (cf. Mt. 5:13)
    [15:4-7 The parable of the lost sheep (cf. Mt. 18:12-14)]
    16:13 On serving two masters (cf. Mt. 6:24)
Sayings about the Law
    16:16-18 The Law and the Prophets until John; on divorce (cf. Mt. 11:12, 13; 5:18, 32)
    17:1, 2 On offenses (cf. Mt. 18:6, 7)
    17:3, 4 On forgiveness (cf. Mt. 18:15, 21, 22)
    17:6 On faith (cf. Mt. 17:20b)
The coming *parousia*
    17:23, 24, 26, 27, 34, 35, 37b The *parousia* (cf. Mt. 24:26-28, 37-39; 10:39; 24:40, 38)
    19:12, 13, 15b-26 The parable of the entrusted talents (cf. Mt. 25: 14-30)
    [22:28-30 The apostles' thrones (cf. Mt. 19:28)]

III. PASSAGES OF MATTHEW ASSIGNED TO M
AND OF LUKE ASSIGNED TO L

The following lists of passages assigned to M and L were prepared by C. S. C. Williams for the Revised Edition of *Peake's Commentary on the Bible*, eds. Matthew Black and H. H. Rowley (London: Thomas Nelson & Sons Ltd., 1962), and are used by permission. As in the case of Q, scholars are not agreed as to what should be included, but here we have a representative listing of the passages drawn from the written—or, in the case of M, possibly oral—sources from which Matthew and Luke drew respectively.

Passages Assigned to M

1:1-2:23	Infancy stories
3:14f.	Reason for the Baptism
4:13-6	Fulfillment of Isa. 9:1f.

5:1, 5, 7-10
14, 16f,
19-24, 27f.,
31, 33-7,
38-9*a*, 41,
43
6:1-4, 5-8
10*b*, 13*b*,
16-18, 34
7:6, 12*b*, 15,
19f., 22 } Passages in Mt.'s Sermon on the Mount, some of it editorial but much of it from reliable sources, if not from Q from which Lk. has omitted it.

8:17	Fulfillment of Isa. 53:4
9:13*a*	Fulfillment of Hos. 6:6
9:27-31	The healing of two blind men (cf. Mt. 10:46ff.)
9:32-6	The healing of the dumb demoniac, and preface to the Mission of the Twelve
10:5*b*	Command to go to the House of Israel

10:8*b*, 16*b*,
23, 25, 36,
41 } Sayings chiefly of a missionary character

11:1	? editorial
11:14f.	(cf. Mk. 9:13)
11:20	? editorial
11:28-30	The invitation to the heavy-laden (cf. Sirach 51:23-7)
12:5-7	Probably three sayings of Jesus spoken at different times, here expanding the story of the plucking of corn
12:17-21	Fulfillment of Isa. 42:1-4
12:36f.	Judgment on idle words
12:40	(cf. Lk. 11:30)

13:24ff.,
44, 45f.,
47ff., 51f. } Parables of the tares, hidden treasure, pearl of great price, draw-net, with an ending (to a parabolic source?)

14:28-31	Peter on the water
14:33	(cf. Mk. 6:51*b*)
15:12-14*a*	The Pharisees and the blind
15:23f.	Pro-Jewish-Christian expansion of the story of the Syro-Phoenician woman
16:12	Explanatory note about the "leaven"
16:17-19	Probably three separate sayings attributed to Jesus, bearing on Peter and inserted here to expand the commission to him (cf. on 12:5-7)
17:6f.	Expansion of Mk's story of the Transfiguration
17:13	Explanatory note about "Elijah"
17:24-7, 18:4	The coin in the fish's mouth, which reads like Jewish-Christian Midrash (but cf. Lk. 14:11, 18:14)

18:10	Introduction to the story of the lost sheep (cf. 18:14, a conclusion to it)
18:16-20	Expansion of the duties to fellow-Christians
18:23-35	Parable of the unforgiving servant, no doubt authentic
20:1-16	Parable of the laborers in the vineyard, also authentic
21:10*b*f.	Introduction to the story of Christ in the Temple
21:14-16	Healings in the Temple and the fulfillment of Ps. 8:3
21:28-32	Parable of the two sons, no doubt authentic
21:43	Explanatory note
22:6f.	A late addition to the parable of the wedding-feast, and 22:11-14, the parable of the wedding-garment, probably a different parable, the beginning of which is lost, that Mt. has conflated awkwardly
23:2f., 5	
23:7*b*-10	
23:15-22	An expansion of the woes against scribes and Pharisees
23:27*b*-28	
23:32f.	(but for 33 cf. Lk. 3:7)
24:10-12	Three sayings, probably originally separate, serving here to expand the beginnings of the messianic woes
24:14*b*	A conclusion to a section or lection
24:20*b*	'Flight . . . on the sabbath,' a Jewish-Christian addition
24:30*a*	An expansion based on Dan. 7:13
25:1-3	Parable of the ten virgins, probably authentic
25:31-46	The picture of the last assize, no doubt authentic also
26:1	Introductory to the Passion narrative
26:25	A secondary addition to show that Jesus knew the betrayer (cf. Lk. 22:23, which seems more primitive)
26:50	(cf. Lk. 22:48)
26:52*b*-54	(cf. Rev. 13:10)
27:3-10	Death of Judas and fulfillment of Zech. 11:12 (cf. Ac. 1:15ff.)
27:19, 24f., 62-6 and 28:11-15	A cycle of Christian Midrashic stories about Pilate, much of which may be secondary
27:43	A fulfillment of Ps. 22:9
27:51*b*-53	Portents at Jesus' death, also Midrashic in character
28:2-4	The earthquake and the angel at the tomb, possibly three originally separate phrases, the second of which may have at one time referred to Christ, brought together here by Mt. to expand the story of the Resurrection (cf. on 12:5-7, 16:17-19 above)
28:11-15	The bribing of the soldiers, which may be secondary material
28:16-20	The command to baptize

Passages Assigned to L

1:5-2:52	Infancy narratives
3:10-14	Teaching of John the Baptist
3:23-38	The genealogy of Christ
4:16-30	Christ's rejection of Nazareth
5:1-11	Draught of fishes and Simon's call
5:39	Old and new wine (but cf. the variant reading of Mk. 2:22)
7:11-17	Raising of the widow's son at Nain

7:36-50	The woman who was a sinner
8:1-3	The ministering women
9:51-6	Rejection in the Samarian villages
10:1	Mission of the seventy(-two)
10:17-20	Their return
10:25-8	The lawyer's question (but cf. Mk. 12:28-31)
10:29-37	The good Samaritan
10:38-42	Martha and Mary
11:1-8	Teaching on prayer (but cf. Mt. 6:9-13)
11:27f.	Blessedness of the Mother of Christ
11:37-41, 53-4, 12:1	Inward as against outward purity
12:13-21	Parable of the rich fool
12:35-8	On watchfulness (but cf. Mt. 25:1ff.)
13:1-9	Call to repentance
13:10-17	The woman with a spirit of infirmity healed
13:31-3	Departure from Herod and Galilee
14:1-6	The man with dropsy healed
14:7-14	Teaching on humility
14:28-33	On counting the cost
15:1-32	Parables of the lost sheep, the lost coin and the lost (prodigal) son
16:1-13	The shrewd steward
16:14f., 19-31	Misuse of wealth and Dives and Lazarus
17:7-10	The servant's wages
17:11-19	Healing of ten lepers
17:20f.	Kingdom of God (but cf. Mk. 13:21)
18:1-8	The importunate widow and unjust judge
18:9-14	The Pharisee and the publican
19:1-10	Zacchaeus
19:11-27	Parable of the pounds (but cf. Mt. 25:14-30, the parable of the talents)
19:37-40	Entry into Jerusalem (cf. Mk. 11:9f.)
19:41-4	Lamentation over the city
20:18	The strength of the stone
21:5-36	The Apocalyptic discourse (cf. C. H. Dodd, *Journal of Roman Studies* 37 [1947], 47-54); cf. Mk. 13

CHRONOLOGICAL CHART

ROMAN EMPERORS	PROCURATORS OF JUDEA	CHRISTIAN WRITINGS
Augustus, 30 B.C.		

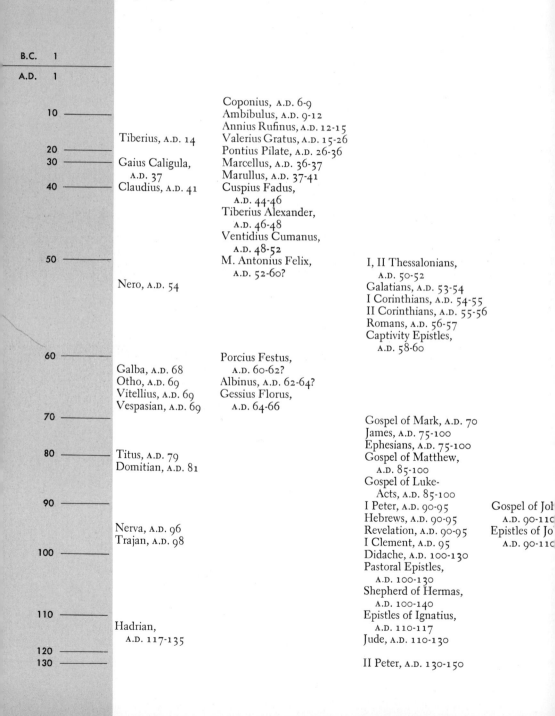

	ROMAN EMPERORS	PROCURATORS OF JUDEA	CHRISTIAN WRITINGS	
B.C. 1				
A.D. 1				
10		Coponius, A.D. 6-9		
		Ambibulus, A.D. 9-12		
		Annius Rufinus, A.D. 12-15		
20	Tiberius, A.D. 14	Valerius Gratus, A.D. 15-26		
30	Gaius Caligula,	Pontius Pilate, A.D. 26-36		
	A.D. 37	Marcellus, A.D. 36-37		
40	Claudius, A.D. 41	Marullus, A.D. 37-41		
		Cuspius Fadus, A.D. 44-46		
		Tiberius Alexander, A.D. 46-48		
		Ventidius Cumanus, A.D. 48-52		
50		M. Antonius Felix, A.D. 52-60?	I, II Thessalonians, A.D. 50-52	
	Nero, A.D. 54		Galatians, A.D. 53-54	
			I Corinthians, A.D. 54-55	
			II Corinthians, A.D. 55-56	
			Romans, A.D. 56-57	
			Captivity Epistles, A.D. 58-60	
60		Porcius Festus, A.D. 60-62?		
	Galba, A.D. 68	Albinus, A.D. 62-64?		
	Otho, A.D. 69	Gessius Florus, A.D. 64-66		
	Vitellius, A.D. 69			
	Vespasian, A.D. 69			
70			Gospel of Mark, A.D. 70	
			James, A.D. 75-100	
80	Titus, A.D. 79		Ephesians, A.D. 75-100	
	Domitian, A.D. 81		Gospel of Matthew, A.D. 85-100	
			Gospel of Luke-Acts, A.D. 85-100	
90			I Peter, A.D. 90-95	Gospel of Joh[n] A.D. 90-11[0]
	Nerva, A.D. 96		Hebrews, A.D. 90-95	Epistles of Jo[hn] A.D. 90-11[0]
	Trajan, A.D. 98		Revelation, A.D. 90-95	
100			I Clement, A.D. 95	
			Didache, A.D. 100-130	
			Pastoral Epistles, A.D. 100-130	
			Shepherd of Hermas, A.D. 100-140	
110			Epistles of Ignatius, A.D. 110-117	
	Hadrian, A.D. 117-135		Jude, A.D. 110-130	
120				
130			II Peter, A.D. 130-150	

IMPORTANT EVENTS IN EARLY CHURCH	IMPORTANT EVENTS IN JEWISH HISTORY	
	Maccabean Revolt, 167 B.C. Dead Sea Sect at Qumran, 105 B.C.(?)-A.D. 66 Pompey takes Jerusalem, 63 B.C. Herod the Great (King of Judea), 37 B.C.-4 B.C.	
Birth of Jesus, 6-4 B.C.?	Herod Antipas (Tetrarch of Galilee), 4 B.C.-A.D. 39	1 B.C.
	Archelaus (Ethnarch of Judea), 4 B.C.-A.D. 6	1 A.D.
	Philip (Tetrarch of Iturea), 4 B.C.-A.D. 34	
		——— 10
	High Priest Caiaphas, A.D. 18-36	
Preaching of John the Baptist, A.D. 27-29?		——— 20
Ministry of Jesus, A.D. 29-33?		——— 30
Crucifixion, A.D. 30-33?		
Conversion of Paul, A.D. 33-35?		——— 40
Peter imprisoned by Herod Agrippa, A.D. 41-44?	Theudas' revolt, A.D. 40? Herod Agrippa I (King of Judea),	
Execution of James, son of Zebedee, A.D. 44	A.D. 41-44 Jews banished from Rome by Claudius, A.D. 41-49?	
Paul in southern Galatia, A.D. 47-49?		——— 50
Paul in Corinth, A.D. 50-51		
Paul in Ephesus, A.D. 52-54		
Paul arrested in Jerusalem, A.D. 56		
Paul in Rome, A.D. 60—		——— 60
Death of James, brother of Jesus, A.D. 62		
Flight of Christians to Pella, A.D. 66-67	War with Rome, A.D. 66-73	
	Jerusalem and Temple destroyed, A.D. 70	——— 70
		——— 80
	Council of Jamnia, A.D. 90?	——— 90
		——— 100
		——— 110
Martyrdom of Ignatius, A.D. 117?		
		——— 120
		——— 130

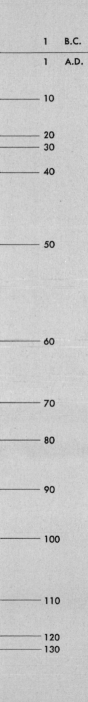

Index

Hermon, Mount, 355
Herod Agrippa I, 44, 154, 165–66, 235, 240,
    241, 391
Herod Agrippa II, 166
Herod Antipas, 43, 44, 126, 192n, 375
Herod Antipater, 43
Herod the Great, 16, 43, 126, 351
Higgins, A. J. B.: *Lord's Supper*, 362n
High Priest, role of, 49–50
"High Priestly Prayer," of Jesus, 366–67
Hippolytus: *Refutation*, 268n
Hitler, Adolf, 404
Holy of Holies, 49, 50, 110, 303, 307–309
Holy Spirit, 222–23
"Homilies" (Clement), 233
Horace, 25
Hosea, 46, 47
Hour, concept of, in John, 348, 361, 366
Humility, of Jesus, 288
Hymns, 276, 378
Hyrcanus, John, 42, 53, 59
Hyrcanus II, 43

Idumea, 43, 122
Ignatius of Antioch, 247
    Letters of, 265n, 265–66, 268, 276, 278,
        315, 316
Illyria, 22, 162
Incest, in Paul, 178, 194
Ipsissima verba, of Jesus, 90
Irenaeus of Lyons:
    Against Heresies, 5, 29, 30, 146, 146n,
        240, 268n, 289
    Detection and Overthrow of Gnosis, 250
Isaac, 175
Isaiah, 46, 47, 61, 170, 207, 290, 354
    and Mark, 116–17
Isis, cult of, 34, 35
Israel, 207 (*see also* Palestine; Jews;
        Judaism)
    disobedience of, in Paul, 226
    God's rejection of, 379–80
    restoration of, 226–27
    and the sin of David, 210
Iturea, 43

Jacob, 294
Jairus' daughter, healing of, 125
James Apostle (brother of Jesus), 94, 129,
        133, 134, 150, 154, 156, 157, 391
James (son of Zebedee), 154, 235, 236, 240
James, Book of, 290
James, Letter of, 5, 291–98
    authorship of, 293–95
    on faith and works, 297–98

and Hellenistic Judaism, 294
and Judgment, concept of, 292, 297, 298
on the rich and the poor, 295–96
on sin, 291–92
structure of, 292–93
on the "tongue," 295
James, M. R.: *Apocryphal New Testament*,
    253n
Jannaeus, Alexander, 42, 59
Jason, 39
Jehovah (*see* Yahweh)
Jeremiah, 15, 46, 47, 137, 170, 208, 307
Jeremias, J.:
    Infant Baptism, 279n
    Parables of Jesus, 93n, 328n, 330n, 331n
Jericho, 130, 131, 376, 377
Jerome, 314
Jerusalem, 38–39, 154–57, 165–66, 233–34
    fall of, 134–35, 156, 234, 237–39, 342,
        376
    Jesus' entry in, 131, 337
Jerusalem Council, 241
Jesus:
    on adultery, 325
    Ascension of, 367–77
    baptism of, 117–18
    as bearer of divine wisdom, 31
    biographies of, 90
    birth story of, 87, 319–20
    at Capernaum, 76, 119–21
    as the "Christ," 124, 128, 217
    Cleansing the Temple, 6, 131, 348–49
    as cosmic redeemer, 176–77
    Crucifixion of, 109, 112–13, 140–41, 190–
        92, 196–97, 212–13, 337, 366, 368
    and David, lineage of, 130, 131, 132, 136,
        139, 321
    death of, 122, 137–38, 139–40, 173–76,
        320
    and the demoniac, 119–20
    and his disciples, 362–63
    on divorce, 102, 325, 326
    and the End of the Age, predictions of,
        112–13
    feeding the multitude, 126
    Flesh and Blood of, 355–56
    and the Foot-washing, 362–63
    at Galilee, 375
    at Gethsemane, 304
    and Gnosticism, 30–31
    as the "good shepherd," 359
    healing and exorcisms of, 119–21, 124–25,
        352–53
    and the heavenly voices, 119, 129
    in Hebrews, 302–309
    historical person of, 89–93
    as a human being, 217, 344